Imaginary Athens

This book comprehensively examines architecture, urban planning, and civic perception in three modern cities as they transform into national capitals through an entangled, transnational process that involves an imaginative geography based on embellished memories of classical Athens. Schinkel's classicist architecture in Berlin, especially the principle of tectonics at its core, came to be adopted effectively at faraway cities in East Asia, merging with the notion of national polity as Imperial Japan sought to reinvent Tokyo and mutating into an inevitable reflection of modern civilization upon reaching colonial Seoul, all of which give reason to ruminate over the phantasmagoria of modernity.

Jin-Sung Chun is a professor of history at Busan National University of Education.

Routledge Studies in Cultural History

91 **Cultures and Practices of Coexistence from the Thirteenth Through the Seventeenth Centuries**
Multi-Ethnic Cities in the Mediterranean World, Volume 1
Edited by Marco Folin and Antonio Musarra

92 **Controversial Heritage and Divided Memories from the Nineteenth Through the Twentieth Centuries**
Multi-Ethnic Cities in the Mediterranean World, Volume 2
Edited by Marco Folin and Heleni Porfyriou

93 **History as Performance**
Political Movements in Galicia Around 1900
Dietlind Hüchtker

94 **The Cultural Life of Risk and Innovation**
Imagining New Markets from the Seventeenth Century to the Present
Edited by Chia Yin Hsu, Thomas M. Luckett, and Erika Vause

95 **Popular New Orleans**
The Crescent City in Periodicals, Theme Parks, and Opera, 1875–2015
Florian Freitag

96 **Science in the Metropolis**
Vienna in Transnational Context, 1848–1918
Edited by Mitchell G. Ash

97 **Imaginary Athens**
Urban Space and Memory in Berlin, Tokyo, and Seoul
Jin-Sung Chun

For more information about this series, please visit: www.routledge.com/Routledge-Studies-in-Cultural-History/book-series/SE0367

Imaginary Athens

Urban Space and Memory in Berlin, Tokyo, and Seoul

Jin-Sung Chun

Translated by Youngjae Josephine Bae

Routledge
Taylor & Francis Group
NEW YORK AND LONDON

First published in English 2021
by Routledge
52 Vanderbilt Avenue, New York, NY 10017

and by Routledge
2 Park Square, Milton Park, Abingdon, Oxon, OX14 4RN

Routledge is an imprint of the Taylor & Francis Group, an informa business

This book is a revised, supplemented, and translated edition of *Sangsang ui Atene, Perullin, Tok'yo, Soul: Kiok gwa konch'uk i pijonaen purhyop'waum ui munhwasa [Imaginary Athens in Berlin, Tokyo, and Seoul: A Cultural History Shaped by the Discord Between Architecture and Memory]* published in Korean by Imagine 1000 (2015). Published in Japanese by the Hosei University Press (2019).

Library of Congress Cataloging-in-Publication Data
Names: Chŏn, Chin-sŏng, 1966– author.
Title: Imaginary Athens : urban space and memory in Berlin, Tokyo, and Seoul / Jin-Sung Chun ; translated by Youngjae Josephine Bae.
Other titles: Sangsang ŭi At'ene, Perŭllin· Tok'yo· Sŏul. English
Description: New York, NY : Routledge, 2021. | Series: Routledge studies in cultural history ; 97 | "This book is a revised, supplemented, and translated edition of Sangsang ui Atene, Perullin, Tok'yo, Soul: Kiok gwa konch'uk i pijonaen purhyop'waum ui munhwasa [Imaginary Athens in Berlin, Tokyo, and Seoul: A Cultural History Shaped by the Discord Between Architecture and Memory] published in Korean by Imagine 1000 (2015). Published in Japanese by the Hosei University Press (2019)" | Includes bibliographical references and index.
Identifiers: LCCN 2020028930 (print) | LCCN 2020028931 (ebook) | ISBN 9780367639921 (hardback) | ISBN 9781003121701 (ebook) | ISBN 9781000262216 (adobe pdf) | ISBN 9781000262230 (mobi) | ISBN 9781000262254 (epub)
Subjects: LCSH: Comparative architecture. | Architecture—Korea (South)—Seoul—History. | Architecture—Japan—Tokyo—History. | Architecture—Germany—Berlin—History.
Classification: LCC NA203.5 .C4613 2021 (print) | LCC NA203.5 (ebook) | DDC 720.943/155—dc23
LC record available at https://lccn.loc.gov/2020028930
LC ebook record available at https://lccn.loc.gov/2020028931

ISBN: 978-0-367-63992-1 (hbk)
ISBN: 978-1-003-12170-1 (ebk)

Typeset in Sabon
by Apex CoVantage, LLC

To my parents

Contents

Figures

Preface

This book is a revised, supplemented, and translated edition of *Sang-sang ŭi Atene, Perŭllin, Tok'yo, Sŏul: Kiŏk gwa kŏnch'uk i pijŏnaen purhyŏp'waŭm ŭi munhwasa* [Imaginary Athens in Berlin, Tokyo, and Seoul: A Cultural History Shaped by the Discord Between Architecture and Memory], published in 2015 through the Korean publisher Imagine 1000. As the title suggests, the book features Berlin, Tokyo, and Seoul, a rather unlikely combination of three capital cities. Berlin and Tokyo have both been capitals of more recent empires that achieved "top-down modernization." Tokyo and Seoul have been part of two countries that were once in an empire–colony relationship amid their long history within the same cultural sphere. Although Seoul and Berlin seem to have nothing in common, it was possible to pair them because, as the capital of Imperial Japan, Tokyo served as a medium for a unique geographical imagery that reached across the barriers of time and space. A near-religious yearning for ancient Greece turned the Prussian capital Berlin into an imaginary Athens, which became a model for Japan in envisioning Tokyo as the capital of an emerging empire and ultimately left indelible traces upon the colonial primate city Keijō/Seoul during the Japanese rule of Korea.

Mainly through a narrative representation of architecture and urban planning, this book shows how memories linked to a certain geographical imagery can heavily impact the creation of a country's capital. Architecture and urban planning are about engineering but more fundamentally part of a discourse and political technology. Commonly remembered by the name "Capitol Hall" among Koreans, the former Japanese Government-General Building of Korea wholly reflected Karl Friedrich Schinkel's sublime, upright architectural style that decorated the heart of Berlin. Since the Athens Schinkel pictured involved authoritarian Prussian ideals of uniting the king with his subjects, it was no coincidence that such an inordinate vision's impact reached as far as colonial Korea. The transcontinental genealogy of modern capitals can therefore be considered an approach based on cultural history in terms of focusing on the formation of urban discourses that transcend the history of intercity connections and impacts, including discourses on architectural reproduction.

At a glance, this book may appear to be an attempt to trace fragments of modern Western civilization disseminated from Germany to Japan and on to colonial Korea. If so, the book would seem to be on a fairly predictable path featuring the dwindling flames of a glorious civilization. It may, then, not seem the least bit strange for a distorted version of Western modernity to surface at a remote colonial city in East Asia. However, turning this process upside down launches a completely different portrayal of history. Would it be possible to interpret the unprecedented turmoil that unfolded in modern Seoul not as a lack of modernity but an inevitable outcome of it? What if modernity only revealed glimpses of its self-contradictory nature in the West, which grew explicit by the time it reached the other side of the world? If so, would it be possible to identify Tokyo as the most dramatic demonstration of modernity's light and darkness and Seoul as the ruins of modernity due to the intensification and eruption of modernity's self-contradictory nature?

Instead of typical narratives of modern history that examine cultural dissemination from the West to the East, this book attempts to trace Western modernity backwards by taking as its halfway point not a city of one of the Western empires but Seoul, a colonial city of a neighboring East Asian empire. Such an approach demonstrates the split character of Tokyo, a city that served as a model for modern Seoul. The two-sidedness of Tokyo, posing as the spokesperson of Western civilization to its Asian neighbors while introducing itself as a representation of the East to Western powers, inevitably brings into question the city that Tokyo was modeled after. Despite having once served as a model for Tokyo, Berlin itself did not represent the original form of Western modernity, which is the proposition marking the beginning and end of this book. By being paranoid about a deep-rooted national culture, Berlin only managed to realize an imaginary original form, or an imaginative geography called Athens.

At the basis of the discourse on reproducing ancient Athens was a far more comprehensive, fundamental discourse called modernity. This formidable discourse demanded revolutionary change from the peripheral kingdom Prussia, as well as Meiji Japan and colonial Korea in the Far East, and even provided them with an anti-revolutionary logic to suppress such change. Imaginary Athens played a part in modernizing authoritarian Prussia's appearance and established itself as the absolute, valid presentation of modern civilization at Japanese colonies, thereby sealing off rejection from the subjugated in advance and colonizing their minds. Imaginary Athens was, in fact, but a shadow of reality faintly reflected in the radiant display of Western-style buildings. The wretched reality of colonies had been covered up by the phantasmagoria of modern cities. This bare face of modernity is what we call coloniality.

To scholars studying European history on the peripheries, the recent theory about modernity's inseparable relationship with coloniality does not sound at all awkward. This book defines coloniality not as a distorted, discolored form of modernity but as the true province of it. Coloniality refers to a harsh reality that cannot be concealed by the impressive mantle of modernity. The phantasm(agoria) of Athens that unfolded dramatically at the center of the (post)colonial city Seoul cast a heavier shadow upon the city's dilapidated surroundings. Western-style buildings and urban planning visualizing a new civilization were visual legacies of control and oppression justifying political, epistemological discrimination against colonies. Nevertheless, an order imposed by power tends to be incapable of embracing all of reality. The reason this book specifically explores architecture and urban planning is because they are most useful in baring not only the avant-garde of modernity but, through modernity's unique corporeality, the gap between the demand of power and social reality, historical memory and spatial inertia, and modernity and coloniality. The entangled history of Berlin, Tokyo, and Seoul based on this methodological principle is a different description of time and space at the limit of histories about vertical, unilateral relations, in other words, a description that subverts modern history generally bound to a consolidated spatiotemporal frame or, on a more provocative note, eschews the Western notion of modernity and history.

This book does not specialize in architectural history, nor does it present a general study of urban history. Rather than reverting an undeniable reality to a certain discourse, architectural style, social fact, or structure, this narrative of cultural history zooms in on the gap between all sorts of social, cultural reproductions and reality as the threshold of such reproductions. From Berlin's Forum Fridericianum to Tokyo's Kasumigaseki district of government offices and the Imperial Palace Outer Gardens, Keijō's boulevard along a north-south axis, Manchukuo's Datong Plaza, and the May 16 Square in Yŏŭido, this book brings together all these incomplete "centers" under the keyword "imaginary Athens" yet does not claim that such spaces represent the whole of reality. The irregular appearance of such spaces may instead be considered a genealogy of political utopias or exhausted/wasted phantasm(agoria)s forcibly awakened at each historical transition.

This book's adoption of a genealogical method inspired by Michel Foucault does not require any inevitability between the factors composing a genealogy. There is no reason the composition cannot be "Berlin, Moscow, and P'yŏngyang" instead of "Berlin, Tokyo, and Seoul." Considering the constant infiltration of and changes to the demarcation between representation and reality, it would essentially be ahistorical to judge history from a single standard or approach. This book's narrative has been arranged in chronological order, yet logically, the order goes against time. Rather than giving an explanation about Berlin to prescribe Seoul as an inescapable outcome, this book features a different logical development that begins with Seoul and then goes back in time to explore historical inevitability. This is why the book's prologue reviews the present Seoul and why the present Berlin is discussed in the epilogue. The entangled, irregular road from Berlin to Tokyo to Seoul is hence a path that traverses a phantasm called Western modernity. It is a path ultimately for those in search of a past different from the sociopolitical order controlling the present. The moment the past is liberated is when the future will be liberated as well. It is now up to the readers to determine whether this challenging journey has fulfilled its purpose in transcending the narrow schemes of advanced versus underdeveloped, West versus East, central versus peripheral, and national versus regional/global to uncover the future's potential amid ruins of the past.

Jin-Sung Chun from Busan
January 2020

Acknowledgments

I began to explore the theme of this book after giving a presentation titled "Prussian Classicism in Postcolonial Lieux de Mémoire" to Korean, Chinese, and Japanese scholars of German history at a symposium held in Osaka, Japan, in November 2008. Although the book project was launched with the aspiration of presenting a new dimension of cultural history, it ran into all sorts of complications. The research climate in Korea did not make it easy to unwaveringly pursue the Chōsen theme. Not only did I fall into an aimless drift from rashly jumping into an unfamiliar academic field, my high spirits plummeted due to the icy reaction from an academia that regards venturing into other domains as sinful. It took a considerable amount of time before the project made it onto a certain course, and until then, I remained unsure about the project's theme. Were it not for the kind help and support from those around me, I would have been quite tempted to give up writing for this project.

First and foremost, I would like to thank Professor Sung-Yong Joh, the leading Korean architect, who opened my eyes to architecture, and Professor Wolfgang Hardtwig, my doctoral dissertation advisor, who awakened my interest in historical culture. I would also like express my deepest gratitude to the following people who directly and indirectly helped me write and publish this book: Michael Geyer, Bruce Cumings, Roger Chartier, Jim Tierney, Arpad von Klimó, Gerd Herzog, Ingmar Arnold, Naoki Odanaka, Shuichi Shindo, Kazuhiro Takii, Masafumi Kitamura, Shizuka Sato, Shigemi Inaga, Joanne Miyang Cho, Hanook Cho, Young Paik Chun, Jie-Hyun Lim, Jung-hee Kim, Jeongho Park, Jinbin Park, Hoi-eun Kim, You Jae Lee, Sung-ho Kang, Jin-sam Chun, Jaeyeon Chung, Kwi-Weon Chung, Yeonkyung Lee, Soo-Hyun Mun, Mi-jung Kim, Jae-Kyeong Kim, Chun-Shik Kim, Inho Na, Yong-gyu Kim, Shin-Koo Woo, Doojin Hwang, Baek Yung Kim, Byung-il Yang, Yong-min Kim, Kyung-hee Kim, So-young Ko, Sam-hun Park, Wan-kyu Sun, and Seung-won Lee. In addition, I would like to convey my appreciation to the Routledge editor Max Novick and editorial assistant Jennifer Morrow, as well as the

Project Manager Sathish Mohan from Apex CoVantage and the translator Youngjae Josephine Bae, for making it possible to publish this book's English translation. Last but not least, I would like to dedicate words of love to my parents who continue from afar to encourage their son now in his fifties, as well as my wife and children, Minjung, Seyun, and Celine for always giving me the energy to keep going.

Prologue

The Phantasm(agoria) of Modernity

Every people have gods to suit their circumstances.

Henry David Thoreau, *A Week on the Concord and Merrimack Rivers* (1849)

1. A Shadow Looming Over Central Seoul

At times, like a recurring phantom, the spot where Capitol Hall/Japanese Government-General Building once was seems onerous to Koreans. Citizens of Seoul at least in their forties or older remember the towering, overwhelming building that used to stand on the spot. Neither the flashy unveiling of the signboard for the palace gate Kwanghwamun nor the busy movement of cranes signaling Kyŏngbokgung Palace's ambitious restoration have been enough to dismiss the phantom of hefty stones reminiscent of a phallus. While it remains more or less vacant until its renewal, the lot obscured by the restored Kwanghwamun Gate still manages to capture the gaze of Koreans and serve as a vanishing point in gauging where they stand.

Demolished Capitol Hall, Restored Kwanghwamun Gate

Removing the overwhelming phallus brought mountainous outlines into view. The features of Mount Pugaksan are lordlier than any other mountain, but they almost seem maternal when compared to the massive stone building that used to barricade it. The mountain's benevolent arms now embrace and invigorate the restored Kwanghwamun Gate and Kyŏngbokgung Palace still being restored. Although the gate and palace appear far more natural and open than before, they somehow still seem insufficient to function as the pivot of Seoul, the capital of the Republic of Korea. After all, they do appear to be newer than the modern buildings around them.

Although Kwanghwamun Gate has already been restored and Kyŏngbokgung Palace's restoration is under way, it is a well-known fact that such restorations have been based not on what they originally looked like when they were first built in 1395 (the fourth year of King Taejo's reign) but on what they looked like when they were rebuilt in 1868 (the fifth year of King Kojong's reign), about 270 years after they were ruined during the Imjin War with Japan. Moreover, it is an open secret that they sustained several fires after being rebuilt, and that less than a decade since their reconstruction, they were abandoned when King Kojong moved with the crown prince to Kyŏng'ungung Palace (Tŏksugung Palace) in early 1896. Even tigers would come down from Mount Inwangsan to roam around the deserted palace until it conveniently fell into the hands of Imperial Japan. The palace was then severely vandalized, and an overwhelming Western-style stone building was erected on its grounds, which the Japanese Government-General used as a headquarters for colonial rule and a pivot in rearranging the spatial order of Seoul. What do these facts tell us? Do they justify the Korean belief that restoring Kwanghwamun Gate and Kyŏngbokgung Palace is a shortcut to recovering the "national spirit" of Koreans and properly reinstating themselves as the true owners of the Korean peninsula? Apart from the arguments for and against restoration, the rationale that it should be able to correct the distorted history as well as dissonant spaces of the Korean capital Seoul does not seem all that convincing.

After Korea's liberation, the Japanese Government-General Building retained its status as the center of not only Seoul but of the Republic of Korea as it went on to house the United States military government, the Republic of Korea's government, even the government of the Democratic People's Republic of Korea for a brief period, and finally the National Museum of Korea. More than anything, the building was where the Republic of Korea's foundation was proclaimed on August 15, 1948, and photos of the celebration that day were circulated widely enough to be published in elementary school textbooks. The photo of the Korean flag being raised at the building on September 28, 1950, the day Seoul was recaptured during the Korean War, etched in people's minds the fact that Korea is a democratic republic. Reflecting on the aforementioned circumstances of the not-so-far-away past makes it difficult to relate to the mysterious nostalgia for a historic site from Chosŏn, a dynasty that grew so detached from public sentiment that its collapse failed to give rise to any substantial movements for its revival. It is equally difficult to relate to the contrasting, deep-rooted animosity toward the place from which the Republic of Korea's modern history originated.

The notion that tradition is "invented" by the needs of today rather than "restored" to a pre-existing condition is an established approach in academia that does not warrant further discussion. What becomes problematic is whether it is acceptable to make certain "political decisions" to choose or exclude specific traditions as society's diverse needs cause conflicts, discrepancies, and even entanglements between multiple traditions:

Figure 0.1 Left: Celebration of the Foundation of the Republic of Korea's Government at Capitol Hall on August 15, 1948. Right: Recapture of Seoul on September 28, 1950.

Source: Left: From National Museum of Korea, *Ku ch'ongdokpu kŏnmul shilch'ŭk mit ch'ŏlgŏ pogosŏ* (1997), vol. 1, 337. Korea Open Government License. Right: Courtesy of the National Archives of Korea, management no. CET0048186.

Why is it necessary for a democratic republic to retain a royal palace? Although there can be no objection to carefully preserving a nation's proud "cultural heritage," why must it be restored at a huge expense when it has long been defiled? Is it to restore the self-esteem of a nation that was trampled by foreign powers? Can civic rights and public awareness be uplifted without causing any issues in a city that has at its heart a royal palace requiring a hefty amount of precious taxpayers' money to restore? Save for some minor contradictions, can such preservation be justified for the sake of future benefits to be reaped from tourism?

What is certain is that demolishing Capitol Hall and restoring Kyŏngbokgung Palace are matters too weighty for discussions about them to be concluded by a single political decision. Koreans are indeed weighed down by the substantiality of a topic such as the memory and identity of their capital city. Historical issues involving heritages of colonial rule are bound to emerge, especially on the clash between different cultures and the dissolution of national identity. On a more realistic level, issues would naturally arise over the gap between urban planning, which determines the spatial order and landscape of a capital city, and what the residents in that city experience on a daily basis. From a comprehensive standpoint, the tricky questions yet to be answered would involve the properties belonging to the notion of "modern" or "modernity" that still culturally and politically govern today's reality. Across the heart of all these issues looms a certain shadow. The faint shadow that haunts the spot emptied from demolishing Capitol Hall. It is a phantom that appears and sucks out the distinct rays of history from not only the Republic of Korea's capital Seoul but from all "post-colonial cities."

Capitol Hall and Athena

With no concept to clearly define this faint shadow or any signifier capable of faithfully reproducing it, the shadow can only be exposed indirectly through ideological fragments relevant to the spot. One such fragment is the revival of ancient Athens. The Athens that gave birth to a classical culture forever youthful as the cobalt blue waters of the Aegean Sea. This historic city was gifted with olive trees by its patron Pallas Athena, and word is that the trees budded even amid the ravages of the Persian War, serving as an oracle of victory and prosperity. They are indeed a symbol of revival that transcends extinction and corruption. Yet, isn't it bizarre to be reminded of Athena and her majestic resurrection in a radiant gold helmet amid gloomy memories of Capitol Hall? An overflow of imagination is to blame for this effect, or it could be easily denounced as malicious whitewashing. Upon the very spot that once served as the center of national humiliation and suffering, how could one possibly mention olive trees and the revival of ancient Athens? No matter how grand and handsome a stone building Capitol Hall may have been, how could it ever be permissible to liken to the Parthenon of Athens a building that flaunted its power on the spot where another country's royal palace was demolished? At least for the typical Korean national sentiment, it makes no sense to attempt to draw a comparison between a great cultural heritage of mankind and the remains of the vicious Japanese empire.

Capitol Hall is clearly too far apart from the Parthenon in terms of time, place, and, most of all, political and historical value. However, it becomes a different story when Capitol Hall is viewed as a travesty rather than an imitation of the original. It is a well-known fact that in establishing its national identity, modern Japan was greatly influenced by the Prussian model of Germany. Japan's emulation of Prussia was not limited to legal and military systems or areas of science and technology but extended even to the innermost core of Japan's national identity. Yet modern Germany is an extremely rare case when it comes to national identity. For the German-speaking region that used to be divided into countless countries, a common national root was uncovered not at a place of memory based on natural experiences but at a separate, ideologically designated space. That space was none other than ancient Greece! Though geographically and periodically far apart, modern German intellectuals yearned for ancient Greece and sought an imaginary homogeneity. What stood at the forefront of the "Greek fever" back then was Prussia, a rapidly rising military power in the German region. The epitome of this trend was Prussian classicism (preußischer Klassizismus), which flourished in Berlin, a city that saw itself as the Athens of central Europe. The realm in which Prussian classicism most vividly exhibited the revival of ancient Greece was architecture, which was partially transplanted in a fairly similar form to the Japanese capital Tokyo that sought to be the Berlin of the East. And as Japan turned Tokyo into an imaginary Athens, it transplanted, out of its own necessities, the systematic, political, spatial, and aesthetic principles of Prussian classicism to the heart of its decaying colony Korea. The Japanese Government-General Building's domineering appearance, status, and function were no doubt the exhibition of a new Weltanschauung. The building cast a shadow as long and dark as a wintry night upon the capital of a dynasty that had grown as inglorious as possible. Inadvertently, Pallas Athena became the patron of Keijō, the primate city of a Japanese colony.

Nevertheless, as Thoreau once said, "every people have gods to suit their circumstances."[1] The attempt to link an utterly distant foreign idea to the Korean capital Seoul is not just to show that Japan's dissemination of German culture in Korea contributed to the formation of a modern Korean culture. As much as ancient Greece cannot be modern Germany, modern Germany cannot be modern Japan, nor can Korea be ancient Greece. Koreans do not worship Athena. This is not because each national culture is fundamentally different but because there is no substance to a national culture that can be disseminated. Rather than being a ready-made substance, German, Japanese, or Korean culture is no more than an outcome of various material, mental practices wrapped in an aura of divinity. So, no matter how much attention is paid to the mutual influence between such cultures, as long as national culture is postulated as a historical constant that goes beyond the confines of a certain epoch, one is bound to become trapped under an essentialism of sorts. This is a methodological error that studies on cultural history should avoid.

Many scholars already agree with the view that national culture and national identity are dictated more by how they are seen by others than how they are recognized by their subjects. As the American critic of Chinese culture Rey Chow explained through contemporary Chinese films, the state of being viewed is more crucial to the establishment of a national culture than the act of viewing. This proves more apparent in non-Western cultures that cannot help but always take Western views into account. In Zhang Yimou's film *Red Sorghum* that sought to present the essence of Chinese culture to a Western audience, "the 'viewed object' is now looking at the 'viewing subject.'"[2] Since Germany, Japan, and Korea each have a different "viewing subject," it is only natural for cultural developments to unfold differently in each country.

2. The Flip Side of Modernity

Prussian classicism's influence spreading from Berlin to Tokyo and on to Seoul raises the matter of "translation" between cultures, whether it be viewed as acculturation, deculturation, or Fernando Ortiz's concept of mutual "transculturation."[3] Translation is the process of allowing the heterogeneous to affect or contaminate the indigenous. Therein, however, lie two assumptions. One is that incommensurability exists between one cultural community and another, and the other is that an undeniable hierarchy is formed between the original and the translation or between the addresser and the addressee.[4] An unequal relationship clearly exists between Athens as the original and its Prussian imitation, between Prussian classicism and its Japanese imitation, and between Japan's modern civilization and its transfer to colonial Korea. Such relational imbalances can at last be settled when the reductionism between the two sides comes into question and both sides are recognized as products of the imagination or an intricately staged phantasmagoria that turns out to be a mere faint shadow.

Is "Modernity" a Maverick?

The aforementioned approach then leads to the matter of how obvious "nation (national culture)" is, as well as the correlation between nations (national cultures). A discussion involving correlation assumes that a distinguishable counterpart can be identified and admits that influence is being wielded, perhaps not reciprocally, but at least bilaterally. This is the very stance taken by "transnational history," which has recently gained a voice in historical studies. Redefining a predominant power structure like the nation-state system as an explanandum rather than an explanans in order to reestablish national history within a transversal network can be, theoretically or empirically, a convincing attempt. A fairly useful example of this would be the relationship between Germany and Japan. After belatedly joining the modern global trend of establishing and expanding nation-states, the way Germany and Japan struggled to recover sovereignty and become subjects instead of objects of history, the process through which the two countries aggressively realized their excessive desire for internal and external domination, had a tremendous impact upon the formation of Germany and Japan's state, society, and national self-identity. This is what makes it most interesting to compare and analyze their similarities and differences or examine whether they were mutually affected by one another.[5]

The equality of a relationship, however, does not guarantee its coevalness. Even if a national culture's incommensurability could be decomposed to expose its inner fissure and insecure boundaries, and even if the fluidity of diverse "co-existing" cultures can be recognized, a transversal history of nations would not be enough to embrace the synchronic exchanges and struggles at a global scale. Assuming that colonial Korea's modernity was in a mutual relationship with the modernity of Germany or Japan would still leave a certain temporal gap between the modernities, and the colony's resistance would be reduced to fit into the system of empires or, at best, be about such a system. A colony can never be regarded as an equal competitor in seeking breakthroughs for modern civilization.

The nature of modernity is originally like a maverick or a commander's unrelenting call to follow his lead. Yet the commander never allows himself to be noticed. In general, modernity is used as a concept to refer to a historical period, but it cannot be pinned down as a neutral descriptive concept when it comes to its relation to the term "modern," because the sound-value of modern is actually interlaced with images that stir people's fear and imagination.[6] Modern is in itself a powerful demand and burden. It is a sense of needing to remain current with the latest. The perpetual demand for a new current pushes reality aside and endlessly generates differences with those deemed "non-modern." Subject versus object, reality versus imaginary, original versus translation ultimately creates a division between East and West.[7]

Such a rationale of excessive self-expression and intervention causes a revolutionary rearrangement of time and space and derives the most typical and obvious expression from the concept of history. History takes advantage of the present accelerating newness so as to continue placing pressure on time. The endless flow of progress from one present to the next forms a homogenized mold of linear time and rearranges geographical space. All territories of nation-states line up from the highest to lowest stage along the path to advancement. The binary developmental schema of arbitrary/constitutional rule, medieval/modern, feudalism/capitalism transforms into a regional division of the world, giving rise to a grand narrative of world history that blatantly reveals a most unilateral, practically imperialistic desire to expand first across Europe and then to other regions. As world history of mankind is shaped by depriving and absorbing "others" outside Europe, the coevalness between East and West is denied, turning history into a waiting room of sorts where all nations wait for their turn. As the Indian-American historian Dipesh Chakrabarty aptly pointed out, "not yet" is the primordial manner of existence for history created by the modern West.[8] What is truly paradoxical is that, as history comes to completely depend on the future, the empirical space of the present is inevitably marginalized.[9] Modern always demands a new present, rendering it practically impossible for the present to exist.

Considering the semantic property of the term "modern," the non-Western world's intellectual attempt to seek an "alternative modernity" after experiencing the sorrows of colonization still fails to attain coevalness despite arguing for an equal share in modern civilization. Because modernity remains normalized as an inevitable stage of history, prospects on the outside are basically precluded. An alternative modernity cannot stand as an independent present without being weighed against Western modernity. A methodological reification such as this obscures the fact that modernity is always a new representation, an insecurely designated boundary, and an excessive imagination about collective constructs and identities like nation, people, civil society, and national economy that appear to be solid. Insisting that modern civilization in the West is a product of encountering other civilizations merely identifies premodern elements in non-Western regions as premature developments. It is similar to arguing that modern division of labor originated from running colonies in the New World prior to the Industrial Revolution, which only manages to secure a bit more ground in the West's singular history. This convenient pluralism overlooks the fact that "modern" is originally no more than a displacement, dislocation, and delay from overly restructuring time and space, not to mention a mechanism of concealment that pretends to be a universal truth without any issues. Postcolonialism is also not free from the aforementioned issue. The prefix "post" implicitly assumes linear time and incorporates the world outside Europe into a single history of meeting Europe.[10]

The Korean discourse on colonial modernity is fundamentally based on the assumption that modernity is a historical inevitability.[11] Going beyond the crude argument that Japan provided the foundation for Korea's modernization and acknowledging that modernity has both liberating and oppressive aspects makes it possible for colonial modernity not to be underestimated as a mutation or deviation of Western modernity. However, such an approach unwittingly ends up cementing the preconception that the outside of modernity does not exist.[12] The most noteworthy point in the Korean discourse on colonial modernity is that resistance and cooperation are not viewed dichotomously in order to meet the social demand for weeding out pro-Japanese Koreans. The discourse instead regards resistance and cooperation as entanglements and contradictions across various dimensions including class, race, culture, and language, based on a new awareness that it would have been difficult in reality to clearly separate colonization from modernization. Such an awareness allows colonial realities to be viewed as complex and multidimensional but simultaneously foreshortens their primordial incommensurability. Can the colonial natives' resistance only be seen as a renunciation, discontinuance, replacement, or extension of cooperating with a modern empire? Did it continue to be truly modern? The colonial modernity discourse primarily tends to fix its gaze upon structural inequality within a modern social system, thereby excessively underlining the ideological collusion between the colonial ruling power and the native ruling class.[13] Is ethnic, racial discrimination in colonies merely a logical extension of social discrimination prevalent in the mainland of an empire? Per postcolonial cultural theorist Homi K. Bhabha's remark, was the natives' resistance a "mimicry" of sorts "almost the same, but not quite," appearing to be radical but simply meant to "immanently threaten" and "disavow" an empire's authority?[14]

The Korean discourse on colonial modernity is unique in that, instead of discussing an alternative modernity, it starts from the assumption that all modernities are a colonial modernity. Such an assumption may enrich the conception of modernity but, as in the case of the alternative modernity discourse, prevents alternatives to modernity from being envisioned. Then is there really no way out? Is it impossible for an outside of modernity to exist? The Argentinean cultural theorist Walter D. Mignolo's mention of "colonial difference" unlatches the gate to new reasoning. According to Mignolo, emphasizing an irreversible colonial difference signifies the demotion of modernity to myth, a myth that specifically pertains to the West. Mignolo instead suggests the concept of "coloniality" as the "darker side of Western modernity." "If there cannot be modernity without coloniality, there cannot either be global modernities without global colonialities."[15]

The Prison of Coloniality

Coloniality refers to a political, cultural, racial, and epistemic power structure that lasts even after colonialism ceases to be a political order. Discrimination and resistance in colonies are not mere imitations of those in the metropoles but products of an entirely different structure. Recognizing coloniality goes beyond criticizing and decomposing modernity led by the West and attempts to bring to the surface of history various others that have been suppressed and concealed. However, Mignolo's argument does not suggest for coloniality to replace modernity. It rather suggests for coloniality to be established as the outside of modernity, which is, of course, not completely separate but more like an external component. "Simultaneity of the non-simultaneous," which the German philosopher Ernst Bloch pointed out long ago as a characteristic of modernity, then is re-appropriated by the establishment of a new relationship between modernity and coloniality.

Coloniality causes modernity to be viewed differently. The moment the differences of (post)colonies are discussed, it takes stability away from all sorts of modern values and norms that have long been considered universal. Modernity is no longer a normative concept that embodies historical inevitability. It becomes a self-reenacted discourse by the West setting out for colonial rule, a generic term for all the traumatic memories directly and indirectly caused by such discourse, an inevitable name that refers to the simultaneity of all non-simultaneous others. In that sense, modernity is reestablished as a "trans-modernity" that traverses the inside and outside of modernity, the East and West, empires and colonies, and modernity and anti-modernity. The prefix "trans" implies a constant fluidity. Mignolo, who played a leading role in suggesting this theoretical alternative, is part of a Latin American cultural research group called "Grupo modernidad/colonialidad." The group aims to overcome Latin America's dismal reality through transversal thinking that goes beyond existing discourses on modernity. According to the philosopher Enrique Dussel, who inspires the research group, the view that considers modernity a purely European phenomenon is no more than a myth. "Modernity is, in fact, a European phenomenon, but one constituted in a dialectical relation with a non-European alterity." In the eyes of Dussel, an Argentinean of German descent working in Mexico, a non-European alterity represents the "ultimate content" of modernity. The new category called trans-modernity is a "process of mutual creative fertilization" in which "both modernity and its negated alterity co-realize themselves," essentially making it possible to envision a "co-realization of that which it is impossible for modernity to accomplish by itself."[16]

Such a pursuit, however, is far from a simple theory of harmony. This is made apparent by the "coloniality of power" theory suggested by Anibal Quijano, a principal member of Grupo modernidad/colonialidad. Quijano's theoretical framework takes note of the fact that as the global power model Europe introduced came to be regarded as a universal principle undeterred by time and space, it has persistently operated beyond the boundaries of colonialism. The so-called paradigm of rational knowledge that regards the West as the subject and the rest of the world as the object engenders a "colonization of imagination of the dominated" that internalizes racial, ethnic discrimination. Such deep-rooted coloniality of power/knowledge is the very cradle that breeds colonial differences that cannot be reverted to modernity. For the theoretical basis of a Western power model, Quijano turns to the idea of social totality, which involves atomistic, structural functionalism and romantic organicism. The latter presumes that each part of society has a distinct hierarchy and that a single complete totality is formed of one part that rules over the other parts that cannot exist without the ruling part. This kind of logic is none other than a "prison of coloniality" that locks the imagination of the dominated within a framework of colonial rule. "Nothing is less rational, finally, than the pretension that the specific cosmic vision of a particular ethnie should be taken as universal rationality."[17]

Despite having originated from his distress over the postcolonial reality of Latin America, Quijano's theory on the coloniality of power can be applied more broadly. The Prussian classicism that came to be transplanted to Seoul forms a familial resemblance to a distinctly German romantic organicism, which justified Imperial Japan's authoritarian political system and oppressive colonial rule and provided a rationale that annihilates the difference of a colonial space. Transforming a certain area's cultural ideas into a universal language for different ruling powers shows how the coloniality of power typically operates.

The distorted modernity of the South Korean capital Seoul casts considerable doubt on the purity of Prussian classicism that blossomed in the German capital Berlin. The faint shadow of Athena looming over Berlin, Tokyo, and Seoul is actually a phantasmagoria silently pressing upon those modern capitals. The goddess demanding absolute trust and obedience is self-righteous and may well be reactionary. Resurrected under the glorious prospects of classicism, Pallas Athena is an utterly modern goddess who bestows sacrosanctity upon German national culture and, at the same time, is the goddess of trans-modernity delivering a harsh oracle called the coloniality of power. With irresistible power, Athena demands all sorts of sacrifices from Berlin, Tokyo, and Seoul. Berlin sacrifices revolutionary fervor, while Tokyo sacrifices Asian traditions, and Seoul sacrifices its indigenous culture. These disparate appearances of the goddess debase her divine sanctity. Her bare face in Seoul puts her brilliant presence in Berlin to shame. It is thus made clear that the Athens in central Europe is an imaginary Athens no different from Keijō, the primate city of a Japanese colony, in being a space of brutal reality where a reactionary ideology prevails. This is how the hidden side of modernity comes to light through an outside perspective called coloniality. Even if Prussian classicism hadn't been directly involved with colonialism, its modernity made brutal colonialist appropriation possible. Radiant modernity and pitch-dark coloniality, or the inside and outside of modernity, are inextricably entangled.

3. Architecture, Cityscape, and Political Technology

Is it possible for a phantasmagoric image of indeterminate substance to establish itself as a solid object of historical narrative? A methodological way out of this question can be found through the concept of "imaginative geography" adopted by Edward Said, the author of *Orientalism*. Imaginative geography refers to a discursive strategy that European civilizations employed to solidify their identity, which ideologically highlights to the extreme the geographical distance and cultural difference between European and Oriental civilizations. Despite being a completely arbitrary concept, it managed to secure actuality, and, according to Said, making the discourse be considered as fact was crucial for the discursive strategy.[18] As if to demonstrate the superiority of Western civilizations, a German imaginary geography called imaginary Athens paraded an overwhelming visual authority as it was realized in Japanese colonial cities. Such a rationale of excessive intervention and disguise specific to modernity inevitably accompanied backlashes such as schism and contradiction, hybridization, and obliteration.

Imaginative Geography Etched in Modern Capitals

Modern capitals are the places that most explicitly exhibit features of Western imaginative geography and trans-modernity. Starting in the late eighteenth century, Western capitals were cradles of democracy and national culture advocated by the bourgeoisie. Major political upheavals like the French Revolution turned spaces for religious, royal rituals into public spheres. Public rallies and rational discussions took place in urban spaces, turning them into a model of civic publicity. And even though new institutions like museums looked no different from old palaces or temples on the outside, they settled at the sacred center of cities as guardians of a nation's communal memories and cultural ideals. Capitals serve as the most typical representation of modern cityscapes. Boulevards, plazas, public monuments, residential areas, arcades, the constant throng of passersby provide visual unity from being managed and sequentially repeated by a functional order. Openness and authority, dynamism and standardization, diversity and homogeneity are structured/symbolized into a utopian whole. However, such external unity cannot conceal the reality of cities as spaces of harsh exclusion. Its citizens never share a uniform set of interests or propensities. Cities spatially reproduce political differences. Those on the outside of utopia such as the poor or immigrants from colonies coexist in cities as shaded peripheries. Because such segmented, disparate modern capitals are compounds of diverse acts and fantasies, representing urban history as a uniform series of national events is no more than creating a myth.[19]

What contributed decisively to creating the myth of modern capitals was urban planning. According to the intentions of a ruling power, a group of experts mobilize all sorts of ideological emblems and technological means to choose locations for buildings and facilities, design a road network, and designate a city's boundaries. Modern capitals display overwhelming authority and technological proficiency through well-formed urban infrastructures and linear streets. The decorative façade of individual buildings lining streets demonstrates aesthetic unity and supplements the formation of a cityscape's aerial view. Modern urban planners didn't stop at having the architectural style of buildings materially realize the citizens' collective identity but arranged such styles so that they would symbolize new perspectives of such an identity. Architecture thus came to take the initiative in bringing change to the world.

Even before urban planning began to fundamentally change urban landscapes, Western architecture was realizing a new symbolic order. What is referred to as the "law of perspective" originated from architecture. "Linear perspective" is a geometric perspective that makes parallel lines converge to a single vanishing point that draws in its surrounding spaces. This perspective was inspired by a law the Florentine architect Filippo Brunelleschi devised to overcome the challenge of building a grand dome. On the ceiling of the famous Duomo in Firenze that Brunelleschi designed, geometric parts meet at an intersection, which also serves as a center for all imaginary lines that connect a viewer's gaze with individual dots representing the sacred universe. Perspective space, blossomed from the spirit of architecture, is formative space imagined from a fixed monocular view and is infinitely open, continuous, and uniform. Perspective space is a microcosm of holistic space in which partial spaces surrounding the world revolve around a central point. All objects within a linear coordinate are bound to find their own place based on a calculated assessment of elements forming the universe.[20]

Although the modern law of perspective for arranging space is based on a mathematical formula, it is in fact an extremely subjective configuration. In the widely recognized *On Painting*, authored by Leon Battista Alberti, who theorized the law of perspective, the pyramid of vision appears that shows how vertical coordinates of a space can be linearly projected upon a flat surface. The relative location of the pyramid's vertex residing within eyesight determines where each coordinate is to be placed on a two-dimensional drawing. Perspective space created by human eyes, the object they view, and the distance between the two is, in fact, artificially formed according to a subjective perspective. Homogenized space, created from a symmetry between the eyes and the viewed object, actually obscures the fact that eyeballs are not flat but round. So, as the difference (and entanglement) that naturally occurs between the point of viewing and being viewed is denied, the subject gains control over the object it views.[21] Perspective space hence serves as the best historical source to substantiate the coloniality of power. The law of perspective has been fully realized at dignified baroque-style urban spaces in modern capitals. The monumental procession of wide boulevards and buildings stretched out according to the perspectival vista of a pyramid of vision overwhelms the eyes of pedestrians by making them appear as if their sole purpose is for military parades celebrating glorious anniversaries. In such spaces, monuments of victory or triumphal arches tend to serve as a vanishing point under the law of perspective. The citizens' mediocre everyday life is thereby obscured from view.[22]

From empires to (post-)colonies, perspective spaces offered by modern capitals are utterly modern for using mathematical truths to cover up the subjective intent of ruling powers. Such spaces are at the same time transmodern for embodying indelible scars left by memories of harsh exclusion at colonies due to the forced demolition of slums or native constructions. This sparks the urge to reconsider the scope of space in principle. Space originally possesses a correlative nature. It is not just a container for or background to human experiences. Space is widely involved in the relationship between humans and goods, built environment, daily practices and political strategies, or processes of symbolization related to perception, representation, and memory.[23] Space itself is a reproduced spatiality. As the German philosopher Martin Heidegger formalized, space is never given to human beings beforehand. On the contrary, human imagination assigns various objects in the world to a place they each belong, establishing a pure representation of "spatiality" (Räumlichkeit). "Space can be made only through the granting of place (Einräumung)."[24]

If space is a practice of assigning objects to where they belong per Heidegger's argument, or reproduced spatiality that emerges from the granting of place, modern spatial concepts such as territory, national boundary, and region that essentialize geographical differences deserve to be reconsidered. Presuming that such spaces are permanent substances instead of reproductions proves how persistently the coloniality of power has been at work. A city's topology produced through urban planning and architectural styles thoroughly reflects a (colonial) ruling power's intentions rather than pure functional necessity. Yet, the outcome reflects the citizens' own acceptance of such intentions rather than being brainwashed by them, thereby forming a new premise for the outcome. To borrow a term used by the Marxist cultural theorist Henri Lefèbvre, "representations of space," created by experts as was the law of perspective, function autonomously as "spaces of representation" in reality due to emotional assimilation from the bottom up using images, symbols, sentiments, and memories.[25]

As long as space is seen as an arena of perpetual, practical intervention, focusing on cityscapes can be an effective way to overcome the coloniality of power. The multiple layers that give life to a city are wholly etched into the style of streets, byways, and public buildings, as well as the endless flow of people and traffic within a cityscape. A visual-centric approach toward cities offers the advantage of being able to examine the complex relationships between different layers, as long as one does not become absorbed in an aerial or perspectival view of rule and control. Architectural styles in particular are more like testimonies than explanations. They reveal aspects of changing realities in a symptomatic rather than straightforward way that confesses much about the modernity and coloniality of modern cities.[26]

Architecture carries a political, technological aspect in that it uses its own method of granting places to influence and domesticate our bodies and daily lives, thereby making it possible to socially control individuals. Walls and roofs stand silently yet speak to and attract certain people. The visual clarity of a building's style conveys a certain meaning. A building standing right before our eyes forms a magnetic field stronger than any other profound idea or political statement. However, a building along a street is not only visible to certain people.[27] As it elicits shock, interest, envy, or even anger from uninvited passersby, a building eventually evolves into an autonomous space of representation per Henri Lefèbvre's suggestion.

Cityscape as a Discursive Formation

In any city, there is a certain gap between the macroscopic system dictated by the logic of power or capital and the microscopic space of daily life in reality. Daily life reflects the logic of power and capital that demands repetitive, regular actions and simultaneously hosts all sorts of individual actions, which introduce differences and conflicts. Daily life draws a curtain of invisibility that cannot be penetrated by the ruling power's aerial or perspectival view. Hence, instead of remaining content with a perspectival view, a visual-centric approach focusing on architecture and cityscape exposes the gap between daily life and control upon which a perspectival view rests and gently lifts the curtain of invisibility. After all, is it not a virtue of cultural history narratives to focus on the invisible?

A visual-centric approach seems all the more necessary for (post)colonial cities where realms of visibility and invisibility breed more serious conflict. While architecture and urban planning contributed to visualizing the glory and historical identity of Western empires in their metropoles, the use of architecture and urban planning at colonial cities was to negate the history of the natives and demonstrate the cultural superiority of colonialists. A disparity inevitably occurs between the legacy of colonialism and the newly established topology, and left within that disparity would be the daily lives of citizens that transform a city's existing topology, despite having been domesticated by that very topology. Most citizens of Seoul tend to accept the modern buildings and straight boulevards left behind by the Japanese as a natural part of their built environment, and each uses them for their own material pursuits. At the same time, they generally react positively toward removing Japanese legacies and restoring Kwanghwamun Gate and Kyŏngbokgung Palace. Such contradictory reactions originate from the gap between modernity and coloniality. The spectacle of a modern urban space can never dispel horrid colonial memories.

Built for the Japanese Government-General, only to be used for other purposes after Korea's liberation, Capitol Hall was, in fact, a monument of Prussian classicism transplanted to East Asia. This grand building and the spot where it used to stand leave a strong impression bound to clash with faith in a nation's glorious history. An obsession to fill that clashing point with something else might be the manifestation of an undeniable desire to conceal uncomfortable memories. Yet this sort of clash between memory and history can generally be found in cities today. Since the exceedingly modern idea of capitals as public spaces defending national legacies gradually lost its timeliness, urban spaces have been disconnected from their past to momentarily flicker or be replaced. As per cultural theorist Andreas Huyssen's explanation, fragmented memories are endlessly inscribed and erased on palimpsests called cities. This exposes homogeneous, sequential times throughout history to rifts and contradictions.[28]

Are modern/contemporary architecture and cityscapes the last bastions to defend history or hotbeds of fragmented memories? Are they ideological tools of the ruling class or autonomous spaces of representation standing up to them? Even if they don't necessarily fall on either side, architecture or built space are indeed products of material practice that cannot fully coincide with a certain ideology. They are therefore forever new, temporary, and incomplete representations. "The real," as an object that triggers a cultural historian's intellectual desire to conquer, only furtively reveals itself amid differences or rifts between dissimilar representations. This indicates that the ideology of modernity that propounds itself as the one and only representation, as if there were nothing before it, is indeed far beyond "the real."

The friction with history that contemporary cities clearly suffer from is a unique form of representation the French historian Pierre Nora has incorporated under the broad concept of "sites of memory" (lieux de mémoire). As the antipode of history, the concept refers to spaces that evoke the absence rather than the preservation of memories. Once "environments of memory" (milieux de mémoire) holding vivid memories of the past vanish, unoccupied sites of memory can only subsist by being artificially presented as national memorials or tourist attractions or by becoming objects of academic study.[29] Cities like Seoul that have lost their original environment of memory through the vicissitudes of history tend to artificially select and edit their jumbled memories to create historic, national sites of memory. The exhaustion of history reluctantly gives birth to a costly substitute.

The demolished Capitol Hall and Kyŏngbokgung Palace undergoing restoration can both be considered sites of memory. Cities with a colonial past are bound to produce sites of memory that tend to be more artificial and ideological. For Western metropolises, environments of memory gradually disintegrate as they are relatively carefully replaced by sites of memory, whereas postcolonial cities purposefully destroy environments of memory from colonial times. Uncomfortable links to a disgraceful past lead to an extreme rupture in memory that requires an even more extreme method to overcome it. Postcolonial Seoul can be characterized by an asymmetric coexistence of tradition lacking context and modernity of unknown nationality, as well as the absence of a modern heritage to serve as a medium between the two coexisting characteristics. This leaves its citizens with fractured memories like a stratum buried under fairly well-polished remains and super skyscrapers. Despite its external vitality, Seoul remains structurally empty.

The nature of architecture and urban planning as an art of memory and oblivion is fundamentally a matter of discourse rather than technology. The process through which Berlin, Tokyo, and Seoul were turned into modern capitals amid the memory and oblivion of ancient Athens and its clone Prussian classicism can be considered through discursive formation in the sense of Michel Foucault, which comprehensively embodies architectural design, urban planning, and how citizens react to them. Despite having been suggested by Foucault quite long ago, the theory of discursive formation remains an appealing methodological strategy that equally considers the material process and the process of political acts as matters of representation. Rather than focusing on the object of representation, the theory focuses on the process of representation that constantly creates a new principle, medium, scope, and criterion of representation.[30] This sort of strategy allows the overall aspects of Prussian classicism's historical stature to be discussed without having to be overwhelmed by essentialism from national history or expertise in architectural history. Thoughts on the nature of architecture central to forming the discourse on Prussian classicism are not simply regarded as matters of architectural history but as a representation tied to the formation of a discourse on modernity that underlines unity and rationality. Likewise, the process through which the utterly European attempt to revive the cultural essence of ancient Athens was transformed according to the East Asian spatiotemporal framework can be discussed at a level different from distortion or corruption. The ideological, visual symbols of German culture etched upon Seoul's Capitol Hall can be examined not as a sequential dissemination of national culture but as a certain discursive formation's sporadic relocation, meaning another coeval representation. Ultimately, the road to discovering an imaginary Athens resembles, rather than an embryology that traces an origin, a "genealogy" that attempts to restore a network of relations based on alliances, exchanges, and key points.[31]

Prussian classicism that blossomed in Berlin is a discourse basically formed by geographically imagining ancient Athens. An imaginative geography called "imaginary Athens" can be effectively analyzed with a methodology proposed by Edward Said. Said referred to "contrapuntal reading" as an approach that focuses on the paradox in which the intensification of stereotypes toward others in the East solidifies the identity of the West.[32] As much as Prussian classicism has been an utterly German discourse, Prussian classicism transplanted in Seoul has been an utterly Japanese discourse. The Japanese empire's imaginative geography objectified the German empire as well as its Asian neighbors, thereby securing its own stature within such contrapuntal relations.[33] In the end, the deceased becomes the only thing fixed. When a colonialist's imaginative geography is transplanted to a space inhabited by the colonized in reality, it may resemble the original on the outside but transforms into something entirely different on the inside. The city Tsingtau – today's Qingdao – colonized by the German Empire could never become a miniature of Berlin, nor could Imperial Japan's colonial capital Keijō become an imitation of Tokyo. Prussian classicism is an imaginative geography that transformed nearly beyond recognition during its continental traverse and was reborn as new (anti-)national sites of memory.

The three capitals Berlin, Tokyo, and Seoul are therefore not given geographical substances but rather spaces of representation that renew themselves over each phase. This justifies approaching the cities as an entangled process in which spaces keep featuring different representations depending on the ruling power, while such demand for new representations clash endlessly with a topology that has already domesticated the citizens' senses.[34] Discourse of a nation's deep-rooted capital becomes no more than an awkward joke. In fact, while it remains undetermined as to where their long histories each belong, Berlin, Tokyo, and Seoul may be alive and well, but perhaps they are capitals yet to come into existence.

Notes

1. Henry David Thoreau, *A Week on the Concord and Merrimack Rivers* (1849; Mineola, NY: Dover Publications, 2001), 39.
2. Rey Chow, *Primitive Passions: Visuality, Sexuality, Ethnography, and Contemporary Chinese Cinema* (New York, NY: Columbia University Press, 1995), 180–181.
3. In the 1940s, Fernando Ortiz proposed the concept of transculturation as an alternative to the concept of acculturation and deculturation. His alternative approach was based on the idea that this conceptual couplet merely represents the interests of the metropoles. On this point, see Mary Louise Pratt, *Imperial Eyes: Travel Writing and Transculturation* (New York, NY: Routledge, 1992), 245. Pratt reformulated the problematic of transculturation with the following set of heuristic questions: "What do people on the receiving end of empire do with metropolitan modes of representation? How do they appropriate them? How do they talk back? What materials can one study to answer those questions?" Ibid., 7–8.
4. On the incommensurability of the addresser and the addressee, see Naoki Sakai, *Translation and Subjectivity: On Japan and Cultural Nationalism* (Minneapolis, MN: University of Minnesota Press, 1997), 11–15.
5. For a similar argument, see Michael Geyer, "Deutschland und Japan im Zeitalter der Globalisierung. Überlegungen zu einer komparativen Geschichte jenseits des Modernisierungs-Paradigmas," in *Das Kaiserreich transnational: Deutschland in der Welt 1871–1914*, ed. Sebastian Conrad and Jürgen Osterhammel (Göttingen: Vandenhoeck & Ruprecht, 2006), 68–86.
6. Dipesh Chakrabarty, "Provincializing Europe in Global Times," in New Preface to *Provincializing Europe* (Princeton, NJ: Princeton University Press, 2007), xiiii–xiv.
7. Timothy Mitchell, "The Stage of Modernity," in *Questions of Modernity*, ed. Timothy Mitchell (Minneapolis, MN: University of Minnesota Press, 2000), 1–34; Dipesh Chakrabarty, *Habitations of Modernity: Essays in the Wake of Subaltern Studies* (Chicago, IL: Chicago University Press, 2002).
8. Dipesh Chakrabarty, *Provincializing Europe: Postcolonial Thought and Historical Difference* (Princeton, NJ: Princeton University Press, 2000), 27–46.
9. Reinhart Koselleck, *Vergangene Zukunft* (Frankfurt am Main: Suhrkamp, 1989), 17–37.
10. For a critical assessment of postcolonialism, see Mitchell, "The Stage of Modernity," 2–3; Frederick Cooper, *Colonialism in Question: Theory, Knowledge, History* (Berkeley, CA: University of California Press, 2005), 116–117, 142–148; Yi Kyŏng-wŏn, "Talshingminjuŭiŭi kyebo wa

chŏngch'esŏng," in *Talshingminjuŭi iron'gwa chaengjŏm*, ed. Ko Bu-ŭng (Seoul: Munhakkwajisŏngsa, 2003), 23–58.

11. Yun Hae-dong et al., *Kŭndaerŭl ta-si ingnŭnda: Han'guk kŭndae inshigŭi saeroun p'aerŏdaimŭl wihayŏ* (Seoul: Yŏksabi'yŏngsa, 2006).
12. See the argument in Cho Hyŏng-kŭn, "Kŭndaesŏngŭi naejaehanŭn oeburosŏ shingminjisŏng/shingminjijŏk ch'aiwa pyŏniŭi munje," *Sahoewa yŏksa* 73 (2007): 385–418.
13. For a similar argument, see Tani E. Barlow, "Eugenics, Woman, Semi-Colonialism, and Colonial Modernity as Problems for Postcolonial Theory," in *Postcolonial Studies and Beyond*, ed. Ania Loomba (Durham, NC: Duke University Press, 2005), 372.
14. Quoted from Homi K. Bhabha, *The Location of Culture* (New York, NY: Routledge, 1994), 86.
15. Walter D. Mignolo, *Local Histories/Global Designs: Coloniality, Subaltern Knowledge, and Border Thinking* (Princeton, NJ: Princeton University Press, 2012), 91, 96–99. Quoted from Walter D. Mignolo, *The Darker Side of Western Modernity: Global Futures, Decolonial Options* (Durham, NC: Duke University Press, 2011), 3.
16. Enrigue Dussel, "Eurocentrism and Modernity (Introduction to the Frankfurt Lectures)," *boundary 2* 20, no. 3, The Postmodernism Debate in Latin America (1993): 65–76, quoted from 65, 75–76.
17. Anibal Quijano, "Coloniality and Modernity/Rationality," *Cultural Studies* 21, no. 2 (2007): 168–178, quoted from 177–178; Anibal Quijano, "Coloniality of Power, Eurocentrism, and Social Classification," in *Coloniality at Large: Latin America and the postcolonial debate*, ed. Mabel Moraña, Enriqué Dussel and Carlos A. Jáuregui (Durham, NC: Duke University Press, 2008), 181–224.
18. Edward W. Said, *Orientalism* (New York, NY: Vintage Books, 1994), 49 ff.
19. Gyan Prakash, "Introduction," in *The Spaces of the Modern City: Imaginaries, Politics, and Everyday life*, ed. Gyan Prakash and Kelvin M. Kruse (Princeton, NJ: Princeton University Press, 2008), 6–10.
20. Pierre Francastel, *Misulgwa sahoe*, trans. Oksŭng Ahn-Bron (Seoul: Minŭmsa, 1998), 29–31. The origin of perspective can also be traced back to the Mercator map, which rendered the world to be surveyed on the same scale by substituting the visible world within a uniform coordinate scale.
21. Erwin Panofsky, *Perspective as Symbolic Form* (Brooklyn, NY: Zone Books, 1997), 27–31, 67–72; Chu Ŭn-u, *Shigakkwa hyŏndaesŏng* (Seoul: Hannarae, 2003), 137 ff., 191 ff.
22. On perspectival representations of urban spaces since the Renaissance, see Siegfried Giedion, *Space, Time and Architecture* (1941; Cambridge, MA: Harvard University Press, 1967), 55 ff.
23. Martina Löw, *Raumsoziologie* (Frankfurt am Main: Suhrkamp, 2001), 158.
24. Martin Heidegger, *Sein und Zeit* (Tübingen: Niemeyer, 2001), 102–113; Martin Heidegger, *Bemerkungen zu Kunst – Plastik – Raum* (St. Gallen, Switzerland: Erker, 1996), 14.
25. Henri Lefèbvre, *The Production of Space* (Hoboken, NJ: Blackwell, 2007), 33 and more generally, see Doreen Massey, *For Space* (Thousand Oaks, CA: Sage, 2008).
26. Maiken Umbach, "Urban History: What Architecture Does, Historically Speaking . . .," *The Journal of the Society of Architectural Historians* 65, no. 1 (2006): 14–15. For a visual-centric approach, see notably Martin Jay, *Downcast Eyes: The Denigration of Vision in Twentieth-Century French Thought* (Berkeley, CA: University of California Press, 1993).
27. Michel Foucault, *Discipline & Punish: The Birth of the Prison*, trans. Alan Sheridan (New York, NY: Vintage Books, 1995), 195–230, characterizes

architecture as a manifestation of power in terms of its typically modern panopticism. See also Mark Crinson, *Empire Building: Orientalism & Victorian Architecture* (New York, NY: Routledge, 1996), 7–9.

28. Andreas Huyssen, *Present Pasts: Urban Palimpsests and the Politics of Memory* (Redwood City, CA: Stanford University Press, 2003); Mark Crinson, ed., *Urban Memory: History and amnesia in the modern city* (New York, NY: Routledge, 2005), Introduction; Christian M. Boyer, *The City of Collective Memory: Its Historical Imagery and Architectural Entertainments* (Cambridge, MA: The MIT Press, 2001), 4.
29. Pierre Nora and Lawrence D. Kritzman, eds., Volume 1 of *Realms of Memory: Rethinking the French Past: Conflicts and Divisions*, trans. Arthur Goldhammer (New York, NY: Columbia University Press, 1996). On Nora's concept of lieux de mémoire, see Chŏn Jin-sŏng, *Yŏksaga kiŏkŭl marhada: Iron'gwa shilch'ŏnŭl wihan kiŏgŭi munhwasa* (Seoul: Humanist, 2005), 56–59.
30. Michel Foucault, *The Archeology of Knowledge and The Discourse on Language* (New York, NY: Barnes & Noble Books, 1993), 31 ff., 47–48.
31. Michel Foucault, "Nietzsche, Genealogy, History," in *The Foucault Reader*, ed. Paul Rabinow (New York, NY: Pantheon, 1984), 76–100.
32. Edward Said, *Culture and Imperialism* (New York, NY: Vintage Books, 1994), 66, 51–52.
33. For a critique of imaginative geography of the Japanese Empire, see Kang Sang-jung, *Orient'allijŭmŭl Nŏmŏsŏ* (Seoul: Isan, 1998), 77–109.
34. On histoire croisée or entangled history, see Michael Werner and Bendicte Zimmermann, "Beyond Comparison: Histoire Croisée and the Challenge of Reflexivity," *History and Theory* 45 (2006): 30–50.

1 In Search of Prussian Classicism

> The bulk of the Berlin of today has about it no suggestion of a former period. The site it stands on has traditions and a history, but the city itself has no traditions and no history. It is a new city; the newest I have ever seen.
>
> Mark Twain, *The Chicago of Europe* (1892)

1. Berlin, the Athens of Central Europe

"View Into the Heyday of Greece" (Blick in Griechenlands Blüte) is a nineteenth-century engraving by Karl Friedrich Schinkel, a prominent architect favored by the Prussian king. The panoramic view of a temple being constructed in an ancient city was a work Schinkel began creating in 1824 ahead of his second trip to Italy. On the right, a couple of unclothed men exude a warrior-like, heroic presence as they move a marble part of the temple's frieze atop its columns in Ionic order. The sight of an ideal ancient city and coastal landscape subtly unfold in the backdrop. It is a motif and atmosphere that fully reflects the times. Prussian youths and intellectuals at the time had been heavily influenced by the war Greeks fought for years to gain independence from the lengthy Ottoman rule as well as the war of liberation that took place only a few years ago to cast off the yoke of Napoleon. Could the sight of ancient Greeks full of vigor have come across as the portrayal of a new age, promising freedom and liberation? However, the actual motive for creating the work had little to do with liberation. The work was commissioned by the City of Berlin as a wedding gift for Princess Louise of Prussia and Crown Prince Frederick of the Netherlands. After its completion in 1825, the work was kept at the national gallery in Berlin for a long time until it was destroyed from an air raid by the Allied Forces in 1945. Although what now remains of the work is a copy made with oil on canvas by August Wilhelm Julius Ahlborn in 1836, the copy is known to be an exact representation of the original.[1]

What the work offers is the promise of a new city rather than liberation. Being an architect's creation, architectural metaphors permeate the

Figure 1.1 *View Into the Heyday of Greece* by August Wilhelm Julius Ahlborn (1836), oil on canvas, 94 × 235 cm.

Source: Public domain via Wikimedia Commons.

work, and even the backdrop's coastal landscape itself is overwhelmed by a man-made stone setting. Yet the work features the dynamic process of constructing a building instead of a completed version of it. The lower left side depicts what appears to be groundwork, whereas the dizzying sight on top of the colonnade to the lower right side seems to portray a challenging stage of construction in need of herculean abilities. The firm Ionic columns; the gods and heroes embossed on the pure white frieze; and the sturdy, unclothed men at work all seem to hint at some sort of authority overseeing the operations. As its title suggests, the work embodies the vision of an omnipotent authority that longs for utopia. That vision demands a capital for a new nation, an utterly masculine, well-planned, organized city full of prosperous energy similar to the golden age of ancient Greece.

Often referred to as "Athens on the River Spree" (Spree-Athen), Berlin was the new capital city where the featured painting's imaginative geography was realized to a certain degree. In Berlin is a historic boulevard where an aura of ancient Greece lingers. True to its name, Unter den Linden, meaning "Under the Linden Trees," the long, wide boulevard lined with linden trees is comparable to Champs-Élysées in the French capital Paris. With the rectangular park simply named Lustgarten at the center, one end of the boulevard is occupied by the square Alexanderplatz, a name also well known as the title of a novel by Alfred Döblin, and at the other end is Brandenburg Gate (Brandenburger Tor), a landmark akin to Sungnyemun gate in Seoul. The boulevard thus extends between this grand gate resembling the Propylaea at the Acropolis of Athens and the nearby Potsdam City Palace. Like the vanishing point of Unter den Linden, the Lustgarten's empty space is surrounded by a series of public buildings.

Right in front of the park stands the Altes Museum, with a stately colonnade decorating its façade. Opposite the museum is Berlin Palace (Berliner Schloß), undergoing reconstruction long after being destroyed under the former East German regime. The palace thereby forms a circular band alongside the magnificent neo-Baroque Berlin Cathedral (Berliner Dom), the German Historical Museum (Zeughaus) that was once an arsenal, the University of Berlin (Friedrich Wilhelm Universität) that served as an institutional model to the Tokyo Imperial University and the University of Chicago and is now called the Humboldt University of Berlin, and the Berlin State Opera (Staatsoper) standing like an ancient Greek temple. These buildings seem to represent a spatial unity between art, history, scholarship, religion, and state authority.

The one to play the most crucial role in building the topology of Unter den Linden was the Prussian state architect Friedrich Schinkel. Having sensed from ancient Greek architecture an ideal balance between beauty and virtue, Schinkel launched a series of projects to transform Berlin, the lackluster capital of the military power Prussia, with the intention of reviving ancient Athens in central Europe. The most urgent task at hand was to develop Unter den Linden into an epicenter of power and culture worthy of being admired by all in Europe. Turning the historic boulevard into Athens on the River Spree therefore required not only the introduction of new architectural techniques and an extensive rearrangement of space but a new historical identity as well.

Spree-Athen: Greek Fever and German National Culture

What inspired Schinkel to come up with such an ambitious imaginative geography? Why did Prussians so admire the periodically and spatially distant ancient Greece? Admiration for classical antiquity was a trend prevalent in Europe at the time. Unlike classicism that embraces all the various directions it branched out into since the Renaissance, neoclassicism refers to a mid-eighteenth-century trend involving art and ideas inspired by the revival of classical antiquity.[2] The excavation of the remains of Pompeii, Herculaneum, and Paestum triggered greater interest in classical cultures unaltered by European aristocracy. They aroused a desire for solemn, objective, straightforward expression that defied the exuberant, decorative, and excessively hedonistic style of Baroque and Rococo art. Yet, rather than going back in time to mindlessly imitate antiquity, such interest involved a surging desire to break free from listless formalism, readily acknowledge the difference between past and present, and create current representations of antiquity's classicality. Per the description of Walter Pater, one of the greatest nineteenth-century British prose writers, the "essentially classical element" in classical art and literature is none other than the "quality of order in beauty," which embodies the "qualities of measure, purity, temperance."[3]

The demand for classicality was especially prominent in architecture. To many European architects who had grown tired of exemplars of Renaissance, Baroque, and Rococo art, the excavation of ancient ruins provided the perfect opportunity to stray from textbook Renaissance-style ancient architectural precepts and directly explore real examples of ancient architecture. Without being overwhelming or needlessly extravagant, the far more concise, functional style of ancient architecture was worthy of becoming a new exemplar. Neoclassical architecture was the beginning of modern architecture that came to learn not only form but rational thinking from antiquity and recognize architecture as a physical actuality. This new notion was understood as a moral ideal that would suit the coming age of great revolutions and nation-states. As Jean-Baptiste Rondelet finished the Panthéon upon the foundations his teacher Jacques-Germain Soufflot designed, neoclassical architecture professing "revolutionary architecture" imitated the aesthetic ideal of ancient Rome, pursuing an absolute harmony between part and whole in order to express a new revolutionary nation's ideal.[4] The moderated use of decorations, adoption of straight lines and right angles, unified geometric spaces, and the sense that structures should fulfill their architectural function were highly appropriate for civic buildings such as museums, libraries, theatres, banks, and government offices. From Napoleon's Arc de Triomphe to middle-class Victorian residences, diverse forms of neoclassicism dominated modern European metropolises.[5]

The forerunners of neoclassical architecture were the Bavarian court architect Leo von Klenze and the Prussian architect Schinkel. Their works were typically neoclassical for stressing form and function over external ornamentation and for valuing simplicity and dignity above all else. Yet when compared to the revolutionary architecture represented by the Parisian École des Beaux-arts, something different can be noticed from the works of von Klenze and Schinkel, who attended the Building Academy in Berlin. More than anything, the two architects were completely engrossed in classical Greece. Their works were in a vein different from the rediscovery of ancient Greece that had already fairly progressed throughout Europe. Deifying classical Greek art as absolute beauty led to an unprecedented fall in ancient Rome's stature.[6]

The Germans' exceptional enthusiasm for classical Greece is most vividly demonstrated through the art historian Johann Joachim Winckelmann, who led the eighteenth-century cultural transition toward classical Greece. Winckelmann rejected extravagant Baroque art and emphasized that the imitation (Nachahmung) of classical Greek art was the only true path worth pursuing. Of course, his suggestion was not to merely imitate. It was to place Greek art within the overall image of classical Greek culture, uncover its spiritual superiority compared to other civilizations, and adopt it as an ideal standard. Through *Reflections on the Imitation of Greek Works in Painting and Sculpture* published in 1755, Winckelmann stressed that a city-state where Greek art used to be utterly free is in itself a combination of utmost beauty and morals.[7] This contrasts with how the French took ancient Rome's Latin culture as their cultural exemplar. Now the golden age of ancient Greece instead of ancient Rome had become the exemplar of neoclassicism.

This Greek fever broke out not just in Germany but grew into a general cultural trend across Europe between the late eighteenth and nineteenth centuries. The fever particularly struck Britain as hard as Germany. In the mid-eighteenth century, architects James Stuart and Nicholas Revett already published *The Antiquities of Athens* that includes detailed drawings of ancient Greek buildings. By the nineteenth century, the British Museum appeared in the heart of London, its Ionic colonnade casting the aura of an ancient Greek temple. Displaying at the museum the Elgin Marbles that used to decorate the Parthenon was a clear indication of how much Britain had actually been caught up in the Greek fever.[8] Nevertheless, Winckelmann's art history had to precede in order for romantic sentiments to be present in John Keats's *Ode on a Grecian Urn* and Percy Bysshe Shelley's *Prometheus Unbound*, for Winckelmann was the pioneer who bestowed classical Greece with a modern image and historical value.[9]

Born near the Prussian borders as the son of a cobbler, Winckelmann was naturally talented, enough to receive patronage from the Kingdom of Saxony, which was at the forefront of German Baroque court culture, and allow him to rise to the position of Prefect of Roman Antiquities in the Vatican. Yet he went ahead with a Promethean resistance against the ostentation of court culture. To the spiritually thirsty Winckelmann, ancient Greek culture represented a utopia of nature without pretense, spiritual freedom, and genius liberated from social customs. The free, open civic life of ancient Greeks seemed to suggest an exemplar for modern individuals and societies.[10] Needless to say, such an idea carried radical political undertones. By a generation later than Winckelmann, building nation-states turned into a prevalent trend across Europe, and ancient Greek republics served as the fountainhead of freedom and democracy for radicals. In revolutionary France, Sparta was actually considered the birthplace of equality, while Athens was considered the birthplace of freedom.[11] However, in German regions that had been the stronghold of restored monarchy, such revolutionary vigor was replaced by a near-religious faith in the unique origin and mission of German culture.

Greek fever in Germany was intimately merged with German new humanism (Neuhumanismus) that originated from evangelical traditions starting in the Reformation. Unlike the earlier Renaissance humanism, German new humanism assigned religious sanctity to art and literature and infused them with strong political aspirations.[12] This closely involved the particularly German ideal of self-cultivation (Bildung). Sharing an affinity with the Greek term "paideia" (παιδεία), the notion of Bildung basically applied to a limited elite class but still managed to successfully live up to the demands of the times. Against the great cause of the French Revolution, Bildung offered the finest justification for German conservatism that emphasized individual spiritual liberation. Linguist Wilhelm von Humboldt, who led Prussia's educational reform while serving as head of the Directorate of Education, fully expected the principle of Bildung to encourage individuals to conduct self-directed learning so as to evolve from natural immaturity to voluntary citizenship, thereby instilling themselves with civic responsibility and patriotism.[13] From a Prussian perspective, such a course might be regarded as a balance between cosmopolitanism (Weltbürgertum) and the exclusive nation-state principle,[14] but in reality, it would be more appropriate to say that the demands of nation-states subdued cosmopolitanism.

For self-cultivation based on new humanism, it was considered essential to gain an in-depth understanding of classical Greece. After the dissolution of the Holy Roman Empire that once kept German-speaking regions under a loose confederacy, a political center for those regions to unite under remained absent. Moreover, the religious divide between the Catholic Church and Protestants primarily made it difficult to picture a unified homeland. These were the circumstances under which a pagan civilization such as classical Greece was summoned. Friedrich Hölderlin's epistolary novel *Hyperion* that sings of a near-religious fervor for classical Greece, the periodical *The Propylaea* (Die Propyläen)[15] launched to penetrate art as the "innermost sanctuary" by Johann Wolfgang von Goethe who followed Winckelmann in regarding Greek sculpture as an eternal artistic ideal, and the science of antiquity (Altertumswissenschaft) studied at the University of Berlin and the University of Göttingen that later took root in Britain and the United States as a new field of study called "classics" were all but a fraction of the widespread Greek fever's influence at the time.[16]

The early Greek enthusiasts remained in aristocratic contemplation of the ideal truth, goodness, and beauty, whereas in the nineteenth century, states built the foundation to systematically study them. Ancient Greek syntax and poems continued to be mandatory subjects of study at institutions of higher education, including universities and gymnasiums. Other various public institutions such as museums and research institutes also helped spread knowledge about and interest in classical Greece, which greatly contributed to forming a uniquely German educated bourgeoisie (Bildungsbürgertum). This trend continued until the early twentieth century and led to the smuggling of parts of a temple from the ancient kingdom of Pergamon, as well as the amateur archaeologist Heinrich Schliemann's excavation of the site of Troy.[17] Why did Germans fix their gaze upon classical Athens when it had been far more ancient and distant than classical Rome?

In every respect, the German view of classical Greece was based on need rather than fact. German writers indeed made exaggerations as if they had been the first to discover classical Greece, even though they had to rely on ancient Roman writers, Roman-era replicas of Greek sculptures, or works by Italian humanists and French philosophers. Winckelmann was typical of such German writers. He had never actually been to Greece.[18] Although masked by the modern science of paleology, philology, history, or ethnology, the affinity between the German and Greek languages or the Aryan blood lineage based on such an affinity is now merely regarded as a historical episode. The more modern science propounds objectivity and depoliticization, the more it is accused of being an ideology that defends actual power. The logic of paleologists that excludes politics and only highlights the ideal truth, goodness, and beauty when discussing classical Greece is just as ideological as the logic of republicans that sets ancient Greek democracy as the exemplar of modern democracy.[19] The "invention" of Greece by German intellectuals pursuing German new humanism was in fact closer to historical distortion. Excessive ideality is merely a fear of revolutionary change, an expression of political frustration toward an unpredictable future. Modern Germany's image of classical Greece was definitely far from democratic ideals. *The Tyranny of Greece Over Germany* is a famous book title that cynically hints at how such a tyranny determined modern Germany's cultural topography.[20]

This German recognition of classical Greece gained support from the current of romanticism with a basically anti-revolutionary tone. German romanticism sprung as writers and artists rebelled against the French philosophers' revolutionary dogmatism that refused to recognize the inherent culture of other countries. Irrepressible impulses and enthusiasm gave birth to dreams, ideas as well as sentences and rhythms of a new, bizarre beauty. The mysticity of medieval religions was reborn from the spirit to rebel against the crude reality.[21] German romanticists deeply admired not only their roots that went back to the Middle Ages but classical Greece as well. This dual admiration may appear contradictory at first, but the two were able to coincide well since they were facing a common enemy. German intellectuals had such profound antagonism toward natural law originating from ancient Rome as well as French Enlightenment ideas based on that natural law so that to defy them, they would have gone as far as to shake hands with the devil.[22] To Germans, classical Greece psychologically felt far closer to the Middle Ages than classical Rome or even their neighbor France. So, it was no coincidence when Friedrich Schiller and Friedrich Schlegel, the writers who sparked romanticism, referred to Germans as "modern Greeks."[23]

The Walhalla is a memorial on a valley overlooking the Danube River in southeast Germany. The German temple reminiscent of the Parthenon in Athens was meant to memorialize Germany's liberation from Napoleon in 1814. However, it was not until 1830 when its construction began and took twelve years to finish under the supervision of Leo von Klenze, one of the most prominent architects at the time. The building's conception actually occurred much earlier. In 1806, when Napoleon's forces dissolved the Holy Roman Empire that had lasted for more than a millennium, a considerable number of German states ended up being incorporated under Napoleon's Confederation of the Rhine (Rheinbund). The acute national humiliation of allowing France to take over the left side of the Rhine prompted Ludwig Karl August, the crown prince of the Kingdom of Bavaria, to conceive a national memorial signifying the revival of Germans. Once he ascended the throne as Ludwig I in 1825, he was finally able to push forward with the Walhalla's construction.[24]

Caught up in the Greek fever at the time, Ludwig I sought to express the German national identity through peripteros, a type of ancient Greek temple surrounded by marble columns. However, the building was named Walhalla after a war hero who appears in a German myth. Since a non-existent national identity had been found in an imaginary world in the faraway past, the difference between German and Greek myths did not matter. At the center of the building that opened in 1842 is the Hall of Fame (Ruhmestempel). Installed in the hall are rows of commemorative plaques and busts featuring two hundred artists, politicians, scholars, and monarchs representative of the two-thousand-year-old German history.[25] Like ancient heroes, they don a veil of remote times. The proud descendants of Athena have been resurrected upon a holy altar of nationalism.

Prussia and Athens

The romantic yearning for ancient Greece was in fact a desire for a new political center. And what filled the lack of politics in the absence of a unified country was none other than culture. The mother tongue, traditional culture, and pride in a common history were what stirred up the fervent yearning for a fatherland. However, it was difficult to find a unique cultural homogeneity other than language among German-speaking regions. Amid the religious strife between Catholicism and Protestantism, the pagan civilization of classical Greece offered an alternative image of a fatherland. Classical Greece emerged as the embodiment of a new Germany free from devastating memories of religious wars.

What was most Greek became the most German. The German combination of romanticism and classicism was practically the product of an unsatisfactory reality, like the notion of the Middle Ages, the notion of classical Greece, namely an ideal image of it provided a baseline for criticizing reality. Inasmuch as the romanticist writer Friedrich Schlegel lamented as if he had lost his homeland, classical Greece came to be remembered as an irreversible "golden age" and poems from that age the "prototype of art and taste" that attained a perfect harmony.[26]

Romanticism with an intersecting view of the Middle Ages and ancient Greece thrived all over Germany. Its former capital, Heidelberg, where first love blooms for the crown prince in *Old Heidelberg*, particularly served as an infinite source of inspiration. However, the true capital of romanticism newly emerged according to the topography of power: Berlin, the capital of Prussia that established itself as the leader of Germany. If the strongholds of classicist literature were Goethe's second hometown Weimar and Jena, where Schiller worked as a university professor, Berlin was the stronghold of romantic literature.[27] The relocation of Ludwig Achim von Arnim, the author of the collection of German folk songs *The Boy's Magic Horn* (Des Knaben Wunderhorn), from Heidelberg to Berlin in 1809 turned out to be quite a symbolic occasion. Arnim was the one who led the foundation of the Christian-German Table Society (Christlich-Deutsche Tischgesellschaft) in 1811, which played a decisive role in establishing Berlin as a pivot of the German romantic movement. Among the prominent intellectuals who led the society's foundation alongside Arnim were the theorist of the state Adam Heinrich Müller, the Prussian general and military theorist Carl von Clausewitz, the theology professor Friedrich Schleiermacher, the law professor Friedrich Karl von Savigny, Clemens Brentano who co-authored *The Boy's Magic Horn* with Arnim in Heidelberg, and the young architect Schinkel. The political directionality the Christian-German Table Society aimed for was clear: inheriting and developing the German people's inherent culture so as to achieve national liberation and unification.[28]

Romanticism and classicism solemnly entered into wedlock in Berlin and were thus able to conceive a hale and hearty child named Prussian classicism. The arduous task of shaping a German national culture with imagined images of classical Greece unfolded in various fields, including literature, humanities, music, painting, sculpture, crafts, and architecture. It would, of course, be a stretch to say only Prussia strived to invent classical Greece, since it had been a general trend throughout Germany as well as Europe. Yet there was indeed something unique about Prussia. To the culturally weak Kingdom of Prussia on the rise in terms of military power, reproducing classical Greece went beyond the realm of culture to be recognized as a geopolitical inevitability. To stand up to the stronghold of Catholicism and the ancient Rome-oriented, Latin-based culture dominant in western Europe at the time, Prussian intellectuals came up with a cultural lineage between ancient Greece and Germany that had strong Protestant overtones. Unlike the states of southern Germany that remained in the Catholic realm, the Kingdom of Prussia professed to be the guardian of "cultural Protestantism" (Kulturprotestantismus) aimed at a more open, enlightened church, making it possible to imagine a "pure" ancient Greece with no traces of ancient Rome. This alternative cultural course pursuing a spirit far more pure and upright than that of the Latin-based realm presented the rising power in central Europe with a national identity and mission.[29] And to form an entirely new center, it became necessary to introduce a completely new imaginative geography.

This trend was also facilitated by international circumstances in the early nineteenth century. The war Greeks went through in the 1820s to gain independence from the Ottoman Empire reminded Germans of the wars of liberation they recently had to fight against Napoleon's empire. Around the time, philhellenism swept across Germany and Europe to surface as a stage of competition for various political ideologies such as republicanism, liberalism, democracy, and even racism.[30] In the Kingdom of Prussia, philhellenism took an extremely conservative, nationalistic turn and maintained its course throughout the Prussian-led unification of Germany that resulted in the German Empire. The rather crusade-like idea of establishing a Greco-German civilization had been carried out by internally promoting a single national culture and externally taking advantage of a gap in power left by the Ottoman Empire's fall. The German Empire's enthusiastic excavation of Olympia and Pergamon was not merely an archaeological achievement but clearly part of an imperialistic advancement.[31]

The underlying nature of philhellenism in Prussia can be gauged from Wilhelm von Humboldt, a symbolic figure of early nineteenth-century neohumanism. Humboldt was an intellectual too balanced to be engrossed in a particular political ideology, yet he failed to remain free from Prussian nationalism. Through *The History of the Decline and Fall of the Greek Republics* published in 1807, he projected the history of ancient Athens onto that of his homeland Prussia and equated the fate of Germans with the tragic fate of ancient Greece, which flourished culturally but was divided politically.[32] To Humboldt, ancient Greece was not of the past but more like an oracle forewarning Germans of their fate. Now that classical Athens reestablished its dominion in central Europe, its great cultural achievements would continue to stand firm. According to Humboldt's confessional description, only from knowledge about ancient Greece "can we find the ideal of what we ourselves aspire to become or strive to create."[33] Hence, classical Greece served as an imaginary center, a reference point from which to consider and transcend all things in the mundane world.

Forum Fridericianum

Even before classical Greece was established as the ideological standard for German nationalism, Prussian classicism was already budding in various areas. It was yet to come up with ideas or forms that would distinguish it from neoclassicism in other parts of Europe, but the soil had already been prepared for them to blossom later on. Architecture was no doubt the area that led the neoclassical culture in eighteenth century Berlin, and at its forefront was Baron Georg Wenzeslaus von Knobelsdorff. As court architect, Baron Knobelsdorff was not strictly a neoclassicist since he had been deeply influenced by Andrea Palladio's "High Renaissance" (Cinquecento) architecture and favored French Rococo décor. Yet he distanced himself from the flamboyant silhouette and excessively embossed, engraved façade of Baroque architecture and instead pursued plain and simple outlines, as did many eighteenth-century architects of northern European protestant states. The Forum Fridericianum he designed by order of the king became a monumental place that proclaimed the beginning of Prussian classicism.[34]

The Prussian kingdom's capital Berlin had long been a twin city since the thirteenth century from forming loose ties with a medieval fortress town called Cölln along the river to its left. In the early fifteenth century, Frederick of the House of Hohenzollern in southern Germany spent a fortune to become the elector of and thereby take over the Margraviate of Brandenburg from the Holy Roman Emperor who ruled central Europe. Previously the Burgrave of Nuremberg, Frederick had been quick in rising to the position of elector, one of only seven in the Holy Roman Empire. And as the elector of Brandenburg built a new palace in northern Cölln during the mid-fifteenth century, the twin city Berlin-Cölln came under the control of the House of Hohenzollern. By the early seventeenth century, the Margraviate of Brandenburg expanded into Brandenburg-Prussia when it came under the control of the same elector who governed the Duchy of Prussia established on the Baltic coast by Teutonic Knights.[35]

While the twin city went through three decades of religious war in the seventeenth century, a fortress was built around it. After the war, new quarters were added to the city: the elector's domain Friedrichswerder on the west side of Cölln, the lengthy Lindenallee leading to the elector's hunting ground, Dorotheenstadt on the north side of Friedrichswerder, and Friedrichstadt below Dorotheenstadt. An old map from the mid-seventeenth century shows the layout of Berlin-Cölln surrounded by the fortress with the river Spree running in between. To the bottom left is Lindenallee that later develops into Unter den Linden. As the Kingdom of Prussia was established through a political arrangement of sorts by the early eighteenth century, the king Frederick I merged Berlin-Cölln with its surrounding quarters to transform it into an administrative city where the Prussian army would be stationed. Berlin was thus reborn as the capital of the Kingdom of Prussia. Compared to Paris or Rome, Berlin near the border was practically barren, but the city evolved over the eighteenth century into a center of industry and commerce, mainly the textile industry with the royal family's support. And under the rule of Frederick II, better known as Frederick the Great (Friedrich der Große), Berlin finally gained an aura befitting the capital of a civilized country.[36]

After leading in the Seven Years' War to victory in the mid-eighteenth century, Frederick II sought to build a palace dignified enough to reflect Prussia's rise to power and comparable to palaces in any other European city. Berlin, however, already had a royal palace. An old castle the House of Hohenzollern built in the center of Berlin had been transformed into a palace when Frederick I had the court architect Andreas Schlüter expand

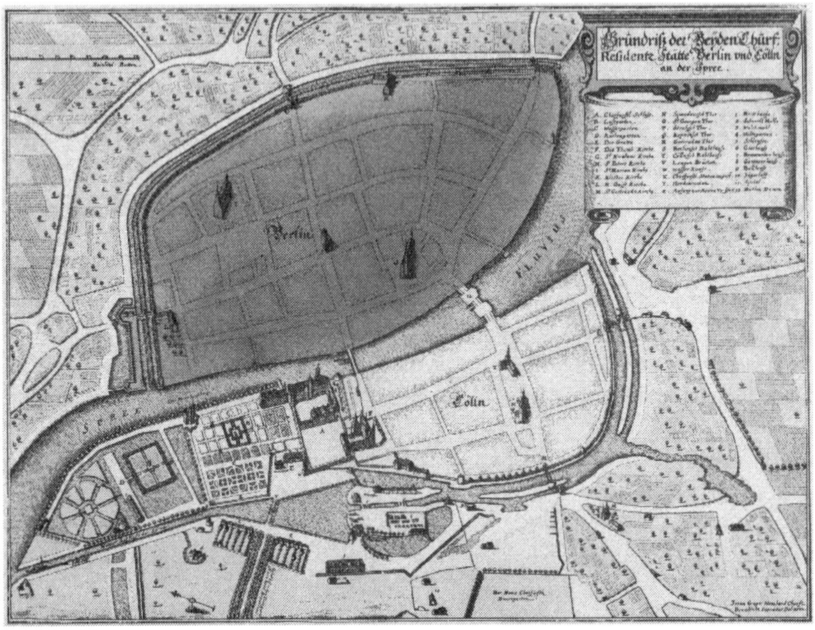

Figure 1.2 Layout of Berlin-Cölln by Johann Gregor Memhardt (1652), copperplate.

Source: Public domain via Wikimedia Commons.

the castle in 1698. Since then, the royal palace standing opposite the Lustgarten was further expanded and came to be referred to as the "Berlin Palace" (Berliner Schloß).[37] Nevertheless, the royal palace Frederick II had in mind was far grander. The new palace would be lavishly decorated with sculptures and reliefs for the sole purpose of glorifying the king's great achievements. But this plan was soon scaled down and altered into constructing a row of Baroque-style buildings to form the "Square at the Opera House" (Platz am Opernhaus). Per the king's orders, Knobelsdorff designed a cluster of Baroque-style buildings widely spread out on a plot of land at the northern end of Lindenallee.

The Square at the Opera House was intended to resemble the Forum Romanum of ancient Rome as well as the Agora of ancient Athens, which had been a public space that also served as a marketplace. If the intention had been realized, the square would have become a grand central plaza comparable to Place de la Concorde in Paris or Trafalgar Square in London. Of course, it wasn't as if Berlin was without a square. There was one alongside Friedrichstraße, one of Berlin's main streets, where, by royal order, the stables of the "Gens d'armes" cuirassier regiment had been turned into the marketplace Gendarmenmarkt. However, the square came to be primarily used for military parades and never managed to settle down as the center of the city. Despite having been a heroic king who did much to improve Prussia's fate, Frederick William I, the father of Frederick II, eventually failed to follow through on his plans to turn the royal family's private garden Lustgarten into a palace square called Schloßplatz and to create another square similar to Place Royale in Paris, which included a monument dedicated to his predecessor standing upon the slope outside the city's fortress walls.[38]

The plans Frederick II had for the Prussian capital Berlin indeed served as a turning point for the city's development. Whereas previous plans had been centered upon a medieval city built around a fortress, the new Forum Fridericianum was aimed at building the capital's true center, fit to rule a modern state in terms of appearance as well as function. Plans for this large-scale construction project launched right after Frederick II rose to the throne had already been in the making since the king was crown prince, which was when he began to form close relations with Knobelsdorff, who oversaw the expansion of the crown prince's residence Rheinsberg Castle. Despite being launched in 1740 as soon as Frederick II rose to the throne, the grand project failed to proceed as originally planned due to a series of impediments. A distant relative of the king who owned a small palace at the center of the project site refused to sell his property; then the Silesian Wars in which Prussia struggled with other European powers to gain hegemony led to delays in the construction schedule. Furthermore, the king later shifted his interest away from the complexities in Berlin and grew more attached to the new palace being built in Potsdam. Nevertheless, the original design for Forum Fridericianum was partially realized in an altered form. Since 1747, classical-style buildings began to appear on a rather slanted rectangular site not too far away from the project's initial site.

Starting with the Royal Court Opera (Königliche Hofoper), buildings emerged one by one from St. Hedwig's Cathedral, reminiscent of the Roman Pantheon, on the southwestern corner of the Court Opera, and the baroque Supreme Parish Church on the Lustgarten's east side. With a Corinthian colonnaded façade similar to that of the Court Opera, Prince Henry's Palace (Palais des Prinzen Heinrich) later came to serve as the main building of one of Germany's finest universities. Opposite the Court Opera's west side appeared the Royal Library (Königliche Bibliothek) that earned the nickname "Kommode" for its curved façade. Among these buildings, the Court Opera (presently the State Opera) was the only one built according to Knobelsdorff's original design and thus was monumental for signaling the true beginning of Prussian classicism.[39]

Although its stature changed due to the frequent corrections made to the square's original design, the Court Opera maintained its central position and lived up to the name Square at the Opera House as the most faithful realization of Knobelsdorff's architectural aesthetics. Inspired by the British Palladian style,[40] the building's portico with six columns was simple without being too grand, making the building look just like an ancient Greek temple. The numbers of floors, functions, and decorations varied between the building's three different sections, but the sections still meshed naturally with one another like an ancient Greek amphitheater. The building was designed so that for occasions such as banquets, the doors to the Apollo Hall, the balcony for saluting the crowd, and the stage could all be opened to form a single, larger space. Barely a year after its construction began, the building ended up hosting its first performance in December 1742 despite being incomplete.[41]

Designed to be admired from all four sides, the features and central location of the Court Opera overtly revealed the motive for creating the Forum Fridericianum. It was dedicated as a temple to worship art. To create the opera house's Greek aura, it is said that Palladio's Villa "La Rotonda" in Italy served as a reference, a building famous for taking its motif from ancient Roman temples. Frederick II had been most fond of the architectural style preferred by the Italian nobility, which is probably why he personally drafted a basic layout of the opera house and asked Knobelsdorff to faithfully realize his vision. Built right next to the Crown Prince's Palace (Kronprinzenpalais), the opera house's distinctly neoclassical portico with six columns adheres to proportions of its own that are disparate from those of the building's interior, while the stairs leading to the building's entrance on either side or the roughly finished architrave have been arranged to accommodate the conditions of the street in front of building rather than the building itself. Upon the pediment supported by columns are the god of music Apollo flanked by the muse of tragedy Melpomene and the muse of comedy Thalia, which is more of a Rococo rather than neoclassical motif.[42]

Once the Silesian Wars ended, the Prussian king lost interest in the Forum Fridericianum and was more eager to build the Sanssouci Palace in Potsdam. The petite pink-and-white French Rococo–style palace that surfaced in the city of royal and noble residences took the spotlight away from the vast public square at the heart of Berlin. Moreover, the king considered himself an architect and had an unwavering, outdated taste that was bound to clash at every step with Knobelsdorff's neoclassical pursuits. This eventually prompted the king to instead hire the Baroque-style architect Johann Boumann the Elder to design the palace for the crown prince Henry. Such were the limitations of the times that inevitably led to a chaotic outcome.[43]

The ambitiously planned Square at the Opera House hence was reduced to having Prince Henry's Palace at its northern end and St. Hedwig's Cathedral at its southern end. The reason the square lacked the typical symmetry and harmony of Baroque style urban spaces was partly because of the failure to acquire Palais Schwedt, standing at the center of

Figure 1.3 Top Left: The Court Opera and Berlin's Square at the Opera House by Joseph Maximilian Kolb (1850), Steel Plate. Top Right: A Current View of the Former Royal Library on Bebel Square. Bottom: Military Parade at the Opera Square (circa 1825).

Source: Top Left: Public domain via Wikimedia Commons. Top Right: Photo by author (2018). Bottom: Artist unknown, aquatint, from *Karl Friedrich Schinkel: Eine Ausstellung aus der Deutschen Demokratischen Republik* (Berlin: Henschelverlag, 1982), Illustration no. 5.6.

the project's initial site. Yet, more fundamentally, it was because a grand Catholic church like St. Hedwig's Cathedral dedicated to the patron of Silesia was belatedly fitted into a narrow corner of the square to politically demonstrate Prussia's religious tolerance after the Silesian Wars. Also, the construction project ultimately devoted less attention to the overall arrangement of the square's space and more to the exterior of individual buildings such as Prince Henry's Palace or the Supreme Parish Church.[44]

Although various factors prevented the Square at the Opera House's construction from accomplishing its original goal, the Forum Fridericianum served as an opportunity to completely reshape Berlin's appearance as a capital city. The addition of unparalleled buildings created a new cityscape where academics and art would live and breathe. What gave vitality to the new scene akin to a revived ancient city was Unter den Linden. This boulevard running through the much-reduced square had been developed since the mid-seventeenth century as a passage connecting the elector's former hunting ground Tiergarten to Berlin Palace. The elector's private passage was elevated to a boulevard in the early eighteenth century when Frederick William I declared the section beyond Tiergarten heading west up to the queen's summer residence Charlottenburg Palace (Schloß Charlottenburg) a public road. Over the eighteenth century, Unter den Linden evolved into a grand boulevard full of public offices and residences and eventually became the vanishing line for the perspective of a newly imagined geography reinforced by the construction of the Forum Fridericianum.[45]

An anonymous etching from circa 1825 depicts an almost photographic view of the Square at the Opera House. On the panorama's left is Prince Henry's Palace that was already occupied by the University of Berlin and the Court Opera standing opposite the former palace. On the center left is the New Guardhouse (Neue Wache) designed by Schinkel and the Arsenal (Zeughaus) built beforehand, while the Crown Prince's Palace stands on the center right. Partially visible in the background is the Berlin Palace to the right and trees in the Lustgarten to the left.

Considerably reduced from the original plan, Forum Fridericianum failed to gain much recognition among the public and underwent a complete change of image two centuries later when the East German socialist regime renamed it Bebel Square (Bebelplatz) after the socialist politician August Bebel.[46] Nevertheless, the square wasn't necessarily a failed project. The Court Opera's construction raised the curtain on the extensive "invention" of Berlin as the capital of the new military power Prussia.

Apart from working on the square, Frederick II ordered Knobelsdorff to build a symbolic park for Berlin. Knobelsdorff had previous experience in collaborating with the king on creating a French-style garden back at Rheinsberg Castle. A park comparable to those in Paris was to be formed as "Parc de Berlin" at Tiergarten stretching out to the west beside the Brandenburg Gate, the entrance to Berlin. Ditches were dug to drain the marshy grounds of Tiergarten, which literally means "zoo" in German. A central axis was formed for the park, an axis which then served as a node in building a long, wide boulevard linking Unter den Linden to Charlottenburg Palace in western Berlin.[47] A victory column (Siegessäule) was later erected sky high upon the node to commemorate Prussia's victory in the Franco-Prussian War, which is now the center of a junction where a grand boulevard, named the 17th of June Street (Straße des 17. Juni) to commemorate the 1953 workers' uprising in East Germany, splits into eight different lanes. Tiergarten's appearance changed considerably thereafter, but it remains the first German park specifically created for public use. Along with Forum Fridericianum signifying the power of an absolute monarchy, the park had been part of a plan to completely transform Berlin into a modern city. This indicates that even before the French Revolution, the basic spatial order of Prussian classicism had already been settling down.

By the time the reign of Frederick was nearing its end, a new architectural trend was thriving in Prussia. Frederick the Great's taste shifted from French Rococo and Italian Palladio toward a German style influenced by ancient Greece. And the Brandenburg Gate built right after his death was established as a new exemplar. The monument designed by the Silesia-born architect Carl Gotthard Langhans was originally named the "Peace Gate" (Friedenstor). Inspired by the Propylaea of Athens, the gate's horizontal entablature decorated with bas-reliefs exhibits the austere aura of archaic Greece. The quadriga atop the gate driven by a winged goddess of peace is a masterpiece by Johann Gottfried Schadow, one of the most prominent sculptors at the time. However, the sculpture was soon swept up in historical turmoil. When Berlin was occupied by Napoleon's army, the quadriga was taken away to Paris, then restored to its original position upon Prussia's liberation, only to be transformed into a chariot of triumph. The original design by Schadow had the goddess of peace holding a laurel wreath as a trophy, but the wreath was replaced by a hostile lance bedecked with an iron cross and imperial eagle, turning the goddess of peace into a goddess of victory. The one responsible for the replacement was Schinkel, a young obscure architect whose name would be made immortal from creating "Athens on the River Spree" (Spree-Athen).[48]

2. Between a Nation and Its King: The Prussian State Architect Schinkel

The French Revolution and repeated wars of aggression had a definitive impact upon Prussian classicism as much as they did on the political course of Prussia. Crushed by Napoleon's boots, Prussia sought to attain power and prosperity by hurriedly carrying out top-down modernization and struggling to forestall all sorts of rebellious movements rising from the bottom up. In terms of culture, Prussian classicism was at the heart of a search for values entirely different from Revolutionary France. Originally placing more weight on continuity rather than an abrupt disconnection between past and present, neoclassicism was able to fully manifest in a unique tone different from Revolutionary France once it reached conservative Germany.

Prussian Classicism as an Aesthetic Revolution

While Parisians stormed Bastille, the Brandenburg Gate was being peacefully built in Berlin. Political upheaval was for the French, not the Germans. Rather than changing external circumstances, a true revolution meant a revolution in the mind for Germany. The French built a new state, but Germans created great everlasting works of art by giving birth to Goethe instead of Robespierre. This notion was most obviously expressed through what the romanticist Friedrich Schlegel expounded as "aesthetic revolution."[49]

Prussian classicist architecture was an aesthetic upheaval of sorts that replaced a political upheaval, seeking to shape the capital into a symbolic center of Prussia. Hence, the ordinary capital Berlin was to turn into an icon of Prussia's rise and even started to be envisioned as a cultural pivot for the entire German nation.[50] Architects like Carl Gotthard Langhans, who designed the Brandenburg Gate; Heinrich Gentz; and David Gilly and his ingenious son Friedrich Gilly took the lead in realizing an imaginary Athens at the Prussian capital. Their infatuation with the modest and simple yet grand style of ancient Greek architecture was a reaction against the so-called "empire style" of Napoleonic neoclassicism that professed the new Roman empire's pretentious splendor.[51] And as the king's approval in 1799 elevated the private architecture school run by David Gilly to the Building Academy in Berlin (Berliner Bauakademie), a stronghold of Prussian classicism was established to stand up to the École des Beaux-Arts in Paris.

The one truly worthy of representing Prussian classicist architecture was, however, not David Gilly but his student and future state architect Karl Friedrich Schinkel. Born in 1781 in the town of Neuruppin, Schinkel later moved to the nearby capital where he succeeded in becoming an architect and civil servant. His personal success went in tandem with the progress the Prussian state made by liberating itself from the fetters of Napoleon and solidifying its position as a European power. Schinkel served as state architect and headed the Prussian Department of Public Works during the reign of Frederick William III (1797–1840). Frederick William III's successor Frederick William IV also placed full confidence in Schinkel starting when he was crown prince. After Schinkel's death, Frederick William IV remained at the forefront of realizing the great architect's ideas by continuing to actively support pupils of Schinkel like Friedrich Ludwig Persius and Friedrich August Stüler. Historically, the period when Schinkel was active is known as the Restoration that followed the fall of Napoleon. Just as Knobelsdorff worked closely with Frederick II in Rheinsberg, Schinkel launched large-scale projects with Frederick William IV to build public monuments and spaces in Berlin, contributing to spatially realizing the Prussian monarchy's traditional ideals of being the guardian of German national culture and the Protestant church.[52]

The neo-classicist Schinkel was originally a proponent of Gothic architecture. Like any other young Prussian intellectual who dreamt of breaking free from Napoleon, Schinkel as an artist considered Gothic the style representative of Germany as a nation. On the other hand, he tended to be critical of the geometric proportions devoid of individuality that eighteenth-century neoclassicism pursued. He was convinced that Gothic was a style fundamentally capable of bringing endless freedom that went beyond the limitations of life in order to organically bridge the divide among members of the German nation. Schinkel was, after all, a member of the Christian-German Table Society (Christlich-Deutsche Tischgesellschaft), a well-known group of romanticists in Berlin.

Schinkel's belief, however, experienced a significant shift as Napoleon exited the stage of history and the Restoration occurred. In 1815, he rose to the senior position of Privy Building Officer (Geheimer Oberbaurat) in charge of overseeing all of Prussia's state construction projects. From thereon, he abandoned his former Gothic taste and turned into a neo-classicist. The transition was practically the result of having compromised with political power. Because the Prussian monarchy did not welcome the revolutionary spirit nationalism advocated and preferred the more orderly style of classicism, Schinkel came to describe himself as a neo-classicist pursing "artistic peace" so as to gain the king's trust and be charged with supervising major construction projects.[53]

Should Schinkel's transition be understood as betrayal for the sole sake of a successful career? Or was it the inevitable fate of an architect with no choice but to conform to power? Or was it simply because he had grown cleverer with age? For whatever reason, there is no question that he turned away from his belief to chase the radiance of power. Besides, there were no other paths for architects to choose from at the time. Nevertheless, it is necessary to take note of the fact that Schinkel's neoclassicism had originally been quite nationalistic and based on a world view that contrasted with French revolutionary architecture. So, although he switched from Gothic to neoclassicism, Schinkel's architecture remained anti-French to the end.

There is one thing that may offer a clue to understanding Schinkel's rather ambiguous ideological position. Throughout the 1820s, Schinkel was fascinated by the German neoclassicism the great writer Goethe and his pupils advocated,[54] which was a German mixture of romanticism and classicism.[55] Discontent from having been driven into a new reality by the French Revolution gave birth to an endless nostalgic yearning for an idealized past. While neoclassicism used the classicality of the ancient past as a source to pursue the revival of a humanist culture, romanticism replaced the principle of criticism based on nature and reason propounded by Enlightenment thinking with a new principle of religion called history. What neoclassicism and romanticism had in common, though, was that they both idealized the past. And like any other pre-existing religion, history thereby settled as a transcendental basis providing order to all things current. Rather than being a journey of revolutionary progress, history came to be distinctly recognized as a story of humans discovering their own individual value and identity from taking part in an ethical community that uniquely unfolds through cultural practices such as language, customs, myths, and art. And to think how exciting it must have been to travel upstream back to remote times in search of a nation's roots![56] To put it the way the romanticist Schlegel did, a historian was fit to be "a prophet looking backward" rather than a hopeful preacher of a revolutionary future.[57]

A manifestation of such a romantic spirit was the Gothic fever that had captivated young Schinkel's soul. Gothic was not just a style but a gospel awakening the spirit of a nation. Gothic buildings, including the Strasbourg Cathedral (Straßburger Münster) much praised by Goethe and the Malbork Castle (Ordensburg Marienburg) in eastern Prussia, which began to be restored in 1815 based on the design from 1794 by Schinkel's teacher and friend Friedrich Gilly, were regarded as expressions of a national culture's incommensurable individuality. To Schinkel, Gothic and neoclassicism, or medieval religion and ancient reason, were not necessarily rivals but elements that could be combined into a modern synthesis, not through a confusing impulse from the bottom up but through the Prussian "state order." By devoting most of his efforts toward designing buildings for the public or the royal family, urban planning, and the preservation of historical remains, Schinkel used Gothic or neoclassical styles to help envision the national culture of Germany.[58]

In no way did the switch to neoclassicism therefore signify Gothic's discontinuation. On the contrary, Schinkel began to construct in 1824 a Gothic building called the Friedrichswerder Church (Friedrichswerdersche Kirche) at the center of Berlin per the king's orders. Developed long ago as the elector's domain and later serving as the site of a huge public market at one point, the Friedrichswerder area was brimming with residential houses and government offices. An overly grand building would have found it difficult to blend into the area. The Friedrichswerder Church, finished in 1828, is a simple, rectangular building made of the typical red bricks of northern Germany and is divided vertically by low but distinct towers. The building's façade is overwhelmed by a large, lengthy pediment window at the center with a belfry standing on either side.[59]

Instead of being resurrected in its medieval form, Gothic experienced a glorious revival across Europe in the nineteenth century that came to be referred to as "neo-Gothic," a Gothic suitable for an entirely new age. British buildings were mainly responsible for making the neo-Gothic style internationally known, a notable example being the Palace of Westminster in London.[60] Neo-gothic gave modern political meaning to a style with a rich history. The neo-Gothic style's broad application to not only chapels but public offices throughout the nineteenth century demonstrates the reality that in the modern world, the authority of the church had been replaced by that of the state, and the state had established itself as the church's substitute in administering life and death for the people.[61] Neo-Gothic was therefore not too far from neoclassicism in that it was inspired by the continuity between past and present. The Friedrichswerder Church by Schinkel also falls under the neo-Gothic architectural

Figure 1.4 Elevation and Floor Plan of Friedrichswerder Church.

Source: From Carl Friedrich Schinkel, *Sammlung architektonischer Entwürfe* (Berlin: Ernst & Korn, 1858), plate 86. Courtesy of the Smithsonian Libraries. https://library.si.edu/digital-library/book/sammlungarchite00schi

style that began in Britain and grew predominant in northern Europe. To design the church, Schinkel himself also admitted that he had referred to English chapels.[62] Yet what is characteristic about the church is not the style but rather the theme it attempted to convey, which was to use planarity and verticality to visually reproduce a balance between the Protestant church and the Prussian state power. Such an intention can easily be recognized from the following comment Schinkel left.

> In this eternally extraordinary time, a great sacred monument, a church is to be built in the poignant style of old German construction, though its completion will be left for the times to come when wonderful and beneficent reviews of antiquity interrupt the development of construction, thereby demonstrating that the world will have to become masterful enough to absorb the elements still necessary for this art to attain completion.[63]

Despite the fairly palliative tone, Schinkel's words reveal his level-headed prediction that the "old German," "poignant" Gothic style will be replaced by neoclassicism based on "wonderful and beneficent reviews of antiquity," as well as his firm belief that only when the two styles are mixed together can architectural art at last attain completion. Underneath lies the sense that be it Gothic, neoclassical, or any other style, an architect's true challenge is to uncover the hidden potential in old styles that have retreated into the deep, wide abyss of history and make such potential meet and serve new historical developments. What seemed necessary was not to borrow individual forms but to reorganize the entire iconographic order that blends everything together.

With an exterior that gives an early medieval vibe, the Friedrichswerder Church was positioned so that it would overlook Schinkel's other works nearby: the neoclassical building Neue Wache (New Guardhouse) and the Altes Museum (Old Museum) at Berlin's symbolic center Lustgarten. The Neue Wache was to represent the Prussian state's authority and glory, while the Altes Museum was to serve as an educational venue for Prussian citizens. In many ways, the two buildings were in contrast to the Friedrichswerder Church. Such representations of religious or secular culture and the rivalry between them reflected what formed the basis of Prussia's ideology as a Protestant state. Unlike the self-contained, natural, static tone of classicism, the steepled Gothic church appears to be dynamic, self-transcendent, and full of Christian spirituality. Having the two contrasting styles face one another from afar can be regarded as a spatial embodiment of a balance between national liberation and sacred tradition, or between civic liberty and state power.[64] What, then, did such a balance nested in the heart of Berlin mean in reality?

Far from being radical or revolutionary, Prussian classicist architecture clearly headed toward a conservative direction that Friedrich Gilly turned to early on. Before dying young, the genius architect who profoundly influenced Schinkel projected his bold ideals through a design in 1797 for a monument dedicated to Frederick the Great, which included a new gateway to Berlin as well as a grand plaza reminiscent of the Acropolis of Athens. Placed upon a high, massive rectangular podium was a typical peripteral temple surrounded by a basic, geometric arrangement of Doric columns. In short, Friedrich Gilly's design accentuated a primitive vigor specific to ancient Greece. The ambitious design suggested a blueprint for the Kingdom of Prussia's unlimited power and cultural achievements. Although the design was never realized, it demonstrated alongside Malbork Castle an ideal combination between a romantic sense of a nation's history and neoclassical aesthetic norms.[65] However, this sort of portrayal of power wholly reflected an oppressed reality far from a revolutionary fervor for liberty and democracy. When the Greek War of Independence broke out in 1821, many volunteers headed to Greece to join the fight in pursuit of ideals of freedom, but people in the kingdoms of Prussia, Austria, and Saxony, where the influence of the Restoration prevailed, were banned from traveling to Greece. Such kingdoms had sought to prevent the impact of revolutionary uprisings from spreading, making the glorification of Greece no longer a rationale of liberation but against it.[66]

Neue Wache, the Dawn of Prussian Classicism

The first commission Schinkel received from the Prussian king was to design the Neue Wache, or the New Guardhouse. The building that may well go down as the first construction of Prussian classicist architecture had been conceived by Frederick William III himself. It was primarily meant to be used by the guards on duty around the Crown Prince's Palace. At the onset of the Restoration, however, it was to also serve as a national memorial to commemorate Prussia's glorious victory in the Napoleonic Wars, or Wars of Liberation. This, in fact, made the Neue Wache the first public building planned since the end of the Napoleonic Wars. Since opening in 1818, its harmonious combination of practical and symbolic functions allowed the Neue Wache to be considered a perfect realization of Prussian classicism's spatial, historical ideals.[67]

In terms of style, the Neue Wache delivers an adequate variation of ancient Roman and Greek architectural motifs. The square-shaped building's courtyard-style arrangement with hefty corner risalits allowing all four sides to be exposed is reminiscent of an ancient Roman castrum,[68] whereas the portico made of a pediment and upright, giant Doric columns undoubtedly gives the impression of an ancient Greek temple. Schinkel once said that the Doric order "carries the character of the serious, the powerful, and the strong."[69] The six Doric columns are an exact imitation of the grand Propylaea at the entrance to the Acropolis of ancient Athens. This sort of entrance was introduced earlier through the Brandenburg

Gate, but that of the Neue Wache was closer in form to the original of Athens. Then again, the Neue Wache was not simply a facsimile of an ancient entrance. Unlike the Doric order that originally uses three vertical bands called triglyphs to divide the frieze and decorates the spaces in between with metopes, the Neue Wache's frieze was evenly divided by six small figures of the victory goddess Nike. The figures were created by the Prussian court sculptor Schadow, who was previously responsible for the quadriga upon the Brandenburg Gate. The triangular gable above the entablature featured in bas-relief Prussia's triumphs during the Napoleonic Wars.

At a glance, the Neue Wache was a building that presented a subdued magnificence. It could have easily been dwarfed by Prince Henry's Palace and the old arsenal Zeughaus towering on either side, but the building's presence was sustained by its overwhelming portico and tightly arranged features that left nothing to waste. What was also extraordinary about the building was that, contrary to its organized, balanced exterior, it actually had an asymmetric floor plan that allowed it to accommodate multiple purposes, and some of the chestnut trees that were once part of a forest still surround the building today as if they are on guard. To serve its originally practical purpose, the Neue Wache exhibited a very straightforward exterior devoid of unnecessary decorations, but through a balanced combination of columns, frieze, pediment, statuary, and bas-relief, it still managed to beautifully project the greatness of Prussia and convey historical motifs befitting of a national monument. The building thereby achieved a harmony between temporal power and religion or between modern cities and history that adorned the Prussian state with an unprecedented divine resplendence as it triumphantly proclaimed its authority and mission.[70]

The Neue Wache was part of a plan to transform Berlin's central boulevard Unter den Linden into a Via Triumphalis for parading Prussia's victory in the Napoleonic Wars. The marble statues of the Prussian generals Gerhard J. D. von Scharnhorst and Friedrich Wilhelm Freiherr von Bülow, who served during the Napoleonic Wars, that used to stand in front of the building's left and right corner clearly stated why the Neue Wache was built. Statues of other generals soon appeared on the opposite side of the boulevard to complete a visual representation of the Prussian state's authority.[71] The new temporal, spatial order etched upon the Neue Wache went on to demonstrate a lengthy perseverance against all sorts of historical hardships that ensued. The fact that such perseverance remained in motion to exercise its influence beyond the unification of East and West Germany in the late twentieth century was made obvious when the Helmut Kohl administration designated the Neue Wache as the central memorial (Zentrale Gedenkstätte) of the Federal Republic of Germany in November 1993.[72]

As the German Empire collapsed from being defeated in World War I, the Neue Wache lost its purpose and instead served as a cenotaph (Ehrenmal) in memory of the German war dead. The building was heavily damaged during World War II and came close to being demolished as a symbol of Prussian militarism and imperialism once it fell under the control of East Germany.

Its value in propaganda, however, was eventually recognized and allowed it to become a memorial to the victims of fascism and militarism. The East German soldiers' exaggerated moves during the change of guard in front of the Neue Wache is a sight now part of distant memories of the bygone East German regime. And after weathering many vicissitudes, the building's purpose changed yet again with Germany's reunification by being charged with the rather unusual purpose of serving as a central memorial. Per the advice of Director Christoph Stölzl of the German Historical Museum housed in the Zeughaus right next door, the Neue Wache was internally remodeled by removing miscellaneous attachments and installing the sculptor Harald Haacke's quadrupled replica of Käthe Kollwitz's 1937 work *Mother With Her Dead Son*. Despite facing considerable opposition, the remodeling was carried out as planned, quite possibly out of the urge to escape the ambiguity of being a nation neither glorious nor remorseful and establish as soon as possible the new Federal Republic of Germany's national identity.[73]

Although conflicting ideologies caused complications, the Neue Wache's history of change is evidence that there is an inertia of motion in the spatial, historical order of Schinkel's work. Hence, the Neue Wache in the heart of Berlin is a site of memory (lieu de mémoire), namely a faded image of the true German nation-state that remains a challenge to this day.[74]

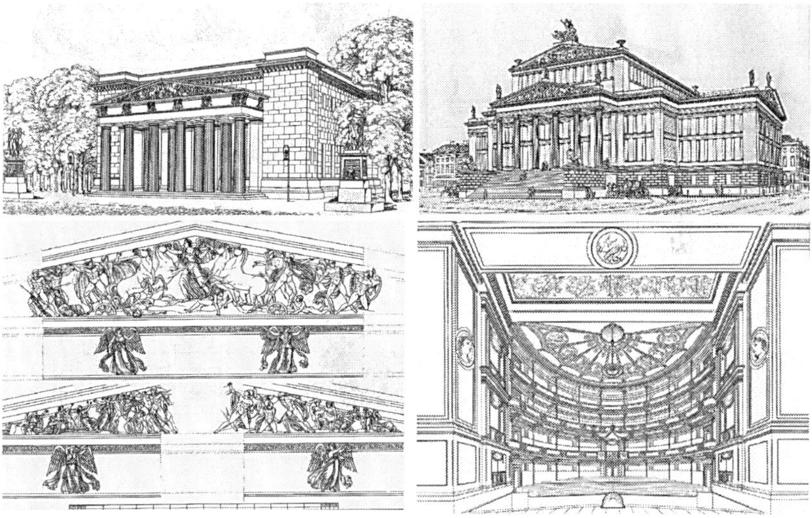

Figure 1.5 Top Left: Perspective of the New Guardhouse. Bottom Left: Frieze Decorations and Bas-Relief on the Neue Wache's Pediment. Top Right: Perspective of the Königliches Schauspielhaus. Bottom Right: Perspective of the Royale Theatre's Auditorium.

Source: Courtesy of the Smithsonian Libraries. https://library.si.edu/digital-library/book/sammlungarchite00schi. Top Left: From Schinkel, *Sammlung*, plate 2. Bottom Left: From Schinkel, Sammlung, plate 3. Top Right: From Schinkel, Sammlung, plate 7. Bottom Right: from Schinkel, Sammlung, plate 13.

The Royal Theatre, Altes Museum, and Lustgarten

Instead of following the Roman architect Marcus Vitruvius Pollio's idea that architecture should imitate nature, which deeply influenced French neoclassical architecture, Prussian classicist architecture exemplified by Schinkel chose to go for the horizontal Greek architrave as opposed to the Roman arch. A typical example would be Schinkel's second masterpiece in Berlin, the Royal Theatre (Königliches Schauspielhaus). The building that appeared at the Gendarmenmarkt square in 1821 creatively adopted the ancient Greek language of architectural form to suit current purposes, thereby serving as a guide to understanding Schinkel's architectural works. When a fire in the summer of 1817 destroyed the theatre designed by Langhans, Berlin authorities asked Schinkel to build on the site a new theatre for staging classical drama. With the new royal theatre, Schinkel explained that he "tried to follow as closely as possible the forms and construction of Greece."[75] Placed upon the captivating portico supported by six Ionic columns was a gable covered with bas-reliefs and statuary to portray mythic scenes, and three muses stood atop the gable as the sun god Apollo looked down at them from his stunning quadriga on the roof.

The building faithful to the grammar of classical architecture had some highly innovative features as well. One of them was the grand staircase leading up to the portico at the center of the building's façade. The stairs offered the audience direct access to the main hall, while the two semi-basement level doors on either side of the staircase served as entrances to rehearsal halls in the north wing and a smaller concert hall in the south wing. Overall, the building was a compound of horizontal architraves and vertical pilasters on the outside that almost made it appear to be a pyramid-like mass. Its colossal rectangular foundation made the building look sprawled out without losing proportion. The building was in fact made up of a central avant-corps flanked on either side by a pavilion of equal height with its own pediment. The upper floor of the central avant-corps accommodated a semi-circular arrangement of seats facing the stage like an ancient amphitheater, which was innovative for making it easier for the actors' voices to reach the audience. This sort of partitioning also satisfied the need to prevent the theatre from being destroyed again by fire. And while the building may have been functionally divided into three parts, those parts were united by the cornices skirting the entire theatre that added to its aesthetic completion. In any case, what stood out most were the main hall's stage protruding from the center of the façade and the large rectangular windows allowing plenty of sunlight to pour in to create a festive aura.[76]

As Schinkel himself mentioned, his design of the royal theatre was inspired by the choragic monument of Thrasyllus located on the south side of the Acropolis in Athens.[77] Like the Acropolis, the theatre was situated at the heart of Berlin in the Gendarmenmarkt. It formed a triangular composition with the French Cathedral (Französischer Dom) and the German Church (Deutscher Dom) standing to its right and left, which can be considered a realization of Prussian classicism's architectural ideals that preferred reconciliation over revolutionary confrontation and a balance between civic life and historical traditions.[78]

Among the many masterpieces of Prussian classicist architecture is another designed by Schinkel: the Altes Museum sprawled across the Lustgarten's north end beside a narrow canal that runs to the river Spree. The grand rectangular building used to be called the "New Museum" when it first opened opposite the royal palace. With the palace now gone, the Altes Museum at first sight is bound to appear even more grandiose to visitors. Unlike the relatively smaller Neue Wache nearby, the building with a palatial exterior was meant to be a cultural venue for the public rather than the king. Of course, it was originally built to house the Prussian monarchy's art collection and retained the name "royal museum" for quite some time, but Schinkel's vision for the building had been clear from the beginning. He designed the museum as an institute of higher education for the public, which reflects his lofty ideals of art embodying moral authority and civic cause.[79]

In 1823, Schinkel received the commission to build a new museum for the art treasures of Prussia. The Prussian Royal Academy of Arts had already reached its limit for housing its increasing collection, and with Napoleon's fall in 1815, the return of the treasures he once took from Prussia raised an even more dire need to create a new space. Schinkel strongly appealed for a new building to be raised. In coming into a new age after defeating Napoleon in the Wars of Liberation, he felt that a central museum would be necessary to reform the Prussian nation, one that would cater to public education rather than only to scholars and artists like the existing royal academies did. Schinkel's proposal on constructing a new public building to exclusively house works of art was accepted. The Prussian state, of course, had different reasons for accepting Schinkel's proposal. By allowing public access to the recovered treasures, Prussia sought to declare its rising political and cultural authority. It was therefore no coincidence that the Altes Museum was dedicated to celebrating the sixtieth birthday of Frederick William III. This, however, shouldn't warrant any reason to disparage the spirit of the times that resonates throughout the building, because it is necessary to acknowledge the fundamental difference between architecture and paintings or sculptures that rely solely on an artist's imagination. Although architecture may contribute to the reinforcement of power, shouldn't it still be credited for creating a universal beauty that power cannot achieve on its own? Whatever the case, the Altes Museum, built upon the intersection of a state's political needs and Schinkel's lofty ideals toward moral

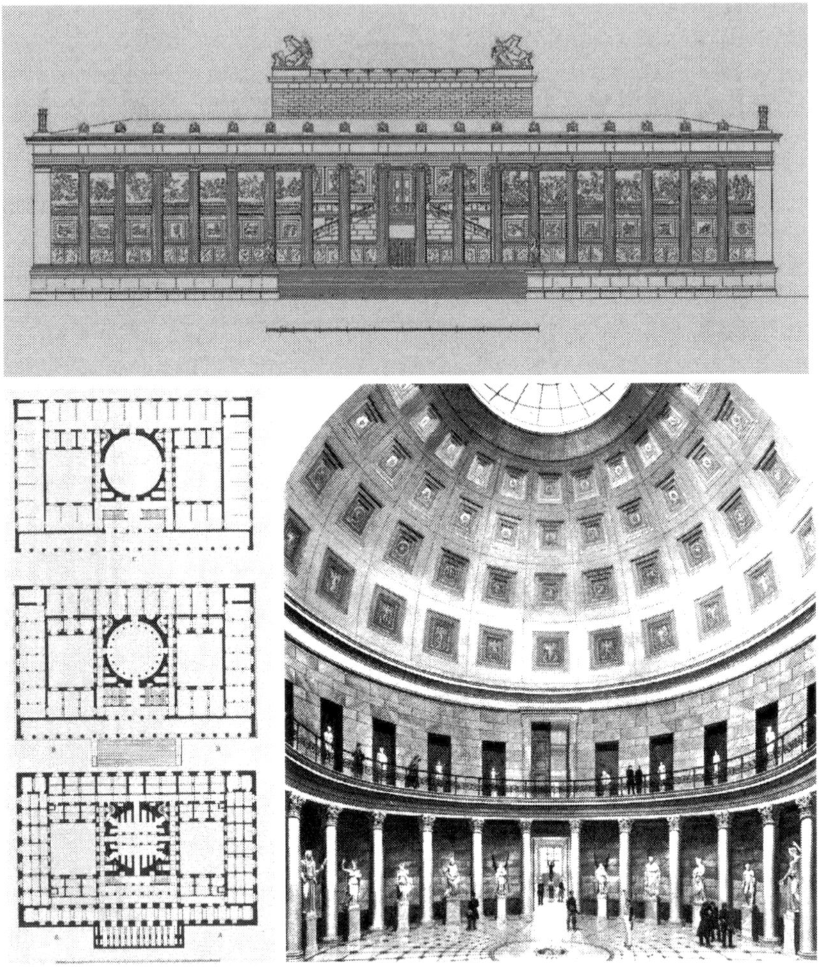

Figure 1.6 Top: Elevation of the Altes Museum. Bottom Left: Basement, Ground, and Upper Floor Plan of the Altes Museum. Bottom Right: *Rotunda of the Altes Museum in Berlin* by Carl Emanuel Conrad (1830s).

Source: Courtesy of the Smithsonian Libraries. https://library.si.edu/digital-library/book/sammlungarchite00schi. Top: From Schinkel, *Sammlung*, plate 38. Bottom Left: From Schinkel, *Sammlung*, plate 39. Courtesy of the Smithsonian Libraries. https://library.si.edu/digital-library/book/sammlungarchite00schi. Bottom Right: Opaque watercolors, 45.7 × 42.1 cm. Public domain via Wikimedia Commons.

authority and civic cause, became an incomparable landmark of Prussian classicism in terms of architectural completion.[80]

Building museums emerged as a trend across Germany in the 1820s and 1830s. Opened in southern Munich in 1830, the same year the Altes Museum's construction was finished, the Glyptothek was an Ionic building typical of neoclassicism that was designed by Klenze and used to be privately owned by the king of Bavaria, Ludwig I. In Germany, civic "publicness" was not attained through revolutions like France but born through a gradual change in court culture. As time went by, the purpose of collecting art shifted from heightening a monarchy's glory at a Baroque palace to serving as a means to reform the people.[81]

This is perhaps why the planning and construction of the Altes Museum in Berlin was carried out by the Prussian administration rather than the royal family. It was a step forward compared to the Glyptothek in Munich, which was the king's private property. What Schinkel aimed for in supervising the Altes Museum's construction was to rearrange works of art so that they could be "instructive to the public and contribute to the nation's reformation."[82] Hence, the Altes Museum's neoclassical appearance was not merely an external style but the portrait of a new order of rectangular buildings resembling the Stoa of Attalos in the Agora of Athens. Beyond a sweeping staircase stood a total of eighteen Ionic columns, nearly 12 meters tall and 1.5 meters wide, forming a colonnade of 83 meters between two corner pillars. The reason this monumental colonnade seemed grand was not due to its imposing size but its orderly, controlled beauty. The flat wall behind the colonnade was at a distance but stood close enough to maintain a certain degree of spatial tension. Accentuating the corner pillars gave a sense of stability to the building's overall structure. The two equestrian bronze statues placed on either side of the front staircase complimented the symmetrical beauty of the building. Flat squares dominated the museum's façade, and undecorated, flat cornices lined the roof above the colonnade to let the museum blend in with other buildings nearby.

As much as the façade, the museum's interior space exuded a neoclassical presence. Except for the alcove near the entrance, the interior was completely hidden under a cubic exterior, giving a sanctuary-like touch to the building that transcended the city's secular everyday life. This became more apparent from stepping further into the building. The two-story rotunda modeled after the Pantheon in Rome displayed a proportion and unity perfect enough to invoke religious awe. A vault more than 20 meters high allowed natural light to flow into the rotunda surrounded by twenty Corinthian columns and sculptures of ancient gods placed in between them. The rotunda wall's beige tone complemented the Greek gods, made of pure white marble, and managed to both structurally divide and consolidate the space, which was an utterly modern element of Schinkel's architectural works. The rotunda connected two inner courtyards that led to different exhibition halls.

The museum's ground floor was completely dedicated to sculptures. Instead of only lining the works against walls or niches, sculptures were arranged orderly along the columns, dividing the space into three parts. Each sculpture was placed upon a pedestal so that the works could be viewed from a comfortable height and at adequate intervals. The upper floor was completely dedicated to paintings. Like the pedestals installed for the sculptures on the ground floor, each painting was displayed in a different frame that suited it best and added to the painting's individuality. Wooden partitions were installed in each hall to divide the space into several sections. Such a division of space reduced the risk of visitors feeling overwhelmed by a massive collection lying ahead and instead allowed them to focus on each work in separated spaces. The museum also introduced a new formula for planning exhibitions. Rather than being preoccupied with a certain theme or decorative principle, works of true masters worthy of representing a period and style were selected to offer exhibitions that showed the development of art over time. Still, what Schinkel concentrated on most was showing how much Western art had been influenced by the ideal beauty of ancient Greek art.[83]

Schinkel's historical awareness was made more obvious through the cycle of massive fresco murals he designed to decorate the museum's exterior wall behind the colonnade of Altes Museum's façade as well as the vestibule indoors where a staircase led to the upper floor. This was a pioneering attempt at an open-air art museum and served as a new attraction to Berlin's citizens and visitors alike. A total of six cycles on the "Educational History of Mankind" was sketched by Schinkel between 1828 and 1834, which took until 1855 to finish painting under the supervision of the history painter Peter von Cornelius. The murals were sublime portrayals of ancient Greek myths, early human culture, the primal power of nature, and the tragedies mankind suffers from it. The cycle on the museum's upper vestibule particularly featured a lengthy progression of mankind's mental development: the civilizational history of mankind represented through ancient Greece's linear development into the European, or more specifically the German civilization at the time. From mainly relying on allegorical expressions rather than specific events, the paintings were more mythic than historical descriptions that nevertheless clearly communicated Prussia and Berlin's awareness of their stature within the history of mankind. Such was the historical awareness that pervaded the Altes Museum as well as the topology of Berlin where the museum was situated.[84]

The notion that, as a public institution, a building can function as a stage for historical drama significantly changed the form and structure of architecture.[85] Past the Altes Museum's entrance was a central grand staircase with two sets of stairs meeting on the upper floor to form a platform that offered a view from indoors of the Lustgarten and other parts of Berlin. The Royal Palace facing the museum seemed to give a visual oratory of the balance between state power and civic culture. The Friedrichswerder Church and Gendarmenmarkt could also be glimpsed from afar. Overall, the Altes Museum could be characterized as a cubic building structurally divided so that the façade's colonnade, outer wall, and interior space appeared separate but still formed a perfect harmony all together. Schinkel said that "the most superb point of view" is "the simplicity of main forms" that prevails as "the one giant order" throughout the museum. And considering the fact that the building was "erected in one of the nicest and most monumental areas of the city,"[86] the Altes Museum was no doubt a rare case in which an architect's lofty ideals were realized through substantial support from the state. Power and art thereby achieved an organic union within a new horizon called history.

At this point, it is necessary to take a closer look at the Lustgarten where the Altes Museum stands. During the early eighteenth century, Frederick William I tried to turn the Lustgarten into a palace square (Schloßplatz), but as the Altes Museum appeared a century later, the Lustgarten turned into a destination along the road between the Brandenburg Gate and the Royal Palace. The newly repaired boulevard Unter den Linden, or Schinkel's "road to victory," realized to a certain degree the ideals Frederick the Great once had for the Forum Fridericianum. However incomplete it may be, a symbolic center was thus built for the capital.

Alongside the Altes Museum, the Lustgarten itself stood out for its extraordinary landscape. The one who played a decisive role in turning the Lustgarten into a utopia of Prussian classicism was Peter-Joseph Lenné, a leading landscape architect and lifelong colleague of Schinkel. For the Lustgarten, Lenné combined the British nature-friendly spirit with the aesthetic ideals of Prussian romanticism and classicism. The prominent landscape architect, with whom even the great writer Goethe aspired to take a stroll, wholly embraced the central axis running through the Altes Museum rotunda when designing the Lustgarten so that a symmetrical order could be established between the museum building and the landscape full of life around it.[87] Hence, the Lustgarten was taken to be a portrait of the Prussian kingdom in which each part formed an organic whole amid vibrant social change.

3. Tectonics and the Prussian Idea of State

Although he worked under the protection of an absolute monarchy, Schinkel's architectural taste was far from the Baroque extravagance exhibited by buildings of the old order. Schinkel was indeed loyal to the restored monarchy, but unlike previous monarchies, the one he devoted his services to had been a historical consequence of revolutions. Schinkel was an innovative, modern architect who lived in the early nineteenth century as a high-ranking bureaucrat of the Prussian state. He broke away from pretentiously indulging in beauty under the old order and sought new values, which the state eagerly supported within the boundaries of an existing order.

Tectonics

The neoclassicist Schinkel aesthetically aimed for the uprightness in ancient Greek buildings, which the art historian Johann Joachim

Winckelmann famously characterized as "a noble simplicity and sedate grandeur" through his review of the statue *Laocoön and His Sons*. Through one of his major publications, *Reflections on the Imitation of Greek Works in Painting and Sculpture* (1755), Winckelmann claimed that *Laocoön and His Sons*, discovered by chance at a vineyard in early sixteenth century Rome, possessed an utterly stoic virtue that contrasted with the art of Winckelmann's time. Despite "excruciating pains," such pains "exert not themselves with violence, either in the face or gesture" of Laocoön. The statue's depiction of "the struggling body and the supporting mind" speaks of the dignity of mankind.[88] Later, through the *History of Ancient Art* (1764), Winckelmann raved about how Laocoön's "suppressed outburst of feeling" was meant to "retain and keep within himself the pain" and stated that "in the parts where the greatest pain is placed he shows us the greatest beauty."[89] This idea of beauty and order as a state having overcome inner anxieties was wholly passed on to Schinkel. By incorporating Gothic's surging fervor into the strict order of classicism, Schinkel's architectural aesthetics emphasized an impeccable compositional order instead of eye-catching exterior appeal, marking the emergence of a value criteria or aesthetic principle endemic to architecture and distinguishable from other genres of art.

An awareness of architectural autonomy had already been budding in neoclassicist architectural theories prior to Schinkel's time. The phrase "back to nature" by Jean-Jacques Rousseau inspired the Jesuit priest Marc-Antoine Laugier to suggest in his 1753 *Essay on Architecture* that the original form of architecture lies in the "primitive hut" that takes four tree trunks to support a horizontal beam and a pitched roof. The suggestion was highly innovative for emphasizing a building's structural frame while touching upon the purity of architecture in terms of its harmony with ornamentation, which is why it caused a considerable sensation among German intellectuals across the border. Although Goethe had a refined taste that didn't identify much with the primitive hut theory, he did share Laugier's distaste toward the excessive ornamentation of Rococo art. This also left a definitive impact upon Gilly's circle in Berlin steeped in ancient Greek architecture.[90] And, as a member of that circle, Schinkel clearly defined the new architectural credo as follows.

> European architecture is but a progression of Greek architecture. No masquerade. Making the essentials of construction aesthetically pleasing is the basic principle of Greek architecture, and this must be upheld in its continuation.[91]

What is worth taking note of from these words is that Schinkel defines "making the essentials of construction aesthetically pleasing" as the core principle of Greek architecture and uses the word "masquerade" in contrast. At first glance, this can be considered antipathy toward Baroque and Rococo architecture, but it actually hints at much more. In the history of Western architecture, Schinkel is known as the one who discovered the tectonic order. As a term that first settled in German architecture, the word "Tektonik" came from a carpenter named "Tecton" in Homer's *Illiad* and referred to an architectural principle that values a perfect harmony between form and function. Schinkel himself never used the term "tectonics," but he was the first to capture the idea of tectonics by identifying the purpose of architecture as realizing an "ideal purposiveness" (ideale Zweckmäßigkeit).[92] Whereas architecture under the old order went as far as to regard columns as ornaments that best serve the purpose of elevating a monarch's dignity, tectonics discarded excessive ornamentation and only acknowledged the "elements essential to construction."[93] This new architectural principle that placed inner construct above outer appeal of course had nothing to do with functionalism and instead aimed for an organic unity between purposiveness and aesthetic form. And by being defined according to internal nature rather than external style, architecture could at last be recognized as a distinct, physical actuality.

By the mid-1830s, at the top of his career in his later years, Schinkel came to recognize the three basics of architectural form: forms of construction, forms of historical significance, and forms modeled after nature. Architectural art may have various roots, including construction, history, and nature, but whatever the case, Schinkel believed and considered it his lifelong mission to liberate architecture "entirely from practical purposes and structural elements" and work toward reviving "two essential elements, the historical and the poetic."[94] The emphasis on "the historical and the poetic" hints at Goethe's view of art, which understood works of art as an organic whole, an organism that is conceived and evolves like a product of nature. Such a notion was not a revival of romantic tendencies from Schinkel's youth. It was an oration preaching that architectural art should not isolate "practical purposes and structural elements" characteristic to architecture but rather sublimate them to a historical, poetic level. For instance, the Altes Museum undeniably demonstrates that functional and dramatic (poetic) elements can simultaneously be implemented by organically combining a fabricated structure like the portico with a functional structure like the walls. That was what the basics of tectonics was about.[95]

What supplied the idea of tectonics in the field of architectural design with a more logically advanced system was the publication of *Tectonics of the Greeks* (1844–1852) by Karl Bötticher, an architect and archaeologist in Berlin who was once a pupil of Schinkel. The book exploring the history of ancient Greek tectonics narrowly defined tectonics as an "act of building and interior decoration" yet sought to reveal the "internal history of tectonics" by contemplating the structural principle beneath each Doric or Ionic component or ornament. The starting point of Bötticher's contemplation was the complementarity of external form and internal idea. As does nature, "the concept of each edifice is expressed in its form." And the "law of form" is what serves as a source for creation. A construction is born out of the interaction between core-form ruled by mechanical necessity and art-form that clads core-form with symbolism. And the relationship between the two forms tends to change over history. Whereas core-form, or structural form, may vary to suit arising needs, art-form only continues to intensify. Ornaments were undermined by religious symbolism and rituals in ancient Egypt, but in ancient Greece, the weakening of religious precepts allowed a balance to be attained between structure and ornamentation, or between form and concept, and finally awarded autonomy to architecture. According to Bötticher, every single component of a Greek temple, from the stylobate to the angle of the roof, is a symbol. Be it a column capital or molding, each ornamental form symbolizes a religious belief and simultaneously represents its specific location within a building, signaling that each component is joined to the building as an organic whole.[96]

What Bötticher meant to underline as necessary during his time was to understand the universal law of tectonics practiced in ancient Greece to be able to imitate not only the styles of Greek architecture but the unity of idea and form in them. Despite his narrow definition, Bötticher characterized tectonics as a historical principle representing the trend of a certain period instead of pigeonholing it as a technical principle. At the same time, his emphasis on the organic unity of buildings was a political principle reflecting the reality of his time.

State Tectonics

Architectural autonomy provided a foundation for architectural politicality. Tectonics literally referred to the aesthetic, technical principle of neoclassical architecture, but Schinkel's notion of it went beyond architecture. What he had in mind was "state tectonics." A state should be an organically structured construction. Its form ought to change with the circumstances of the times, but the underlying principle of its structure should not change. Whatever the circumstances, each part of a state should serve the whole, like the components essential to supporting a building. All subjects must fulfill their duty to the king.[97] This was no different from the state ideology behind the Prussian kingdom. The sense that tectonics obsessed over a tightly knit principle of unity made it difficult to avoid being criticized for defending a state historically stipulated as an "authoritarian state" (Obrigkeitsstaat).

The authoritarian state Prussia was a strong constitutional monarchy based on a well-organized bureaucracy and military, a distinct combination of aristocratic and democratic elements. Per Frederick the Great's orders, judicial reform transformed Prussia's class society and established a Prussian constitutional system by fusing an authoritarian state with a civil society based on the social contract theory's legal principles. The General State Laws for the Prussian States (Allgemeines Landrecht für die Preußischen Staaten) promulgated in 1794 turned the Prussian king from the absolute sovereign into the head of state and sought to mediate all social ranks, including the landed nobility called *Junkers*, through professional associations (Berufsverbände) officially recognized by the state. The class system in reality thus was absorbed into a bourgeois, individualistic constitutional system. This clearly aimed for a coexistence between tradition and new order. Besides allowing the Prussian state to establish itself as both a guardian of civil society and a civil servant, the laws also allowed the state to carry out planned social reforms while remaining autonomous from interest politics pursued by the Prussian National Assembly.

Prussia's choice to go for top-down reform helped it overcome the disintegrative tendency of feudal societies and achieve national unity. Bureaucracy served as a medium between different social ranks undergoing reform, making bureaucrats the bearers of the middle way. Alongside officers, bureaucrats were the only stand that guaranteed the state's unity and continuity. The state offered its people opportunities to climb the social ladder as bureaucrats and instill themselves with a bourgeois, civic spirit. As bureaucrats took the lead in social reform, Prussia's economic sphere experienced change as well. Debt previously dispersed across social ranks and regions was combined into national debt, thereby disbanding the existing feudal economic order and creating opportunities to establish capitalistic ownership.[98]

The organically integrated Prussian authoritarian state became a realistic power structure that received theoretical support, typically from the philosopher Georg Wilhelm Friedrich Hegel's idea of the state. Hegel took note of personality (Persönlichkeit) emerging in modern civil society that breaks away from traditional social ties to have free will and recognized a potential crisis for modern society in personality's tendency to absolutize freedom. In Hegel's eyes, freedom without mediation was no more than abstract freedom, which is why the only way to wholly realize freedom was through and within the boundaries of the state.[99] According to Hegel's work *Elements of the Philosophy of Right*, civil society gives birth to a private person, the first among mankind to follow only self-interests. However, for each private person to actualize their ownership, they need to establish ties with one another. Those ties can be formed through contracts that recognize common will and rights as well as the transfer of one personality's ownership to another personality. Contracts work upon the premise that the parties entering a contract mutually recognize one another as a personality and owner. When a personality enters into a relationship with another personality, the subjective desire of a personality is mutually restricted by that of the other personality. Hegel referred to this sphere of mediation as a "system of needs," allowing the individual's subjective selfishness to contribute to creating an abstract universality.[100]

Universality achieved in civil society, however, is bound to become a formality, because it is formed of purposes specific to each individual. The institutionalization of universality realized through all sorts of professional associations within a civil society becomes integrated into a "political state."[101] According to Hegel, a political state is a state purely formed out of a civil society's internal strength, making it impossible to go beyond its intrinsic nature as a "state of necessity and of the understanding."[102] The reality of modern civil society is thereby once again dualized into an individualized personal sphere and a political state's universal order.

> If the state is confused with civil society and its determination is equated with the security and protection of property and personal freedom, the interest of individuals as such becomes the ultimate end for which they are united; it also follows from this that membership of the state is an optional matter.[103]

The way Hegel saw it, the political state that emerged as an alternative to the issues of civil society remained relative in terms of its universality and therefore could not serve as the ultimate alternative. What could instead realize absolute universality was the "ethical state." In the sense that an individual's subjective will is unified within an ethical whole, the ethical state is a universal state "in and of itself" (an und für sich).[104] Hegel's conservative idea of state originated from thoughts on the issues of modern civil society that revolves around the private individual. Realizing that universality created through mutual recognition among individuals would not be able to outweigh individual self-interests, Hegel employed a methodological reversal to make it necessary to call for absolute universality. The state was thereby elevated from performing a political role to an entity also charged with an "ethical" mission.

The utterly idealistic notion that the state is an ethical unity "in and of itself" met with traditional German romanticism that regarded the state as an organism. Although Hegel himself was critical of romanticism for only glamorizing medieval individual rights and failing to acknowledge state unity,[105] the romanticist concept of state did share a common denominator with Hegel's concept of state in that they both identified the state as an end in itself. Highlighting an ethnic community's cultural vibrancy as opposed to the Enlightenment's bland concept of global citizenship, romanticism rejected all theoretical attempts like the social contract theory seeking to explain why the state is functionally necessary and instead elevated the state as a spiritual entity embodying a divine mystery.[106] For instance, in his 1809 work *Elements of Statecraft*, the renowned theorist of romanticism Adam Heinrich Müller assumed that "there is no (generalized) concept of state" and called for a different approach toward the state.

> Should our contemplations on such a sublime object become expanded, and grow and move as does the object, we may refer to such contemplations not as a concept about the issue, but as an idea of the issue, of the state, and of life.[107]

Instead of being a neatly defined concept, if the state indeed "grows and moves" like a living organism, contemplations to grasp the "sublime object" should not simply remain a suggestive concept. They should be exalted to the level of an "idea" encompassing all aspects of our lives. The state is a boundless mystery beyond rational judgment. Rather than an object of scientific study, it is therefore an all-embracing idea that may well be closer to a divine revelation. Sufficiently combining Hegel's idealism with this romantic idea of regarding state as an organism was achieved by none other than Lorenz von Stein. It was through Von Stein's works that a more detailed state tectonics began to reveal itself.

After being immersed in the Hegelian doctrine of state, Lorenz von Stein worked as a professor of political economy at the University of Vienna. Von Stein understood the state as a unified entity, or a supreme personality. A personality would first have a body and spirit followed by a self-determining nature. For the state as a superior personality, its territory and people would be its body and spirit. A state is a community elevated to an independent, self-conscious, and self-acting personality. Regarding the state as a living organism leads to the discussion of functions essential to sustaining it: the head of state who represents the state's existence, will, and unity; the will of the state that recognizes within its unity the individual self-determination of its people; and the actions of the state that resolve ongoing conflicts. These essential functions require a state institution to take responsibility over them. Hence, a state's unified self-understanding is maintained by the head of state, while the legislature formulates a state's will, which is carried out by the administration.[108]

What Von Stein accentuates through his state theory is public administration. In particular, the notion of internal administration (innere Verwaltung) serves as a theoretical backbone. Internal administration is what provides the conditions for personal development that an individual cannot attain solely through their own power and exertion. Supporting each individual to reach their highest possible development thus falls under the inherent duty of an organic state. And an ideal convergence of each individual's free self-determination into the state as a whole results in a constitution (Verfassung), which is the consummation of the concept of state and state activities. However, a constitution alone does not guarantee the organic unity of a state. A communal society (Gemeinschaft), which unfolds as a whole of individuals with equal rights and personalities, becomes threatened by the reality of an associational society (Gesellschaft) where a principle of disparity dictates. This is why the role of administration is important. Compared to an assembly mired in never-ending debates, Von Stein believed an administration made up of cabinet members and bureaucrats had the advantage of being more agile in responding to the changing reality. He argued that when an administration serves as an intermediary to constantly interact with reality, an organic state can answer social questions arising in an associational society's reality.[109] Only through an administration's leadership can an associational social order solely highlighting disparities be substituted with a legal order that realizes organic unity.[110]

Lorenz von Stein's strict constitutionalism eventually leads to his unique idea of monarchy. In a constitutional state, a monarch is someone who maintains the constitution's unity but is not bestowed with the actual authority to give orders to the administration or legislature. Nevertheless, for old European state systems, monarchy remains "the purest expression of the state as an autonomous personality."[111] As an Austrian professor of law, Von Stein presented the concept of "social kingdom" that differed from the Prussian authoritarian state's absolute monarchy. In a social kingdom, monarchy establishes itself as the only institution capable of protecting the subjugated class from tyranny of the ruling class. For seeking an organic totality between a monarch and its subjects, or between state and society, the idea of a social kingdom may as well be the purest expression of the state organism theory.[112]

In that Lorenz von Stein's notion of a social kingdom aims for complete structural unity, it shares a commonality with Schinkel's neoclassical architecture that sought ideal purposiveness. Neither reflected reality itself, but both embodied a certain ideal that could be dreamt about in reality. To borrow Aristotle's expression, they were potentiality (dunamis) within an actuality (entelecheia) called the Prussian – Austrian Habsburg – kingdom. Such ideal types of power evoke the notion of governmentality (gouvernementalité) Michel Foucault refers to. Rather than through stipulations about sovereignty in legal provisions or the individualized regulation of bodies, the types of power in modern states can be explained through the ways human lives are collectively governed. With the emergence of "biopolitics," all previous power structures were integrated and supplemented so that the state came to be governed like one massive body. Each part forming the state is organically segmented, allocated, and presented as chunks like the "population," thereby completely denying the presence of an "outside."[113] The governmentality of modern states operates through a variety of technological means, a typical example being Prussian state tectonics, which gained its architectural expression from Schinkel.

The ideal purposiveness shown through masterpieces representative of Prussian classicism like the Neue Wache, the Royal Court Opera, and the

Altes Museum was undoubtedly an expression of Prussian governmentality. Such buildings brought a representation – imaginative geography – called ancient Greece into the heart of the Prussian kingdom for the sake of achieving national unity. The ancient Greece revived as a savior was utterly anti-revolutionary and revealed an authoritarian state's threatening claws, exhibiting an imperial overtone starkly different from its original appearance. An ideal, purposive ancient Greece was a fabrication that never actually existed, a mere upside-down reflection of an authoritarian state in reality.

History, the Tectonics of Time

As tectonics spread from the realm of architecture to the realm of state governance, it metastasized from the dimension of space into that of time. Pieces of memory dispersed across individual spaces of experience were assembled into a single whole like a unified state. To Schinkel, Gothic and neoclassicism, or medieval religion and ancient reason, didn't rival one another but made it possible to achieve a modern synthesis within Prussia's cultural landscape. Underneath such thinking lay a temporal schema. Ancient Greece was used like Archimedes's lever to instantly support an infinite amount of time. And that mass of infinite time came to be named "history," signifying an overall rearrangement of experienced times.

The foremost inspiration for such a major intellectual revolution was the works of Johann Joachim Winckelmann. Winckelmann's *The History of Art in Antiquity* was different from the biographical style of writing Giorgio Vasari conventionalized through *The Lives of the Most Eminent Painters, Sculptors, and Architects*. Instead of simply describing a periodical background, *The History of Art in Antiquity* sought to relay the internal history of art.

> The history of art should inform us about the origin, growth, change, and fall of art, together with the various styles of people, periods, and artists, and should demonstrate this as far as possible by reference to the remaining works of antiquity.[114]

The history of art Winckelmann pursued was indeed unique for intertwining internal changes in art with a nation's political changes. His work therefore imparted aesthetic as well as historical knowledge. Attempting to serve as a historical narrative as well as a textbook about ideal examples of art presented Winckelmann's history of art with a formidable challenge. If ancient Greek art represented a great community of its time, would it be possible to restore that original artistic spirit after that community disappeared like a distant dream? As a convinced classicist, Winckelmann couldn't abandon his norms, but he was simultaneously aware of their temporal limitations. He seriously considered whether the eternal ideals of beauty ancient Greek art attained could serve as an imitable source for different periods. It was a purely theoretical matter that could not be solved by presenting more empirical data. In any case, Winckelmann lived in a time when he mainly had to rely on written sources and copies produced in the Roman era because Greece was still under the Ottoman rule. What Winckelmann had to compete against was the fundamental conundrum called modernity. In the face of an unprecedented period of transition where past ideals grew starkly unfamiliar, it was definitely paradoxical to search for a set of norms capable of serving as a guide. So, Winckelmann eventually chose to focus on the change process of styles. Since this involved a combination of systematic and historical analysis, it was an impossible attempt to discover an unchanging set of norms amid change. Based on this approach, ancient Greek art went through the archaic style, the high or sublime style, the beautiful style, and the decadent style, and throughout the process, it was dependent upon the spiritual and political circumstances as well as the climatic and geographical conditions of each period. Being redefined as a history of style gave the history of art a system no longer divided by period, which made it possible for ancient Greek art to jump over time to serve as a model for modern art. As the end – decadence – of a series of styles from the Renaissance to the Rococo came to be considered a historical inevitability, the arrival of a new cycle launched by the art of classical antiquity's revival was a fait accompli.[115]

Winckelmann's stylistic history of art was suggested as a way out of the impossibility of imitating Greek art. Absolutely normalizing yet historically relativizing beauty was certainly a paradoxical path, but that paradox was resolved to a certain degree from structurally reorganizing the entire history of art. Instead of being part of the past, Greece was now repositioned as a possibility of the future. The galaxy of history came to revolve around an inimitable blank space.[116] If Foucault, through *The Order of Things*, sought the classical episteme's characteristic from a mixture of differences in the actual absence of a center,[117] history took that absence as an axis to inversely construct a unified order of different spaces and times. Still, the fact that such a completely unified system resulted from unilateral restructuring and austere exclusion should not be overlooked. Even the spirit of "freedom" Winckelmann always emphasized when discussing ancient Greek art tends to cave under the unilateral order of history and be diminished to an aesthetic freedom trapped in a sans revolutionary, empty schema.[118] To make matters worse, this even gives rise to an absurd logic of racial exclusion. According to Winckelmann's argument, races like the Greeks who have the right physique and live in an adequate climate are the only ones capable of creating beautiful art. "The flattened nose of the Kalmyk, the Chinese, and other distant peoples, is likewise a deviation: it interrupts the unity of the forms according to which the other parts of the body are shaped."[119]

The falsehood in the order of Winckelmann's stylistic history was ruthlessly exposed by the German Enlightenment thinker Gotthold Ephraim Lessing, who was against Winckelmann's normative interpretation of Laocoön. Based on Lessing's criticism, Laocoön didn't internally overcome pain. He couldn't cry out no matter what, because crying bore the risk of distorting his face, a primordial limitation of plastic arts being unable to surpass spatial imagery. Therefore, Laocoön could never become an eternal ideal of beauty but deserved his own specific place along the road of manmade art's development over history.[120]

The order of history that remained incomplete for Winckelmann gained the most solid system thanks to the philosopher Hegel. The paranoid philosopher's exhaustive dialectics disintegrated the classicist frame of understanding and allowed the order of history to take root. Hegel's *Lectures on Aesthetics* shows the order of history in its most ideal form. The central axis throughout history is the "idea of beauty" that springs from the "beauty of nature" and passes various stages in the "beauty of art" until it becomes complete under the concept of "fine arts" (schöne Künste). Through such a process, the idea of beauty attains complete freedom from the distinct materiality that used to restrict each realm of art. The process of how the idea of beauty historically unfolds offers the most pure, abstract presentation of a new history's order. Each of the genres of art from all periods is thus each assigned its own position within the overall order of history. As a medium that tends to be ruled by materiality, architecture represents a symbolic form of art that belongs to the early stage of the beauty of art and can be considered to have already arrived at the stage of completion by the end of ancient Greece. By then, the idea of beauty and corporeal form were combined into a "child-like harmony." When that harmony is later broken, ancient Greece's harmonious beauty of art is like a child growing up over a long historical process before it reaches the "romantic" German world and is reborn upon a new horizon.[121]

Hegelian aesthetics completely detached the stylistic history of art launched by Winckelmann from classicism rooted in aesthetic norms and rearranged it into a course of history tightly packed from beginning to end. Aesthetic value was determined only by historical value, or its stature within the overall order of history. This made it impossible to discuss everlasting norms now that the order of history itself was the only thing everlasting. It was no different from the human frame that could function from gaining flesh yet sustain itself without gaining more flesh. Only when that frame broke would an organism meet death.

Having gained the clearest philosophical expression from Hegel, the modern sense of history had to do with exercising control, to even place time under unified control. The reality of modernity plagued with all sorts of revolutions and innovations leads to the self-contradiction of allowing everything, including the future, to be swept away into the past. History is the sublimation of temporality's contradiction, or the gap between past, present, and future, to a higher level. It is to apply creative, contrarian thinking to reorganize temporality's contradiction into a consistent historical narrative. Expectations for the future, legacies from the past, and severe conflicts between subjective values and objective perceptions of reality each turn into opportunities for history to formulate its overall system. Such opportunities allow subjective hope for the future to travel back in time and discover a possibility in a distant, bygone past. This is what Schlegel pointed out when he suggested that "the historian is a prophet looking backward."

History drove a wedge into the tradition of theology and natural law, which believed in an everlasting, ultimate order and settled as a modern world view hinting at the impermanence of all things and the permanence of change. Such a trend could be characterized as "the triumph of becoming" over "being" per the words of Franklin L. Baumer, an American historian of ideas. History was, needless to say, an innovative world view.[122] It tore down the absolute authority of the past. The French Enlightenment thinkers' so-called "philosophy of history," which truly employed history as an innovative world view, brought into history rigorous legal categories. Such thinkers summoned reality to the court of history to be judged by the law of "reason" and called for it to constantly change for a better future. To them, history's progression was not the passing of everyday reality but the fulfillment of a revolutionary plan. This sort of philosophical history was bound to result in a "crisis" that endlessly sacrifices today for tomorrow.[123] It should therefore come as no surprise that an authoritarian state like Prussia took such a crisis seriously when it was firmly resisting revolutionary change.

It was a timely choice for the most eminent Prussian intellectuals, including Hegel, to suggest the order of history as the principle most effective in unraveling the chaos caused by revolutions and wisely reconciling past and present. The Prussian state architect Schinkel chose to take the same path. Schinkel's alternative to French neoclassicism, which was faithful to the principle of natural law, was the principle of history. Despite idealizing ancient Greek architecture, Schinkel's choice was based on a level-headed awareness of the cultural situation at a time when classical norms were collapsing. Tectonics pursuing the ideal purposiveness of space in fact shared an affinity with the order of history. In other words, history could be described as the tectonics of time.

What Schinkel's Prussian classicist architecture tried to overcome was the crisis brought on by progressive ideas of history. The buildings this immortal maestro created proposed as an alternative a new spatial, temporal principle that went beyond Enlightenment thoughts and their adversary romanticism. That principle sought an ideal way to reconcile the past with the future, or ancient stylistic models with a modern city's new functional demands. Schinkel clearly expressed that he didn't intend to vaguely admire the new or blindly adhere to the past. Ancient Greek architecture and art were not prescribed norms but an unlimited source where new inspirations for building a great nation and city would always be available. By replacing unchanging rules with principles of origin, formation, and development, or by supplanting normativism with teleology, Schinkel's architectural stance can be considered to have been among the first to embrace the so-called historicism that dominated the Western psyche starting in the mid-nineteenth century.[124]

Schinkel's life-long interest in panorama imparts the core characteristics of his historical view. Ever since he first visited Paris during his youth, Schinkel had been fascinated with panorama. When there were no construction projects to work on under Napoleon's rule of Prussia, Schinkel went around working as a stage designer and created dioramas. Between 1815 and 1820, his use of perspective in the stage design for the opera *The Magic Flute* (Zauberflöte) attracted the audience's attention. Unlike Baroque-style stages that placed individual decorations in a crisscross pattern, Schinkel's stage resembled a diorama, completely surrounded by a huge background painting. Panorama takes a single viewpoint that summarizes an entire story, offering an overview of developments that go beyond individual incidents.[125] This was precisely what the core principle of tectonics was about, not to mention the principle of history as the tectonics of time. And this was fully carried through to Schinkel's historical illustrations across the Altes Museum's façade.

Such a panoramic totality, however, is actually no more than a phantasm(agoria). Schinkel's tectonic architectural art sought a harmony between reality and ideals but at the same time concealed conflicts in reality. His art therefore showed where the Prussian kingdom stood as a tectonic authoritarian state. A tectonic unity between state and subject, power and art, function and form, past and present was only possible when their conflicts were concealed under a phantasmagoria of ancient Greece. The organic unity the immortal maestro pursued through architecture from his youth was a tightly knit, closed unity instead of a unity for vigorous freedom and liberation.

Schinkel as a Historicist

Although he was a classicist faithful to neo-humanist ideals, Schinkel was certainly a maestro for having the historical sensibility to read the trend of the times. As shown through the Neue Wache, the Royal Opera House, and the Altes Museum, Schinkel never remained content with imitating or compromising and used inherited stylistic techniques to create new exemplars. This drew a stark line between Schinkel and Professor Alois Hirt, who taught art history and archaeology at the University of Berlin and believed ancient Greek architecture represented the universal rules of architecture.[126] Schinkel's later works diverged even further from the classicist style to meet new demands of the times. And as he neared the stage of mastering neoclassical architectural techniques, Schinkel met a radical turning point when he went to survey England and Scotland for a couple of months in the late 1820s. The trip was groundbreaking for him in that it opened his eyes to the new built environment of industrial societies and its negative consequences.

At industrial cities like Manchester, Schinkel was fascinated by factory buildings made of bricks and roofs finished with cast iron. He expressed great interest in tenement houses for the working class. However, he strongly disapproved of the overall formation of such cities. In his eyes, dull buildings constructed purely to satisfy function without considering basic architectural principles could never serve as a future alternative. Architecture's innate mission had to lie in bringing individuals together as enlightened members of a humane, historically conscious community. Once he returned to Berlin, Schinkel tried to realize his belief by working on buildings essentially different from his previous works such as a department store (Kaufhaus) and a customs warehouse (Packhof).[127] However, his new belief came to be most eloquently expressed through the new building for his alma mater, the Berlin Building Academy (Bauakademie).

While traveling around England for several months, Schinkel was accompanied by his high school friend Peter Christian Wilhelm Beuth. As a high-ranking bureaucrat working for the Prussian Ministry of Finance, Beuth had seriously been considering ways to successfully lead his nation's belated industrialization. He generally agreed with his friend Schinkel in that new building material and industrial technologies should be combined with historical knowledge and aesthetic sensitivity. They also shared the same political views from participating in the Christian-German Table Society. And their shared beliefs eventually materialized through the Building Academy in Berlin. In 1822, jurisdiction over the academy was transferred from the Royal Academy of Arts to the Department of Industry and Trade under the Ministry of the Interior, which was being headed by Beuth. Beuth was thus able to lend his support to Schinkel, the head of the Prussian State Building Commission, in internally reorganizing the academy and constructing a new building for it based on a different style.[128]

Finished in 1835 after its construction was launched in 1832, the new academy building catered to a functionality aimed specifically at housing engineers, as if to protest against the absolute norms of ancient classical architecture. Square windows lining the building's red brick wall like a colonnade substituted all other forms of decoration for the building, highly innovative in terms of allowing its framework and material to dominate its façade.[129] This made the building appear much more British than Greek but still feel unmistakably Schinkel. Having the building's form take after its structural frame can be considered an even purer representation of tectonics than Schinkel's previous works that display a Greek temple-like aura. The square floor plan based on a structural grid pattern, the rectangular inner court, and the terrace on the uppermost floor demonstrated the highlight of Schinkel's architectural aesthetics that blended structural spatial division into a monolithic construct.

Figure 1.7 Top: Elevation of the Bauakademie. Bottom: Sketched Design for the Berlin Bauakademie's Main Entrance.

Source: Courtesy of the Smithsonian Libraries. Top: From Schinkel, *Sammlung*, plate 117. Bottom: From Schinkel, *Sammlung*, plate 120. Courtesy of the Smithsonian Libraries. https://library.si.edu/digital-library/book/sammlungarchite00schi.

Of course, the building didn't entirely relinquish the language of classical form. Elements ranging from structural to independent and purely decorative were applied to window frames, door frames, and the roof. What is distinctive about those elements is that they mainly used terracotta. The only decoration on the otherwise plain brick wall was placed around the window frames, lining the top arched with spandrels as well as the jambs and muntins. Beneath each window frame, a terracotta panel was attached, featuring a series of architectural, technological developments in the history of mankind. The series included many motifs in the shape of beasts and angels that have historically represented nature and culture, quite possibly to show "the historical and the poetical" side of architecture and to cater to the building's educational purpose. This series was continued along the frames of the building's entrance doors.[130] Schinkel particularly refrained from fully using arches to create a decorative effect, which is why the arches above the window frames were almost flat. Using a flat architrave and terrace instead of a dome on the roof reflected the architect's unwavering faith in the tectonics of Greek architecture. Greek symbols were engraved like cryptograms upon the corbels supporting the cornice along the top of the building.[131]

Schinkel spent his last years at the Berlin Building Academy, where he took residence in the building's top floor. This makes it safe to conclude that the building embodied the conclusion the great architect arrived at after a lifetime of research during a period of transition. At first glance, the building may seem dissimilar to the others Schinkel previously designed, but it in fact stands closest to the essence of classical architecture as Schinkel understood it. The neoclassical architecture Schinkel originally had in mind was about losing the artificial decorations of Baroque or Rococo architecture and employing the simplest geometric form inspired by nature. Since nature continued to create and evolve, there was no reason for architecture to adhere to one particular form. Assuming that ancient Greek architecture sought a harmonious unity between nature and human culture, its underlying spirit must have been able to experience a glorious revival by forming a harmony with the new modern environment.

> Each work of art should introduce a "new element" to its construct. Even if the work's nature has been inspired by a well-known aesthetic style from the past. Without a "new element," a work of art cannot truly attract its creator or spectators.[132]

Historical thinking was therefore necessary not because of an obsession with the past but to take note of the endless changes various styles went through over time. Through such thinking, Schinkel firmly believed a certain period's functional demands could be incorporated into the ideals of an inclusive ethical community. Schinkel's tectonics was too grand to be limited to a certain style or building. The Building Academy's new main building was located at the heart of Berlin, quite close to the Friedrichswerder Church. Although the church and the new academy building exhibited different styles that each represented the past and the future, the two still appeared to be a well-matched pair for their simple cube-shaped construction finished with red bricks. Against the distant sight of the landmark buildings along Unter den Linden as well as the Altes Museum, it seemed obvious that the new academy building not only had value as an individual construction but was also a work that took into consideration a new urban tectonic order. Clearly, the academy building and the church nearby reflected Schinkel's imaginative geography.

Of course, Schinkel's imaginative geography was not limited to Berlin. In fact, Schinkel had been in charge of building or renovating most of Prussia's royal residences. Babelsberg Palace (Schloß Babelsberg), built beside the lake connecting southern Berlin and Potsdam, was dedicated to the Crown Prince Frederick William's younger brother Prince William. Glienicke Palace (Schloß Klein-Glienicke) was dedicated to Prince Charles of Prussia. The Prinz-Albrecht-Palais standing along the thoroughfare Wilhelmstrasse in Berlin was dedicated to Prince Albert of Prussia and later served as a headquarters for Nazi Germany's secret police Gestapo.[133] Charlottenhof Palace at the edge of Sanssouci Palace in Potsdam, considered the highlight of palace architecture by Schinkel, was built on a small piece of land King Frederick William IV received when he was crown prince as a wedding gift from his father. A work from Schinkel's later years, the palace, exuding an Italian air, also reveals Prussian simplicity. Surrounding the palace is a quaint garden presenting an idyllic pastoral scene that was landscaped by Schinkel's lifelong colleague Peter Joseph Lenné. Schinkel's collaboration with Lenné actually went beyond the aforementioned palaces to planning and carrying out a comprehensive landscaping project all around the lake between Potsdam and Berlin.[134] Having one architect's imaginative geography create the entire scene of a nation's capital like Berlin is something unlikely to be witnessed again.

The geographic scale of Schinkel's projects was as extensive as his imaginative geography. His projects crossed the Prussian borders and even went beyond the boundaries of Western Europe to reach Athens in Greece. Schinkel once launched an ambitious plan to build a new palace upon the ruins of the Acropolis of Athens. He had been officially commissioned to design the palace for Otto I, the Duchy of Bavaria, who became the Greek kingdom's first ruler. It must have been a dreamlike opportunity for the neoclassicist Schinkel, and he indeed drafted highly detailed plans, but they ultimately were never realized due to the domestic circumstances in Greece.[135]

Another meaningful design by Schinkel that was never realized was the Orianda Palace (Schloß Orianda) in the Crimea. The official commission to build an ancient Greek-style palace on the shores of the Black Sea in southwest Crimea came from the Russian Empress Alexandra Feodorovna. As the daughter of Frederick William III of Prussia, the empress's choice to hire an architect from her home country was not at all out of the ordinary. It was also natural for the Prussian-born empress to favor Greek-style architecture, but Schinkel actually planned to take a step away from typical neoclassicism in an attempt to create a building inspired by the Arabian Nights. Russia's aggravating fiscal circumstances forced the project to be cancelled without even giving the architect a chance to defend his plan before his client,[136] but the incident hints at what Schinkel's architecture may have looked like when realized outside Europe. His style would have ranged freely between classicism and its Oriental variations, yet Prussian imaginative geography would have surely run underneath them. The clues leading to this supposition can be found in the impression Schinkel drew as he was designing the Orianda Palace. The impression depicts the sight of a terrace where Erechtheion caryatids overlook the Black Sea, which is reminiscent of a typical ancient Greek temple. However, considering the spot where the building was supposed to stand, the direction the building is facing in the scene seems to hint at something else. Would it be an overstatement to say that the direction appears to be aligned with Prussia's gaze abroad?

Figure 1.8 Seaside Terrace of the Orianda Palace by Schinkel (1838), watercolor, 48 × 49.2 cm.

Source: Muesse/Public domain via Wikimedia Commons.

Whatever the case, Schinkel's architecture was not preoccupied with one stylistic form. It broadened from neoclassicism and neo-Gothic to modernism and even Orientalism, and in terms of function, it was applied to a wide range of buildings, including a guardhouse, opera house, museum, educational facility, commercial facility, and residences. They can be considered to have stood at the forefront of nineteenth-century historicism for relying on ancient exemplars yet striving to adapt them to current purposes.[137] To more freely make use of such ancient exemplars, it would have been no doubt necessary to tour through all the styles that ever existed in history. It took new ideas and their implementation before the so-called "historicist architecture" could emerge. Not only was historicism's hybrid nature effective in applying architectural legacies of Western antiquity to the reality of modern industrial societies, it helped form favorable conditions for disseminating heterogeneous spaces and civilizations.[138] The immortal architect Schinkel was certainly among the first to pick up the trend. And his grand imaginative geography and unfulfilled dream of building an Orianda Palace overseas came back to life decades later under the name of the German Empire.

4. The German Empire's Historicist Architecture

The nineteenth century, often dubbed the "age of revolution" by historians at the time, was a period when all legacies were shattered. As an alternative, history provided a new chance to discover the significance of the present through the meaning of the past in its entirety. Historicism, which swayed the minds of nineteenth-century Europe, was not an idea or style with a specific agenda but an inclination to keep its ties with the past amid waves of rapid change. And it made a huge impact on disciplines of human science (Geisteswissenschaften), such as history, theology, and jurisprudence, as well as the arts and architecture.[139]

"Kulturnation" and Historicist Architecture

Historicism "historicized" everything, including seemingly unshakable aesthetic norms. As fine arts became an independent realm with its own values, purpose, meaning, and history, traditional aesthetic norms lost their absolute value and were relativized as individual historical styles. Instead of imitating specific stylistic exemplars, art was thereby able to holistically treat all preceding styles as a reservoir to freely quote or pick and choose from whenever necessary. Art itself had turned into an exploration of art history.[140] This so-called historicization of art prompted art to stand on its own feet and forge a new cultural mission. Against the reality of modern times where everything was changing, art projected a temporary, individual entity as a synecdoche for an entire period and thus became charged with the task of recovering lost cultural identities.[141]

While the constant use of allegory in traditional religious paintings spurred the dominance of historical paintings depicting monumental episodes or figures from the past,[142] a single independent style was created in the realm of architecture. Typical narratives of architectural history will describe historicist architecture as a style between Biedermeier and Art Nouveau that covers a spectrum of neo-styles, including neo-Gothic, neo-Renaissance, and neo-Baroque. Period-wise, historicist architecture covers between the 1840s, when the bourgeoisie secured their political, social hegemony, and the early 1910s, when World War I broke out.

Historicist architecture rejected the doctrine of classicism, favoring architecture that adhered to the unchanging laws of nature, and believed that exemplars could be found from the classical architecture of antiquity. Instead of dwelling on a specific stylistic exemplar, it went with the eclectic approach of using such exemplars to suit current needs. The true nature of historicist architecture therefore lay in the multiplicity of several different styles mixed in a single building. It originated from the historicist way of thinking, which acknowledges that the present is a result of the past but also possesses a specificity of its own. So, historicist architecture was about constructing buildings that met present purposes but in forms that evoked historical styles. In-depth historical research allowed details of historical styles to be realized through the construction of historically unprecedented buildings that served new purposes such as train stations, operating offices, and even mining plants. Mixing new material and techniques with historic languages of architectural form made the possibilities for architecture to seem endless.[143]

This trend wholly reflected the interests of the bourgeoisie as the driving force of nineteenth-century Europe. From the 1840s until a major stock market crash occurred in Vienna, Austria, in 1873, western and central Europe saw liberal albeit incomplete civil revolutions take place and achieved economic prosperity with the onset of full-scale industrialization. The region to exhibit the most notable change was Germany, where development in the machine and electrochemical industries allowed it to outpace other regions in all aspects, including industrial production and population growth.[144] Often referred to as the "Founders' Period" (Gründerzeit) in German history, it was a time when the bourgeoisie solidified as the middle class in German society.[145] And this middle class served as a basis for the birth of the German idea of culture (Kultur). Germany's middle class took pride in being an "educated class of the bourgeoisie" that was apolitical yet heavily nationalistic. Such tendencies had stemmed from a fundamental antagonism toward a Western civilization represented by France and served as a cause for establishing a German national identity.[146] It was therefore not surprising to see Friedrich Meinecke, an influential German historian of the early twentieth century, define the German nation as a cultural nation (Kulturnation), a cultural community different from the French state-nation (Staatsnation) as a political community.[147]

In 1871, the Kingdom of Prussia subdued its archrival France and gave birth to the German Empire. The dramatic fulfillment of Prussia's long-held ambition to unify the German states brought an end to lengthy discussions as to which city should be the nation's capital. Berlin naturally became the capital of the German Empire. However, rather than functioning as a pivot of national consolidation, the city carried on with its traditional role as the old royal capital. The German Empire's formation had in fact been an extension of Prussia rather than an outcome of political unification.[148] Such political circumstances served as a condition for Schinkel's architectural legacies to exercise a long-lasting influence. Schinkel didn't particularly pay attention to forming a school of his own, but his legacies certainly dominated the German Empire's architecture.[149] Prussian classicism's spatio-temporal principles modeled after ancient Greece evolved in tandem with the changing circumstances of the times. History, which emerged as the tectonics of time, offered an optimal world view to the bourgeoisie, familiar with dynamic change but fearful of the iconoclastic turmoil of revolutions. Historicism was quite attractive for smoothly connecting the past with the future. Although it was at odds with classicism for not absolutizing past styles as timeless canons, historicism and classicism did share more commonalities than differences in cases like Schinkel who readily acknowledged the difference between past and present and tried to infuse the present into past styles.[150]

The bourgeoisie's desire to express themselves played a major role in allowing historicist architecture to flourish. Housing construction thrived and political optimism overflowed during the Founders' Period. It was no surprise that the bourgeoisie pushed functional efficiency aside in favor of antique villas with large gardens or multistoried houses with façades decorated as flamboyantly as royal palaces.[151] Houses were spaces where the bourgeoisie unreservedly revealed their antiquarian taste by filling them with imitations of art styles, decorations, and furniture used by the old aristocracy. This indicated a social situation in which the bourgeoisie was becoming assimilated with the aristocracy.[152] Yet the bourgeoisie was progressive enough not to remain satisfied with merely dabbling in the antiquarian taste. They did not hesitate in applying to historical-style buildings modern technology that drove industrialization. For instance, the advancement of iron smelting technology enabled romantically shaped spires to be placed atop buildings, and glass started to be used as the main material for buildings like the Crystal Palace in London.[153]

Historicism was certainly a mode of self-representation or a form of collective memory for the European bourgeoisie attempting to gain a political, social, and cultural foothold amid the currents of rapid change. Such attempts paraded their bold, adventurous spirit but also exposed their rather self-contradictory nature of sticking to old forms that lacked timeliness. A balance between past and present was but a figure of speech. A gap between artistic form based on historical exemplars and practical function in real life tends to be a trait that can typically be glimpsed from historicist architecture. Over the nineteenth century, practice and theory continued to drift apart in architecture, giving birth to various mutations and deviations.[154]

Schinkel's Successor Gottfried Semper

The applicable range of historical styles widened over the nineteenth century to embrace the entire span of Occidental architectural history. As appraisals and interpretations of historical artistic styles grew more subjective, a new architectural trend emerged around the 1840s. Stylistic streams using neo- as a prefix came to vie with one another for supremacy. Based on an understanding of their original iconological meaning, historical styles were freely "quoted" for different purposes. Churches mainly adopted the neo-Gothic style, while upper-class bourgeois residences mostly went for the neo-Renaissance style. Palaces or theatres for the nobility followed the neo-Baroque style, and main buildings of factories usually took on British classicism referred to as the Georgian style. All sorts of old styles were mined like mineral from the vast quarry of history.

Historicist architecture gradually discarded classical elements as it went through the romantic neo-Gothic style. The German round-arched style (Rundbogenstil) was something that appeared during this transition. The style that can be described as a passive alteration of classicism mainly grew popular in pro-French states of western Germany belonging to the Confederation of the Rhine. It partially accepted exemplars from ancient Roman architecture, discarded excessively monumental elements, and actively adopted functional elements that catered to modern civic life. Such aspects of the style seemed to architecturally represent the political status of the confederated states stuck between Napoleon's revolutionary France and the anti-revolutionary Prussia. Similar to the preceding Romanesque style on the outside, the round-arched style was theorized by Heinrich Hübsch, who deemed conformability (Schmiegsamkeit) the style's distinctive feature. Conformability referred to how the style didn't fixate on a particular stylistic model from the past and made various styles replaceable at any time, mainly depending on the practical function they could each serve. Through his 1822 publication *On Greek Architecture*, Hübsch argued that even the tectonics of Greek architecture originated from construction material and methods shaped by a climate and social environment specific to the region. This meant that a style is formed out of a purposiveness inherent in architecture to live up to a society's demands. Based on this viewpoint, absolutizing columniation as an architectural norm or insisting that pointed arches are a German feature are no more than ideas lacking conformability.[155]

Hübsch's semicircular arch was suggested as an architectural alternative capable of meeting the desperate need for light under northern

European climatic conditions as well as newly arising needs of industrial societies. At the heart of a modern city with increasing numbers of barrack-like tenement houses built with cheap machine-made bricks and decorated with ready-made goods, Hübsch's suggestion had been formulated from grappling with the question and title of a booklet he authored in 1828: "In What Style Should We Build?" No matter how shabby those houses were on the inside, Hübsch believed their façade on the outside should imitate a historical style to enhance the city's dignity. To him, the round-arched style was a timely alternative capable of satisfying both the artistic and functional values of architecture.[156]

Rather than being a sufficient alternative, Hübsch's suggestion hinted at the collapse of stylistic exemplars commonly employed up until then. It had grown difficult to locate a common ground between historically inherited forms and their practical functionality. The gap between the two became more evident in the face of the so-called neo-Renaissance style of architecture. Through his 1851 publication *Science, Industry, and Art*, Gottfried Semper, a German architect well-known for practicing the neo-Renaissance style, severely criticized that the art of his time had either become dependent upon the commercial profit of the bourgeoisie or fallen to the status of decorations for public spaces. Art, Semper stressed, should contribute to strengthening the organic unity of urban life. To do so, Semper believed that the best model could be found from old Italian Renaissance architecture, since it had contributed to the formation of a unity between the artistic features of a city-state and the practical lives of its citizens.[157]

If Schinkel represents the first half of nineteenth-century German architecture, Semper is often named as the architect who represents the second half. Like Schinkel, Semper primarily designed museums, libraries, and theaters. He also fully upheld Schinkel's belief that public architecture can turn a city into an urban theater. Semper was not like Friedrich August Stüler or Friedrich Ludwig Persius in Berlin, who were taught by Schinkel. Still, Schinkel's works were turning into common property for Semper and his contemporary architects as the Schinkel Festival (Schinkel Fest) was established as an annual memorial to honor Schinkel after his death. What Semper learned foremost from Schinkel's architecture was that a similarity could be found in ancient Greek architecture between the forms of art and nature. As with any organism, Semper's architecture basically presumed that a building's form should not be disengaged from its functional structure. Yet Semper did more than remain an imitator of Schinkel. He immersed himself in Bötticher's theory of tectonics, and instead of idealizing ancient Greece, he treated it strictly as an object of archaeological study. He also turned his gaze toward French architecture to enthusiastically embrace new stylistic trends. And he became a pupil of the German architect Franz Christian Gau, who was a naturalized French citizen.[158]

Through his two-volume book *Style in the Technical and Tectonic Arts; or, Practical Aesthetics*, published in 1861 and 1863, Semper used natural science as a model to cast light upon the history of architectural styles. According to the book, the motives of architectural style fall under four different material or functional categories: textiles, ceramics, carpentry, and masonry. As these categories meet with the social conditions of each period, architectural transformations occur. What forms the origin of architectural art is the curtain wall that symbolizes spatial division. And architecture began as the curtain wall transformed into walls made of wood or stone. This constitutes Semper's well-known theory of *Bekleidung*, the principle of clothing, which regards architecture as the stylization of space akin to dressing a naked body. New architectural styles emerge as existing motifs such as the curtain wall undergo physical transformations due to changing social conditions. For example, Greek Ionic architecture became stylized as the tectonic structure for wooden constructions had to be transformed to be applied to stone buildings. Fluting was originally applied to columns as decorations to demonstrate the solidity of columns until it settled as an art form that obscured the structural role of columns. Hence, decorations were not mere supplements overlaid on a building's structure. In Semper's eyes, the nature of monumental architecture, or art itself, lay in the formalization and concealment of all essential structural components. Through such an embryological analysis, Semper drew the conclusion that architecture is formed not out of a contest but a compromise between being purely artistic and entirely functional, or between being utterly independent and completely dependent upon society. Rather than simply copying styles, imitation in architecture was to recreate time and again by reinterpreting stylistic motifs that each once satisfied certain functional or symbolic needs.[159]

Semper's principle of clothing allowed Schinkel's neoclassical principle of tectonics to be more flexibly applied in a new reality by placing it within the context of Western architectural history. Even the color of buildings came to be regarded as the best clothes for them, more so than metals or jewels. Semper's theory of polychromy indicates that his principle of clothing disallowed one-sided idealistic interpretations and focused on the materiality of architecture. Although he wasn't the first to do so, Semper attempted to squarely challenge Winckelmann-like preconceptions deeming pure white marble a distinctive characteristic of Greek architecture. Ever since the archaeologist and art historian Quatremère de Quincy published *Jupiter Olympius, or, The Art of Antique Sculpture Considered in a New Point of View* in 1815, the pure white image of Greece began to waver and then became impossible to maintain by the 1820s when trips to Greece could be made more frequently. It was French architects like Jacques-Ignace Hittorff who led the movement to apply newly discovered colors and decorations of ancient architecture to nineteenth-century neoclassicism, but Semper was the one who attempted to more systematically theorize the movement in Germany.

Semper's teacher Gau was friends with Hittorff, which is probably why Semper was aware of the latest trends in French architecture.[160]

To formulate an architectural theory of his own, Semper delved into architectural history, art history, aesthetics, and even archaeology and anthropology. However, instead of managing to merge theory with practice, his empirical, scientific approach accentuated pluralism and led to the contradictory outcome of dissociating style from practical functionality, reducing it to a perpetually replaceable ornament. The buildings Semper designed came across as too monument-like compared to those designed by Schinkel. The domineering entrance, exaggerated proportions, and excessively heavy rustication gave the actual effect of Semper's profound theory a reputation similar to that of Heinrich Hübsch's architecture, which emphasized façades.[161] But regardless of how it is regarded, there is no doubt that Semper's architecture was at the forefront of German historicist architecture. The idea that architectural style can be historically created and sublimated into an organic whole, or a total work of art (Gesamtkunstwerk), representative of an entire period, served as an ideological core to Schinkel's neoclassical architecture as well as historicist architecture. And Semper, more than anyone, was responsible for allowing that idea to be equipped with theoretical systemicity and applied to architecture.[162]

The Neo-Renaissance Style: The Quintessence of Historicist Architecture

The most historicist among historicist architecture was the neo-Renaissance style represented by Semper. Unlike classicism that relies on time-honored aesthetic norms or romanticism that mystifies the past, the neo-Renaissance style tends to historically explore the architectural language from the peak of the Renaissance (cinquecento) and reproduce it as it is. It most typically reveals the characteristics of historicist architecture in which the reproduction of architectural history itself becomes architecture. By the mid-nineteenth century, romanticism's sentimental fervor abated and began to be replaced by academic rigor. As it grew common to more objectively reproduce old styles through detailed historical research and holistically reviewing traditions from the past instead of blindly accepting them, classical architecture's basic elements and motifs such as columns, pilasters, cornices, friezes, sculptures, mansard roofs, dormers, spires, and domes regained their Italian aura. This, in turn, did not bridge but made more conspicuous the gap between form and function.

The neo-Renaissance style was adopted by constitutional monarchies in the 1830s when the refined Italian style was seen and favored as truly upper class. However, as the revolutions of 1848 occurred, the bourgeoisie, filled with desire to climb the social ladder, gradually acquired the style, which thereafter settled as a style of self-representation for the bourgeoisie by the 1870s. What the neo-Renaissance style sought was not to restore a forgotten past but to revive uninhibited individuality. Various stylistic elements of Renaissance architecture reproduced through rigorous historical research were ultimately used by the bourgeoisie for self-representation and to gain commercial profits. Individualism, urbanity, science, modernity, and classicality were the core elements that characterized neo-Renaissance architecture.[163] The Swiss historian Jacob Burckhardt's famous travel guide *The Cicerone* (1855) and *The Civilization of the Renaissance in Italy* (1860), his masterpiece on cultural history, kindled among the bourgeoisie at the time a fondness for the Italian Renaissance, despite Burckhardt's aristocratic pessimism.[164]

The place where the neo-Renaissance architectural style first blossomed in Germany was not "Spree-Athens" Berlin where Schinkel's neoclassical style ruled, but Dresden, known as "Florence on the Elbe." The Kingdom of Saxony's capital, Dresden was infused with a new vigor as the obscure young architect Semper arrived in 1834 to work as Professor of Architecture at the Royal Academy of Arts. The Royal Theater (Königliches Hoftheater) Semper designed and built in Dresden between 1838 and 1841 signaled the beginning of German neo-Renaissance architecture. A tragedy by Goethe was performed for the opening of the ornate theater with a semicircular façade that dovetailed with the arches of the Zwinger, a symbolic Baroque-style palace in Dresden. Round walls and arched windows were stretched out across the building's first and second floor, an elaborate display far from German rigidity. The building's form reflecting Semper's French taste also fulfilled the building's function. Its round façade made the theater appear inviting to people passing by through the square in front of it and at the same time functioned as a round wall for the indoor space with seats arranged along the wall in a semicircular pattern. The three-story-high left and right wings with square-shaped façades served as the stage area. The Dresden Royal Theater was indeed an object of bold experimentation. The Renaissance style realized through the theater was quite different from Schinkel's legacy in Berlin and unlike the neo-Gothic or round-arched styles popular at the time. Semper had regarded the Renaissance style as a profound source of stylistic motifs capable of offering an alternative in terms of form and function.[165]

At one point, Semper incorporated the royal theater's construction into a more comprehensive plan. He soon began working on a plan to build a massive cultural forum (Kulturforum) by expanding the Zwinger north toward the riverside. While devising this large-scale plan, Semper sought advice from Schinkel in Berlin and is said to have received enthusiastic support from the great architect.[166] However, financial issues forced that ambitious plan to be reduced to building a picture gallery (Gemäldegalerie) on the Zwinger's northeastern side. The gallery that opened in 1855 wasn't finished by Semper, but it was nevertheless named the Semper Gallery (Sempergalerie) for having been largely based on his design. Unlike Semper's original design, the gallery was built at a right angle to

Figure 1.9 Top: Elevation of the Royal Theater Dresden. Middle: The Gemäldegalerie. Bottom: The Gemäldegalerie and the Zwinger.

Source: Ludwig Neumann, Hermann August Richter, Otto Siebdrat, Richard Steche, Robert Wimmer/CC BY-SA (https://creativecommons.org/licenses/by-sa/4.0). Top: From *Die Bauten, technischen und industriellen Anlagen von Dresden*, ed. Sächsisches Ingenieur- und Architekten-Verein und vom Dresdener Architekten-Verein (Dresden: Meinhold, 1878). Middle: Photo by author (2013). Bottom: Photo by author (2013).

the Zwinger like a fence to the palace. The building's protruding central part resembled the shape of a Roman triumphal arch, which served as a passage leading to the street in front of the riverside royal theater. The building, plainly divided into left and right, assumed a distinctively neo-Renaissance, horizontal form. Its façade was dominated by a rusticated finish around the ground level and was trimmed with decorative moldings and balustraded cornice.

What makes the gallery highly original is that the arrangement of its space reflected its exhibition themes. The northern side adjacent to the riverside royal theater represented classical themes, whereas the southern side facing the Zwinger represented the history of early modern art. On the northern side above the cornice of the building's protruding center were statues of the ancient Greek sculptors Phidias and Lysippos, as well as the Greek hero Pericles and Alexander the Great, juxtaposing art and politics or tradition and transience. Medallions and reliefs featuring Greek myths lined the windows stretched out along the façade. The southern side, on the other hand, was adorned with more delicate ornaments and statues of Giotto di Bondone, Hans Holbein, Albrecht Dürer, and Peter von Cornelius, depicting the Italian origin of modern painting and its German successors. The two central alcoves above the arch were occupied by Raphael and Michelangelo, personifying the apogee of European art. The gallery's interior once again delivered the building's message about art history. Once visitors stepped inside, they would face the reliefs upon two long friezes, one featuring the history of Italian painting between the middle ages and the eighteenth century, the other featuring German and northern European painters and their patrons. The painting on the ceiling illustrated, among other religious themes, the birth of Christian art from ancient ruins. Each time visitors stepped into a different room, they would be encouraged to explore the lengthy history of art that leads from one style to another.[167]

Semper's picture gallery was an architectural reenactment of Western art history to which the Renaissance was key. Its façade, sculptures, and even the spatial arrangement of the rooms featuring a series of styles all demonstrated an ideal implementation of historicist ideas. The neo-Renaissance style certainly seemed to be suitable for museum buildings. Unlike other public offices, museums were civic, public institutions that markedly embodied bourgeois initiative. As the Altes Museum by Schinkel previously showed, museums were places that helped associate history with notions of origin, formation, or development rather revolution in order to preach that the present is a logical, inevitable result of the past. This trait of museums corresponded ideally to the desire of the bourgeoisie that was rapidly growing conservative as it pursued cultural hegemony. The monumental neo-Renaissance style equipped with functional rationality was truly a perfect fit for the bourgeoisie's self-representation.[168]

German neo-Renaissance architecture reached its peak with Semper's final work in Dresden. When a fire in September 1869 destroyed the monumental royal theater Semper had designed, a pressing need arose for a replacement, and Semper was once again commissioned to build it. The opportunity to relive the passion from his youth came unexpectedly for Semper, who by that time had long left Dresden after his involvement in the March Revolution of 1848. Once Semper finished the design, it took nearly seven years, until February 1878, for his son Manfred Semper to complete the new Hoftheater (Neues Hoftheater), often referred to as the Semper Opera House (Semperoper) that came to represent the peak of German neo-Renaissance architecture.

The Semper Opera House stands out for its rational arrangement of space that embodies both aesthetic form and the utmost acoustic quality. In terms of style, the building incorporates some fairly eclectic elements in order to reinforce its functionality. In particular, the combination of arches and pillars is a unique part of Semper's architectural language that cannot be found in neoclassicism, neo-Gothic, or even the German round-arched style.[169] The most eye-catching aspect is the massive exedra set into the building's façade with a quadriga on top, creating a crown-shaped space for conversation. Amid lustrous marble facing and mosaic, the exedra displays an actualization of polychromy that Semper studied his whole life. The curvy façade and the rusticated lower-level pilasters; the pairs of Corinthian half-columns and arched windows on the upper level; and the staircases, foyers, and auditorium inside have all been put together to achieve a highly dramatic effect.

Compared to the old royal theater, the new Hoftheater Dresden was situated further away from the picture gallery, giving its façade and wings a bit more space to spread out. In terms of formativeness or size, the building was no less monumental than the Zwinger standing nearby. The

Figure 1.10 Left: Elevation of the New Hoftheater Dresden. Right: The Main Entrance and Exedra of the New Hoftheater.

Source: Photos by author (2013).

stage house facing northwest beyond the building's façade was covered with a gable roof, where a classical touch was given by placing a Greek lyra upon the ridge and gryphons on either edge. The stage house's front section facing southeast was shaped like a horseshoe, with the auditorium located three levels below and staircases running two more levels down to the front foyer. The building's wings extended even lower to accommodate ground-level carriage porches. The building's structure could therefore be characterized as a tense unity between the front and rear as well as between horizontal and vertical lines. Its rusticated finish gave the building's lower level a rugged texture that appeared almost brutal. The arched windows and double pilasters shaped like a tightly pulled back piece of fabric seemed to echo Semper's principle of clothing.[170]

In April 1878, not long after the building's completion, the architecture journal *Deutsche Bauzeitung* published in its thirtieth issue an article about the new Hoftheater Dresden, along with its elevation and floor plan for the ground floor. Through the article, the journal's editor, Karl Emil Otto Fritsch, highly praised Semper as "the master who has continued to profoundly influence German architecture since Schinkel."[171] Unlike the former royal theater's elegance, the new Hoftheater Dresden may have appeared in the eyes of Fritsch too rigid and lacking organic unity due to its starkly divided sections, but such potential criticism was summed up under the word "unfamiliar." The way Fritsch saw it, the theater revealed "the truth behind architectural organism that has been internally sought through the emergence of ideal purposiveness and beauty," making it "a monument in the utmost sense of the word." Above all, Fritsch underscored that the exedra served as a central pivot that tied the building's divided sections together and satisfied the "tectonic conscience" of architects.[172]

Wholly accepting Fritsch's argument published in *Deutsche Bauzeitung* surely allowed Semper's neo-Renaissance architecture to be considered a creative successor to the Prussian classicism Schinkel represented. And Schinkel in fact did react enthusiastically toward Semper's plan to build a cultural forum in Dresden. The transition from Schinkel to Semper could be described as a Greek stoa's transformation into a Renaissance palace.[173] While both are monumental as well as functional, there are differences between them that cannot be taken lightly. Through his final masterpiece, Semper featured the sight of the Greek god of wine Dionysus and his bride Ariadne riding a quadriga up Mount Olympus. The statue could come across as an architectural representation of Friedrich Nietzsche's *The Birth of Tragedy* (1872) and stood in contrast to the god of light and reason Apollo on a quadriga that Schinkel placed upon the roof of the Royal Theatre (Königliches Schauspielhaus) in Berlin. Greece had thus been turned into an image of Dionysian divide rather than Apollonian harmony.

This sort of divide was inevitable for historicist architecture. Like the Rococo style of the eighteenth century, the neo-Renaissance style indicative of nineteenth-century upper-class culture sought to satisfy the contradictory bourgeois desire to take a serious interest in historical traditions yet aim for functional rationality. The process through which neo-Renaissance settled as a dominant architectural style involved the evolution of Prussian spatio-temporal tectonics into a new discourse formation. The contradictory unity between past and present, or form and function, attempted through Semper's principle of clothing had practically resulted from excluding and suppressing a disintegrated exterior. It reflected the reality of the German Empire established by overcoming political and social divides. As the German Empire expanded overseas, developed industrial technologies, and saw an increase in economic and cultural demands from its middle class, rigorously reproducing past styles grew incompatible with the times and raised the need to employ an eclectic style that further catered to functionality.[174] The contrast had grown too stark between heavily ornamented façades and practical interior spaces or sunny bourgeois residences and the gloomy working-class shacks behind them. Change was therefore inevitable. After Semper's new Hoftheater Dresden appeared, the neo-Renaissance style gradually fell out of favor as historicist architecture moved on to a new stage.

Neo-Baroque Architecture: The Spearhead of Imperialism

Historicism showed signs of overheating right before its flames began to die down. Around the 1890s, the spread of imperialism spurred nationalism and undermined objective approaches toward history. Historicism thus turned into a means of propagating imperial cultural superiority. No longer capable of representing a harmonious combination of past and present, history instead transmuted into a narration of apocalyptic salvation and self-transcendence. Economically, a prolonged recession shifted the flow of capital from the private consumer goods market toward the public sector that guaranteed greater profits. Architecture accordingly expanded its scale and used historical materials or styles purely to present a spectacle rather than to serve practical purposes. It was, of course, historicism's nature to memorialize the past in a public capacity. The difference was that whereas early historicism was about the bourgeoisie's collective admiration for a disappearing culture of nobility, late historicism fell to an unabashed tool of imperialist propaganda.[175]

Since the 1830s, train stations and auxiliary facilities started to be built in cities, gradually disintegrating the existing urban structure and giving rise to new urban nuclei. As the bourgeoisie struggled to secure control over the vast space in the suburbs of traditional urban centers, historical identity once more began to matter. It was no coincidence that populated public spaces like train stations were used as venues for exhibiting technological and industrial progress as well as the cultural achievements of the bourgeoisie. The more the acceleration of change drove past and present apart, the greater the desire to compensate for a sense of loss by ostentatiously restoring past cultural traditions.[176] On the one hand, late historicism praised past glories but on the other hand extremely flaunted the technological and cultural feats of modern civilizations. This resulted in hybrid forms based on combinations of disparate architectural motifs. Historical allegories were appropriated regardless of their original meaning and even led to the appearance of grandiose, abstract forms reminiscent of ancient Egyptian or Mesopotamian remains. History had turned into a domain of distant myths instead of specific periods, which suggests, in a way, a self-dissolution of historicism.[177]

This new trend in historicist architecture is usually referred to as the neo-Baroque style for attempting to create a holistic visual effect by introducing grandiose Baroque elements such as arched awning windows, domes or cupolas, and protruding balconies while adopting dynamic lines embodying diverse stylistic elements. The style is sometimes mockingly referred to as Wilhelminism (Wilhelminismus) for resembling the autocratic ruling style, ostentation, and vanity of the German Emperor Wilhelm II. In France, the neo-Baroque style was called the "Second Empire style" for being reminiscent of the times of Napoleon III, while in Britain, it was referred to as the "Queen Anne style" or "neo-Palladianism." Neo-Palladianism attempted to apply mathematical ratios to the dynamic asymmetry of mannerism, which is the precursor to the Baroque style. Neo-Palladianism can be characterized by rusticated pilasters dividing a façade into different sections and cornices of differing heights. Buildings formed like a disintegrated mass of individual sculptures despite their artificially determined mathematical harmony can be regarded as symbolic of the British Empire stretched out across the five great oceans and six continents.[178] Overall, neo-Baroque architectural works share a megalithic structure based on tension created from the contrast between horizontal and vertical lines. In other words, neo-Baroque was an architectural style sustained by an unstable partnership between exaggerated form and functionality.

Generally known as a formalist art historian, Heinrich Wölfflin described through his 1888 work *Renaissance and Baroque* that the two styles were different in terms of their form as well as their spiritual roots. Compared to the Renaissance style's essentially sculptural nature, he underscored that the truly pictorial Baroque style possessed a notably profound inwardness, a manifestation of a truly northern European spirit that could be traced back to medieval Gothic art.[179] Rather than being an art historian's personal opinion, Wölfflin's view reflected to a certain degree the cultural trend of the times. Indeed, the neo-Baroque style emerged with the loft historical mission of reviving national spirit. The style sought to establish buildings and urban spaces not as technological achievements but as grand national monuments. This, of course, didn't mean a social consensus had been formed on what constituted a national style, which is why competition for hegemony was endless between the neo-classicist, round-arched, neo-Gothic, and neo-Renaissance styles. Hence, rather than recognizing neo-Baroque as a distinct, individual style, it can be regarded as a discursive formation involving such a style.

A distinct example of neo-Baroque architecture would be the Reichstag Building constructed to house the German Empire's imperial Diet. Ruling forces kept casting looks of doubt upon the building at the heart of Berlin that would come to symbolize the German Empire's political unity. Otto von Bismarck, the chancellor who played a leading role in unifying the German Empire but retained his Prussian noble identity, even suggested for the Diet building to be constructed in Kassel, a small midwestern city far away from Berlin.[180] Completed in 1894 in a partially modified version of the publicly recruited architect Paul Wallot's design, the Reichstag Building was the outcome of exhausting discussions about what constituted the German architectural style. The standard Gothic style was too Catholic, the northern German style too Protestant, the Renaissance style too bourgeois, and the Baroque style too aristocratic. The desperate solution turned out to be a mixture of several different elements of Western classicist architecture, causing the Reichstag Building to be identified as either the neo-Renaissance or neo-Romanesque style depending on the viewer. Critics at the time gave harsh reviews of the stylistically hybrid building. Wilhelm II, who disapproved of the imperial Diet itself, referred to the building as "the Reich's Monkey House."[181] And because the emperor refused to allow the building to be built near the royal palace or on Wilhelm Street, it ended up beside the Brandenburg Gate.[182]

Although it failed to completely satisfy the ruling class, the Reichstag Building was authoritarian enough to provide access only through its

Figure 1.11 The Reichstag Building.

Source: Photo by Georg Pahl (1926). Courtesy of the Bundesarchiv, Bild 102–03034.

main entrance. More than anything, the massive dome made of steel and glass demonstrated the German Empire's power. Reborn from the neo-Renaissance style, the dome's motif based on the sky originally carried religious implications, its hemispherical shape suggesting the most complete possible representation of the sky embracing the earth. Built from the ground up toward the sky unreachable to mankind, the dome substantiates the earth's existence as well as salvation from heaven. The glass dome rising from the building's center to reflect the sunlight seemed to elevate the building to a divine status.[183] This was certainly perfect for elevating the empire's divine authority. However, the dome was also the most modern element throughout the entire building and therefore embodied the duality of imperial authority and open, transparent democratic politics.[184] The building differentiated itself from other brick buildings featuring Wilhelminism, but its natural, sturdy construction combined with the dynamic form from the period of imperialism represented the spirit of the times. The Reichstag Building's projection of Wilhelminism blended in with the stringent architectural undertone originating from Prussian classicism yet remained open enough to adapt to a different building environment. It was therefore not surprising when a refined, condensed version of it emerged decades later in an unfamiliar space far away from Germany.

5. Historicism and Urban Planning

Prussian classicism's ideal to actualize the tectonic unity of architectural space went beyond individual buildings and facilitated an overall reorganization of urban space. For Schinkel, it was most natural to work on urban planning for a city while designing individual buildings in that city, because he oversaw all public construction projects in Prussia and his architecture always involved an imaginative geography that encompassed an entire city. While constructing the Neue Wache, Schinkel presented the Prussian king with a large-scale construction plan for downtown Berlin in 1817. Having critically considered the eighteenth-century plan for Forum Fridericianum, the new plan sought to achieve an entire city's perspectival unity rather than being preoccupied with individual buildings.[185]

As Prussia's capital, the population of Berlin, including soldiers, jumped from 50,000 to nearly 170,000 throughout the eighteenth century, making it imperative to rearrange the city's layout. By the mid-eighteenth century, the old fortress walls were falling apart from no longer being able to serve their original purpose, but the transportation circumstances remained poor between the city's nucleus and suburban areas to its west. Schinkel's plan served as a practical intervention for Berlin in such a transitional state. Although his rather idealistic plan eventually met a fate similar to the former plan for Forum Fridericianum by managing to only partially repair downtown Berlin's layout,[186] it was still meaningful for establishing the tectonic construct as a new direction for the city of Berlin.

Schinkel and Lenné's Neo-Classicist Urban Architecture

What stood out most from Schinkel's plan was how it aimed to establish the heart of an organism called Berlin by fully tearing down the fortress wall in the downtown area and completing Unter den Linden, the road to victory between the royal palace and the Brandenburg Gate. To achieve this goal, a stone bridge was built in 1824 to link the Lustgarten facing the royal palace with Unter den Linden across the river. The king ordered for the old bridge built according to the eighteenth-century plan for the Palace Square (Schloßplatz) to be demolished and had the so-called Palace Bridge (Schloßbrücke) built in its place. Since Schinkel had made clear that his primary goal was aesthetic, the new bridge had to be fit for a kingdom's capital: elegant in form and adorned with symbolic sculptures so that it blended in with buildings such as museums that would later surround it and helped the river's water flow more smoothly through the city.[187] Four solid granite pedestals formed low arches along either side of the Palace Bridge, topped with arabesque cast-iron railings. Perched above between the railings were four pairs of statues of warriors and goddesses of victory, signaling that memories of the Wars of Liberation had dictated the bridge's construction as they had when the statues of Gerhard J. D. von Scharnhorst and Friedrich Wilhelm Freiherr von Bülow were placed in front of the Neue Wache. Although the statues were installed on the bridge only after Schinkel's death due to cost issues, the Palace Bridge was nevertheless monumental for declaring that Schinkel's hands had given birth to the heart of Berlin.[188]

Figure 1.12 Design for the Palace Bridge.

Source: From Schinkel, *Sammlung*, plate 24. Courtesy of the Smithsonian Libraries. https://library.si.edu/digital-library/book/sammlungarchite00schi

The construction of the Palace Bridge finally helped the Lustgarten assume the look it was meant to exhibit. The royal palace, the Supreme Parish Church built by Johann Boumann the Elder in the eighteenth century, and the addition of the Altes Museum by Schinkel later on allowed an ensemble of buildings representing different periods to unfold around the Lustgarten. The pathway formed along the riverside also turned into an attraction for the citizens of Berlin.[189] However, it remains uncertain as to whether an organic union had truly been achieved between the urban space and the individual buildings along Unter den Linden or between the Prussian state and its citizens. Schinkel certainly seems to have tried to create a steady, unified urban space by completing Unter den Linden. Yet hadn't the autonomy of that urban space been sacrificed to produce a representation of power? Was the cityscape's stage-like display not merely a phantasmagoria rather than a realization of harmony?[190] These fundamental questions prompted by Schinkel's urban architecture led to an aporia of historicism later on.

Schinkel continued to devote his efforts to construction and landscaping projects in the central Mitte district of Berlin, which included Unter den Linden. By the final stage of his life, Schinkel took part in more comprehensive urban design projects led by his lifelong colleague Peter-Joseph Lenné. In 1825, the Berlin urban planning authority Baupolizei launched a construction project at an undeveloped district in downtown Berlin. The crown prince, or the future Frederick William IV, took the lead and was enthusiastic enough to suggest a blueprint of his own for the project, but Schinkel rejected it and adhered to the Baupolizei's original plan. Full-scale construction began as soon as the crown prince ascended to the throne in 1840, most likely because housing had turned into a highly urgent matter that had to be addressed. Rapid industrialization triggered a massive influx of the rural population into cities, including Berlin, where its population of approximately 160,000 around 1810 doubled by 1840. According to the king's orders, Lenné collaborated with Schinkel on devising a new plan aimed at extensively rearranging the layout of Berlin. The famous blueprint for the "Projected Embellishment of Berlin and Its Immediate Vicinity" (Projectirte Schmuck-und Grenzzüge von Berlin mit nächster Umgebung) proposed to pave a wide, looped boulevard lined with trees and embellish it with buildings, sculptures, and parks to serve as the summation of a lengthy process of transforming Berlin into Prussia's capital, not to mention the starting point to newly establishing Berlin's foundation as an industrial city.[191]

When Schinkel passed away from a chronic illness not long after the enthronement of Frederick William IV, Lenné was entrusted with the plan's execution. As a renowned Prussian landscape architect, Lenné had been responsible for redesigning the Sanssouci Palace garden in Potsdam. Since 1833, he had been focused on completely rearranging the Tiergarten in Berlin. Lenné transformed the marshy park covered with wild vegetation into a garden full of flowers with a lake and streams. The garden's pathways gave the impression of having been naturally formed, but behind their creation were in fact geometric calculations. Demonstrating a combination of the naturalness of English gardens and the flowing elegance of Italian and French gardens, Lenné's style of landscape gardening came to be adopted throughout Berlin. Although his style was never fully realized, it certainly left an exemplar to refer to for urban planning in the future.[192] Despite rapid growth due to industrialization, Berlin managed to secure a road network embellished with classical architecture as well as space for greenery without becoming swept up in rampant development by private developers, which seems to reflect the way Schinkel's tectonics evolved into historicism. This series of developments may not have been intended from the beginning, but they did lay the groundwork for Berlin on its way to becoming an imperial capital.

As the garden director charged with overseeing Berlin's landscaping projects, Lenné tried to uphold Schinkel's desire to elevate the central Mitte district of Berlin into a new Athens as he applied the same approach in developing districts that were newly incorporated into Berlin. Lenné was basically a neo-classicist, but, like Schinkel, he preferred to modify various old styles to suit individual functions rather than adhering to a particular stylistic form. Instead of pruning nature for the privileged few, Lenné's landscaping meant to provide a green lung to a city where commoners lived and breathed. This underlying idea was what fueled the application of historicism's principle of utilizing a massive quarry of stylistic resources from the past, even partially to the suburbs of Berlin. For instance, the Landwehr Canal, a 7.4-kilometer canal named after the frontier guards, was built and lined with vegetation between southern Berlin and the Tiergarten. In addition, a street network and green area on par with those of downtown Berlin were constructed in the fields of Köpenick (Köpenicker Feld) on the southeastern outskirts of Berlin, forming what may as well be called the Unter den Linden of the proletariat.[193]

Lenné's ambitious plans often ended up remaining on paper due to technological and social insufficiencies, but he was at least able to achieve a certain degree of progress on one project from his 1840 plan that he had continued to treat as a priority. That project involved the loop road that ran along the canal around the outskirts of southwestern Berlin. Although Frederick William IV actively supported the project by ordering monumental plazas to be built at every intersection, the project was realized in a modified form as someone with a different set of expertise took the lead in the 1860s after the king's death. That someone was James Hobrecht, a certified architect specializing in railways and waterways at the Berlin police headquarters who rose to the position of head of the Commission for the Preparation of Building Plans for the Environs of Berlin in 1859 at the age of thirty-three.[194]

The Hobrecht Plan

The wave of industrialization that surged since the 1830s drastically changed the size of Berlin's population. According to a census conducted at the time, Berlin's resident population amounted to around 430,000 in 1855. That number increased by 20,000 to 30,000 each year, so that by the time Germany was unified in 1871, the capital's population was above 825,000. In 1880, Berlin's population exceeded one million and reached nearly two million when including those in the environs of Berlin in the early 1890s. This rapid population growth led to the city's expansion as the districts of Moabit and Wedding to the northwest of the Tiergarten were newly incorporated into Berlin in 1861, mainly to serve as residential areas for the incoming rural population, especially workers from East Prussia.[195]

Baroque urban architecture was no longer capable of meeting realistic demands. For metropolises of the nineteenth century, a systematic, smooth transportation network became essential in order to handle the population spike caused by industrialization, not to mention the increasingly multilateral interactions among that population. New means of transportation, including railways, made it meaningless to simply decorate small downtown areas. New urban architecture for industrial societies therefore had to focus on functionality rather than artistic form. There were, however, possibilities moving into new times to utilize the Baroque form language as exemplified by the seventeenth-century Palace of Versailles. Monumental buildings integrating long, wide main roads, public squares, and radial street systems under a single view – vista – was a key component of metropolises in the nineteenth century that gained its most pioneering and typical expression during the transformation of Paris under the rule of Napoleon III.

In 1853, Georges-Eugène Haussmann was appointed as the prefect of the department Seine, which included Paris. According to the French emperor's order, Haussmann embarked upon the historic task of transforming the medieval city of Paris into the capital of a new empire. As land expropriation and redevelopment became possible through government decrees without having to obtain votes of approval from the national assembly, hundreds of buildings were instantly torn down in central Paris, and shabby alleyways disappeared in no time. Until the end of the 1860s, extensive long-term construction projects gave rise to a modern capital equipped with radial or cross-shaped wide boulevards lined with trees, lights, and benches, a water supply and sewage system, and communication facilities. Paris was reborn as a bright, clean, well-lit and well-ventilated city with a smooth transportation system. What stood out most about Haussmann's design was the road that meant to function as the city's aorta, which physically secured a transportation route, demonstrated the prestige of Paris as the French Empire's capital, and improved the city's hygiene. More than anything, the arterial road sparked a boom in the construction and real estate industry that yielded profit margins for the upper middle class and jobs for the working class.[196]

Haussmann's renovation of Paris, however, entailed a fundamental issue related to imperial authoritarian rule, or Bonapartism. A practically surgical operation on a living city may have had the positive effect of fostering commerce and industry to improve the city's infrastructure, but it proved too brutal toward the city's lower class. The practice of covering the construction cost by forcibly acquiring target areas as well as their adjacent areas at a low price and reselling those areas at a higher price once construction was completed came to be referred to as "excess condemnation" in the realm of urban planning. Instead of preventing speculation from causing the value of land to soar, this unprecedented practice forced landowners to bear the cost of public projects and shaped circumstances so that only the upper class could afford to reside in the downtown area. Even after acknowledging that the rise in real estate prices and rent would have been inevitable, the emergence of wide boulevards clearly made it more difficult for the public to install barricades to carry out uprisings and thereby caused politics to more quickly grow conservative. Barricades were replaced by monumental buildings parading imperial grandeur, and the boulevards of Paris turned into a stage where all sorts of spectacles unfolded.[197]

Of course, Baron Haussmann and Bonapartism are not entirely to blame for causing such outcomes. As much as it was inevitable for the value of land and rent to rise with the concentration of population in industrial cities, this irreversible trend made it inevitable for the working class to be pushed out to the suburbs. Suburbanization also occurred as means of transportation advanced and mechanization caused factories and their workers to relocate to more spacious suburban areas. Yet such unsupervised rural exodus turned suburban areas into slums, which tends to be marked as an indelible flaw in Haussmann's policy.

London presented a case that stood in contrast to that of Paris. By respecting individual interests and becoming only partially involved in making urban improvements, London's authorities used suburbanization as a means to relieve chronic overpopulation in downtown London and resolve issues related to traffic congestion, crime, and sanitation. Unlike Paris, planned public housing projects were carried out in London's suburbs based on expectations for new means of transportation. The loss owners could possibly suffer from having their land confiscated was minimized by requiring real estate or construction companies to offer compensation for price differences caused by speculation or to grant a new building lot. London's utterly liberal policy turned out to be more effective at preventing extreme disorder than Paris's centralized policy.[198]

In the mid-nineteenth century before full-scale urban planning was established, policymakers in Berlin ran into the same fundamental issue that those in Paris and London had experienced: how to preserve Berlin's dignity as the capital of Germany while building a layout efficient enough to accommodate the reality of industrial society. To a city like Berlin, ruled by the aesthetic legacies of Schinkel and Lenné, the case of Paris appeared to be a more convincing model than that of London. The idea of using symbols of civilization and progress such as boulevards and buildings to turn a city into a stage definitely had something in common with Prussia's classicist tradition. However, London's practical approach offered far more merits in terms of living up to the reality of industrial society. And the foremost task Berlin had to deal with was to expand the means of transportation connecting downtown Berlin to its suburbs and supply more housing to the working class so as to prevent slums from spreading.[199]

Taking care of this task was precisely why the Hobrecht Plan was devised. Berlin's boundary had come to be mainly defined by the customs wall since the fortress wall built in the seventeenth century mostly fell apart by the end of the eighteenth century. However, administrative changes proved inevitable for Berlin as a sharp population increase during the nineteenth century prompted the development of its transportation system. The railway line between Berlin and Potsdam introduced in 1838 was rapidly extended so that a looped line connecting existing train stops emerged by the 1850s. The railway thus settled as an indispensable part of Berlin's urban space. When major enterprises like Borsig began to build factories in Berlin, the city ran into a more desperate need to secure land for commercial as well as housing purposes. However, a medieval city like Berlin was not yet equipped to handle such social and economic demands.[200]

The Development Plan for the Environs of Berlin, often referred to as the Hobrecht Plan, was officially approved in 1862 and announced by the Berlin police headquarters. The plan that would affect Berlin's layout for the next few decades focused on paving new roads and constructing buildings per the king's request that the Prussian capital should be as splendid and dignified as Paris. However, whereas constructing new roads was a priority that caused buildings to be renovated or torn down in Paris, Berlin focused on developing newly incorporated districts into residential areas and sought to replicate in those areas the way street blocks had been divided in the downtown area. The Hobrecht Plan's inclusion of crossroads, loop roads, and densely populated tenement buildings was modeled after Paris, while its consideration for urban sanitation and a canal system in the city's outskirts was modeled after London.[201] The plan was not only comprehensive but ambitious. It was unprecedented to plan for one hundred years ahead in the nineteenth century so that the city would be able to accommodate a population of up to four million. Of course, in reality, that population estimate was exceeded within the next five decades or so.[202]

One of the most major issues for Berlin in the mid-nineteenth century did not have to do with the old downtown area that Schinkel had formed but the Tiergarten beside it and the Moabit district that used to house a firearm factory. Since the 1830s when he was crown prince, Frederick William IV had experienced friction with bureaucracy over his plan to fill the vacant space in the Moabit district with military-related facilities. By 1862, a considerable compromise was made through the Hobrecht Plan. With the new king and the Berlin police headquarters' support, the plan sought to preserve the old downtown area's neoclassical cityscape and surround it with a transportation network, offices, houses, and amenities befitting the reality of modern industrial society. Hobrecht was not an artistic architect but a civil engineer, so it was natural for him to propound functionality. Road types were mainly determined by the railway system, while constructing high-rise building complexes was permitted as long as the builder agreed to bear the increased land price. The system of wide roads practically secured enough space for constructing canals, which justified the construction of a sewage system and greatly contributed to improving the city's sanitation.[203]

The construction of canals was launched in 1873. As an expert on canals, Hobrecht intended to create a network of them throughout Berlin to dispose sewage. An irrigation system was adopted to preserve the river's water quality by preventing domestic sewage from flowing into the river and dispersing wastewater toward the city's outskirts. However, this technological reasoning suffered from a lack of architectural guidelines. Despite its official title, the Hobrecht Plan had no clear-cut architectural blueprint. Without any guidelines on the form of buildings, it only contained regulations on building lines (Fluchtlinien) that defined the width of avenues, the size of squares, intersections, or street blocks, and the distinction between sites for buildings and roads.[204] Because the Architectural and Police Act for Berlin and the Other Police Districts (Bau-Polizei-Ordnung für Berlin und den weiteren Polizei-Bezirk), promulgated on April 21, 1953, stipulated that only a building's outer wall rather than an entire building had to observe building lines, the act left a window open for indiscriminate development along the city's streets unless the act could be supplemented with a subsection stipulating further details.[205] It was therefore only a matter of time before private contractors began to engage in rampant speculation, and barrack-like tenement houses (Mietskasernen) sprung up in residential areas for workers. This was later sharply criticized by Werner Hegemann in his book *Berlin, City of Stone* published in 1930. The book pointed out that Hobrecht's architectural plan, which only controlled floor plans and left elevations unregulated, was originally to blame for causing indiscriminate development.[206]

Hobrecht had nevertheless already defended his approach in the 1860s. He claimed that dense tenement houses allowed various social classes to live together as a closely knit community and therefore reinforced national unity. Instead of excluding the poor from society, Hobrecht stressed that they should be "under the care of an ethical state," clearly indicating that his plan had taken this great cause into consideration.[207] Indeed, the Hobrecht Plan did show consideration for members of each social class, including the poor. For instance, the policy of giving landowners a certain degree of discretion by permitting joint investment for the purpose of improving or reallocating land slated for development was unlike Paris, which used state authority to confiscate land, or London, which completely relied on the commercial interests of landowners.[208]

The Hobrecht Plan was practical yet clearly a product of Prussian conservative thinking. The attempt to guide an industrial city's aggressive growth onto a disciplined track and subsume excluded members of society under state authority came into contact with the issue Schinkel had been conscious of. Although the plan presented a technological solution instead of a Schinkelian artistic alternative, it wholly inherited Schinkel's tectonic ideas and further shaped them to suit the times. In fact, not only did Hobrecht manage to leave the downtown area designed by Schinkel and Lenné intact while carrying out construction projects, he was able to realize the formation of canals along with the loop road connecting the southwestern outskirts of Berlin that was part of the 1840 plan for urban beautification.[209]

A city's reality is, however, not to be discerned only through the eyes of a conservative bureaucrat. To the poor, considered objects to be subsumed under the state, the reality projected through *Berlin, City of Stone* was harsh. The dark, damp backstreet scenes of Berlin the realist novelist Wilhelm Karl Raabe described in *The Chronicle of Sparrow Lane* made it hard to believe they were indeed part of the German Empire's glorious capital in the late nineteenth century. The contrast between the dim, winding Sparrow Lane and the wide, brightly lit Unter den Linden stretched out nearby featured the two different faces of Berlin. "At sunset and midnight, the lamplight and moonlight cast a peculiar glow here." In Raabe's eyes, the dingy underground chambers or attics full of cigarette smoke hidden in the backstreets of Berlin were "a valuable stage in the real world, reflecting all the antinomies of life including war and peace, misery and happiness, and famine and glut." The shadowy lives led in those backstreets signified what was excluded by the ideal purposiveness of Schinkelian tectonics.[210]

Backstreets were not the only problem. Even the magnificence of the tallest monument of triumph in Berlin failed to show the imperial capital's ideal purposiveness. Walter Benjamin's confession in his book *Berlin Childhood Around 1900* hints at how the citizens of Berlin actually regarded the grand column erected at a newly created intersection to commemorate Germany's victory in the Battle of Sedan during the Franco-Prussian War. In the eyes of an unprejudiced child, the victory column donned in gold seemed far from glorious and more like a "funerary stele" standing merely for ritualistic purposes like parades on anniversaries. Berlin was nothing but an inescapable prison to an innocent child like Benjamin. "Not to find one's way around a city does not mean much. But to lose one's way in a city, as one loses one's way in a forest, requires some schooling."[211] A space of suffocating integration and heartless exclusion: Was this not the rational conclusion of tectonics?

The Advent of Modern Urban Planning

Urban planning in the modern sense is commonly known to have originated from Britain and the United States, where large industrialized cities emerged early on. The term and technique appeared in the late nineteenth century and were established with the passing of Britain's first urban planning act in 1909. Linked directly to this trend was the idea of a "garden city" that left a long-lasting impact, since it was proposed at the turn of the century by a former parliamentary stenographer named Ebenezer Howard, as was the City Beautiful Movement carried out by the American architect Daniel Burnham when he devised a master plan for the lake city Chicago in 1909 after serving as director of the 1893 World's Columbian Exposition. The particularly influential idea of garden cities emulated the British policy's use of suburbanization to solve urban issues but proved to be fundamentally different in that the idea targeted small satellite cities likely to attract the educated middle class rather than the working class. In 1903, the first garden city was created up north of London in Letchworth, aiming to integrate the city center, the residential area, and the industrial and agricultural zones into a middle-class community without the interference of any speculative craze from the outside.[212]

This rather bourgeois and practical urban planning in Britain and the United States was in fact bred out of the idea and techniques of city planning (Städtebau) that emerged earlier in central Europe. Through his 1889 book *City Planning According to Artistic Principles*, the Austrian architect Camillo Sitte caused a major sensation by opposing the functionalistic tendency prevalent in large European cities during the nineteenth century and instead advocating a pictorial approach to urban planning. The book's fame helped Sitte rise to the position of director at the newly opened school of applied arts in the Austrian capital Vienna. In 1903, Sitte launched the journal *Der Städtebau* with a German architect and bureaucrat named Theodor Goecke. The journal was Sitte's attempt to realize in architectural design what his book preached about the harmony between functionality and aesthetics, which had an impact that went beyond continental Europe and reached Britain. The British architect Raymond Unwin served as proof of that impact from publishing the book *Town Planning in Practice* in 1909 and designing the first-ever garden city in Letchworth. Unwin's town planning is known to have critically succeeded Sitte's city planning in terms of shunning overcrowded cities in favor of cities with organic unity.[213]

Alongside his lifelong colleague Richard Barry Parker, with whom he jointly designed Letchworth Garden City, Unwin devoted himself to the

Arts and Crafts movement that had captivated young artists at the time and played a leading role in applying the movement to the practice of architecture. The movement that started in Britain, the cradle of industrial revolution, advocated the revival of medieval craftsmanship within the new reality of industrial society. However, the movement instead resulted in liberating aesthetic preferences from traditional restrictions as it attempted to overthrow the modern boundary between pure art and crafts. The nature of the movement was different from the historicist directionality of Sitte's city planning in that the movement embraced the beauty of French Art Nouveau's vivacious, natural curves combined with flatness while aiming for designs helpful to commoners in real life.[214] Letchworth Garden City was certainly not a place ruled by traditional architectural styles. Nevertheless, city planning in the German-Austrian sense and town planning in the British sense both originated from growing critically aware of the issues related to overcrowded industrial cities, and they both rejected functionality devoid of aesthetic values. In fact, they were disparate paths that both led to modernism.

Modernism had already been newly emerging as a major trend across Europe. It referred to art and literature that defied modernity, which basically gave modernism a self-contradictory nature. As did Charles Baudelaire, who regarded modernity as temporary and coincidental and believed art was the only alternative capable of cross-connecting such transient qualities with perpetuity, modernism embraced radical or conservative responses toward the conventional "modern" bourgeois culture.[215] The German-speaking part of central Europe was no exception to this trend. In Berlin, Munich, and Vienna, a group of impressionist artists stirred up secession movements to escape from conventional academies and institutions at a time when the German Art Nouveau called Jugendstil was budding. Such developments were meant to raise an objection against the one-sidedness, conventionality, and rigidity of established art and culture.[216] However, this trend cannot be fully explained by viewing it as a stylistic contest between modernism and historicism, because historicism, at least in its German sense, was already quite modern on its own. This can clearly be witnessed through the case of the *Deutscher Werkbund*, the German Association of Craftsmen that can be considered Germany's reaction to the Arts and Crafts movement in Britain.

Founded in 1907 in the southern German city of Munich, the Deutscher Werkbund sought to live up to the new needs of industrial society while infusing designs with the traditions of Germany's national culture. The association was made of up elite members of the German Empire such as professors, craftsmen, artists, architects, industrialists, and politicians. Yet it was characterized foremost as an alliance between artists and industrialists who criticized the handicraft romanticism advocated by the British Arts and Crafts movement and sought to actively utilize the machine civilization's potential for the sake of national prosperity.

According to Hermann Muthesius, who played a leading role in the Deutscher Werkbund's foundation, a broad range of interest "from sofa cushions to urban planning" was arising toward the use of machines in crafting, or applied arts.[217] As the birthplace of new architecture and applied arts that later came to be referred to as industrial design, the Deutscher Werkbund pushed for an unprecedented ideal, which was to revive a German national culture that can in short be described as conservative modernism.[218]

Having served as the Deutscher Werkbund's second president, Muthesius was someone who represented the nature of the association. Born in 1861, Muthesius studied philosophy, art history, and architecture at the University of Berlin. He worked for a time in the office of the architect Paul Wallot, who would later design the Reichstag Building. He then found a job at a construction firm in Berlin, which sent him to work in Tokyo for four years. After returning to Germany, Muthesius briefly worked as an official at the Prussian Ministry of Public Works before coming across the opportunity to serve as the cultural and technical attaché to the German Embassy in London between 1896 and 1903. While experiencing the Arts and Crafts movement in London, Muthesius established himself as an expert on English architecture but never turned into an advocate of it. He instead defended German values, and through his book *Style-Architecture and Building-Art*, published in 1902, he even criticized Semper's architecture for failing to be German due to the incorporation of French styles and preached the value of Nordic art's heavily ideological undertone. Nevertheless, Muthesius was not backward looking like any other conservative. He formed cooperative ties with Peter Behrens, the pioneer of German modernist architecture, that reinterpreted Schinkel's classicism to suit modern industrial society. An architect working for a leading German electricity company named AEG at the time, Behrens had been experimenting with an architectural style for factory buildings that left out unnecessary decorations to focus on producing a solid form. Muthesius and Behrens came to share the belief that "quality work" and healthy tastes should be actively encouraged for Germany's industrial development.[219]

While the early stages of the Deutscher Werkbund were led by Muthesius, a proponent of "great tectonic complete art" that integrates crafts and architecture,[220] modernist architects such as Walter Gropius and Ludwig Mies van der Rohe led the association's later stages from 1919 right after the end of World War I until the association was disbanded by the Nazis in the 1930s. These modernist architects distinguished themselves from Muthesius's conservative course in order to pursue a more universal aesthetics. They sought to form transatlantic, transnational solidarity through the International Congresses of Modern Architecture (Congrès internationaux d'architecture modern). By leading the so-called internationalism that dominated the European and American realms of architecture in the

1920s, such architects played a definitive role in the naissance of modern architecture and urban planning. Despite such a difference in approach between the members of the old and new generations, the fundamental nature of the Deutscher Werkbund remained unchanged.[221]

Also at the forefront of internationalism was Le Corbusier. The Swiss-born architect advocated purism from being inspired by Cubist art and pursued Descartes's rationality of pure lines and surfaces uninhibited by historical traditions.[222] Yet he willingly kept in step with the Deutscher Werkbund's attempt to integrate functionality with aesthetics. He had briefly worked at Peter Behrens's construction firm and was therefore christened with the strict classical modernism Behrens was pursuing. Le Corbusier's functionalistic approach in regarding a house as a "machine for living in" can be said to have been rooted in Schinkel's tectonics. As a matter of fact, internationalism was more of an introspective response to rather than an unconditional affirmation of the newness of modern industrial society, seeking a new order to patch up conflicts between form and function, or art and industry. Le Corbusier's approach aligned with how his German colleague Walter Gropius tried as master of Bauhaus to develop the newly founded art school into a cradle of modern architecture and industrial design that would answer to people's everyday needs.[223] The summation of this trend was New Functionalism (Neue Sachlichkeit), a critical rationalism that dominated the minds of central Europe in the 1920s and created a solid platform for the emergence of modernism.[224]

There were, in fact, more commonalities than differences between historicism that preferred traditional styles and the utterly modern Deutscher Werkbund that pursued mass production and standardization. The Deutscher Werkbund showed signs of reintroducing traditional cultures to the material culture of the bourgeoisie, while historicism had shown signs since the 1860s of utilizing various form languages of the past in the construction of modern industrial facilities. What Muthesius newly demonstrated was to no longer attempt to conceal the industrial aspects of architecture and design, which could be regarded as the Deutscher Werkbund's succession of historicism.[225]

Historicist architecture had already begun to use materials favored by modernist architecture, such as iron and concrete. The introduction of such new material rendered bearing walls unnecessary and freed interior spaces from having to serve structural functions, making it possible for such spaces to take on aesthetic form. The combination of iron structures and artistry had already been discussed exhaustively in the mid-1840s through Karl Bötticher's theory of tectonics. Bötticher infused classicism's stringent aesthetics with an open mind toward physical structures and material. He believed iron had the potential to formulate styles superior than those of Greek or medieval architecture because it was light and solid enough to allow structures to be freed from walls. Instead of constraining tectonics, modern construction material granted the possibility to better realize it.[226]

The neo-Baroque style representative of late historicist architecture was able to serve various functions, because it produced a monumental visual effect while being stylistically eclectic. Whereas early historicism believed a cityscape and the stylistic form of individual buildings should be preserved for generations because they symbolize civic spirit and the historical achievements of ancient sages, late historicism attempted to turn monumental public buildings into landmarks of metropolises serving as nodes of a nation's industrial activity and transportation network, which had a distinct impact upon individual buildings as well as a cityscape's overall arrangement.[227]

Christened with late historicism's neo-Baroque urban planning, European metropolises gradually grew familiar with the spirit of modernism that appeared to be in stark contrast to historicism.[228] Intensifying stylistic eclecticism paradoxically resulted in generalizing the value of rigid tectonic composition. Jugendstil, German Art Nouveau, and its natural beauty of curves was no exception.[229] The harmonious combination of historicism and Jugendstil architecture earned its most dramatic expression upon the loop road Ringstrasse in Vienna, the capital of the Habsburg Empire. Designed in 1859 to surround the city along the Danube, the wide road soon developed into a site for a string of new buildings, including a university, a parliament building, a city hall, an opera house, and museums.[230]

The Ringstrasse around central was one significant example of late historicist architecture. As the 5.2-kilometer-long road's construction began in the 1860s, individual apartment buildings, public offices, and university buildings were constructed in the neo-Renaissance style favored by the bourgeoisie until Jugendstil was introduced around 1900 while revamping Vienna's waterways, adding a much more eclectic overtone to buildings along the road. The Ringstrasse was considerably less centralized than the avenues in Paris reconstructed by Baron Haussmann under the rule of Napoleon III. The Ringstrasse's horizontal formation with no center earned it the impressive description of being "an iconographic index to the mind of ascendant Austrian liberalism," according to Karl Schorske, who studied the urban culture of Vienna.[231] The coexistence of historicism and modernism at the Ringstrasse therefore suffered no major strains. The railway and roads were designed to spread out in a radial pattern from the city's center like Paris, while modern modular buildings came to coexist with the neo-Gothic city hall and the neo-Baroque Kaiserforum designed by Semper.

Major implications can be drawn from the fact that Semper participated in the Ringstrasse's construction after having implemented tectonics at the center of Dresden. Semper's participation clearly proves that modern urban planning was rooted in historicist urban design or city planning. Semper's Kaiserforum served as the pinnacle of the Ringstrasse. The mammoth square was designed to expand and revive the Hofburg as Vienna's nucleus after having served as the monarchy's home for centuries. In 1869, Semper was commissioned to design the square, and with help from a young colleague named Carl Hasenauer, he completed and submitted a blueprint for the Kaiserforum to the Austrian emperor Franz Joseph I. According to Semper's blueprint, the Hofburg stood in the center of the square's upper edge at the beginning of a 500-meter-long path across the middle of the square leading to the old castle gate Burgtor. Along either side of the central path, the square was to house monumental buildings that would come to represent Vienna. The Kunsthistorisches Museum (Art History Museum) and the Naturhistorisches Museum (Natural History Museum) would be at the front of the square, overlooking the Hofburg across the square at the vanishing point between the two museums. With the Ringstrasse running in between, the emperor's residence would be situated on the right, and on the left would be the imperial reception hall. Overall, the Hofburg housing the emperor's throne occupied the center of the blueprint, controlling the square's architectural style and having the palace wings intervene in Vienna's urban space so that a hierarchy may be sensed from the rigid symmetrical layout.

This blueprint for the Kaiserforum, however, was never realized, nor did it manage to settle as the sole center of Vienna.[232] The ground plan printed in the February 17, 1917, edition of *Deutsche Bauzeitung* shows how Semper's plan actually turned out. The Ringstrasse that ran through

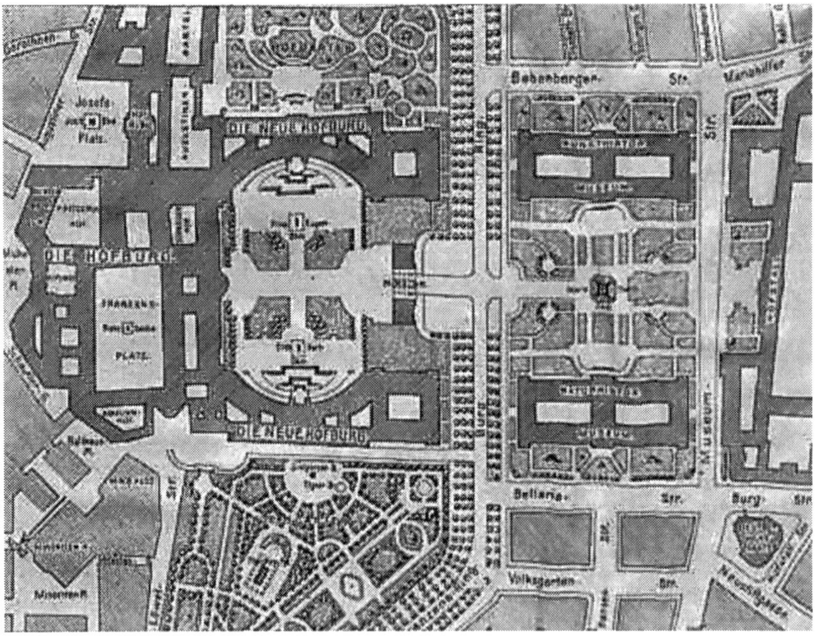

Figure 1.13 Ground Plan of Die neue Hofburg.

Source: From *Deutsche Bauzeitung* 51, no.14 (1917): 68.

the square in the blueprint does not seem as conspicuous, but traces of Semper's original plan such as the two museums facing each other to the right can be detected from the general layout of the square named Die neue Hofburg instead of Kaiserforum.[233]

From Spree-Athens to Spree-Chicago

It would not be a stretch to consider the Ringstrasse, which once sought to turn Semper's Kaiserforum into its nucleus, the true starting point of modern urban planning. Although the boulevard's modern aspect annoyed backward-looking urban planners like Camillo Sitte,[234] historicism and modernism formed a relatively natural mixture upon the boulevard. Then what did urban planning involve in Berlin, where the Prussian classicist traditions of Schinkel and Lenné remained alive while the city was brimming with the Deutscher Werkbund's enthusiasm? Did the Hobrecht Plan, which emerged not long after the plan for the Ringstrasse, engage any aspects of modern urban planning? On the surface, the reality of Berlin seemed to be a failure to learn from in terms of urban planning. With the city's center surrounded by duplex barrack-like tenement houses, Berlin was not functional, nor was it graceful like Paris or Vienna. Nevertheless, the city did have relatively bright industrial prospects, because it was home to all sorts of businesses, and a massive pool of workers were on standby at their cheap tenement houses.

Despite its glorious architectural legacies, the reason Berlin fell to the state of a drab city full of tenement houses more or less had to do with issues involving architectural regulations. Article no. 10 of the 1853 Architectural and Police Act for Berlin and the Other Police Districts placed the supervision of buildings' lines, a regulation key to construction in Berlin, entirely under the purview of the city's police headquarters.[235] This use of police forces to regulate construction was based on authoritarian state traditions established through the Prussian Civil Code promulgated in 1794.[236] These authoritarian measures nevertheless incited reckless development, for as long as building lines were observed, there was absolutely no need to consider the cityscape. What served as a turning point was the Prussian Building Line Act of 1875. The twenty-article act legalizing the development of master plans is regarded as one of the first in Europe to involve urban planning. By having the head of the municipal executive board determine building lines with the consent of the landowners association and the approval of the local police authority, the act gave local communities more autonomy in carrying out construction projects so as to accommodate local conditions and address their financial difficulties. Private associations were willing to relinquish a portion of their land, hoping that overheated speculation would boost land values, while proprietors who purchased land were to bear the cost of construction and maintenance.[237]

Being authoritarian yet excessively commercial, the Prussian Building Line Act failed to mesh well with the architectural traditions of old downtown Berlin, but it did possess some forward-looking aspects. Most significantly, the act went through several amendments to eventually establish a zoning system that introduced a new mode of regulating land use.[238] Based on a district's size and location, the system was to determine the use of each district and accordingly dictate the height and occupation density of buildings, thereby putting a stop to the spread of barrack-like tenement houses. However, this system came to be more actively adopted in other German cities instead of Berlin. In 1899, Franz B. E. Adickes, the mayor of the midwestern German city of Frankfurt am Main, submitted to Landtag, the Prussian State Parliament, a bill for *Lex Adickes*, a law to enable urban extension and zoning for land development. The bill aimed for urban extension projects to concentrate tall buildings and dense construction within the inner city and pursue the opposite in the outer city. It also sought to reasonably divide and assign market values to land so as to stimulate development but ran into fierce resistance from landowners. The Prussian Law on Land Readjustment in Frankfurt am Main (Preußisches Gesetz betreffend die Umlegung von Grundstücken in Frankfurt am Main) was finally enacted in 1902 and made its mark in the history of modern urban planning as a law that encouraged more rational use of land to accelerate urban growth.[239]

Compared to other metropolises in Germany as well as Europe, Berlin's urban planning may not have been successful, but at least it did not fall behind the times. The German Empire's establishment in 1871 turned the city into an imperial capital that had to deal with rapid population growth as it evolved into Germany's largest industrial city. Yet it managed to maintain its checkerboard street grid and equip itself with an advanced urban infrastructure in terms of waterways, electricity, transportation, and communication.[240] When the famous American writer Mark Twain visited Berlin in the early 1890s, he was greatly impressed by its straight, wide boulevards lined with streetlamps lit by gas or electricity. Through a series of essays Twain published in the *New York Sun* about his trip, he went as far as to describe Berlin as "the Chicago of Europe." "For there are many old-looking districts in Chicago, but not many in Berlin. The main mass of the city looks as if it had been built last week, the rest of it has a just perceptibly graver tone, and looks as if it might be six or even eight months old."[241]

However, unlike the superficial impression the American writer received, many German intellectuals were not so impressed by Berlin's modern features. They criticized that Berlin had been Americanized or turned into the spearhead of Americanism (Amerikanismus). Their sentiment at the time can be discerned from how the politician Walther Rathenau opined that "Spree-Athens is dead, and Spree-Chicago has arrived." By the time Rathenau was serving as the Foreign Minister of the Weimar Republic, even harsher criticism was directed toward Berlin's Americanization.[242]

Ancient Greece crept back into the current of cultural criticism that prevailed upon the turn of the century. Amid changing circumstances, Greece was reborn as an icon of cultural regeneration. August Julius Langbehn's *Rembrandt As Teacher*, which created a sensation among central European intellectuals, adopted a blunt, reprimanding tone to criticize the social circumstances at the time and used logical exaggerations to place Greek culture in the spotlight once again. Way before Rathenau, Langbehn had likened Berlin, swarming with migrants, to the American capital Washington D.C., denouncing the commercial spirit for hindering the independent spiritual life of people in both countries. Regarding the prevalent tendency in American-style cities to hastily accept or hunt for various cultural programs, he disparaged it as no more than an illegal mining of culture. Langbehn found fault with higher education and the science of antiquity at the time for leaning heavily toward classicism. Yet he had been an archaeologist who wrote about ancient Greek works of art in his doctoral dissertation. On Johann Joachim Winckelmann, Langbehn pointed out how Winckelmann only valued Greece and neglected German art. Still, if it was possible to discern which aspects of Winckelmann's vision were useful or detrimental to Germany and which remained pure or had become corrupted, Langbehn added that such discernments might be able to serve as a catalyst for the positive transition from the Latin Baroque culture to the Rembrandt-Nordic-German culture.[243] This claim seems to hint at Langbehn's understanding of ancient Greece as the foundation of German national culture.

Rembrandt As Teacher had a tremendous influence upon young intellectuals at the time, including Hermann Muthesius, the founder of the Deutscher Werkbund.[244] As the association's conservative modernism alluded, ancient Greece and modernism, or Spree-Athens and Spree-Chicago, were actually not that far apart. Berlin's urban planning was deeply rooted in none other than Schinkelian tectonics, which was why the city's barrack-like tenement houses could never be completely free of the imaginative geography of Spree-Athens. It should therefore come as no surprise that even while a massive number of tenement houses were being built, an extensive museum complex that would later be called the Museum Island (Museuminsel) was simultaneously formed as an extension of the Altes Museum. This attempt as ambitious as Semper's plan for Dresden displayed conservative tendencies from adhering to the neoclassical style of Schinkel, because it had been led, among others, by his pupil Friedrich August Stüler. Nevertheless, the Neues Museum built right behind the Altes Museum was already modern enough from using iron in its construction.[245]

The profound interest in Greece seemed to instantly wane as the German Empire grew increasingly explicit about its imperialistic desire to expand and accentuate its German traits. For instance, through a speech given at a school conference in 1890, the Emperor Wilhelm II deplored how most gymnasiums (high schools) in Germany placed far too much emphasis on teaching Latin and Greek and thereby neglected instruction in the German language.[246] However, the Greek fever was soon rekindled as it merged with German racism. The Winckelmann Renaissance popular among scholars during the Nazi period grew more ideologically extreme with the German army's expedition to Greece, while a simplified image of Greece was spread among the German public for propaganda purposes. Greek fever once again dominated German culture as it morphed into monumental classicism, or an anti-modernist, fascist form.[247]

This reactionary claim over Greece was, of course, not something entirely new. Philhellenism had originally been established to justify the old German order as opposed to the oppressive rule by the Ottoman Empire and Napoleon, and the fact that it was used as a logical device to culturally criticize industrial cities at the turn of the century rendered philhellenism fairly conservative if not reactionary. Then again, it had already been imperialistic in many cases since the early nineteenth century. Johann Gustav Droysen, the prominent nineteenth-century German historian who advocated Prussianism (Borussianismus), projected an image of Prussia upon Macedonia in northern Greece through his 1833 publication *History of Alexander the Great*. Although less civilized than southern Greece, including Athens, Alexander the Great's kingdom of Macedonia ended the conflicts among small southern city states and spread the brilliance of Greek civilization to the world by venturing upon an eastward expedition, which seemed to offer a preview of Prussia's future. Readers of the book would have been able to sense Droysen's enmity toward Napoleon's empire from his descriptions of ancient Persia.[248] Through the conclusion of *History of Hellenism*, published in 1836, Droysen even argued for Germanization of the Slavic regions as he discussed the establishment of colonial cities in Asia Minor during the Hellenistic period.[249]

Even so, treating all strands of German philhellenism as the same would be misleading. The idea was, after all, imaginary, so trying to discover logical clarity within it would be a futile attempt. Regarding philhellenism as no more than a logic that cemented the West's superiority over the East and justified colonial domination would be able to offer only half of the truth, because well-known philhellenists such as Goethe, Schlegel, and Humboldt had simultaneously been fascinated by the spiritual world of India. To German romanticists who claimed that a connection between India and Europe could be found in Sanskrit, the ancient Orient and Greece were pools of inspiration that would eventually flow into a single stream. What they regarded with hostility was Frenchified court culture, the feudal landed nobility, and the dogmatic clergy. Only since World War I did German classicists begin to outwardly support imperial expansion, and even then, they had not yet begun to explicitly advocate racism.[250]

Although imaginary Greece boiled down to a logic of domination, it would be an overly consequential interpretation to say that it had colonial implications from the beginning that corresponded to the power politics of Prussia or the German Empire. Only as it traveled across the boundaries of Germany and Europe was imaginary Greece modified into a logic of harsh colonial rule. The Prussian classicism that held the architect Schinkel's dreams was assigned a new meaning and purpose as it encountered extraneous circumstances and ended up magnifying its latent paranoid logic of domination. This cannot be described as an exception, since culture is something that essentially is adopted rather than disseminated. Whether diachronic or synchronic, "continuity of culture" is not an obvious logic. Continuity of culture itself is discontinuous for being an ideology used differently in different contexts. A Berlin realized outside Europe was therefore bound to be an imaginary Berlin.

Notes

1. Adolf Max Vogt, *Karl Friedrich Schinkel. Blick in Griechenlands Blüte: Ein Hoffnungsbild für Spree-Athen* (Frankfurt am Main: Fischer, 1985), 18–21.
2. Originally, the term "Neo-Classicism" was used in France and England to distinguish it from the Palladianism since the Renaissance. This is quite different from current usage. See Kŭm Yo-ch'an, "Karl Friedrich Schinkelŭi kŏnch'uge kwanhan koch'al: kŭ kŏnch'ukkubŏpkwa hyŏngt'aerŭl chungshimŭro," *Tongyangdaehakkyo nonmunjip* 7 (2001): 11.
3. Walter Pater, "On Classical and Romantic" (1889), in *Romanticism: Points of View*, ed. R. F. Gleckner and G. E. Enscode (Upper Saddle River, NJ: Prentice-Hall, 1970), 21.
4. This building was originally the church of St. Geneviève, whose design began in 1755 by request of the French Royal Academy of Arts, and its construction was repeatedly delayed. In the heat of revolution in 1791, the still-unfinished church was changed to Panthéon in honor of the heroes of the French people. Its designer J.-G. Soufflot died in 1780 long before its completion, and eventually his protégé J.-B. Rondelet completed the work. See Harry Francis Mallgrave, *Modern Architectural Theory: A Historical Survey, 1673–1968* (Cambridge: Cambridge University Press, 2005), 15–19, 69.
5. Barry Bergdoll, *European Architecture 1750–1890* (Oxford: Oxford University Press, 2000), 9–41; Peter Pütz, "The Renaissance to the Romantic Movement: An Outline of Ideas," in *Neoclassicism and Romanticism: Architecture – Sculpture – Painting – Drawings 1750–1848*, ed. Rolf Toman (Potsdam: H. F. Ullmann, 2008), 6–13.
6. Mallgrave, *Modern Architectural Theory*, 24–43, 91–113.
7. Johann Joachim Winckelmann, *Gedanken über die Nachahmung der griechischen Werke in der Malerei und Bildhauerkunst* (1755; Ditzingen: Reclam, 1969), 8–9.
8. Richard Jenkyns, *The Victorians and Ancient Greece* (Cambridge, MA: Harvard University Press, 1980), 10–14.
9. David Ferris, *Silent Urns: Romanticism, Hellenism, Modernity* (Redwood City, CA: Stanford University Press, 2000).
10. Johann Joachim Winckelmann, *Geschichte der Kunst des Altertums* (1764; Darmstadt: Wissenschaftliche Buchgesellschaft, 1993), 332 ff.; Alex Potts,

Flesh and the Ideal: Winckelmann and the Origins of Art History (New Haven, CT: Yale University Press, 1994), 16–17, 54–55; Suzanne L. Marchand, *Down From Olympus: Archaeology and Philhellenism in Germany, 1750–1970* (Princeton, NJ: Princeton University Press, 2003), 9.

11. Pim den Boer, "Neohumanism: Ideas, Identities, Identification," in *The Impact of Classical Greece on European and National Identities*, ed. Margriet Haagsma et al. (Amsterdam: J. C. Gieben, 2003), 10.
12. Ibid., 7, 3–5. According to Pim den Boer, the term "neohumanism" was not used until the late nineteenth century, while the term "Humanismus," which refers to the revival of classical antiquity in the Renaissance, had been used in Germany since the early nineteenth century. In other words, there was a certain temporal gap between the use of terms and the flow of reality. Ibid., 1–3.
13. Herwig Blankertz and Kjeld Matthiessen, "Neuhumanismus," in *Pädagogische Grundbegriffe*, ed. Dieter Lenzen (Berlin: Rowohlt, 2001), 1092–1103.
14. Friedrich Meinecke, *Weltbürgertum and Nationalstaat: Studien zur Genesis des deutschen Nationalstaates* (Munich: R. Oldenbourg, 1919), 39–61.
15. Friedrich Hölderlin, *Hyperion* (1797; Ditzingen: Reclam, 2013). Quoted from Mallgrave, *Modern Architectural Theory*, 92.
16. Marchand, *Down From Olympus*, 16–24, 36 ff.; Frank M. Turner, *Contesting Cultural Authority: Essays in Victorian Intellectual Life* (Cambridge: Cambridge University Press, 1993), 322 ff. The establishment of the German *Altertumswissenschaft* was a sheer effort to defend the normativity of classicalism, which had been declining over the course of the nineteenth century, by consecrating it as an academic dogma. See, notably, Esther Sophia Sünderhauf, *Griechensehnsucht und Kulturkritik: Die deutsche Rezeption von Winckelmanns Antikenideal 1840–1945* (Berlin: Akademie Verlag, 2004), XI.
17. Thomas Nipperdey, *Deutsche Geschichte 1800–1866: Bürgerwelt und starker Staat* (Munich: C. H. Beck, 1983), 455–456; Marchand, *Down From Olympus*, 25, 34–35.
18. Marchand, *Down From Olympus*, 4.
19. Ibid., 34–35, xix, 152–187. According to Suzanne Marchand, German archaeologists were forced to ride on the logic of national chauvinism as long as they were in dire need of government support for large-scale excavations such as in Olympia and Pergamon. Ibid., 75 ff.
20. Eliza Marian Butler, *The Tyranny of Greece over Germany: A Study of the Influence Exercised by Greek Art and Poetry Over the Great German Writers of the Eighteenth, Nineteenth, and Twentieth Centuries* (1935; Boston, MA: Beacon Press, 1958).
21. H. J. C. Gierson, "Classical and Romantic. A Point of View" (1923), in *Romanticism: Points of View*, ed. R. F. Gleckner and G. E. Enscode (Upper Saddle River, NJ: Prentice-Hall, 1970), 47–49.
22. Martin Bernal argues that the idea of ancient Greece as the source of Western civilization was backed up by the German academic discipline of *Altertumswissenschaft* that was strongly influenced by the romantic tradition opposing to enlightenment, rationality and the French Revolution. See Martin Bernal, Volume 1 of *Black Athena: Afro-Asiatic Roots of Classical Civilization: The Fabrication of Ancient Greece* (New York, NY: Vintage Books, 1991), 204–206, 215–223. On the relationship between German romanticism and classicism, see, notably, Jane K. Brown, "Romanticism and Classicism," in *The Cambridge Companion to German Romanticism*, ed. Nicholas Saul (Cambridge: Cambridge University Press, 2009), 119–131.
23. Hans-Ulrich Wehler, *Nationalismus: Geschichte, Formen, Folgen* (Munich: C. H. Beck, 2001), 66.

24. Jörg Träger, ed., *Die Walhalla: Idee, Architektur, Landschaft* (Regensburg: Bernhard Bosse, 1979). The original shape of this building is documented, especially on the web site https://commons.wikimedia.org/, under the designation of *Walhalla-Memorial*.
25. Andre Rank, *Die Walhalla im Zeitalter des romantischen Nationalismus* (Munich: GRIN Verlag, 2008), 28–29.
26. Friedrich Schlegel, *Kritische Ausgabe seiner Werke*, ed. Ernst Behler et al., vol. 1 (Paderborn: Schöningh, 1958), 287–288. See also Ernst Behler, *Ironie und literarische Moderne* (Paderborn: Schöningh, 1997), 92–104.
27. Hagen Schulze, *Staat und Nation in der europäischen Geschichte* (Munich: C. H. Beck, 1995), 179–187.
28. Stefan Nienhaus, *Geschichte der deutschen Tischgesellschaft* (Tübingen: Niemeyer, 2003).
29. David Watkin and Tilman Mellinghoff, *German Architecture and the Classical Ideal* (Cambridge, MA: The MIT Press, 1987), 59–83; Marchand, *Down From Olympus*, xxiii.
30. den Boer, "Neohumanism," 7–8.
31. Dirk van Laak, *Über alles in der Welt: Deutscher Imperialismus im 19. und 20. Jahrhundert* (Munich: C. H. Beck, 2005), 30.
32. Wilhelm von Humboldt, "Geschichte des Verfalls und Untergangs der griechischen Freistaaten," in Volume 2 of *Werke in fünf Bänden, Schriften zur Altertumskunde und Ästhetik: Die Vasken*, ed. Andreas Flitner and Klaus Giel (1807; Stuttgart: Klett-Cotta, 2010), 73–124, 118–119.
33. Ibid., 92.
34. Hans-Joachim Kadatz, *Georg Wenzeslaus von Knobelsdorff: Baumeister Friedrichs II.* (Leipzig: E. A. Seeman, 1983).
35. Christopher Clark, *Iron Kingdom: The Rise and Downfall of Prussia, 1600–1947* (Cambridge, MA: Harvard University Press, 2008), 1–18.
36. Jürgen Angelow, "Residenz und Bürgerstadt: Das 17. und 18. Jahrhundert," in *Berlin: Geschichte einer Stadt*, ed. Julius H. Schoeps (Berlin: Bebra Verlag, 2012), 28–53; Waltraud Volk, "Die Stadterweiterungen in Berlin im 17. und 18. Jahrhundert," *Studien zur Geschichte Berlin: Jahrbuch für Geschichte* 35 (1987): 93–118; Clark, *Iron Kingdom*, 67–77.
37. Goerd Peschken and Johannes Althoff, *Das Berliner Schloß* (Berlin: Bebra Verlag, 2000), 28 ff.; Sepp-Gustav Gröschel, "Antikenrezeption in Architektur und Plastik des Berliner Schlosses zur Zeit Friedrichs III./I.," *Pegasus: Berliner Beiträge zum Nachleben der Antike* 6 (2004): 54–62.
38. Martin Engel, *Das Forum Fridericianum und die Monumentalen Residenzplätze des 18. Jahrhunderts*, Ph.D. diss. (Freie Universität Berlin, 2001), 36–52.
39. Ibid., 91, 67 ff.
40. In designing this building, Knobelsdorf is known to have referred to "Vitruvius Britannicus, or The British Architect" (1715–1725), the famous three-volume folio of architectural engravings compiled by the Scottish architect Colen Campbell, who is the founder of the so-called "Georgian style" architecture. See Hans Lange, *Vom Tribunal zum Tempel: Zur Architektur und Geschichte Deutscher Hoftheater zwischen Vormärz und Restauration* (Marburg: Jonas, 1985), 206, note 26. Campbell's folio contained several prints of English-style Palladian architecture. On English Palladianism and Campbell's folio, see Mallgrave, *Modern Architectural Theory*, 47–51.
41. Brian Ladd, *The Ghosts of Berlin* (Chicago, IL: University of Chicago Press, 1997), 53; Claudia Terne, "Friedrich II. von Preußen und die Hofoper," in *Friedrich der Große und der Hof*, ed. Michael Kaiser and Jürgen Luh (Berlin: Stiftung Preußische Schlösser und Gärten Berlin Brandenburg, 2009), 1–23.

42. Bruno Forment, "Frederick's Athens: Crushing Superstition and Resuscitating the Marvellous at the Königliches Opernhaus, Berlin," *Cambridge Opera Journal* 24, no. 1 (March 2012): 1–42; Engel, *Das Forum Fridericianum*, 96–114.
43. Engel, *Das Forum Fridericianum*, 9–10, 121–122, 157–165.
44. Ibid., 123–155; Martin Engel, "Das 'Forum Fridericianum' in Berlin: Ein kultureller und politischer Brennpunkt im 20. Jahrhunderts," *Kunst und Politik* 11 (2009): 35–39.
45. Günter de Bruyn, *Unter den Linden* (Berlin: Bebra Verlag, 2004), 18 ff.; Elke Kimmel and Ronald Oesterreich, *Charlottenburg im Wandel der Geschichte: Vom Dorf zum eleganten Westen* (Berlin: Berlin edition, 2005), 24.
46. Engel, "Das 'Forum Fridericianum' in Berlin," 39–44; Brian Ladd, "Socialism on Display: East Berlin As a Capital," in *Berlin – Washington, 1800–2000: Capital Cities, Cultural Representation, and National Identities*, ed. Andreas W. Daum and Christof Mauch (Cambridge: Cambridge University Press, 2005), 221; Jörn Düwel, "Am Anfang der DDR: Der Zentrale Platz in Berlin," in *Moderne Architektur in Deutschland 1900 bis 2000: Macht und Monument*, ed. Romana Schneider and Wilfried Wang (Berlin: Hatje Cantz Verlag, 1998), 176–180.
47. Engel, *Das Forum Fridericianum*, 77; Kimmel and Oesterreich, *Charlottenburg*, 34.
48. Bruyn, *Unter den Linden*, 167–172; Mallgrave, *Modern Architectural Theory*, 94.
49. Walter Jaeschke, "Ästhetische Revolution: Stichworte zur Einführung," in *Früher Idealismus und Frühromantik: Der Streit um die Grundlagen der Ästhetik 1795–1805*, ed. W. Jaeschke and Helmut Holzhey (Hamburg: Felix Meiner, 2013), 1–11; Nipperdey, *Deutsche Geschichte*, 30 ff.
50. Wolfram Siemann, "Die deutsche Hauptstadtproblematik im 19. Jahrhundert," in *Hauptstadt: Historische Perspektiven eines deutschen Themas*, ed. Hans-Michael Körner and Katharina Weigand (Munich: dtv, 1995), 255.
51. Watkin and Mellinghoff, *German Architecture*, 59–83.
52. John Edward Toews, *Becoming Historical: Cultural Reformation and Public Memory in Early Nineteenth-Century Berlin* (Cambridge: Cambridge University Press, 2008), 19 ff., 117, 197 ff.; Andreas Kahlow, "Karl Friedrich Schinkel und David Gilly: Aufklärung, Technik und Neuhumanismus in der Architektur," in *Karl Friedrich Schinkel: Aspekte seines Werkes*, ed. Susan M. Peik (Fellbach: Edition Axel Menges, 2001), 20–26.
53. Toews, *Becoming Historical*, 129 ff., 142; Mallgrave, *Modern Architectural Theory*, 96.
54. Maria Erxleben, "Goethe and Schinkel," in *Karl Friedrich Schinkel und die Antike: Eine Aufsatzsammlung*, ed. Max Kunze and Jürgen Kraeft (Stendal: Winckelmann-Gesellschaft, 1985), 20–32.
55. Siegfried Giedion, a pioneering architectural historian, points out that Western architecture has undergone qualitative changes since the 1800s, as demonstrated by the bifurcation of classicism into late Baroque and Romantic classicism. See Siegfried Giedion, *Spätbaroker und romantiker Klassizismus* (Ann Arbor, MI: University of Michigan Library, 1922).
56. Isaiah Berlin, *The Root of Romanticism* (Princeton, NJ: Princeton University Press, 2013), 54–78, 107–136.
57. Friedrich Schlegel, *Der Historiker als rückwärts gekehrter Prophet* (Ditzingen: Reclam, 1991).
58. Heinz Ohff, *Karl Friedrich Schinkel oder Die Schönheit in Preußen* (Munich: Piper, 2007), 25–27; Mitchell Schwarzer, *German Architectural Theory and the Search for Modern Identity* (Cambridge: Cambridge University Press, 1995), 64.

59. Carl Friedrich Schinkel, *Sammlung architektonischer Entwürfe* (Berlin: Ernst & Korn, 1858), 7; Kurt Milde, *Neorenaissance in der deutschen Architektur des 19. Jahrhunderts* (Dresden: Verlag der Kunst, 1981), 115. In the original design, there were four towers, but at the request of the king, two were withdrawn. See Ohff, *Karl Friedrich Schinkel*, 132–133.
60. Christian Baur, *Neugotik* (Munich: Heyne, 1981), 110–124. The building is commonly called the House of Parliament.
61. Ernst-Heinz Lemper, "Historismus als Großstadtarchitektur: Die städtebauliche Legitimierung eines Zeitalters," in *Historismus: Aspekte zur Kunst im 19. Jahrhundert*, ed. Karl-Heinz Klingenburg (Leipzig: E. A. Seemann, 1985), 66; Thomas Nipperdey, "Der Kölner Dom als Nationaldenkmal," in *Nachdenken über die deutsche Geschichte* (Munich: C. H. Beck, 1992), 189–207; M. Brix and M. Steinhauser, "Geschichte im Dienste der Baukunst," in *Geschichte allein ist zeitgemäß: Historismus in Deutschland*, ed. Brix and Steinhauser (Wetzlar: Anabas, 1978), 243–244.
62. Hans-Joachim Kunst, "Die Friedrichswerdersche Kirche in Berlin: Die bürgerliche Vorstadtkirche als fürstliche Hauptkirche," in *Karl Friedrich Schinkel*, ed. Peik, 39. Conversely, the neo-Gothic architecture of England grew out of competition with the German neoclassical architecture represented by Schinkel and Klenze. On this point, see John Steegman, *Victorian Taste: A Study of the Arts and Architecture* (Cambridge, MA: The MIT Press, 1971), 83–84.
63. Karl Friedrich Schinkel, *Aus Schinkels Nachlaß: Reisetagebücher, Briefe und Aphorismen* (1862), quoted from Baur, *Neugotik*, 31.
64. Toews, *Becoming Historical*, 182 ff.
65. Ohff, *Karl Friedrich Schinkel*, 34; Nikolaus Pevsner, *A History of Building Types* (Princeton, NJ: Princeton University Press, 1976), 15–16; Bergdoll, *European Architecture*, 69–71. The original shape of this design is documented on the web site https://commons.wikimedia.org/, under the designation of *Gilly Denkmal*.
66. Marchand, *Down From Olympus*, 32–33.
67. Martin Steffens, *K. F. Schinkel 1781–1841: Ein Baumeister im Dienste der Schönheit* (Cologne: Taschen, 2003), 25–27; Toews, *Becoming Historical*, 141 ff., 144.
68. Schinkel, *Sammlung architektonischer Entwürfe*, 1.
69. Quoted from Erik Forssman, "Schinkel und die Architekturtheorie," in *Karl Friedrich Schinkel*, ed. Peik, 13.
70. Steffens, *K. F. Schinkel*, 25–27; Toews, *Becoming Historical*, 141 ff., 144; Ohff, *Karl Friedrich Schinkel*, 106–107.
71. Jürgen Tietz, "Schinkels Neue Wache Unter den Linden: Baugeschichte 1816–1993," in *Die neue Wache Unter den Linden: Ein deutsches Denkmal im Wandel der Geschichte*, ed. Christoph Stölzl (Leipzig: Koehler & Amelang, 1993), 10–21.
72. Wallis Miller, "Schinkel and the Politics of German Memory: The Life of the Neue Wache in Berlin," in *A User's Guide to German Cultural Studies*, ed. Scott Denham et al. (Ann Arbor, MI: University of Michigan Press, 1997), 227–256.
73. Reinhart Koselleck, *Zur politischen Ikonologie des gewaltsamen Todes: Ein deutsch-französischer Vergleich* (Basel: Schwabe & Co Ag, 1998), 51–53.
74. Friedrich Dieckmann, "Schinkels Wachgebäude als nationales Mahnmal: Bundesprojekt und Denksmalspflege im Widerstreit," *Die neue Wache*, ed. Stölzl, 204–211.
75. Schinkel, *Sammlung architektonischer Entwürfe*, 1.
76. Ibid., 2.

77. Ibid., 1.
78. Mallgrave, *Modern architectural Theory*, 97–98; Harry Francis Mallgrave, *Gottfried Semper: Architect on the Nineteenth Century* (New Haven, CT: Yale University Press, 1996), 86, 122.
79. James J. Sheehan, *Museums in the German Art World: From the End of the Old Regime to the Rise of Modernism* (Oxford: Oxford University Press, 2000), 70–81.
80. Steffens, *K. F. Schinkel*, 47–51.
81. Sheehan, *Museums in the German Art World*, 27 ff.
82. Schinkel, *Sammlung architektonischer Entwürfe*, 4–5.
83. Theodore Ziolkowski, *German Romanticism and Its Institutions* (Princeton, NJ: Princeton University Press, 1992), 314 ff.
84. Monika Wagner, *Allegorie und Geschichte: Ausstattungsprogramme öffentlicher Gebäude des 19. Jahrhunderts in Deutschland* (Tübingen: Ernest Wasmuth, 1989), 103–126; Steffens, *Schinkel*, 47–51. The frescoes on the outer walls of the Altes Museum were never restored after they were destroyed during World War II. It is now replaced by a flat marble plate.
85. Mallgrave, *Modern Architectural Theory*, 89.
86. Schinkel, *Sammlung architektonischer Entwürfe*, 5, 4.
87. Heinz Ohff, *Peter Joseph Lenné: Eine Biographie* (Berlin: Jaron, 2012), 28–39, 96–98.
88. Johann Joachim Winckelmann, *Gedanken über die Nachahmung der griechischen Werke in der Malerei und Bildhauerkunst* (1756; Ditzingen: Reclam, 1995), 20–22.
89. Winckelmann, *Geschichte der Kunst des Altertums*, 324–325.
90. Mallgrave, *Modern Architectural Theory*, 19–23; Kim Chŏng-rak, "P'ŭrangsŭ shin'gojŏnjuŭigŏnch'ugirone taehan koet'eŭi nonp'yŏngŭrosŏŭi togilgŏnch'uge taehan sogo (1771–1772)" *Sŏyangmisulsahak'oenonmunjip* 40 (2014): 39–61.
91. Quoted from Forssman, "Schinkel und die Architekturtheorie," 17.
92. Ibid., 13.
93. Goerd Peschken, "Schinkels Klassizismus," *Karl Friedrich Schinkel*, ed. Paik, 18–19. According to James Sheehan, the basic principles of tectonics had already been completely manifested in Friedrich Gilly's Design for the Monument to Frederick the Great. See Sheehan, *Museums in the German Art World*, 52 ff. On the other hand, French theorists such as Jean Rondelet and Jean-Louis Durand attempted to disclose architecture of classical antiquity in terms of its utility and economic feasibility. On this point, see Schwarzer, *German Architectural Theory*, 44–45.
94. Karl Friedrich Schinkel, *Das architektonische Lehrbuch*, documented by Goerd Peschken (Berlin: Deutscher Kunstverlag, 1979), 149–150.
95. Kŭm, "Karl Friedrich Schinkelŭi kŏnch'uge kwanhan koch'al," *Tongyangdaehakkyo nonmunjip*, 22–23; Ohff, *Karl Friedrich Schinkel*, 57–63; Schwarzer, *German Architectural Theory*, 171 ff.
96. Quoted from Karl Gottlieb Wilhelm Bötticher, Volume 1 of *Die Tektonik der Hellenen: Zur Philosophie der tektonischen Form* (Potsdam: Ferdinand Riegel, 1852), XIV–XV, 76–78.
97. Peschken, "Schinkels Klassizismus," 18–19; Toews, *Becoming Historical*, 117 ff.
98. Reinhart Koselleck, *Preußen zwischen Reform und Revolution: Allgemeines Landrecht, Verwaltung und soziale Bewegung von 1791 bis 1848* (1975; Stuttgart: Klett-Cotta, 1989), 23–51.
99. See the pioneering argument of Joachim Ritter, *Hegel und die Französische Revolution* (1957; Frankfurt am Main: Suhrkamp, 1996).

100. G. W. F. Hegel, Volume 7 of *Werke in 20 Bänden: Grundlinien der Philosophie des Rechts (oder Naturrecht und Staatswissenschaft in Grundrisse)* (Frankfurt a. M.: Suhrkamp, 1986), §182, §71, §181–188, §198–199.
101. Ibid., §195, §236, §230–241, §249–255, §260.
102. Ibid., §183.
103. Ibid., §258, quoted from *Hegel: Elements of the Philosophy of Right*, trans. H. B. Nisbet (Cambridge: Cambridge University Press, 1991), 276.
104. Ibid., §257, §258 Zusatz.
105. The idea that the logic of individualization espoused by romanticism reflect the German reality that fails to achieve national unity was revealed in Hegel's early writings. See, for example, G. W. F. Hegel, "Die Verfassung Deutschlands (1800–1802)," in *G. W. F. Hegel Werke in 20 Bänden*, vol. 1. (Frankfurt a. M.: Suhrkamp, 1986), 451–581.
106. Isaiah Berlin, *Against the Current* (Princeton, NJ: Princeton University Press, 2001), 10–12; Berlin, *The Root of Romanticism*, 144 ff.
107. Meinecke, *Weltbürgertum and Nationalstaat*, 132.
108. Lorenz Jacob von Stein, *Handbuch der Verwaltungslehre und des Verwaltungsrechts mit Vergleichung der Literatur und Gesetzgebung von Frankreich, England und Deutschland: Als Grundlage für Vorlesungen* (1870; Boston, MA: Adamant Media Corporation, 2004), 4–7; Lorenz Jacob von Stein, *Gegenwart und Zukunft der Rechts-und Staatswissenschaft Deutschlands* (1876; Boston, MA: Adamant Media Corporation, 2004), 132 ff.
109. Lorenz von Stein, *Handbuch der Verwaltungslehre*, 43–45, 401, 440, quoted from 45.
110. Lorenz von Stein, *Gegenwart und Zukunft*, 134–138.
111. Lorenz Jacob von Stein, Volume 1 of *Geschichte der socialen Bewegung in Frankreich. Von 1789 bis auf unsere Tage: Der Begriff der Gesellschaft und die sociale Geschichte der französischen Revolution bis zum Jahre 1830* (1850; Salt Lake City, UT: Ulan Press, 2012), 37.
112. Lorenz Jacob von Stein, Volume 3 of *Geschichte der socialen Bewegung in Frankreich. Von 1789 bis auf unsere Tage: Das Königtum, die Republik und die Souveränität der französischen Gesellschaft seit der Februarrevolution 1848* (1850; Salt Lake City, UT: Ulan Press, 2012).
113. Michel Foucault, *Security, Territory, Population: Lectures at the Collège de France, 1977–1978* (New York, NY: Palgrave Macmillan, 2007); Mathew Coleman and John A. Agnew, "The Problem with Empire," in *Space, Knowledge and Power: Foucault and Geography*, ed. Jeremy W. Crampton and Stuart Elden (Aldershot: Ashgate, 2007), 317–339.
114. Winckelmann, *Geschichte der Kunst des Altertums*, 9, quoted from *History of the Art of Antiquity*, trans. Harry Francis Mallgrave (Los Angeles, CA: Getty Publications, 2006), 71.
115. Ibid., 207–237; Potts, *Flesh and the Ideal*, 67–112, 23–25.
116. According to David Ferris, the Greek revival was not merely an accidental archaeological discovery but a cultural phenomenon imbricated with the formation of modernity. See David Ferris, *Silent Urns: Romanticism, Hellenism, Modernity* (Redwood City, CA: Stanford University Press, 2000). In this respect, Ferris relates the impossibility of representing Greek art to the birth of the modern conception of history. Ibid., 16–51.
117. Michel Foucault, *The Order of Things: An Archaeology of the Human Sciences* (New York, NY: Vintage Books, 1973), 3–16.
118. Potts, *Flesh and the Ideal*, 4, 57–60.
119. Winckelmann, *Geschichte der Kunst des Altertums*, 35–41, 146–147, quoted from *History of the Art of Antiquity*, 194.

120. Gotthold Ephraim Lessing, *Laokoön oder über die Grenzen der Malerei und Poesie* (1766; Ditzingen: Reclam, 1987), 7, 20, 26 ff.
121. G. W. F. Hegel, Volume 13 of *Werke in zwanzig Bänden: Vorlesungen über die Ästhetik I.* (Frankfurt am Main: Suhrkamp, 1970), 13–124; G. W. F. Hegel, Volume 14 of *Werke in zwanzig Bänden: Vorlesungen über die Ästhetik II* (Frankfurt am Main: Suhrkamp, 1970), 25–27, 302–326, 231–242.
122. Franklin Le Van Baumer, *Modern European Thought: Continuity and Change in Ideas, 1600–1950* (New York, NY: Macmillan, 1977), 402–416.
123. Reinhart Koselleck, *Kritik und Krise: Eine Studie zur Pathogenese der bürgerlichen Welt* (Frankfurt am Main: Suhrkamp, 1992).
124. Thomas Nipperdey appraises neoclassical architecture as an attempt to guarantee continuity and sustainability in the age of great disruption. See Nipperdey, *Deutsche Geschichte*, 554.
125. Birgit Verwiebe, "Schinkel's Perspective Optical Views: Art Between Painting and Theater," in *Karl Friedrich Schinkel: The Drama of Architecture*, ed. John Zukowsky (Chicago, IL: Art Institute of Chicago, 1994), 49–52.
126. Alois Hirt, *Die Baukunst nach den Grundsätzen der Alten* (Berlin: Realschulbuchhandlung, 1809), vii.
127. Toews, *Becoming Historical*, 164–165; Ohff, *Karl Friedrich Schinkel*, 156–176.
128. Toews, *Becoming Historical*, 161 ff; Ohff, *Karl Friedrich Schinkel*, 190; Mallgrave, *Modern Architectural Theory*, 98.
129. Schinkel, *Sammlung architektonischer Entwürfe*, 8.
130. Mallgrave, *Modern Architectural Theory*, 101–102; Ohff, *Karl Friedrich Schinkel*, 192–193; Bergdoll, *European Architecture*, 192–194.
131. Kurt Milde, *Neorenaissance in der deutschen Architektur des 19. Jahrhunderts*, 115; Mallgrave, *Gottfried Semper*, 89–91.
132. Karl Friedrich Schinkel, *Briefe, Tagebücher, Gedanken*, ed. Hans Mackowsky (Berlin: Propyläen, 1922), 190.
133. Ohff, *Karl Friedrich Schinkel*, 203–204.
134. Rand Carter, "Gartenreich Potsdam: Schinkel's, Persius's and Lenné's Summer Retreats for the Prussian Princes," in *Karl Friedrich Schinkel*, ed. Peik, 71–81.
135. Ohff, *Karl Friedrich Schinkel*, 214–215.
136. Ibid., 232–236.
137. Mitchell Schwarzer defines this large denotation as "constructive eclecticism" in that it was based on the principles of tectonics rather than sheer openness. See Schwarzer, *German Architectural Theory*, 64–67.
138. Maiken Umbach, "Memory and Historicism: Reading Between the Lines of the Built Environment, Germany c. 1900," *Representation* 88 (2004): 26–54, 31–32.
139. Hermann Fillitz, ed., *Der Traum vom Glück: Die Kunst des Historismus in Europa*, vol. 1 (Wien: Brandstätter, 1996).
140. Nipperdey, *Deutsche Geschichte*, 556–558. Werner Busch traces the birth of modern art back to the inherent crisis of the eighteenth-century art. See Werner Busch, *Das sentimentalische Bild: Die Krise der Kunst im 18. Jahrhundert und die Geburt der Moderne* (Munich: C. H. Beck, 1993), 9–18.
141. Wolfgang Hardtwig, "Kunst und Geschichte im Revolutionszeitalter: Historismus in der Kunst und der Historismus-Begriff der Kunstwissenschaft," *Archiv für Kulturgeschichte* 1 (1979): 154–190.
142. Wagner, *Allegorie und Geschichte*, 31–40; Matthew Jefferies, *Imperial Culture in Germany 1871–1918* (New York, NY: Palgrave Macmillan, 2003), 118.
143. Robert Jan van Pelt, *Architectural Principles in the Age of Historicism* (New Haven, CT: Yale University Press, 1993).

144. Hans-Werner Hahn, *Die industrielle Revolution in Deutschland* (Munich: R. Oldenbourg, 1998), 24–48.
145. For an overall cultural aspect of German society in this period, see, notably, Jefferies, *Imperial Culture in Germany*.
146. Wolfgang J. Mommsen, *Bürgerliche Kultur und künstlerische Avantgarde: Kultur und Politik im deutschen Kaiserreich 1870–1918* (Berlin: Propyläen, 1994), 7 ff.
147. Meinecke, *Weltbürgertum and Nationalstaat*, 1–22.
148. Siemann, "Die deutsche Hauptstadtproblematik," 256–257.
149. Brix and Steinhauser, "Geschichte im Dienste der Baukunst," 208. For an overview of German historicist architecture, see Dieter Dolgner, *Historismus: Deutsche Baukunst 1815–1900* (Leipzig: E. A. Seemann, 1993); Lemper, "Historismus als Großstadtarchitektur," 50–72.
150. Alan Colquhoun, *Modernity and the Classical Tradition. Architectural Essays 1980–1987* (Cambridge, MA: The MIT Press, 1991), 4–18; Erxleben, "Goethe and Schinkel," 20–32.
151. Maiken Umbach, *German Cities and Bourgeois Modernism 1890–1924* (Oxford: Oxford University Press, 2009), 27–36.
152. Mommsen, *Bürgerliche Kultur*, 35. See also Jörg Bahns, *Zwischen Biedermeier und Jugendstil: Möbel des Historismus* (Munich: Keysersche Verlagsbuch, 1987).
153. Suzuki Hiroyuki, *Sŏyang kŭnhyŏndae kŏnch'ugŭi yŏksa: Sanŏp'yŏngmyŏnggiesŏ hyŏnjaekkaji*, trans. (from Japanese into Korean) U Tong-sŏn (Seoul: Sigongsa, 2003), 54–55.
154. Nipperdey, *Deutsche Geschichte*, 558; Bergdoll, *European Architecture*, 269–279.
155. Milde, *Neorenaissance in der deutschen Architektur*, 116–124; Schwarzer, *German Architectural Theory*, 51–53; Mallgrave, *Modern Architectural Theory*, 106–108.
156. Dagmar Waskönig, "Konstruktion eines zeitgemäßen Stils zu Beginn der Industrialisierung in Deutschland: Historisches Denken in H. Hübschs Theorie des Rundbogenstils (1828)," in *Geschichte allein ist zeitgemäß*, ed. Brix and Steinhauser, 93–105.
157. Mallgrave, *Gottfried Semper*, 165–227; Schwarzer, *German Architectural Theory*, 72–74; David Waktin, *A History of Western Architecture* (London: Laurence King Publishing, 2005), 487–488.
158. Mallgrave, *Gottfried Semper*, 91, 220–225.
159. Gottfried Semper, Volume 1 of *Der Stil in den technischen und tektonischen Künsten oder praktische Ästhetik, Ein Handbuch für Techniker, Künstler und Kunstfreunde: Textile Kunst* (1860; Munich: Bruckmann, 1878), §61, §62. For a discussion of Semper's ideas, see Brix and Steinhauser, "Geschichte im Dienste der Baukunst," 258–260; Mallgrave, *Gottfried Semper*, 274–308; Mari Hvatum, *Gottfried Semper and the Problem of Historicism* (Cambridge: Cambridge University Press, 2004), 72–75.
160. Semper, *Der Stil*, §58; Mallgrave, *Modern Architectural Theory*, 77–77, 132, 130.
161. Milde, *Neorenaissance in der deutschen Architektur*, 174 ff.
162. Hvatum, *Gottfried Semper*, 167.
163. Thomas Nipperdey, *Deutsche Geschichte 1866–1918: Arbeitswelt und Bürgergeist* (Munich: C. H. Beck, 1990), 718–719; Walter Krause, ed., *Neorenaissance: Ansprüche an einen Stil* (Dresden: Verlag der Kunst, 2001); Iain Boyd Whyte, "Modern German Architecture," in *The Cambridge Companion to Modern German Culture*, ed. Eva Kolinsky and Wilfried van der Will (Cambridge: Cambridge University Press, 1998), 282–301.

164. Jacob Burckhardt, *Der Cicerone: Eine Anleitung zum Genuss der Kunstwerke Italiens* (1855; Stuttgart: Kröner, 1986); Jacob Burckhardt, *Die Kultur der Renaissance in Italien* (1860; Stuttgart: Kröner, 2009). On the influence of these works, see Jefferies, *Imperial Culture in Germany*, 95–98.
165. Mallgrave, *Gottfried Semper*, 120–123, 356–357.
166. Ibid., *Gottfried Semper*, 95–98.
167. Ibid., 109–117; Sheehan, *Museums in the German Art World*, 127–131.
168. Sheehan, *Museums in the German Art World*, 137; Ulrich Großmann, "Renaissance der Renaissance-Baukunst," in *Renaissance der Renaissance: Ein bürgerlicher Kunststil im 19. Jahrhundert*, ed. Ulrich Großmann and Petra Krutisch (Berlin: Deutscher Kunstverlag, 1992), 201–219.
169. Milde, *Neorenaissance in der deutschen Architektur*, 137.
170. Mallgrave, *Gottfried Semper*, 339–353; K. E. O. Fritsch, "Das neue Hoftheater zu Dresden," *Deutsche Bauzeitung* 12, no. 34 (1878): 167.
171. K. E. O. Fritsch, "Das neue Hoftheater zu Dresden," *Deutsche Bauzeitung* 12, no. 30 (1878): 145.
172. Fritsch, "Das neue Hoftheater zu Dresden," no. 34: 167, 168.
173. Mallgrave, *Gottfried Semper*, 117.
174. Mommsen, *Bürgerliche Kultur und künstlerische Avantgarde*, 35.
175. Umbach, "Memory and Historicism," *Representation*, 26–54.
176. Lemper, "Historismus als Großstadtarchitektur," 50, 60.
177. Umbach, "Memory and Historicism," *Representation*, 39–43; Valentin W. Hammerschmidt, *Anspruch und Ausdruck in der Architektur des späten Historismus in Deutschland 1860–1914* (Frankfurt am Main: Peter Lang, 1985).
178. Umbach, *German Cities*, 33; Jefferies, *Imperial Culture in Germany*, 183–228.
179. Heinrich Wölfflin, *Renaissance und Barock: Eine Untersuchung über Wesen und Entstehung des Barockstils in Italien* (Basel: Schwabe, 2009).
180. Siemann, "Die deutsche Hauptstadtproblematik," 256.
181. Jefferies, *Imperial Culture in Germany*, 83 ff.; Whyte, "Modern German architecture," 285. The socialist politician August Bebel's praise for the Reichstag building seems to be based on his political antipathy toward the emperor rather than a purely architectural evaluation. See Brix and Steinhauser, "Geschichte im Dienste der Baukunst," 298.
182. Wolfgang Hardtwig, *Nationalismus und Bürgerkultur in Deutschland 1500–1914* (Göttingen: Vandenhoeck & Ruprecht, 1994), 202. The Construction of the Reichstag building was the outcome of a compromise between parliamentary democracy and constitutional monarchy, embodying the hope and frustration of German democracy. On this point, see Michael S. Cullen, *Der Reichstag: Im Spannungsfeld deutscher Geschichte* (Berlin: Bebra verlag, 2004), 9–10; Utz Haltern, "Architektur und Politik: Zur Baugeschichte des Berliner Reichstags," in *Kunstverwaltung, Bau-und Denkmal-Politik im Kaiserreich*, ed. Ekkehard Mai and Stephan Waetzoldt (Berlin: Gebr. Mann Verlag, 1981), 75–102.
183. Christian Norberg-Schulz, *The Concept of Dwelling: On the Way to Figurative Architecture* (New York, NY: Rizzoli, 1985), 34.
184. Cullen, *Der Reichstag*, 32–34; Milde, *Neorenaissance in der deutschen Architektur*, 303.
185. Jean-François Lejeune, "Schinkel and Lenné in Berlin – from the Biedermeier flâneur to Beuth's Industriegroßstadt," in *Karl Friedrich Schinkel*, ed. Peik, 84–85.
186. Thomas Hall, *Planning Europe's Capital Cities: Aspects of Nineteenth Century Urban Development* (New York, NY: Routledge, 2010), 190.
187. Schinkel, *Sammlung architektonischer Entwürfe*, 2–3.

188. Peter Springer, *Schinkels Schloßbrücke in Berlin: Zweckbau und Monument* (Berlin: Propyläen, 1984).
189. Engel, *Forum Friedericianum*, 183.
190. For a similar argument, see Kŭm, "Karl Friedrich Schinkelŭi kŏnch'uge kwanhan koch'al," *Tongyangdaehakkyo nonmunjip*, 29–31.
191. Hall, *Planning Europe's Capital Cities*, 187–200; Lejeune, "Schinkel and Lenné in Berlin," 96–97. On Berlin's population growth, see Ingrid Thienel, "Verstädterung, städtische Infrastruktur und Stadtplanung: Berlin zwischen 1850 und 1914," *Zeitschrift für Stadtsoziologie, Stadtgeschichte und Denkmalpflege* 4 (1977): 63.
192. Ohff, *Peter Joseph Lenné*, 117–125.
193. Ibid., 118, 134, 130–131. The construction plan for the fields of Köpenick adopted a modified version of the 1830 plan drafted by Schmid, the chief building official in Berlin. His original plan stood out for very simple and rough grid blocks based on financial considerations. See Walter Kieß, *Urbanismus im Industriezeitalter: Von der klassizistischen Stadt zur Garden City* (Berlin: Ernst & Sohn, 1991), 69; Jean-François Lejeune, "Schinkel and Lenné in Berlin, from the Biedermeier flâneur to Beuth's Industriegroßstadt," in *Karl Friedrich Schinkel*, ed. Peik, 91–97.
194. Ohff, *Peter Joseph Lenné*, 132–135; Ingrid Thienel, "James Hobrecht," in *Neue Deutsche Biographie*, ed. Historische Kommission bei der bayerischen Akademie der Wissenschaften, vol. 9 (Leipzig: Duncker & Humblot, 1972), 280–281; Hall, *Planning Europe's Capital Cities*, 192–193; Kieß, *Urbanismus im Industriezeitalter*, 250.
195. Peter Ring, "Bevölkerung," in *Berlin Handbuch: Das Lexikon der Bundeshauptstadt*, ed. Horst Ulrich et al. (Berlin: FAB Verlag, 1992), 237; Horst Matzerath, "Berlin, 1890–1940," in *Metropolis 1890–1940*, ed. Anthony Sutcliff (Chicago, IL: The University of Chicago Press, 1984), 293–294; Kieß, *Urbanismus im Industriezeitalter*, 238.
196. Hall, *Planning Europe's Capital Cities*, 63–77.
197. David Harvey, *Paris, Capital of Modernity* (New York, NY: Routledge, 2003), 121–136; Norma Evenson, "Paris, 1890–1940," in *Metropolis*, ed. Sutcliff, 259–287.
198. Patricia L. Garside, "West End, East End: London 1890, 1940," in *Metropolis*, 235–243.
199. Gerhard Brunn, "Stadtumbau im 19. Jahrhundert. Zwei Modelle: London und Paris," in *Die Stadt als Moloch? Das Land als Kraftquell? Wahrnehmungen und Wirkungen der Großstädte um 1900*, ed. Clemens Zimmermann and Jürgen Reulecke (Basel: Birkhäuser, 1999), 95–115.
200. Thienel, "Verstädterung, städtische Infrastruktur und Stadtplanung," 79 ff.; Kieß, *Urbanismus im Industriezeitalter*, 228–229.
201. Anthony Sutcliffe, "Planung und Entwicklung der Großstädte in England und Frankreich von 1850 bis 1875 und ihre Einflüsse auf Deutschland," in *Stadterweiterungen 1800–1875: Von den Anfängen des modernen Städtebaues in Deutschland*, ed. Gerhard Fehl and Juan Rodriguez-Lores (Hamburg: Hans Christians Verlag, 1983), 35–53. Floor plans of Berlin from the Hobrecht plan to the 1990s are documented on the web site www.stadtentwicklung.berlin.de/planen/fnp/pix/historie/Berliner_Plaene_1862_bis_1994.pdf (accessed January 15, 2020).
202. Hildegard Schröteler-von Brandt, *Stadtbau-und Stadtplanungsgeschichte: Eine Einführung* (Berlin: Springer, 2014), 104.
203. Daniel Ehebrecht, *Der Hobrechtplan von 1862 und seine Einflüsse auf das Stadtbild von Berlin* (Munich: Grin Verlag, 2008), 11; Kieß, *Urbanismus im Industriezeitalter*, 70–71, 230–232, and more generally, see Harald

Bodenschatz, *Berlin Urban Design: A Brief History of a European City* (Berlin: DOM Publishers, 2013), 18–26.

204. James Hobrecht, *Die Canalisation von Berlin* (Berlin: Ernst & Korn, 1884), 4 ff, 55 ff.
205. Kieß, *Urbanismus im Industriezeitalter*, 227–228. The act had some positive aspects, particularly in terms of fire protection, which was facilitated by setting the minimum area of the backyard (Hinterhof) of the building to 5.34 × 5.34 meters. See Jürgen Reulecke, *Geschichte der Urbanisierung in Deutschland* (Frankfurt am Main: Suhrkamp, 1985), 52.
206. Werner Hegemann, *Das steinerne Berlin, Geschichte der größten Mietskasernenstadt der Welt* (Berlin: Gustav Kiepenheuer, 1930), 207 ff. Hegemann blames even Schinkel's urban architecture for helping to ruin Berlin due to its self-satisfying "romantic" propensity. Ibid., 181–182.
207. James Hobrecht, *Über öffentliche Gesundheitspflege und die Bildung eines Central-Amts für öffentliche Gesundheitspflege im Staate* (Stettin: Th. von der Nahmer, 1868), 14–17.
208. Sutcliffe, "Planung und Entwicklung," 50.
209. Kieß, *Urbanismus im Industriezeitalter*, 231–232.
210. Wilhelm Raabe, "Die Chronik der Sperlinsgasse," in *Wilhelm Raabe Sämtliche Werke*, Braunschweiger Ausgabe, vol. 1 (1908; Göttingen: Vandenhoeck & Ruprecht, 1980), 16–17.
211. Walter Benjamin, *Berlin Childhood Around 1900*, trans. Howard Eiland (Cambridge, MA: Belknap Press of Harvard University, 2006), 46, 54.
212. Kieß, *Urbanismus im Industriezeitalter*, 400 ff, 427 ff.; Edward C. Relph, *The Modern Urban Landscape: 1880 to the Present* (Baltimore, MD: Johns Hopkins University Press, 1992), 49–64; Mervyn Miller, *Letchworth: The First Garden City* (Chichester: Phillimore, 1989).
213. Kieß, *Urbanismus im Industriezeitalter*, 393–409; Mallgrave, *Modern Architectural Theory*, 193; Carl E. Schorske, *Fin-de-Siècle Vienna: Politics and Culture* (New York, NY: Vintage Books, 1981), 62–72.
214. Mallgrave, *Modern Architectural Theory*, 170–177.
215. Matei Calinescu, *Five Faces of Modernity: Modernism, Avant-Garde, Decadence, Kitsch, Postmodernism* (Durham, NC: Duke University Press, 1987), 41, 46–58. For a conceptual history of modernity, see Hans Ulrich Gumbrecht, "Modern, Modernität, Moderne," in *Geschichtliche Grundbegriffe: Historisches Lexikon zur politisch-sozialen Sprache in Deutschland*, vol. 4, ed. Otto Brunner et al. (Stuttgart: Klett-Cotta, 1978), 93–131.
216. Peter Paret, *The Berlin Secession: Modernism and Its Enemies in Imperial Germany* (Cambridge, MA: Belknap Press of Harvard University, 1989).
217. Quoted from Joan Campbell, *The German Werkbund: The Politics of Reform in the Applied Arts* (Princeton, NJ: Princeton University Press, 2015), 3.
218. Muthesius's aspirations had a close affinity with the "national liberalism" represented by the moderate politician Friedrich Naumann, who insisted on achieving a successful industrialization without losing a national harmony. Obviously, Naumann's commitment to the Deutscher Werkbund was predicated on his aspirations to social reform. On this point, see Campbell, *The German Werkbund*, 16–22, and more generally, see Hardtwig, *Nationalismus und Bürgerkultur*, 246–273.
219. Campbell, *The German Werkbund*, 12–16, 24–29. On the relationship between Behrens's and Schinkelian architecture, see Stanford Anderson, "Schinkel, Behrens, an Elemental Tectonic, and a New Classicism," in *Karl Friedrich Schinkel*, ed. Peik, 116–124; Mallgrave, *Modern Architectural Theory*, 226–234.

220. Hermann Muthesius, *Kunstgewerbe und Architektur* (1907), quoted from Schwarzer, *German Architectural Theory*, 250.
221. Relph, *The Modern Urban Landscape,* 112–113; Maiken Umbach, "The Deutscher Werkbund, Globalization, and the Invention of Modern Vernaculars," in *Vernacular Modernism: Heimat, Globalization, and the Built Environment*, ed. Maiken Umbach and Bernd Hüppauf (Redwood City, CA: Stanford University Press, 2005), 114–140; Werner Durth, *Deutsche Architekten: Biographische Verflechtungen 1900–1970* (Munich: dtv, 1992), 67–73.
222. Mallgrave, *Modern Architectural Theory*, 254–255.
223. Siegfried Giedion, *Space, Time and Architecture* (1941; Cambridge, MA: Harvard University Press, 1967), 496; Peter Gay, *Modernism: The Lure of Heresy* (New York, NY: W. W. Norton & Company, 2008), 298–318; Francesco Passanti, "The Vernacular, Modernism, and Le Corbusier," in *Vernacular Modernism*, ed. Umbach and Hüppauf, 141–156, esp., 142; Alan Colquhoun, *Modernity and the Classical Tradition*, 89–119.
224. On New Functionalism during the Weimar Republic, see Jost Hermand and Frank Trommler, *Die Kultur der Weimarer Republik* (Frankfurt am Main: Fischer, 1988), 116. On the underlying tendencies of New Functionalism in German architecture after Peter Behrens, see Nipperdey, *Deutsche Geschichte 1866–1918*, 727–729.
225. On the historical aspects of the Deutscher Werkbund, see Umbach, *German Cities and Bourgeois Modernism*, 51 ff.; Schwarzer, *German Architectural*, 120–127.
226. Karl Bötticher, "Das Prinzip der hellenischen und germanischen Bauweise," *Allgemeine Bauzeitung* 11 (1846): 119. On this point, see Mallgrave, *Modern Architectural Theory*, 111; Schwarzer, *German Architectural Theory*, 184, 187–188.
227. Christian M. Boyer, *The City of Collective Memory: Its Historical Imagery and Architectural Entertainments* (Cambridge, MA: The MIT Press, 2001), 4.
228. Maiken Umbach emphasizes the continuity between bourgeois modernism and historicism. See Umbach, *German Cities and Bourgeois Modernism*, 32.
229. Schwarzer, *German Architectural Theory*, 84.
230. Schorske, *Fin-de-Siècle Vienna*, 24–46.
231. Ibid., quoted from 27.
232. Andreas Nierhaus, "Schauplatz und Handlungsraum: Zur visuellen und räumlichen Inszenierung des Wiener Kaiserforums," *Kunst und Politik* 11 (2009): 48–53; Mallgrave, *Gottfried Semper*, 314–339.
233. *Deutsche Bauzeitung* 51, no. 14 (1917): 68.
234. Schorske, *Fin-de-Siècle Vienna*, 66.
235. Kieß, *Urbanismus im Industriezeitalter*, 227 ff.
236. Koselleck, *Preußen zwischen Reform und Revolution*, 23–51.
237. The full title of the law is "Gesetz, betreffend die Anlegung und Veränderung von Straßen und Plätzen in Städten und ländlichen Ortschaften. Vom 2. Juli 1875 [Law on the Creation and Modification of Streets and Squares in Cities and Rural Areas. July 2, 1875]." The full-text of the law is documented on the web site https://digital-beta.staatsbibliothek-berlin.de/werkansicht?PPN=PPN682742007&DMDID=DMDLOG_0002&PHYSID=PHYS_0033 (accessed January 15, 2020). On this law, see Helmuth Croon, "Staat und Städte in den westlichen Provinzen Preußens 1817–1875: Ein Beitrag zum Entstehen des Preußischen Bau-und Fluchtliniengesetzes von 1875," in *Stadterweiterungen*, ed. Fehl and Rodriguez-Lores, 55–79, esp. 72–75. See also Dorothea Berger-Thimme, *Wohnungsfrage und Sozialstaat: Untersuchungen zu den Anfängen staatlicher Wohnungspolitik in Deutschland 1873–1918* (Frankfurt a. M.: Peter Lang, 1976), 213–220.

238. Ehebrecht, *Der Hobrechtplan*, 14–15.
239. See the construction report drawn up by the then–Civil Engineering Bureau of Frankfurt, Städtisches Tiefbauamt, ed., *Umlegung von Grundstücken in Frankfurt am Main* (Frankfurt am Main: Schirmer & Mahlau, 1903), also web site, https://archive.org/stream/umlegungvongrun00tiefgoog#page/n4/mode/2up (accessed January 15, 2020). See also a contemporary report from the Frankfurt district court judge, C. Merlo, *Der Gesetzentwurf Betreffend Stadterweiterungen und Zonenenteignungen: Lex Adickes* (1894; Whitefish, MT: Kessinger Publishing, 2010). On the enactment of this law, see Anthony Sutcliffe, *Towards the Planned City: Germany, Britain, and the United States and France, 1780–1914* (Oxford: Basil Blackwell, 1981), 32, 37. On the effects of this law, see Dorothea Berger-Thimme, *Wohnungsfrage und Sozialstaat: Untersuchungen zu den Anfängen staatlicher Wohnungspolitik in Deutschland 1873–1918* (Frankfurt a. M.: Peter Lang, 1976), 213–220. On Franz Adickes, see, notably, Lothar Gall, *Franz Adickes: Oberbürgermeister und Universitätsgründer* (Frankfurt a. M.: Societäts Verlag, 2013), and more generally, see Jin-Sung Chun, "The Lex Adickes in East Asian Contexts: The Introduction of Land Readjustment and Spatio-political Effects," in *Transnational Encounters Between Germany and East Asia since 1900*, ed. Joanne Miyang Cho (New York, NY: Routledge, 2018), 101–122. Long before drafting the Lex Adickes, Frankfurt Mayor Adickes created a municipal zoning act. Drafting the 1891 zoning act was mainly indebted to Reinhard Baumeister, a pioneering German city planner. For further details, see John Robert Mullin, "American Perceptions of German City Planning at the Turn of the Century," *Landscape Architecture & Regional Planning Faculty Publication Series* 35 (1976): 9–10.
240. Matzerath, "Berlin, 1890–1940," 297–298. Berlin's advanced water supply system, for example, evidenced a drastic reduction of typhoid fever mortality. See Reulecke, *Geschichte der Urbanisierung in Deutschland*, 60–61.
241. Mark Twain, "Berlin – The Chicago of Europe," *New York Sun*, April 3, 1892, quoted from Mark Twain, *Berlin – The Chicago of Europe* (Berlin: Berlinica Publishing LLC, 2013), 77. On these reports, see Ralf Thies and Dietmar Jazbinsek, "Berlin – das europäische Chicago: Über ein Leitmotiv der Amerikanisierungsdebatte zu Beginn des 20. Jahrhunderts," in *Die Stadt als Moloch?* ed. Zimmermann and Reulecke, 53–94.
242. Thies and Jazbinsek, "Berlin – das europäische Chicago," 70–73; Na In-ho, *Kaenyŏmsaran muŏshin'ga: Yŏksawa ŏnŏŭi saeroun mannam* (Seoul: Yŏksabip'yŏngsa, 2011), 225–261. Walter Rathenau's statement in his 1902 writing *Die schönste Stadt der Welt* [The most beautiful city in the world] is quoted from Thies and Jazbinsek, "Berlin – das europäische Chicago," 69.
243. August Julius Langbehn, *Rembrandt als Erzieher* (1890; Leipzig: C. L. Hirschfeld, 1925), 264, 280–281. For further details on the "cultural pessimism," see Chŏn Jin-sŏng, *Posuhyŏngmyŏng: Togil chishigindŭrŭi hŏmujuŭijŏg isang* (Seoul: Ch'aeksesang, 2001), 25–29.
244. Fritz Stern, *The Politics of Cultural Despair: A Study in the Rise of the German Ideology* (Berkeley, CA: University of California Press, 1974), 174.
245. Nikolaus Bernau, *Museuminsel Berlin* (Berlin: Stadtwandel, 2010); Mallgrave, *Gottfried Semper*, 105.
246. Marchand, *Down From Olympus*, 136.
247. Sünderhauf, *Griechensehnsucht und Kulturkritik*, 295–364, 55 ff., 128–138; Joachim Petsch, *Kunst im Dritten Reich: Architektur-Plastik-Malerei-Alltagsästhetik* (Potsdam: Vista Point, 2002), 47–49.

248. Johann Gustav Droysen, *Weltreich des Alexander des Großen* (1833; Dresden: Paul Aretz, 1934).
249. Johann Gustav Droysen, Volume 3 of *Geschichte des Hellenismus: Geschichte der Epigonen* (1836; Darmstadt: Wissenschaftliche Buchgesellschaft, 2008), 434.
250. Marchand, *Down From Olympus*, 238 ff.; Suzanne L. Marchand, *German Orientalism in the Age of Empire: Religion, Race, and Scholarship* (Cambridge: Cambridge University Press, 2009), 53–55.

2 Beyond the Prussia of Asia

> Were the thrifty Dutch to cultivate the rich plains of China, who knows how many hundred Hollands could be born in the East? Could the Japanese compare themselves to the Dutch in diligence or are we, from the outset, more akin to the indolent Chinese?
>
> Kume Kunitake, *The Iwakura Embassy, 1871–73: A True Account of the Ambassador Extraordinary & Plenipotentiary's Journey of Observation Through the United States of America and Europe*, ed. Graham Healey and Chūshichi Tsuzuki

1. Qingdao, the Epitome of German Historicist Architecture

Schinkel's Prussian classical architecture originally sought to advance the culture of Germans, but its influence turned out to be international, reaching beyond Prussia and the German Empire. Schinkel pursued an architecture of refined form that exercised a subtle and long-lasting rather than explosive influence. The secret to such an extended impact may be gathered from the following two factors.

First, the tectonic harmony between part and whole, form and function, and past and present perfectly suited colonial ruling powers as an ideology. As European and American powers entered the age of imperialism starting in the mid-nineteenth century, neoclassicism traveled beyond the European continent to take root in colonies around the world, evolving into a typical architectural and decorative style for public buildings at colonies, especially those in Southeast Asia and the Pacific coasts.[1] The solid, firm impression tectonic unity gave was perfect for visually demonstrating the superiority and prestige of Western modern civilization. Rather than future-oriented French Revolutionary architecture, architecture with historicist elements far better suited the purpose of colonial rule. Depending on the circumstances of each colony and its ruling power, buildings and urban planning would sometimes adopt the Greek neoclassical style or assume the neo-Renaissance or neo-Baroque style, encroaching on the colonial terrain. The neat, north German style of neo-Renaissance architecture in particular contributed significantly to transforming the bourgeois belief in scientific objectivity and heritage into a logic of universal civilization. At the epicenter of such rapid waves of transformation was, of course, Schinkel. As proved through Semper's architecture, German neo-Renaissance architecture had evolved over time from Prussian classical architecture.

Second, tectonics conceived through Schinkelian architecture created a common sphere that rose above minute stylistic differences to touch upon the essence of building (Bauen) and profoundly influence the formation of architectural modernism. German architects like Walter Gropius, Mies van der Rohe, and Bruno Taut were heavily critical of historicist architecture during their time, but they did subscribe to Schinkel's belief in the simplicity, unity, and monumentality of architecture. It was through Schinkel's works that they learned the objectivity, functionality, aesthetic sensitivity, and tectonics essential to modernist architecture before they went on to lead architectural internationalism that played a definitive role in the birth of modernist architecture and urban planning. To them, the Prussian state architect's great achievements seemed to be on a par with the influence Palladio had exercised upon Western architecture for 450 years.[2]

Cultural Imperialism

If Prussian classical architecture and the German Empire's historicist architecture were the source of modernist architecture and an efficient instrument of colonial rule, they should be regarded as homogeneous rather than contrasting styles. Tectonics excluding elements nonessential to building and the logic of modernity concealing the inevitable conflict between form and function were actually two sides of the same coin. Tectonics served as a catalyst for modernity and made possible the trans-modern prosperity of Prussian classicism. The way Schinkel emphasized the façade more than interior space opened a broad range of possibilities for it to be utilized instead of being a weakness.

It would, of course, be an exaggeration to say that Prussian classical architecture itself carried colonial implications. During Schinkel's time, Prussia was no more than a medium-sized power without any colonies overseas. Even after the German Empire's establishment, Chancellor Bismarck's foreign policies remained focused on defending the economic interests of Germans. The desire to solidify its belated political unification had been stronger than the imperialistic urge to expand. Based on the Iron Chancellor's hard-edged realpolitik stance, the German Empire had to be involved in the Western powers' reorganization of territories throughout the world but only when it accompanied specific profits unrelated to the French "*mission civilisatrice*." Bismarck is known to have preferred the term protectorate (Schutzgebiet) as opposed to colony, which explicitly entails territorial despoliation.[3]

Germany's colonial administration began the year after the German Colonial Society (Deutsche Kolonialverein) was launched in 1883 as

Bismarck designated as protectorates the territories German merchants or conquerors individually acquired in the eastern and southwestern regions of Africa.[4] However, the German Empire lacked its British and French counterparts' lengthy tradition of building colonies and met its demise earlier than they when it was dissolved upon the end of World War I. Over a mere thirty or so years of colonization, the German Empire did not promote a distinct mission like other empires and instead focused on securing for its people "living space," or *Lebensraum*, which also served as the title of an essay the German geographer Friedrich Ratzel published in 1901. In other words, the German Empire did not fit into the typical profile of a colonial empire. It did not bother to make efforts to teach the German language to the natives in its African colonies.[5]

It would, however, be misleading to draw conclusions about German colonialism by examining only the actions Germany took in its colonies or protectorates between 1884 and 1918. Colonialism refers to a series of actions taken to relocate people from their homeland to a faraway region, which involves more than economic, political, or military purposes. German colonialism in particular was far more advanced in discourses or academic studies on colonialization, as well as the accompanying fantasies toward the Orient, and this had a greater impact upon the German Empire itself than its colonies.[6] Ideological, cultural, and psychological factors beyond practical purposes were commonly employed for colonial rule by all empires, especially by an unsuccessful colonial empire like Germany. Excessive idealization or disdain toward the subjugated, suppression and commercialization of native cultures, and ideologies based on crude exploitation and patriarchal discipline were too stilted and contradictory to utilize as instruments of colonial rule.[7] Colonialism was ultimately a concoction of extreme ideas and implementations, constantly clashing with the reality of colonial natives.[8] The German Empire could not have been entirely free from these general issues of colonialism, no matter how early it was dissolved. Although it did not suffer from decolonization wars like Britain or France, Germany eventually caused an even graver tragedy from attempting to deal with an uncontrollable fever of nationalism within the boundaries of Europe. German colonies comparable to the British colonial India or the French colony Algeria were not Cameroon or Togo but Eastern Europe.[9]

The colonialism of the German Empire was no different in principle compared to that of other empires, but Germany was mindful of rivals like Britain or France as it strived to develop ideas of its own. Since Germany's unification was based on the idea of a cultural nation, the German Empire's emphasis on cultural spheres should come as no surprise. Because late nineteenth-century Germany had been at the European forefront in the academic realms of humanities, social sciences, medicine, natural sciences, and technology, it was able to propound "scientific" colonial rule dissimilar to the French civilizing mission or Anglo-Saxon commercialism.[10]

However, the reality was somewhat different from the propounded slogan. The German Empire's rule in southwestern Africa was utterly practical, spontaneous, and extremely brutal, as can be sensed from the genocide committed against the Herero, whereas a completely different approach was taken toward the South Pacific Samoa Islands by patriarchally offering to protect the islands' native cultures and help form a tropical paradise.[11]

The only case in which the German Empire disseminated its idea of a cultural nation and adopted tectonics derived from Prussian classicism for scientific colonial rule can be found in China, a sophisticated civilization with a climate similar to Germany. As with any other colony, coercive rule based on racial antipathy did take place, but Germany also adopted more detailed planning, professional administration, and official supervision in China. Yet this change seems to have been spurred not necessarily by ideas but by Germany's competition with Britain and France that began prior to Germany's advancement into China. German Oriental studies focused on old documents and languages that contributed little to Germany's colonization, and prior to the twentieth century, colonialist culture had not yet permeated German society as it had in the societies of other imperialist powers.[12] Moreover, Germans in general lacked interest in and were ignorant of the Far East. The famed Chinese House (Chinesisches Haus) on the grounds of Frederick the Great's Sanssouci Palace in Potsdam was no more than a polished demonstration of the Chinoiserie motif the Rococo court culture had been swept up in at the time. Once the craze died down, the motif was soon replaced with a fascination for Greek neoclassicism and India's spiritual heritage. Even after Japan's victory in the First Sino-Japanese War, the thoughts of German politicians remained confined within the context of competition among European powers. Instead of awakening such politicians, the German emperor Wilhelm II's "yellow peril" argument further incited racial prejudice. German leaders only began to recognize Japan and East Asia as genuine participants in international politics upon being shocked by the Russo-Japanese War's outcome.[13]

Before it started to take note of East Asia, the German Empire made the politically calculated move of seeking to build a colonial city of a new dimension in mainland China. Unlike its protectorates in Africa and the South Pacific, the German Empire secured a ninety-nine-year lease over a territory in China and placed it under the German Naval Ministry's government. A model colony (Musterkolonie) to show the German Empire's greatness was thus built as rapidly as the German military tactic called "lightning war" (Blitzkrieg).

Qingdao, the German Empire's Naval Base in East Asia

In 1897, amid the scramble for colonies, the murder of two German Catholic priests in the Shandong Province served as an excuse for the

German Empire to dispatch cruisers from Shanghai and occupy the Kiautschou (Jiaozhou) Bay on November 14. The German Empire thereafter pressured the Chinese government into signing a treaty leasing a 50-kilometer-wide zone around the bay to the Germans for ninety-nine years. The treaty also awarded the German Empire the rights to railroad construction and coal mining in China. Wilhelm II thereby installed a German government in Qingdao, or "Tsingtau" to Germans, in order to turn the area into a commercial and military port.

Qingdao was originally the name of a small island facing Qingdao Bay of Shandong Province. Before the German Empire stuck its flag in the area, the bay already had a small but established administration and defense system. Nevertheless, for large steamships to be able to anchor, it was necessary to build a port and breakwater. Based on a comprehensive construction plan formulated by 1899, Qingdao was systematically transformed into a naval base for the German Empire. By 1904, the railway connecting the port at Kiautschou Bay to the coal mines in Jinan was completed.[14]

Germany first set foot in East Asia during the Prussian expedition to the Far East in the 1860s. Charged with the king's commission to conclude treaties with China, Japan, and Siam (present-day Thailand) and find potential sites for Germans to relocate, Count Friedrich Albrecht Graf zu Eulenburg headed to East Asia on warships, arriving in the image of a conqueror.[15] Nevertheless, East Asia might as well have been on another planet as far as Prussia was concerned, since Prussia had been preoccupied with a series of wars to unify Germans in Europe at the time. The German geographer Ferdinand von Richthofen's proposal in the early 1870s to create a bridgehead and military port in East Asia for the German navy and thereby establish a "German Hong Kong" went unheeded.[16]

After its foundation, the German Empire began to more actively advance into East Asia once the domination of Chancellor Bismarck and his classical foreign policy drew to an end. By securing Togo and Cameroon as its African protectorates in 1884, the German Empire could have joined the ranks of imperialist states, but its diplomacy continued to gravitate toward maintaining a balance between powers in Europe. At the height of a frenzy among powers to secure markets and territories, the young emperor Wilhelm II forced the old chancellor to resign in 1890, no longer able to hide his desire to expand and search for a "place in the sun." Under the slogan Weltpolitik, the German Empire thus started to pursue the path of imperialism, driven above all by the Flottenpolitik policy. This naval policy was first tested as the German Imperial Naval Office led by Admiral Alfred von Tirpitz attempted to secure and maintain bridgeheads all over the world for the German Imperial Navy so as to boost the empire's economic interests and political influence.[17]

The German Empire governed the Kiautschou Bay for seventeen years, until Japan took over within months after World War I broke out in

1914. The area was practically a semi-colony of the German Empire, serving as its East Asian base, industrial channel, and a source of raw material and coal for the German navy stationed in Qingdao. The fact that Qingdao evolved into a prosperous international port in East Asia demonstrated that Germany's plan had been fairly successful, apart from failing to fully exploit its ninety-nine-year leasehold. Geopolitical considerations did play a part in the German Empire's decision to take a lease of the Kiautschou Bay, but the abundant amount of coal at the Shandong peninsula was the foremost reason. The bay was necessary for not only the German navy stationed in East Asia but for the German Empire's entry into the Chinese market. Despite such practical purposes, Germany had to demonstrate Qingdao's true worth as a model colony comparable to the British-ruled Hong Kong, so it built a hospital, school, and weather station in Qingdao and opened their doors to Chinese locals for the most part. These actions were somewhat different from those the German Empire exhibited at its African colonies but not entirely different in the sense that the empire unilaterally treated the natives as subjects of rule.[18]

Chinese locals in the Qingdao area were deprived of their land, forced to relocate, and, above all, had their sovereignty violated from racial segregation. They heavily resisted the railroad construction, because it involved only the interests of foreigners and had nothing to do with theirs. The land policy enforced from the day German cruisers arrived and took over Qingdao prohibited civilians from buying and selling land in the Kiautschou Bay area. This reinforced the German Empire's administrative monopolization and control over the area's land so as to be able to preclude speculation from the outside and cheaply acquire land. The German governor of Kiautschou Bay swiftly surveyed and measured the area's land, then set out to purchase lots. By half forcing native villagers to bargain, the German governor was easily able to secure spacious lots for public construction. The German conquerors' ruthless conduct and the Qing government's submissive attitude seriously violated China's legal order, frustrating even local officials enough to take part in a widespread resistance movement. It was therefore no coincidence that the German Empire's occupation of the Kiautschou Bay eventually triggered the Boxer Rebellion that occurred in the Huabei region in 1900.[19]

The Chinese also resented the German Empire's missionary policy. To them, German missionaries arriving on warships loaded with artillery and opium was a sight that appeared as negative as their earlier impression of Catholic missionaries.[20] German protestant missionaries primarily worked in the southern parts of the Shandong peninsula. The region happened to be where Confucius of the Lu dynasty was born, and Jinan at the peninsula's center had long functioned as an administrative city that took pride in its tradition of thorough Confucian education. These circumstances made it challenging for missionaries to operate in the region and forced the German Empire to employ cleverer cultural policies. Fierce competition among powers made it all the more necessary for Germany to carry out a differentiated colonization program in the semi-colonized mainland China. The German Protestant Missionary Council thus launched extensive education projects in Qingdao with the establishment of a German-Chinese Confucian academy called Dehua shuyuan in 1898. Once the Boxer Rebellion was suppressed, the Germans switched from oppressive to cultural rule, focusing on missionary work and projects involving education and sanitation. The German governor formed ties with pro-German Chinese elites in order to further facilitate long-term commercial and political interests for his homeland. By jointly establishing the German-Chinese college Dehua daxue in 1909, Germany sought to appeal to the Chinese through its outstanding spiritual culture, which was no doubt a means of imperialist invasion.[21]

Distinction From British and French Colonial Cities

What set the German-controlled Qingdao apart from cities colonized by other Western powers such as Britain and France was its appearance, which looked like an exact copy of a city in mainland Germany. It had been a strategic decision aimed at promoting Germany's outstanding culture. This was antipodal to the case of Britain, which apparently showed respect for the indigenous culture of its colonial cities. Qingdao was no exception in that the conqueror's perspective dictated the establishment of the city's center and the cityscape's reorganization according to ideal purposiveness. The architectural façade's diversity did not guarantee open-mindedness in spatial order. Allowing superficial diversity could instead be considered to have attained an advanced degree of unity.[22] Also, it was not uncommon for such outcomes of technological, ideological experimentation in colonial cities to be adopted in metropolises in the imperial homeland and have a long-term effect.[23] Urban planning was an intricate strategy to demonstrate how developed and modern Western civilizations were, like a magic wand that makes it natural to destroy and dominate everyday life. And the so-called German culture was no exception to this global trend that fell under the concept of the coloniality of power.

Employing both explicit colonial rule and "informal" imperialism exercising actual control from behind the scenes, the British Empire took a practical approach to architecture and urban planning. A typical example of this would be the Anglican Saint Mark Church that James William Wild built in the 1840s in the residential district for Europeans at Alexandria, Egypt. By combining the eclectic neo-Gothic and mosque style, the church seemed supportive of the Egyptian royal family's modernization policy. After turning Egypt into its protectorate, Britain grew more conscious of other imperialist competitors than the Egyptians' regional interests. It nevertheless failed to develop a specific architectural style at its colonies. Instead, fusing orientalism with the diversity and flexibility characteristic of the Victorian era emerged as a nativized form in each colonial region.[24]

In the British colony of India loomed a more obvious version of a colonial city. Since 1857, the British viceroyalty installed within it a public works department to carry out full-fledged construction work for public buildings and urban planning. The city to be newly developed was New Delhi. The strategy was, as usual, to combine the British with the indigenous. Although the indigenous remained only in decorations, the basic characteristics of a British colonial city were preserved in New Delhi. The architects to take charge of newly developing the city were Edwin Landseer Lutyens and Herbert Baker. The most ambitious part of their plan was Rashtrapati Bhavan, which was once the viceroy's house and now serves as the presidential residence of India. The building at the top of the New Delhi plateau was constructed right after the decision was made to relocate India's capital from Calcutta to New Delhi. The original plan the leading British urban planner Lutyens sent to Baker in 1912 was overall classical with an Indian flavor mixed into the colors and details. Lutyens is said to have originally gone for a starkly classical building until he eventually caved under political pressure. The Rashtrapati Bhavan is a massive four-story building with a total of 340 rooms. Its tall copper dome is the most eye-catching feature of the building, which exhibits stylistic elements of Mughal architecture visible through other local buildings such as the Taj Mahal. Shaped like a *stupa* or Buddhist burial mound, the dome is above the point where the diagonals of the square building meet, rising twice as high as the rest of the building's height.[25]

Figure 2.1 Rashtrapati Bhavan Upon the New Delhi Plateau.

Source: Photo: Ronakshah1990/CC BY-SA (https://creativecommons.org/licenses/by-sa/4.0).

Compared to British colonial cities that reinterpreted indigenous traditions, France stayed far truer to the definition of a colonial city. Based on the mission of civilization, the French Empire's assimilation policy sought to integrate colonies with the mainland by introducing identical systems and allowing colonial subjects to enjoy the same rights and educational and cultural benefits as those in the mainland. This, however, was only a stratagem for efficient colonial rule. The districts for Westerners and the colonial natives were strictly segregated, forming a "dual city" per the suggestion of Hubert Lyautey, the resident-general of the French protectorate Morocco. The Westerners' district served as a test bed for mainland France. This contradictory combination of assimilation and segregation was characteristic of the French policy for its colonial cities.[26]

France's colonial rule of North African Islamic regions began with its occupation of Algeria in 1830, followed by the French occupation of Tunisia in 1881, and Morocco was taken as a protectorate in 1912. While the early French colonization projects in Algeria were based on a stringent assimilation policy, France gradually shifted its approach toward preserving indigenous cultures. Actively developing districts for Westerners while retaining the médina, or old parts of the city occupied by the Muslims, for the purpose of being romantically consumed could be considered a typical manifestation of France's dual city policy.[27] Nevertheless, there were definitely new aspects to urban planning done by Henri Prost in the 1910s for the French colonial city Casablanca in Morocco and by Le Corbusier for Algiers, the capital of the French protectorate Algeria. More standardized construction, more reasonable industrial frameworks and public services, efficient thoroughfares, and greater attention paid to ventilation and lighting for urban hygiene were indications of modernism at colonial cities that had not yet even blossomed in mainland France.[28]

Packed with white houses along the Mediterranean coast, Casablanca was an experimental city sometimes referred to as the "French Chicago." Ever since the French army landed in Morocco in 1907, the French Empire expressed tremendous interest in the beautiful port city. Rather than the city's médina, such interest had more to do with newly developing the area around the pier. To the French Empire, the area seemed to be an optimal point of access to the Moroccan inlands. Starting with the installation of a new breakwater along the city's northernmost fortification in 1910, the restructuring of Casablanca formally began in 1915 by the renowned architect Henri Prost, who studied at École des Beaux-Arts. Upon the enactment of the French urban planning law Les lois Cornudet in 1919, the leading urban planner Prost launched a more comprehensive plan that later earned him the title Baron Haussmann of Casablanca. Prost's plan boldly wiped out the médina near the pier and built a district for Europeans divided into three zones: central, industrial, and residential. To carry out his plan, Prost pioneeringly implemented a modern land ownership system in addition to the German zoning system. It was an attempt to build rational city blocks that went beyond a simple road network. The most monumental aspect of Prost's blueprint was the Place Administrative situated at the new town's center. The public square was not part of Prost's original plan but made its way into his design with enthusiastic administrative support from the Resident-General Lyautey. This grand plan was realized piece by piece, including a central post office, office of military affairs, theater, victory monument, hotel, Catholic church, commercial district, residential district, and a new médina. The traffic artery traversing the Place Administrative was central to Prost's plan because it extended toward the pier, allowing Boulevard de la Gare between the city's center and the new train station to prosper.[29]

The fresh breeze of modernism that blew in Casablanca in the 1920s not only failed to liberate the new town from the underlying notion of a dual city but further intensified the idea. Most colonial natives could not be beneficiaries of modern urban planning, and Prost further marginalized them by touting the traffic artery as a sanitary cordon (cordon sanitaire) protecting Europeans from endemic and infectious diseases.[30] This brutal measure was wholly replicated in French Indochina. Compared to the experimental image of Casablanca, a more classical cityscape unfolded in French Indochina. In the city of Hanoi, public buildings typically served as focal points in shaping uniform boulevards, and public squares and parks were newly constructed. Examples of this were the Hanoi Opera House and the arterial road Pho Trang Tien, one of the first the colonial government paved to run from east to west.[31] Slight changes did occur over time, including those between 1923 and 1931 when Ernest Hébrard oversaw construction and urban planning in French Indochina. Hébrard was an architect with experience in construction projects in Casablanca, but instead of installing a sanitary cordon, he sought a way to reinforce a zoning system while struggling to develop a new Indochinese style. However, Hébrard had no objection to the need for a dual city.[32]

The idea of a dual city, which facilitated the demonstration of the French civilization's superiority without showing any consideration for indigenous traditions, was explicitly and commonly pursued among the French Empire's colonial cities, albeit to different extents. This suggests that France took an approach closer to that of Germany than Britain. The fact that Prost's design of the Place Administrative realized the idea Camillo Sitte expressed through *City Planning According to Artistic Principles* carries significant implications.[33]

The German Empire was even more fundamentalist than France, but on the other hand, as can be witnessed through its colonial cities in Africa, was as practical as Britain. A clear example of cultural imperialism can be found through Strasbourg (Straßburg), the capital of Alsace-Lorraine that was in some ways the German Empire's colonial city in Europe. Upon falling into German hands in 1871 after the Franco-Prussian War, this city that had long been situated along the border between France and

Germany was Germanized at a pace rapid enough to cause a nationalistic backlash among the French, which can be sensed through the French writer Alphonse Daudet's story *The Last Lesson*. Such Germanization was carried out in tandem with modern urban expansion projects. Built in the middle of a new road network formed slightly away from the old city center, the main square Kaiserplatz came to be surrounded by monumental Prussian-style buildings constructed with light-colored sandstone. The university library, public offices, and cultural facilities forming a circle around the square appears to be a condensed reproduction of the center of Unter den Linden in Berlin. Urban planning for Strasbourg realized Schinkelian tectonics to a degree worthy of being nominated over Berlin as the city representative of the early German Empire's architectural culture.[34] Signs of such urban transformation surfaced a century earlier when the writer Goethe visited Strasbourg and praised the Strasbourg Cathedral (Straßburger Münster), "originating from a strong, rugged German soul," as the epitome of German architecture through which "countless parts face toward the whole."[35]

The liberal form language of historicism was incapable of accentuating German colors within Europe, which may have been a practical reason for a colonial European city of the German Empire like Strasbourg to be obsessed with the form language of classicism. Yet it would be difficult to say that Strasbourg's choice had nothing to do with the Prussian principle of tectonics permitting no deviations past the boundary of a uniform order of dominance. This becomes more obvious when comparing Strasbourg with other colonial cities far outside Europe. Buildings in British colonial cities in East Asia such as Hong Kong, Shanghai, or Singapore adopted the "treaty port style," a variation of the European neoclassical form language so as to cater to warm, humid local climates. On the other hand, Qingdao, the only German colonial city in East Asia, realized a thoroughly German historicist style. In its African colonies, the German Empire developed stylistic elements from late Wilhelminism to suit the local climate such as wrap-around verandahs, well-ventilated attics, and open corridors.[36] As if to achieve an optimal balance with such alterations, tropical bungalows gradually lost their popularity from the early stage of British colonies, and the neoclassical style instead grew dominant by the end of the nineteenth century.[37] Yet in China, where the climate was similar and the culture far from unsophisticated, the extreme obsession over the "original form" of national culture was none other than a realization of a German imaginative geography called imaginary Athens within a colonial space.

Competition with Britain certainly continued to be a sensitive matter. Criticizing Anglo-Saxon commercialism and declaring to all nations the German culture's spiritual superiority was the greatest mission of all to German colonialists. The German Club, built in 1907 in the Shanghai International Settlement's Waitan area full of Western buildings, remained the tallest building in the city until 1920. A combination of the German neo-Renaissance and neo-Baroque styles, the building with a huge bronze spire exuded a strictly German air.[38] Around the same time, a full-fledged German-style urban district was nearing its completion in Qingdao of the Shandong Province, which made the city closer to a Chinese Hamburg rather than a German Hong Kong. German historicist architecture realized in Qingdao heavily leaned toward tectonic fundamentalism. Historicism may not have exclusively belonged to German culture, but it was able to develop into a unique discursive formation in Germany and its colonial city.

Urban Planning and Historicist Architecture in Qingdao

Historicist architecture at the turn of the century had already transcended the original boundary of historicism. Depending on functional purposes, late eclectic historicism was mixed with modernist tendencies like Jugendstil as it became involved in entire cityscapes. The unique historicist ideal of pursuing a balance between form and function, part and whole, and past and present came to be overshadowed by intensifying eclecticism. The final flames of historicist architecture blazed in colonial cities of Europe. As the Catholic church turned to non-European parts of the world to regain the dominance it lost in Europe through the Reformation, historicism was revived in European colonies with the global spread of European imperialism. Instead of being purely faithful to a particular style, Western buildings in colonies displayed eclectic tendencies out of consideration for the individual sociocultural, environmental circumstances of each colony in addition to reflecting European cityscapes at the turn of the century.

The German Empire's late historicist architecture assembled in the faraway city of Qingdao, fully demonstrating its unique cultural potential. The realization of tectonic unity between efficient functionality for colonial rule and time-honored aesthetic form had been an achievement unattained in Germany. Regardless of its geographical position, the model colony that emerged out of an extremely brief but extensive construction project presented the most distinct, condensed version of the German Empire's imaginative geography. The colonial city Tsingtau was more German than any other city in Germany.[39]

In building Tsingtau, the port and railroad were priorities because of their potential to contribute to the national interests of the German Empire. For this purpose, the Land Order of Kiautschou (Die Landordnung von Kiautschou) was promulgated in September 1898. Modeled after the policy Britain practiced in Hong Kong, the order provided the legal basis for German capitalists to cheaply acquire land from the Chinese in central Tsingtau for construction. The German colonial government concluded purchase contracts directly with the locals to amass lands it would exclusively resell and whose use it would continue to supervise through the imposition of specific rules and regulations. And by precisely surveying the land, the colonial government also began to draft blueprints for building the port and city. A construction plan for Tsingtau was devised in 1898 by German naval officials in the city, including Georg Franzius, the chief port engineer who had surveyed the area the previous year. Beginning with a massive breakwater, the port's construction involved building state-of-the-art facilities, leveling out the shore, and dredging the seabed. A semi-circular embankment was built at the center of the port so that piers built upon it would be able to accommodate large ships and lead directly to the railway. Many German banks and firms rushed in to acquire the rights to construct railroads and manage coal mines, which helped in promptly constructing two railways as planned.[40]

According to a twice-drafted plan, the construction of roads, a sewage system, transportation facilities, and dikes was carried out without any setbacks, and old buildings along the harbor were instantly demolished in the process.[41] Building the residential district for Europeans was a matter as crucial as building the city's infrastructure. The construction plan for Tsingtau was the first to implement the German zoning system in East Asia, dividing the entire city into a residential district for Europeans, a commercial district, and a couple of residential districts for laborers. Considering the change of seasons and temperatures, the southeastern side of Tsingtau was designated as the residential district for Europeans. The area had beautiful scenery, clean air, and few native residents, which made it easier to develop a living environment suitable for Europeans. The city's center was naturally built near the southern shore of Guanhai Mountain, which offered a pleasant view of the sea. The German Kiautschou government office stood with its back to the mountain and a square formed in front through which an arterial road running east to west converged and led to churches built at either end. Residential districts were developed on the south side adjoining the Qingdao Bay, while the east side was devoted to business facilities and the west to hotels and villas. A hospital and elaborate residences settled at the western foot of Guanhai Mountain. The construction plan specified the width of roads, the height of buildings, the size of building areas, and the proportion of building lots. The building ordinance promulgated in 1898 stipulated that buildings could not rise more than three stories high or occupy more than fifty-five percent of a construction site so as to prevent property speculation and encourage the creation of neat and pleasant living spaces. These strict regulations had been impossible to implement in Germany, yet they were able to be enforced at a leased territory far away from it.[42]

Such measures did not, however, apply to the residential district for the Chinese locals. It was located north of the port, strictly separated from the residential district for Europeans. This segregation policy was

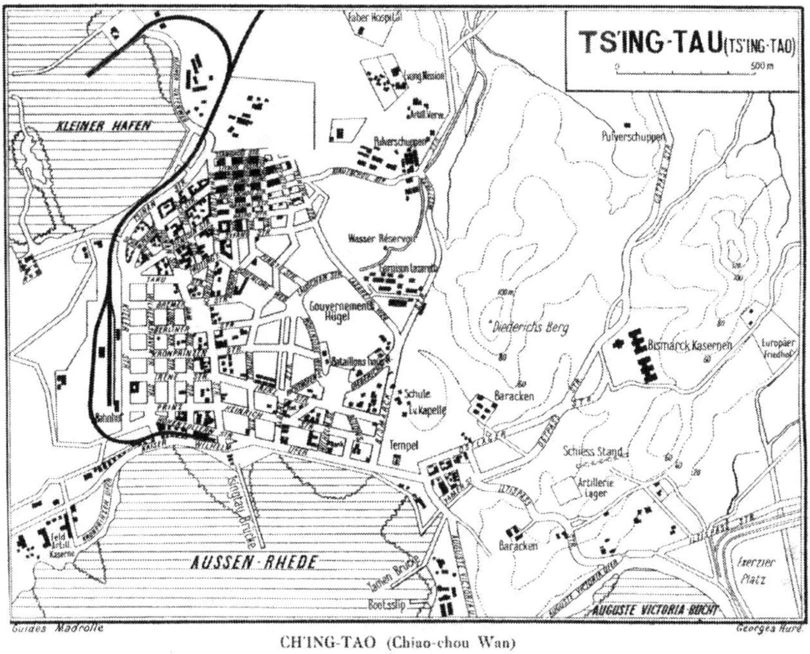

Figure 2.2 City Map of Qingdao (1912).

Source: From the Perry-Castañeda Library Map Collection. Public domain via Wikimedia Commons. Courtesy of the University of Texas Libraries, The University of Texas at Austin.

justified under the pretext of minimizing the risk of infections originating from the unsanitary Chinese, but it would be more plausible to understand the policy as having resulted from the rise of Japan and the yellow peril argument prevalent in the West. Still, it would be a stretch to assume such segregation shared commonalities with German racism that later surfaced. Yet it is undeniable that the experience of colonial rule essentialized race and culture to a biological dimension over the long run and therefore encouraged exclusive, hostile ideas.[43]

German-style buildings were rapidly constructed in the residential district for Europeans in southeast Tsingtau under the enthusiastic supervision of Governor Oskar von Truppel. The area's climatic conditions were similar to those of Germany, and the abundant amount of granite buried in the mountains at the city's outskirts definitely contributed to transplanting the late historicist architecture of Germany to Tsingtau. Bricks, stone, and wood were mainly used for building structures. Qingdao granite was used for decorative purposes, and pale yellow was the color primarily used on plastered walls. German neo-Renaissance and neo-Baroque styles clearly different from their British equivalents flourished mainly through government offices in Tsingtau. They typically featured steep titled mansard or domed roofs, imposing towers, and red tiles. And boldly mixing those with Jugendstil elements at their climax in Germany and Austria at the time managed to produce an open, modern atmosphere suitable for a port city. Jugendstil was adopted at the governor's residence, chapels, and even pharmacies. In other words, Tsingtau architecture exhibited an eclectic tendency of mixing historicism and Jugendstil. It was a prototypical reflection of German architecture at the time, including the German rigidity of keeping decorations to a minimum.[44]

The German Kiautschou government office (Gouvernements-Dienstgebäude) that later came to serve as Qingdao's city hall was designed in the neo-Baroque style by Friedrich Mahlke in 1904 and completed two years later in April 1906. Situated on the southern slope of Guanhai Mountain, the five-story building was 20 meters tall, and the wings on either side of the central avant-corps indicated that the building followed Western classical traditions of centrality and symmetry. The rectangular bricks made of Qingdao granite gave the office a distinct façade and earned the building the nickname "ink bottle" among the locals. The interior space was dominated by a massive semi-circular vault. The building's entrance could be approached by crossing a bridge, giving the impression of a medieval castle gate. To fulfill its purpose as the administrative center of Tsingtau, the building was placed at the center of the city with a public square unfolding before it.[45]

The Jugendstil-style German governor's residence on the slope of Signal Mountain in southern Tsingtau is now used as a museum and reception hall for the city of Qingdao. It was jointly designed by Friedrich Mahlke and Karl Strasser, then head of the construction department under the German Kiautschou government's civil engineering bureau. Completed at the perspectival center of Tsingtau in 1907, the building was an experimental piece of work rarely seen even in Europe. The square granite blocks forming the exterior gave the three-story building an elegant touch, and the absence of an outer wall made it perfect for hosting receptions. Attached to the grayish-green gabled canopy protruding from the main entrance were anchor chain–like iron decorations fixed with stone nails, and the gable's edges were shaped like sailor knots to accentuate the image of a port city. The building incorporated many Jugendstil elements, such as the granite panels in two different shades forming the façade beside the main entrance, the shape of the gables, and the square pattern dominating the interior space. Three sides of the building were made of granite, while the use of iron and glass to construct the greenhouse attached to the building's back side added a notably modern touch.[46]

Among the Jugendstil-style buildings in Tsingtau, the works by Curt Rothkegel were particularly eye-catching. The Christ Church completed in 1910 based on Rothkegel's design was built for German protestants and occupation forces in the city. It was located upon a shallow

Figure 2.3 Top: German Kiautschou Government Office. Bottom Left: German Governor's Residence in Tsingtau. Bottom Right: Christ Church in Tsingtau.

Source: Top: Courtesy of the Bundesarchiv, Bild 137–003364. Bottom Left: Courtesy of the Bundesarchiv, Bild 137–023557. Bottom Right: Courtesy of the Bundesarchiv, Bild 137–003847.

hill at the city's eastern edge populated by villas for Europeans. The green clock tower and chapel sprawled over an extensive site were topped with red tiles and finished with a pale-yellow plastered stone wall on the outside. The church itself looked like the remains of an old building, and the cornices seemed to have been hastily shaped into scrolls, presenting a unique compromise between historicism and Jugendstil. Rothkegel is known to have also participated in designing the German Club at the Shanghai International Settlement and even left his traces upon a Korean treaty port across the sea in Inchŏn.[47]

The architecture of Tsingtau was conservative and austere yet modern and open. This may have been an ideal-typical expression of the German Empire during the days of Wilhelm II. The Imperial Court hinting at the secession movement, the central train station in the typical

German neo-Renaissance style with a decorative gable and grand clock tower visible from afar, and the neo-Romanesque Saint Michael's Cathedral with twin towers supporting massive crosses, a sight reminiscent of the Friedrichswerder Church by Schinkel,[48] all proved that Tsingtau was the orchard where the German Empire's late historicist architecture bore fruit. Construction over a short period of time with no restrictions other than the German governor's supervision allowed the styles that dominated major public buildings in the German Empire to come together in a foreign city. Buildings in Tsingtau featured the eclectic tone popular at the time but overall actualized tectonics more faithfully than in any other place in mainland Germany, all because Tsingtau had been a German colony.

Yet one point that should not be overlooked is the simple fact that Tsingtau cannot be Berlin or Vienna. Tsingtau had been considered a model colony and featured German traces purer than mainland Germany. However, in Tsingtau, tectonics was not a principle of structural unity as in Germany but instead functioned as a principle of structural separation. It strictly separated central from peripheral, subject from object, and the present of the colonizers from the past of the colonized. Rather than unifying such contradictory aspects, one could only be subordinate to the other. This should be regarded not as a colonial, tectonic distortion but a logical conclusion of it or a maximization of tectonics' paranoid disposition.[49]

From the viewpoint of the Chinese, the German navy's occupation of Kiautschou Bay was a major turning point worthy of being noted as the beginning of modern Chinese history. Frustrated by the stagnant pace of reform, the Chinese took to the streets when their country had fallen into a semi-colonial situation. The Hundred Days of Reform in 1898 and the Boxer Rebellion that broke out in 1900 may have been brutally subdued by Yuan Shikai's iron-fist rule with support from the allied forces led by the Field Marshal Alfred von Waldersee, but this failed to silence cries of anger in China. Farmers and rural officials engaged in armed resistance against issues such as railroad construction that went against their interests. Merchants developed traditional goods to compete with imported goods, while miners received support from the government to develop a modern means of transportation. Government officials outside the capital struggled not to lose their cultural hegemony to local elites.[50]

As soon as World War I broke out in 1914, Imperial Japan attacked Tsingtau and engaged in months of combat until it eventually occupied the city on November 7. After eight years of Japanese rule, the city the Japanese called Aoshima or Seito was returned to China through the Washington Naval Conference in 1922. However, Japan seized Qingdao once more in 1938 and ruled the city until it lost the war in 1945. Throughout those years, many Japanese came across the sea to Qingdao, and in no time, the city became Japanized.[51] The Japanese gained opportunities to directly experience and learn about German architecture and urban planning at Qingdao or through German captives transported from Qingdao to Japan. One such captive was the German architect Curt Rothkegel, who was taken to a prisoners' camp in Japan and released only after the Paris Peace Conference was held in 1919.[52]

Yet Japan had already been considerably exposed to German politics and culture since signing a treaty with Prussia in 1861. The German city in China therefore had nothing particularly new to offer to the Japanese. Moreover, by the 1910s, modernism grew dominant in major cities in mainland Germany, rendering Tsingtau more of a showcase of modernity than a laboratory of modernity influencing mainland Germany.[53] Imperial Japan had already stepped too far into the shop to be awed by the showcase up front. It had long since entered the competition with Western powers for the hegemony of modernity. There was, however, a conundrum difficult to solve. Although Germany relied on the phantasmagoria called Greece, it was able to declare that its national culture was modern, but Japan was unable to do the same. What was modern was part of heterogeneous Western cultures, not Japanese culture. Qingdao's modern cityscape could be German but not Japanese. How could something be modern yet Japanese? The choice made to bridge this overwhelming gap involved none other than Prussia.

2. Meiji Japan and Prussia: In the Eyes of the Iwakura Embassy

Japan was the only non-Western imperialist state. By taking advantage of a void of European and American powers in East Asia, it solidified its position and actively adopted Prussian tectonics to join the ranks of great powers. Meiji Japan chose to go with the Prussian-style top-down modernization and, as widely known, headed toward the path of militarism. The object of interest among Japanese advocates of westernization, including Fukuzawa Yukichi, who campaigned for civilization and enlightenment, shifted from the Netherlands to Britain before moving on to Prussia as in the case of Itō Hirobumi. And, as allies during World War II, Japan and Germany naturally seemed to share an affinity.

The Westernization of Japan

The degree to which Japan actually preferred Prussian culture and institution is not as obvious as it may seem. Many objections have been raised against the existing view[54] that Meiji Japan's anti-feudal, authoritative, nationalist tendency was influenced by the extremely conservative German historical school of political economy.[55] Japanese intellectuals during the Meiji period displayed more interest in British, French, and American models of modernization as part of the civilization and enlightenment movement at the time.[56] After the Iwakura Embassy returned from its nearly two-year trip throughout European countries and the United States between December 1871 and October 1873, the Meiji government sent people overseas to study in Europe or the United States and invited a diversity of experts from abroad to train local experts. Having gained a detailed grasp of the status as well as strengths and weaknesses of each country, it made perfect sense for the Meiji government to selectively acquire what was necessary from different countries rather than relying on a single country. During its early stages, the Meiji government acquired practical expertise on industry, railways, and naval operations from Britain and adopted legal, police, and education systems and tactics from France; the military system from Prussia; and American farming methods in order to colonize Hokkaido. It was long after the Meiji period when Imperial Japan came to maintain a strong affinity with conservative German forces and launch a full-fledged counterattack against Western modernity.[57]

In terms of architecture and urban planning, there were just as many cases like Josiah Conder, a Briton who went over and taught pupils in Japan, or Yamaguchi Hanroku, a Japanese trained in Haussmann-style urban planning in Paris, as there were cases like the German architects Wilhelm Böckmann and Hermann Ende, who designed a new government complex for Tokyo. Some think that although Meiji Japan learned urban planning techniques from Germany, it was more influenced by Britain and the United States when it came to architectural ideas.[58] Japan gained the opportunity to experience the reality of German architecture and urban planning through its occupation of Qingdao in 1914, but by then, European neoclassical architecture had already been almost completely localized in Japan. The central train station in Tokyo, finished in the French neoclassical style by the end of 1914, could be considered a culmination of such Japanization. And the following year, construction commenced for the Tokyo Imperial Hotel, a monumental work designed by the American modernist architect Frank Lloyd Wright. By the 1920s, modernism had come to dominate the Japanese realm of architecture.[59]

To precisely gauge the weight Prussia carried for Meiji Japan, looking into the experience of the Iwakura Embassy has proved to be quite useful. This is because the Embassy played a pivotal role in the formation of modern Japan after going through an instinctive experience of the West filled with curiosity, shock, awe, regret, and enlightenment. Nearly three years after its establishment, the Meiji government appointed Iwakura Tomomi as the plenipotentiary ambassador on November 12, 1871, to head a delegation of forty-six members that included key government figures such as Kido Takayoshi, ōkubo Toshimichi, Itō Hirobumi, and Yamaguchi Naoyoshi. The Embassy amounted to an entourage of one hundred and seven, including forty-three students, five of them female, as well as dozens of attendants that joined in visiting the United States and eleven European countries over a span of one year and ten months.[60] If their official mission was to engage in preliminary negotiations to revise treaties, why was it necessary to dispatch such a massive delegation for such an extended period of time? When building a foundation for their nation must have been a matter of the utmost urgency after only a few years into the establishment of a historically unprecedented government, what could have prompted key Japanese figures to travel abroad for almost two years?

Between July 8, 1853, when the American Commodore Matthew Calbraith Perry arrived at Tokyo Bay with the threatening black ships and January 3, 1868, when the Meiji Restoration began, Japan was swept up in numerous waves of change. Under the rule of the Edo Bakufu, Japan opened its ports and entered into unfair trade treaties with Western powers. Enraged by such developments, low-ranking samurai in the southwestern regions of Japan launched the *Sonnō jōi* movement demanding the emperor be revered and the barbarians expelled. They managed to overthrow the Bakufu and restore the emperor's power. Over this process, extremely conservative forces that had called for barbarians to be expelled gradually lost their power as a new wave of civilization and enlightenment came to prevail throughout the Japanese archipelago. It strongly occurred to the Japanese that to revise degrading, unfair treaties, Japan had to be reborn into a state that fit the Western norm of a civilized nation.[61]

"Civilization and enlightenment" was a thoroughly political proposal. The term was coined by Fukuzawa Yukichi, the ideological godfather of modern Japan, who described through his work *An Outline of a Theory of Civilization* that civilization refers to "the progress of man's knowledge and virtue" and emphasized that "civilization is not a matter of the knowledge or ignorance of individuals but of the spirit of entire nations." Fukuzawa even went as far as to write that "national independence is the goal, and Japan's present civilization is the means of attaining that goal." On the matter of Japanese civilization heading toward universality, he claimed that "I have only considered our national independence as the first necessary step in the process, with everything else only secondary, to be left for some later day."[62]

Above all, the newly established Meiji government sought to sketch an outline for building an autonomous nation-state. And this was precisely the mission the Iwakura Embassy had been charged with. The Embassy was to promulgate the birth of modern Japan while grasping the overall framework of Western nation-states so as to formalize a program for Japan's national reform. It should therefore come as no surprise to find that the Embassy's object of interest was not civilized people but civilized states.[63] After returning from the journey, a member of the delegation named Kume Kunitake soon published an extensive five-volume report titled *A True Account of the Ambassador Extraordinary and Plenipotentiary's Journal of Observation Through the United States of America and Europe* (hereafter referred to as the True Account).[64]

The True Account's Basic Approach

Kume Kunitake, a professor at Tokyo Imperial University until being dismissed for criticizing the Japanese traditional religion Shinto, had little to do with nationalism. Instead of admiring major Western powers, he is thought to have paid attention to small countries that fostered patriotism and preserved their autonomy. In fact, a considerable number of pages of the True Account are dedicated to small countries such as Belgium, the Netherlands, and Switzerland. The True Account is indeed noteworthy for making an argument for economic prosperity without mentioning the need for military power, contrary to arguments that would typically push for both. However, it is difficult to overlook the fact that the True Account also conveys Fukuzawa Yukichi's infamous theory of three stages of development, from primitive to semi-developed to civilized, not to mention his pro-Western, anti-Asian ideas.[65] Since the True Account was not a personal work, Kume seems to have tried to faithfully represent the position of the Japanese ruling class at the time.

Does the True Account then reveal a particular interest in Prussia? On the surface, it seems not. The True Account is a highly practical report. It can be considered the ultimate book the Japanese compiled to learn the syntax of a foreign language called modernity. It encompasses the technologies, economic principles, social institutions, laws, art techniques, geographical perceptions, and the rise and fall of states throughout history that dictated modern Western civilizations. Yet, the text not only imparts the prescribed syntax but assigns new meaning to it. The True Account is an account of what occurred while traveling to the United States and European countries as well as a record of how modern Japan's view of the world changed. It wholly embodies the process of an object called modern Western civilization and a subject called modern Japan becoming established upon the blueprint of a new imaginative geography. Where, then, did Prussia stand within that process?

If the True Account's publication was part of a political proposal to establish a modern nation-state, it may not be an exorbitant attempt at all to consider the True Account not as a mere report but as a major opportunity for discursive formation in the sense of Foucault.[66] Rather than having discourse deal with a given subject, Foucault believed that a subject emerges from discourse and sought to unveil the structure of interactions between rules that form the conditions of such an emergence. To do so requires dealing comprehensively with various terms, concepts, and enunciations within a certain time and place, but it is also possible to approach a body of text from the perspective of discursive formation. In a single body of text, different locutions as well as dispersed, disparate enunciations coexist according to rules of order, correlation, position, function, and transformation. These rules are what generate subjects, concepts, modes of enunciation, and conditions of thematization. Hence, the need to approach text as a discursive formation is because it is impossible to accept the common notion of an author conveying a prescribed message. It would be more accurate to consider the author and message not prerequisites but results of discourse. As such, the major concepts such as civilization, sovereignty, autonomy, world peace, and the people that Kume employs in the True Account as well as his use of referents like East and West, or Germany and Japan, need to be considered in terms of the structural order they form rather than the direct message the author seeks to convey.[67] They are all inscribed in a comprehensive imaginative geography. Of course, if their meaning and identity are relative and vary depending on the context, that could be regarded as a manifestation of a compositional defect intrinsic to imaginative geography.

According to the third volume of the True Account, on March 15, 1873, Chancellor Bismarck of the German Empire invited the Iwakura Embassy staying in Berlin to dinner. The speech the chancellor of the newly established empire gave for the occasion included the following symbolic words.

> So while Japan may now have amicable diplomatic relations with a number of countries, its friendship with Germany should be the most intimate of all because of the true respect in which we hold the right of self-government.[68]

Considering that the new German Empire was desperate to make as many allies as possible, Bismarck's remark can be regarded as a common diplomatic rhetoric. Yet Japan had been a country at the edge of Asia struggling to revise its unfair treaties with Western powers, which makes it unusual for a dominant player in continental Europe like the German Empire to court it. Then does the record of Bismarck's speech in the True Account constitute sufficient evidence that Japan held a special position in the geopolitical configuration the German Empire had been trying to form? Most likely not. When Count Friedrich Albrecht zu Eulenburg, the Prussian ambassador extraordinary and plenipotentiary, outmatched the Austrian delegation in concluding a trade treaty with Japan in January 1861, Prussia was mainly focused on pursuing commercial interests for the German Customs Union and securing an upper hand in the German Confederation over Austria.[69] It is therefore hard to believe the German Empire's ancillary interest in East Asia changed abruptly over a mere decade. The Iwakura Embassy may have been deeply impressed by German hospitality, but it is not surprising to find that Germany failed to display any reaction out of the ordinary. A couple of local dailies, including Kölnische Volkszeitung and Neue Preussische Zeitung, published fairly detailed reports about the dinner, but there were no noteworthy comments.[70] Hence, it would be more reasonable to focus on the position of Japan rather than Germany when discussing Kume's records.[71]

When analyzing the discourse in the True Account, a tricky methodological issue arises due to the reversed relationship between the referent of the text Prussia and the subject Japan. In the text, Japan's attitude toward Prussia overlaps with Prussia's attitude toward Japan. Then which side is referring to which? The author of the text is Japanese. Bismarck and Prussia solely reveal themselves in the text through the eyes of the Japanese. To be exact, the referent of the text would therefore be Prussia in the eyes of the Japanese, directing a friendly gaze upon Japan. Foucault believed that rather than referring to something, discourse travels between things and words, thereby overseeing the referent's establishment and assigning a position for the speaking subject. This always creates a gap between the referent and words. Words cause instability in meaning by constantly referring to the referent in excess or insufficiently.

In the 1870s when the True Account was authored and published, Japan had not yet explicitly chōsen to pursue a pro-German path. To the Iwakura Embassy, Germany must have seemed like a region lagging or not quite at the forefront of continental Europe. Germany was described as an incompletely unified country, and although Prussia held hegemony, there was still a want of customs and competitiveness as a nation. What, then, was the source of familiarity the Embassy felt for the middlemost country in Europe in terms of its location or status? There was not much about Prussian self-identity that Japan was likely to regard as familiar. The experience with Napoleon of France played a decisive role in prompting Prussia to build its national identity, which led to an imaginary familiarity toward ancient Greece in opposition to the Latin civilization rooted in Rome. This imaginative geography of Prussia is not apparent in the True Account, most likely because it would have been impossible for the Japanese to gain an in-depth understanding of the overall circumstances of a particular Western country.

Descriptions of Prussia in the True Account very much revolve around phenomena. Rather than Athens, Berlin is described as more similar to Paris or London. A general overview and three chapters are devoted to descriptions of Berlin, following the typical style of reports, albeit with relentlessly criticizing statements occasionally inserted. Compared to London or Paris, Berlin was still a "second-rate" city and the only one in Europe to publicly sell obscene pictures on the streets. Students in the city are denigrated for being raucous to the point where even the police would avoid them. The True Account even points out how people in Berlin lacked respect for women, unlike other European countries or the United States. "In Berlin, even the ladies scoff at American and British men for their servile demeanor in front of their womenfolk, which they dismiss as a curious habit."[72] Yet, despite such immature aspects, the emerging country Prussia and its emerging capital Berlin are repeatedly identified as places where the future is open. The True Account reveals that the worth of Prussia and "its ascendant power," was recognized only recently when Japan concluded a treaty of amity and trade with it in January 1861. And with the Iwakura Embassy's visit, Japan had been able to officially recognize Prussia's potential.[73]

Discourse analysis originally presupposes the constant polysemy and impermanence of meaning in linguistic constructs.[74] However, it would be impossible to consider the speaking subject Japan merely as a discursive effect. The subject instead represents a structural deficiency, a dimension that cannot be fully expressed through discourse. The psychoanalytic theory of Jacques Lacan deals with a subject that constantly remains redundant, invisible, and unconscious. A subject that is structured through the metaphorical, metonymical play of signifiers and thereby says more than intended may be constructed linguistically and defined by the structure of a chain of signifiers, but the subject does not begin from it. Within the contradiction of a symbolic order, a subject instead marks itself as an independent product of such an order. The desire of a historical subject fails to remain satisfied from identifying with its assigned position within a symbolic order and turns its eyes upon the gaze from the original object that assigned its position. That gaze, of course, is like an opaque curtain, always out of reach.[75] Based on a hypothesis formed out of this theory, Prussia in the eyes of the Japanese could be the gaze constructing a subject called the Japanese as well as an unattainable object desired in order to overcome the position the Japanese have been assigned to. This is heavily implied through the following remark Kume made in the True Account's part about Prussia.

> Yet in terms of the determining features of national policy, it actually bears a close resemblance to Japan, and there is more to be gained from studying the politics and customs of this country than conditions in Britain and France.[76]

Instead of lavishing praises on or devaluing Prussia, the True Account's part about the country maintains an appropriate balance between positives and negatives based on a cool-headed evaluation of the reality of Prussian politics, economy, society, and culture. Upon arriving at Prussia, the Embassy was finally able to look into the eyes of the object called modern Western civilization. Rather than being seen as an expression of aloofness and indifference, the levelheaded review made from attempting to be a fair judge is counterevidence of the fact that the Embassy would no longer be intimidated by the object. It may not have gazed at the same eye level, but the Embassy had become capable of understanding and communicating with an object that entered its range of vision from the subjective viewpoint of an observer. Assuming that modern Japan's identity oscillated due to this eye contact's partial match and inevitable mismatch, the part about Prussia occupies a special status within the overall imaginative geography laid out through the True Account.[77]

The Experience in the West

As previously mentioned, the True Account is documentation of how modern Japan's world view changed. The process of broadening its knowledge of Europe and the United States was none other than the process of defining modern Western civilization within Japan's vision of the world, thereby using the relationship with it to establish the subject of modern Japan. Every time the Japanese envoys would come across something to take note of or learn from during their long journey, they would constantly draw comparisons with Japan and question themselves about their own people. This dialectic interaction continued to intensify, primarily due to the distance between the civilizations of the East and West. Such a distance fundamentally refers to a difference in the level of civilizational development, but geographical distance is also involved like a functional relation. As subject and object become established and their status is determined, a new imaginative geography reveals itself.

After departing Japan and sailing across the boundless Pacific, the Iwakura Embassy realized upon reaching the United States that it would basically be impossible to compare the country with Japan. The United States is identified as a country at the extreme opposite of Japan in every respect. "When we look at our own country of Japan, its 'great treasure' of population is about the same as America's, but the country is one hundred times older. The size of the country is less than three-hundredths that of America."[78]

This experience of an entirely different time and space was none other than a déjà vu of the shock Japan must have felt upon encountering modern Western civilization. While descriptions related to Europe revolve around cities, descriptions of natural or artificial regional environments occupy a greater proportion than cities in the True Account's first volume covering the United States. From personally witnessing the vastness of the uninhabited wilderness and the roar of raging waterfalls through an extended railroad trip, the Embassy was able to examine the overall circumstances in land development; the industries of agriculture, mining, and shipping; and the use of irrigation water. While describing his impression of a suspension bridge nearby Niagara Falls, the True Account's author makes the following point.

> Crossing this suspension bridge made viewing the three falls even more exciting. Here we found the landscape, with its steep gorge and wild natural appearance, exciting in its beauty. What thrill would there have been if it were a grand and elegant iron bridge?[79]

For laying bare sensations from encountering such overwhelming beauty, Kume's reaction could be categorized as one toward the sublime. In fact, Kume compared the wild horse-like flow of the Mississippi River, the

Great Lakes, and the Niagara Falls to Japanese landscapes, citing the Seto Inland Sea as a typical example.[80] Such sublimity represented an original experience of modernity, a category already established in the West to refer to new experiences like the French Revolution that obliterate the existing political, aesthetic order in the face of unprecedented realities. And encountering overwhelming scenes of nature such as waterfalls reminiscent of the shock from historical incidents constitute as a typical motif of such sublimity.[81] While traveling across the vast North American continent, the Iwakura Embassy came to discuss the sublimity of the modern West, which was dramatically different from the beauty of the traditional East. The Embassy's tour through nature took place because issues related to treaty renegotiation forced them to stay longer in the United States than expected,[82] but it helped establish a structural order for imaginative geography within the True Account's text.

What captivated the Iwakura Embassy in the United States, the first destination covered in the True Account, was new time and space rather than individual institutions or technologies. The "crude, large-scale method" used to pioneer "a new world of liberty called America" came to be accepted as a new ethic. The unyielding determination to overcome nature, that "independent spirit," was the virtue Japan should foremost emulate. "The great treasure of the world lies not in material things such as money but in the force of [human] physical energy."[83] This new approach toward space naturally led to the recognition of a temporal distance between the progressive West autonomously spearheading its future and the East falling behind.

> Likewise, even in the fertile lands of the East, national wealth does not come by itself and harvests do not produce value without human effort. Two thousand years have passed in a dream.[84]

A near self-deprecating assessment shows that the Embassy was overwhelmed by the experience. And it is easy to anticipate how such a state of excitement must have accelerated a shift in awareness. If traveling across the United States was a shocking entry into the atmosphere of an unfamiliar planet called modernity, the trip to European countries was a flight to the galaxy where that unfamiliar planet belonged. The True Account starts to cover Europe from its second volume, mainly describing cities. Hence begins an exploration of the fountainhead of modern Western civilization.

The second volume is entirely devoted to Britain. A parade of praises adorns the text from beginning to end. Britain is considered the greatest commercial country mediating world trade, the motherland of capitalism, and a symbol of historical progress in terms of industry, technology, political and social institutions, and most importantly, in terms of admirable spirit. Through the True Account, Britain is featured as an unquestionably ideal model of modernity. The obscure outlines of modernity finally emerge into sight through the second volume to be able to discuss the encounter between modernity and Japan.

The Iwakura Embassy delves into how an island country like Britain, similar to Japan in size, was able to become the world's most wealthy nation. The True Account's second volume on Britain devotes a majority of its pages to introducing various industrial technologies that even include the beer brewing process. From visiting factories all around Britain, the Embassy arrives at the realization that coal and iron are the substance of Britain's wealth. More important, though, is human will, as they previously discovered in the United States. In Britain, the Japanese envoys further realize that the secret to modern civilization lies in refusing to remain content with (natural) circumstances and proactively reorganizing them according to self-determining, autonomous will. The True Account hints here and there that such a principle applies not only to industry but to the operation of state and society. By that point, modernity is no longer considered a fiercely gushing waterfall but a visible target that can be carefully and steadily approached. While describing the Embassy's visit to the British Museum in London, the author more confidently shares his view of modern time and space. "Progress does not mean discarding what is old and contriving something which is entirely new."[85]

It should not come as a surprise to find an unreserved display of the Embassy's political conservatism through the part about Britain in the True Account. Since modernity was no longer an object of fear, it had become possible to contemplate grafting it on mainstream Japanese values. It was time for autonomy to meet with the logic of laws instead of being regarded as a value to be pursued by the people. This was based on the belief that Britain was able to obtain great national wealth because it "exercised autonomous power within legally permissible boundaries."[86] Such a change in approach is not explicitly stated but can be detected from the description of the Embassy's trip to the Scottish Highlands. Unlike the sublimity sensed from American nature, the beauty of the highlands is recognized as similar to that of Japan. This implies that it had finally become possible to draw individual comparisons between Japan and Western countries. Nevertheless, in terms of imaginative geography, Britain's beautiful balance between civilization and nature was still too distant from Japan, a willpower-lacking member of the East. Britain was strictly a model to learn from and catch up with. The Japanese envoys found it difficult to break away from the sense that they were but wanderers searching for a way while roaming through a vast galaxy called modern Western civilization.

> When Japanese people think of the West they imagine some distant galaxy. When Western merchants view the world, however, they see it as a single city. With this attitude, they cannot fail to prosper.[87]

On their way to continental Europe, the Iwakura Embassy's perception of the West grew more detailed and individualized. Having been overwhelmed by modern Western civilization's sublimity on the American continent and discovering an ideal of modernity in Britain, the third and fourth volumes of the True Account attempt to take a more objective approach toward the characteristics of and differences between individual countries. When the Embassy arrived in France, its first destination in continental Europe, the country was still being haunted by its defeat in the Franco-Prussian War, and news of Napoleon III's death in Britain reached France during their stay. The Embassy's estimation of France is much less generous than that of Britain. The volumes highly regard France's commodity market, with finer jewelry, chinaware, and fabric than those of Britain. There is no shortage of compliments on sophisticated French architecture, urban planning, and art when compared to Japan, which was tantamount to the difference between "a great mansion" and "a straw hut." However, the language, industrial goods, and cityscape drenched in an "empty sham" of royal authority were viewed coldly. Surprisingly enough, the disparity between Japan and a Western country is partially dismissed for the first time in the True Account's part about France. Although they are all Europeans, the "vivacious" French have a temperament opposite from the British or Germans, are "akin to the Japanese, invariably excelling in their weakness for reckless daring and their lack of diligence and perseverance." This harsh review of France may have to do with a bias toward a defeated country as well as the Embassy's conservative mindset. The spirit of revolution was a value the Embassy fundamentally denounced. In particular, the radical idea of equality brought on by the revolution was disparaged as no more than a "extremely foolhardy premise." "Affluent gentlemen unversed in the basics of economics who exhort their colleagues to seek justice and adhere only to ideals of humanity and benevolence are quick to put forth such arguments."[88] Despite such a negative impression, visiting France allows the Embassy to take one step closer to understanding Western capitalism. Consequently, a rather loose imaginative geography is established in which the United States is a land reclaimed by Europeans, Britain is the center of world trade, and France is the largest market in Europe.[89]

After leaving France, the Iwakura Embassy stopped by Belgium and the Netherlands before reaching Prussia, which is less negatively described in the True Account than France but regarded as considerably inferior to the United States or Britain. Prussia is regarded even more negatively than Belgium or the Netherlands. However, as previously noted, it would be impossible to fully ascertain the Embassy's appraisal of Prussia from textual descriptions alone. For instance, the description of Unter den Linden, the main boulevard in Berlin, may appear much more detached compared to the stream of exclamations toward the Boulevard Champs-Élysées in Paris, but a closer look at the passage reveals careful observations made on the road with four lanes facilitating different purposes and the flourishing sight of shops and buildings lining the boulevard, proving that the Embassy had sensed the power of Prussian civilization.[90] As far as the Embassy saw it, Prussia was not yet as culturally sophisticated as Britain or France, but it was already at the center of Europe in terms of trade, agricultural productivity, science and technology, and military power. And historically, Prussia had been the most European of Europe. It was at the heart of everything in Europe. Compared to Britain and France, Prussia had remained well within the boundaries of Europe and therefore possessed both the light and shade of it. By including detailed descriptions of Prussia and the three other kingdoms of the German Empire in addition to the seven grand duchies, eight duchies, and three Hanseatic cities, the True Account recognizes that Germany is indeed "a vitally important part of Europe."[91] Considering that the True Account devotes nine chapters to France that mainly center around Paris, it is noteworthy to find that Prussia as well as the entire German Empire has been broadly covered over a total of ten chapters. Such great interest in Germany formed a contrapuntal relationship with the perception of Japan's status. Through the True Account, Japan, despite its many insufficiencies, is increasingly perceived as a country that deserves to become the leader of East Asia for being the only one in pursuit of sovereignty and autonomy.

Prussia's Status in the True Account

The third volume about Prussia takes a rather neutral position compared to the fourth volume of the True Account, which covers the Embassy's journey through East Prussia to reach Russia and begins to discuss a West distant from modern civilization. After reviewing the United States and Britain positively and France somewhat negatively, the Embassy assembles an almost overly neutral impression of Prussia. This comes into stark contrast to its utterly negative appraisals of Russia and southern Europe as well as the African and Asian regions the Embassy stops by on the way back home, as described through the fifth volume of the True Account.

A brief examination of records created beyond the Embassy's tour of Prussia offers a clearer indication of where the part on Prussia stands. The "cold and barren" Russia may have been as extensive as the United States, but unlike the United States, the land was reserved for the state to reclaim, and the people lacked a spirit of autonomy. Although religiously devout, the Russians were unable to overcome ignorance. The sparse dwellings natives lived in throughout the vast lands of Russia even led the author to think they were similar to "the houses of the natives in Hokkaidō." Such sights should not have come as a surprise, since the Russian economy, even with flamboyant cities of its own, remained in bad credit. Through their visit to Russia, the Japanese delegation became convinced that fearing Russia more than other Western countries had been a mere "delusion" on the part of Japan due to its closed-door policy.[92]

The critical review of lesser developed regions in the West is maintained while discussing countries besides Russia. On Austria, expelled from the German Confederation after its defeat to Prussia, the True Account denounces the country for being no different from Russia in that the people "lack a spirit of independence." This view is maintained toward southern Europe. "Even the great civilised countries of Europe are divided by the Alps into northern and southern regions, one marked by diligence, the other by idleness. This shows itself clearly in their relative wealth and poverty." The description of the southern Italian city Naples is particularly negative, as it mentions how filthy urchins roam around begging for money along streets littered with excrements and trash. Such a portrayal serves as a premonition for the negative review of North African cities across the Mediterranean.[93]

The account of the Embassy's long journey around the hemisphere toward home is full of descriptions of the squalid, shabby living circumstances the Embassy witnessed as they bid the West adieu in crossing the Mediterranean and traveled in the direction of China through Egypt and the waters of the Red and Arabian Seas. Moving scenes of natural beauty occasionally emerged, but non-Westerners were generally regarded as people steeped in rigid "customs, far removed from civilization" and thereby neglecting to "undertake new enterprises."[94] A typical expression of this view would be the following description of the Arabians living in tropical regions around the Red Sea.

> They are content, wastefully, simply to continue to live, and so in thousands of years they have not advanced one step in civilisation. They merely pass their days, almost like beggars. The ancients said that the people of fertile lands were lazy.[95]

In comparison, the achievements Westerners made outside the West are awarded with quite generous reviews. The French diplomat Vicomte de Lesseps's herculean efforts are highlighted in describing the construction of the Suez Canal, while India under British rule is more highly regarded than its surrounding regions. "The Indians are tough and courageous. For many years they have been trained by the British, who now have one million sturdy [Indian] soldiers." Hong Kong under British rule also earns a generous review. "The streets are clean even though most of the inhabitants of the city are Chinese." Such a description is in stark contrast to the negative impressions about other Chinese regions including Shanghai. "There is much here for those who admire China and take at face value the high reputation of its products to reflect on."[96]

Narratives in the True Account are therefore not simply factual records of a journey but include a civilizational ranking of all countries in the northern hemisphere. Previously independently dispersed time and space are rearranged according to a single perspective. And at the spatial and temporal nodal point of this global imaginative geography is Prussia. The part about Prussia, which may instantly come across as a dry description based on facts, has the potential to be read in a completely different light by considering the overall imaginary arrangement of countries in the northern hemisphere. Having slightly narrowed their distance with the West from visiting France, the Japanese grow capable of accepting hospitality with a bit more enthusiasm by the time they arrive in Prussia. Their eyes that seemed to peek at others would no longer avoid the others' gaze and instead tried to look directly into the eyes of others. This Japanese view is different from their condescending view of others that emerged upon arriving in Russia. Making eye contact with others ultimately renders them an objective whole. Modern Western civilization is constructed as an object, which assigns a fixed position for the subject looking at the object. And the world lying between object and subject naturally falls back to a peripheral position. Even ahead of visiting them, rankings had already been assigned to Africa, Asia, and non-Western parts of the West, like Russia lying between Japan and the West.

This global imaginative geography is wholly reproduced through the description of a museum in Berlin. As it did in every other European city, the Iwakura Embassy visited the finest museum in Berlin. Although the museum is not specifically named, descriptions of a "famous building" that was "so immense in construction that it surpasses even the British Museum in scale" and has "a wide square in front with paving stones and lawns surrounded" certainly seem to refer to the Altes Museum in front of the park Lustgarten on the east side of Unter den Linden. The description of the museum unfolds in the order of exhibits. It begins with ancient Greek and Roman sculptures on the ground floor and moves on to oil paintings on the upper floor. The passage about "exhibits from Arabia and lands farther east, from India to the South Seas and places throughout the Orient" near the end of the description conveys an intensity by drawing an obvious distinction between the "fine artefacts" from Japan and China and the "barbarous custom" in the South Sea islands. The statement that Japan and China are "the most civilised lands in the South Seas and the East" takes on a different meaning when considering the fact that it is part of a description of a museum in central Berlin.[97]

The Altes Museum undoubtedly represented the imaginative geography of the newly established German Empire. The relatively high status the Japanese civilization occupied there, along with Bismarck's hospitality, would have been enough to reassure the Iwakura Embassy. Had there actually been a point of overlap between the imaginative geography reproduced at the heart of Prussia and the imaginative geography of Japan that came to acknowledge Prussia's extraordinary status? The True Account only reveals Prussia's imaginative geography through the eyes of the Japanese. It is but a gaze that establishes the Japanese as a subject and forms a contrapuntal relationship with the viewpoint of the Japanese. The distance between the two will never be dissipated.

Unlike the aforementioned descriptions, the part about Prussia in the True Account makes an almost too cool-headed estimation of the country's reality. This paradoxically alludes to a communion with Prussia. It means the Japanese delegation was able to no longer be intimidated by the object and more actively respond to the hospitality of others. For them to be keenly aware of Prussia's hospitality is indicative of a self-determination to build a character that can readily respond to hospitality from others, which can be seen as direct evidence that the Japanese envoys were past the stage of being in awe of modern Western civilization. Despite being at the heart of the West, the fact that Prussia had not yet sufficiently ascended to meet the standards of modern Western civilization carried major implications for Japan. By designating Prussia as a vanishing point that mediates between Western and non-Western, or advanced and underdeveloped, Japan was able to objectify modern Western civilization and determine its own position in a new imaginative geography. Hence, the part about Prussia in the True Account can be regarded as a vanishing point for the Japanese to construct an independent imaginative geography as well as a record about their rediscovery of Prussia. Rather than limiting itself to the practical purpose of providing accurate information about Europe and the United States, the True Account was an arena of fierce competition where various concepts and enunciations interacted as they intermittently rearranged the existing order of discourse.

3. Imperial Constitution as State Tectonics

Until the end of the 1870s when the True Account was published, Japan had not yet fully adopted the German model of modernization. Yet, assuming that the part about Prussia occupies a special position in the imaginative geography featured through the True Account so that Prussia could be rediscovered as a discursive occasion for modern Japan to establish itself, it would not be farfetched to conclude that the True Account can offer a glimpse into Japan's "switch onto the German path" in the 1880s when it began to pick up steam. The Iwakura Embassy's discovery of Prussia, which used to be overshadowed by Britain and France, may have been a rediscovery of Japan.

Nevertheless, the fact that Japan of the East and Germany of the West belonged to entirely different political, historical, and discursive contexts should not be overlooked. As Edward Said pointed out, "The relationship between Occident and Orient is a relationship of power, of domination, of varying degrees of a complex hegemony."[98] This applies to both Orientalism and Occidentalism.[99] A fissure thus inevitably materializes between the stature of Germany in Europe and that of Japan in East Asia. If modern Japan's identity wavered due to that fissure, Prussia can be identified as a discursive formation that both generated a modern subject called Japan and caused that subject's structural deficiency. The Japanese Orientalism, or the contradictory discourse about Japan's East Asian neighbors, that soon emerged can therefore be regarded as a reverse image of an internally unstable Prussian discourse. Meanwhile, such discourse may have been responsible for inducing Japan's contradictory conduct of attempting to do away with its unequal treaties with Western powers while forcing Chōsen to sign an unequal treaty on Ganghwa Island.

Dreaming of an Asian Prussia

As previously illustrated, the exemplar of modern civilization Japan had been seeking was Britain, not Prussia. Britain was indeed an exemplar but not a role model available for Japan to adopt. Japan was still tied to unequal treaties, making it impossible to ever dream of becoming the Britain of Asia. Neither the United States or France were suitable models, nor Austria or Russia, which left Prussia as the only candidate among Western powers. What, then, did choosing the Prussian model signify for Japan's political reality?

Japan's switch onto the German path cannot be fully explained at an ideological level. For instance, political friction among the Japanese ruling class also played a major role, namely the conflict between the domains of Chōshū and Satsuma that evolved into friction between the army and navy. Among the three great nobles who led the Meiji Restoration, Kido Takayoshi was from the Chōshū Domain, while ōkubo Toshimichi and Saigō Takamori were from the Satsuma Domain. Saigō Takamori in particular is well known as an advocate of the *Seikanron*, an argument for a punitive expedition to Korea. The one who joined hands with Kido Takayoshi to subdue the *Seikanron* and channel the government's attention toward the West was Itō Hirobumi, the up-and-coming statesman from the Chōshū Domain who guided the Meiji government toward the German path. Also from the Chōshū Domain was the Foreign Minister Inoue Kaoru. Inoue continued to follow the same political line as Itō Hirobumi throughout his life and is known to have supported Chōsen reformists such as Yu Kil-chun and Yun Ch'i-ho.[100] Even Yamagata Aritomo, Itō's political rival who likewise served as prime minister, was from the Chōshū Domain. Having been dispatched to Europe in 1869 ahead of the Iwakura Embassy, Yamagata took the lead in remodeling the Imperial Japanese Army after the Prussian military in 1873.[101]

As the pro-German faction from the Chōshū Domain gained power, the Prussian course of modernization firmly settled as an exemplar for modern Japan. This shift can easily be noticed from the fact that eighty-six percent of Japanese students, or five hundred thirty-nine out of the six hundred twenty-three who went abroad on government scholarship, went to Germany for their studies. The Meiji government awarded most of its scholarships to students headed to Germany, especially those who intended to study medicine, law, economics, philosophy, or education at the University of Berlin (Friedrich Wilhelm University). The government also encouraged enrollment in the Prussian Military Academy (Preußische Kriegsakademie).[102]

While the circumstances that led Japan to weigh between different countries before leaning toward Germany for top-down modernization are fully understandable, the fact that feudal power relations were at work underneath the process requires further explanation. It implies that the Prussian model of nation building applied to Japan was actually not an application but an entirely new discursive formation. This can be sensed from the following remark the Prussian field marshal and politician Helmuth Karl Bernhard von Moltke made during a parliamentary speech.

> What I wish for now is not simply to keep peace, but to control the peace and make all nations say that it is Prussia, situated in the heart of Europe, which is preserving peace throughout the continent.[103]

The True Account offers a fairly detailed description of Moltke's speech. Although the Iwakura Embassy did not actually hear the speech, since it was given after their visit to Prussia, the fact that it was nevertheless described in detail proves that the speech's content had resonated with the Japanese and their position. This suggests that after the Iwakura Embassy's journey to the United States and Europe, Japan may have no longer been satisfied with defending itself against the West and began to aspire to become the leader in Asia the way Germany sought to become the center of Europe. At least in the True Account, Prussia is featured as the object of Japan's desire, or the object that stirs a desire in Japan.

The description of the Embassy's visit to an aquarium in Berlin is another passage in the True Account that gives reason to dwell on the significance of the Prussianization of Japan. The author expresses pure amazement at the "world's largest" aquarium and its interior arrangement "in the shape of natural caves" inside a building near the Brandenburg Gate in Berlin. Considering that it wasn't the Embassy's very first visit to an aquarium during their journey, the intensely vivid description sprinkled with personal emotions seems rather unusual for a publication meant to be a formal report.

> We had seen a number of large snakes during our travels but nothing quite the size of this. A small rabbit, which had been released inside this tank, hesitantly climbed atop the snake's slithering back. In a flash the reptile lifted its neck, embraced the rabbit in its coils and fastened its teeth on its prey. The rabbit let out a shriek and its eyes started out of its head in agony, but the snake did not release its grip as it sucked the lifeblood from the creature. In three or four minutes

> the rabbit was quite dead, leaving nothing but a lump of skin and fur. It was a despicably cruel spectacle.[104]

Depending on the interpretation, this almost sensational passage can be read as a tacit display of the suppressed subconscious of the Japanese faced with harsh international relations in the age of imperialism. Although the shock the Embassy received early on would have worn off considerably by the time it reached Germany, it would not have died down easily. Yet, what is more significant is that the Embassy was aware that this cruel scene was not part of a natural phenomenon but a staged spectacle in an artificial setting. "These large snakes live mostly in the tropics, and in Western countries they are kept in underground tanks and fed a diet of rats."[105] Through descriptions of the United States, Britain, and France, Japanese readers of the True Account were bound to understand the violence of Western empires not as a primitive, perpetually destructive power but a productive power. Regardless of whether the author Kume intended, within the text's discursive order, the snake in the aquarium served as an allegory of modernization that dismantles old systems so that a new world may unfold. The fact that a large snake was in central Berlin instead of a tropical forest implied that Prussia was the power of the future poised to take the lead in such creative dismantlement. This is highlighted through several mentions about the country's unpolished customs which inversely function as a discursive device.

As hinted through descriptions in the True Account, taking Prussia as a model for modernization was a declaration that Japan would actively dismantle its old systems and those of its neighbors in order to create a new East Asia. It would be more accurate to regard it not as a simple transplant of Prussia as a nation but Japan's choice of a new national strategy in East Asia. Japan's view of Prussia had been more parallel with its gaze toward Korea, China, and other East Asian neighbors than with Prussia's gaze toward Japan. By the time Prussia did become the model of modernization for Japan while Japan was trying to take the lead in the East to realize the world peace advocated by Moltke, the East was already being rapidly colonized. This boiled Japan's options down to imperialist encroachment. Japan thus turned itself into an imperialist state in order to escape imperialism.[106]

The Establishment of a Prussian-Style Constitution

There is nothing new to the interpretation that the transformation of Fukuzawa Yukichi's liberalistic ideas of civilization and enlightenment into an argument for Japan to end its relations with bad Asian neighbors and leave Asia to enter Europe was a reaction to developments in reality such as the failure of the 1884 coup d'état in Chōsen and, more fundamentally, an inevitable consequence of the notion of civilization in

Fukuzawa's *An Outline of a Theory of Civilization*.[107] The civilizational view of history was problematic for postulating Asia as semi-civilized and Africa as barbarous. However, it was even more problematic for thoroughly converging freedom, which Fukuzawa himself translated and posited as a core value of civilization, into the goal of forming a modern nation-state. It was as if the Right Hegelians of Prussia had been reborn in East Asia.

In founding a modern nation-state, the task that surfaced as a top priority for Meiji Japan was none other than to establish a constitution. That was the foremost task it postulated to be able to proclaim itself a civilized nation. Establishing a constitution provided justification for Japan to defend its independence as a civilized country, meaning it could revise unequal treaties and become a respectable member of international society. The Iwakura Embassy's original mission may as well have been to gather information to establish a constitution.[108] After returning to Japan in late July 1873 from his journey as a key member of the Embassy, Kido Takayoshi immediately published an editorial titled "Speech by Councillor Kido Upon Returning to Japan" in the October edition of the political periodical *Shinbun zasshi*. By the following year, he submitted a proposal based on his editorial to the royal court in July. Through his proposal, Kido suggested that the most urgent task was to form a country in which the ruler unaffected by parliament works through a cabinet-backed government to unite the people's will within a constitutional framework. This practically pointed toward a heavily absolutist constitutional monarchy.[109] Kido's proposal was followed by a variety of political proposals, each made by other key members of the Embassy.[110]

Constitutions were the tectonics forming a solid construct called modern state. And Prussia proved to be a source of inspiration in establishing such constitutions. While staying in Berlin, Councilor ōkubo Toshimichi, another key member of the Iwakura Embassy, sent letters on March 21, 1873, to Saigō Takamori and Yoshii Tomozane. ōkubo specifically mentioned in his letters that, unlike other Western countries, Germany had a more "rough-hewn and honest aspect" and produced "such great teachers as the famous Bismarck and Moltke," who suggested a path to him when he was feeling lost.[111] These remarks by ōkubo are unlikely to have been purely personal impressions. The course of realpolitik that drove Prussian politicians like Bismarck or Moltke to seek an exit from harsh international relations instead of remaining satisfied with ideological pacifism must have come as a refreshing shock to the political elites of Meiji Japan who wished to revise their country's unequal treaties with Western powers.[112]

There is room for debate regarding the weight the Prussian model carried in Japan's modernization, but since the Iwakura Embassy's dispatch at the earliest or the 1880s at the latest, it is a plain fact that Meiji Japan attempted to follow the German path. Prussia's military success and national unification, supported by the efficient system of an authoritarian state and its deeply patriotic people, was more than enough to attract the attention of ruling Japanese elites such as Itō Hirobumi, who dubbed himself the "Karl August von Hardenberg of Japan"; the first Japanese foreign minister Inoue Kaoru; and Yamagata Aritomo, the founder of the Imperial Japanese Army. To a latecomer like Japan seeking to quell all modern revolutionary spirits that emerged in places like France and converge such political, social vitality into the sole objective of strengthening national capability, a Prussian-style military establishment and constitution must have seemed more necessary than anything else. Japanese elites noticed that politics in the German Empire was a product not of national majority decision-making but of state tectonics built out of blood and iron. It was not by chance that in September 1881, Inoue Kaoru took the lead in launching the German Studies Association, which influential figures of the Meiji government joined as members.[113]

Imperial Constitution as a Realization of National Polity

As Prussian state tectonics was refashioned to suit Japan, one of the contradictory outcomes turned out to be the emergence of *kokutai*, or the concept of "national polity." Through *An Outline of a Theory of Civilization*, Fukuzawa clearly defines that "polity means a framework or a format," thereby highlighting a country's unity and singularity, more specifically, a national polity involved "living under the same government, enjoying self-rule, and disliking the idea of being subject to foreign rule."[114] The year after the Meiji Constitution's proclamation, this abstract concept was officially recognized on October 31, 1890, through the issuance of the Imperial Rescript on Education, which defined the people's loyalty and filial piety toward the imperial throne as the "glory of the fundamental character of our empire" and the "source of our education." Such an idea sprung from the view of Japanese history revolving around the emperor and the *Bansei ikkei* argument claiming that the Japanese nation has been and will continue to be reigned by an unbroken imperial lineage. As if the emperor most high and his people were one body, the view postulated the two as a harmonious whole and immediately condemned as anti-national and anti-historical any political idea or act going against the emperor's will.[115] Governmentality distinctive of modern states seems to have been adopted by this conservative and even reactionary idea of national polity in that it governs the state as one massive body, a Japanese twist to an utterly Western biopolitics.

The establishment of modern Japan's constitutional system clearly demonstrates how Japan faced and dealt with the principles of Western civilization. Accepting Prussian state tectonics on the one hand led to the active adoption of conservative Prussian statism and on the other hand reverted the image of Japan back to a mythicized impression far from

German rationality. Having been too immersed in the course of realpolitik, the way to go must have appeared an excessively defensive, thoroughly apathetic modernization. In this sense, the Prussian legacy seems to have continued yet discontinued throughout the process of Japan's modernization.

It is common knowledge that not only was the German legal advisor Hermann Roesler consulted in drafting the constitution of the Empire of Japan known as the Meiji Constitution, proclaimed in 1889 and enacted the following year, but that the constitution wholly reflected Lorenz von Stein's theory highlighting the state's patriarchal role rather than unlimited individual freedom.[116] As a matter of fact, drafting the Meiji Constitution turned out to require years of effort. Under the emperor's orders, Home Minister Itō Hirobumi, who practically led the pro-German faction in Japan, headed a mission sent to Germany and Austria for nearly eighteen months between 1882 and 1883. The mission sought consultation from Rudolf von Gneist and his pupil Albert Mosse, the leading theorists in constitutional law in Berlin, and from Lorenz von Stein in Vienna, who had been propounding the idea of "social kingdom" at the time. However, Itō ran into an unexpected hurdle in Berlin. Having learned state theories from the philosopher Hegel himself at the University of Berlin, Von Gneist insisted that constitution was a highly spiritual product incomparable to other individual laws. He thereby expressed skeptical views about establishing a constitution in a peripheral East Asian country such as Japan and had his pupil Mosse handle the consultative discussions Itō had regularly scheduled with himself. Discouraged by such a condescending reaction, Itō turned his footsteps toward Vienna, where he was able to gain his greatest supporter. What most helped Itō Hirobumi connect with Lorenz von Stein was the view they both shared on a monarch's role in reconciling new social conflicts with state authority.[117]

Itō Hirobumi's choice to head to Germany actually had to do with an internal threat. The waves of modernization triggered a political crisis by 1881 as the Freedom and People's Rights Movement demanded the establishment of a constitutional government and an elected assembly. In March 1881, Councilor Ōkuma Shigenobu submitted a proposal to Prince Arisugawa Taruhitō. The proposal radically suggested the adoption of a British-style parliamentary system by establishing a constitution by the end of that year, forming a cabinet based on the majority in parliament, and having an assembly elected within two years.[118] This was practically a rebellion from within the government, sparking a sense of crisis among the ruling forces tantamount to that during the 1877 military revolt Satsuma samurai caused under Saigō Takamori's lead. This situation that occurred at a crossroads of the nation's future ended with the dismissal in October 1881 of all government officials involved, including Ōkuma Shigenobu. It was a crude way of patching the affair up, but the ruling forces did give way to some degree by agreeing to establish an assembly within the next nine years until 1890. And behind all such arrangements was none other than Itō Hirobumi.[119]

Yet the waves of the Freedom and People's Rights Movement did not easily die down. Although popular rights thinkers mostly valued the independence of national sovereignty and regarded the reinforcement of popular rights as a means to achieve such independence, it was difficult to reconcile the desire for a British, American, or French-style bourgeois revolution for democracy with Meiji Japan's authoritarian system. Still, such thinkers had already created a bridgehead in the Japanese legal terrain. The modern civil code of Japan contained many liberalist elements from having been based on the French civil code translated by Mitsukuri Rinshō in the 1870s.[120] Upon the 1880s, the Freedom and People's Rights Movement showed distinct signs of morphing into a political force. Itagaki Taisuke, who once advocated the *Seikanron* alongside Saigō Takamori, formed the Liberal Party in 1881, and the following year, Ōkuma Shigenobu, after having been dismissed from his government position, formed the Constitutional Reform Party. Amid such chaotic domestic circumstances, Itō Hirobumi's choice to explore the German political system, in stark contrast to that of Britain, carries major implications. Itō's trip to Germany not only contributed to his own success as a politician who played a leading role in the Meiji Constitution's establishment later on but also symbolized the choice modern Japan went with at a historical crossroads.

Previously, the True Account had already made note of the negative aspects of the political reality in modern Western countries and considered some alternatives. Western parliamentary democracy that politically operated according to individual pursuits of interest was deemed unsuitable for Japan's political climate. A unique racial theory advanced in the fifth volume of the True Account predicated that Caucasians are greedier than Asian and that assuming all Caucasians are civilized is a supposition that should be discarded.[121] The theory acknowledged that races may engender differences, but race itself cannot be a standard for assigning a hierarchy. A political theory was formed based on such a racial theory. The following shows how the True Account's author Kume underlined political principles of the East as opposed to those of the West.

> The Eastern races are less inclined to greed; they submit themselves to moral governance; their sovereigns are conscientious and frugal and thus have raised their people to great heights. . . . The Western races, by contrast, are given to rampant greed and are slow to correct their conduct; and as for their rulers, it would not be a calumny to say that they tax the people on their lands heavily and make themselves wealthy by keeping the revenue for themselves, and that they are all but tireless in their cupidity and rapacity. The people of the East and the West are different in character; they are almost opposites.[122]

If the ethos dominating a certain country and civilization is what breeds differences, the inevitable conclusion of discourse for Japan would be to opt for an alternative course. The True Account's conservative directionality that gauged the potential of moral politics in the East continued to trickle down to the ruling forces of Meiji Japan. The shock from Ōkuma's proposal in June 1881 prompted the then–Minister of the Right Iwakura Tomomi to order the Chief Cabinet Secretary Inoue Kowashi to conduct preliminary research on establishing a constitution. From reviewing Ōkuma's proposal, Inoue was able to grasp the issues related to British parliamentary democracy and thereafter consulted the Prussian constitution instead to draft a proposal for a Japanese constitution. During this process, he received considerable aid from the German legal advisor Hermann Roesler.[123]

Itō Hirobumi's return from his trip to Berlin and Vienna, however, brought a major change to Japan's previous approach toward constitutional law. Armed with expert insights he personally acquired from prominent European scholars, Itō exercised charisma back home. He stressed that establishing a constitution does not merely involve creating a draft on paper but must also entail comprehensive institutional reform. If establishing a constitution was aimed at building a modern nation-state as well as boosting national wealth and military power, Itō had learned from Lorenz von Stein that establishing an executive branch capable of promptly responding to historical changes had to be a priority. A prominent professor's unique idea about public administration from Vienna hence was conjoined with the keynote of a Prussian-style Japanese constitution. An executive branch backed by the cabinet had to maintain its autonomy against parliamentary and political parties as well as remaining independent from the monarch, which would in turn allow the monarch to be detached from the crude reality of politics and preserve himself as a unique national symbol. In short, the Japanese constitutional monarchy pursued a balance between the legislative and executive branches under the monarchy instead of placing the monarch's power in opposition to parliamentary power. This was fundamentally different from the Prussian constitutional monarchy, where the monarch retained control over the parliament. These new elements introduced by Itō Hirobumi helped accelerate and intensify the Japanese adoption of a Prussian-style constitution.[124]

After returning to Japan from Germany in 1883, Itō Hirobumi created the Bureau for the Investigation of Constitutional Systems within the Imperial Household Agency in March 1884, and, as the bureau's director, he took charge of creating a draft for the constitution. To complete most institutional reforms ahead of establishing a constitution, Itō also launched a cabinet system in 1885 and became the first prime minister of Japan. In 1888, he became the first president of the Privy Council, newly created as a consultative body with authority to review constitution drafts and advise the emperor. In January 1889, the Privy Council finished reviewing the constitution draft and, on February 11, the Constitution of the Empire of Japan was finally promulgated at the royal council hall of the imperial palace newly built on the spot where the Edo Castle once stood. The lengthy conflict surrounding the constitution's establishment was concluded with a victory for constitutional gradualism that pursued the middle course between absolute and constitutional monarchy.[125]

Proclaimed as an "immutable fundamental law" through the Imperial Rescript on the Promulgation of the Constitution, the Meiji Constitution took the form of being granted by the sovereign instead of having been politically acquired by the people.[126] It must have had in mind moral politics that would not be hindered by crude special interest politics. This unusual constitution stipulating the mighty authority of the sovereign, or emperor, and the administration may have approved of establishing a two-chamber Diet with a House of Peers and a House of Representatives but awarded almost all authority to the cabinet, the center of the administration, leaving no need for the cabinet to recruit from the ruling party or be responsible for the House of Representatives. The government budget did not require the Diet's approval. The House of Representatives only had the right to oppose increasing taxes, and in cases where the budget was not finalized, the constitution specified that the cabinet was to take responsibility and obtain the emperor's approval. The poisonous clauses in the Meiji Constitution's sixth chapter that made it easy for the government to arbitrarily use the budget entirely reflected suggestions Itō had received in Berlin from Rudolf von Gneist and even the German emperor Wilhelm I.[127]

Yet not everything about the Meiji Constitution granted by the emperor to his subjects was reactionary. Rejecting the emperor's direct rule and proclaiming the emperor a state institution instead of a sovereign was an argument by Itō Hirobumi clearly different from what the Iwakura faction believed in and partially reflected the idea of social kingdom Itō had learned about from Professor Lorenz von Stein at the University of Vienna. The emperor would, of course, be strictly isolated from society, allowing him to hide behind a mythical curtain. In form only, the emperor would be the one and only ruler with imperial authority, meaning he would nominally have the prerogative to exercise supreme command over the army and navy, diplomatic and legislative authority, and even the authority to issue emergency imperial ordinances. However, such authority would actually be with the Privy Council, and the emperor would serve as a prerequisite for legislation instead of acting as an absolute ruler above the law. This certainly differs from a standard constitutional monarchy in which the monarch also falls under the purview of the law. Symbolizing national unity by using the first-person pronoun "I," the emperor was not to be involved in pending political issues and only perform the perfunctory role of offering his final approval. The framework for the Constitution of the Empire of Japan was completed around a hollow core called the emperor and thereby legalized the Japanese national polity.[128]

The emperor's legal status continued to leave room for dispute. One of the typical controversies that ensued over the constitution was between Uesugi Shinkichi, who presumed the emperor to be the subject of sovereignty, and Minobe Tatsukichi, who argued that sovereignty belongs to the state as a corporate body that then allows the emperor to exercise that sovereignty on behalf of the state as its highest organ. Instead of encouraging wider public discussion, such fierce debates sparked violent right-wing attacks that led to an act of terror upon Minobe, putting a gag on his argument. This swept sensitive issues under the rug and created an excuse for military and government officials to wield power in the name of imperial authority.[129] Imperial Japan with an utterly ambiguous nucleus of power curiously corresponds to the idea of absolute nothingness proposed by the philosopher Nishida Kitarō. Through *An Inquiry Into the Good* published in 1911, Nishida discusses self-awakening, a more introspective stage than intuition in Western phenomenology, to suggest a new philosophical horizon that transcends subject and object, or existence and nonexistence. Absolute nothingness, or the horizon of absolutely contradictory self-identity, is a logic that takes the notion of nothingness from Zen Buddhism as a basis to invert the Hegelian absolute spirit. The logic predicates a religious state in which subject and object become one without being hindered any more by reason. This logic leaves open the possibility to regard the Japanese people as a subject that is dissolved into an object called empire. In that case, the absolute nothingness that transcends subject and object would, of course, be the emperor.[130]

In fact, Imperial Japan's politics and culture were heading toward a far more authoritative, repressive direction than specified in the constitution. In 1882, prior to the Meiji Constitution's establishment, the Japanese emperor issued the Imperial Rescript to Soldiers and Sailors and ordered that the rescript pledging their loyalty solely to the emperor be memorized. Making such a pledge deemed it logically impossible for soldiers and sailors not to oust a civilian government for going against the emperor's wishes. As the Prussian-style military reform of 1885 adopted a modern universal conscription system for Japan, what proved to be as a formative experience for almost all young Japanese men was not the idea of civilization and enlightenment but compulsory military service that depended on discipline and obedience.[131]

At the forefront of such a trend was not Japan's first prime minister, Itō Hirobumi, but his rival for the position, Yamagata Aritomo. Yamagata was a major political figure who first served as home minister before serving as prime minister twice after Itō's term. With a far more conservative inclination than Itō, Yamagata believed that military training and education were crucial to his nation's survival. The education he had in mind focused on internalizing loyalty, obedience, and discipline and thus eradicating individualism.[132] Since Itō Hirobumi's visit to Lorenz von Stein, it became popular to embark on intellectual excursions called the "Stein pilgrimage," and Yamagata joined the trend by visiting Rudolf von Gneist. The Prussian jurist maintained a stance far more conservative than Lorenz von Stein. For two hours a day over a course of nearly two weeks in May 1889, Yamagata received private tutoring from Gneist, who mainly advised it was too early to establish a parliament in Japan and emphasized extreme government control. This approach was implemented in Imperial Japan by the end of that year as Yamagata rose to the position of prime minister and formed a cabinet. As the true successor of Prussian militarism, Yamagata's conservative approach was applied not only to domestic affairs but diplomatic policies, which eventually gave rise to an explicit argument for territorial expansion primarily based on securing a "line of sovereignty" and a "line of interest."[133]

Westernization and Japanization

The Meiji Constitution strongly imparts the impression that it is a parody instead of a realization of modern constitutionalism. Despite having fulfilled the same formal conditions as any other Western constitution, the Meiji Constitution was focused on a single goal: to internally as well as externally solidify the ruling power of Japan. The political task the Meiji government saw as a top priority was to revise the fourteen unequal treaties Japan held with Western powers. Boosting military power, accepting Western fields of study, and even Westernizing attire and manners were all basically aimed at achieving that single goal. By 1899, the Meiji government eventually succeeded in abolishing consular jurisdiction that had allowed Western diplomats in Japan to be tried and sentenced in consular courts. Over the previous year, Japan had already managed to partially obtain tariff autonomy. After gaining most of what it set out to from the West, why did Japan go on with, or become even more fiercely obsessed with, Westernization?

The national identity of modern Japan was highly complex. Its switch onto the German path and adoption of state tectonics signifies that Japan did not remain satisfied with protecting itself from the West and sought to establish itself as a modern Western power. This formed a colonial topology in which Asian neighbors, including Korea and China, were deemed the "Orient of Japan."[134] However, Westernization should not be misunderstood as what bred Japanese Orientalism. A logical causality could be established between the two, but they fail to fit into a historical sequence. The typical interpretation of modern Japanese history tends to divide that history into developmental stages, where the stage of Westernization between the Meiji Restoration and the formation of a state through the establishment of a constitution and parliament (1887–1896) was followed by the stage of self-reflection on mindless Westernization and then the stage of restoring national dignity and territorial expansion. Such an interpretation overlooks the fact that mindless Westernization was carried out by suppressing the *Seikanron* professed by Saigō Takamori, among others. All national polices were consistently aimed at increasing the national wealth and military power of Meiji Japan, while the tip of its sword was pointed at its neighboring countries. The only inconsistency was that each political faction prioritized such policies differently.

The Western aspect of Japanese identity was but a consequence from the toiling process of discursive formation, struggling to figure out Japan's position in the world. Prussian classicism was part of that consequence. Rather than assuming that Japan transformed into the Prussia of Asia, it may be more accurate to conclude that as a new topological order settled during the modern times, Japan took advantage of the spatio-temporal principle from Prussia while seeking to become the subject instead of the object of change. The spatio-temporal order Prussian classicism conceived was converted into the basis of an entirely new topology in Japan.

In that sense, Westernization and Japanization were inseparable, and Japanese Asianism did not exactly conflict with Fukuzawa Yukichi's suggestion to leave Asia and enter Europe. Japanese Asianism originated from a sense of having been victimized by Western powers, not from Japan's relations with its Asian neighbors.[135] Inversely, the Westernization of Japan had proceeded within its relationship with Asia, particularly within a relationship of disconnection from and competition with China. In other words, Japan's pursuit of the West and of Asia were not stages in a process of development but were rising in counterpoint to one another. Therefore, it was a matter of time before Japan's argument for Asian solidarity turned into an argument for Asian hegemony. This perhaps explains how the prominent literary critic Takeuchi Yoshimi discovered Japanese Asianism from the subtle union and separation between an aggressive policy and a sense of solidarity. To Takeuchi, the idea of placing Japan above Asia and using its superiority to drive away European and American forces seemed thoroughly contradictory. The Great East Asia War had been "the ultimate point where the 'escape from Asia' absorbed the 'revival of Asia' and took advantage of it until only its skeleton was left."[136] However, the distance Japanese intellectuals tried to create between prewar and postwar Japan did not make it very far. Even Takeuchi merely regarded Fukuzawa's argument for leaving Asia as an effort to draw closer to civilization and failed to notice that civilization was necessary in order to leave Asia.

Architecture best reveals the truth behind the Westernization the Meiji government pursued. Like any other realm, mixed forms of unknown nationality were rife in architecture during the early Meiji period. Western architecture was only adopted by factories or shipyards as part of the early stages of industrialization. Western-style buildings nevertheless did exist in Japan prior to the Meiji Restoration. Embassies, churches, commercial facilities, and residential areas for foreigners that intermittently emerged in the mid-1860s had already attracted attention, and at the center of it was Nagasaki, where Dejima, Japan's window of exchange with the West, used to be. Urakami Cathedral, the largest of its kind in the East until it was destroyed by atomic bombing, was built between 1862 and 1864, and the residence of the Scottish merchant Thomas Blake Glover was finished in 1863 upon a broad hill overlooking the Nagasaki Harbor. The cathedral was built in the Romanesque style, while the Glover residence displayed an eclectic mix of the British Georgian and native Japanese styles. In 1859, an open port was built in Yokohama near Tokyo, which soon settled as the cradle of the Meiji civilization. The Western buildings in Nagasaki and Yokohama were influenced by precedents of the Chinese "treaty port style" in areas like Hong Kong.[137]

Such a trend, however, changed course as semi-colonial cities formed out of unequal treaties with Western powers gradually transformed into cities of prosperity and military power. The new course sought to imitate the West as much as possible in the hopes of reaping the same political and cultural effects. Even when architectural advisors invited from the West recommended mixing Western styles with native styles, the Japanese tended to prefer purely neoclassical or neo-Renaissance styles.[138] An example of this was the stone bridge at the imperial palace's main gate called Nijūbashi. Despite having been built as a symbolic part of the palace's reconstruction in 1888 ahead of the Meiji Constitution's promulgation, the fact that the bridge featured a German neo-Renaissance instead of a traditional Japanese style made a profound statement.[139] The bridge, supported by two gentle arches, was lined with embellished rails and three bronze lamps on each side. The name Nijūbashi, which means double bridge, actually referred to a different steel bridge laid beyond it that was designed by the German engineer Wilhelm Heise in 1888. This single arched bridge had a relatively plain form, with four lamps imported from Germany placed at each corner. While the stone bridge remained in place, the steel bridge was rebuilt in 1964, and one of the four lamps was taken to be preserved at the Meiji Village Museum on the outskirts of Nagoya.[140]

A more direct expression of a new imaginative geography was the Japanese vertical datum in the Western-style park formed in front of the Diet building. Installed in May 1891, the benchmark derived from mean sea level was meant to serve as a reference point on land used to measure heights above surface without being influenced by the sun, moon, weather, or subsidence. The spot where the benchmark was situated was not an actual vertical datum but where the Japanese military's land survey department used to be located. This small monument designed by Satachi Shichijiro, a first-generation architect of Meiji Japan, had Dorian

Figure 2.4 Left: Stone Bridge at the Imperial Palace's Main Gate. Right: Japanese Vertical Datum Made of Stone.

Source: Photos by author (2015).

pillars, a decorated gable, and on the front, an entablature adorned with triglyphs and metopes in addition to stairs at the center. Apart from the label "vertical datum" and the bronze chrysanthemum seal below it, the simple but altogether thoroughly solid appearance made the monument an unmistakable legacy of Prussian classicism. Even the benchmark on land in modern Japan had turned into a portrayal of Prussia.

These developments were quite in contrast to the case of Thailand, which was swayed by Western powers just like Japan but maintained its independence. Japanese politicians had architectural advisors from the West teach the essence of Western architecture in Japan, and once the purpose was achieved, such advisors were immediately driven away. The ruling power of Thailand, on the other hand, offered their full support to Western architects and granted them far more opportunities and privileges than to local architectural craftsmen. The outcome was the domination of an eclectic style, as can be seen through the Chakri Mahaprasad Hall in Bangkok with Western classical pillars under traditional Thai spires.[141] Where did such a difference stem from? How was Japan able to form a new imaginative geography in which even the West revolved around itself and engage in tectonic thinking?

The Cultural Nationalism of Japan

Modern Japan's topological order was what caused the transition from superficially accepting the West to obsessing over Westernization. The order was forced to remain unstable from constantly being surrounded by contradiction. Therefore, fusing an obsession over Westernization with an obsession over Japan's original culture was an inevitable contradiction. Fukuzawa Yukichi's notion of civilization in essence aimed for national wealth and military power, which had difficulty maintaining its normative position because it ranked Japan as "semi-civilized." Being semi-civilized stirred fear and anxiety over falling to a colonial status and at the same time endlessly generated a distance from others presumed to be barbaric.[142] The notion of civilization that simply bestowed a relative position upon Japan soon lost timeliness and was replaced by a concept of culture. Used as a translation of the German concept "Kultur" since around 1890, the Japanese concept of culture initially exhibited no particular difference from the concept of civilization, but it gradually took on the German connotation of spiritual depth and historical legitimacy as opposed to material abundance.[143] By the Taishō period (1912–1926), culturalism was widespread, stressing the uniqueness of Japan that distinguishes it from the West. This is perhaps why the leading critical cultural theorist Nishikawa Nagao pointed out that modern Japan's idea of culture has always been about an exclusive "national culture."[144]

The German notion of culture in modern Japan seemed to actually gain international legitimacy by receiving wholehearted support from one of the most prominent German intellectuals. Bruno Taut was an architect who represented the later stages of the Deutscher Werkbund and was considered a pioneer of modern German architecture. During his stay in Japan, Taut published *Japanese Art Seen With European Eyes* in 1936, through which he raved about traditional Japanese architecture. On the Ise Shrine, built with Hinoki cypress wood, Taut described how the building's form matching its structure, as open and simple as a farmer's hut, made the shrine the quintessence of the virtues of Japanese culture. The Katsura Imperial Villa was a "work of classic Japanese architecture on par with the Acropolis of Athens as well as the Parthenon and Propylaea in it." Like the bamboo rain gutter at its entrance, the villa altogether eschewed ostentation so that everything down to the finest detail fulfilled a purpose, demonstrating a classic simplicity and clarity. The way Taut saw it, such Japanese buildings were entirely modern in that they sought the simplest forms capable of fulfilling functions as well as unified scales and proportions. On the contrary, the American-style skyscrapers and modern buildings like the Imperial Hotel by Frank Lloyd Wright increasingly appearing in the Japanese capital Tokyo left much to be desired in Taut's eyes for being immersed in the subjectivism of form and thereby displaying non-Japanese inclinations. Taut claimed that by wholly embracing the proportions of nature, traditional Japanese architecture demonstrated the "absolute purity of its arrangement" and coincided with the modern architecture he was aiming for.[145]

In 1940, the Japanese translation of Taut's extraordinary book was published by the publisher Meiji shobō under the title *A Personal View of Japanese Culture*. The translation created a tremendous sensation and engendered countless mutations of Taut's view of Japanese culture. For excluding "non-Japanese" influences from the West as well as from Buddhism and China and for acknowledging only Shintōism and the emperor as the basis of Japanese culture, the extreme obsession over purity was to Taut as much as to Japan linked directly to a certain design involving the future.[146] Taut began to gain fame since jointly designing the glass pavilion Glashaus for an international exhibition the Deutscher Werkbund hosted in Cologne, Germany, in 1914. He mainly worked in Berlin until fleeing to Switzerland to escape Nazi persecution. When he was officially invited to join the International Architectural Association of Japan, Taut sought asylum in Japan in 1933. As can be sensed from his career, Taut was deeply related to the Deutscher Werkbund through which modern German architecture originated, and interestingly enough, positioned himself as a mediator between the Prussian classicist tradition of Berlin, modernism, and traditional Japanese architecture.[147] The key factor Taut discovered from the Ise Shrine or the Katsura Imperial Villa and attempted to emulate in modern architecture was the tectonic unity between aesthetic form and function.

Taut was not the only one to discover such a connection. There was another case far from Japan that revealed a connection between the utterly classical (Western) and the utterly Japanese (traditional). While building his reputation in Dresden, the architect Gottfried Semper once submitted a plan to renovate the Japanese Palace (Japanisches Palais). Built in the Baroque style in 1715 as the oldest and largest palace along the river Elbe, the building had already undergone an expansion in order to house the Japanese porcelain collection of Augustus II, or Augustus the Strong. Renovations on this major architectural work in Dresden continued throughout the eighteenth century and even involved Matthäus Daniel Pöppelmann, the architect who designed the cultural city's landmark Zwinger. Having been commissioned for a renovation in the spring of 1835, Semper adorned seven of the palace's rooms with multiple bright colors. He assigned different themes to each, such as the Pompeii Room, the Greek Room, and the Renaissance Room, an approach that caused a huge sensation at the time.[148] It is unknown whether Semper had particularly been interested in Japan, but at the very least, it seems certain there were no specific conflicts between Japan and Western classicism in his imaginative geography. Perhaps Japan was a blank slate upon which Westerners could freely visually express their impressions without being influenced by the aversion and discomfort they felt toward other civilizations. The French literary critic Roland Gérard Barthes's excessively creative misinterpretation characterizing the faraway Japan as a "cabinet of signs," "tapestried with openings, framed with emptiness and framing nothing,"[149] appears to be in line with the view of Japan that persisted from the preeminent German architect Semper down to Bruno Taut.

Unlike common Orientalism, Japonism meshed well with classical and modern designs of the West, which is why it was able to avoid becoming fossilized and left futureless. The fact that French impressionist paintings owe much to exotic Japanese woodprints by artists like Katsushika

Hokusai or Ando Hiroshige for their simplicity, clarity, isometric projection, and unique mix of colors only manages to partially explain the imaginary view of Japan that deeply took root in Western cultures.[150] In any case, these inadvertent favorable circumstances provided the Japanese with an opportunity to engage in Occidentalism, tweaking Western civilizations to suit their own taste.

Okakura Kakuzō was a pioneer of Japanese Occidentalism who established the Japanese system of studying art history. Before going to the United States to serve as head of the Asian arts division at the Museum of Fine Arts in Boston, Okakura served as director of the fine arts section at the Imperial Museum launched in 1889 and as head of the Tokyo School of Fine Arts, which later became the Tokyo University of the Arts. *The History of Japanese Art*, published posthumously based on Okakura's notes for his lectures at the Tokyo School of Fine Arts between 1890 and 1891, argued that the origin of exceptional Japanese art such as the murals of the golden hall Kondō at Hōryū-ji temple built in Nara during the reign of Emperor Tenji (626–671) or the statue of Guanyin could be traced back to ancient Indian and Greek art. By doing so, the book underscored that Japanese art was eligible for appraisal based on the same criteria applied to Western art. Such an approach attempted to liberate Japanese culture from the Sinocentric cultural sphere so as to newly establish it within a global context.[151] Now Asia and the West all had to be incorporated into a new imaginative geography revolving around Japan.

Okakura's view of art history is known to have been influenced by Ernest Francisco Fenollosa, an American who launched an academic exploration into the history of Japanese art. While teaching at Tokyo Imperial University, Fenollosa, despite not having been formally trained in art history, attempted to systematize the study of Japanese art history using Hegelianism, with which he had been deeply impressed with as a student at Harvard University. His posthumous book *Epochs of Chinese and Japanese Art: An Outline History of East Asiatic Design*, published in English in 1912, faithfully followed Hegelian aesthetics in line with the idea that the horizon reached during each period continues to expand over the development of art history. At the same time, the book revealed fresh aspects that went beyond Hegelian Eurocentrism in order to enthusiastically appraise East Asian art. However, because he wasn't an expert in art history, Fenollosa's analysis remained at the level of drawing one-on-one comparisons between the East and West. For instance, the Chinese city Hangzhou was compared to Venice in Italy, while the statue of Guanyin's mysterious smile was compared to the smile of Mona Lisa.[152]

Okakura began studying art history as he helped Fenollosa organize related material. Okakura managed to systematize Japanese art history by adopting Western methodologies. He classified cultural assets, assigned rankings among which national treasures would be at the top, and categorized them into genres such as sculptures, paintings, buildings, and crafts. He then became the first to propose a methodology of classifying art works by period according to the Hegelian *Zeitgeist*, or "spirit of the times."[153] Through one of his major works, *The Ideals of the East* (1903), Okakura used Hegelian aesthetics to divide the history of Japanese art into the three stages of "symbolic, classic, and romantic." This corresponded exactly with the periodical division between ancient, medieval, and modern in historical studies. Such a periodical division depended on Buddhism: the ancient Nara period identified with Theravada Buddhism that recognizes a dichotomy between this world and the pure land, the medieval Heian period identified with Esoteric Buddhism that places Buddhahood at an approachable distance to people, and the early modern Ashikaga period during which Zen Buddhism emphasized the state of enlightenment.[154]

Okakura's methodology and view were hence thoroughly Western, and he was clearly aware of it. Like *Bushido*, originally written in English by Nitobe Inazō, Okakura's notes for the lectures he gave in English at Boston's Museum of Fine Arts were published as *The Book of Tea*, which became an instant bestseller. Both books touched upon and fulfilled precisely what Western readers sought from the East. Having been well versed in the English language and Western customs, Okakura sensed that Westerners were already skeptical toward their civilization, which the Japanese had been keen to learn from, and were instead interested in learning from the East.[155] This was indeed a golden opportunity for Japan to improve its national destiny. Whether it be tea rituals or samurai ethics, the time had come for Japanese culture to claim for global hegemony. What now became necessary was not unconditional loyalty or a return to Japanese traditions but a forward-looking plan for Japan to lead and rise above modern civilization. It was hence no coincidence when Okakura mentioned that "Art is the flowering of a nation" at the beginning of a statement to launch the art magazine *Kokka* in 1889.[156]

Rather than remaining satisfied with fulfilling the Western desire for Japonism, Okakura Kakuzō took a step further by trying to turn it into Occidentalism. Written in English and published in London in 1903, *The Ideals of the East* propounded Eastern-centrism as opposed to Western-centrism and placed Japanese culture at its core. Famous for its first line, "Asia is one," the book argued that Indian religions, including Buddhism and Hinduism; Chinese philosophies revolving around Confucianism and Taoism; and Japanese art form a trinity that realizes the ideals of the East. The argument deemed the spiritual culture of the East superior to military power or the science-centered Western civilization, suggesting what seemed to be a reverse take on the Hegelian philosophy of history. This view reflected the strategy of being firmly aware of and intentionally otherizing the Westerners' gaze toward the East. With respect to otherizing, the East was actually no different. Despite claiming that the East is a single cultural community, the unquestionable leader of that community had to be Japan. "The unique blessing of unbroken sovereignty, the proud self-reliance of an unconquered race, and the insular isolation, which protected ancestral ideas and instincts at the cost of expansion, made Japan the real repository of the trust of Asiatic thought and culture." Okakura regarded the "spirit of living Advaitism which welcomes the new without losing the old" as a unique attribute of Japanese culture and succinctly named the reason Japan, "a museum of Asiatic civilization," should be the leader of Asia. "It is the glory of Continental Asia that her touch upon Japan has made always for new life and inspiration."[157]

In some ways, the Okakura-type switch from Western-centric Japonism to Eastern-centric Occidentalism shared a connection with the essence of the European spirit of historicism. If the nature of historicism lay in reorganizing the relationship between past and present and creating a new spatio-temporal order, for Japan, reinterpreting the glorious culture of the East within a modern horizon created by the West may have been something that corresponded with the spirit of historicism. As Germany broke away from the influence of Rome and discovered ancient Greece, Japan broke away from China and directly formed its own link with ancient Greece.

Having been deeply influenced by Fenollosa and Okakura, the one who reinterpreted the style of inherently Japanese shrines and temples as the horizon of pure neoclassicism was Itō Chūta, the first architectural historian of Japan. Through the paper "An Architectural Study of Hōryū-ji," authored as a doctoral student of the Imperial College of Engineering and published in 1893 in the Journal of Architecture *Kenchiku zasshi*, Itō argued that the world's oldest wooden building Hōryū-ji altogether preserved the essence of various styles, including Western classical styles, that were dominant during the ancient times. Although Fenollosa may be credited for recognizing the true value of Hōryū-ji, Itō pointed out that Fenollosa was only interested in individual paintings or sculptures, whereas he himself attempted to understand architecture as a whole that embraces such individual works of art per se. The main gate, standing out among the architectural components for its grand scale and ornate embellishments, resembled an ancient Etruscan temple in terms of the proportional consistency maintained between the height of stories and distance between pillars as well as between the diameters of the main and corner pillars. The slope of the gate's tiled roof looked extremely similar to a gable. As for the magnificent golden hall, the columns were shaped like an entasis in ancient Greek architecture. In the end, Itō recognized Hōryū-ji as the ultimate legacy demonstrating a history of ancient exchange between the East and West.[158]

Itō was the first in Japan to approach architectural history as a history of styles involving architectural art or artistic architecture. What is distinctive about Itō's argument is the claim that among the mix of various styles at Hōryū-ji, the Tang Chinese style, a fusion of the Six Dynasties style and

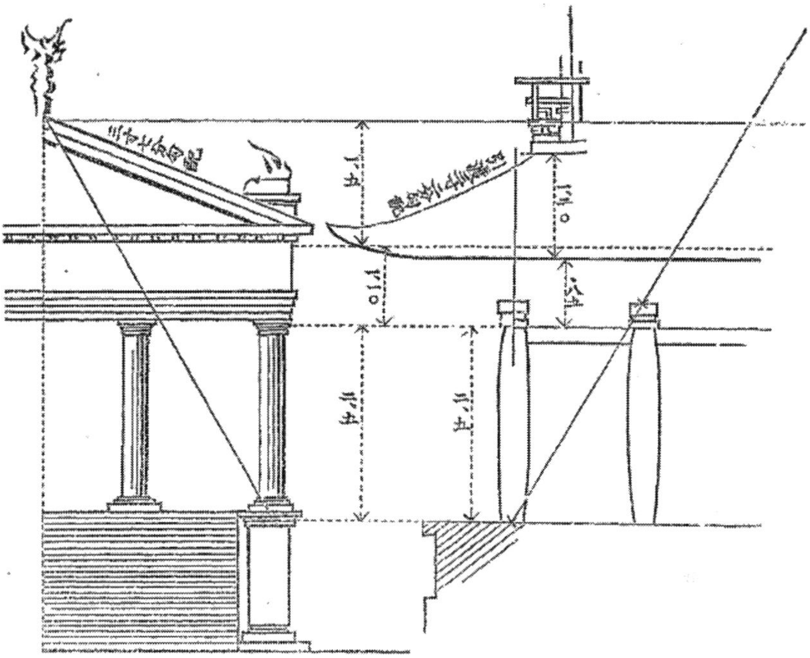

Figure 2.5 Comparison of Proportions Between Hōryū-ji's Main Gate and an Etruscan Temple.

Source: From Itō Chūta, "An Architectural Study of Hōryū-ji," *Kenchiku zasshi* [Architectural Journal] 82 (1893): 328. Courtesy of the Library of the Architectural Institute of Japan.

the Greco-Indian style, was markedly different from the Korean style of the three Han states. In other words, the argument suggests that ancient Western cultures reached Japan without passing through the Korean peninsula. The main purpose for suggesting so was to forge a direct link between ancient Japan and Greece rather than to demonstrate Japan's cultural superiority against Korea. Hōryū-ji, where the antiquity of Asia is well preserved, had become the Parthenon of the East. Etched into such an unconventional idea was Hegelian aesthetics. As ancient Greece was reborn within modern German culture, ancient Japanese culture, which brought forth a beautiful ray of light like Hōryū-ji upon waking from its natural state, experienced countless vicissitudes of foreign cultures before returning to itself. As an authentic work from the distant past, Hōryū-ji was a vivid legacy of Japanese culture that had managed to keep pace with the West and establish itself as a dialectic opportunity for the Japanese national culture's current advancement.[159] Itō eventually developed the paper published in 1893 into his doctoral dissertation submitted in 1898.

"An Architectural Study of Hōryū-ji" by Itō Chūta revealed the Western-centric prepossession that Greece was the origin of all cultures and an obsession to associate Japan with that origin. On the other hand, researching the history of the East, which evolved into an academic discipline in the twentieth century, adopted the strategy of otherizing not only neighbors in the East but the West as well. With Shiratori Kurakichi at the forefront, positivists conceived an identity of its own for Japan, one that would be distinguishable from nations on continental Asia like China or India and stereotyped even the West for comparison with Japan. However, *toyoshi*, or the history of the East, basically failed to escape the Western idea of linear stages of development, exposing certain limitations to completely incorporating the West into a Japanese imaginative geography. Japan was special, but it could not readily find an escape route from its past as a part of Asia.[160]

In the opinion of the Japanese theorist Karatani Kojin, modern Japan failed to wholly secure its place within the frame of modernity created by the West and eventually had to call that frame into question. Okakura Kakuzō's theory of Japanese art history or Nishida Kitarō's philosophy not only turned the tables on the Western-centrism of Hegelian historical dialectics but overcame that dialectics to restructure the Japanese world view and plant a seed for the theory on overcoming modernity developed by the Kyoto School. The way Karatani saw it, overcoming modernity was the ultimate conclusion Japanese intellectuals arrived at since the Meiji Restoration. It was the only way Japan could leave its trace in the modern world.[161] This course set out on a mission impossible to achieve with Shiratori's history of the East. As a second-generation Kyoto School philosopher who studied under Nishida Kitarō, Miki Kiyoshi advocated a "unified idea of world history," representing the Japanese postmodern response against Hegelian historical dialectics. Although he personally met the fate of dying in prison from an anti-establishment charge, Miki and the Kyoto School's idea was used by Japan as a logic of justification during the Second Sino-Japanese War and World War II.[162]

Yet the logic the Japanese used was overly similar to German cultural nationalism. It was as if German criticism toward the Anglo-Saxon civilization or "Americanization" had been wholly transferred to Japan. The praises the German architect Bruno Taut sang for pure Japanese culture and the reproach he expressed toward its Westernized mutation were no coincidence. It is worth taking note of how the Japanese *Buraiha* (Decadent School) writer Sakaguchi Ango made a travesty of Taut's praises for Japan by publishing a book with a title identical to Taut's bestseller *A Personal View of Japanese Culture*. Sakaguchi remarked that tradition was but a coincidental product and that the Katsura Imperial Villa would not be missed, provocatively declaring that vulgar urban culture was what he needed and loved.[163] This sort of switch in thinking gained support only after the Japanese Empire sustained tremendous sacrifices and collapsed.

4. The Invention of Tokyo

Forming modern Japan's imperial capital Tokyo upon the base of the Edo Bakufu was the first and most notable case of using the tectonics of Prussian classicism to establish a new topological order for Japan. Tokyo was a city with historical traditions and a well-organized system. Right before the Meiji Restoration, Japan was one of the most urbanized countries in the world. Tokyo was an economically and culturally sophisticated metropolis populated with more than one million people, although the environment was still medieval in that it was frequently exposed to fire and had poor road conditions. For nearly two and a half centuries from when Tokugawa Ieyasu established the Edo Bakufu in 1603 after the 1592–1598 Japanese invasions of Korea to 1868, when the Meiji Restoration occurred, Edo was extensively developed as the Bakufu practiced a strong centralization policy and rearranged the city's residential districts. A notable example of this would be the *Sankin kōtai* system, a system of alternate attendance in which the *daimyō*, or feudal lords, would switch on an annual basis between tending to their own domain in the countryside and fulfilling their duty to serve the government at Edo. This system helped Edo maintain its population and naturally led to the development of the city's economy and transportation network. The central government directly governed Edo, Osaka, and Kyoto, and the Genna edict of 1615 limited the number of castles to one per domain, further strengthening the position of the central government while weakening that of the daimyō. According to this almost radically readjusted order, officials were dispatched by the central government to govern each rural district. This led to the custom of autonomously settling everyday matters within the purview of feudal agricultural societies, shaping the ultimately Japanese aspect of enjoying economic and cultural vitality but lagging behind in developing into an autonomous civil society and public sphere. In any case, the prevailing social order laced with a certain rationality left Japan in no rush to adopt Western urban planning or make it easy to do so.[164]

From Edo to Tokyo

Had Meiji Japan sought to comprehensively govern society at large through the military, elementary schools, Shinto shrines, vocational groups, and even licensed quarters for prostitution, it could be seen as an extension of traditional benevolence from above and mutual assistance among people from the days of the Tokugawa Bakufu. At least until the Taishō period, the Japanese state system of promoting self-sufficiency or self-management as the moral responsibility of each village and thereby encouraging voluntary participation to achieve state goals worked relatively smoothly without the need to explicitly apply pressure.[165] The Meiji Restoration was clearly what transformed the Japanese society of mutual assistance into a uniform modern state. The coup d'état on January 3, 1868, for imperial restoration merely shifted power from one group to another within the uppermost ruling class, so it was absolutely necessary to deal with the domains the daimyō ruled outside the capital in order to truly achieve direct rule by the emperor. In July 1869, the daimyō immediately returned their domains and its people back to the emperor, which were then divided into districts for each daimyō to govern called *han* and districts governed by the central government called *fu* and *ken*. Two years later in August 1871, the han system was altogether abolished and replaced by the prefecture (ken) system, placing the entire nation under the central government's direct supervision. Major cities were divided into boroughs (shiku), and by 1872, all the castle gates around Edo were torn down.[166] Such radical administrative reforms are thought to have established the foundation for a modern state with centripetal force. They were revolutionary yet conservative for reshaping a tradition from the days of the Tokugawa Bakufu into a modern system of agency-delegated functions where the central government passes instructions down to officials in different regions for them to carry out locally.[167]

The new state was now in need of a detailed blueprint, for which a number of options were in the race, including direct rule by the emperor, centralism, and egalitarianism favored by the people. Having suddenly transformed into the imperial capital where the emperor resides, Tokyo had to be rebuilt into a space that would visually convey Japan's new state ideology. However, there was no consensus or prior knowledge as to how to proceed with such an urban transformation. Japanese cities hadn't particularly been underdeveloped, for the concept of urban planning only settled in Europe by the mid-nineteenth century. Traditional castle towns called *Jōkamachi* were typically formed around a daimyō's castle, which would be encircled by spaces like *buke-chi* where samurai resided, *chōnin-chi* where merchants resided, and *jisha-chi* where Buddhist temples and Shinto shrines were situated. A modern reorganization of such spaces transformed old castle sites and *buke-chi* into lots for local government offices or military reservation. According to the central government's plan for land use, some rural cities that once served as the headquarters of the daimyō were preserved with the installation of prefectural or county offices, while some were dismantled for complete reorganization.[168]

What accelerated such change was the Japanese political leaders' trip to Europe. After witnessing European cities with their own eyes, they could no longer remain satisfied with their reality back home. When the Iwakura Embassy visited Paris in 1872 during Napoleon III's rule of France, its members were greatly impressed by Haussmann's renovation of the city that had just finished working on boulevards, public buildings, and a transportation network.[169] Yet, in order for such impressions to actually set things into motion in reality, there were many factors to consider. The Meiji period was a time of rapid social change that left little energy to push forward with urban planning. To instantly boost its national power, there were much more urgent matters at hand for Japan, such as establishing political order, increasing government funds, and spurring economic growth.

Industrial growth, innovations in transportation technology, and the rising fatality rate from infectious diseases all pointed to a dire need for fundamental change in urban order, but lending priority to urban planning had to be directly linked to the great cause of boosting national power. To impart a modernized impression to foreigners and convince them to revise unequal treaties, the Meiji government decided it was necessary to change the capital's landscape and took the lead in launching renovation projects. The most urgent tasks involved laying paved roads as straight as possible to prevent fires and repairing the water and sewage system. It was not by chance that planning for Tokyo became synonymous with urban planning in nineteenth-century Japan.[170]

The Advent of Ginza Bricktown

Rather than transforming into a modernized Edo, the imperial capital Tokyo became a newly invented historical space. Tokyo itself could be considered a discursive formation of sorts.[171] The emperor's arrival on October 13, 1868, from Kyoto to the shōgun's former residence Edo Castle was an incident that merged actual power with the authority that comes with historical legitimacy, serving as a fanfare declaring the beginning of an invention. In July, a few months prior to the incident, the newly established Meiji government announced Tokyo as the new name of Edo, along with its intention to turn the city into an imperial capital. However, the sharp decline in the city's population from 1.3 million at the height of the Edo Bakufu's reign to 0.57 million by 1872 indicated that it would be difficult to dispel the confusion during a period of transition and instantly subvert the loyalty locals felt toward the shōgun.[172] The Meiji government assumed a very active, uncompromising approach toward constructing a new institution because it was directly linked to the establishment of a new national identity. So, a dual policy settled in, pushing for a massive renovation of Tokyo's appearance and structure while in other cities focusing on advancing the local economy without tending to the urban structure.[173]

To transform a former shogunal base like Edo Castle into a modern imperial capital, it was imperative to create a new identity and urban structure. Tectonics disguised as the concept of national polity was summoned for the "invention" of Tokyo. Such an invention was, of course, not to be instantly achieved. The construction of Ginza Bricktown, known as the first public construction project since the Meiji Restoration, was a case that demonstrated the absence of a consensus as to the new capital's identity.

It was by chance that there was an opportunity to launch the project. In late February 1872, a fire that started at the imperial palace's south gate Sakuradamon ate up a wide area as it spread with a northwesterly breeze. Included in that wide area was the Ginza district, where the Tokugawa shogunate's silver coin foundry used to be. The fire completely destroyed a total of three thousand buildings that used to house fifty thousand people.[174] The Ginza district adjacent to the historic bridge Nihonbashi had the commercial Marunouchi district to its north; the Tsukiji district's foreign settlement to its east; and to its south Shinbashi Station, scheduled to be completed in the fall of that same year. The station was the terminus of Japan's first railroad, which connected the port of Yokohama to Tokyo, and the Ginza district was likely to unfold before foreigners as soon as they disembarked at the port. So, rather than restoring the burnt-down district to its former state, the Meiji government sought to newly produce a more fire-resistant, dignified sight befitting an imperial capital. The officials at the Ministry of Treasury took the initiative and with unprecedented swiftness came up with a plan in a mere six days. Inoue Kaoru, a pro-German bureaucrat who later served as the Japanese Minister of Foreign Affairs, particularly regarded the project as an opportunity to practice his Westernization policy and made a rather bold attempt at the time by designing long streets lined with Western-style brick buildings. Luckily, there were no regulations or agency primarily in charge of such projects since the Meiji government had not yet stabilized by then, which provided the few samurai elites who took down the Bakufu ideal circumstances to pursue whatever they pleased.[175]

As the very first public construction project carried out since the Meiji Restoration, rebuilding a commercial area such as the Ginza district in Tokyo entailed much controversy as well as trial and error. However, the fundamental issue of the project was in its ultimate goal, not in technological, institutional limitations or incomplete sociopolitical circumstances. The identity of the newly invented imperial capital was ambiguous. Blindly imitating the West was as undesirable as an eclectic fusion with the indigenous. The circumstances were quite different from Berlin, the Athens of central Europe, where a certain consensus regarding Berlin's historical identity had been formed between the middle and ruling-class Prussians. Berlin had to clearly demonstrate that it was the "Athens on the river Spree." Such a consensus remained intact despite political strife, at least among the middle to upper class until they were hit by the catastrophe of World War I. To the German Empire, ancient Greece hadn't seemed as far off compared to its internal and external enemies. However, there was no such consensus over Tokyo. Not only was Tokyo not a modernized Edo, it was not the Berlin of Tokyo Bay nor the London of East Asia.

The Meiji government reached the conclusion that the Ginza district should present an expressly European image. The architect chōsen for the job was Thomas J. Waters, who had been active in Japan since the 1850s. Officially commissioned by the Ministry of Construction, which was designated as the authority in charge of the project, Waters designed a straight Victorian-style street lined with a series of two-story brick buildings and trees on either side. Making the district more accessible to foreigners by increasing the street's width and more fire-resistant by using bricks were choices that had taken both appearance and function into consideration and were surely consistent with what Japanese officials like Inoue Kaoru had in mind. In just over a year since drafting the plan in 1872, most of the district's key parts emerged into view, and Ginza Bricktown running from the first street, itchōme, to the eighth street, hatchōme, was finished in 1877 to display a highly civilized presence no longer under the frequent threat of fire. The brick buildings mostly had windows and balconies on the second floor and steel-framed roofs supported by trusses, and the ground floor formed an arcade adjoining the sidewalk. The overall façade's continuous unity was more valued than individual buildings. The streets were widened into four different widths of 27 meters, 18 meters, 14.4 meters, or 5.4 meters. The sidewalks were paved with bricks, and trees separated them from the roads macadamized with broken stone. The streets of Ginza Bricktown were the first in Japan to have 6-meter-wide sidewalks and gas lamps installed alongside the trees. The light cast from the gas lamps seemed to signify civilization and enlightenment. What was most suggestive, though, was how the back side of the streets adopted a mix of Western and Japanese styles, while the front side strictly assumed a modern Western style, plainly demonstrating the fundamental nature of this large-scale construction project.[176]

Ginza Bricktown is said to have been inspired by John Nash's design for a cluster of buildings with curved colonnades called the Quadrant on Regent Street in central London.[177] Regent Street dividing the city north and south is known as the mecca of Georgian architecture, formed with the intention of outdoing Napoleon's Paris by George IV, since he was prince regent before rising to the throne in 1820. The Quadrant was part of a commercial district situated in the middle of that long thoroughfare. In terms of architecture, the Quadrant stood out for living up to the demands of a new age: steering clear of gaudy ornaments, displaying Greek regularity through evenly placed colonnades along the road, and occasionally adding a few pronounced features to create a rhythmic sensation.[178] The Quadrant was still, of course, different from Ginza Bricktown in many ways. Most of all, second-floor balconies demonstrated that early Meiji Japan had been under the indirect influence of the "treaty port style," an exotic, eclectic motif popular in places like Hong Kong or Shanghai.

Yet determining which architectural style Ginza Bricktown was based on may not carry much meaning. What carries more significance is the fact that while serving as a foreign government advisor, Waters adopted the form language of British neoclassical architecture from two generations ago in an entirely different environment like Japan. It is easy to imagine how shocked pedestrians may have felt at the time from encountering a straight brick-laid street lit with gas lamps.[179] Strictly speaking, style was not an issue. Since coming to Japan, Waters showed a highly flexible attitude toward stylistic forms as long as they didn't impair functionality while he supervised the construction of a spinning mill that used steam engines and built the Osaka Mint Bureau around the time the Meiji Restoration occurred.[180] The streets of Ginza had an impact upon Japanese carpenters accustomed to wooden buildings and thereafter spawned all sorts of variations which were generally referred to as *giyōfū*, the pseudo-Western style, or *kaikashiki* among experts, meaning a restoration mode.[181]

Ginza Bricktown ended up with about one-third of the nine hundred thirty-three buildings originally planned. Not only did the expenses far exceed the budget, the project failed to attract locals who assumed brick buildings would be too damp to live in during the hot summers of Tokyo, thereby forcing the project into early termination. The plan had disregarded the locals' opinion from the beginning so that most tenants who couldn't afford the rising price of houses in the district were eventually evicted. Yet, it is difficult to say that the original plan ultimately failed because, in the long run, Ginza Bricktown did settle down as a commercial district specializing in imported goods and developed into the most prominent commercial area in Tokyo.[182] What is more important is that Ginza Bricktown had originally been planned as a display case to attract the eyes of Westerners.[183] And because the exhibition was an enthusiastic attempt made by a few elite bureaucrats, it lost touch with reality. The brick buildings did receive praise among intellectuals for presenting a physical realization of civilization and enlightenment, but they were not enough to dispel the dominant belief that giyōfū architecture was no more than a signboard, an ostensible display to satisfy the interests of foreigners. In a reality where foreigners had extraterritoriality in Japan, the young elites' immature infatuation with the West could not avoid gazes of suspicion. Ginza Bricktown's construction in central Tokyo was the first and practically the last attempt to build according to the aesthetic principles of European cities.[184]

Concentrating Government Offices in Central Tokyo

After the Ginza Bricktown project of the 1870s did not turn out to be as successful as expected, contrasting proposals vied for the upper hand during the 1880s. The first to set foot into the arena was the proposal "Tokyo Central District Demarcation Issues" the Governor of Tokyo Matsuda Michiyuki submitted to the central government on November 2, 1880. Modeled after Paris, the center of nineteenth-century urban planning, Matsuda's proposal mainly focused on reconstructing central Tokyo. Its emphasis on economic growth by expanding major roads, regenerating central commercial areas, or building a new port was likely to appeal to the city's middle class. What particularly stood out in the proposal was the plan to lay a new road through a densely populated area and drive the slum full of old wooden buildings out of the city's center to make room for the construction of an upscale neighborhood. The proposal was, however, soon discarded. It failed to gain any support from politicians, and the administrative organ in charge of its execution had run out of funds.[185]

What the proposal had overlooked the most was the symbolic aspect necessary for an imperial city. The symbolic center of Tokyo was practically vacant during the early days of the Meiji period when the city's stature as a capital was unclear. After a fire completely destroyed the Nishinomaru section of Edo Castle, the Meiji government planned to use the site to build an imperial palace and government offices. However, not only did foreign consultants warn that the site was unsuitable for brick buildings, opinions varied on which architectural style the new imperial palace should exhibit. A compromise was eventually reached in which the imperial palace would be built in a traditionally Japanese style, while its annexes would adopt the giyōfū style. Completed in 1888, the imperial palace was composed of purely Japanese wooden constructs on the inside, while the wooden entrance displayed *wayoshiki*, a mixture of Japanese and Western styles, and a Western brick building was built for the Imperial Household Ministry.[186] Such stylistic choices were as much in flux as the circumstances at the time. While the palace's construction experienced delays, there were no buildings or thoroughfares at the regime's center worthy of symbolizing the empire. Something extraordinary was in order between the historical Edo Castle transformed into an imperial residence and the civilized Ginza commercial district.

Thus emerged a monumental plan that succeeded the cause for building Ginza Bricktown but overall far better fulfilled the center of the regime. Once again, Inoue Kaoru took the lead. As foreign minister at the time, Inoue had been devoting all his energy to revising unequal treaties with Western powers around May 1886 and felt the dire need for the imperial capital to appear dignified to foreign envoys. As opposed to Matsuda's overly practical plan, Inoue proposed in 1887 a plan to build a wide boulevard south of the imperial palace in central Hibiya and concentrate major government offices in the adjacent Kasumigaseki district. Such urban planning in the neo-Baroque style, new even for Europe at the time, was aimed at forging a dignified appearance for the Japanese imperial capital. With the Bakufu and its retainers gone, the empty sites surrounding the old Edo Castle were perfect for constructing public buildings. The government therefore sought to invent a new topological order for the imperial capital by adding to its center a monumental boulevard, public buildings including a parliamentary building, a park, and a central train station connecting the northern and southern parts of the city.[187]

In 1886, Inoue established and became head of a temporary architecture bureau under the cabinet's direct supervision. The bureau took charge of the project while it lasted, for four years until 1890. Hoping for a cluster of Western buildings that would blend in well with the Tokyo cityscape, the pro-German Inoue consulted the German Empire. With help from the likes of Aoki Shūzō, who served for years as a minister at the Japanese embassy in Berlin, Inoue was able to be officially introduced to the Berlin-based architectural firm Ende & Böckmann. The firm won second place in the competition for designing the Reichstag Building of the German Empire and had been participating actively in all sorts of public construction projects around the new German imperial capital. The firm's founding director, Wilhelm Böckmann, went to Japan in 1886 and spent several months there, and his partner Hermann Ende, visited the following year in 1887. James Hobrecht, a high-ranking bureaucrat who oversaw the project for Berlin's expansion, accompanied Ende to Japan and spent about a month and a half there to work on simplifying Ende & Böckmann's design. Such involvement of German architects and bureaucrats turned Berlin into a model for the invention of Tokyo.[188] Wilhelm Böckmann came to refer to his plan for Tokyo as "Forum Japanum."[189]

Around the time he visited Tokyo in late April 1886, Böckmann was a key figure among mainstream German architects as co-editor of the architecture journal *Deutsche Bauzeitung* who once served as the director of the Berlin Building Academy. Böckmann's work and position made him worthy of being considered an architectural successor of Prussian classicism. The Chinese-style buildings he designed for the Berlin Zoological Garden (Zoologischer Garten) demonstrated that Böckmann was

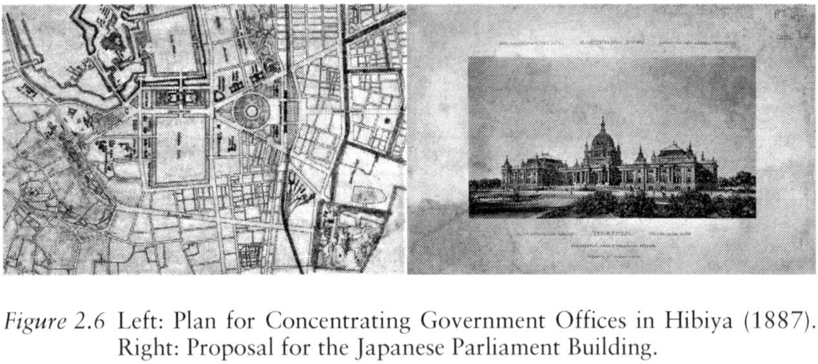

Figure 2.6 Left: Plan for Concentrating Government Offices in Hibiya (1887). Right: Proposal for the Japanese Parliament Building.

Source: Left: From Tsumaki Library. Right: From Tsumaki Library, *Architects Ende & Böckmann* 10/15. Courtesy of the Library of the Architectural Institute of Japan.

also capable of practicing historicist eclecticism.[190] The Japanese government decided to appoint him as the supreme architectural advisor for five years and officially commissioned him to design an entire complex of government buildings, including those for the National Diet, the Tokyo Court, the Ministry of Justice, and the National Police Agency. Once the Japanese government approved the project's blueprint he had submitted, Böckmann took the blueprint back to Berlin to add the final touches. When Hermann Ende brought the finished version to Japan in early May the following year, the blueprint appeared to take after the Ringstrasse in Vienna rather than Berlin filled with tenement houses.[191]

The blueprint showed a horizontal line extending from the Tsukiji district to the Kasumigaseki district, serving as a central axis. Taking the right end of the central Japan Avenue as the vertex, Emperor Avenue and Empress Avenue spread out to each form sides of a triangle that would be completed by the central train station. Government offices would unfold along the streets of the Kasumigaseki district to the left of Japan Avenue, and beyond the hill, Parliament Avenue would lead up to the National Diet building, then turn with a gradual curve onto Europe Avenue running eastward along the bottom of the blueprint. This layout must have been a realization of the Meiji government's imaginative geography for a new Japan. Japan, born out of the emperor and empress's union, was stepping out with a new state system to meet the enlightened world.[192]

At the core of this detailed initial plan was the building for the Japanese Imperial Diet. Given their experience in attempting to design a parliament building for Germany, Ende & Böckmann was considered the firm most eligible to design a building that may prove to be a national monument for Japan. The result was a 180-by-70-meter building with a sloped mansard roof surrounding a dignified crown-shaped dome at the center. The pairs of pillars along the façade accentuated a stark bilateral symmetry, which continued inside where an octahedral hall with a stairway would be flanked by wide corridors on either side. Much of this design was borrowed from the firm's 1872 design for the Reichstag building.[193] A brief report about the project in Japan along with its elevation published in issue no. 25 of *Deutsche Bauzeitung* in 1891 indicated that the building was to be mainly built with polished natural stone in the neo-Renaissance style and deemed it a satisfactory case of overseas activities by German architects.[194]

The plan, however, failed to gain final approval for lacking uniquely Japanese features. The architectural firm devised another plan in an eclectic style with a wooden roof based on its experience of designing Chinese-style buildings for the Berlin Zoological Garden, although this second plan also suffered rejection. In the end, Adolph Stegmüller, a partner at Ende & Böckmann who visited Japan with Ende in 1887, was charged with the building's design. The result was a more simplified version of the initial plan using a mixture of granite and bricks to cut costs.

On November 29, 1890, the Imperial Diet convened its opening session at the new building in the presence of the emperor himself. Unfortunately, about two months after its completion, the building was destroyed by an electrical fire in January 1891. The incident was even mentioned in *Deutsche Bauzeitung*.[195] It took another several decades until a proper parliament building was able to emerge.

Such an unexpected incident was not entirely to blame for the difficulties in realizing the concentration of government offices. The high cost and the idea of leaving the construction of the capital's heart in the hands of foreigners did not sit well with the Japanese ruling class. When Inoue resigned as Minister of Foreign Affairs for failing to revise Japan's unequal treaties, the plan to concentrate government offices met its demise. The new administration closed the temporary architecture bureau, drastically pared the plan down, and, as of March 1893, terminated all contracts the Japanese government had made with German architects.[196] It was a symbolic incident announcing an end to the Westernization Japan had continued to pursue since the Meiji Restoration.

Although Forum Japanum never materialized, the desire to build the new empire's heart persisted and continued to leave its traces around Tokyo over the long run. Some of Ende & Böckmann's original plan was realized along the streets of Kasumigaseki, namely the Tokyo Court and the Ministry of Justice. These buildings turned out to provide a new generation of Japanese architects with opportunities for growth. Tsumaki Yorinaka and Kawai Kōzō, respectively, participated in designing the Tokyo Court building and the Ministry of Justice building after studying in Berlin. Tsumaki went on to firmly establish himself as the top bureaucrat in terms of architecture in Japan.[197] Along with giving birth to a new generation of architects, the plan to concentrate government offices left another distinct institutional legacy. While the plan was under way, the Japanese Home Ministry and the Metropolitan Police Board took the lead in inviting Wilhelm Höhn from Germany to help Japan adopt the German police system, which later led to the adoption of German building regulations as well.[198]

The Tokyo City Improvement Ordinance

After experiencing gossip and turmoil from the very beginning, the far-fetched attempt to concentrate government offices was replaced with a much more practical alternative. In fact, the Tokyo City Improvement Ordinance enacted in 1888 had been in the making long before the plan to concentrate government offices. As soon as the Home Ministry was established in 1873, a city improvement committee was launched to research urban planning for Tokyo. The committee members, who included the economist Taguchi Ukichi, referred to as the "Adam Smith of Japan," used their expertise to prepare a plan to improve the capital city.[199] By 1876, even before Ginza Bricktown was completed, the Japanese Home Ministry finished creating a draft of the plan for *shiku kaisei*, or city improvement specifically aimed at improving the existing infrastructure of downtown Tokyo.[200]

The city improvement plan was less ambitious than the plan for Ginza Bricktown but had a far more practical goal. Although Ginza Bricktown proved a good chance to experience building modern infrastructure and improving roads, extending it to the entire city was impossible considering the cost as well as institutional and cultural aspects. Up until 1890, Tokyo had failed to regain the population it used to maintain in the 1850s before the days of the Edo Bakufu came to an end, eventually bringing the city's expansion to a standstill. Meiji Japan's plan therefore focused on projects that would directly revitalize the city, such as widening, straightening, and paving roads; improving water supply facilities; repairing bridges; and improving rivers. Modeled after Haussmann's reconstruction of Paris, the city improvement plan contained rudimentary components of urban planning and building codes that placed the city's commercial value ahead of decorating it as a grand and glorious capital.[201]

When the governor of Tokyo, Matsuda Michiyuki, who proposed a general plan to reconstruct Tokyo in 1880, suddenly passed away from an illness, his successor Yoshikawa Akimasa submitted a new draft of the city improvement plan to the central government in November 1884, which featured the sixteen-article Tokyo City Improvement Ordinance. The ordinance was, however, difficult to put into effect immediately in Japan's domestic political landscape. Ever since the concentration of government offices led by the Foreign Ministry was abandoned after creating a storm, various offices competed fiercely against one another to take charge of Tokyo's reconstruction until the Home Ministry managed to take the lead. After further complications, the bill for the Tokyo City Improvement Ordinance was at last presented to the Privy Council in March 1888 for a final review. However, another obstacle awaited. As head of the Privy Council, Itō Hirobumi opposed the bill for being overly pragmatic. Itō was a political ally of Inoue Kaoru who once led the concentration of government offices. Nevertheless, Home Minister Yamagata Aritomo and Finance Minister Matsukata Masayoshi, both political enemies of Itō, ignored the Privy Council's decision and gained approval for the bill through a cabinet meeting in August, which ultimately led to the ordinance's promulgation. Officially aimed at smoothing "urban administration involving commerce, public hygiene, fire prevention, and transportation in all municipalities," the Tokyo City Improvement Ordinance was Japan's first urban planning act that governed the spatial order of Tokyo for the next thirty or so years until the Urban Planning Law was formally established in 1919.[202]

In the 1880s, when the Tokyo City Improvement Ordinance was established, full-fledged change began to occur in the economy and urban structures across the Japanese archipelago. Top-down reform gave momentum to the economy and led to an actual increase in urban population. Administrative streamlining drastically cut back the number of prefectures and reshuffled local governments. The Land Tax Act established in 1873 launched a series of reforms that stripped daimyōs and samurai of their right to collect tax from their domains and established modern ownership of farmland, which in turn greatly helped vitalize urban economies. The railway network formed along the Japanese Pacific coastline also played a crucial role in urban growth during the late 1880s. Since opening a railway between Yokohama and Tokyo in 1872, building a railway network gained further impetus once the Iwakura Embassy returned from traveling by train throughout Europe and the United States. During the 1890s, Japan was equipped with a nationwide railway network homologous to its new administrative grid. The network built with British technology had military as well as economic purposes.[203] The Tokyo City Improvement Ordinance had therefore been devised to administer the imperial capital at a pace that would be able to match such rapid economic growth.

The initial plan to build and expand three hundred fifteen streets, improve canals, extend the main railway from the terminus Shinbashi to Ueno, build the Tokyo Station as well as countless bridges, forty-nine parks, eight markets, five crematoria, and six cemeteries nevertheless had to be scaled down due to a lack of funds. Tokyo still had no mayor with independent authority, nor did it have any dedicated civil servants or an office building.[204] The successive outbreak of the First Sino-Japanese War and the Russo-Japanese War also contributed to the untoward circumstances. Although the 1888 Tokyo City Improvement Ordinance failed to sufficiently achieve its goal, it was still significant for being Japan's first urban planning act and for being a comprehensive plan aimed at Tokyo's reconstruction. Despite being an extremely practical plan, the lengthy research and discussions involved in its formation infused the plan with aspirations to be grandiose, eternal, and monumental, all of which were part of Haussmann's reconstruction of Paris.[205] In that sense, the ordinance could be considered an extension of the plans for Ginza Bricktown or the concentration of government offices. The invention of Tokyo was no longer an exhibit in a display case but was truly heading toward the establishment of a new topology.

With the Tokyo City Improvement Ordinance's implementation, the Western features and layout Inoue Kaoru originally envisioned were realized to a certain degree through the Chiyoda district of central Tokyo. Of course, Inoue would have never allowed commercial buildings and practicality to predominate over government offices and authoritativeness. Nevertheless, that was the case, and the Marunouchi business district to the east of the imperial palace was a notable example. Since the Mitsubishi Ichigokan building was completed in the district in 1894, a series of Victorian neo-Gothic buildings appeared nearby so that Tokyo citizens came to refer to the street as the "one-block London." Despite having been delayed by a series of wars, the long-cherished desire to build a central train station in Tokyo was finally realized in the Marunouchi district by 1914. This was also when the commuter rail Yamanote Loop Line was constructed. Streetcars imported from the United States started to operate in Kyoto in 1895, and they also appeared in Tokyo in August 1903. The operation of streetcars brought a major change to the spatial structure of Tokyo. Arterial roads emerged to transform peripheral areas into suburbs of the city.[206]

The predominantly practical Tokyo City Improvement Ordinance inherited Inoue Kaoru's policy by designating the districts Hibiya and Kasumigaseki as sites for government offices.[207] However, several of the details specified in Inoue's original plan were placed on the back burner, one of them being the formation of parks. Most of the insufficient funds went into building Hibiya Park, which appeared in Tokyo as a miniature version of the Tiergarten in Berlin. The park was, however, the outcome of a precautionary measure to secure space between the imperial palace and the commercial Ginza district so that the palace would remain out of reach from any fires in the district.[208]

In the meantime, the imperial palace's construction was still an enigma. The main hall was completed in time for the promulgation of the constitution, but the palace itself remained incomplete. Once landscaping the immediate space outside the palace walls was finished in 1888, it was labeled the "Imperial Palace Outer Gardens," but Itō Hirobumi's policy forbade any structures from being installed in that space for a long time.[209] As time went by, the space was opened to the public as the "Imperial Palace Square,"[210] but the palace continued to be an unfinished project. It possessed dignity, or perhaps too much dignity, which prevented it from functioning as the vanishing point of Tokyo. Even before most of central Tokyo, including Ginza Bricktown, was destroyed in the Great Kantō earthquake of 1923, or perhaps even after the area was successfully restored from the earthquake, the center of Tokyo continued to be empty.

Another major aspect the Tokyo City Improvement Ordinance failed to cover was the regulation of buildings. The ordinance concentrated too much on expanding roads and creating waterways to build an infrastructure that it almost completely neglected building codes and regulations. The one who translated newly established German building codes into Japanese was Mori Ōgai, a surgeon and writer who was also a member of the Tokyo City Improvement Committee. Mori had studied public hygiene in Germany for four years at a time when the country was considered to have the most advanced urban planning system in Europe. His suggestion that building codes should be established for Tokyo was not accepted, but the German-style urban planning did turn out to have a long-term impact upon the city's spatial characteristics.[211]

Mori Ōgai wielded greater influence through his literary works than translations of legal codes. After returning from Germany in 1888, he published the novel *The Dancing Girl* in 1890, which contained a thorough portrayal of Berlin in the 1880s and thereby engraved the city's urbanity in the minds of the Japanese. In the work that became a best-seller and has since joined the ranks of classics in Japanese literature, the protagonist Ōta Toyotarō, a Japanese student on a government scholarship, arrives at Unter den Linden "in the middle of this most modern of European capitals" and is dazed by the Baroque space decorated with countless monuments. There were "groups of men and women sauntering along the pavements that line each side of that great thoroughfare as it runs, straight as a die, through the city" while "carriages ran silently on asphalt roads." The boulevard with "towering buildings" stretched beyond the Brandenburg Gate toward a victory column upon which a goddess seemed to be "floating halfway to heaven." Only after he passes "through that sea of lights" and suddenly turns into a "gloomy passage" does the protagonist Ōta come across the heroine Elise. The poor dancing girl Elise represented the dark side of the imperial capital Berlin. Unlike the grand, ostentatious Unter den Linden, the street Klosterstraße where the girl lived and fell in love with Ōta was kept under a mysterious veil in the story.[212]

> Opposite it stood some houses with the washing hanging out to dry on poles on the roofs, and a bar where an old Jew with long whiskers was standing idly by the door.[213]

The Dancing Girl allowed readers of Meiji Japan to understand Berlin not from the perspective of a visitor but that of a resident of the city. Berlin was no longer an unknown imaginary place but a harsh reality. The Japanese man who abandons his lover Elise is overwhelmed with sadness and despair in the story but at the same time alludes to the new stature of the Japanese Empire capable of treating a Western empire as it sees fit. This, however, also painted a self-portrait of the Japanese endlessly torn by diverging views at the heart of their empire and its capital. The protagonist Ōta experiences inevitable conflicts between the ideal and reality of Westernization as well as between his modern conscious and feudal subconscious self.

The admiration the Japanese had for the German spatio-temporal principle does not prove that Japan was the Asian Prussia. On the contrary, it proves there was a lack of historical identity. Efforts to invent the topology of modern Japan and turn Tokyo into a symbolic center kept ending in failure. Tokyo had no center in the strictest sense.[214] The imperial palace was too veiled to be the city's central landmark, and the Imperial Palace Square was too vast and empty to function as a central plaza. And the watchtower of Edo Castle, revealing glimpses of itself as it remained buried among trees, served as a reminder of that void.

5. Victoria or Wilhelm? Meiji-Era Public Buildings

The Japanese ruling class's determination to modernize was shown most obviously through Meiji-era public buildings. They must have been the most convincing way to realize a new spatio-temporal principle at the heart of the Japanese Empire. The success of this unprecedented attempt depended on cultivating Japanese experts by sending students to Europe and the United States to study architecture and urban planning or inviting experts from abroad referred to as "surveyors" to provide training in Japan. Surveyors were paid far more than their Japanese colleagues, but such preferential treatment proved to be temporary. The Japanese government's plan was to eventually replace them all with trained local experts, showing that the government had only been interested in acquiring what was necessary from Westerners.

Influence of the British Architect Josiah Conder

The civil engineering bureau established under the Japanese Ministry of Industry in 1870 invited various foreign experts in architecture, civil engineering, urban planning, and art. Among them were the architects Charles Alfred Chastel de Boinville from France, Giovanni Vincennzo Cappelletti from Italy, Richard Perkins Bridgens from the United States, and Josiah Conder from Britain. A young British architect with experience in the Gothic revival, Conder went to Japan in 1877 at the age of twenty-five and came to represent the early architectural lineage between Britain and Japan. The Iwakura Embassy's visit to Edinburgh and Glasgow in late 1872 eventually led to an invitation for Conder to come to Japan, where he was the first to be hired as professor of the Department of Architecture at the Imperial College of Engineering and went on to make a profound impact on modern Japanese architecture.[215] Among the many buildings he designed, the Rokumeikan, meaning Deer Cry Pavilion, was a banquet hall built in the style of an Italian villa where foreigners and the high-ranking Japanese used to socialize. The building was conspicuous enough to leave a strong impression among not only Japanese architects but the ruling class in Japan as well.[216]

Architects and civil engineers from the West contributed to the introduction of Western building techniques in Japan, which were impressive but not understood well enough. Japanese architects familiar with wooden buildings found Western-style buildings extraordinary but were unable to grasp the significance their form language carried. The giyōfū style's appearance served as proof of such a lack of understanding. Western architects, on the other hand, did not stick to a certain style once they set foot in Japan. Architectural style was a mere signboard and did not carry the same sociocultural value as it did in Europe. Most Western architects in Japan tended to freely employ decorative elements of Western architecture to accommodate a building's purpose.[217]

A typical example of this is the buildings Thomas J. Waters designed for Ginza Bricktown. Then again, Professor Conder's design for the office building Mitsubishi Ichigokan in the Marunouchi business district was by no means less eclectic. Constructed between 1892 and 1894, Mitsubishi Ichigokan was unusual red brick building with simple pilasters surrounding the entrance, window frames made of white stone, and random balconies that made it difficult to define stylistically. Yet the narrow, decorated dormer windows and ornaments along the ridge displayed features of Victorian architecture.[218] Far from being purely neoclassical, the building appeared to be closer to the "Queen Anne style." During in the 1870s and 1880s, this uniquely named style pursued neo-Baroque grandeur through long rows of windows, triangular gabled roofs at the center, quoining, and elevations modified to cater to existing streets, thereby distinguishing itself from the Victorian Gothic style that had previously dominated Britain for decades.[219] Unlike the buildings by Waters, those by Conder definitely set themselves apart from the treaty port style and drew landscapes from the British Empire into the heart of Tokyo. Nevertheless, it remained impossible to identify the nationality of the exceedingly eclectic sight Mitsubishi Ichigokan presented. This trend, of course, didn't last for long, as circumstances changed with the return of Japanese students who had gone to study in Europe and the United States.

Figure 2.7 Currently Restored Façade of Mitsubishi Ichigokan, 2009.

Source: Photo: Wish.F/CC BY (https://creativecommons.org/licenses/by/3.0).

British architects played a prominent role in isolation from political developments in Japan, but they did grow politically symbolic over time. This change was primarily caused by a scarring conflict Japan experienced with Germany, a country it once admired. In 1895, the Japanese became greatly disappointed in Germany. When the Japanese army won the First Sino-Japanese War and took over Port Arthur in Lushun, China, the German Empire joined forces with Russia and France in pressuring the Japanese army to immediately withdraw from the Liaodong Peninsula. The incident went down in history as the "Triple Intervention." It was an imperialistic move no doubt made to acquire more concessions from China and clearly demonstrated that Germany was willing to abandon Japan whenever necessary. The incident was enough for the fondness Japan had for Germany to turn into a sense of betrayal and prompted Japan to instead pursue an Anglo-Japanese Alliance.[220] Considering such political developments, it was natural for British influence to grow within the architectural realm of Japan.

Tatsuno Kingo, a Symbol of Modern Japanese Architecture

The year 1886 is a truly meaningful year in the history of modern Japanese architecture. According to the Imperial University Ordinance promulgated in March that year, the Imperial College of Engineering (Kōbu Daigakkō), founded in 1877, was absorbed by the newly established university as its College of Engineering. The following month, graduates of the Imperial College of Engineering founded a professional organization for engineers called the Building Institute and selected Tatsuno Kingo, a professor at the Imperial College of Engineering, to head the institute. At the suggestion of Itō Chūta, the institute replaced the word building (zōka) with architecture (kenchiku) in 1894 to add a more artistic, creative nuance to its name. Changing the institute's name to the Architectural Institute of Japan led to a name change from the Department of Building to the Department of Architecture for the Imperial University. By then, however, the term architecture was already in use in the monthly *Journal of Architecture*, published since 1887.[221]

As a pupil of Professor Conder at the Imperial College of Engineering, Tatsuno Kingo later went to study at the University of London and became a professor at his alma mater upon his return to Japan. When the college was absorbed by the Imperial University, he served as a professor at the university's College of Engineering. Tatsuno is thought to have been influenced by the Queen Anne style while studying at the University of London, where Josiah Conder's grand-uncle Thomas Roger Smith taught architecture. Conder, three years older than Tatsuno, spent two years working for the prominent neo-Gothic architect William Burges before heading to Japan and teaching at the Imperial College of Engineering, but he never turned into an exponent of the Gothic style like Burges.

Unlike his teacher Conder, Tatsuno mixed Burges's strand of Gothic with the neo-Baroque Queen Anne style and pursued a path that resembled neo-Palladianism. This allowed Tatsuno to keep up with the times as well as with late historicism in Europe.[222]

Tatsuno Kingo is regarded as the first modern architect of Japan. The College of Engineering building at the Imperial University's Hongō campus where he used to teach was one of his early works, built in 1888. The round towers on either side of the entrance and equilateral triangular gables were a combination of Gothic and neoclassicism that heavily suggested a neo-Gothic influence from Burges. The triple arched entrance and cubic shapes were typical neo-Palladian features that managed to form an adequate balance between disparate elements. The building strongly gave the impression of having been influenced by the time Tatsuno spent in London.[223]

Another representative work was the Bank of Japan's headquarters Tatsuno began designing in 1890. This public building, completed in 1896, had the largest committee of all the construction projects in Japan during the 1890s. Among the project's sponsors was Shibusawa Eiichi, the founder of the national Dai-Ichi Bank, regarded as a pioneer of Japanese

Figure 2.8 Top: College of Engineering Building at Tokyo Imperial University. Bottom Left: Bank of Japan (2014). Bottom Right: Courtyard of the Bank of Japan.

Source: Courtesy of the Library of the Architectural Institute of Japan. Top: From *Meiji-Taisho architectural photography collection* (1936), no.58. Bottom Left: Photo by author (2015). Bottom Right: Photo by author (2015).

capitalism. Tatsuno spent years abroad working on the building's design and is said to have received assistance from Burges's firm.[224] However, the Bank of Japan's headquarters went down in history as the first French-style neo-classical building in Japan. Separated from the street by a narrow moat, the building, primarily made of bricks and steel, was shaped overall like a square made by joining at right angles three three-story rectangular sections and one single-story section. On either end of the single-story section was a double-arched entrance, a small entrance paired with a visibly larger one side by side. Beyond the entrances was a courtyard and a classicist two-story portico with balustrades on the second floor. Installed behind these was an octagonal domed roof, the first of its kind on record for Japan, topped with a lantern and lucarnes.[225] The combination of several cubic shapes made the Bank of Japan headquarters seem similar to the Imperial University's College of Engineering building, but the bank building stood out more due to its refined proportions and balance. Whereas the elegant French-style neoclassicism running through the entire building symbolized the capitalist prosperity of modern Japan, the heavily neo-Baroque octagonal dome visualized the imperial authority that supported such prosperity. Most importantly, the building was the work of a Japanese architect.[226]

Tatsuno continued to create a unique style of his own. Rather than modifying the elevation to accommodate the existing street, the works of Tatsuno maintained the symmetrical façade of the original Queen Anne style, and, as can be witnessed through Tokyo Station, domes were placed on corners to make buildings stand out from the street.[227] As the first Japanese architect to master Western architecture and add his own stylistic touch, Tatsuno Kingo serves as testament that Japan had thoroughly embraced the complex aspect of Western historicist architecture and was especially influenced by British architecture.

At the turn of the century, thoroughly imitating Western architectural styles was established as a general trend in Japan. Many public buildings raised at the time commonly featured the basic form language of classical European architecture through Palladian porticos, delicate moldings, applied pilasters, and grandiose Baroque pediments.[228] Just as in Europe, architectural styles in modern Japan came to eagerly embody a spatio-temporal principle and play a major role in establishing a topological order. Of course, unlike the West, such architectural styles could not represent the collective memory or self-revival of a particular social class but only function as the tectonics of state power in Japan. This fundamental difference was responsible for the lack the Japanese somehow felt in British-style architecture. Instead of external grandiosity or delicacy in details, Imperial Japan was in dire need of an image revealing the Japanese spirit of an iron hand in a velvet glove in order to make its state ideology apparent. It was therefore inevitable for Prussian classicism and the neo-Renaissance style of north German cities like Berlin, Hamburg, and Bremen to form an axis of Tokyo's architectural realm because of the calmer and more solid impression they offered compared to the British Queen Anne style or the French Second Empire style.

The Pro-German Architect Tsumaki Yorinaka

Tsumaki Yorinaka was an architect in many ways at the opposite end of the architectural spectrum from Tatsuno Kingo. The relationship between the two architects not only represented a competition for superiority between the pro-British and pro-German factions in Japan but a subtle conflict between academia and government.[229] To be exact, though, the competition was not about architectural directions. Records indicate that Wilhelm Böckmann maintained a friendship with Josiah Conder during his stay in Japan and the distance between their views had not been substantial.[230] Conder and his Japanese pupils were pursuing an eclectic strand of late historicism, making it unnecessary for them to struggle to defend their choice of style. The problem was about power. Ever since Inoue Kaoru launched the plan to concentrate government offices, some within the Japanese central government strongly called for buildings and urban planning that embodied Prussian nationalism. This opened a channel for a group of pro-German architects like Tsumaki Yorinaka to climb the government ladder as bureaucrats involved in the architectural sector.

The Tokyo Court and the Ministry of Justice building designed by Ende & Böckmann were cases that reconciled a heavily Prussian image with practical functionality, displaying splendor as if to specifically justify the abandoned plan to concentrate government offices. The Tokyo Court generally leaned toward the neo-Renaissance style. At the center of the façade was an open loggia rising toward a huge dome in between a round, protruding tower on either side. Both the ground and upper level of the loggia were supported by three arches, which made Wilhelm Böckmann the first to feature this kind of loggia in Japan. The building was formed of four wings and two courtyards connected to each other with shorter connecting wings.[231] The construction of this grand and delicate building began in 1888, the year the German architect Richard Seel, working for Ende & Böckmann, came to Japan and was appointed as the project's supervisor. Seel's Japanese associate on the project happened to be Tsumaki Yorinaka, who had just returned to Japan from Berlin that same year. When the Japanese government fired all the architects invited from Germany in 1893, including Seel, the project was left solely in the hands of Tsumaki. The Tokyo Court was completed in 1896.[232]

The Ministry of Justice building constructed across the street from the imperial palace's south gate Sakuradamon marked an entry point into a government office district and served as the most obvious reminder of a discarded plan to concentrate government offices. Instead of natural stone, the building was made of granite and red bricks, distinctively

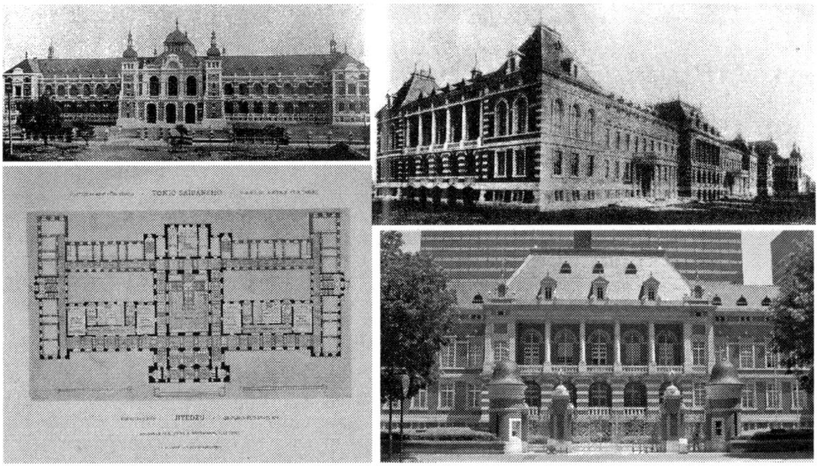

Figure 2.9 Top Left: The Tokyo Court. Bottom Left: Ground Plan for the Tokyo Court. Top Right: The Ministry of Justice. Bottom Right: The Central Avant-Corps of the Ministry of Justice.

Source: Courtesy of the Library of the Architectural Institute of Japan. Top Left: From *Meiji-Taisho Architectural Photography Collection* (1936), no.106. Bottom Left: From the Tsumaki Library, *Architects Ende & Böckmann* 7/15. Top Right: From *Meiji-Taisho Architectural Photography Collection* (1936), no. 102. Bottom Right: Photo by author (2015).

Meiji-era materials. Its modest pilasters, steep mansard roof, and protrusions at the façade's center, as well as the building's corners, were typical of a north German, neo-Renaissance architectural language. Yet the building was also full of highly original elements. Such elements included the markedly simplified Baroque-style dormers, the five bays dividing and neutralizing the façade excessively elongated for functional purposes, the two-and-a-half instead of three-story structure, E-shaped elevation, and the loggia with Tuscan-style columns perched above large arched pillars at ground level. Also considered out of the ordinary were the neoclassical, flat-roofed porticos at the entrance on either side of the façade's central protrusion; the additional loggias featured along the side wings; and the verandas that rarely appeared in north German neo-Renaissance buildings. Ende & Böckmann's design of the Japanese Ministry of Justice building revealed a historicist mix and match without relinquishing an overall sense of unity and stability. The building's construction was overseen by Richard Seel, who worked on the Tokyo Court, while a German architect named Oscar Tietze took the lead in actually running the construction project. Among the Japanese involved in the project was Kawai Kōzō.[233] Kawai was taught by Josiah Conder before going on to study in Berlin, and as a graduate student, he took part in the construction of the German Renaissance-style bridge Nijūbashi.[234]

The Tokyo Court and the Ministry of Justice were buildings in Tokyo that distinctly portrayed Prussian statism. German architecture carried significance for its implications rather than the impact it actually made. Although Prussian public buildings were dictated more by style than functionalism, their exclusion of extravagant motifs and unnecessary ornaments to present a rock-solid organic union between individual parts was perfect for illustrating the authoritativeness of an empire. In fact, brick masonry was one of the major techniques Japanese architects specifically acquired from Germany and later used to build the basic structure of Japanese government office buildings.[235]

Tsumaki Yorinaka was something of a leader among Japanese architects who studied in Berlin and came to establish a collective presence on Meiji Japan's architectural stage. He thereby played the role of defending the government's position against academics like Tatsuno Kingo. The ultimate goal behind such defense was to build monumental buildings based on brick masonry.[236] Tsumaki entered Josiah Conder's tutelage later than Tatsuno and then went to the United States to earn his bachelor's degree from Cornell University. When he returned to Japan in 1885, Tsumaki briefly worked for the Tokyo prefectural government before moving on to the temporary architecture bureau created by Inoue Kaoru, where he took part in the plan to concentrate government offices alongside Kawai Kōzō and Watanabe Yuzuru. With support from Ende & Böckmann, he was able to further his studies in Berlin, but by the time he returned to Japan in 1888, the plan to concentrate government offices had already been discarded and the Tokyo City Improvement Ordinance was established.[237]

From 1905, Tsumaki served as director of the Bureau of Public Works under the Ministry of the Treasury, which provided him with a perfect opportunity to realize his own architectural vision at the heart of Tokyo. The most notable among his designs involved the reconstruction of the historic bridge Nihonbashi, which literally means "Japan Bridge." Since the Edo period, the wooden bridge in a densely populated area served as a crucial control point for measuring the distance between the capital and any other location in Japan, despite having been repeatedly destroyed by fire and reconstructed. The Meiji period gave rise to a more acute need to smooth the traffic flow in and out of the heart of the capital. On April 3, 1911, a newly constructed stone bridge finally emerged on the anniversary of the death of Emperor Jimmu, who was considered the founder of Japan. The bridge, built with granite, had two gentle voussoir arches, pedestals to support sculptures, and decorative rails. It was only 48 meters long, but its width of 27 meters highly improved the bridge's usefulness in accommodating greater volumes of traffic. Placed on the pedestals were lavish candle-shaped bronze lamps and bronze sculptures of mythical creatures like qilins and lions personally designed by Tsumaki, signaling that the bridge was the symbolic center of the imperial

Figure 2.10 Left: Nihonbashi. Right: Tokyo Prefectural Government (1912–1926).

Source: Unknown author/Public Domain via Wikimedia Commons. Left: From a postcard image (1911). Right: From Mainich Newspapers Co., *Ichi oku nin no Shōwashi*, vol. 11 (1975). Unknown author/Public Domain via Wikimedia Commons.

capital. The gentle arches, the position of the sculptures, and the fact that it was a monumental stone bridge at the heart of the city made Nihonbashi in many ways similar to the Palace Bridge (Schloßbrücke) designed by Schinkel, which Tsumaki must have come across often during his time in Berlin.[238]

Whereas pro-German bureaucrats within the Japanese central government promoted architecture that dignified the state, Japanese architectural scholars represented by Tatsuno Kingo preferred a more open, practical approach to architecture.[239] Naturally, at least until the middle of the Meiji period, pro-German Japanese architects ended up playing an active role mainly in building government offices and infrastructure. A typical example of this was the Tokyo prefectural government building designed by Tsumaki and completed in 1894. The building with an intricate steeple featured a north German neo-Baroque style, and its horizontal emphasis could certainly be considered an influence of German architecture from Schinkel onward. Yet the elaborate pilasters and combination of individual cubic shapes indicative of neo-Palladianism and the overall façade's nearly neo-Renaissance look with gabled windows made it difficult to stylistically distinguish the Tokyo prefectural government building from the works of pro-British architects like Tatsuno Kingo.[240]

The German architect Heinrich Hübsch alluded to the flourishing of historicist architecture as an "architectural carnival,"[241] which also seemed apt for describing Japan at the turn of the century, even if only on the surface. Tokyo was, however, not Berlin. The one who may be able to offer a clue to discerning the significance Schinkel-inspired German historicist architecture carried for Japan would be Hermann Muthesius, the founder of the Deutscher Werkbund. As a young man, Muthesius once headed Ende & Böckmann's Tokyo branch office.[242] The Deutscher Werkbund's foundation is commonly known to have been prompted directly by the Arts and Crafts Movement Muthesius witnessed while working in London, but what caused the promising architect to distance himself from historicism dominant in Europe at the time must have been the far more exotic experience he went through in East Asia. What requires further examination would then be the fact that the experience Germans like Ende, Böckmann, or Muthesius went through in Japan had been quite different from the experience the Japanese like Itō Hirobumi or Tsumaki Yorinaka went through in Germany. While Germany had been focused on introducing and disseminating its national culture abroad, the Japanese inversely discovered their alter ego from cultures overseas. An alter ego tends to produce the effect of mistaking a nonexistent image of oneself for true and induces an obsession with that alter ego to sustain the illusion. In that sense, rather than being the result of a distinct ideological choice, the Japanese obsession over German culture can only be regarded as counterevidence of the rarely identified shame and emptiness the Japanese felt toward themselves.

Architecture as an Imperial Instrument and Icon

During the Meiji period, public buildings increasingly pursued pure neoclassicism, going as far as to imagine commonalities between Greek and Japanese architecture. How can such a retrogression be explained? When traces of historicist eclecticism, including the Queen Anne style, the Second Empire style, and Wilhelminism, were disappearing in Europe as they mutated into avant-garde architecture throughout the 1910s, why did the Japanese cling to neoclassicism in particular? Had they intended to create the Athens at Tokyo Bay by returning to the purity of Prussian classicism? That does not seem to be the case. Over the course of architectural history, the styles adopted by empires grew abstract and simpler during the early twentieth century transition from historicism to modernism, which consequently triggered a return to early neoclassicism.[243] In that sense, it would be possible to conclude that Japanese architects had faithfully kept up with the international trend. However, what is far more important than this historical context is that while Western-style buildings in Japan may have been conscious of the eyes of Westerners during the early years of the Meiji period, they certainly grew conscious of something else later on. Perhaps Japan adopted symbols of Western civilization with the eyes of its Asian neighbors in mind. In other words, it could have been part of efforts to establish its stature in Asia. The true intention behind the Japanese desire for pure neoclassicism later became apparent beyond doubt through Japanese colonial architecture.

Japan's assertive approach toward its Asian neighbors, however, was not rooted in self-confidence but was closer to a manifestation of derangement from placing too much faith in an uncertain subject.[244] The leaders of an empire claiming to be the center of East Asia were troubled by the fact that the very core of that empire remained incomplete. As political and fiscal circumstances even caused the imperial palace's construction to be delayed repeatedly, the only building capable of preserving Imperial Japan's dignity in front of foreign envoys was the palace of the crown prince called Tōgū-gosho. The construction of the building, which later came to be known as the Akasaka Detached Palace after the crown prince moved to a different residence, was initially funded by reparations from the First Sino-Japanese War until the Russo-Japanese War forced the project to be suspended. When it was finally completed in 1909, the building became Japan's first Western-style palace and represented the Meiji government's uncompromising policy of Westernization.

The architect who designed Tōgū-gosho was Katayama Tōkuma, who studied alongside Tatsuno Kingo under Josiah Conder. Records indicate that Katayama earned his doctoral degree in architecture from the Imperial University in Tokyo after Tatsuno. Known as an advocate of the French Second Empire style, Katayama modeled Tōgū-gosho, one of his final works, after the Palace of Versailles and the Louvre Palace to produce a thoroughly elegant neo-Baroque building with neoclassical elements such as columns and pediments. As implied by the name Akasaka, the building was made of bricks and covered with pinkish granite panels. The wings on either side of the central façade gracefully stretched forth like the arch of a bow, while a connecting wing divided the courtyard behind the façade into half. At the end of each front wing was an entrance crowned with a cupola featuring star-shaped ornaments.[245]

Katayama Tōkuma was as much a leader of modern Japanese architecture as Tatsuno Kingo. The Red Cross Central Hospital in Shibuya, Tokyo, was one of Katayama's early works, modeled after the Heidelberg University Hospital in Germany. Katayama also designed the Central Post and Telegraph Office, imperial museums in Nara and Kyoto, and finally the Hyōkeikan, a gallery of the Tokyo National Museum standing to the right of the museum's main building. His works mainly featured

Figure 2.11 Akasaka Palace.

Source: From *Meiji-Taisho Architectural Photography Collection* (1936), no.152. Courtesy of the Library of the Architectural Institute of Japan.

the French Second Empire style, which was starkly different from the German neo-Renaissance style. Katayama was a recognized master in the Japanese realm of architecture but was in fact part of a minority. Perhaps his works brought closure to an era instead of leading it, because after the Tōgū-gosho and Hyōkeikan were completed in 1909, his career as well as the era of Western classical architecture in Japan drew to an end.[246]

The curtain came down on public architecture of the Meiji period without being able to uncover a "national style" amidst pure neoclassicism, eclectic historicism, and other German and British styles.[247] At least in the architectural realm, Japan failed to realize the idea of national polity and create an iconic center for its empire. Nevertheless, a consensus on architectural style was formed to a certain extent. There was a primary motif that emerged across modern Japanese architecture regardless of whether the style was British, French, or German, which happened to be double-layered, ribbed domes. If red brick buildings were an icon of civilization and enlightenment, domes offered a far more powerful visual impression. There seemed to be no other architectural language more suited for displaying the dignity of an empire.

Domes and cupolas have always been symbols of power in Europe. In the Christian cultural sphere, they were a reminder of heaven since they prompted people to gaze up at an invisible vanishing point and let their spirits soar beyond life and death. Domes had the visual effect of suggesting continuity, transcendence, and powerfulness. A classic example would be the cathedral Berliner Dom, designed by Julius Carl Raschdorff and finished in 1900. The towering dome at the heart of Berlin spoke volumes about the German Empire riddled with social conflict. Rather than its original purpose, the building served more as an extension of the palace across the river Spree and sought to secure a slot that would prevent the city from being taken over by residential buildings. The Berliner Dom was the empire's reaction to an urban space's transformation into a citizen-centric space. It lived up to the emperor's intention to visually declare state power and exerted a tremendous impact upon the cityscape of Berlin.[248]

The Japanese seem to have precisely understood the symbolic value domes carried. The first dome in Japan appeared upon the Bank of Japan headquarters. The building's heavily German neo-Baroque octagonal dome appeared once again upon Tokyo Central Station. Originally referred to as the Central Station, this work by Tatsuno Kingo is the most well-known domed building in Japan. After the project was conceived in 1896, Tatsuno started working on the design from 1903 until the project was delayed by the First Sino-Japanese War and the Russo-Japanese War. Full-scale construction began in 1908, and the station was finally finished in December 1914.[249] As a long-held desire of Meiji Japan, the plan for its construction had already been drafted by Ende & Böckmann in 1887.[250] The three-story French-style neoclassical building that emerged decades later had a steel frame with red brick walls and a large neo-Baroque ribbed dome atop the left and right entrance. The domes were further highlighted by its distinctly French Baroque bull's-eye windows. Situated squarely across the imperial palace with the Marunouchi district lying in between, the station's central entrance was reserved for the royal family, while the entrances on the left and right side were open to the public.

There is much implied by the use of domes on a train station that would function as a base to propel modern industrialization. The Tokyo Central Station's construction was filled with the intent to centralize state power and make the empire's new technological prowess known at home and abroad. The significance of railways at the time was different from today. As can be noted from Karl Marx's famous words, "revolutions are the locomotives of history," locomotives or railways signified the progress of history and were the force that actually drove capitalism. The station's construction may have been delayed, but it kept pace with the

Figure 2.12 Top Left: Berlin Cathedral. Bottom: Tokyo Central Station. Top Right: Front of the Japanese National Diet.

Source: Courtesy of the Alt-Berlin-Archiv. Bottom: From *Meiji-Taisho Architectural Photography Collection* (1936), no.179. Courtesy of the Library of the Architectural Institute of Japan. Top Right: Photo by author (2015).

global trend. In Europe, plazas in front of train stations were surrounded by hotels, offices, and shops to form a hub of urban life, showing a contrast with former patterns of symbolic urban hubs usually formed around a church or city hall. Likewise, in Japan, railways and train stations created a new platform for modern technological achievements as well as the unprecedented circulation of people, commodities, and information, thereby settling down as bases for economic, political, and military expansion. In that sense, it would not be a stretch to regard the Tokyo Central Station as the cradle of Japan's colonization of East Asia.[251]

Domes were a means to manifest the power of the Japanese Empire and a motif widely used by modern Japanese architects, but no consensus was reached on other stylistic matters. Like the iconic center of its capital Tokyo, there was still no architectural style to characterize modern Japan. The lengthy controversy surrounding the Japanese Diet building's design was major proof of such a lack of consensus. After the rejection of the two blueprints submitted by Ende & Böckmann, the building was completed in 1890 based on Adolph Stegmüller's design, only to be destroyed by fire. By the time a proper Diet building could be reconstructed decades later, the architectural trend in Japan had changed significantly.

The wave of international modernist architecture had swept into Japan. The Japanese found the German and Viennese Secession movements that created geometric designs out of combinations of straight lines more to their taste than the curvy Art Nouveau. The first modernist architectural movement in Japan launched the *Bunriha kenchikukai*, or the Secessionist Architectural Group. The foreign term "secession" was established as a keyword signifying modernism in Japanese architecture between the late Meiji period and the early Taishō period.[252] The change in construction methods also affected the architectural trend in Japan. After the Great Kantō earthquake of 1923, the replacement of red bricks, the symbol of civilization and enlightenment during the Meiji period, with ferroconcrete brought about drastic change.[253] Moreover, the intervention of Western architects exerted considerable impact as well. Bruno Taut's argument drawing a direct connection between traditional Japanese and modernist architecture as well as Frank Lloyd Wright's organic prairie style, emphasizing horizontal lines from being inspired by Japanese architecture, provided opportunities for the Japanese architectural realm to break away from historicism.[254] Buildings designed by foreigners were referred to as "emerging architecture" at the time in Japan, and when architects in the Kansai region launched the International Architectural Association of Japan in 1927 in Kyoto, it caused a sensation by having ten renowned foreign architects, including Walter Gropius and Bruno Taut, join as members.[255]

Amid such innovative change, Forum Japanum cast its final spell. The Imperial Diet building's location was the same as where Ende & Böckmann had based its blueprint. A competition held in 1918 received entries twice before deciding on the final design. The winning design by Watanabe Fukuzo remained fairly faithful to the outline of Ende & Böckmann's earlier design, featuring a classic portico, a Jugendstil wing on either side, and a grand dome rising above the pediment of the colonnaded entrance. In addition, a pyramidal roof was introduced from the third-place entry's design by Takeichi Shinshichi. Construction did not, however, proceed smoothly. The temporary Diet building was destroyed by fire in 1925 while undergoing improvement, and other predicaments kept unfolding until a ceremony for the building's completion could finally be held in November 1936.[256]

The Japanese Diet building made of steel frame and ferroconcrete was officially proclaimed to be of an "early modern style," but the building was too eclectic to be pinned to a specific style. The pyramidal roof merged with a neoclassical framework made it challenging to clearly define the building's style. Its overbearing presence was reminiscent of buildings designed by the Nazi architect Albert Speer.[257] This would not be an overstatement considering the way Adolf Hitler's extremist propaganda about the "German tectonics" demonstrated that the basic characteristics of fascist aesthetics was a combination of modernism and neoclassicism and that excessive self-display always resulted in kitsch.[258] The abuse of empty form language bearing no connection to any distinct memories of the past certainly made the Diet building an icon of modern Japan's split identity. After all, apart from the concealed imperial palace, it was the most central building among those that represented the imperial capital. At the heart of the empire, the solemn principle of national polity that was supposed to ensure the empire's unified identity had somehow fallen to the state of a caricature of Prussian tectonics.

Notes

1. David Irwin, *Neoclassicism* (London: Phaidon, 1997), 297–358; Bak Sun-kwan, *Tongnama kŏnch'ungmunhwa sanch'aek* (Seoul: Han'guk'aksulchŏngbo, 2013), 207–209.
2. Stanford Anderson, "Schinkel, Behrens, an Elemental Tectonic, and a New Classicism," in *Karl Friedrich Schinkel: Aspekte seines Werkes*, ed. Susan M. Peik (Fellbach: Edition Axel Menges, 2001), 116–117; Wolfgang Pehnt, "Schinkel after Schinkel: Heirs of the Prussian Master Architect," in *Karl Friedrich Schinkel: The Drama of Architecture*, ed. John Zukowsky (Chicago, IL: Art Institute of Chicago, 1994), 134.
3. Dirk van Laak, *Über alles in der Welt: Deutscher Imperialismus im 19. und 20. Jahrhundert* (Munich: C. H. Beck, 2005), 10; Hartmut Pogge von Strandmann, "The Purpose of German Colonialism, or the Long Shadow of Bismarck's Colonial Policy," in *German Colonialism: Race, The Holocaust, and Postwar Germany*, ed. Volker Langbehn and Mohammad Salama (New York, NY: Columbia University Press, 2011), 200–202; Sebastian Conrad, *Deusche Kolonialgeschichte* (Munich: C. H. Beck, 2012), 18, 23.
4. Horst Gründer, *Geschichte der deutschen Kolonien* (Stuttgart: UTB, 2004), 55 ff.

5. Russel A. Berman, "Der ewige Zweite Deutschlands Sekundärkolonialismus," in *Phantasiereiche: Zur Kulturgeschichte des deutschen Kolonialismus*, ed. Birthe Kundrus (Frankfurt am Main: Campus, 2003), 23–24.
6. For a discussion of German colonialism, see, notably, Michael Perraudin and Jürgen Zimmerer, eds., *German Colonialism and National Identity* (New York, NY: Routledge, 2010); Sara Friedrichsmeyer, Sara Lennox, and Susanne Zantop, eds., *The Imperialist Imagination: German Colonialism and Its Legacy* (Ann Arbor, MI: The University of Michigan Press, 1998).
7. Birthe Kundrus, "German Colonialism: Some Reflections on Reassessments, Specificities, and Constellations," in *German Colonialism*, ed. Langbehn and Salama, 34.
8. Edward Said distinguishes between imperialism and colonialism, with the former referring to the ideological dimension and the latter referring to its practical execution. See Edward Said, *Culture and Imperialism* (New York, NY: Vintage Books, 1994), 8. Contrary to Saidian dichotomy, both of them can be viewed as a part of contradictory practices. On this point, see Robert C. J. Young, *Postcolonialism: An Historical Introduction* (Hoboken, NJ: Willey-Blackwell, 2016), 15–24. For further details on various implications of colonialism, see Jürgen Osterhammel, *Colonialism: A Theoretical Overview* (Princeton, NJ: Markus Wiener, 2009).
9. David Blackbourn, "Das Kaiserreich transnational: Eine Skizze," in *Das Kaiserreich transnational: Deutschland in der Welt 1871–1914*, ed. Sebastian Conrad and Jürgen Osterhammel (Göttingen: Vandenhoeck & Ruprecht, 2006), 323.
10. Dirk van Laak, *Über alles in der Welt*, 15–23.
11. Ariane Isabelle Komeda, "Kolonialarchitektur als Gegenstand transkultureller Forschung: Das Beispiel der deutschen Bauten in Namibia," in *Kulturerbe und Denkmalpflege transkulturel: Grenzgaenge zwischen Theorie und Praxis*, ed. Michael Falser and Monica Juneja (Bielefeld: Transcript, 2013), 119–137; George Steinmetz, *The Devil's Handwriting: Postcoloniality and the German Colonial State in Qingdao, Samoa, and Southwest Africa* (Chicago, IL: University of Chicago Press, 2007).
12. Suzanne L. Marchand, *German Orientalism in the Age of Empire: Religion, Race, and Scholarship* (Cambridge: Cambridge University Press, 2009), 334–336.
13. Gerhild Komander, "China in Sanssouci? Die Chinamode in friderizianischer Zeit und deren Rezeption durch Friedrich II," web site, www.gerhildkomander.de/kuenste/134-brandenburg-chinamode.html (accessed January 15, 2020); Marchand, *German Orientalism*, 367–377.
14. Jork Artelt, "Die Befestigungsanlagen Tsingtau und deren Bewaehrung im Ersten Weltkrieg," in *Tsingtau: Ein Kapitel deutscher Kolonialgeschichte in China 1897–1914*, ed. Hans-Martin Hinz and Christoph Lind (Neu-Isenburg: Edition Minerva, 1999), 62–63; Kim Chun-sik, "Togilchegukkwa pada: Togirŭi tongashia haeyangjŏngch'aekkwa shingminji kŏnsŏlgyehoekŭl chungshimŭro," *Daegusahak* 91 (2005): 157–187. For further details on the current state of research, see Bernd Martin, "Gouvernement Jiaozhou: Forschungsstand and Archivebestände zum deutschen Pachtgebiet Qingdao (Tsingtau) 1897–1914," in *Deutschland und China: Beiträge des Zweiten Internationalen Symposiums zur Geschichte der Deutsch-Chinesischen Beziehungen*, ed. Kuo Heng-yü and Mechthild Leutner (Munich: Minerva-Publikation, 1994), 375–398.
15. Heiko Herold, *Deutsche Kolonial- und Wirtschaftspolitik in China 1840 bis 1914: Unter besonderer Berücksichtigung der Marinekolonie Kiautschou* (Cologne: Ozeanverlag Herold, 2006), 21–25.

16. Jürgen Osterhammel, "Forschungsreise und Kolonialprogramm. Ferdinand von Richthofen und die Erschließung Chinas im 19. Jahrhundert," *Archiv für Kulturgeschichte* 69 (1987): 172.
17. Wolfgang J. Mommsen, *Großmachtstellung und Weltpolitik 1870–1914: Die Außenpolitik des Deutschen Reiches* (Berlin: Ullstein, 1993), 107 ff.; Herold, *Deutsche Kolonial- und Wirtschaftspolitik*, 26–28; Conrad, *Deutsche Kolonialgeschichte*, 33–34; Chŏng Sang-su, "Togilchegukchuŭiwa kyojuman chŏmnyŏng 1897/98nyŏn," *Yŏksahakpo* 194 (2007): 327–362.
18. Mechthild S. Leutner and Klaus Mühlhahn, "Interkulturelle Handlungsmuster: Deutsche Wirtschaft und Mission in China in der Spätphase des Imperialismus," in *Deutsch-chinesische Beziehungen im 19. Jahrhundert: Mission und Wirtschaft in interkultureller Perspektive*, ed. Leutner and Mühlhahn (Münster: LIT Verlag, 2001), 9–42.
19. Kim Hyŏng-ryŏl, "Togirŭi ch'ingdao kyŏngnyakkwa shingmin'gongganŭi hwakchang (1898–1914)," *Chungguksayŏn'gu* 70 (2011): 266–268; Gründer, *Geschichte der deutschen Kolonien*, 228–231.
20. Gisela Graichen and Horst Gründer, *Deutsche Kolonien: Traum und Trauma* (Berlin: Ullstein, 2005), 212.
21. Kim Hyŏng-ryŏl, "Sandong kŭndae toshiŭi sŏgumunhwa suyonggwa kyoyuk'wan'gyŏng: Ch'ingdao, chinan esŏŭi munhwashingminjuŭi sŏnggyŏkŭl chungshimŭro," in *Tongashia kyoryuwa munhwabyŏnyong: Sahoe-munhwa-pŏnyŏkŭro pon tongashia kŭndaesang*, ed. Dong-Eui Taehakkyo Inmunsahoeyŏn'guso (Seoul: Pangmunsa, 2013), 147–148, 153–161, 169–173; Kim Chun-sik, "Togilchegugŭi chungguk kyojuman shingminji munhwajŏngch'aek 1898–1914" *Yŏksahakyŏn'gu* 32 (2008): 379–407; Gründer, *Geschichte der deutschen Kolonien*, 232–235.
22. Maurice Amutabi, "Buildings As Symbols and Metaphors of Colonial Hegemony: Interrogating Colonial Buildings and Architecture in Kenya's Urban Spaces," in *Colonial Architecture and Urbanism in Africa: Intertwined and Contested Histories*, ed. Fassil Demissie (Aldershot: Ashgate, 2012), 325–346.
23. Jonathan Schneer, *London 1900: The Imperial Metropolis* (New Haven, CT: Yale University Press, 1999); Felix Driver and David Gilbert, "Imperial Cities: Overlapping Territories, Intertwined Histories," in *Imperial Cities: Landscape, Display and Identity*, ed. Felix Driver and David Gilbert (Manchester: Manchester University Press, 1999), 1–17.
24. Mark Crinson, *Empire Building: Orientalism & Victorian Architecture* (New York, NY: Routledge, 1996), 114–120, 167–168, 267. Conversely, Brenda Yeoh, *Contesting Space in Colonial Singapore: Power Relations and the Urban Built Environment* (Singapore: Singapore University Press, 2003), provides a case study of the British colonial cities from the perspective of indigenous people.
25. Andreas Volwahsen, *Imperial Delhi: The British Capital of the Indian Empire* (Munich: Prestel, 2002), 22–28; Robert Grant Irving, *Indian Summer: Lutyens, Baker, and Imperial Delhi* (New Haven, CT: Yale University Press, 1981), 17 ff.
26. Gwendolyn Wright, "Tradition in the Service of Modernity: Architecture and Urbanism in French Colonial Policy, 1900–1930," in *Tensions of Empire: Colonial Cultures in a Bourgeois World*, ed. Frederick Cooper and Ann Laura Stoler (Berkeley, CA: University of California, 1997), 328 ff.
27. Song Do-yŏng, "Sangjinggongganŭi chŏngch'i: P'ŭrangsŭŭi pugap'ŭrik'a shingmin toshijŏngch'aek," *Han'gungmunhwaillyuhak* 35, no. 2 (2002): 127–155; Song Do-yŏng, "Tamunhwajŏk kwanjŏmesŏ pon chijunghae isŭllam toshi: Morok'o p'esŭŭi saryeyŏn'gu," *Chijunghaejiyŏkyŏn'gu* 10,

no. 4 (2008): 59–83; Hassan Radoine, "French Territoriality and Urbanism: General Lyautey and Architect Prost Morocco (1912–1925)," in *Colonial Architecture and Urbanism*, 11–31.

28. Wright, "Tradition in the Service of Modernity," 325–326.
29. Jean-Louis Cohen and Monique Eleb, *Casablanca: Colonial Myths and Architectural Ventures* (New York, NY: The Monacelli Press, 2002), 12–13, 51–119.
30. Wright, "Tradition in the Service of Modernity," 330.
31. U Sin-ku, "Shingminshidae hanoiŭi chegukchuŭijŏk kyŏnggwan: Toshi karogujowa kinyŏmbijŏk kŏnch'ukŭl chungshimŭro," *Taehan'gŏnch'uk'ak'oenonmunjip kyehoekkye* 24, no. 2 (2008): 175–184.
32. Wright, "Tradition in the Service of Modernity," 334–335; U Tong-sŏn, "Hanoiesŏ kŭndaejŏk toshi shisŏrŭi kiwŏn," *Taehan'gŏnch'uk'ak'oenonmunjip kyehoekkye* 23, no. 4 (2007): 154.
33. Cohen and Eleb, *Casablanca*, 96.
34. "Die Stadterweiterung von Straßburg," *Deutsche Bauzeitung* 12, no. 68 (1878): 343–347, esp. 346; "Die Stadt-Erweiterung von Straßburg," *Deutsche Bauzeitung* 12, no. 80 (1878): 411. On Strasbourg (Straßburg), a border city of the German Empire, see, notably, Jefferies, *Imperial Culture in Germany*, 79–80.
35. Johann Wolfgang von Goethe, "Von deutscher Baukunst," in Volume 12 of *Goethes Werke: Schriften zur Kunst, Schriften zur Literatur, Maximen und Reflexionen* (1772; Munich: C. H. Beck, 2005), 14, 12.
36. Winfried Speitkamp, *Deutsche Kolonialgeschichte* (Ditzingen: Reclam, 2005), 119.
37. Bak Sun-kwan, *Tongnama Kŏnch'ungmunhwa Sanch'aek* (Seoul: Han'guk' aksulchŏngbo, 2013), 218.
38. Paek Chi-un, "Shingminjiŭi kiŏk, kŭ chaeyŏngt'ohwarŭl wihayŏ: Chonsŭt'ŏn pyŏlchangŭl t'onghae pon tongashia chogye net'ŭwŏk'ŭ," *Chungguk' yŏndaemunhak* 42 (2007): 220–224. On Waitan, the waterfront thoroughfare unique to East Asian port cities, see Kim Chu-kwan, "Kaehangdoshi kongganŭi chŏnhyŏng, oet'an," in *Chungguk kaehangdoshirŭl kŏtta: Sot'onggwa ch'ungdorŭi konggan, kwangjuesŏ sanghaekkaji*, ed. Kim Nŭng-gu et al. (Seoul: Hyŏnamsa, 2013), 27–43; Leo Ou-fan Lee, *Shanghai Modern: The Flowering of a New Urban Culture in China, 1930–1945* (Cambridge, MA: Harvard University Press, 1999), 7–13.
39. Pouyan Shekarloo, *Musterkolonie Kiatschou: The Expansion of the German Empire into China* (Munich: Grin Verlag, 2013); Klaus Mühlhahn, *Herrschaft und Widerstand in der "Musterkolonie" Kiautschou: Interaktionen zwischen China und Deutschland, 1897–1914* (Munich: R. Oldenbourg, 2000).
40. Kim Chun-sik, "Chegukchuŭi konggan'gwa yunghap: Togilchegugŭi chunggukshingminji toshigŏnsŏlgyehoekkwa kŏnch'ukŭl chungshimŭro," in *Kwahakkisulgwa kongganŭi yunghap*, ed. Yim Kyŏng-sun and Kim Chunsik (Seoul: Han'guk'aksulchŏngbo, 2010), 238–239; Mechthild Leutner and Klaus Mühlhahn, eds, *"Musterkolonie Kiautschou": Die Expansion des Deutschen Reiches in China. Deutsch-chinesische Beziehungen 1897–1914, Eine Quellensammlung* (Berlin: Akademie Verlag, 1997), 176.
41. Gert Kaster, "'Image-Pflege' Geschichte und lokale Aneignung von deutschem Architekturerbe in Qingdao, China," in *Kulturerbe und Denkmalpflege transkulturell: Grenzgänge zwischen Theorie und Praxis*, ed. Michael Falser and Monica Juneja (Bielefeld: Transcript, 2013), 168–169.
42. Torsten Warner, "Der Aufbau der Kolonialstadt Tsingtau: Landordnung, Stadtplanung und Entwicklung," in *Tsingtau: Ein Kapitel deutscher*

Kolonialgeschichte in China 1897–1914, ed. Hans-Martin Hinz and Christoph Lind (Berlin: Deutsches Historisches Museum, 1998), 84–86; Kim, "Chegukchuŭi konggan'gwa yunghap," 241–242; Yi Han-sŏk et al., "Hanggudoshi ch'ingdaoŭi shingminji shidae toshi pyŏnch'ŏn'gwa kŭndae kŏnch'ung hyŏngsŏnge kwanhan yŏn'gu," *Han'guk'anghaehangmanhak'oeji* 34, no. 5 (2010): 357–358; Kim Hyŏng-ryŏl, "Sandong kŭndae toshiŭi sŏgumunhwa suyonggwa kyoyuk'wan'gyŏng," 169–171.

43. Kim Chun-sik, "Chegukchuŭi konggan'gwa Injongjuŭi: Togilchegugŭi injongwisaenggwa shingminji kyojumanŭi injongjŏngch'aekŭl chungshimŭro," *Yŏksawa munhwa* 23 (2012): 113–137; Speitkamp, *Deutsche Kolonialgeschichte*, 109; Kundrus, "German Colonialism," 31–32.
44. Kim, "Chegukchuŭi konggan'gwa yunghap," 249–250; Paek, "Shingminjiŭi kiŏk, kŭ chaeyŏngt'ohwarŭl wihayŏ," *Chungguk'yŏndaemunhak*, 232; Kim Hyŏng-ryŏl, "Sandong kŭndae toshiŭi sŏgumunhwa suyonggwa kyoyuk'wan'gyŏng," 169–173; Kaster, "'Image-Pflege' Geschichte und lokale Aneignung," 167–180; Wang Hŭm, "Togil chŏmnyŏng shigi palchŏndoen chungguk ch'ingdao kŏnch'uge kwanhan yŏn'gu," *Taehan'gŏnch'uk'ak'oe haksulbalp'yodaehoe nonmunjip* 33 no. 1 (2013): 129–130; Winfried Speitkamp, *Deutsche Kolonialgeschichte*, 119.
45. Torsten Warner, *Deutsche Architektur in China: Architekturtransfer* (Berlin: Ernst & Sohn, 1994), 210–212.
46. Ibid., 206–208.
47. Ibid., 244–246, 288; Paek, "Shingminjiŭi kiŏk," *Chungguk'yŏndaemunhak*, 229–232; Kim Chŏng-tong, "Ashiaŭi chakŭn togil, ch'ŏngdo(ch'ingdao) esŏ kŏnch'ukka rot'ŭk'egerŭi kŏnch'ukŭl ch'annŭnda," *Kŏnch'uk* 45, no. 7 (2001): 59–62.
48. Warner, *Deutsche Architektur in China*, 214–216, 222, 248; Kim, "Sandong," 172–173.
49. On this point, see Kim Hyŏng-ryŏl, "Kŭndae sandongŭi toshigŏnsŏl yuhyŏnggwa sahoegaltŭng kujo: Ch'ingdaowa chinanŭi toshi kŭndaehwarŭl chungshimŭro," in *Toshihwawa sahoegaltŭngŭi yŏksa*, ed. Kim T'ae-sŭng et al. (Seoul: Shimsan, 2011), 135–186.
50. Mechthild Leutner, "Kiautschou: Deutsche 'Musterkolonie' in China?," in "*. . . Macht und Anteil an der Weltherrschaft": Berlin und der deutsche Kolonialismus*, ed. Ulrich van der Heyden and Joachim Zeller (Münster: Unrast, 2005), 206.
51. On Qingdao under Japanese rule, see Kim, "Sandong," 173–178.
52. Paek, "Shingminjiŭi kiŏk," *Chungguk'yŏndaemunhak*, 231.
53. Dirk van Laak, "Kolonien als 'Laboratorien der Moderne'?" in *Das Kaiserreich transnational*, 257–279; An Yŏng-chin, "Togil kongganjŏngch'aegŭi pyŏnhwagwajŏnggwa inyŏmsange kwanhan yŏn'gu," *Chirihakyŏn'gu* 33, no. 2 (1999): 121–136.
54. Kenneth B. Pyle, "Meiji Conservatism," in Volume 5 of *The Cambridge History of Japan: The Nineteenth Century*, ed. Marius B. Jansen et al. (Cambridge: Cambridge University Press, 1989), 704–710; Wolfgang Schwentker, "Fremde Gelehrte. Japanische Nationalökonomen und Sozialreformer im Kaiserreich," in *Intellektuelle im deutschen Kaiserreich*, ed. Gangolf Hübinger and Wolfgang J. Mommsen (Frankfurt am Main: Fischer, 1993), 172–197.
55. Erik Grimmer-Solem, "German Social Science, Meiji Conservatism, and the Peculiarities of Japanese History," *Journal of World History* 16, no. 2 (2005): 187–222.
56. Hirakawa Sukehiro, "Japan's Turn to the West," in *The Cambridge History of Japan*, 432–498.

57. Tetsuo Najita and H. D. Harootunian, "Japanese Revolt Against the West: Political and Cultural Criticism in the Twentieth Century," in Volume 6 of *The Cambridge History of Japan: The Twentieth Century*, ed. Peter Duus (Cambridge: Cambridge University Press, 1989), 711–774; Minamoto Ryoen, "The Symposium on Overcoming Modernity," in *The Rude Awakening: Zen, the Kyoto School, and the Question of Nationalism*, ed. James W. Heisig and C. Marajdo (Honolulu: University of Hawai'i Press, 1995), 197–229.
58. Henry D. Smith II, "Tokyo As an Idea: An Exploration of Japanese Urban Thought Until 1945," *Journal of Japanese Studies* 4, no. 1 (1978): 60–61.
59. Fujimori Terunobu, Volume 1 of *Nihon no kindai kenchiku: Bakumatsu-Meijihen* (Tokyo: Iwanami shinsho, 2010), 206 ff.; David B. Stewart, *The Making of a Modern Japanese Architecture: 1868 to the Present* (Tokyo: Kodansha International, 1987), 90 ff.
60. Tanaka Akira, *Meijiyushin'gwa sŏyang munmyŏng: Iwak'ura sajŏltanŭn muŏsŭl poannŭn'ga*, trans. (from Japanese into Korean) Hyŏn Myŏng-ch'ŏl (Seoul: Somyŏngch'ulp'an, 2006), 18–19; Ch'oe Yŏn-sik and Yi P'il-yŏng, "Iwak'ura sajŏltani pon sŏyang: Mobanggwa sŭp'ap," *Tongsŏyŏn'gu* 25, no. 2 (2013): 35–63. For further details, see Nishikawa Nagao and Matsumiya Shūji, eds., *Bei-Ō kairan jikki o yomu: 1870 nendai no sekai to Nippon* (Kyoto: Hōritsubunkasha, 1995).
61. Haga Toru, *Myŏngch'iyushin'gwa ilbonin*, trans. (from Japanese into Korean) Son Sun-ok (Seoul: Yeha, 1989), 20 ff., 146 ff.; Inoue Katsuo, *Mangmal yushin*, trans. (from Japanese into Korean) Yi Wŏn-u (Seoul: Ŏmunhaksa, 2013), 14–21, 103–115; Ian Buruma, *Inventing Japan 1853–1964* (New York, NY: Modern Library, 2003), 9–62.
62. Yukichi Fukuzawa, *An Outline of a Theory of Civilization*, trans. David A. Dilworth and G. Cameron Hurst III (New York, NY: Columbia University Press, 2008), 48, 59, 256–257.
63. Kazuhiro Takii, *The Meiji Constitution: The Japanese Experience of the West and the Shaping of the Modern State* (Tokyo: International House of Japan, 2007), 1–48; Sŏng Hŭi-yŏp, "Iwak'ura sajŏltanŭi kukkagusang yŏn'gu: Miguhoeramshilgie nat'anan kukkagusangŭl chungshimŭro," *Kukchejiyŏk'angnonch'ong* 4, no. 1 (2011): 23–47.
64. Kunitake Kume, *The Iwakura Embassy, 1871–73: A True Account of the Ambassador Extraordinary & Plenipotentiary's Journey of Observation Through the United States of America and Europe*, ed. Graham Healey and Chūshichi Tsuzuki, 5 vols. (Chiba: Japan Documents, 2002).
65. Akira, *Meijiyushin'gwa sŏyang munmyŏng*, 75–80, 170–192; Fukuzawa, *An Outline of a Theory of Civilization*, 17.
66. Michel Foucault, *The Archeology of Knowledge and The Discourse on Language* (New York, NY: Barnes & Noble Books, 1993), 31 ff., 47–48.
67. This sort of discourse analysis is closely related to "historical semantics." For a methodological discussion of this field, see Reingard Eßer, "Historische Semantik," in *Kompass der Geschichtswissenschaft*, ed. J. Eibach and G. Lottes (Göttingen: Vandenhoeck & Ruprecht, 2002), 281–292; Dietrich Busse, *Historische Semantik: Analyse eines Programms* (Stuttgart: Klett-Cotta, 1987); Na In-ho, *Kaenyŏmsaran muŏshin'ga: Yŏksawa ŏnŏŭi saeroun mannam* (Seoul: Yŏksabip'yŏngsa, 2011), 27–67.
68. Kume, *The Iwakura Embassy*, vol. 3, trans. Andrew Cobbing (Chiba: Japan Documents, 2002), 324.
69. Josef Kreiner, *Deutsche Spaziergänge in Tokyo* (Munich: Iudicium, 1996), 71–74.
70. Ulrich Wattemberg, "Germany," in *The Iwakura Mission in America and Europe: A New Assessment*, ed. Ian Nish (Richmond, VA: Japan Library,

1998), 74. The report in *Kölnische Volkszeitung* was published on March 7, 1873, and the *Neue Preussische Zeitung* published reports on March 11 and 26 of the same year. The dinner was also mentioned in articles of other newspapers, such as *Vossische Zeitung* and *Spenersche Zeitung*.

71. Josef Kreiner, *Deutsche Spaziergänge in Tokyo* (Munich: Iudicium, 1996), 71–74. Bismarck's dinner with the Iwakura Embassy can be verified from reports in the German press, but the speech he made for the occasion has only been documented in Japanese records. The speech was later included in Volume 8 of *Bismarck: Collected Works* (Die gesammelten Werke von Otto von Bismarck), which was only possible because Itō Hirobumi, a former member of the embassy, stated that there were Japanese notes of the speech during his visit to Berlin in 1901 as the Japanese Prime Minister. For further details, see Ulrich Wattemberg, "Germany," 76.
72. Kume, *The Iwakura Embassy*, vol. 3, 277–278.
73. Ibid., 296–304, quoted from 302.
74. Philipp Sarasin, *Geschichtswissenschaft und Diskursanalyse* (Frankfurt am Main: Suhrkamp, 2003), 10–60; Luise Schorn-Schütte, "Neue Geistesgeschichte," *Kompass der Geschichtswissenschaft*, ed. Joachim Eibach and Günther Lottes (Stuttgart: UTB, 2011), 270–280.
75. On the Lacanian concept of "gaze (le regard)," see Jacques Lacan, *The Four Fundamental Concepts of Psycho-Analysis*, trans. Alan Sheridan (New York, NY: WW Norton & Co., 1998), 72 ff.
76. Kume, *The Iwakura Embassy*, vol. 3, 291–292.
77. On the Iwakura Embassy's particular interest in Germany, see, notably, Pang Kwang-sŏk, "Meiji kwallyoŭi 'munmyŏng' inshik: Iwak'ura sajŏltanŭi chaejomyŏng," in *Tongashia yŏksa sogŭi yŏhaeng 2: Net'ŭwŏk'ŭ, chŏngch'esŏng*, ed. Yim Sŏng-mo et al. (Seoul: Sanch'ŏrŏm, 2008), 359–360.
78. Kume, *The Iwakura Embassy*, vol. 1, trans. Martin Collcutt, 160.
79. Ibid., 298.
80. Ibid., 290–299.
81. The most classical view on the modern sense of sublimity was expressed in Edmund Burke's well-known treatise, entitled *A Philosophical Enquiry Into the Origin of Our Ideas of the Sublime and Beautiful*, first published in 1757.
82. Chŏng Ae-yŏng, "Shinsaeng migukkwaŭi mannam," in Kume Kunitake, *T'ŭngmyŏngjŏn'gwŏndaesa miguhoeramshilgi*, vol. 1, trans. (from Japanese into Korean) Pak Sam-hŏn (Seoul: Somyŏngch'ulp'an, 2010), 30.
83. Kume, *The Iwakura Embassy*, vol. 1, 393–394, 248–250, quoted from 160.
84. Ibid., 161.
85. Kume, *The Iwakura Embassy*, vol. 2, trans. Graham Healey, 109–110.
86. Ibid., 261.
87. Kume, *The Iwakura Embassy*, vol. 1, 245.
88. Kume, *The Iwakura Embassy*, vol. 3, 55, 43, 22, 75.
89. Ibid., 157.
90. Ibid., 295–296.
91. Ibid., 260.
92. Kume, *The Iwakura Embassy*, vol. 4, trans. P. F. Kornicki, 9, 14–16, 20, 30, 99.
93. Kume, *The Iwakura Embassy*, vol. 5, trans. Graham Healey et al., 11, 290.
94. Ibid., 327, 289.
95. Ibid., 289.
96. Ibid., 274–276, 295, 341, 351.
97. Kume, *The Iwakura Embassy*, vol. 3, 319–320.
98. Edward W. Said, *Orientalism* (New York, NY: Vintage Books, 1994), 5.
99. Considered a twin of Orientalism, Occidentalism generally refers to the non-Western world's bias toward the modern West, which counters the

West's bias toward the non-Western world. See the argument in Ian Buruma and Avishai Margalit, *Occidentalism: The West in the Eyes of Its Enemies* (London: Penguin Books, 2005).

100. Yun Ch'i-ho, *Kukyŏk Yunch'i-ho ilgi*, vol. 1, trans. Bak Chŏng-shin (Seoul: Yonsei University Press, 2005), 224–227; Hwang Ho-tŏk, *Kŭndae neisyŏn'gwa kŭ p'yosangdŭl: T'aja, kyot'ong, pŏnyŏk, ek'ŭrit'wirŭ* (Seoul: Somyŏngch'ulp'an, 2005), 233–248.
101. W. G. Beasley, "Meiji Political Institutions," in Volume 5 of *The Cambridge History of Japan: The Nineteenth Century*, ed. Marius B. Jansen et al. (Cambridge: Cambridge University Press, 1989), 635–636.
102. On the overall circumstances surrounding Meiji Japan's "switch onto the German path," see Bernd Martin, *Japan and Germany in the Modern World* (New York, NY: Berghahn Books, 1995), 20–27. The numbers involving Japanese students who studied overseas have been quoted from page 22 of the same book.
103. Kume, *The Iwakura Embassy*, vol. 3, 337.
104. Ibid., 306.
105. Ibid.
106. On the transition of modern Japan's diplomatic policy to attacking its East Asian neighbors, see Inoue, *Mangmal yushin*, 229–250; Akira Iriye, "Japan's Drive to Great-Power Status," Volume 5 of *The Cambridge History of Japan*, 747 ff.
107. Yaskawa Junoske, *Huk'ujawa yuk'ich'iŭi ashia ch'imnyaksasangŭl munnŭnda*, trans. (from Japanese into Korean) Yi Hyang-ch'ŏl (Seoul: Yŏksabip'yŏngsa, 2011), 167–184, objects to the political scientist Maruyama Masao's account of Fukuzawa as a "typical civil libertarian." See also Nishikawa Nagao, *Kukkyŏngŭl nŏmnŭn pangbŏb: Munhwa, munmyŏng, kungmin'gukka*, trans. (from Japanese into Korean) Han Kyŏng-gu and Yi Mok (Seoul: Ilchogak, 2006), 119, 206–209.
108. Takii, *The Meiji Constitution*, 2–6.
109. Nippon shiseki kyōkai, ed., *Kido Takayoshi bunsho*, vol. 8 (Tokyo University Press, 2003), 118–124. Regarding Kido Takayoshi's understanding of and enthusiasm for establishing a constitution, see Pang, "Meiji kwallyoŭi 'munmyŏng' inshik," 364–367.
110. For instance, Ōkubo Toshimichi took a more liberal stance than Kido Takayoshi, stressing the need to enlighten the people and envisioning a country in which the monarch shares sovereignty with the people. See Nippon shiseki kyōkai, ed., *Kido Takayoshi bunsho*, vol. 4 and vol. 5.
111. Nippon shiseki kyōkai, ed., *Kido Takayoshi bunsho*, vol. 4, 492, quoted from Takii, *The Meiji Constitution*, 41.
112. On this point, see Takii, *The Meiji Constitution*, 41–43, 47–48.
113. On Doitsugaku kyōkai, or the German Studies Association, see, notably, Katada Tsuyoshi, *Doitsugaku kyōkai to Meiji hōsei* (Tokyo: Bokutakusha, 1999). See also Ienaga Saburo, ed., *Kŭndae ilbon sasangsa*, trans. (from Japanese into Korean) Yŏn'gugonggan suyu+nŏmŏ ilbon'gŭndaesasangt'im (Seoul: Somyŏngch'ulp'an, 2006), 43.
114. Yukichi Fukuzawa, *An Outline of a Theory of Civilization*, p. 30.
115. Louis Frédéric, *Japan Encyclopedia* (Cambridge, MA: Belknap Press of Harvard University Press, 2005), 552; Hirakawa Sukehiro, "Japan's Turn to the West," in Volume 5 of *The Cambridge History of Japan*, 495–498; Michael Wachutka, "Der *Kokutai*-Diskurs im Staatsverständnis des 19. Und frühen 20. Jahrhunderts: Kerngedanken und Entwicklung der Idee von Japans einzigartigem Nationalwesen," in *Staatsverständnis in Japan: Ideen und Wirklichkeiten des japanischen Staates in der Moderne*, ed. Kazuhiro

Takii and Michael Wachutka (Baden-Baden: Nomos, 2016), 65–88; Ch'oe Kyŏng-ok, "Ilbone issŏsŏŭi kyoyukkibonbŏbŭi sasangjŏk paegyŏng," *Hŏnbŏp'akyŏn'gu* 12, no. 5 (2006): 303–328.

116. Pak Sŏk-sun et al., *Ilbonsa* (Seoul: Taehan'gyogwasŏjushik'oesa, 2005), 303 ff.

117. Ch'oe Kyŏng-ok, "Ilbonŭi Hŏnbŏpchejŏnge issŏsŏŭi oeguginŭi yŏnghyang," *Hŏnbŏp'akyŏn'gu* 7, no. 1 (2001): 233–266; Shimizu Shin, Volume 1 of *Meiji kenpō seiteishi: Doku Ō niokeru Itō Hirobumi no kenpō chōsa* (Tokyo: Hara shobō, 1971); Takii, *The Meiji Constitution*, 49–89. According to Takii, Lorenz von Stein had been interested in Japan even before Itō Hirobumi arrived on his doorstep. He probably had hopes that although his theory failed to gain recognition in Europe, it could be put to practice at an emerging nation such as Japan. Stein had been subscribing to the magazine *Japan Weekly Mail* published in Yokohama and corresponding with Fukuzawa Yukichi. See Takii, *The Meiji Constitution*, 72–73. Based on a series of letters, Takii also confirms that Rudolf von Gneist resumed his consultations with Itō Hirobumi upon Itō's return to Berlin from Vienna and eventually came to maintain a close relationship with Meiji Japan. From this, Takii concludes that Itō's own position lay between Gneist and L. von Stein. See the argument in Takii Kazuhiro, *Itō Hirobumi: Japan's First Prime Minister and Father of the Meiji Constitution*, trans. Takechi Manabu (New York, NY: Routledge, 2014), 49–51.

118. Ōkuma sangi kokkai kaisetsu kengi, or Councilor Ōkuma Shigenobu's proposal on establishing a parliamentary system, can be accessed online through the Waseda University Library's web site, http://archive.wul.waseda.ac.jp/kosho/wa09/wa09_06404/wa09_06404.html (accessed January 15, 2020).

119. Ienaga, ed., *Kŭndae ilbon sasangsa*, esp. chapter 1, section 2; Pang Kwang-sŏk, *Kŭndaeilbonŭi kukkach'eje hwangnipkwajŏng: It'o hirobumiwa "chegukhŏnbŏpch'eje"* (Seoul: Hyean, 2008), 89–100.

120. Maki Hidemasa and Fujiwara Akihisa, *Nippon hōseishi* (Tokyo: Seirin shoin, 1993), 332; Ienaga, ed., *Kŭndae ilbon sasangsa*, 62–63.

121. Kume, *The Iwakura Embassy*, vol. 5, 148–149, 322–323.

122. Kume, *The Iwakura Embassy*, vol. 4, 58–60.

123. Pang, *Kŭndaeilbonŭi kukkach'eje*, 111–121; Ienaga, ed., *Kŭndae ilbon sasangsa*, 68–69.

124. Takii, *The Meiji Constitution*, 69–84; Pang, *Kŭndaeilbonŭi kukkach'eje*, 133–158.

125. Ōishi Makoto, *Nippon kenpōshi* (Tokyo: Yūhikaku, 1995), 61 ff.; Pang, *Kŭndaeilbonŭi kukkach'eje*, 197–219.

126. Ienaga, ed., *Kŭndae ilbon sasangsa*, 71.

127. Regarding the advice that not only Rudolf von Gneist but also the Emperor Wilhelm I gave to Itō Hirobumi, see Takii, *The Meiji Constitution*, 60–64.

128. Martin, *Japan and Germany in the Modern World*, 31 ff.; Ch'oe Kyŏng-ok, "Ilbonŭi myŏngch'ihŏnbŏpsang ch'ŏnhwangŭi pŏpchŏng chiwi," *Hŏnbŏp'akyŏn'gu* 10, no. 3 (2004): 487–510. Lorenz von Stein is known to be the one who recommended to Itō Hirobumi that the king use the pronoun "I" to represent the state. See Shimizu, *Meiji kenpō seiteishi*, 353.

129. Ienaga, ed., *Kŭndae ilbon sasangsa*, 198–201; Buruma, *Inventing Japan*, 126.

130. For an overview of Nishida Kitarō's philosophy, see Ōkubo Takaki, *Ilbonmunhwaronŭi kyebo*, trans. (from Japanese into Korean) Song Sŏk-wŏn (Seoul: Sohwa, 2012), 124–137.

131. Buruma, *Inventing Japan*, 53–55.

132. Ibid., 55.

133. Pang Kwang-sŏk, "Meiji kwallyoŭi yurŏp 'chishiksullye'," in Kim Yu-ch'ŏl et al., Volume 1 of *Tongashia yŏksa sogŭi yŏhaeng: Kyŏnggye, chŏngbo, kyoryu*

(Seoul: Sanch'ŏrŏm, 2008), 343–352, 359–360; Takii, *The Meiji Constitution*, 107–130; Iriye, "Japan's drive to great-power status," 763–764.

134. Stefan Tanaka, *Japan's Orient* (Berkeley, CA: University of California Press, 1993), 115–152.
135. Kim Kyŏng-il and Kang Ch'ang-il, "Tongashiaesŏ ashiajuŭi: 1870–1945 nyŏnŭi ilbonŭl chungshimŭro," *Yŏksayŏn'gu* 8 (2000): 269–332. For more practical approaches toward Asianism, see Matsuura Masataka, "Soilbonjuŭi, min'ganjaegyejuŭi, taeashiajuŭi: Kŭndae ilbonesŏŭi ashiajuŭiŭi sekaji kanŭngsŏng," in *Tongashiaŭi chishikkyoryuwa yŏksagiŏk*, ed. Tongbugayŏksajaedan (Seoul: Tongbugayŏksajaedan, 2009), 115–175.
136. Takeuchi Yoshimi, *Ilbon'gwa ashia: Tak'euch'i Yoshimi p'yŏngnonsŏn*, trans. (from Japanese into Korean) Sŏ Gwang-dŏk and Paek Chi-un (Seoul: Somyŏngch'ulp'an, 2006), 101, 213–216, quoted from 213–214.
137. Fujimori, *Nihon no kindai kenchiku*, 22–28; Stewart, *The Making of a Modern Japanese Architecture*, 13 ff.
138. Stewart, *The Making*, 13–32; K. Abe, "Early Western Architecture in Japan," *Journal of the Society of Architectural Historians* 13, no. 2 (1954): 13–18.
139. Takashi Fujitani, *Splendid Monarchy: Power and Pageantry in Modern Japan* (Berkeley, CA: University of California Press, 1998), 79.
140. Dallas Finn, *Meiji Revisited: The Sites of Victorian Japan* (New York, NY: Weatherhill, 1995), 148–150.
141. Pak, *Tongnama Kŏnch'ungmunhwa*, 265–306.
142. Komori Yōichi, *P'osŭt'ŭk'olloniŏl*, trans. (from Japanese into Korean) Song T'ae-uk (Seoul: Samin, 2002), 35; Hwang, *Kŭndae neisyŏn'gwa kŭ p'yosangdŭl*, 248–254.
143. Suzuki Sadami, *Ilbonŭi munhwanaesyŏnŏllijŭm*, trans. (from Japanese into Korean) Chŏng Chae-chŏng and Kim Pyŏng-chin (Seoul: Sohwa, 2008), 39–40.
144. Nishikawa, *Kukkyŏngŭl nŏmnŭn pangbŏb*, 113, 120, 212 ff.; Maruyama Masao, *Pŏnyŏkkwa ilbonŭi kŭndae*, trans. (from Japanese into Korean) Yim Sŏng-mo (Isan, 2000).
145. Bruno Taut, *Japans Kunst mit europäischen Augen gesehen*, ed. Manfred Speidel (1936; Berlin: Gebrüder Mann Verlag, 2011), 8, 18–28, 114–118.
146. For a critical discussion of this approach, see Nishikawa, *Kukkyŏngŭl nŏmnŭn pangbŏb*, 258–304. See also Carola Hein, "The Transformation of Planning Ideas in Japan and Its Colonies," in *Urbanism: Imported or Exported?* ed. Joe Nasr and Mercedes Volait (Chichester: Wiley-Academy, 2003), 65–66.
147. Fujimori Terunobu, Volume 2 of *Nihon no kindai kenchiku: Taisei-Shōwahen* (Tokyo: Iwanami shinsho, 2010), 156–157; Werner Durth, *Deutsche Architekten: Biographische Verflechtungen 1900–1970* (Munich: dtv, 1992), 123.
148. Harry Francis Mallgrave, *Gottfried Semper: Architect on the Nineteenth Century* (New Haven, CT: Yale University Press, 1996), 92–94.
149. Roland Barthes, *Empire of Signs*, trans. Richard Howard (New York, NY: Hill and Wang, 1983), 3, 107.
150. Gordon Millan et al., "Industrialization and Its Discontents, 1870–1944," in *French Cultural Studies*, ed. Jill Forbes and Michael Kelly (Oxford: Oxford University Press, 1996), 19–20.
151. Kim Yong-ch'ŏl, "Ok'ak'ura t'enshin'gwa ilbon misulsaŭi sŏngnip," *Ilbonsasang* 7 (2004): 185, 188.
152. David Carrier, *Museum Skepticism: A History of the Display of Art in Public Galleries* (Durham, NC: Duke University Press, 2006), 126–145.
153. Takagi Hiroshi, "Ilbon misulsawa chōsen misulsaŭi sŏngnip," in *Kuksaŭi shinhwarŭl nŏmŏsŏ*, ed. Yim Ji-hyŏn and Yi Sŏng-si (Seoul: Humanist, 2004), 165–196.

154. Kakuzō Okakura, *The Ideals of the East with Special Reference to the Art of Japan* (New York, NY: Stone Bridges Press, 2007), esp. 102–102. On Okakura Kakuzō's acceptance of Hegelian aesthetics, see Tanehisa Otabe, "Ilbonŭi mihak hwangnipkie issŏsŏ tongsŏgyosŏpsa: Tongyangjŏk yesurŭl chungshimŭro pon Ok'ak'ura t'enshin', Wach'ŭji t'ech'ŭro, Oonishi yoshinori," *Mihak yesurhakyŏn'gu* 27 (2008): 239–241.
155. Ōkubo, *Ilbonmunhwaronŭi kyebo*, 58.
156. Kim, "Ok'ak'ura t'enshin'gwa ilbon misulsaŭi sŏngnip," *Ilbonsasang*, 179.
157. Okakura, *The Ideals of the East*, quoted from 9–13, 20. For an argument from intellectual history, see, notably, Inaga Shigemi, *Kaiga no rinkai: Kindai Higashiajia bijutsushi no shikkoku to meiun* (Nagoya University Press, 2014), 149–163.
158. Itō Chūta, "Hōryūji kenchikuron," *Kenchiku zasshi* 82 (1893): 318–350. On Itō Chūta's works, see Fujimori, *Nihon no kindai kenchiku*, vol. 2, 7–8; Cherie Wendelken, "The Tectonics of Japanese Style: Architect and Carpenter in the Late Meiji Period," *Art Journal* 55, no. 3 (1996): 30–34, esp. 32.
159. Stefan Tanaka, *New Times in Modern Japan* (Princeton, NJ: Princeton University Press, 2004), 170–175.
160. Tanaka, *Japan's Orient*, 11–13, 58–62.
161. Karatani Kojin, "Misulgwanŭrosŏŭi yŏksa: Ok'ak'ura tenshin'gwa p'enollosa," in *Ch'angjodoen kojŏn*, ed. Haruo Shirane and Suzuki Tomi, trans. (from Japanese into Korean) Wang Suk-yŏng (Seoul: Somyŏngch'ulp'an, 2002), 299–321; Karatani Kojin, "Kŭndaeŭi ch'ogŭge taehayŏ," in *Kŭndaech'ogŭngnon*, ed. Hiromatsu Wataru, trans. (from Japanese into Korean) Kim Hang (Seoul: Minŭmsa, 2003), 239–247. For further details on Nishida Kitarō's idea of the East, see Fujita Masakatsu, "Tetsugaku to sekai ninshiki: Nishida Kitarō okeru 'tōyō' to 'sekai'," in Volume 8 of *Teikoku Nippon no gaku chi: Kūkan keisei to sekai ninshiki*, ed. Yamamuro Shinichi (Tokyo: Iwanami shoten, 2006), 77–110.
162. Hiromatsu, *Kŭndaech'ogŭngnon*, 208–209; Takeuchi, *Ilbon'gwa ashia*, 104–121. On Miki Kiyoshi's Marxist philosophy of history, see Hirako Tomochō, "Nippon marukusu shigi tetsugaku no tōtatsuten: Miki to jun," in *Teikoku Nippon no gaku chi*, 112–126, 145–147.
163. For an overview of this book, see Ōkubo, *Ilbonmunhwaronŭi kyebo*, 197–209.
164. André Sorensen, *The Making of Urban Japan: Cities and Planning From Edo to the Twenty-First Century* (New York, NY: Routledge, 2002), 11 ff., 36 ff.; Ōishi Manabu, "Ilbon kŭnsedoshi edoŭi kinŭnggwa sŏnggyŏk," *Toshiinmunhakyŏn'gu* 1, no. 1 (2009): 123–137.
165. Sheldon Garon, *Molding Japanese Minds: The State in Everyday Life* (Princeton, NJ: Princeton University Press, 1997), 3–59.
166. Inoue, *Mangmal yushin*, 202–215.
167. Sorensen, *The Making of Urban Japan*, 52–57.
168. Ibid., 22–36; Kim Paek-yŏng, "Sangjinggonggganŭi pyŏnyonggwa chip'apkiŏgŭi palmyŏng: Sŏurŭi shingminji kyŏnghŏmgwa minjogŭi changsosŏng chaegusŏng," *Konggan'gwa sahoe* 28 (2007): 195–196.
169. On this point, see Min Yu-ki, "Iwak'ura sajŏltanŭi p'ŭrangsŭ kŭndae toshi ch'ehŏmgwa inshik," *Sach'ong* 80 (2013): 66–71.
170. Sorensen, *The Making of Urban Japan*, 50, 60 ff.
171. Smith II, "Tokyo As an Idea," *Journal of Japanese Studies*, 45–80.
172. Narita Ryuichi, *Kŭndae toshigongganŭi munhwagyŏnghŏm: Toshigongganŭro ponŭn ilbon'gŭndaesa*, trans. (from Japanese into Korean) Sŏ Min-kyo (Seoul: Ppuriwa ip'ari, 2011), 24. The sharp decline in Tokyo's population can be attributed largely to the return of daimyōs and their retainers since the Meiji Restoration to their respective domains in the countryside after

being obligated to remain in Edo under the *Sankin kōtai* system. See Okata Junichiro, "Kŭndae tok'yoŭi toshigyehoek: Kyooehwawa toshibyŏnshin," in University of Seoul Sŏurhakyŏn'guso, *Sŏul, peijing, sanghai, tok'yoŭi taedoshiroŭi sŏngjanggwajŏng pigyoyŏn'gu*, vol. 1 (Seoul: Sŏurhakyŏn'guso, 2006), 104; Shun-Ichi J. Watanabe, "Metropolitanism As a Way of Life: In Case of Tokyo, 1868–1930," in *Metropolis 1890–1940*, ed. Anthony Sutcliffe (Chicago, IL: University of Chicago Press, 1984), 407.

173. Narita, *Kŭndae toshigongganŭi munhwagyŏnghŏm*, 73–79.
174. Fujimori Terunobu, *Meiji no tōkyō keikaku* (Tokyo: Iwanami shoten, 2012), 57–59.
175. On Ginza Bricktown, see, notably, Fujimori, *Meiji no tōkyō keikaku*, 1–55; Nagamatsu Sakae, *Zusetsu toshi to kenchiku no kindai: Pure-modanizumu no toshi kaizō* (Kyoto: Gakugei shuppansha, 2008), 176–179; Sorensen, *The Making of Urban Japan*, 60 ff.
176. Ishida Yorifusa, *Nippon kindai toshi keikaku no hyakunen* (Tokyo: Jichitai kenkyūsha, 1987), 39; Kim Kyŏng-ri, "'Munmyŏnggaehwawa' kinjaŭi toshigonggansŏnge kwanhan nishik'ie yŏn'gu: Kinjaren'gadorinishik'ierŭl chungshimŭro," *Toshiyŏn'gu: Yŏksa, sahoe, munhwa* 10 (2013): 45–49.
177. Stewart, *The Making of a Modern Japanese Architecture*, 22.
178. John Steegman, *Victorian Taste: A Study of the Arts and Architecture* (Cambridge, MA: The MIT Press, 1971), 102, 105; Barry Bergdoll, *European Architecture 1750–1890* (Oxford: Oxford University Press, 2000), 132–133; Thomas Hall, *Planning Europe's Capital Cities: Aspects of Nineteenth Century Urban Development* (New York, NY: Routledge, 2010), 86.
179. Yumoto Koichi, *Ilbon kŭndaeŭi p'unggyŏng*, trans. (from Japanese into Korean) Yŏn'gugonggan suyu+nŏmŏ Tongashia kŭndae seminat'im (Seoul: Kŭrinbi, 2004), 152–153.
180. Fujimori, *Nihon no kindai kenchiku*, vol. 1, 70, 77–80.
181. Ibid., 118 ff.; Stewart, *The Making of a Modern Japanese Architecture*, 13 ff., 22.
182. Watanabe, "Metropolitanism As a Way of Life," 408; Sorensen, *The Making of Urban Japan*, 62; Fujimori, *Meiji no tōkyō keikaku*, 43 ff. According to Fujimori, Ginza has been the commercial district with the highest rent in Japan since the 1870s. The plan for Ginza Bricktown's construction contributed to the rise of real estate prices in central Tokyo. And with the help of changes in land ownership, the district was able to secure a foundation for long-term economic prosperity.
183. Smith II, "Tokyo As an Idea," *Journal of Japanese Studies*, passim.
184. Stewart, *The Making of a Modern Japanese Architecture*, 31; Hein, "The Transformation of Planning Ideas," 56–57.
185. Ishida, *Nippon kindai*, 55–56; Fujimori, *Meiji no tōkyō keikaku*, 100–101.
186. Finn, *Meiji Revisited*, 94; Fujitani, *Splendid Monarchy*, 101–115; Hatsuda Toru, *Mobanggwa ch'angjoŭi konggansa*, trans. (from Japanese into Korean) Kim Tong-yŏng and Cho Kŭk-rae (Seoul: Bomoondang, 2003), 20.
187. Hein, "The Transformation of Planning Ideas," 58; Fujimori, *Meiji no tōkyō keikaku*, 277 ff.
188. Fujimori, *Nihon no kindai kenchiku*, vol. 1, 195–197; Koshizawa Akira, *Tōkyō no toshi keikaku* (Tokyo: Iwanami shoten, 1991), 27–30; Josef Kreiner, *Deutsche Spaziergänge in Tokyo*, 107–122; Sorensen, *The Making of Urban Japan*, 38 ff.
189. Wilhelm Böckmann, *Reise nach Japan* (Berlin: Reichsdruckerei, 1886), 56, 97.
190. For further details regarding the careers of Hermann Ende, Wilhelm Böckmann, and their firm Ende & Böckmann, see Horiuchi Masaaki, *Meiji no o yatoi kenchikuka: Ende Bekkuman* (Tokyo: Inoue shoin, 1989), 60–169;

Franziska Pagel, *Ende & Böckmann: Ein Berliner Architekturbüro im 19. Jahrhundert* (Berlin: Gebr. Mann Verlag, 2019), esp. 105–112.

191. Horiuchi, *Meiji no o yatoi kenchikuka*, 172–194; Josef Kreiner, *Deutsche Spaziergänge in Tokyo*, 114.
192. Fujimori, *Nihon no kindai kenchiku*, vol. 1, 198–199; Fujimori, *Meiji no tōkyō keikaku*, 316–319; Michiko Meid, *Europäische und nordamerikanische Architektur in Japan seit 1542* (Cologne: Abteilung Architektur des Kunsthistorischen Instituts Köln, 1977), 213–215; Hermann Josef Stübben, *Der Städtebau* (Stuttgart: Alfred Kröner Verlag, 1907), 291–298.
193. Meid, *Europäische und nordamerikanische Architektur in Japan*, 222; Horiuchi, *Meiji no o yatoi kenchikuka*, 240–244.
194. "Deutsche Entwürfe für japanische Monumental-Bauten. I.," *Deutsche Bauzeitung* 25, no. 21 (March 14, 1891): 121–122.
195. "Der Brand des provisorischen Parlamants-Gebäudes in Tokio," *Deutsche Bauzeitung* 25, no. 26 (March 31, 1891): 157; Meid, *Europäische und nordamerikanische Architektur in Japan*, 225.
196. Fujimori, *Meiji no tōkyō keikaku*, 304–311; Meid, *Europäische und nordamerikanische Architektur*, 203–221.
197. Fujimori, *Nihon no kindai kenchiku*, vol. 1, 200–201.
198. Kreiner, *Deusche Spaziergänge in Tokyo*, 137–152.
199. Taguchi Ukichi was one of the leading figures of the civilization and enlightenment movement. He authored the acclaimed *A Brief History of Japanese Civilization* (Nihon kaika shōshi) and followed Britain's precedent by launching the *Tokyo Journal of Economics*. In 1894, he was elected as a member of the House of Representatives. See Sorensen, *The Making of Urban Japan*, 63 ff.; Fujimori, *Meiji no tōkyō keikaku*, 127 ff.
200. Ishida, *Nippon kindai*, 51.
201. Fujimori, *Meiji no tōkyō keikaku*, 247–255.
202. Yi Myŏng-kyu, "Han'gung kŭndae toshigyehoeng chedoŭi paltalgwa soul," in Ch'oe Sangch'ŏl et al., *Tongyang toshisa sogŭi sŏul* (Seoul: Sŏulshijŏnggaebaryŏn'guwŏn, 1994), 432–435; Sorensen, *The Making of Urban Japan*, 71–74; Nagamatsu, *Zusetsu toshi to kenchiku no kindai*, 179–183; Fujimori, *Meiji no tōkyō keikaku*, 138 ff, 242 ff.
203. Inoue, *Mangmal yushin*, 251–253; Sorensen, *The Making of Urban Japan*, 55 ff.
204. Watanabe, "Metropolitanism As a Way of Life," 411, 407.
205. Smith II, "Tokyo As an Idea," *Journal of Japanese Studies*, 54–55.
206. Sorensen, *The Making of Urban Japan*, 71 ff.; Fujimori, *Meiji no tōkyō keikaku*, 263 ff.
207. Itō Takeshi, "Kŭndae tok'yoŭi toshigonggan," in *Sŏul, peijing, sanghai, tok'yoŭi taedoshiroŭi sŏngjanggwajŏng pigyoyŏn'gu*, 198.
208. Fujimori, *Meiji no tōkyō keikaku*, 249–250; Yumoto, *Ilbon kŭndaeŭi p'unggyŏng*, 428–429.
209. Koshizawa Akira, *Tok'yo toshigyehoek tamnon*, trans. (from Japanese into Korean) Chang Chun-ho (Seoul: Kumisŏgwan, 2007), 110–113.
210. On the Imperial Palace Square, see Fujimori Terunobu, *Kenchiku tantei no bōken: Tōkyōhen* (Tokyo: Chikuma shobō, 1989), 155–191.
211. Sorensen, *The Making of Urban Japan*, 69–71.
212. Mori Ōgai, "Muhŭi," in *Mori ogai tanp'yŏnjip*, trans. (from Japanese into Korean) Son Sun-ok (Seoul: Chishikŭlmandŭnŭnjishik, 2012). For literary criticism that relates this work to Berlin's urban space, see Maeda Ai, "Berlin 1888: Mori Ōgai's 'Dancing Girl'," in Maeda Ai, *Text and the City: Essays on Japanese Modernity*, trans. Leslie Pincus (Duke University Press, 2004), 295–328, quoted from 298–299. Maeda's critique from the perspective of

urban cultural history has its advantages, but when it comes to the matter of Japanese identity, it fails to recognize the implications of a Japanese man's domination over a German woman.

213. Quoted from Maeda, "Berlin 1888," 313.
214. Barthes, *Empire of Signs*, 30–32; Maet'i p'orŏ (Matthi Forrer), "Toshi sangjingjuŭi," in Kim Chu-kwan et al., *Sasanggadŭl toshiwa munmyŏngŭl marhada* (Seoul: Han'gilsa, 2014), 171.
215. Fujimori, *Nihon no kindai kenchiku*, vol. 1, 169 ff.; William H. Coaldrake, *Architecture and Authority in Japan* (New York, NY: Routledge, 1996), 217–218.
216. Hozumi Kazuo, *(E de miru) Meiji no Tōkyō* (Tokyo: Sōshisha, 2010), 70–72; Fujimori, *Nihon no kindai kenchiku*, vol. 1, 169–171; Toshio Watanabe, "Josiah Conder's Rokumeikan: Architecture and National Representation in Meiji Japan," *Art Journal* 55, no. 39 (1996): 21–27; Coaldrake, *Architecture and Authority in Japan*, 21–27. The Deer Cry Pavilion (Rokumeikan) completed in 1883 was named after a passage in the *Book of Songs* that begin with "the deer call to one another." True to its elegant name, the lavish building for people of the highest ranks symbolized the Europeanization of Japan. In 1885, the Western banquet the Foreign Minister Inoue Kaoru hosted at the building's grand hall to celebrate the emperor's birthday became the talk of the town as the guests enjoyed ballroom dancing and card games. For further details, see Haga, *Myŏngch'iyushin'gwa ilbonin*, 350–355; Buruma, *Inventing Japan*, 46; Finn, *Meiji Revisited*, 97.
217. Nakatani Norihito, "Kindai (Meiji-Taisei-Shōwa zenki)," in *Nippon kenchiku yōshikishi*, supervised by Ōta Hiroshi and Fujii Keisuke (Tokyo: Bijutsu shuppansha, 2010), 137–139.
218. Finn, *Meiji Revisited*, 188–190.
219. On the Queen Anne style, see Mallgrave, *Modern Architectural Theory*, 174; Stewart, *The Making of a Modern Japanese Architecture*, 37–38.
220. Iriye, "Japan's Drive to Great-Power Status," 768–769, 773 ff.
221. Hatsuda, *Mobanggwa ch'angjoŭi konggansa*, 15, 25; Meid, *Europäische und nordamerikanische Architektur in Japan*, 204–206. The original School of Engineering established in 1873 taught eight different subjects, one of which was building (zōka). This school was restructured into the Imperial College of Engineering in 1877.
222. Fujimori, *Nihon no kindai kenchiku*, vol. 1, 219–224; Stewart, *The Making of a Modern Japanese Architecture*, 37–38. On the imperialist nature of British neo-Gothic architecture, see Crinson, *Empire Building and Orientalism*, 48–61.
223. Fujimori, *Nihon no kindai kenchiku*, vol. 1, 224–227.
224. Coaldrake, *Architecture and Authority in Japan*, p. 235.
225. Stewart, *The Making of a Modern Japanese Architecture*, pp. 52–54.
226. Fujimori, *Nihon no kindai kenchiku*, vol. 1, 228–231; Finn, *Meiji Revisited*, 101.
227. Nishizawa Yasuhiko, "Kenchiku no ekkyō to shokuminchi kensetsu," Volume 8 of *Teikoku Nippon no gaku chi: Kūkan keisei to sekai ninshiki*, ed. Yamamuro Shinichi (Tokyo: Iwanami shoten, 2006), 244.
228. Fujimori, *Nihon no kindai kenchiku*, vol. 1, 210–218.
229. Ibid., 238–241; Finn, *Meiji Revisited*, 158; Hatsuda, *Mobanggwa ch'angjoŭi konggansa*, 24.
230. Böckmann, *Reise nach Japan*, 93.
231. Ibid., 97; Horiuchi, *Meiji no o yatoi kenchikuka*, 245–252.
232. Meid, *Europäische und nordamerikanische Architektur in Japan*, 228.
233. "Deutsche Entwürfe für japanische Monumental-Bauten. III.," *Deutsche Bauzeitung* 25, no. 35 (2. Mai 1891): 209–210; Horiuchi, *Meiji no o yatoi kenchikuka*, 252–263.

234. Finn, *Meiji Revisited*, 95.
235. Fujimori, *Nihon no kindai kenchiku*, vol. 1, 204; Meid, *Europäische und nordamerikanische Architektur in Japan*, 236–237.
236. Meid, *Europäische und nordamerikanische Architektur*, 274.
237. Fujimori, *Nihon no kindai kenchiku*, vol. 1, 236–238.
238. Tokugawa Yoshinobu, *Nihonbashi kinenshi* (Tokyo: Tōkyōbu, 1911). Some argue that Tsumaki Yorinaka's design for Nihonbashi was inspired by the bridge Pont Alexandre III Tsumaki saw while attending the 1900 Paris Exposition, but even if he did, Schinkel's influence cannot be disregarded altogether. See the argument in Finn, *Meiji Revisited*, 148–150.
239. Hatsuda, *Mobanggwa ch'angjoŭi konggansa*, 18–19, 24.
240. Fujimori, *Nihon no kindai kenchiku*, vol. 1, 246.
241. Thomas Nipperdey, *Deutsche Geschichte 1800–1866: Bürgerwelt und starker Staat* (Munich: C. H. Beck, 1983), 557.
242. Joan Campbell, *The German Werkbund: The Politics of Reform in the Applied Arts* (Princeton, NJ: Princeton University Press, 2015), 12.
243. Suzuki Hiroyuki, *Sŏyang kŭnhyŏndae kŏnch'ugŭi yŏksa: Sanŏp'yŏngmyŏnggiesŏ hyŏnjaekkaji*, trans. (from Japanese into Korean) U Tong-sŏn (Seoul: Sigongsa, 2003), 228 ff.
244. See the argument in Karatani Kojin, *Neisyŏn'gwa mihak*, trans. (from Japanese into Korean) Cho Yŏng-il (Seoul: Tosŏch'ulp'an b, 2009), 232.
245. Coaldrake, *Architecture and Authority in Japan*, 214–215; Stewart, *The Making*, 55–59; Hozumi, *(E de miru) Meiji no Tōkyō*, 218–220.
246. Fujimori, *Nihon no kindai kenchiku*, vol. 1, 249–257; Finn, *Meiji Revisited*, 114–115.
247. Hatsuda, *Mobanggwa ch'angjoŭi konggansa*, 24–26.
248. Iain Boyd Whyte, "Modern German Architecture," in *The Cambridge Companion to Modern German Culture*, ed. Eva Kolinsky and Wilfried van der Will (Cambridge: Cambridge University Press, 1998), 285.
249. Fujimori, *Kenchiku tantei no bōken*, 117–154.
250. Meid, *Europäische und nordamerikanische Architektur in Japan*, 278.
251. Coaldrake, *Architecture and Authority in Japan*, 222 ff.; Stewart, *The Making*, 37–38; Yumoto, *Ilbon kŭndaeŭi p'unggyŏng*, 362–363.
252. Hatsuda, *Mobanggwa ch'angjoŭi konggansa*, 141–142, 160–161; Fujimori, *Nihon no kindai kenchiku*, vol. 2, 1, 170 ff.
253. Fujimori, *Nihon no kindai kenchiku*, vol. 1, 129–131.
254. Yun In-sŏk, "Ilbonŭi kŭndaehwa kwajŏnggwa ilbon kŭndae kŏnch'ugŭi pyŏnch'ŏn kwajŏng," *Kŏnch'uk* 40, no. 8 (1996): 13–14; Stewart, *The Making*, 75–76.
255. Hatsuda, *Mobanggwa ch'angjoŭi konggansa*, 167.
256. Fujimori, *Nihon no kindai kenchiku*, vol. 1, 235–241; Jonathan M. Reynolds, "Japan's Imperial Diet Building: Debate Over Construction of a National Identity," *Art Journal* 55 (1996): 46.
257. Albert Speer, *Kiŏk: Che3chegugŭi chungshimesŏ*, trans. Kim Ki-yŏng (Seoul: Mat'i, 2007), 93–142, 275–276; Alan Tansman, *The Aesthetics of Japanese Fascism* (Berkeley, CA: University of California Press, 2009), 22; Graham Pakes, "Heidegger and Japanese Fascism," in *Japanese and Continental Philosophy: Conversations with the Kyoto School*, ed. Bret W. Davis et al. (Bloomington, IN: Indiana University Press, 2010), 247–265.
258. Adrian von Buttlar, "'Germanische Tektonik'? Leo von Klenzes patriotische Interpretation des Klassizismus," in *Klassizismus-Gotik: Karl Friedrich Schinkel und die patriotische Baukunst*, ed. Annette Dorgerloh et al. (Berlin: Deutscher Kunstverlag, 2007), 281. More generally, see Paul P. Jaskot, *The Architecture of Oppression: The SS, Forced Labor and Nazi Monumental Building Economy* (New York, NY: Routledge, 2000).

3 An Eerie Phantasmagoria of Athena

> All things shall remain but an eerie phantasmagoria until the lives of our people evolve into congruous works of art, analogous or even superior to those of Greece during its brief golden age. Once this happens, every riddle shall be solved! Where are the ones who have been pondering the possibility?
>
> Gottfried Semper, *Style in the Technical and Tectonic Arts; or, Practical Aesthetics*, Volume 1 (1860; Munich: Bruckmann, 1878)

1. Urban Planning and Colonialism

A phantasmagoria is mysterious because of its insurmountable distance from ourselves here and now. The yearning for a perfect world far beyond petty reality is what guides us to a world of futile shadows. Then again, the silhouette of those shadows turns out to be that of our own from leaning against the sun. With their inaccessible brilliance, the futile shadows make our present seem pitiful and encourage us to dream of the future, but they remain forever out of reach. So, unless that vague yearning for the world on the other side disappears, our petty reality persists. And the perfect Hegelian "end of history" with no more need for art never arrives.

Imperial Japan's Paranoia and Schizophrenia

Athens and Prussia were shadows, each reflecting the reality of central Europe and East Asia. Rather than being true portrayals of reality, such shadows were compelled by reality to be staged. This therefore constantly created a gap between those shadows and reality. Out of a yearning for the Athens on the other side, the German Empire became obsessed with an imaginary origin of national culture and tried to uncompromisingly actualize it everywhere. That same paranoia can also be found to a certain degree in Japan, which staged the "Prussia of Asia." By projecting all its desires onto the West on the other side, Imperial Japan intentionally mistook itself as the West and tried to disparage and rule its "half-civilized" neighbors. The conceit of the Japanese, however, proved they were no different from their neighbors, who were semi-colonized by the West, and revealed a sense of shame among the Japanese from being unable to become Westerners no matter how hard they tried. This excessive faith in one's uncertain identity, or a sense of inferiority entangled with conceit, is typical of schizophrenia. Unlike the Athens of central Europe, the Prussia of Asia failed to discover an image of itself solid enough to uncompromisingly actualize anywhere.

West and East were dichotomous notions representing Japan's vacillating identity. Imperial Japan modeled its alter ego after Western powers, especially Prussia, and created an insurmountable distance between itself and its neighbors. However, as joining the Western framework of modern civilization proved to be impossible over time, Japan had to newly create an East that could compete with the West. A new topology was envisioned in which the East revolving around Japan would first be established before incorporating the West. Yet the difference between paranoia and schizophrenia tends to be paper thin. Representing Western civilization while emphasizing solidarity in the East was not only hypocritical but a manifestation of impulsive self-division. It was an act of backpedaling after failing to find an exit. In that sense, overcoming modernity was closer to an outpour of despair than an ambitious ideal.

Such haphazard behavior resulted in an utterly aggressive construction of colonies. In a sense, the tectonics of Prussian classicism may have been truly realized not in the colonies of the German Empire but those of the Japanese Empire. If tectonics was not an aesthetic or technological matter but purely a logic of domination, the adjacent colonial spaces Imperial Japan risked almost everything to build were the true imaginary Athens rather than a peripheral showcase like Qingdao. Such spaces seemed to be ruled by a pure modern civilization instead of Japan or Germany, which was something that had been impossible to realize at the imperial capital, Tokyo. In colonies, there was no need to struggle for leadership or interests while carrying out reform, nor was it necessary to argue over a national architectural style. There was only the inevitability of world history that could not be defied.

The reason modern urban planning and public architecture failed to fulfill their intended purpose in mainland Japan was because of the self-contradictory ruling class. With a firm grip on absolute power, the Meiji government continued to focus on symbolic construction projects to embellish the capital or large-scale urban plans instead of accommodating the long-term development of civil society. Local governments were under the direct control of the Home Ministry so that most of them were headed by the ministry's veteran bureaucrats. As the autonomous development of civil society was delayed, the interests of the establishment and local community leaders were not particularly violated while government offices struggled from a chronic lack of funds. Moreover, fierce competition between government offices over bills or budgetary matters hindered their operational efficiency. The Home Ministry succeeded in warding off competition from the Ministry of Treasury, which carried out the Ginza Bricktown project, and in monopolizing the administration of urban planning. However, whereas the Home Ministry drafted a plan to comprehensively reconstruct the capital, the Ministry of Foreign Affairs proposed a plan to concentrate government offices within the capital. Specific cases of city improvement show that the Home Ministry, with administrative power, tended to be held back by the Ministry of Treasury, with its grip on the purse strings. Compared to the friction between government offices, there was less marked conflict and tension between the state and the bourgeois civil society in Japan than in the United States or Europe. This, of course, did not mean confusion was minimal for Japanese society. Restricted autonomous communality always carried the risk of maximizing disorder in everyday life. A stark example was the absence of regulations for individual buildings, so that up until the early 1900s, no comprehensive building codes had been established in Japan, except for a few cities such as Osaka.[1]

As if to vent its spite for being unable to practice comprehensive urban planning at home, Imperial Japan took an aggressive approach and mobilized violent means to carry out such urban planning in its colonies. It is therefore not surprising to find that various innovative plans were tested in colonies before they were exported back to mainland Japan. A classic example of this was the Imperial Diet building, the most central building in Tokyo, which put an end to the controversy over the national architectural style of Japan once it was finally completed in the late 1930s. The spatio-temporal principle of German tectonics the Meiji government ambitiously implemented was at last able to gain practicality by shifting its modus operandi from rational agenda to ruthless colonialism.

The Birth of Japanese Urban Planning

Through the Taishō period between 1912 and 1926, Japan truly emerged as an industrial nation. Its gross national product doubled between 1910 and 1930, while real output in mining and manufacturing as well as employment in the heavy chemical industries nearly quadrupled.[2] At the same time, Japanese cities experienced explosive growth. The population of 1.12 million in Tokyo as of 1900 jumped to 2.17 million by 1920.[3] However, urban planning established during the Meiji period had been preoccupied with renovating the city center, which was not enough to accommodate new growth. Although the Tokyo City Improvement Ordinance broke away from the idea of concentrating government offices and switched to a practical approach, it was still an ordinance intended to elevate the capital's prestige and failed to improve the infrastructure of areas other than central Tokyo. The rapid increase in the city's population engendered an urban sprawl, or rampant expansion into the suburbs, signaling the advent of a "dark age" for urban planning that became impossible for the city improvement ordinance to handle.[4]

The only regulations the Meiji government had established on urban planning were the Tokyo City Improvement Ordinance of 1888 and the subsidiary Regulations on the Disposal of Land and Buildings of 1889. After lengthy controversy and delay, a plan was drafted in 1918 to extend the existing city improvement ordinance to the five major cities of Osaka, Kyoto, Yokohama, Kobe, and Nagoya, but it was replaced with entirely new legislation the following year. On April 4, 1919, the Urban Planning Law (Law no. 36) and the Urban Building Law (Law no. 37) were passed and promulgated. Unlike the city improvement ordinance, the newly established laws applied to all parts of major cities and focused on giving structure to economic dynamics that had been developing in urban peripheries. The laws remained in effect for nearly half a century until a new urban planning law was established in 1968. These laws of 1919 were major turning points in that they not only emulated similar American and European laws but took the unique circumstances of Japan into consideration.[5] The issues in Japanese society that gave birth to the 1919 Urban Planning Law were in fact ones that all industrial powers were commonly facing at the time. Japan was not alone in having to innovate its transportation system and secure the necessary land and funds to expand its infrastructure such as roads and ditches as it rearranged urban areas. Hence, it was only natural for Japanese leaders to take an interest in ideas and cases overseas related to urban planning. The reason they were particularly attracted to the German model was because instead of leaving urban development to the autonomy of civil society, the German model demonstrated a formula effective when carried out as part of the great cause of achieving national prosperity and military power. The new laws reflected the determination to make cities live up to the prestige of the Great Empire of Japan, which became one of the "Big Five" nations after World War I.

The laws of 1919 took on a new dimension when compared with the Tokyo City Improvement Ordinance. The ordinance had concentrated on improving infrastructure such as roads or sewage arrangements, whereas the Urban Planning and Building Law moved beyond roads to include all land and buildings and thus aim for an overall rearrangement of urban spaces. The Japanese implementation of the German zoning system divided land according to residential, commercial, and industrial purposes and accordingly designated the height, construction material, coverage ratio, and number of windows for each building. The Building Line System, also imported from Germany, stipulated that roads had to be at least 2.7 meters wide so as to avoid the chaotic growth of new suburban towns and organize roads as planned. The bills for the 1919 laws also proposed some fairly radical measures, such as the readjustment of plots for a more reasonable use of land, excess condemnation to effectively secure fiscal resources, and a betterment levy on the increase in land value.[6]

What was likely a world-class bill at the time met with strong opposition from the Japanese Ministry of Treasury and was forced to have several of the proposed measures removed before it could be passed. Excess condemnation, which Haussmann used in the late nineteenth century to renovate Paris, was one of the provisions removed after sparking strong opposition from landowners who would be forced to sell land at a bargain price and pay more to reacquire it. The provision involving betterment levy also had to be deleted, because the Ministry of Treasury opposed it for the sake of the landowners' vested interests.[7] In its original form, the bill would have brought a severe cost burden upon landowners, and they would have sustained a particularly heavy loss if all roads less than 2.7 meters had to be sold at a bargain price. In the end, landowners were able to protect their interests by having existing small roads excluded from the purview of building regulations.[8] This was an enforcement more deformed than that in Germany, where rampant development was excused in Berlin as long as compliance with the cursory building line was maintained. Although private interests were protected to a certain degree, legal recourse was at least secured for expanding public facilities. The regulation on facility designation was a legacy of the Tokyo City Improvement Ordinance and made the Home Ministry's approval mandatory regarding all matters related to operating public facilities including roads, water and sewage systems, parks, and public squares.[9]

Despite being equipped with a legal system, insufficient land reform and fragmentation of land ownership in Germany as well as Japan raised the need for land readjustment in both countries.[10] In Japan, the Agricultural Land Consolidation Law had already been in place since 1899 to divide land according to readjusted ownership, which originated from a tradition of communal land management that can traced back to feudal customs during the days of the Bakufu.[11] With the 1919 establishment of the Urban Planning and Building Law, land readjustment projects called *kukaku-seiri* applied methods of consolidating agricultural land to reorganize new urban districts. Since it was imperative for such projects to increase the utility of urban spaces, land fragmentation had to be resolved by reshaping irregular farming plots into regular building lots and then paving roads and building public facilities nearby. In some ways, such projects had something in common with German urban policies in that they promoted urban growth but also sought to offer patriarchal protection to the population flowing into cities. However, it was only after the Great Kantō earthquake that Japan began to fully adopt *Lex Adickes*, or the German law involving replotting. Still in shock from the earthquake of 1923, the Imperial Capital Reconstruction Project was launched so that the traditional structure of Japanese cities could finally be improved to perform modern functions and their suburban areas could be rearranged in a more orderly fashion. Land readjustment was far more developed in Japan than in Europe or the United States, because reorganization and building in urban districts could be executed almost without relying on public expenditure at a time when public finances were in an extremely fragile state. And the developments Japan achieved were immediately introduced to its colonies.[12]

In Japan, the term "urban planning" is known to have been used since around the 1910s. As a Home Ministry official's 1907 translation of Ebenezer Howard's *Garden Cities of To-Morrow* resonated with Japanese readers, British "town planning" was initially translated as "town layout planning" in Japan before it was soon replaced with "urban planning."[13] Until the Housing, Town Planning, etc. Act was established in Britain in 1909, there had been no consensus on what the term entailed even in a country like Britain at the forefront of the field. Hence, Japan had not been particularly behind the times. Japanese urban planners learned much not only from Britain but from the western parts of the United States as well. Straightforward roads, extensive parks, better public hygiene than Europe, and most of all, the American social atmosphere stressing efficiency prompted the Japanese to look back on the reality of their own society. On the other hand, the zoning system, building lines, and land readjustment were German measures worth studying for less developed capitalist nations like Japan. Nevertheless, what seemed to hold the most potential was the British idea of garden cities. There seemed to be no alternative better at neutralizing the inevitable vice caused by capitalism and at enriching a modern lifestyle.[14]

The ones who played a leading role in establishing ideas on urban planning in Japan were architects and bureaucrats active in Osaka rather than Tokyo. The most notable among them was Seki Hajime, who served as mayor of Osaka for nearly fourteen years starting in 1923. In his previous position as the city's deputy mayor, Seki organized the City Planning Research Committee in 1917 with Kataoka Yasushi, the president of the Kansai Architectural Association, and worked on drafting a bill aimed at improving urban districts. Seki demonstrated a new approach that aimed at understanding cities as a structural whole. His proposal to build satellite cities in order to resolve urban issues such as the chronic shortage of housing and slumism was groundbreaking, although the carefully drafted bill for it was never passed, perhaps for being too ahead of its time. Yet the committee's efforts were not in vain. In the spring of 1918, Kataoka Yasushi and Sano Toshikata, the then–vice president of the Kansai Architectural Association and a pioneer in the study of aseismatic design, launched a campaign together for legislations on urban planning and building.[15]

Accomplishing the mission of their campaign proved easier than expected. Home Minister Gotō Shinpei immediately offered his support by creating an urban planning department and an urban planning research committee within the Home Ministry's secretariat in May 1918. By that time, bureaucrats at the ministry had already formed a consensus on the need for a new urban planning law. Over the previous year, Gotō had established a governmental Urban Research Association, lobbied for the legislation on urban planning, and launched the journal *Toshi kōron*, or Urban Review. Gotō remained the association's president until his death in 1929, which goes to show how much he had been interested in urban planning. The Urban Planning Research Committee formed in 1918 was meant to draft and review bills related to urban planning. The committee's president was Mizuno Rentarō, who had worked for Gotō as vice minister before becoming the new home minister. Among those who played leading roles were Seki Hajime, Kataoka Yasushi, and Ikeda Hiroshi, who was the first to head the Home Ministry's Urban Planning Department and earned enough of Gotō's confidence to serve as the Urban Research Association's secretary.[16] Ikeda is known to have been greatly influenced by German urban planning after conducting a long-term survey in Europe and the United States when he came across the opportunity in 1913 while working for the Civil Engineering Bureau.[17] In July 1918, Ikeda, as head of the Urban Planning Department, submitted a draft of the bill for the Urban Planning Law. Simultaneously, the draft bill for the Urban Building Law was submitted jointly by Professor Uchida Yoshikazu of the Tokyo Imperial University's Department of Architecture, Sano Toshikata, and Kasahara Toshirō, a bureaucrat working for the Home Ministry. The two draft bills were turned over to the newly organized Urban Planning Research Committee for review and was passed the following year.[18]

Home Minister Gotō Shinpei was at the center of this lightning-fast process. Known as the father of Japanese urban planning, Gotō was originally a doctor until he began to work at the Hygiene Bureau of the Home Ministry. Recognized for his exceptional administrative skills, he became the head of civilian affairs in 1898 to assist the Governor-General of Taiwan. Gotō contributed to transforming Taiwan into a Japanese colony by initiating field surveys or projects for urban improvement. This experience in colonial administration landed him a position as the first director of the South Manchuria Railway Company, often referred to as *Mantetsu*. Mantetsu was one of the companies Japan created with the occupation of Korea and China explicitly in mind. It clearly had the authority to not only manage railway transportation at colonies but the lands called *fuzokuchi* attached to the railway as well. The fact that Gotō was the first to lead an organization upon which the Japanese Empire's rise and fall depended indicates his stature. Gotō Shinpei had turned into an expert in administration. He went on to serve in other key positions, including the Minister of Communications, the director of the Railway Agency, Home Minister, and Foreign Minister, until he became the mayor of Tokyo in 1920.[19]

The approach by a worthy statesman was sure to be reflected in the 1919 laws on urban planning and building. The two laws could be most characterized by pragmatism, hinting that German level-headedness or British practicality held dominance over pretentious French urban planning. As a physician by training, a scientific approach toward cities was what Gotō stressed above all. While heading civilian affairs for the Japanese Government-General of Taiwan, he foremost had meticulous field surveys conducted, arguing that colonial governance should be based on the principles of biology and take into consideration the capacity of the natives. This approach placing science ahead of political logic carried an even more distinct colonialist undertone.[20] In 1922, while Gotō was mayor of Tokyo, he had the newly established Tokyo Institute of Municipal Research invite Charles A. Beard, an American scholar and icon of progressivism. At the time, Beard was someone well worth inviting since he had been serving as director of the New York Bureau of Municipal Research. However, what motivated Gotō to make his acquaintance was Beard's materialistic view based on progressivism, not the title he held.[21] To Gotō, urban planning was not meant to simply reveal the dignity of a nation or serve as a vague means to boost happiness.

Through the preface "The Need to Legalize Urban Planning" in an issue of *Toshi kōron* published in February 1919 shortly ahead of the Urban Building Law's establishment, Gotō Shinpei argued that urban development was the core foundation of national advancement. However, through the contribution Gotō made to the journal the following year, "Improvement of Cities and the Resolve of Citizens," he emphasized that improving cities could promote public participation in civic affairs.[22] In other words, he believed urban development was a way for a nation and its people to become one. Mizuno Rentarō, who had worked under Gotō Shinpei before becoming Home Minister, also made a contribution to the journal, claiming that urban planning was linked directly to national wealth. Sano Toshikata, who drafted the bill for the Urban Building Law, stressed that urban planning was capable of drawing a larger population into a single space and guiding them toward a more efficient, developed society where shelters would be provided to escape natural disasters.[23] To these Japanese pioneers, urban planning guaranteed the formation of a safe country, precluded revolutions by facilitating economic prosperity, and above all, presented a new sort of beauty that was rational and progressive. Their emphasis on national interests and *fūchi bikan*, or beautiful cityscapes, was proof that they were the successors of Prussian tectonics.[24]

From Reconstruction Planning to Colonial Urban Planning

Despite their many limitations, the Urban Planning Law and Urban Building Law of 1919 created opportunities to apply to actual cities a new spatial principle that had been attained over the Meiji period. The

Great Kantō Earthquake that occurred on September 1, 1923, offered a test bed for gauging the future of urban planning. The earthquake struck Tokyo and Yokohama, leaving a dead and missing toll that amounted to one hundred and forty thousand and destroying forty-four percent of the two cities, including the old wooden settlements in them.[25] It did not, however, manage to destroy the new spatial principle and instead created an opportunity to accelerate the modernization and suburbanization of Tokyo. The curtain had risen on the plan to rehabilitate the capital.

The seasoned statesman Gotō Shinpei once again took center stage. The day after the earthquake occurred, the mayor of Tokyo was appointed Home Minister for the second time in his life and spent the next six years overseeing a large-scale project to rehabilitate the imperial capital. Much in the city had fallen apart to a degree that made it pointless to hang onto the old order, allowing Gotō to push forward with what had originally been included in the urban planning legislation. Gotō launched the Imperial Capital Reconstruction Board and took charge of the reconstruction project as the board's president. In less than a month after the earthquake, a plan to rehabilitate the imperial capital was established. Controversy within the government drastically cut the budget down to just over seven hundred million yen, but the project contained innovative elements such as making all major arterial roads in downtown Tokyo more than 50 meters wide and creating a park of nearly 10 million square meters, all of which required a ten percent land contribution from each and every landowner.[26] Such bold measures, no matter how dire the circumstances, could not avoid resistance from those with vested interests. From the landowners' point of view, Gotō Shinpei seemed to take advantage of a natural disaster to see unfulfilled reforms through instead of being interested in the rehabilitation of Tokyo. It was difficult for Gotō's plan to escape such criticism, since it was in fact focused on setting up the city's infrastructure. Itō Miyoji, a member of the Privy Council also known as a major landowner of Ginza, led the anti-Gotō front to put brakes on Gotō's plan.[27] The landowners were ultimately granted their wish, as the Special City Planning Law with an emphasis on urban rehabilitation was passed and promulgated on December 24, 1923.

Although the momentum for reform was slowed, the new legislation allowed the project to push forward with redeveloping previously overcrowded districts without requiring too much cost. There were still many obstacles to overcome in order to practice the zoning system and land readjustment, but the circumstances had indeed changed. The formation of the 73-meter-wide Gyoko street leading straight from the imperial palace to the Tokyo Central Station would have been impossible had it not been for the project's impetus. The sidewalk was separated from the road lined with ginkgo trees, water fountains were installed, and streetlamps were carefully designed.[28] Also, a bill was passed in 1929, nearly four decades after Ende and Böckmann's visit to Japan, in order to revive the old plan of concentrating government offices in the vicinity of the Diet building, which had been undergoing reconstruction.[29] Things had notably changed since the time of the Tokyo City Improvement Ordinance.

There is no doubt that Germany served as an important model in implementing this new spatial principle. The Home Ministry bureaucrat Ikeda Hiroshi, who drafted the urban planning legislation, particularly favored German urban planning techniques, and Gotō Shinpei was eager to employ the German zoning system and land readjustment method as soon as possible. Gotō had, after all, studied in Germany on a government scholarship.[30] Of course, the German model did not have to be the sole source in seeking reasonable solutions to issues of modern urban societies. In fact, it was American progressivism that had inspired Gotō. Yet, as always, reformists within the Japanese central government were not simply in pursuit of civilizational progress or capitalist rationalization. While dealing with the plan to concentrate government offices, the Tokyo City Improvement Ordinance, the Urban Planning Law, and the rehabilitation plan due to the earthquake, the "center" of Tokyo was what continued to occupy their minds. Every time that center emerged as the subject of discussion, Germany never failed to be brought up as well. To modern Japan, Prussia or Germany was definitely more than a technological, political, or military model. It rather symbolized a new spatio-temporal principle Imperial Japan had been in search of. And that principle suggested by Prussian classicism was none other than tectonics. This invisible principle that modern Japanese urban planning and public buildings struggled to realize continued to be resurrected even as it kept bumping into reality. It lifted its head from time to time, including when a 66-meter-wide "street of triumph" running north to south was built through the long-undisturbed Imperial Palace Outer Gardens to facilitate a military parade in celebration of Japan's victory in its war with Russia[31] and when the fervor to rehabilitate the capital led to the creation of Gyoko Street as well as the revival of the plan to concentrate government offices.

After being repeatedly pushed back by reality, tectonics was finally able to prove its true value in Japanese colonial cities. At colonies, it was possible to carry out premature yet ambitious urban plans and public building projects. To Japanese bureaucrats, colonies were empty spaces they could take advantage of to demonstrate newly acquired knowledge and technologies to their heart's content.[32] Urban plans adopted at colonies made it seem normal to destroy and dominate everyday life. What should not be overlooked here is that the Japanese bureaucrats' regard of colonies as empty spaces was basically no different from their regard of Japan and its capital. The invention of a new imperial capital had only been possible by completely denying that something else used to occupy the same space. Such an approach tends to be behind all impulses defined by modernity, including historicism. The only difference is that while such an approach would bump into reality and deflect in mainland

Japan, in the colonies, it was free to eliminate anything that seemed to stand in its way.[33]

In fact, the global phenomenon of importing back to imperial metropoles technologies and ideologies already tested in colonial cities was wholly repeated in East Asia.[34] The process of how Gotō Shinpei used his governance experience in Taiwan to manage Mantetsu, create an urban planning department within the Home Ministry, and plan the imperial capital's rehabilitation shows a typical mechanism between empires and their colonies. Unlike Western powers operating colonies from afar, Japan was an adjacent empire that had no problem taking its experience in colonies and utilizing it back in the metropole. Colonial cities of Japan shared cultural and racial affinities with the indigenous society. And most of those cities had a Japanese community that was not only made of bureaucrats and servicemen but also of migrant families from a diverse social and professional spectrum, which made the composition of such communities practically identical to that of cities in Japan.[35]

Moreover, except for the Shinto shrines and licensed quarters installed in all colonial cities, Japan presented itself as a modern state power in its colonies instead of applying its own national color. This was not merely for disguise. There was actually no difference of opinion between the colonial ruler and its subjects when it came to the goal of Westernizing and thereby modernizing colonies. This is why modernization continued to be pursued even after the end of colonial rule and why simply replacing the signs outside allowed Western-style buildings left by the Japanese to immediately blend into the cityscape of newly independent countries. The basic principle behind what Imperial Japan pursued in its colonies was no different from what it had pursued at home.[36]

There is, nevertheless, no need to especially highlight Japan's character as an adjacent empire. The historical fact that Japan was far more authoritarian and violent in its colonies than at home should never be disregarded. Colonies were spaces where more progressive technologies and legislations could be tested, which meant the indigenous nature of such spaces was thoroughly ignored, while violent methods were employed to carry out urban planning. A ruling ideology and its violence generally tend to be implemented invisibly in an imperialist homeland and visibly in its colonies.[37] Utilizing all sorts of negative images involving violence, inconsistency, immorality, decadence, fragmentation, atypicality, confusion, fissure, and dystopia to accentuate the empire's cultural ideal was the genuine purpose of colonialism, and colonial cities were where it came into full display. Under the banner of civilization or modernization, principles of Western architecture and spatial composition were transplanted to colonial cities to wield material, cultural, and institutional influence and affect their landscape.[38]

The city of Sapporo in Hokkaido where colonization began early on in the Meiji period shows the earliest stage in the evolution of Japanese colonialism. Urban planning was yet to clearly materialize in Japan, let alone Tokyo, but there certainly seems to have been an awareness of modernization through a rational layout of urban spaces. The basic plan to develop Sapporo was drafted in 1873, six years after the Meiji government came into power. A thoroughfare was laid between the city's southern commercial district, equivalent to the old *chōnin-chi* for merchants, and the northern district for public administrators, equivalent to the samurai area *buke-chi*, with a military base and a Shinto shrine situated on either end of the road. At the city's center, government offices, military facilities, educational establishments, drainways, a hospital, botanical garden, cemetery, Buddhist temple, Shinto shrine, and a boulevard leading up to the train station were methodically placed upon a traditional grid. The grid made of 60-ken-by-60-ken square blocks was mostly inherited from the castle town structure of the Shogunate period, but when paired with the address system, it seems to have been inspired by an American model.[39]

As the first formal colony of Japan, Taiwan was where urban improvement was carried out earlier than Tokyo.[40] However, only rudimentary improvements were made to the Taiwanese capital Taipei. It was by the time Japan gained access to Manchuria when Japanese urban planning reached a certain degree of development. Through the Treaty of Portsmouth, concluded on September 5, 1905, as a result of the Russo-Japanese War, Japan took over the Kwantung Leased Territory as well as the operation of the southern branch of the Chinese Eastern Railway. This allowed Japan to gain control over urban areas along the railway, including Mukden, Dalian, Port Arthur, and Changchun, and thereby develop them into focal cities.[41]

Mukden is the Manchu name of a city that was once the capital of the Qing dynasty and is now known as Shenyang. By entering into an unequal treaty with China in 1896 for helping it regain the Liaodong Peninsula, Russia was able to build a railway, train station, and a Russian-style district in Mukden based on the railway concessions it obtained until Japan took over the city in 1905 and built a new urban district around the land attached to Mantetsu. Thus, a new city was formed with basic arterial roads and three public squares, including Shifu Square.[42]

Meanwhile, the headquarters of Mantetsu, the office of the Kwantung Governor-General, and the Kwantung Army headquarters were all located in the port city Dalian, which served as the base for Japan's administration of Manchuria and the bridgehead for Japanese advancement into continental China. Dalian was both the starting and terminal point of a railway network that linked Europe and Asia. It was also a port city modernized through Russian urban planning, so that by the time Japan occupied the city, it already revealed a Western appearance rare in northeast Asia, with a circular plaza, Western classicist buildings, and radial or looped roads. The "Rules on Establishing a Japanese Concession in Dalian" and

"Interim Rules on Housing Construction and Management in Dalian," promulgated in April 1905, focused on dividing the city into three districts for the military, Japanese residents, and Chinese residents and on expanding the city's infrastructure, including roads, bridges, and electricity and water supply system per Russia's initial plan. Of course, Japan did not remain satisfied with merely finishing what Russia had started. It introduced a zoning system in Dalian in 1919, years earlier than the system's implementation in mainland Japan, dividing the city into four zones with the political intention of incorporating the native upper class into the Japanese empire. Furthermore, the already established radial pattern of roads was reshaped into the Japanese grid pattern, and new construction plans were drafted to overwhelm the buildings left by the Russians.[43]

As Nikolayevskaya Square, designed by the Russians, was rearranged under Japanese rule into Zhongshan Square, a series of public buildings emerged around the square. The first among them was the Dalian Police Station, completed in 1908 and designed by Maeda Shōin, a full-time architect at the Kwantung Governor-General's office. Modeled after the north German neo-Renaissance Hamburg City Hall, the police station, with an imposing brick clock tower, visually signified a new architectural style for the Japanese-occupied city.[44] The most noteworthy among the public buildings at Zhongshan Square, however, would be the former Dalian branch of the Bank of Chōsen completed in 1920, which served as the central bank of Dalian under Japanese occupation. Despite the six Corinthian columns dominating its façade, the neoclassical building had a steel-framed brick structure, and its entablature was simplified to the point of appearing abstract. The noteworthy aspect, though, lay not in the building itself but in the person who designed it. Nakamura Yoshihei was a mainstream architect who studied under Tatsuno Kingo at the Tokyo Imperial University. Since 1907, Nakamura had aided Tatsuno in supervising the construction of the Seoul branch of Japan's Dai-Ichi Bank, which later became the headquarters of the Bank of Chōsen. Nakamura was also involved in the construction of multiple buildings throughout the Korean peninsula, including the Kunsan branch of the Bank of Chōsen and the Mokp'o branch of the Oriental Development Company.[45] In fact, many graduates of the Tokyo Imperial University's Department of Architecture besides Nakamura participated in construction projects in major Japanese colonial cities. The portfolio they built in the colonies was considered something of a license by mainstream Japanese architects that would help launch their careers.[46]

In Manchuria, Japan mainly built focal cities around lands annexed to Mantetsu. This practically made the president of Mantetsu perform a role similar to that of a colony's governor-general. As the first president of Mantetsu, Gotō Shinpei took full advantage of his experience in Taiwan to turn Manchuria into a Japanese colony. His main administrative goals in Manchuria boiled down to the following four: transform Dalian into a first-class international port, expand the railway network in

Figure 3.1 A Current View of the Dalian Branch of the Bank of Chōsen (2017).
Source: Courtesy of Yeonkyung Lee. Photo by Yeonkyung Lee.

Manchuria, relocate five hundred thousand people from Japan to Manchuria, and develop Dalian into a pilot city. For the fourth goal, Gotō determined it would be more effective to preserve the districts formed by the Russians yet do away with the Russian-style segregation policy. Like in Taiwan, encouraging the cohabitation of the Chinese and Japanese was a policy basically aimed at allowing people in China to experience the advanced Japanese civilization and naturally accept the idea of being ruled by Japan.[47]

No further explanation should be necessary regarding the fact that the apparently magnanimous idea of Asian solidarity had been preconditioned upon Japanese leadership. Focal cities in Manchuria functioned as exhibition halls that internally and externally promoted modern Japanese civilization. Unlike the German Empire's relationship with Qingdao, such focal cities were directly linked to the formation of urban spaces in mainland Japan. Gotō Shinpei is proof that the 1919 Urban Planning Law established in Japan was an outcome of Japan's administration of Manchuria. And his connections indeed had a long-running influence. Ikeda Hiroshi, a proponent of German urban planning who drafted the urban planning legislation under Gotō's supervision in Japan, later served as an advisor to the Japanese troops that occupied Shanghai. The German-style secessionist architect Sano Toshikata, who drafted the Japanese urban building legislation, became a professor of the Tokyo Imperial University and was appointed as an advisor to the Capital Construction Bureau of Manchukuo.[48] These intertwined connections between the Japanese Empire and its colonies led to the creation of a new, unprecedented city.

Changchun was a geopolitically significant city in China that was within the range of both Russia and Japan's influence. The South Manchuria Railway and the Chinese Eastern Railway, respectively owned by Japan and Russia, both had to pass through Changchun in order to cross northern Manchuria and reach Europe. After the Russo-Japanese War ended in 1905, Changchun therefore surfaced as a key strategic point to Japan in establishing a British-style "informal empire" in Manchuria. Changchun Station was built in the Renaissance style upon land Japan acquired in the area in 1907, and to the station's south, a public square and new urban district began to be built. Compared to the former Qing capital Shenyang or Dalian full of Russian relics, the land attached to Changchun was practically empty, so Japan could shape it any way it saw fit.[49] And just in time, a surprising opportunity came calling. Changchun was renamed Shinkyō, the new capital of the puppet state Manchukuo.

The Conspicuous Modernity of the Manchukuo Capital Shinkyō

> The construction of a capital! Shinkyō! Shinkyō! How bright and cheerful it sounds, for the power and joy of creation is overflowing in a corner of East Asia.[50]

The *Journal of the Manchurian Architectural Association* turned its June edition of 1932 into a special issue to cover the Manchukuo capital Shinkyō. The birth of Manchukuo had resulted from the Mukden Incident that occurred when the Japanese Kwantung Army staged an attack in Shenyang on September 18, 1931. Once the puppet state was established on March 1, 1932, Changchun was designated as its capital a few days later on March 10. The new capital was to be called Shinkyō in Japanese and Xinjing in Chinese. Before the end of that same month, a ban on trading land in Changchun was issued, and an organization affiliated with Mantetsu immediately began drawing up a plan to develop the area.[51] The *Journal of the Manchurian Architectural Association*'s special issue featuring Shinkyō was also part of the process of transforming the city. Through the special issue, Onoki Toshiharu, the chairman of the Manchurian Architectural Association, glamorized Manchukuo as a creation driven by a "motive unprecedented in world history" and pointed out that the significance of its capital Shinkyō lay in using the knowledge and experience the Japanese gathered to launch a "new age" in Manchuria. A graduate of the Tokyo Imperial University's Department of

Architecture, Onoki had once worked in Taiwan and served as the head of Mantetsu's Construction Department, so he was well aware of what was new and what could be traced back to the past.[52]

The foundational motto of Manchukuo, "Five Races Under One Union," advocated cooperation and harmony between the Japanese, Han Chinese, Koreans, Manchus, and Mongols. The circular Datong Plaza became a symbolic representation of that motto at the center of Shinkyō, already full of Western-style public buildings since its affiliation with Mantetsu. The plaza south of the old Changchun Station met with four streets running from east to west to create a total of eight intersecting points that each formed a space suitable for monumental buildings. Beginning with a post office and police agency, buildings of various styles were quickly built to completely ignore indigenous styles and use Western historicism, Art Nouveau, or internationalism to flaunt the colonial ruler's civilizational superiority. As its status elevated from the city of a major railway station to the capital of Manchukuo, the time had come for Changchun to seek a more distinctive style capable of conveying the founding principle of Manchukuo and unifying its people.[53]

The department officially charged with overseeing the construction of Shinkyō was the Capital Construction Bureau, directly controlled by the State Council of Manchukuo. Once the plan was finalized by the end of 1932, the administrative details were worked out, and in April 1933, the "Planning Law for the Capital's Construction" was promulgated. The plan basically aimed for centralization, and although supervision of the construction project was left to the police per the custom in mainland Japan, it was policy for the police not to intervene more than necessary. The plan designed a tightly knit street network with radial, looped, and grid-patterned roads adequately distributed throughout the city. An extensive plaza with an outer circumference of 1 kilometer was to be formed at the intersection where the main roads would meet so as to also serve as a rotary accessible from all directions.[54] To design what was to be called Datong Plaza, all the advanced theories and techniques available at the time were considered, including the Swiss architect Le Corbusier's scheme "Contemporary City for Three Million Inhabitants."[55] And the civic center placed in the middle of Datong Plaza was to serve as a strong testament to the plaza's modernist nature.[56] This construction plan, however, was never realized.

Shinkyō was like a huge testing ground. With the old Changchun Station, renamed Shinkyō Station, serving as a landmark, the thoroughfare Datong Dajie stretched out for several kilometers toward Datong Plaza. The imperial palace of Manchukuo and its gardens were located southwest of the plaza, and a monument for national foundation as well as a university were placed even further south. The older parts of Changchun were situated to the east of the plaza.[57] In the 1932 special issue of the *Journal of the Manchurian Architectural Association* featuring Shinkyō

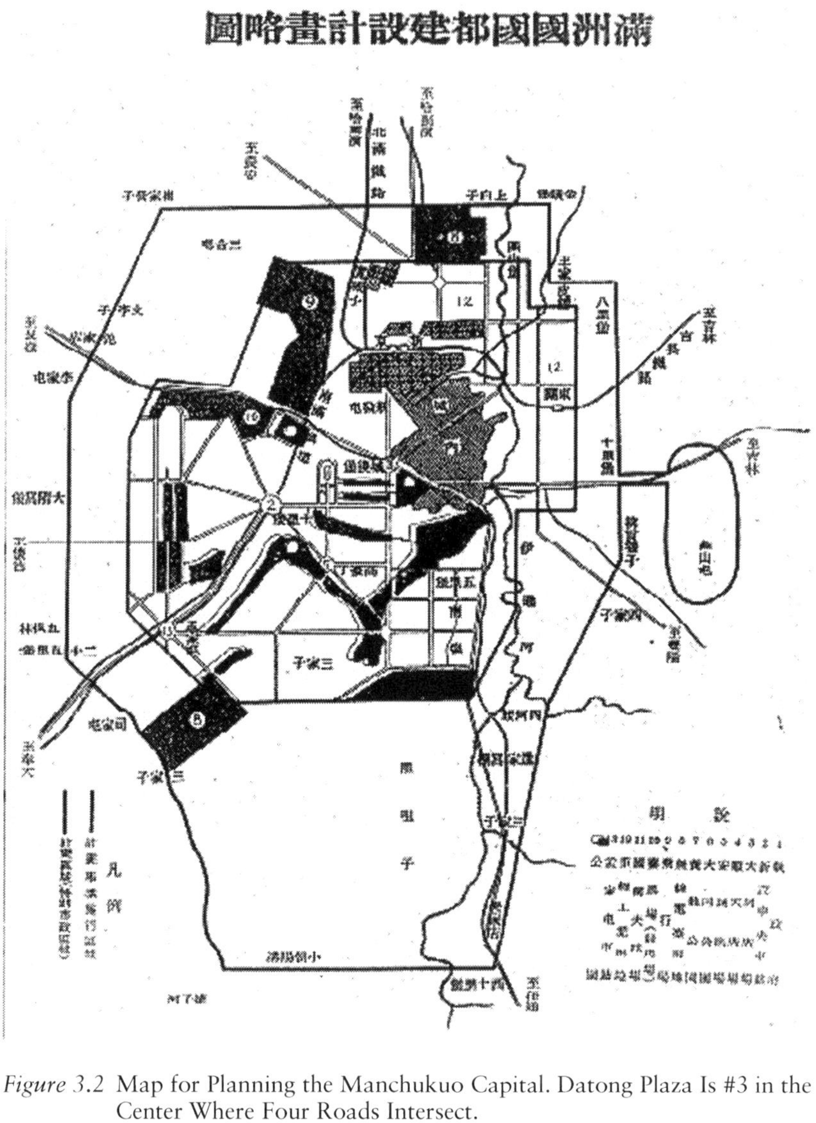

Figure 3.2 Map for Planning the Manchukuo Capital. Datong Plaza Is #3 in the Center Where Four Roads Intersect.

Source: Map adapted from the *Journal of the Manchurian Architectural Association* 13, no. 11 (1933). Courtesy of the Library of the Architectural Institute of Japan.

was a contribution by an official from the local government's construction department about the construction plan for the new capital. The contribution specifically listed the buildings necessary for the city to be acknowledged as a capital, which turned out to be an ambitious list including "a museum, library, art gallery, agricultural museum, industrial museum, transportation museum, zoo, arboretum, and applied chemistry laboratory" for educational purposes; "a track-and-field stadium, baseball park, tennis court, football stadium, swimming pool, skating rink, horse racing track, flying practice field, and shooting range" for the purpose of physical training; and for commemorative, religious purposes "monuments for national foundation and for the nameless patriots sacrificed for national foundation, and Confucian shrines." On the other hand, the contributing author also warned that blindly pursuing ideals should be avoided. The fundamental prerequisite in establishing a law for construction was to comprehensively take the country's natural cultural climate into consideration while focusing on the aspects of security, hygiene, transportation, and aesthetics. The author stressed that the new-born state was not an extension of the Great Qing Empire but an amalgamation of multiple Far Eastern ethnicities.[58]

Although Japanese urban planners at the time all agreed it was necessary to identify a regional tone specific to Manchuria, they did not hesitate to describe Changchun as "wild fields."[59] A city with seemingly nothing was completely recreated as it was divided by function into administrative, industrial, residential, mixed, and undetermined districts.[60] The population of Shinkyō surged, so that by the end of 1933, it reached above one hundred eighty thousand, including the soldiers stationed in the area. The Capital Construction Bureau expected the new capital's population to rise beyond five hundred thousand and established plans accordingly. The construction project covered an area of 200 square kilometers in total, including the old parts of town. This total area was cut back to half as the development of suburban areas was excluded from the plan, and when it proved difficult to make changes to the older parts of town, the total area was further reduced to 79 square kilometers, which was still a vast area to cover.[61]

To young Japanese elites, Manchukuo was a space with endless possibilities where they could unleash their vigor, ideals, or fantasies that had been held back at home. From ambitious bureaucrats specializing in technology to creative scientists, modernist architects, militaristic economists, speculators, and political extremists, all sorts of problematic figures seeking to escape mundane everyday life flocked to the new capital of Manchukuo.[62] Progressivism à la Gotō Shinpei or liberal conservatism was losing timeliness and was followed by the rise of a fascist tone that was more impulsive, extreme, and belligerent. All previous sense of restraint and timidity had been discarded by the eruption of an excessive determination to prove to the world the greatness of Imperial Japan. In the end, what Manchukuo created was not an East Asian modernity but an East Asian destructive urge that oscillated between extreme paranoia and schizophrenia. Manchukuo's mixture of civilizational and nationalist values gave birth not to a civilization or nation but to an aggressive state.[63]

It was therefore no coincidence for Manchukuo to be the first to feature *teikan yōshiki*, or the Imperial Crown style meant to embody the national mission and civilizational universality of the Great Empire of Japan. This new eclectic 1930s style of placing a Japanese roof above a Western ferroconcrete structure can be considered the Japanese response to Western modernist architecture.[64] The idea of merging an Oriental gabled roof with a Western pediment had already been envisioned by Itō Chūta through *An Architectural Study of Hōryū-ji*, but the Imperial Crown style made a rather abrupt debut. A neoclassical façade with a steep gabled roof was an awkward combination that had resulted out of an eagerness to flaunt the authority of an unparalleled empire. Then again, there were no set rules for adventurers who had already crossed the line. To them, contradictory combinations between a pure past and an entirely new future, or the extremely Oriental and extremely Western, was not an issue. A minor logical inconsistency was nothing if such combinations were able to contribute to the creation of a historically unprecedented state and capital.

The first buildings in the Imperial Crown style appeared at Datong Plaza. The construction of the first and second government office buildings began in 1932, and they were respectively finished in May and June of the following year. In November 1933, the two buildings were especially featured in the *Journal of the Manchurian Architectural Association*. The journal's review of the two structurally identical two-story buildings described that each had a twenty-eight-meter dome upon the center of a rectangular symmetrical construct made with ferroconcrete and black bricks. The special issue identified both buildings as the Manchurian style,[65] but the first government building in fact featured internationalism, while the second was done in the Imperial Crown style. Its elongated façade displaying a mixture of the neo-Renaissance and neo-Baroque styles with a pagoda-style roof of indeterminable nationality caused the second government building to be referred to as the Asian Renaissance style, or an architectural rendition of imperial authority as well as the Five Races Under One Union motto. The Imperial Palace of Manchukuo was constructed a bit south of the second government building to form a sense of unity in the landscape. Regardless of how they appeared on the outside, the ground plans for the buildings revealed a fundamental structure no different from any other Western-style building in terms of arrangement or functionality.[66]

A construction representative of the Imperial Crown style in Shinkyō is the Manchukuo State Council building. Its imposing presence along Shuntian Dajie running south from Datong Plaza stood out from the other government buildings lining the boulevard. Like the second government building at Datong Plaza, the rectangular state council building had identically shaped roofs placed on either end. A tower rising from the center was topped with a pagoda-style roof accentuated by a

Figure 3.3 Top: Front View of Manchukuo's Second Government Building. Middle: The Front Gate and Portico of the Manchukuo State Council Building. Bottom: Front View of the Central Bank of Manchukuo.

Source: Courtesy of the Library of the Architectural Institute of Japan. Top: From the *Journal of the Manchurian Architectural Association* 13, no. 11 (1933). Middle: From the *Journal of Manchurian Architecture* 17, no. 1 (1937). Bottom: From the *Journal of Manchurian Architecture* 18, no. 11 (1938).

slightly recessed section beneath it. The portico with robust Tuscan columns complemented the building's overall balance and proportions. The Japanese Diet building in Tokyo built around the same time is known to have served as a major reference for the state council building's construction.[67] With no parliament in Manchukuo, the state council was in fact the highest government organ, making it necessary for its building to appear more grand and authoritative than the Diet building in

Tokyo. While a fascist mutation of Prussian classicism could be detected from the Japanese Diet building, the Manchukuo State Council building seemed to share that mutation in addition to embodying the idea of a "Greater East Asia."

Shinkyō was a city where Japan laid bare its ambition to outshine the West. The Imperial Crown style was the tentative answer to a "new international style based on Oriental architecture" pursued since the inception of plans to build the new capital.[68] With the establishment of Manchukuo, all Japanese architects working in Manchuria were mobilized, and many young architects from mainland Japan also flocked to Shinkyō with expectations.[69] Architects and urban planners in Manchukuo sought to surpass the West instead of simply denouncing it. In other words, they aimed at overcoming modernity. Hence, the construction of Shinkyō was far from traditionalistic and just as modern as fascist architecture in Italy and Germany at the time. The Central Bank of Manchukuo, completed in 1938, was a building that symbolized the modernism of Datong Plaza instead of the civic center that ultimately failed to materialize. The size of the four-story marble building amounted to 30,000 square meters, while the diameter of each column decorating the façade was more than 1 meter.[70] This grand building was between several other buildings constructed earlier around the plaza, including a telephone and telegraph company, police agency, hotel, and the Capital Construction Bureau.[71]

The urban planning of Shinkyō was certainly different from how it was previously practiced in mainland Japan, as well as in Japanese colonies or areas within Japanese jurisdiction, and the difference was not limited to technical matters. Japan had finally come into its own governmentality in Manchukuo. Once it was able to patrol, surveil, control, and intervene, Japan could easily exercise "biopower" over the entire population.[72] In that respect, it was Manchukuo rather than mainland Japan where the solemn principle of national polity was upheld. The urban planning of Shinkyō did not stop at constructing a few monumental buildings but sought to create a thoroughly modern city with infrastructures such as a railway, driveways, and an airfield. The arrangement of a green zone, park, lake, museum (memorial hall), and zoo throughout the city demonstrated the intention to realize an ideal of the Great Empire of Japan through Shinkyō.[73]

In particular, the obsession with museums and parks had major implications. While visiting museums and zoos around Europe, the Iwakura Embassy recognized the fact that such facilities were not spaces meant to merely offer entertainment but had the potential to systematize knowledge and contribute to the rational formation of society. As the Imperial Household Agency took over museum-related affairs in Japan in 1886, it was actively involved in preserving cultural assets so as to elevate the imperial household's prestige. In May 1888, the agency took the lead in conducting a nearly four-month-long survey of ancient works of art in

Japan. This involved a large number of investigators, including Ernest Fenollosa and Okakura Kakuzō, and by the following year, the agency launched a project to build the Imperial Museum.[74] Museums made it possible to look beyond immediate interests by offering an intelligent means of gaining systematic control over the past and present. Zoos had the same effect as well. Unlike a garden, which would typically be part of private property, a public park provided the means to systematically control and manage space at a national level. The notion of "government" had been embedded deep within the Japanese awareness of "public."[75] Considering this would make Shinkyō the assembly of modern Japan's efforts to be able to dictate temporal and spatial changes instead of being dominated by them the way Japan had been up until then.

Having joined the ranks of powerful nations, Imperial Japan arrived at the point where it had to completely redesign its past as well as the future about to unfold. In 1928, the Japanese Ministry of Commerce and Industry established the Industrial Arts Institute to more actively utilize designs in revitalizing stagnant industries. Charged with rationalizing designs and developing them for mass production, the institute eagerly carried out its mission by inviting Bruno Taut to serve as an advisor and introducing to Japan the works of Le Corbusier and Bauhaus artists. The Industrial Arts Institute had a distinct military purpose as well. Industrial rationalization was key to boosting military power. The young bureaucrat Kishi Nobusuke, who led the institute's creation, later built his career in Manchukuo by serving as the deputy minister of industrial development there, and after the war rose to the position of prime minister in Japan. However, the approach Kishi advocated in pre- and postwar Japan was starkly different from that of Gotō Shinpei. Kishi's approach was not pro-Western or pro-Eastern, nor was it modern or anti-modern. It was as extraneous and provocative as the Imperial Crown style and both authoritarian and totalitarian.[76]

In the early 1940s, when the construction of Shinkyō was finished and Japan moved onto a war footing, the Japanese translation of *The New City* by a German urban planner and avid Nazi named Gottfried Feder came to hugely influence mainland Japan. The book was full of desire for a tectonic order capable of preventing chaos in industrial societies. The idea of dividing a city into self-sustainable farming zones to restore a true town community was based on an antimodernist Nazi ideology represented by the "Blood and Soil" slogan, something different in nature from middle-class English garden cities. In postwar Japan, Nishiyama Uzō adopted Feder's idea and actively made use of it in construction projects.[77] Imperial Japan had already begun to cross a critical point with the establishment Manchukuo in the early 1930s. The new image of state and society the empire initially failed to embody had actually originated from an ideal envisioned by the Japanese central government since the Meiji Restoration.

In October 1942, during the height of World War II, a young architect named Satō Takeo described through a short essay published in the *Journal of Manchurian Architecture* that "Manchukuo is a huge testing ground for Japan's self-reconstruction" and that "controllability and planning have been distinct features of Manchukuo since its foundation." Remarking that the Japanese should be thankful for the outcomes of experiments performed in Manchukuo, he claimed that now was the time for them to break free from Western liberalism and establish the authority of a new politics.[78] Satō went on to become well known in postwar Japan as a pioneer of empirical architectural acoustics. The fact that his scientific explorations were the product of a transmodern idea speaks volumes about the reality of the so-called East Asian modernity.

All those experiments, however, only allowed Japan to verify its own desires and could not make it truly embrace those of others. It was all about their own ideals, adventures, reconstruction, science, and overcoming modernity. There was no denying that Satō Takeo's definition of Manchukuo as a testing ground was no more than a reflection of how the Japanese perceived the puppet state.[79] Five Races Under One Union was but a forced union, and by giving precedence to the empire's interests, the Imperial Crown style and the idea of a Greater East Asia ended up excluding a majority of people from an invented national tradition.[80] So, despite having been equipped with infrastructures and environmental circumstances that may have been ideal, it was not difficult to understand why nearly half the population of Shinkyō continued to live in the old town or suburban industrial districts.[81]

What Shinkyō truly looked like grew more apparent in the eyes of those who came to visit the city from other Japanese colonies. Published in colonial Korea in the early 1940s, the short story *Sinkyŏng* by Yu Chin-o conveyed a sense of amazement at the "great modern city." "Mammoth-like buildings emerged into sight here and there across the plain near the southern edge of the new capital, and soon, a grand modern city unfolded." More than anything, the "Oriental roofs on large buildings visible from afar" captured the eyes of the intellectual from colonial Korea, and the "new architectural style" was understood in the story as an "effort made by the East to break away from Western influences and create something of its own." The new capital Sinkyŏng was certainly an admirable sight. To a visitor from another colony, "the large houses neatly lined along a wide street stretching out in all directions and bustling with pedestrians" may well have seemed like a mirage. The sight of his dead friend back home continues to overlap the overwhelming cityscape as the protagonist wanders through the streets.[82] The story itself does not reveal any obvious anti-Japanese sentiments, but it is possible to sense that the author's feelings were quite complex. What hung on the bare face of coloniality was a look of both awe and extreme intimidation.

2. From Hansŏng to Keijō

Korea as a Japanese colony occupies a unique position within the world history of colonization. Having been colonized by a neighboring country, one that has long remained at the receiving end of cultural transmission, continues to be a traumatic memory for Koreans. Modernization was not something Koreans would have rejected, but the problem was that it had been forced upon them by a neighboring country. The contradiction between modernization and colonization weighs on the collective memory of Koreans. Elements of modern civilization are entangled with remnants of painful colonial rule. This, however, should be considered an illusion rather than an overlapping aspect of reality. Modernity is not a term referring to a new reality but rather a unique discursive formation that mythologizes newness, which in turn disparages the colonial past and hastens the future. And there was no place that more acutely revealed the coloniality of modernity than Seoul under colonial rule.

The Urban Renewal of Hansŏngbu

Immediately after the 1910 Japanese annexation of Korea, the Chōsen Sōtokufu, or the Japanese Government-General of Korea, set out to restructure the capital of the Chōsen dynasty. Imperial Japan transformed the dynastic capital Hanyang into a colonial primate city called Keijō in Japanese, or Kyŏngsŏng in Korean. Between the Chōsen dynasty and the Korean Empire, the castle town Hanyang and the immediate areas outside the castle gates were merged into a single metropolitan district called Hansŏngbu. Under colonial rule, however, most areas surrounding the castle town were reassigned to a separate county in the adjacent Gyŏnggi Province, which was also responsible for administering the downsized capital renamed Kyŏngsŏngbu, or Keijō Prefecture. A dignified dynastic capital thus fell to the state of a small provincial city. What stood out the most over the process of this urban restructuring was the emergence of Western-style buildings. They were no doubt a means for Imperial Japan to visually suggest that it shared a prestige on a par with other Western empires. Such new buildings and other disparate spaces introduced by destroying the existing built environment represented the political and spiritual superiority Imperial Japan must have felt toward an old Asian dynasty like Chōsen.[83]

Waves of modernization began to rise in Hansŏng even before Japan gained control over Korea. The Korean Empire transformed Hansŏngbu by changing its closed street structure so that Kyŏng'ungung (later Dŏksugung) Palace instead of Kyŏngbokgung Palace would assume a central position. The castle town Hanyang was originally enclosed by fortress walls. Despite suffering multiple wars, the hierarchical arrangement between the royal palace, the royal family's ancestral shrine Chongmyo, the state altar of soil and grain Sajikdan, the upscale northern village Bukch'on, the southern village Namch'on full of thatched houses, the network of roads, and marketplaces all remained intact since early on in the Chōsen dynasty. The near-revolutionary restructuring of Hansŏngbu occurred late in the Chōsen dynasty when King Kojong decided to return to Kyŏng'ungung Palace instead of Kyŏngbokgung Palace after his flight to the Russian legation. Turning Kyŏng'ungung Palace into the city's center and forming a more open street structure around it indicated a determination to change the disengaged relations between the king and his subjects.[84] Moreover, the restructuring was a fairly ambitious project for the Korean Empire to announce at a time when it was devastated from political humiliation.

Once the Home Ministerial Ordinance no. 9 stipulating road width in Hansŏng was issued on September 28, 1896, King Kojong demonstrated his strong desire for reform by appointing the reformist Yi Ch'ae-yŏn as the magistrate of Hansŏngbu. Yi Ch'ae-yŏn thereby swiftly led the urban renewal of Hansŏngbu, but the idea of it had actually been suggested years earlier. Prior to the Kabo Reform of 1894, the magistrate of Hansŏng Bak Yŏng-hyo once proposed the construction of a modern city as a means to attain ideal governance. Realized by eventually gaining the king's firm support, the urban renewal of Hansŏngbu has been mentioned as a signal to reassess the political ambition and potential of an altogether fragile Korean Empire. The radial and ring roads around Kyŏng'ungung Palace as well as their circumscribing roads particularly attracted attention once they became known for having been modeled after the network of roads in Washington D.C. This was probably because some of the officials responsible for the project, like Home Minister Bak Chŏng-yang or the Hansŏngbu magistrate Yi Ch'ae-yŏn, had experience working as envoys in the American capital.[85]

The developments that unfolded around the time are also referred to as "Kwangmu Reform," which was named after the era name for Emperor Kojong's reign of the Korean Empire. In 1897, Emperor Kojong held a rite dedicated to heaven and earth and built an altar called Wŏn'gudan to announce at home and abroad the establishment of the Korean Empire. The altar was built within the grounds of Kyŏng'ungung Palace,[86] which began undergoing major renovations in 1897 as it became the new residence of Emperor Kojong after his flight to the Russian legation. The new royal council hall Junghwajŏn, finished in 1902, had a presence as dignified as its equivalent named Kŭnjŏngjŏn at the center of Kyŏngbokgung Palace. Two years earlier, Tae'an Gate, the front gate of Kyŏng'ungung Palace, was finished. The fact that a palace gate in close proximity to the daily lives of the emperor's subjects stood face to face with a sacred, unapproachable space like Wŏn'gudan carried profound meaning. It indicated that the Korean emperor sought to secure a power based on both widespread support from his subjects and historical legitimacy in the form of a blessing from the gods.[87]

For a brief while, Hansŏng fluttered its wings to launch itself as an imperial city.[88] The temporary shacks that had inched onto the major roads downtown were torn down to form a circular and radial road around Kyŏng'ungung Palace, and wide, straight roads were built in some parts of the city to partially form a tidy grid pattern. Apart from renovating Kyŏng'ungung Palace and building the altar Wŏn'gudan, transforming the cityscape to befit a new empire also involved repairing and expanding the Three Armies Headquarters, as well as the city's east gate, and forming Pagoda Park. Furthermore, the city started to be equipped with modern urban infrastructures such electricity, trams, and waterworks. Particularly impressive was the construction of the tram system, which Emperor Kojong adopted at the suggestion of Henry Collbran and Harry R. Bostwick. The two American businessmen apparently succeeded in convincing Emperor Kojong by pointing out the financial burden and physical inconvenience the emperor had to bear every time he made way to the Ch'ŏngnyangni area to visit Hongnŭng where Empress Min was entombed. Emperor Kojong awarded Collbran and Bostwick the exclusive right to operate trams, streetlamps, and telephone lines in the city. The two American businessmen thereby led the establishment of the Hansŏng Electric Company in 1898. By April 1899, a tram line running from the city's west gate through Chongno to reach Ch'ŏngnyangni outside the city's east gate was finished and a launching ceremony was soon held on the same day as Buddha's birthday.[89] The line was later extended to the transportation hubs Yongsan and Map'o that linked the lower Han River to downtown Seoul.[90] The construction of a tram line in Hansŏngbu was not the first of its kind in East Asia,[91] but it was definitely remarkable progress considering the overall circumstances of the Korean Empire at the time. The installation of streetlamps proceeded smoothly, so that three lamps along Chongo were lit for the first time in April 1900.[92] As the historian Bruce Cumings pointed out, Seoul became the first city in East Asia to be simultaneously equipped with electricity, trams, waterworks, and telegram and telephone lines.[93]

What was more important than achieving records was, however, their true nature. Building an imperial capital was part of a top-down reform to create a symbolic center for the Chosŏn dynasty. The circular and radial roads revolving around Kyŏng'ungung Palace conveyed a desire for the palace to serve as an axis that brought the hierarchically segmented subjects of the Chosŏn dynasty together as subjects of the Korean Empire. Views may vary on the way Chosŏn desperately flapped its wings when it was in a near semi-colonial state. However, one thing for certain is that as long as the Korean Empire sought to consolidate its subjects on its own terms, the subjects had to become modern citizens, which meant a royal palace could no longer represent them. The rhetoric of an empire incapable of coping with change was nothing but a poor excuse to hold on to power.[94] Some may say that Emperor Kojong's attempt to renew Hansŏngbu shares the spirit of Western absolute monarchy.[95] However, considering the overall circumstances at the time, what Emperor Kojong and those loyal to him exhibited was not the dignified spirit of absolute monarchy but a dismal parody of it.

Keijō City Improvement Project

Despite being a limited attempt from the top down, the door to a changed future had already opened. Calls for enlightenment poured out from the royal family as well as the ruling class in Korea. Evidence of this can be found in the several voluntary implementations of Western architectural styles. The royal family had some buildings built in the traditional style like the Chunghwajŏn Hall or in the Qing style like the Wŏn'gudan Altar but also experimented with foreign styles like the Sŏkcho Hall, designed by the British architect John Reginald Harding,[96] or eclectic styles fusing the Korean style with Western styles, such as the Jŏngkwanhŏn Pavilion designed by the Russian architect Afanasy Seredin-Sabatin.[97] The Independence Gate designed by Sŏ Chae-p'il was a case in which the ruling class outside the royal palace adopted a Western architectural style to declare its desire for enlightenment. Meanwhile, the foreign-style buildings Western forces built one after another according to their own needs, such as the Russian legation building, the German consulate building, and the Sontag Hotel[98] run by the sister-in-law of the German Ambassador to Korea, imparted a modern impression.[99]

From a general standpoint, this trend could be viewed as an entry into modern civilization, but it was in fact a result of weakened royal authority. As restrictions enforced by the national law loosened, foreign countries built taller embassies or legations, mostly in the Chŏng-dong area, and rapidly transformed the capital city's skyline. Rather than such embassies or legations, though, it was Myŏngdong Catholic Cathedral, seemingly unrelated to state power, that turned out to be responsible for neutralizing the restriction on the number of floors. Once the cathedral was finished in 1898, it remained one of the most eye-catching Western style buildings in Seoul for quite some time.[100]

These various developments, however, were completely swept under a strong current called the Japanese Empire. The empire had already joined the trend of Western-style construction in Korea by raising buildings, primarily at open ports such as the Japanese intendance office in Busan or the Inch'ŏn branch of Japan's Dai-Ichi Bank,[101] both of which were completed in 1879. Then a strong architectural current emerged only after the conclusion of the 1905 Korea-Japan Protectorate Treaty and the immediate establishment of a protectorate government called the Japanese Residency-General of Korea. The Residency-General reshuffled the Korean Ministry of Finance in charge of managing all financial affairs for the royal household as well as the government and created an architectural bureau within the ministry. Many Japanese architects were recruited into the bureau to start building a series of government offices and other modern facilities. A larger number of Western-style buildings appeared in Hansŏng and several open ports: the Ŭijŏngbu (Council of State) building (1907), the main building of the Industrial Training School (1907), the main building of Taehan Clinic (1908), the P'yŏngniwŏn (Supreme Court) building (1908), and the Kwangt'ong Hall (1909).[102]

Once the Japanese Government-General of Korea was established in 1910, larger construction projects were launched. The Japanese Empire's transformation of Hansŏng into Keijō essentially took over the Korean Empire's project to build a capital and turned it into one aimed at building the focal city of a Japanese colony. Even after the urban renewal of Hansŏngbu between 1896 and 1898, the Korean Empire continued to carry out construction projects. According to the second volume of *Keijō fushi* (The History of Keijō Prefecture) published by Keijō Prefecture many years later in 1936, the Korean Empire conducted partial road improvements, which included widening the road between Namdaemun (South Gate) and the Namdaemun Railway Station (today's Seoul Station) to 34.54 meters.[103] Such urban reconstruction projects were naturally carried over to the Government-General's urban improvement projects, although it was inevitable for their nature to change due to colonial urban planning.

The foremost change was administrative and turned Hansŏngbu into Keijō Prefecture. The Residency-General had already carried out administrative reform in 1906 when it ordered the rural administrative districts of Korea to be restructured into one capital (*subu*), thirteen provinces (*do*), eleven prefectures (*bu*), and three hundred thirty-three counties (*gun*). This restructuring left the existing framework of one capital and thirteen provinces intact but separated towns (*chon*) and townships (*myŏn*) from prefectures (bu) and placed them under the jurisdiction of adjacent counties. It also elevated places with treaty ports such as Inch'ŏn and Tongnae (Busan) to the status of prefecture. On September 30, 1910, shortly after Japan's annexation of Korea, an ordinance was proclaimed regarding the Government-General's local administrative system, and the very next day, the Government-General issued Ordinance no. 6 and 7 that designated which districts would fall under the jurisdiction of the twelve prefectures throughout the nation. As such, Hansŏngbu was renamed Keijō Prefecture and placed under the jurisdiction of Gyŏnggi Province.[104] On April 11, 1911, the size of Keijō Prefecture was reduced to the area inside the fortress walls in addition to Yongsan where Japanese residents mainly resided and other certain areas alongside the Han River. The five-hundred-year-old castle town that once dreamt of its ascent as an imperial capital thus ended up having to fold its small scrawny wings.[105]

Since the 1914 restructuring of administrative districts, prefectures were considered basic administrative units that purely covered urban areas,[106] and this had to do with conducting new forms of urban renewal. On October 7, 1912, the Government-General notified the governors of each province of Directive no. 9, revealing the intention to extensively reconstruct major cities throughout Korea.[107] A month later, on November 6, the Government-General made public through Announcement no. 78 its plan to improve twenty-nine routes in Keijō. While the directive in October merely shared the Governor-General's intention toward municipal improvement, the announcement made a month later revealed specific plans to realize that intention in a particular area. The map featuring plans to improve Keijō published in the Government-General's official gazette *Chōsen sōtokufu kanpō* showed two roads forming a central axis of symmetry: a radial road around Hwanggŭmjŏng Square (Kōganemachi Avenue) near Kyŏng'ungung Palace and a road running from the Governor-General's official residence up to the northern downtown area central to Koreans. This plan demonstrates a relatively smooth fusion between two disparate facets: a shift of focus in the Korean Empire's renewal of Hansŏngbu from Kyŏng'ungung Palace to the Japanese residential area and the creation of a new urban space around the front gate of Kyŏngbokgung Palace. What is most noteworthy is that the hierarchy between the northern area with the historic Ch'ŏnggye Stream and palaces central to the Chosŏn dynasty and the southern area developed by the Japanese was torn down by the horizontal connection built between them, signifying the disintegration of a historic space.[108]

The Keijō City Improvement Project aimed to systematically repair the network of roads downtown and add a large number of new roads to it. The downtown area was knit into a grid-like pattern, and the construction order and width of each route was determined based on their respective importance. For instance, Route no. 1 between Kwanghwamun Gate and Hwangtohyŏn Square was to be 30 kan (54.54 meters) wide, while Route no. 2 between Namdaemun Gate and Namdaemun Railway Station was to be 19 kan (34.54 meters) wide. The rest of the routes were to be either 15, 12, 10, or 8 kan wide. To appear more urban, a square was to be formed at each major intersection, namely Hwangtohyŏn Square, Taehanmun Square, Taeandong Square, Hwanggŭmjŏng Square, Sŏnŭnjŏn Square, and T'apkol Park Square. These details were not all determined through the first draft of the project's plan but finalized over five revisions carried out to adapt to the project's developments. Two more routes were added in 1917 to make the total number of routes thirty-one. Some roads were already in place before the city improvement project's announcement. Route no. 2, which functioned as the gateway to Keijō, was already finished after its construction began in 1911. So was Route no. 3 between Hwangtohyŏn Square and Kyŏng'ungung Palace, which began to be constructed in early 1912. The project's plan as of November 1912 therefore focused on improving streets around Hwanggŭmjŏng and Bonjŏng (today's Ch'ungmuro), which emerged as Japanese commercial districts in Keijō. In between those two districts, Route no. 9, running north to south through Keijō to directly link Ch'angdŏkkung Palace and the Governor-General's official residence at the foot of Mount Namsan, was newly paved by 1918, thereby completing the first phase of the 1912 plan for city improvement.[109]

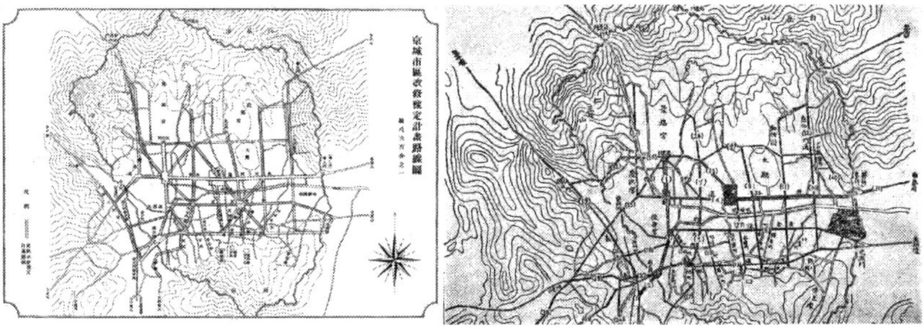

Figure 3.4 Left: Keijō City Improvement Plan of 1912. Right: Keijō City Improvement Plan of 1919.

Source: Left: Map adapted from *Chōsen sōtokufu kanpō* 81 (1912). Right: Map adapted from *Keijō fushi* 3 (1941).

The 1912 plan for the Keijō City Improvement Project was carried out with a certain degree of ambition. By widening and straightening thoroughfares and repairing bridges and waterways, the plan wholly inherited the basic purpose and techniques of Japanese city improvement and referred to Haussmann's renovation of Paris as it attempted to refashion an entire city. The one who led the 1912 plan's execution was Mochiji Rokusaburō. Mochiji had become a leading expert in city improvement from working on a similar project for the Japanese Government-General in Taiwan before he was reassigned as the first director of the Government-General's civil engineering bureau in Korea.[110] Despite bringing in an expert in city improvement like Mochiji, aiming for total renovation was what kept the project from remaining faithful to its original plan. Creating a radial road around Hwanggŭmjŏng Square was an impractical idea to begin with. The site was at the heart of a historic capital with centuries of tradition. Taking it apart immediately after depriving Korea of its sovereignty had to come at a tremendous political cost.[111] The plan was eventually forced to give up its central axis, which in turn affected the horizontal-vertical arrangement of the overall street network. Route no. 9 lost its importance as a major north-south axis, and other routes running from east to west also underwent change. It became uncertain as to whether Route no. 6 connecting Tonhwamun Gate and Ihwa-dong would actually be constructed because it had been designed to cut through Ch'angdŏkkung Palace and Chongmyo Shrine. Even though the palace was the legacy of a fallen dynasty, meddling with it still sparked considerable resistance. The route was opened after overcoming many hurdles, but it ended up greatly delaying the project's overall schedule and brought major political repercussions.[112]

The underlying purpose of the plan, however, did not change. The only thing that did change was the pivot, which shifted from the radial road around Hwanggŭmjŏng Square to Route no. 1 and Routes no. 2 and 3 immediately connected to it. The three routes had been completed prior to the city improvement plan's announcement. Although the numbers they were given made their importance obvious enough, the long thoroughfare stretching past the front of Kyŏngbokgung Palace, through Taehanmun Square, and leading up to Namdaemun Gate went on to claim a unique status as a central axis to the project as it progressed. What was the significance of this thoroughfare running through the heart of a fallen dynasty's capital? According to the historical record *Keijō fushi*, it was in 1912 when the forecourt of Kyŏngbokgung Palace was selected as the site of the new Government-General building that would replace the old Resident-General's residence at the foot of Mount Namsan.[113] This selection seems to have been made before the city improvement plan was announced in November of the same year.[114] So, although the new headquarters for the Government-General may have been a vague part of the project's initial plan, its presence solidified as the plan kept being revised during its execution.

The incomplete construction of Route no. 9 marked the conclusion of the first phase of the Keijō City Improvement Project. On the surface, road reorganization may appear to be all that the project achieved. Compared to the urban planning that later unfolded, the project's first phase indeed failed to go beyond reorganizing existing roads and only covered a small area. Its scale was quite different from that of the Tokyo City Improvement twenty-four years earlier in 1888 which, in addition to reorganizing roads, created other infrastructure such as a water and sewage system for the urban population.[115] However, paying too much attention to the aspect of achievement bears the risk of overlooking the historical cause: oppressive colonial rule immediately after depriving a country of its sovereignty. Considering the changes the project later brought to the urban space of Keijō, its underlying purpose mattered far more than its direct outcome. The site for the Government-General's new headquarters may have been vaguely factored into the city improvement plan at the beginning, but it was nevertheless an inseparable factor. Having the forecourt of Kyŏngbokgung Palace, a place entrenched with memories of a fallen dynasty, serve as the central axis in building a colonial primate city seemed truly contrarian. It involved an entirely new approach to time and space, one that went beyond simply revealing an empire's splendor or practically representing the interests of Japanese residents in Keijō.

The demolition of the fortress walls starkly demonstrated the approach the modern empire Japan took toward the capital of a fallen dynasty. The Japanese Empire mutilated the city by tearing down the walls and the four gates surrounding Hansŏng. The reason the demolition met little resistance was because the Empire of Korea practically provided the pretext for it. In October 1898, the second year of Emperor Kojong's Kwangmu Reform, the Korean government initially planned to tear down the walls on either side of the east, west, and south gates Tongdaemun, Sŏdaemun, and Namdaemun to lay a tram track linking Chongno, Namdaemun Gate, and Wŏnhyŏ-ro. However, it eventually chose to leave the walls intact and went for the unorthodox solution of having trams drive through the gates, which were only 2 kan wide. As the Kyŏngbusŏn Railway began to operate in early 1905, the ninth year of the Kwangmu Reform, railway passengers had to pass through the gates as well, making the walls seem even more cumbersome. By the time the Japanese Residency-General of Korea was established, the old walls around Hansŏng found it difficult to withstand the overbearing political pressure against them.[116]

The demolition of walls around Hansŏng proceeded swiftly. In 1907, the year the last king of Korea, Sunjong, ascended to the throne, the Korean Empire's government launched a committee for the castle walls' disposal and tore down the battlements to the left and right of Tongdaemun and Namdaemun Gate. And as a new road started to be paved, a massive demolition of the castle walls began.[117] The committee dissolved six months later after achieving what it had set out to do. The motivation behind such a swift disposal was much less complex than the circumstances leading up to the decision to dispose of the walls. The streets of Keijō had to be polished enough to welcome the Japanese Prince Yoshihito (the future Emperor Taishō) during his visit to Korea. As if to show off the power of Meiji Japan, the prince came calling on the Korean imperial household with an entourage of prominent figures, including General Katsura Tarō, Admiral Tōgō Heihachirō, and Duke Iwakura Tomosada.[118] The territory of Korea was now purely at the disposal of the Japanese Empire. After Japan's annexation of Korea in 1910, the trend of demolition intensified so that the walls on either side of Tongdaemun Gate as well as Sŏdaemun Gate were torn down, and soon enough, most of the walls around Hansŏng disappeared from sight.[119]

The swift and near-total demolition of the historic walls was surely evidence of the brutality of colonial rule. However, viewing it only as an instance of oppression and disregard for a colony would be missing the point. What the Japanese Empire sought was not to unnecessarily provoke the natives of its colony but to introduce modern civilization to it in a way that would best serve Japan's own interests. It was therefore not about representing the interests of the colonial natives, which exposes the violence in the means Japan adopted to achieve its goal. The fact that the Empire of Korea began tearing down the walls of its own accord suggests that the point of the matter was not in the demolition itself but the creation of a new urban space.

After the treaty concluded on August 22, 1910, completely and permanently ceded all rights of sovereignty over Korea to "His Majesty the Emperor of Japan,"[120] the Japanese Government-General of Korea established a few months later on October 1 had no further reason to hesitate in creating a new urban space. The Japanese military soon became involved in road construction and required the passage of military vehicles to be considered in determining the type and width of roads.[121] The "Land Confiscation Law" promulgated as Regulation no. 3 in April 1911 allowed the colonial government to confiscate and use any land necessary for projects in the public interest.[122] The enforcement rules for Regulation no. 3 issued two months later as Departmental Ordinance no. 80 turned the land confiscation law into reality.[123] The law made the harsh reality of colonial rule feel far more real than the demolition of the walls around Hansŏng. Its uninhibited enforcement and punishment relied on police force and were coercive under the unique conditions of colonial rule. Yet the police played a considerable role in urban planning in Japan as well, from having adopted the Prussian system during the Meiji era. Hence, the Land Confiscation Law promulgated ahead of the Keijō City Improvement Project was part of an administrative plan based on certain principles rather than being a matter of the winner simply taking possession.

To be able to alter roadside buildings and thereby widen roads while the Keijō City Improvement Project was picking up steam, the Government-General promulgated Ordinance no. 11, called "Regulations to Control Urban Construction," in February 1913.[124] The nine-article ordinance covered details that would be stipulated later in building codes, including building coverage ratio, building lines, construction material, supplementary installation, aesthetics, and disaster prevention. It also attempted to rationally reorganize the urban space of Keijō, which would eventually be divided into zones with different purposes such as a fire prevention zone, height control zone, or semi-industrial zone.[125] The ordinance did not, however, manage to rise far above the level of building regulations that focused more on control than development.[126]

Having established a legal, administrative scheme, the city improvement project went from repairing roads and the landscape around them to serving as a foundation for introducing features of modern civilization. In Keijō, such features signaling a new age happened to be trams and trains. The Japanese Empire quickly extended the tram line the Korean Empire started to lay in Hansŏngbu so that even before Japan's annexation of Korea, the line went as far as the Sinyongsan area where a Japanese military base and army headquarters was located, not to mention many Japanese residents. As the project progressed, tram lines running east to west and north to south were newly installed in Keijō. Road repair and the addition of tram lines were the product of a new idea to create a horizontal network in the city.[127] The introduction of railways was carried out according to a bigger picture. The Kyŏnginsŏn Line extended to link Chemulp'o Harbor and Namdaemun Gate. The Kyŏngŭisŏn Line running north along the west side of the Korean peninsula up to Sinŭiju already existed prior to Japan's annexation of Korea. When the railroad bridge over the Amnok River was opened in November 1911, a transportation route between Japan, Korea, and China was secured, doubling the strategic importance of railways. That importance upon which the interests of an entire empire depended did not go unnoticed by the first Japanese Governor-General of Korea, Terauchi Masatake, who also served as minister of the Japanese Army. The Government-General expropriated the land necessary to build railways and accelerated construction to complete the Kyŏngwŏnsŏn and Honamsŏn Line in 1914, establishing an X-shaped railway network with Keijō at its center. The flourishing of railways greatly transformed Keijō. It brought into the city a rapid influx of goods, information, and people, and the newness of railways itself drastically changed the city's structure and landscape.[128]

Once the first phase of the Keijō City Improvement Project was finished, the July 25, 1919, edition of *Chōsen sōtokufu kanpō*, the Government-General's official gazette, announced that the plan for city improvement would be revised. The revised plan reflected all the changes made since the plan was first formed in 1912.[129] The radial road around Hwanggŭmjŏng was gone, and the plan's center was instead occupied by a straight, vertical road that started in front of Kyŏngbokgung Palace, ran past the front of Tŏksugung Palace, and went down to Namdaemun Gate. The prominence of the new Government-General headquarters yet to be built was already secured within the reshaped network of roads. Whereas the 1912 plan featured many diagonal roads, the 1919 plan displayed a more distinct grid pattern stretching out north, south, east, and west, with Route no. 1 and 3 serving as vertical axes. Another notable change was the plan's inclusion of Yongsan and Map'o, which were areas that used to be outside the walls of Hansŏngbu. The straight thoroughfare leading to those areas from Kyŏngbokgung Palace must have been a choice dictated by military reasons and the purpose of maintaining public order. At the time, Sinyongsan was where the Japanese army headquarters and barracks were located, while the Keijō Prison was in Map'o.[130]

The Rationality of Urban Planning?

On the whole, the Keijō City Improvement Project was part of an attempt to build a new modern urban space. The oppressive nature of colonial rule did not contradict such an attempt but rather accelerated it. The more the Japanese Government-General of Korea wielded its absolute power, the more shocking and convincing modern civilization seemed. An editorial titled "City Improvement" published in the November 17, 1912, edition of *Maeil Sinbo*, the daily newspaper that turned into the Government-General's mouthpiece, stated that since roads are directly related to civilizational exchange, straightening and extending them in all directions brought Korea onto the path of civilization. The credit for trying to improve Korea, of course, went to the Japanese Governor-General, who exerted every effort for the project.[131] The account of the project in

Keijō fushi is similar in deeming the project a tremendous success thanks to the governor-general's ceaseless efforts to make transportation in Keijō convenient and timely.[132] The fact that Japanese expatriates in Keijō were fairly satisfied with the project's achievements can easily be sensed from *Saikin keijō an'nai-ki*, or the Latest Guide to Keijō. The book was published in 1915 by Aoyagi Tsunatarō, who had served since 1912 as president of a society to study Korean history called Chōsenshi kenkyūkai and began to serve as president of the daily newspaper *Keijō Shinbun* in 1917. Although the project was still in its early stages around the time the work was published, Aoyagi gave a generous appraisal of the project.

> The streets of Keijō appeared devastatingly depressed. Without vigor and trembling with fear, it was barely surviving. However, as Japan gained sovereignty over the Korean peninsula, the bold reforms the governor-general carried out has transformed Keijō beyond recognition. Now smooth thoroughfares are stretching out east, west, north, and south. The scale and convenience of transportation in the city surpasses that of Japanese metropolises. Downtown Keijō is dotted with grand new buildings showing off their dazzling and stately presence.[133]

It is difficult to take such a generous appraisal at face value considering the positions Aoyagi held at the time and the underlying nature of his books. Yet it does seem certain that change was in the air in Keijō. In the 1910s, the city had already been captivated by the phantasmagoria of modern civilization. It would not necessarily be wrong to claim that such a phantasmagoria did nothing to help to the city's residents in real life, nor did it help explain the situation at the time. What matters more is that the colonial ruler and its subjects alike were obsessed with becoming modern. The new landscape of the colonial primate city Keijō seemed to clearly demonstrate the omnipotence of modernity.

The foremost reason behind modern civilization's undeniable appeal was "rationality." It possessed impartiality that stood in contrast to partiality or voluntary will. Rationality was what made even colonial rule appear to be an act of taking moral responsibility rather than that of a colonial ruler pursuing its own interests. Regardless of how its specific achievements would be viewed, the Keijō City Improvement Project was an attempt to rationally reorganize an urban space. It sought to maximize the effectiveness of colonial rule by improving the transportation infrastructure and polishing the city's landscape. Under the exclusive charge of the Keijō Civil Engineering Branch directly supervised by the Government-General's Bureau of Interior Affairs, the project went on until the late 1920s. It imitated the city improvement of Tokyo by macadamizing crowded intersections and laying sidewalks on either side of the road to separate them from the carriageways and tram lanes running in the middle. The existing network of roads and natural topographical features of Hansŏng were preserved to a certain degree as the knotted streets were transformed into a grid-like pattern.[134] Out of the forty-seven routes planned, twenty-one were realized by 1927.[135] And while carrying out such a long-term project, more specialized, "rational" plans were bound to surface.

The urban planning that grew popular in the West and Japan started to more heavily influence Korea in the 1920s. Junior civil engineering officials at the Government-General and Japanese capitalists in Keijō formed the Keijō Urban Planning Research Society and drew from their collective expertise to discuss the project's future. The society held its first meeting near the end of August in 1921 and decided its purpose would be to work on introducing the 1919 Urban Planning Law of Japan to colonial Korea. It was only natural for the society to set such a goal, considering that the society's creation was led by Mizuno Rentarō, who played a leading role in the establishment of the 1919 Japanese Urban Planning Law as president of the Urban Planning Research Committee until he was appointed as the director-general of political affairs at the Government-General in 1919.[136]

What directly prompted the need for expert urban planning was the petitions from Japanese expatriates who repeatedly suffered from flooding. Yet it was more fundamentally propelled by the clear desire among officials at the Government-General to rationalize urban space. Relying only on force without rational conviction in carrying out its mission to civilize Keijō, the Government-General had to repeatedly revise its plan for city improvement every time it clashed with reality. As military rule tainted with trial and error drew to an end and colonial rule showed signs of settling down, it grew necessary for the Japanese ruling class in Korea to etch the cultural hegemony of the Japanese Empire upon the minds of its colonial subjects. The time had come for "cultural rule," advocated by the third Governor-General, Saitō Makoto.[137] Like Tokyo or Berlin, Keijō also worshiped the one and only god called modernity in the 1920s. That meant there was no other logic capable of standing up to the logic of functional rationality in Keijō.

News of the Imperial Capital Reconstruction Project after the Great Kantō earthquake served as another occasion that fanned the desire for urban planning. Although the project failed to be carried out strictly as planned in the metropole Tokyo, there was still plenty of room to try new things in another urban space where the practice of policies was far more uninhibited. The gap between theory and reality, however, still existed. The Keijō Urban Planning Research Society was a semi-governmental group that had direct ties with the bureaucratic society, enough for the Government-General's director-general of political affairs to serve as an advisor to the society. At the same time, it was a semi-civilian group meant to conduct studies led by civilians and had central figures in Japanese urban planning like Kataoka Yasushi and Sano Toshikata join as honorary members. In actuality, the society functioned as no more than an advisory body in terms of forming and executing policies, which was in contrast to the influence the Urban Planning Research Committee wielded in Japan under the Home Minister Gotō Shinpei's lead.[138]

Between 1926 and 1930, the Keijō Urban Planning Research Society drafted three different plans for Keijō Prefecture, but none of them were adopted during the process of policy making. Many aspects required legal examination, and the enormous cost the plans entailed came across as unrealistic.[139] Nevertheless, the research society's activities and their outcomes did have an impact on the policies formed by the Government-General. *Research for the Urban Planning of Keijō*, published by the Keijō Prefectural Government in February 1927, hinted at a developing interest in the population, climate, transportation, and hygiene circumstances in suburban areas, which was related to what the research society had discussed and proposed for years.[140] The authorities did, of course, carry out investigations of their own to form plans. When the Government-General underwent a reshuffle in 1921, an urban planning section was created under the Bureau of Interior Affairs' Civil Engineering Division. A temporary urban planning section was also installed within the Keijō Prefectural Government in 1926 to take charge of urban planning surveys. In March 1929, the Keijō Prefectural Government asked Okazaki Shōtarō, the chief of general affairs at the city of Osaka's urban planning department, to draft the bill for an urban planning law. Okazaki was, after all, considered a leading authority in Japan on legislations related to urban planning and had played a principal role in carrying out urban planning projects in Nagoya and Osaka.[141]

In the Korean history of urban planning, the 1920s was a time when research and investigations were conducted to establish an urban planning law like Japan. It was also a time when the city improvement project launched in the 1910s was being wrapped up and preparations were being made ahead of the extensive spatial reorganization to come in the 1930s.[142] Such an assessment, however, fails to look beyond the general view that in the history of Korea, the twentieth century was a process of achieving modernization. Rather, it is necessary to note that the Japanese Government-General of Korea made use of state tectonics in transforming Hansŏng into the colonial primate city Keijō. Although the use of state tectonics was justified by the great cause of introducing modern civilization, there are still aspects of it that cannot be explained as a modern form of state governance or a technological response to the demand for industrialization. What kept the rational suggestions of a civilian research society from being acknowledged? The Keijō Urban Planning Research Society certainly had enough connections in the Government-General to make its suggestions be acknowledged. It would also be an insufficient explanation to say the Government-General found it unnecessary to spend fiscal resources on improving the lives of colonial natives.[143] The natives of Korea were not a subject of interest to the society, and the circumstances were no different for Japanese expatriates in terms of being excluded from the Government-General's policies. Among the proposals made by the Japanese Residents' Association of Keijō was one that included a complaint about how the private houses scheduled for demolition around Namdaemun Gate were being bought out at excessively low prices and that the evacuation deadline was too tight.

> The expansion of roads seems to be focused only on certain aspects. The Namdaemun Gate area is one of the most important sites in this city, which is why the area's improvement should be perfected through public-private consensus. . . . Only then can this city maintain its reputation even after a hundred years of further development and expect to prosper commercially.[144]

While the Japanese Residents' Association of Keijō called for modern rationality, the Government-General revealed the coloniality of power. What the Government-General actually emphasized was Imperial Japan as an organic whole. Modern rationality was simply a tool to forge a stronger empire and could not serve as a purpose in itself. In a colony, modern rationality was only summoned for efficient rule and mobilization. In other words, rationality in real life or in industrial technology was of no concern to the colonial ruler unless it particularly contributed to colonial rule and mobilization.[145]

Chosŏn Urban Planning Ordinance

Despite remaining a subject of discussion throughout the 1920s, the establishment of an urban planning law in Korea kept being postponed for a variety of reasons. Nevertheless, it was no surprise that a bill for its enactment suddenly emerged after the Manchurian Incident. With the establishment of Manchukuo in 1932, Najin in North Hamgyŏng Province was selected as the terminus of the shortest, most economic route for transporting natural resources produced in Manchuria to Japan and for sending Japanese industrial products to Manchuria. The Japanese Government-General of Korea rushed to draft a Japanese-style urban planning law for Korea in order to develop Najin into a modern port and the terminus of the South Manchurian Railway. In June 1934, the Government-General promulgated the Chosŏn Urban Planning Ordinance as Regulation no. 18 and subsequently the rules for the regulation's enforcement as Ordinance no. 78 the following month. In September 1935, amendments to those enforcement rules were promulgated as Ordinance no. 105, which specified a ten-page guideline on the restriction of building heights. These legal, administrative measures immediately led to the 1936 plan for Greater Keijō.[146]

As its name suggests, the Chosŏn Urban Planning Ordinance aimed for nationwide urban development. Unlike city improvement projects that concentrated on revamping old downtown areas, the ordinance focused more on expanding cities to suburban areas or developing new cities like the port

Najin while using governmental authority to control the expected surge in land price or population growth. It was an emergency measure the governor-general took based on his strong leadership rather than from considering public opinions. As Article no. 2 and 3 in the first chapter of general rules indicate, the ordinance basically depended on the governor-general, who was the only one allowed to draft and make decisions related to urban development plans.[147] Out of the fifty articles divided into three chapters, Article no. 1 stated that the ordinance basically applied to the planning of major facilities involving transportation, hygiene, security, and the economy. An editorial in the daily *Maeil Sinbo* also confirmed that the ordinance encompassed urban planning, building regulation, and land readjustment.[148] This urgently created set of regulations resembled a combination of the Japanese urban planning and building laws of 1919 as well as parts of the 1923 Special City Planning Law related to land readjustment conducted during the Imperial Capital Reconstruction Project.[149] The colonial government took the lead in urban planning and building regulation, severely limited private participation, and tried to push ahead with land readjustment without considering the residents' opinions, although such readjustment would directly impact the lives of the residents. This was not because of the urgency of the matter but because the authorities were aware of the past trial and error in mainland Japan triggered from falling under the sway of private interests.[150] From the Government-General's point of view, there was no reason not to take advantage of the fact that it was operating in a colony. In colonial Korea, there was no need to consider vested interests, which meant projects could be carried out smoothly at the discretion of the colonial ruler.

Through the second paragraph in Article no. 1 of its enforcement rules, the Chosŏn Urban Planning Ordinance stipulated the implementation of a zoning system in colonial Korea. The system categorized areas as either residential, commercial, or industrial. In each area, zones were classified according to their respective purpose, which would either be scenic, disciplinary, aesthetic, fire prevention, or a special zone within an industrial area. Unlike the 1913 Regulations to Control Urban Construction that mainly focused on control, the ordinance took active urban development into consideration by diversifying its enforcement rules on limiting building heights.[151] Adding rules on urban land readjustment by referring to the Special City Planning Law of Japan was another aspect introduced to colonial Korea through the ordinance. Since the governor-general was invested with full authority, the ordinance met with few administrative difficulties, but the fiscal aspect proved challenging. Various options were explored, including subsidies from central or local government budgets. However, considering the circumstances of colonial Korea, enforcing the ordinance ultimately had to be financed through development charges such as betterment levies. This policy was stipulated in the ordinance's first chapter on general rules.[152]

Among the various proposals made through the Chosŏn Urban Planning Ordinance, the one on land readjustment was key. This scheme of expropriating land "for public interests"[153] without having to individually purchase such land from their respective owners had originated from the faraway land of Prussia, traveled through fissures in Japan created by the great earthquake, and finally arrived upon the barren soil of colonial Korea. The general rules in the ordinance repeatedly stated that it was aligned with the legislative purpose of the Land Confiscation Law that took effect in the early stages of colonial rule. This indicates that the Chosŏn Urban Planning Ordinance was fundamentally a method of colonial rule epitomized by the land readjustment proposal. Land readjustment was primarily carried out at a municipal level in Prussia, while in Korea, it was executed through state power as a government policy. Article no. 42 in the ordinance's third chapter clearly stated that the purpose of land readjustment was to take advantage of the existing land according to government policies. Describing land readjustment as "the exchange, division, consolidation, reclassification of land or its purpose or the installation, alteration, or demolition of roads, squares, waterways, or parks" could be seen as a pursuit of modern capitalist rationality in terms of attempting to appreciate land according to its use value and maximize its efficiency. However, that modern capitalist rationality revealed a coercive aspect by giving only one month for landowners to submit a petition and issuing an order to expropriate land immediately after the deadline based on the excuse of having to cope with a multitude of absent landowners. Moreover, the Government-General's policy to continue pursuing the restitution of development gains and maintain control over land speculation may have raised the efficiency of land readjustment but also made it impossible to identify the public interests it claimed to seek.[154] A revision of the enforcement rules through Ordinance no. 193 issued by the Government-General in September 1938 allowed land readjustment to perform as a method used to newly form building lots or install roads or sewage on undeveloped land.[155]

Keijō Prefecture was no exception to such land readjustment. Its municipal government planned and carried out land readjustment in ten districts, thereby focusing on the development of newly incorporated districts instead of tending to the old downtown area that had already been revamped through the city improvement project. This was in response to the purpose of issuing the urban planning ordinance that particularly sought to develop new sections of the city. Announcement no. 180 made by the Government-General on March 26, 1936, revealed the Keijō districts scheduled for urban planning through the Keijō Urban Planning Project. The details of this project were specified a few days later when the Government-General Ordinance no. 8 issued on April 1 finalized a plan to alter the districts falling under the administrative jurisdiction of Keijō Prefecture. The alteration involved the incorporation of areas leading up to the Chungnyangch'ŏn Stream to the east, Hongjewŏnch'ŏn Stream to the west, and Yŏngdŭngp'o District to the south, as well as parts of neighborhoods like Tongjak-ri, Pŏndaebang-ri, and Torim-ri, resulting in the birth of a "Greater Keijō" three and a half times larger than the prefecture's previous size.[156]

Greater Keijō was already an actively discussed topic during the 1920s among the likes of the Keijō Urban Planning Research Society. The idea

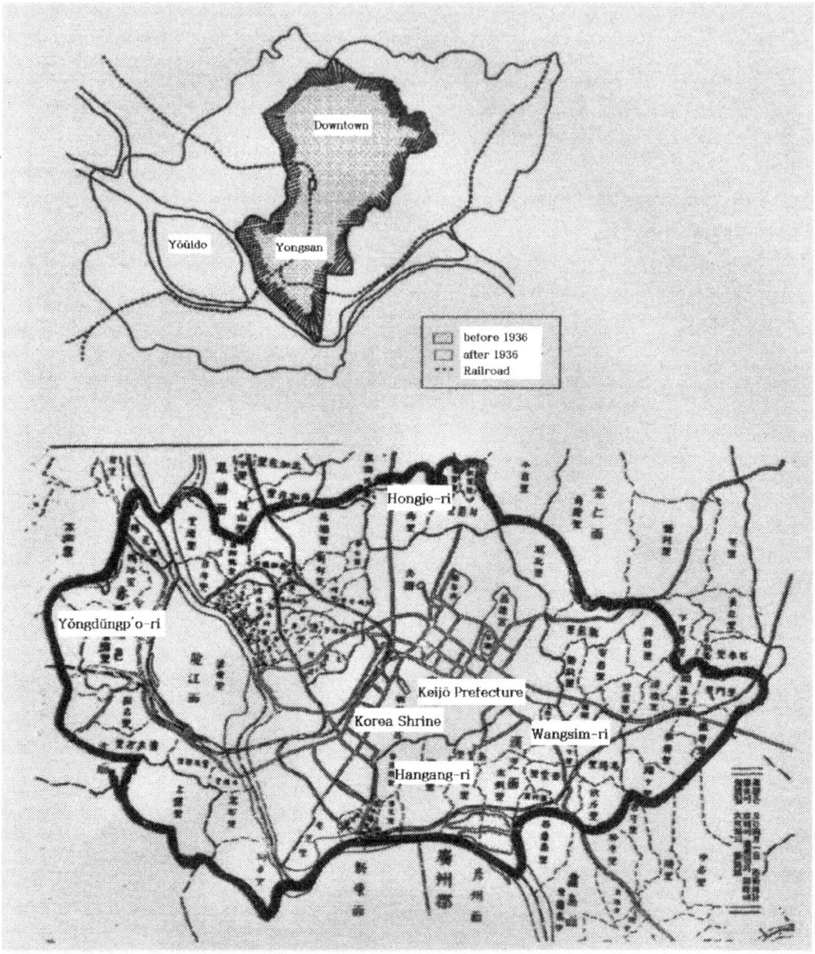

Figure 3.5 Expansion of the Administrative District Keijō Prefecture in April 1936.

Source: Map adapted from *Chosun Daily News* (*Chōsen Ilbo*), January 16, 1936, p. A2, morning edition.

of garden cities popular at the time in Japan prompted the need in colonial Korea for "cultural residences," which referred to upscale residences in green suburban areas.[157] That need was reflected to a certain degree in the expansion of Keijō's administrative jurisdiction in the 1930s. However, land readjustment in colonial Korea generally concentrated on creating new roads, forming sites for factories, and building residences attached to factories. This meant that Keijō Prefecture had also basically aimed at developing industrial areas and building new residential districts capable of taking people in from overpopulated downtown areas. As such, building large standardized residential complexes turned into a priority. Clusters of modified traditional houses built on narrowly subdivided plots like those in the district of Tonam in northeastern Keijō were duplicated en masse and changed the landscape of Keijō Prefecture.[158]

The Brief on Urban Planning Decisions for Keijō published by the Government-General in 1937 made it obvious that developing areas newly incorporated into the city was key to the Keijō Urban Planning Project. The area was largely divided into the eastern section, western section, and the section south of the Han River. These sections were then subdivided into eight areas that would be developed according to their individual characteristics. Areas linked to the railway lines Kyŏngbusŏn, Kyŏnginsŏn, or Kyŏngwŏnsŏn would be developed as industrial districts. Other areas would be developed as residential districts, some of which would be turned into upscale neighborhoods. The new hierarchy determined by purpose and class rearranged the urban space into an organic whole. For instance, one of the three areas in the eastern section was near Han'gang-ri, expanding between the west side of Wangsim-ri and the military reservation in Yongsan. Mount Namsan to the back, the Han River to the front, and a tram line nearby made the area eligible to be developed into an upscale district. Of course, like most suburban areas, the area was dotted with slums that had to be strictly controlled to preclude the possibility of disorderly development. Most of the western areas around Ŭnp'yŏng, on the other hand, were designated as scenic zones where development was to be restricted. Based on such designs, the Keijō prefectural government first built roads in the newly incorporated areas. This was because the subdivided areas had to be organically connected in order for their functions to achieve maximal efficiency. Each area was thus further divided into several transportation zones where roads would form a grid-like pattern, while the old and new downtown areas would be furnished with radial roads. Radial roads spreading out all the way to suburban areas from the Keijō Prefectural Government Building standing opposite to Kyŏng'ungung Palace were a realization of the Chosŏn Urban Planning Ordinance's ideal to create a tectonic unity.[159]

To execute the Chosŏn Urban Planning Ordinance, a smooth administrative system was necessary. The Japanese Government-General of Korea created an urban planning section under its civil engineering division. After having served as the highest review board for construction projects in Korea since its annexation to Japan, the Government-General's Civil Engineering Committee was abolished and replaced by the Urban Planning Committee formed in 1935. Once the committee actually began to operate in 1936, it buttressed the governor-general's decisions, essentially serving as a rubber stamp.[160] Is it possible to regard urban planning realized through the colonial ruler's divine authority as modern? Was it reasonable to mobilize, as if for a wartime operation, a state's capability, resources, and people for a private land improvement project? More than anything, making landowners bear the construction cost while the state retained control over construction seems highly inappropriate.[161] These contradictory aspects, however, lost their acuteness against the logic of public interest. When efficiency and thoroughness are mixed into a clear cause, a more modern, advanced undertone is bound to surface.

The urban planning project in Keijō was heavily armed with rigid scientific rationality. Rational procedures and methods of investigation, analysis, and planning were employed to empirically survey the land, population, traffic volume, and institutional capacity and perform statistical calculations. Natural features such as wind direction, water volume and quality, amount of sunlight, and terrain were carefully considered to determine the purpose of each area. Detailed plans on road widths, building heights, and transportation network were devised upon a fixed scheme. Behind such efforts was the assumption that standardized guidelines could be applied to all target areas of the project.[162] "Value neutrality" unique to modern science keeps its distance from the tyranny of a ruler or an iconoclastic impulse and instead tends to commit ruthless epistemic violence toward the native history and identity of an area.

The urban planning project eventually succeeded in bringing innovational change to the urban space of Keijō. The city was certainly modernized. Through the Keijō City Improvement Project launched right after Japan's annexation of Korea and the urban planning project in the 1930s, Keijō finally appeared to be a modern capital, at least on the outside. More than anything, the straight, grid-like street pattern was crucial to creating such an impression. Streets running north to south were formed during the first phase of the Keijō City Improvement Project, and those running east to west were built in the 1920s during the project's second phase, thereby completing the grid-like pattern before the emergence of Greater Keijō. That pattern was then replicated all across Keijō Prefecture during the 1930s. Those homogenously shaped roads were an undeniable symbol of modernity not just in terms of maximizing efficiency but also in terms of ingraining in the minds of Keijō's citizens a new imaginative geography completely different from that from a traditional, dynastic period.[163] The *Keijō Street Map* printed by a company in the late 1920s called Myŏngsansanghoe to inform clients of its location in Keijō shows that the roads in the downtown area were already shaped into a grid-like pattern at the time. In the map, Kyŏngbokgung Palace up north with extensive vacant grounds is marked as a fairground. The boulevards Kwanghwamunt'ong and T'aep'yŏngt'ong form a long thoroughfare stretching south from the palace to the Shinto shrine Chōsen jingū. In front of Kyŏng'ungung Palace, marked as *Tŏksugung* on the map, a radial road is already formed to a certain degree. The roads from that point leading to Hwanggŭmjŏng Avenue and on to Bonjŏng Street are well linked, indicating that the area had developed into a heavily commercial district.

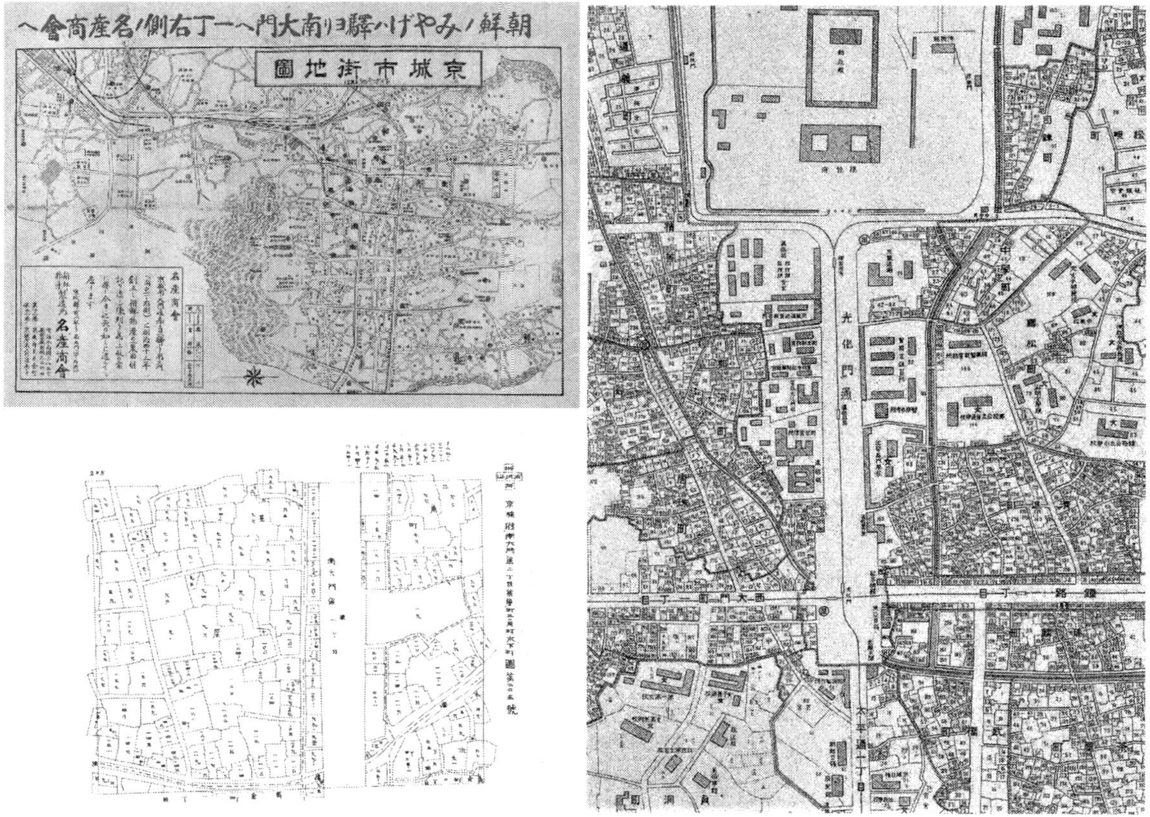

Figure 3.6 Top Left: Keijō Street Map From the Late 1920s. Bottom Left: Detailed Cadastral Map of Keijō Prefecture (1929). Right: Detailed Map of Greater Keijō, *Taegyŏngsŏng jŏngdo* (1936).

Source: Top Left: Courtesy of the Seoul Museum of History, artifact no. seo251. Bottom Left: From the National Library of Korea, classification code. jo65, 205. Right: Courtesy of the Seoul Museum of History, artifact no. seo13639.

The new street names and administrative arrangement also greatly contributed to changing the impression of an urban space. The Korean Empire replaced its age-old system of five sections and forty-nine subsections with the *Dong-Jŏng* System. This institutional innovation was absorbed by the Japanese Government-General through an administrative reshuffle after Korea's annexation. The Government-General's Announcement no. 7 regarding Kyŏnggi Province proclaimed that the basic Japanese planning units of blocks (*chō*) and subblocks (*chōme*) dating back to the Edo period would be transplanted to colonial Korea. Districts were to be subdivided into the standardized administrative units of *jŏng*, *dong*, *tong*, *and ro*. Lot numbers were assigned sequentially from the northeast corner of each *jŏng* or *dong*.[164] A larger jŏng or tong would be further divided into a *jŏngmok* (equivalent to the Japanese unit *chōme*) before being assigned lot numbers. Within a jŏngmok, lot numbers would be assigned sequentially starting with the one closest to Kyŏngbokgung Palace.[165] A typical example reflecting this new system would be Namdaemun-tong, featured in a detailed cadastral map published by Keijō Prefecture in 1929.

This was not the only change that affected people's sense of space in Keijō. The new and impressively straight streets created possibilities for experiences quite different from those along naturally formed roads. By being paved with asphalt, automobiles instead of people became central to roads; tram lines were added; and streets came to be lined with lamps, telephone poles, and bus stops. Neon lamps started to be used on signs and in display windows from the early 1930s.[166] The curtain to the phantasm(agoria) of modernity had been raised.

The Coloniality of Urban Planning

Imperial Japan introduced more than a few conveniences of modern civilization to Keijō. The duplication and expansion of homogenous spaces proved to be a new experience, as was the efficiency of urban infrastructures such as arterial roads, train stations, parks, and a water supply and sewage system. However, the shortage of housing for the urban poor known as "shanty town inhabitants" never made it to the discussion table, and segregation occurred between the residences of colonial natives and those of Japanese expatriates. With Ch'ŏnggye Stream running in between, a Japanese-style Keijō was formed around Honmachi (Bonjŏng) to the south of Kōganemachi (Hwanggŭmjŏng), while a separate old village called Pukch'on above Kōganemachi was relegated to Koreans.[167] This sort of segregation was accelerated by the city improvement project.[168] Considering the unique position colonial Korea occupied within Imperial Japan, such segregation was not consistently practiced as a policy, nor did it materialize in an absolute form in reality,[169] but it was certain that the grid-patterned streets did not guarantee equality in Keijō.

What was truly new to this newly formed urban space was the way in which it was hierarchically divided.

The new urban space physically reproduced the disparities between advanced and underdeveloped, western and eastern, modern and medieval, thereby creating and functionally assigning spatial disparities. The transformed streets were part of that reproduction, and the sight of the modern Namch'on area itself acted as a mechanism that solidified the area's unequal relationship with other areas. Ever since the Japanese government built a legation in Hansŏng in April 1880, Japanese residents lived around the Chin'gogae area, which was known to grow muddy whenever water in the valleys of Mount Namsan overflowed into the neighborhood. The Japanese gradually spread out toward Namdaemun Gate and took the commercial lead in the area.[170] Later, as the Keijō City Improvement Project was carried out, closely knit roads were laid around Namdaemun Gate. Government offices, banking facilities, companies, a department store, and all sorts of commercial facilities settled in the area, turning it into a scene representative of Greater Keijō.[171] A vivid description of what the area looked like at the time can be found in the 1940 novel *Ch'ŏnma*, which means "heavenly horse," authored by the North Korean novelist Kim Sa-ryang.

> Honmachi Street, from the point near Meiji Confectionery to the point where the street ends, was always brimming with people, even in the morning. The Japanese carelessly clacking along in their clogs, native country folk dressed in white as they stare at shops with gaping mouths, old women amazed at dolls with moving eyes beyond display windows, Japanese ladies out to do their daily shopping, errand boys noisily ringing their bike bells, and A-frame porters trying to snatch each other's bundle to earn a mere ten-cent wage.[172]

This modern cityscape seemed to have nothing in common with the grim reality of colonial Korea. Would it be correct to explain the disparity as a product of ethnic discrimination? If so, how could the unequal relationship between the downtown area and the outskirts of Keijō be explained?[173] The formation of a dual city where residential districts are segregated between the ruling and the ruled seemed to be a general trend among colonial cities, but it was in fact a phenomenon that materialized in all modern cities since Haussmann's renovation of Paris. If the Japanese empire's city improvement project was the introduction to Keijō of modern urban planning techniques from the West, shouldn't the way it unfolded in Keijō be considered a colonialist intensification rather than colonialist distortion?[174] It certainly is a typically modernist way of thinking to differentiate between normal and distorted modernity. Yet it is difficult to agree with the view that the "originally Janus-like duality of modernity" is at the heart of the matter.[175] Because the view is in proximity to the approach of colonial rulers, which believes the introduction of modern civilization to colonies is historically inevitable.

Between tectonic urban renewal and modern urban planning lies the quagmire of coloniality. Between Spree-Athens and the Athens of the Japanese Imperial Palace Square were Keijō and Dalian. What was Janus-like was not modern reality but the myth called modernity that caused modern reality to be misunderstood. The illusion that myth creates sometimes made rationality and efficiency stand out and other times made violence and oppression conspicuous. It was an error caused by having that myth take the place of reality. The reality of colonial Korea was that it was turned into a logistics base for the Japanese Empire over the 1930s as the empire increasingly revealed its militarist intentions. With the appointment of Ugaki Kazushige as the sixth Governor-General in 1931, a policy to industrialize colonial Korea was practiced for it form an economic bloc with Japan and Manchuria.[176] The Chosŏn Urban Planning Ordinance was part of that policy as well. As such, it may sound convincing enough to argue that modern urban planning was not simply a product of scientific rationality but was secretly born out of experimentation with urban planning in a colony.[177] Nevertheless, it is necessary to clarify that such urban planning demonstrated the coloniality of power rather than the Janus-like nature of modernity. The modern civilization that colonial rulers habitually mentioned was in fact an effect or a mere byproduct of the pursuit of power instead of a purpose of power.

It was therefore not surprising for the Japanese Empire's power to be expressed unreservedly through the landscape of the colonial primate city, Keijō. The Government-General building was at the center of all changes that took place in Keijō Prefecture after Japan's annexation of Korea. Only through the long-vacant site inside Kyŏngbokgung Palace could all changes find their own place. The notion of func tional efficiency that generally applies to any modern city is not enough to explain why the site was considered as the new location of the Government-General headquarters since nearly the beginning of the Keijō City Improvement Project. As the Street of Six Ministries just outside the front of Kyŏngbokgung Palace was rearranged as Kwanghwamun Boulevard, the diagonal street running between the boulevard and the Shinto shrine Chōsen jingū at the foot of Mount Namsan came to form a central axis symbolic to Keijō Prefecture as well as to colonial Korea. Because the urban planning project in the 1930s primarily aimed for the city's expansion into the suburbs, the space already renewed through the city improvement project was able to take root in the downtown area and serve as a model to be replicated in suburban areas.[178] A detailed map of Greater Keijō from 1936 titled *Taegyŏngsŏng jŏngdo* clearly exhibits the overpowering stature of the Baroque-like space called Kwanghwamun Boulevard that starts from the Government-General building.

That stature made it blindingly obvious that the remains of an old dynasty had lost their footing. Most remains outside palaces turned into nuisances that obstructed the flow of traffic. A satire published in the magazine *Byŏlgŏn'gon* in September 1929 personified the bell pavilion Posin'gak that barely avoids demolition after being forced to relocate and face the wrong direction because of the Keijō City Improvement Project. The following is an excerpt from the satire in which the historic pavilion laments the disturbing times it spent around Kwanghwamun Boulevard.

> A few years ago, I was forced to move here because Keijō Prefecture was expanding roads. The workers placed levers under me and yelled "One two, one two!" as they moved me. If I had a body even a tad weaker than the tough and durable one I actually have, I would have already perished from all that fuss. To think of it now still makes tears of sorrow flow.[179]

3. Homage to Schinkel? The Japanese Government-General Building in Front of Kyŏngbokgung Palace

On May 15, 1910, an article titled "Kyŏngbokgung Palace Is Disappearing" was published in the general news section of *Taehan maeil sinbo*, a daily newspaper that stood by the Empire of Korea on the brink of demise. A few days earlier on May 9 and 10, around eighty Koreans and Japanese attended an auction held by Kungnaebu, the Department of the Royal Household, to "demolish and sell buildings across a nearly 4,000 *kan* area inside Kyŏngbokgung Palace to create a large park."[180] One year later on May 17, 1911, ownership of the palace was officially turned over to the Japanese Government-General of Korea.[181] A few months prior to this, the altars Wŏn'gudan and Sajikdan had already been transferred to the Government-General.[182] It was only a matter of time before the royal palaces and sanctuaries of a fallen dynasty would be at the disposal of the colonial ruler.

"Kyŏngbokgung Palace Is Disappearing"

By that point, Kyŏngbokgung had already lost its function as a royal palace. The palace ceased to be forbidden territory far before the Korea-Japan Annexation Treaty was signed in August 1910. When the Japanese crown prince visited Korea in October 1907, he was accompanied by the Korean Crown Prince Yŏngch'in on a tour of the palaces Kyŏngbokgung and Ch'angdŏkkung.[183] From March 1908, the palaces were open to the public.[184] Once Japan annexed Korea, Kyŏngbokgung's conversion into a park accelerated. Many buildings on the palace grounds were either torn down or sold to individuals or groups, while the section around the pavilion Kyŏnghoeru was relegated to the status of a space to entertain distinguished guests.[185]

The watershed moment of Kyŏngbokgung's destruction was the Chōsen Industrial Exhibition held for fifty days between September 11 and October 31, 1915, to celebrate the first five years of the Japanese Government-General's rule of Korea. According to an official announcement by the Government-General, the elaborate event was held for the purpose of helping Koreans realize the great benefits of colonial rule and allowing the Japanese to develop a better understanding of circumstances in Korea so that they could take the lead in its perpetual growth.[186] In other words, the event was intended to advertise the glorious achievements of Japanese rule so as to encourage voluntary obedience from Koreans and attract investment from Japanese businesses. There must have indeed been multiple purposes for choosing to hold the event at Kyŏngbokgung. The palace was most likely to suffer damage from building exhibition halls and clearing a path for visitors. In fact, a great deal of the palace's buildings and walls either sustained damage or were destroyed. Kwanghwamun Gate served as the main entrance to the exhibition, and the Hŭngnyemun Gate standing behind it was demolished. Hall no. 1 was built in front of the demolished gate, and a series of other exhibition halls were built to its east. The halls were all temporary buildings made of wood, except for the one that was later used as the Government-General Museum. Most of the halls featured the Renaissance style with occasional hints of the Secession style. They were painted a pale white color on the outside, which gave an exotic, modern impression different from the rest of the palace. Extensive demolition took place in the east section of the palace, including Pihyŏn'gak, which used to be the crown prince's office, and Chasŏndang, which was once the crown prince and princess's quarters. The buildings that stood behind Hall no. 1, including Kŭnjŏngjŏn, Sajŏngjŏn, Kangnyŏngjŏn, and Kyot'aejŏn, were remodeled to function as exhibition and reception spaces.[187]

Turning the main royal palace of a bygone dynasty into an exhibition venue open to visitors carried major practical and symbolic implications. The highlight of the event was its opening ceremony that simultaneously celebrated the first five years of the Government-General's rule of Korea. The former Korean emperors Kojong and Sunjong attended the ceremony held at Kŭnjŏngjŏn, where the Governor-General was briefed by an official as he sat upon the throne once reserved for the kings of Chōsen, a scene that could only be regarded as a gesture of cruelty by the Japanese conqueror.[188] Overall, though, the Chōsen Industrial Exhibition was not merely about displaying power. The event was an occasion to level the ground ahead of building the Government-General headquarters and procure funds to finance the project. Although Hall no. 1 was a temporary construction situated in the yard between Kŭnjŏng Gate and where Hŭngnyemun Gate once was, it carried profound significance. It was standing right where the new Government-General headquarters was to be built, blocking a building like Kŭnjŏngjŏn that was central to the palace. Once the headquarters stood upon the heart of a bygone dynasty, its vertical structure with a roof rising toward the sky was bound to cast a shadow on not only the palace but on the colonial city as well.

Pillaging a country's sovereignty and destroying its capital are acts of brutality that cannot be justified for any reason. Whether at a symbolic or practical level, such acts can be nothing but an explicit exercise of violence. However, defining the historical nature of those acts of brutality instead of condemning them is likely to be far more challenging. What do the destruction and alteration of Kyŏngbokgung Palace and its surroundings signify? Can new buildings and cityscapes be regarded as displays of historical progress? Or are they merely products of exploitation and oppression? Did they rob someone else's space or create a new space?

The Ideals Behind Kyŏngbokgung Palace

Even before the Japanese Government-General of Korea took over Kyŏngbokgung, the palace was not the actual center of Hansŏng. Under the rule of the Korean Empire, the city's center was Kyŏng'ungung Palace, situated in the downtown area. Kyŏngbokgung was a symbolic rather than practical center or, to be more precise, a "lieu de mémoire" that would invoke memories as the center of a capital. Nearly five centuries prior to being damaged and demolished by Japan, Kyŏngbokgung was created as an ideological center to the Chōsen dynasty's capital by Chŏng To-chŏn, the very man who orchestrated the dynasty's formation. The centrality of the palace remained a political issue from beginning to end during the Chōsen dynasty and was endlessly associated with memories of the Chōsen dynasty's foundation.

The stature Kyŏngbokgung held within the dynastic capital Hansŏng primarily had to do with the palace's location and its natural surroundings. Backed by layers of mountains to its north and a large river flowing to its south, Hansŏng had long been considered geomantically propitious. That is why the city used to be the southern capital Hanyang during the Koryŏ dynasty and, before that, the place where the ancient Korean kingdom Paekche established one of its capitals called Wiryesŏng. Having originated from the phrase "protect from the wind and procure water," the term *feng shui* (*p'ungsu*), known as Chinese geomancy, was coined by combining the Chinese characters that stand for wind (*feng*) and water (*shui*). Based on the theory of *yin-yang* and the five elements in the *Book of Changes*, feng shui is a methodology used to pinpoint locations (*xue*) where energies (*qi*) flowing underground converge. Feng shui has thus been used for the practical purpose of determining residential or burial sites, but more fundamentally, it has been an approach to space based on the understanding that the universe, earth, man, and artifacts are an organic whole.[189] According to traditional feng shui, propitious sites where energies converge are surrounded by geographical features that represent four mythical creatures: the blue dragon guarding the east, the red phoenix guarding the south, the white tiger guarding the west, and the black tortoise guarding the north.[190] According to such feng shui criteria, Hanyang was a utopia full of energy. To its north was Mount Pugaksan, acting as the black tortoise, while Mount Naksan served as the blue dragon to the east. To the west was Mount Inwangsan, poised as the white tiger, and Mount Namsan to the south, serving as the red phoenix. Ch'ŏnggyech'ŏn Stream originating from Mount Pugaksan flowed through the city's center and on to join the Han River. Mount Kwanaksan situated below the river offered an extra layer of protection for the capital to the south.[191]

What made Hansŏng special, though, was its ideological foundation rather than its geographical conditions. The capital was a rare case, a planned city built according to Confucian ideas from the outset. After founding a new dynasty in Kaesŏng in 1392, its founder and first king Yi Sŏng-gye named Hansŏng, where the royal villa and its pavilion Yŏnhŭngjŏn used to be during the Koryŏ dynasty, as the new capital of the Chōsen dynasty in 1394. Although the construction of the new capital proceeded swiftly and adapted to its natural surroundings, the layout of arterial roads, placement of major facilities, and the royal palace's location and design demonstrated that the new dynasty's ideals had been realized through Hansŏng.

The capital of the Tang dynasty Chang'an served as a model for Hansŏng. The new capital of Chōsen wholly adopted the principles for designing capital cities suggested in "Kaogongji," or Records on the Examination of Craftmanship, included in the sixth chapter of *The Rites of Zhou*. According to those principles, when looking south from the center of a palace, government offices should be placed in front of the palace, while markets belonged behind the palace. Outside the front gate of the palace, the ancestral shrine should be established on the left side, while the altar of soil and grain should be erected on the right side. The king's residence Kyŏngbokgung was placed at the foot of Mount Pugaksan, with the Street of Six Ministries (Yukcho kŏri) just outside the front of the palace. The ancestral shrine was built to the east of the palace, while to its west was Sajikdan, the altar of soil and grain. *Kaogongji* prescribes for fortress walls to surround a capital in the shape of a square, with a gate on each side respectively facing the north, south, east, and west.[192] This prescription was realized in the new capital Hansŏng, as Chŏng To-chŏn arranged for the four gates to the city to be built in addition to a pavilion for a bell at the center of the city. The gates and pavilion were to be named after the five virtues cited in the theory of yin-yang and the five elements, which is why the names Hŭnginjimun, Tonŭimun, Sungnyemun, Sojimun, and Posin'gak each include the Chinese characters that stand for benevolence (*in*), righteousness (*ŭi*), propriety (*ye*), wisdom (*ji*), and trustworthiness (*sin*). The only diversion from this strict adherence to the principles in *Kaogongji* was not to place a market behind the palace due to geographical features unique to Hansŏng. After all, Chang'an was not entirely faithful to the same principles either.[193] Hansŏng was in fact unique for mixing indigenous feng shui factors into a ritual, institutional order based on Confucianism. Kyŏngbokgung Palace was placed in front of the central mountain, Mount Pugaksan, while the other palaces Ch'anggyŏnggung and Ch'angdŏkkung and the royal ancestral shrine were placed at another propitious site where the ridge of Mount Naksan ended. To prevent the flow of energy from being dispersed, arterial roads were arranged so they would not cross over one another. This arrangement influenced by feng shui stood in stark contrast to the modern street layout that later transformed the Street of Six Ministries into Kwanghwamun Boulevard, which ran straight down to the city's south gate, Namdaemun.[194]

In October 1394, King T'aejo relocated the capital of the Chōsen dynasty. The following year, the name of the new capital was changed from Hanyangbu to Hansŏngbu, and a system of administrative districts was set up that consisted of five *pu* subdivided into fifty-two *pang*. This pu-pang system had been inherited from that of the Koryŏ dynasty's capital Kaesŏng and was supplemented by further subdivisions called *kye* and *dong*. By perfecting the division of urban districts, the construction of a new capital drew to an end. With a royal palace at the center, facing government offices to the front, an ancestral shrine to the left, and a state altar to the right, the capital became a powerful ideological symbol declaring the birth of a centralized Confucian state. Furthermore, Kyŏngbokgung Palace, finished along with the royal ancestral shrine in September 1395, emerged as a beacon holding the structural order of the city together. The front gate Kwanghwamun was also erected along the south side of the palace in 1395.[195]

True to its name, which originated from the phrase "tremendously good fortune bestowed from the heavens" in the *Book of Songs*, Kyŏngbokgung Palace was built more with the realization of ideals than functionality in mind. Everything was monumental, from the palace's central location in the city to the arrangement and architectural form of facilities inside the palace. At the core of the palace was Kŭnjŏngjŏn, which housed the royal throne. This building with a name calling for the king to diligently tend to state affairs served as the royal council hall equipped with a courtyard to hold major state events such as the king's enthronement or assemblies where large numbers of civil and military officials gathered. To the south of Kŭnjŏngjŏn were the gates Kŭnjŏngmun, Hŭngnyemun, and Kwanghwamun, while to its north stood Sajŏngmun, Sajŏngjŏn, Hyangomun, Kangnyŏngjŏn, Yangŭimun, and Kyot'aejŏn, all aligned with Kŭnjŏngjŏn in a vertical row. This arrangement is said to have been inspired by the principle of eight steps introduced in the Confucian text *Great Learning*. At the forefront of this sacred section of the palace stood Kŭnjŏngmun, and outside it flowed the stream Kŭmch'ŏn. The bridge named Yŏngjegyo lying over the stream seemed to be at a crossroads between sacred and secular, because once across the bridge, the only gates remaining within the palace grounds were Hŭngnyemun and Kwanghwamun.[196] Kyŏngbokgung Palace was therefore an architectural realization of a strictly hierarchical, Confucian imaginative geography. While buildings in the northern section beyond the royal council hall such as the king's office and sleeping quarters were off limits to most, the eastern section was reserved for the crown prince and other royal family members, and the western section was where the king met with court officials at the pavilion Kyŏnghoeru, the hall of worthies Chip'yŏnjŏn, and other office buildings in the inner courtyard. This symmetrical spatial division between the royal family and state affairs featured a realization of ideology rarely witnessed in the everyday world.[197] A complete map of Kyŏngbokgung created in the second half of the nineteenth century clearly shows Kŭnjŏngjŏn standing upon the central axis between the symmetrical left and right sections of the palace.

The north–south axis of Kyŏngbokgung extended to the Street of Six Ministries outside Kwanghwamun Gate. Modeled after the "Red Phoenix Boulevard" described in *Kaogongji*, the buildings of the six ministries of personnel, taxation, rites, military affairs, justice, and public

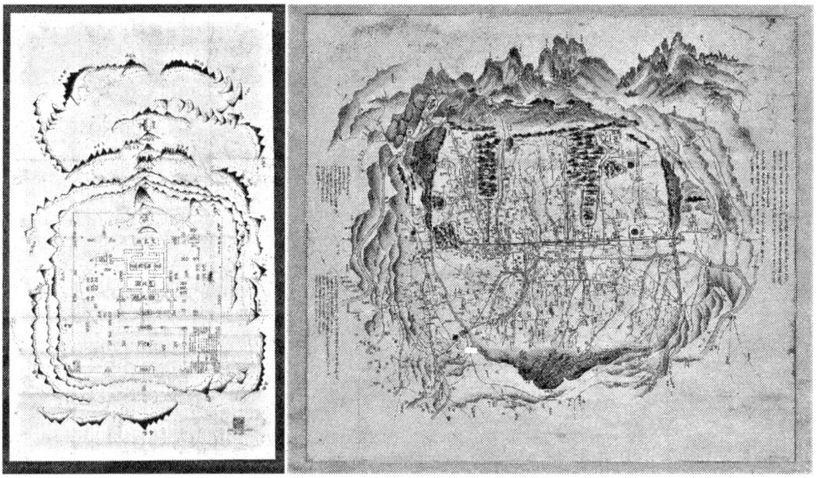

Figure 3.7 Left: Complete Map of Kyŏngbokgung Palace (1866), Paper, 69.6 × 140 cm. Right: Capital City Map (1750s–1760s), Paper, 65.5 × 74.5.

Source: Left: Courtesy of the Seoul Museum of History, artifact no. seo249. Right: From the Collection Database of the National Museum of Korea, artifact no. Mbeon113. Korea Open Government License.

works lined either side of the street immediately outside the palace. Hence, the street was where the magisterial premises came into contact with secular everyday life, a space that encompassed the political ideals of Chŏng To-chŏn, who envisioned a Confucian state.[198] The adjacent Chongno was a secular area where markets opened and a point that split the northern district where the privileged resided from the southern district where the commoners resided. This vertical hierarchy running from north to south intersected with the horizontal line that ran across the bell pavilion Posin'gak situated at the central point from the city's four gates, allowing the entire city to be swathed in the resplendence of the five Confucian virtues.[199]

The capital Hansŏng planned around Kyŏngbokgung Palace was a very special city for combining a vertical hierarchy with horizontal mutual support to form an organic whole. The pivotal position Kyŏngbokgung and the Street of Six Ministries occupied is clearly visible in a map of Hansŏng presumed to have been made in the latter half of the eighteenth century. The arterial roads connecting the multiple palaces downtown formed a central part of the city's street network through which a natural stream flowed. Overall, the mountains in the background, each supporting a different palace, and the balance between the street network and stream created a sight worthy of an ideal dynastic capital.

The Harsh Fate of Kyŏngbokgung Palace

Despite its display of Confucian virtue and harmony, the fate of Kyŏngbokgung Palace as the core of the dynastic capital Hansŏng failed to unfold smoothly. Although it continued to be known as the main palace, Ch'angdŏkkung practically served as the main palace for a considerable period. In fact, Kyŏngbokgung became a site of instability early on, as Yi Pang-wŏn slaughtered his half-brothers at the palace, as well as officials like Chŏng To-chŏn, who heavily contributed to the Chōsen dynasty's foundation, all for the sake of his succession to the throne. Less than five years after King T'aejo relocated the dynasty's capital from Kaegyŏng to Hanyang, his successor King Chŏngjong again designated Kaegyŏng as the capital. Kyŏngbokgung Palace was thus neglected until King T'aejong (Yi Pang-wŏn) moved the capital back to Hanyang six years and eight months later. It seemed as though the palace would finally recover its title as the main palace, but King T'aejong built Ch'angdŏkkung and primarily resided there before moving to Kyŏngbokgung in the eleventh year of his reign. The popular belief that Kyŏngbokgung frequently caught fire from being under the influence of the fiery constitution of Mount Kwanaksan was a testament to the instability the palace continued to suffer from. The palace finally found some stability under the reign of King Sejong. The north gate Sinmumun was built to complete the palace's four-gate layout, and names were given to the rest of the gates and bridge within the palace grounds: Kwanghwamun for the south gate, Kŏnch'unmun for the east gate, and Yŏngchu'mun for the west gate. This turned Kyŏngbokgung into a true main palace spread across an area of around 390 kan.[200]

While Kyŏngbokgung did indeed frequently suffer damage from all sorts of fires, such damages served as occasions for reconstruction and extension. However, the great fire that occurred in the midst of the Imjin War in April 1592, the twenty-fifth year of King Sŏnjo's reign, turned the palace into complete ruins. Then, as soon King Kwanghaegun succeeded the throne from King Sŏnjo, he rebuilt Ch'angdŏkkung and took care of state affairs from there. Kyŏngbokgung was forced to hand over the position of main palace to Ch'angdŏkkung, as it continued to be neglected for two hundred seventy-three years until King Kojong moved his residence to Kyŏngbokgung once it was rebuilt at the order of his father Hŭngsŏn taewŏn'gun.[201] Despite all those hardships, Kyŏngbokgung never completely lost its inherent centrality. To the ruling class of the Chōsen dynasty, the palace continued to serve as a reminder of the dynasty's foundation. It had at least retained its symbolic stature as direct evidence of the Chōsen dynasty's legitimacy. This centrality can be spotted from the previously introduced capital city map presumed to have been made while the palace remained neglected, around the time King Yŏngjo, the twenty-first king of the Chōsen dynasty, rose to the throne.

The reconstruction of Kyŏngbokgung began in 1865, the second year of King Kojong's reign, and King Kojong moved in once it was completed four years later. The restored palace had been expanded to a size of 7,481 kan to accommodate more than one hundred buildings.[202] Two years into the reconstruction, Kŭnjŏngjŏn was restored upon a large double-layered stone platform with a dignified double-layered roof. On the inside, the ceiling was raised as high as possible, while the amount of complex ornaments was reduced. Stones marking sections reserved for different ranks were installed in two rows along the middle of the large courtyard in front of Kŭnjŏngjŏn. Restoration filled the palace with symbols illustrating the authority of the king. It is, after all, a well-known fact that Hŭngsŏn taewŏn'gun, the regent and father of King Kojong, had the palace rebuilt in order to reassert the power of the throne. The reconstruction has also been understood as a strategic attempt by Hŭngsŏn taewŏn'gun to strengthen his position within the royal household.[203] Why, then, did he depend upon the restoration of a ruined palace to achieve such goals? Various possibilities may be worthy of discussion, but what is certain is that Kyŏngbokgung was the optimum symbol of the Chōsen dynasty's legitimacy. The restoration of that symbol was therefore a political statement declaring that attempts to reform the existing system would never be tolerated. The project was not aimed at living up to the popular will, nor was it meant to be the icon of a modern nation, which is probably why Tangbaekchŏn, bronze coins worth one hundred *mun* each, were arbitrarily minted in a struggle to finance the palace's reconstruction.[204]

The reconstruction of Kyŏngbokgung was undeniably a product of the nineteenth century rather than a recovery from an abnormal to normal state. It was a conservative response to unprecedented rapid political change due to the appearance of Western powers and the collapse of a Sinocentric world. Imminent demands of the present had summoned the past. Traditions were not revived but newly created. After all, isn't conservatism essentially a product of resistance against modern change? It should thus come as no surprise that the basic arrangement Chŏng To-chŏn originally designed for the main palace was preserved through the reconstruction of Kyŏngbokgung. Although buildings were newly added and the northeastern and northwestern sections of the palace were greatly enlarged, hardly any changes were made to the layout of the palace's core section. Those behind the palace's reconstruction obsessed over the theory of yin-yang and the five elements described in the *Book of Changes*. The five private quarters, including Kangnyŏngjŏn and the three offices Sajŏngjŏn, Manch'unjŏn, and Ch'ŏnch'ujŏn, were to symbolize the "eight trigrams." A left–right symmetry was strictly observed from the south gate Kwanghwamun up to the king's sleeping quarters Kangnyŏngjŏn. Almost all buildings stood facing the south and in parallel with the palace's central axis. What ruled the renewed Kyŏngbokgung was an authoritative, formalistic sense of beauty.[205]

Even after the reconstruction, Kyŏngbokgung failed to escape its unfortunate fate and turn onto a smoother path. On the contrary, more serious seeds of misfortune were sown. A series of fires destroyed the palace and forced it to be rebuilt, but those were minor episodes compared to the developments that occurred later. Due to a large fire in 1873, King Kojong had to move to Ch'angdŏkkung, and once the Kapsin Coup of 1884 was repressed, he was able to return to Kyŏngbokgung, albeit only for a short while. In 1895, the Japanese brutally assassinated Queen Min at Kŏnch'ŏnggung, a private section newly added deep inside Kyŏngbokgung, which threatened King Kojong seriously enough to flee to the Russian legation in 1896. The regular practice of governing state affairs at either palace was discontinued for the Chōsen dynasty and again turned Kyŏngbokgung into an abandoned royal residence. The following year, King Kojong proclaimed the establishment of the Empire of Korea and began to mainly reside at Kyŏng'ungung, while his son King Sunjong, the last sovereign of the Korean Empire, mainly lived at Ch'angdŏkkung after rising to the throne in 1907.[206] Abandoned once more, Kyŏngbokgung turned into the target of an iconoclastic plunder by the Japanese and ultimately met its demise.

The Japanese Government-General Building's Emergence

Not much is known as to why the southern section of a fallen palace was coveted as the site of a new headquarters for the Japanese Government-General of Korea. Located in an area at the foot of Mount Namsan historically referred to as Waesŏngdae, meaning a Japanese fortress, the two-story brick building once used by the Japanese Residency-General must have become increasingly crowded for the ever expanding Government-General at a time when it desired to have its administrative departments all under a single roof. Taking advantage of a spacious abandoned site downtown could have easily appealed to the Government-General as a convenient solution as opposed to struggling to secure an entirely new site. At the time, Kyŏngbokgung Palace was not a politically sensitive target that would have been difficult to acquire. Moreover, the Japanese rule of Korea itself was surprisingly unorganized and uncalculated so that many measures turned out to be extemporaneous.[207] The initial design for the new Government-General headquarters drafted after the site was decided had the building blend in with the rest of the palace by placing it south of the Yŏngjegyo Bridge and in line with the central axis upon which Kŭnjŏngjŏn and Kwanghwamun Gate lay.[208] This draft was completely revised in a way that outright destroyed the palace, but it is likely that the Government-General sought to eliminate anything considered as an obstacle to its plan instead of aiming for destruction itself. The Japanese chose the contrarian option of laying their "modern" imaginative geography across a meaningful "lieu de mémoire" to Koreans. Such an ideological rather than practical choice continually proved exorbitant or deficient and frequently accompanied administrative setbacks.

There was some degree of initial confusion over deciding the site for the new Government-General headquarters. Possible sites for the building included one in Taehangno where the Keijō Imperial University was later built and another where Seoul City Hall is currently situated,[209] but the final decision went with the forecourt of Kyŏngbokgung Palace. Nearly the entire space between Kŭnjŏngmun and Kwanghwamun Gate was designated as the site of the new Government-General headquarters. The person who played a leading role in making such decisions was Itō Chūta, the Japanese architectural historian who suggested that ancient Japan shared architectural commonalities with ancient Greece.[210] A great deal of analysis will be required to grasp the reason the Tokyo Imperial University professor pinpointed the forecourt of Kyŏngbokgung as the site for the new Government-General headquarters. Itō Chūta was no doubt far from an ignorant destructionist. He was in fact unparalleled in terms of his aesthetic sense in Asian architecture. However, when his vision that linked ancient Greece to ancient Japan overlapped with his vision for the forecourt of the Chōsen dynasty's main palace Kyŏngbokgung, those visions soon transformed into a gaze of power, staring fixedly from an unknown center concealed by curtains. The moment the forecourt was determined as the site for the control tower of colonial rule, the old palace symbolically collapsed. Kyŏngbokgung no longer had a place to stand in the inevitable course of world history.

While making suggestions for the new Government-General headquarters, Itō Chūta is said to have also suggested a site for the Shinto shrine

Chōsen jingū.[211] The shrine had been a definitive part of Japan's assimilation policy that sought to transform Koreans into subjects of the Japanese Empire. As an advisor to the project, Itō Chūta was actively involved in designing and building the shrine that emerged in 1925, one year earlier than the new Government-General Building. While the new Government-General headquarters was within the grounds of Kyŏngbokgung, Chōsen jingū was established on Mount Namsan, the same mountain where Yi Sŏng-gye built the shrine Mongmyŏk sinsa in the hopes of protecting the capital. Along with the Japanese military base in Yongsan, the three locations served as the corners of a new triangular space. Japan's entry into the capital of Chōsen signaled the birth of a new imaginative geography. The new Government-General headquarters built at the forefront of Kyŏngbokgung indicated a dramatic replacement of imaginative geography, changing the symbolic center of a dynasty into the center of a modern state.[212] This, however, was incapable of legitimizing destruction. The phantasmagoria of Athens about to unfold by tearing down an old palace in a colony was tantamount to a euphemism glossing over the reality of East Asia under Japanese oppression. There was but a paper-thin difference between Itō Chūta's intellectual judgment and iconoclastic impulse. How far apart was the Ottomans' religious passion that left Constantinople drenched in blood from an imperialistic sense of civilizational superiority based on a grandiose myth called modernity?

In 1912, the site for the new Government-General headquarters was decided and preparations were made per the plan for the project. During that same year, an engineer was dispatched to Europe,[213] and a civil engineering bureau was created under the secretariat of the Government-General, thereby absorbing the building and repairs division that originally belonged under the accounting bureau. The first to head the newly created civil engineering bureau was Mochiji Rokusaburō, who had been working at the Japanese Government-General of Taiwan. After playing an active role in the architectural bureau under the Japanese Residency-General of Korea's Ministry of Finance, Kunieda Hiroshi was another engineer who participated in designing the new Government-General headquarters as well as in the early stages of its construction.[214] The responsibility of designing the building was entrusted to a German architect. Georg de Lalande was running an architectural firm in Tokyo at the time when he was appointed as an advisor to the Government-General. He had been actively making a name for himself in Japan and was friendly enough with Terauchi Masatake, the first Governor-General of Korea, to design Terauchi's residence in Tokyo.[215] De Lalande also happened to be acquainted with King Kojong from meeting him through his hometown friend Richard Wunsch, who served as the Korean king's physician.[216]

Georg de Lalande is a name nearly forgotten in the history of architecture. He is known to have come from Hirschberg, a small town in Prussian Silesia. Yet considering his unique name, it is possible he was not of pure Germanic blood but a Protestant Calvinist of Huguenot descent who left France to seek refuge in Germany.[217] He studied architecture at an engineering college in Charlottenburg, Berlin, which later became part of the Technical University of Berlin. He traveled to Shanghai and Tianjin in search of work until he went over to Japan in 1903 at the invitation of Richard Seel, a German who was running an architectural firm in Yokohama. Originally from Hirschberg as well, Seel had initially come to Japan as an employee of Ende & Böckmann. Despite opening a practice of his own in Yokohama later on, he soon had to return to Germany, at which point De Lalande took over Seel's practice. As did the architects who came before him, De Lalande carried out the mission of promoting German architectural styles in Japan. To remain current, he especially stood at the forefront of introducing Jugendstil. De Lalande eventually expanded his practice to other major Japanese cities to primarily build residences for foreigners in Japan and also built banks, offices, and hotels.[218]

Among his works was the Oriental Hotel built in Kobe in 1907. The three-story building had a flat roof and a four-story square tower on either end. Between the two towers was another tower with a mansard roof rising to the same height as the towers to its left and right. The façade was dominated by an open loggia, supported by stairs at the lower level and featuring a terrace on the third level. The mixture of Gothic and Renaissance styles created a sturdy impression usually witnessed in government office buildings. De Lalande's foremost demonstration of Jugendstil would be the head office of the Takada Trading Company that opened in 1914. The four-story building seemed almost like a tightly packed box featuring neoclassical simplicity alongside Jugendstil elements such as the roof and eaves reminiscent of traditional Japanese architecture. Both the hotel and the office are now gone, but the sturdiness and simplicity they once displayed as well as the German approach of placing the structural whole ahead of individual design details were replicated through his greatest work ever in a colonial city of the Japanese Empire.

The new headquarters of the Japanese Government-General of Korea was not the only work by De Lalande in colonial Korea. The Western-style building the Japanese referred to as "Chōsen Hoteru" was also designed by De Lalande. The hotel was in fact the first of his works to be completed in Korea. Considered the best hotel in Korea at the time, the Chōsen Hotel run by the Government-General became the talk of the town when it opened. Once Japan annexed Korea, the number of Japanese railway passengers in Keijō increased so that the Bureau of Railway Management under the Government-General felt the need to build a railroad hotel ahead of the 1915 Chōsen Industrial Exhibition. De Lalande was commissioned to design a hotel representative of Korea just as he had begun to design the new Government-General Building. In 1913, the altar Wŏn'gudan used to proclaim to heaven and earth the establishment of the Korean Empire was demolished. From where the altar once stood, the Chōsen Hotel emerged by the following year across a floor space of

Figure 3.8 Top Left: The Oriental Hotel in Kobe (circa 1907). Top Right: Head Office of the Takada Trading Company. Bottom: Chōsen Hotel (before 1945).

Source: Top Left: Uploaded by 663h/Public domain via Wikimedia Commons. Top Right: From *Meiji-Taisho Architectural Photography Collection* (1936), no. 175. Courtesy of the Library of the Architectural Institute of Japan. Bottom: Courtesy of Busan Museum, collection no. guib2872.

1,917 square meters as a four-story building with one basement floor and fifty-two rooms. Through this building, De Lalande was able to demonstrate Jugendstil in colonial Korea, a style alien to the land.[219]

From an architectural viewpoint, the brick masonry building featured a rather stiff version of Jugendstil that could primarily be witnessed in Qingdao, China. Finishing the entire building with brown bricks except for the main entrance and the lower part of the first floor gave it an undeniably monotonous, authoritarian air. Variation was attempted by adding moldings reminiscent of a traditional Chōsen style to some of the windows along the first and second floor, but it was difficult to detect the "youthful" freedom and openness inherent to the Jugendstil style. Yet, in some ways, this exterior well suited the basic purpose of the building. When Kon Wajirō stayed at the hotel in 1923, he gazed at Hwanggungu, a building next to the demolished altar left in the hotel's backyard, and warned the Government-General sternly against self-righteousness.[220] Per the Japanese architect's warning, the hotel could only become the cradle of cultural discrimination that impeded and stunted the subjugated in colonial Korea.

In a short story by Kim Sa-ryang from 1940 titled "Ch'ŏnma," as well as literary works from 1941 such as *The Boundless Blue Sky* by Yi Hyo-sŏk or *Hwasangbo* by Yu Chin-o, the Chōsen Hotel is described as a space detached from the reality of colonial Korea, allowing access only to a special class of people. If the building Hwanggungu in the hotel's backyard was an ornament that induced sentimental emotions for the fallen Chōsen dynasty, the space beyond the hotel grounds where commoners resided came across as a disappointing "filthy reality" to the few privileged hotel guests like Ch'ŏn Il-ma, an international cultural entrepreneur who leads the story in *The Boundless Blue Sky*.[221] Clearly, there was a discrepancy between the mirage called modernity and the trivial everyday lives of urban dwellers.

The aristocratism of the Chōsen Hotel was nevertheless refined compared to the brutality the new Government-General building exhibited. Leaving Hwanggungu intact when demolishing Wŏn'gudan was incomparable to the damage done to Kyŏngbokgung Palace, with the exception of Kŭnjŏngjŏn. The construction of the new headquarters did not proceed swiftly, nor did it concern only a select group of guests from the uppermost echelon of society. It was an infeasible plan to begin with, which is why many issues arose and numerous details had to be additionally sorted out. There may have been some truth to the popular belief that the palace site was under the influence of the fiery constitution of Mount Kwanaksan, because the new headquarters' construction experienced quite a few twists and turns.

By the time he was almost finished with the initial design of the new Government-General headquarters in 1914, Georg de Lalande passed away from acute pneumonia at an inn in Yokohama.[222] Only the previous year, he had been honored with the appointment as Baurat, or Prussian building officer, in recognition of his contributions to enhancing his home country's prestige overseas.[223] The sudden death of this promising architect placed the construction of the new headquarters under new circumstances. The successor of De Lalande was Nomura Ichiro, a Japanese architect with experience in designing the residence of the Japanese Governor-General of Taiwan. An expert in brick construction, Nomura was suddenly commissioned by the Japanese Government-General of Korea around the time the groundwork was coming to an end for the Japanese Government-General of Taiwan's new headquarters.[224] Being resourceful, Nomura brought into the project fellow Japanese architects he had studied with at Tokyo Imperial University,

Figure 3.9 Left: The Japanese Government-General Building in Korea. Right: Grand Main Hall in the Japanese Government-General Building.

Source: Public domain via Wikimedia Commons. Left: Photo by Kadota Fusatarō (1929). Right: From the National Museum of Korea, *Ku ch'ongdokpu kŏnmul shilch'ŭk mit ch'ŏlgŏ pogosŏ* (1997), vol. 1, 234. Korea Open Government License.

as well as seven Korean architects, including Pak Kil-ryong, and managed to finish designing a new headquarters for the Japanese Government-General by 1916. Nomura's design is known to have been faithful for the most part to De Lalande's initial draft. The project was initially set to take five years, but by 1916, its duration was extended to eight years. However, it again ran into a serious delay as Japan's participation in World War I made it impossible for the Imperial Diet of Japan to spare funds for the project. Only ten years after the blueprint was finished did the construction project reach an end. The ceremony to celebrate the building's completion was held in October 1926.[225] The largest building yet in all the territories of the Japanese Empire had emerged at the heart of its colonial primate city.[226]

The Japanese Government-General Building's Architectural Characteristics and Spatiality

The Japanese Government-General Building was built about 84 meters behind Kyŏngbokgung Palace's main entrance Kwanghwamun Gate and a mere 31 meters in front of Kŭnjŏngmun.[227] The gates Hŭngnyemun and Yuhwamun as well as the bridge Yŏngjegyo were demolished and the stream Kŭmch'ŏn was re-routed toward Kwanghwamun Gate. After much debate, it was decided that the direction of the Government-General Building would be shifted 3.5 degrees further to the east than the rest of the palace so that the building would face due south. This decision was no doubt made so that the building would squarely face the Shinto shrine Chōsen jingū on Mount Namsan. That way, the Government-General Building would be at the center of the base axis running through Keijō along Kwanghwamun Boulevard, T'aep'yŏng-ro, past Namdaemun Gate, and up to the entrance of Chōsen jingū.[228] It was an altogether aggressive arrangement but does not necessarily warrant the interpretation that it was part of a Japanese plot to disrupt the layout of Kyŏngbokgung Palace. In 1926, the architectural journal *Chōsen to kenchiku*, published by the Association of Korean Architecture, dedicated its May issue to the new Japanese Government-General Building. According to "An Overview of the Building's Design" published in the issue, Japanese engineers created a survey drawing of all the buildings in Kyŏngbokgung Palace and their relationship with Kwanghwamun Boulevard and T'aep'yŏng-ro. The drawing revealed that the central axis within the palace was slightly titled toward the west and did not coincide with the line running through the center of Kwanghwamun Boulevard. This led to the conclusion that an adjustment would have to be made to the direction the new Government-General Building would face. This explanation was repeated in the *Records on the Construction of the Japanese Government-General Building in Korea* (*Chōsen sōtokufu jōsha shineishi*), published by the Government-General in 1926.[229] In other words, the Japanese had only been interested in faithfully carrying out their plan. The construction of the Government-General Building was not meant to dishearten the vanquished with the building's imposing presence but was part of a plan to reorganize an old dynastic capital. The Confucian city that sought a traditional balance between vertical hierarchy and horizontal mutual support was completely transformed into a modern planned city based on a mathematical, perspectival order.

The fact that the main construction material was completely procured in Korea demonstrates that the Government-General did not view the building's construction as a parallel contest between Japan and Korea. Considering the matter of transportation cost and deciding to use locally procured material hints at bureaucratic rationality and some degree of imperialistic capacity to embrace the various regionalities. The building's exterior was finished entirely with Korean granite as planned, while a bold choice was made to decorate the interior with marble. Once the design was finished in 1916, digging and pile driving began immediately after holding a Japanese-style rite to sanctify the site. Yet many twists and turns caused the construction to take an unexpected ten years until the opening ceremony could be held, and then it took two more years to finish the accessory works.[230] Meanwhile, the former Government-General building at Mount Namsan was, by the Japanese emperor's generosity, turned into a science museum since April 1929.[231]

The new building not only helped the Japanese Government-General of Korea operate more efficiently but also helped display the grandeur of the Japanese Empire. Unlike the blueprint, the floor space was approximately 7,335 square meters, and the total floor space amounted to approximately 31,309 square meters. The four-story building with one basement floor was about 130 meters wide, and its height, including the central dome, was 55 meters. It provided a total of two hundred fifty-seven rooms and was equipped with a central heating system and flush toilets. The central dome, topped with a cupola and lantern, was nearly 31 meters high, thereby completely obscuring the rest of the buildings on the palace grounds.[232] The building was not only vast in size but incomparable in terms of its framework. A building made of gray granite and reinforced concrete was rare even in Japan. While cheap local labor and shipping costs may have influenced the Government-General to risk using such material, the opinion of Mochiji Rokusaburō, director of the Government-General's Civil Engineering Bureau, is likely to have been decisive in taking that risk because he was well aware of the weaknesses of the Japanese Government-General Building in Taiwan from being finished with bricks.[233]

The Japanese Government-General Building in Korea made the most out of its use of stone to form its framework. According to the *Records on the Construction of the Japanese Government-General Building in Korea*, the building's style was to be a "revival of the early modern times," which referred to the neo-Renaissance style.[234] In fact, the building featured mathematical proportions and complete bilateral symmetry around the central section and dome, which were fundamental to the neo-Renaissance style. The neo-Renaissance style was mainly adopted by modern public buildings in Germany, while in modern Japan, it was mixed with the neo-Baroque style and settled as a style suitable for representing the authority of the Japanese Empire. Considering that the Japanese Government-General Building in Korea was finished in the mid-1920s, the building seemingly adopted a style that had gone slightly out of fashion. On closer look, however, the building displayed some eclectic elements that were not identified with a single architectural style. The grand building largely consisted of three sections: the central section, the corner pavilions, and the flanks. The building's cubic shape displayed solidity from the tight balance between the horizontal lines formed by the stairs and balcony and the vertical lines formed by the cupola and portico of the Corinthian order. A strong sense of centrality and hierarchy was conveyed by adding protrusions to the central section and four corners of the building. The dark shadows created by the balconies on the south, east, and west sides of the building gave it the utmost sublimity. Rustication to the lower part of the building reinforced its masculine image. Nevertheless, the most eye-catching feature of the building was the massive bronze ribbed dome. Supported by sixteen pillars, the dome featured German details such as colorless stained glass but was topped with a weighty cupola shaped like the traditional cap worn by the Japanese emperor.[235] Its grand size, bold protrusions, and contrast between vertical and horizontal lines placed the building closer to the neo-Baroque than the neo-Renaissance style. However, the lack of superfluous Baroque details and the formulaic division between each part of the building resembled the Renaissance style.

Although the building widely displayed design elements of Western classical architecture, colonialist elements were interspersed as well. The fact that the protruding portico on the front side is missing a triangular pediment, a feature key to Palladian architecture, seemed to show that the building was not in Europe. Compared to the almost Renaissance façade, the arched pediment raised above the eaves at each corner clearly veered away from the typical Renaissance style. It was a sight reminiscent of the Oriental Hotel in Kobe that Georg de Lalande designed. The ceremonial entrance and vertical windows were elements of the neo-Baroque "imperial" style, while the repetition of simple lines and curves was characteristic of the Jugendstil style De Lalande used to favor. The grandeur and curvy interior demonstrated the neo-Baroque aspects of the building. A large, extremely formal vestibule led to a grand hall glowing with white marble. Above the two wide elaborate staircases leading to the second floor were two triptych murals by the Japanese artist Wada Sanzō, right below the walls supporting a semi-circular ceiling. The mural on the north wall featured *The Fairy and the Woodcutter*, a folktale common to both Korea and Japan, while the one on the south wall featured an interplay of Korean and Japanese customs. To the left and right of this grand hall were rectangular courtyards. The rooms on the underground floor were reserved for the police to conduct interrogations and torture.[236] This eclectic combination of diverse stylistic elements can be regarded as a hybridity unique to colonial architecture. However, it is necessary not to overlook the fact that mixing a variety of classical styles was the trend in Europe and the United States around the time the design for this building was being drafted.

Regardless of the style it was identified by, the Japanese Government-General Building was certainly a massive structure that visually represented the authority of Japan and its imperial household. From the bronze dome to the mural in the grand hall and torture chambers underground, all the architectural expressions employed by the building were visual, physical apparatuses meant to serve the building's purpose. In terms of its form or stature as an urban space, the Japanese Government-General Building was a colonial manifestation of Schinkelian tectonics seeking a powerful centrality and unified layout that left no "surplus" parts. These very aspects are what undermine the credibility of the suggestion that the Japanese Government-General Building in Korea was an imitation of the Secretariat Building in New Delhi built under British control.[237] It would be an oversight to ignore the difference between British imperialism that sought to retain the local style of its colonies and Japanese practices that tried to erase traces of local styles. On the other hand, the suggestion that the Japanese Government-General Building in Korea was modeled after buildings in

Europe, especially the German Reichstag building, sounds more convincing to a certain degree regardless of whether it is true.[238] This is because the two buildings indeed share a great deal in common, such as morphological elements of Prussian classicism like a monumental façade or the distinctive treatment of corners and windows, not to mention their central location in a capital city. Furthermore, Georg de Lalande, who initially drafted the design for the Japanese Government-General Building in Korea, studied architecture in Berlin. There is little chance for him to have been unaware of a building like the Reichstag, when it was the talk of the town during his time in the city. Nevertheless, rather than the superficial features they had in common, the similarity the two buildings shared had more to do with how they both realized the basic principle of Schinkelian tectonics in ways that would best suit their individual circumstances.

The imposing size and exterior of the Japanese Government-General Building made Kŭnjŏngjŏn, a building crucial to the fallen palace, seem extremely small and disconnected from the Street of Six Ministries just outside the palace. Of course, that street was long gone and replaced by a wide boulevard to which the massive stone building that emerged years later was to serve as the finishing touch. Once the building was finished, there was only one complexity left to take care of. Kwanghwamun Gate, standing between the building and Kwanghwamun Boulevard stretching down to Namdaemun Gate and Yongsan, had become intolerable. The Government-General was hesitant about quickly doing away with the symbolic gate, since the matter sparked quite a few debates. However, as the new headquarters began to reveal itself, sentiments shifted to regard it an absurdity to leave the gate intact. Although Kwanghwamun was deeply ingrained in the minds of Koreans as the main gate of Kyŏngbokgung Palace, the gate was struck by misfortune once more only after a few decades after it was restored in 1864 during the palace's reconstruction. Kwanghwamun was dismantled in 1926 around the time the Government-General Building was nearly finished and moved the following year to a spot north of the palace's east gate Kŏnch'unmun. The vertical hierarchy long maintained between Kyŏngbokgung Palace, Kwanghwamun Gate, and the Street of Six Ministries thus was destroyed, and the Japanese Government-General Building finally came face to face with Kwanghwamun Boulevard.[239]

Heated public opinion played a significant role in having Kwanghwamun Gate relocated instead of being destroyed. Even Japanese intellectuals frowned upon violating Kyŏngbokgung and Kwanghwamun. One of them was the Japanese art critic Yanagi Muneyoshi, who published the column "For the Soon to Be Lost Building of Chōsen" in the daily *Dong-a Ilbo* in opposition to demolishing the gate.[240] His sentimental resistance described as "heart-wrenching painful thoughts" requires further critical examination and discussion as to whether it was resistance toward the new order Japan was promoting or rather an argument to internally reinforce that new order.[241] Nevertheless, the violation of the antiquated palace was nearly over by then, and the Japanese Government-General Building surfaced as the embodiment of a new spatio-temporal order.

The appearance of the new headquarters and the removal of Kwanghwamun completed the center of Keijō. Taking pains to usurp the symbolic power of an antiquated dynasty was not exactly what Japan initially had in mind, so the "political spectacle" that ensued was far from what it had intended.[242] There was, of course, no doubt that the Japanese Government-General Building's imposing exterior was the product of a strategic choice to make colonial subjects voluntarily submit themselves to Japan,[243] but at least the focus did not lie on obstructing the palace behind the building. Moreover, Kyŏngbokgung had not been central to the Chōsen dynasty for quite some time. What was paradoxical, however, was that after a long hiatus, the space was able to reclaim a core position by accommodating the Japanese Government-General Building.[244] Shadows of the "Plan to Concentrate Government Offices" that pro-German Japanese politicians sought to carry out at the imperial capital Tokyo loomed around the Japanese Government-General Building in Korea. To put it in Böckmann's way, a "Forum Koreanum" had emerged in the colonial primate city Keijō. The connection Keijō shared with Tokyo seems clear. If the thoroughfare that started from the Government-General Building and ran through Kwanghwamun Boulevard and T'aep'yŏng-ro bridged the gap between the Meiji period plan to concentrate government offices in Tokyo and Gyoko Street that emerged through the Taishō period plan to revive the imperial capital, the obstructed Kyŏngbokgung Palace went on to be transformed into the Hibiya Park of Keijō. The capital of the Chōsen dynasty had at some point turned into an imaginary Tokyo. For envisioning a center that never existed, Itō Chūta, who picked the Japanese Government-General Building's location, shared an uncanny resemblance with Chŏng To-chŏn, who designed Kyŏngbokgung.

Considered "the greatest building in the East,"[245] the Japanese Government-General Building shared affinities with the Japanese Imperial Diet building in terms of its political function and architectural style. Built between 1920 and 1936, the Japanese Imperial Diet Building had a central portico and Jugendstil corners similar to those on the façade of the Japanese Government-General Building in Korea. There were, of course, stylistic differences between the eclectic features of each building. The Japanese Imperial Diet building was influenced by German fascist architecture from the 1930s, while the Japanese Government-General Building in Korea was influenced by the neo-Baroque architecture of nineteenth-century Berlin. The two buildings nevertheless had more common denominators than differences. Standing at the center of the mainland or outland, they both symbolized the Japanese Empire's authority. While one was built as a nucleus according to Inoue Kaoru's plan to concentrate government offices in Tokyo, the other was built as a nucleus in Keijō and became the starting and ending point of the Keijō City Improvement Project overseen by the Government-General.

Ideal realization, however, was not achieved in Keijō, just as much as the plan to concentrate government offices in Tokyo remained an idea. Alike the fate of "Forum Japanum," a proper "Forum Koreanum" worthy of serving as a pivot for Keijō Prefecture as well as the entire Korean peninsula failed to be born. Of course, the circumstances of colonial Korea were different from those of Japan. The Japanese Government-General Building was massive enough to house all the core organs so that less vital organs settled along Kwanghwamun Boulevard, which was once the Street of Six Ministries, including the Kyŏnggi Provincial Government, Bureau of Postal Services, Chōsen Infantry, an annex to the Japanese army headquarters, and, in 1923, the Keijō Central Telephone Office and its Kwanghwamun branch office.[246] However, the more fundamental reason the boulevard was unable to rise to a dominant position was because it had not been the commercial center of Keijō. The southern village Namch'on, which included Hasegawa-chō, the area now called Sogong-dong, and the Honmachi area known today as Ch'ungmuro, was the commercial area where public institutions more immediately pertinent to everyday life settled, such as the Oriental Development Company, the Bank of Chōsen, the Keijō Post Office, and the Keijō Station. The completion of the Government-General Building did open up possibilities for circumstantial changes. As many officials working for the Government-General moved to the vicinity of Kyŏngbokgung Palace, buildings, roads, and access points to public transportation were newly added to the northern village Pukch'on.[247] Ahead of the Government-General Building's completion, a large-scale military parade was held in early 1926 along Kwanghwamun Boulevard, publicizing it as a noteworthy place.[248] In actuality, however, it was difficult to have the demands of power concur with those of everyday life. While state power pursued tectonics efficiency, businesses pursued pragmatic efficiency. And since both were sufficiently "modern" according to their own standards, it was difficult to determine which side was superior. Even in a colony, not everything could be "mobilized" under the state flag.[249] "Governmentality" functioned explicitly yet ambiguously in colonial spaces.

The Colonization of Time and Space

Though not a perfect realization of tectonics, Japan certainly implanted a new spatio-temporal dimension in colonial Korea. Changes in time and space ensued one after the other to build an entirely new imaginative geography. The adoption of "standard time" brought ground-breaking change to the measure of time. Immediately after the Japanese Residency-General of Korea was established, Japanese government offices in Korea began to use Japanese Standard Time starting in June 1906. Japanese Standard Time was a time zone at 135 degrees east longitude that was defined in 1886 based on the prime meridian passing through the Royal Observatory in Greenwich, London. On April 1, 1908, Korean Standard Time was proclaimed with a thirty-minute difference compared to Japanese Standard Time. However, it did not take long for the "modernization" of time to be replaced by the "colonization" of time. Soon after Japan's annexation of Korea, Korean Standard Time was abolished as of January 1, 1912, and Korea thereby reverted to using Japanese Standard Time.[250]

Next to be completely transformed was the structure of time. Memories of the Chōsen dynasty were rearranged into a distant part of the past. The rich details attached to an antiquated dynasty were thrust beneath a glorious history soon to be made by Imperial Japan and swept into the tranquil backyard of the monumental Government-General Building. In June 1902, a team of Japanese investigators led by the nationalistic architectural historian Sekino Tadashi was dispatched to the Empire of Korea to survey historical remains. For a total of sixty-two days, the team surveyed palaces and historical remains in Hansŏng, Kaesŏng, Kanghwa, and Puyŏ. In 1909, Sekino Tadashi again started out from Keijō to conduct a general survey that included research on ancient Korean architecture, which went on for seven years until 1915. His assistant Yatsui Seiichi subsequently left a detailed report about Korean antiquities. Based on the findings from such surveys, the Government-General launched a full-scale five-year project to research Korean antiquities in 1916.[251] By that time, Japan was already equipped with the theoretical expertise and specialists capable of handling such research. For instance, Okakura Kakuzō's utterly modern view of Japanese art history was reflected to a certain degree in the detailed nationwide survey of cultural artifacts conducted in Japan from 1888 to 1897.[252]

When he visited the Korean Empire in 1902, Sekino Tadashi was an assistant professor at the Tokyo Imperial University actively involved in building Shinto shrines and surveying antiquities in Japan. He had studied architecture at the university and participated in designing the Bank of Japan building under the supervision of his teacher Tatsuno Kingo. With recommendations from Itō Chūta, Sekino worked as an architect at the Home Ministry and Nara Prefecture, gaining practical experience in surveying ancient architecture until he was appointed to a position at the Tokyo Imperial University in 1901. In other words, his career showed that he was a mainstream figure in the Japanese realm of architecture. *The Illustrated Guide to Korean Antiquities*, a fifteen-volume work featuring twenty years of his research efforts between 1916 and 1935, was awarded a prize by the Académie française. However, as demonstrated through the case of Itō Chūta, knowledge and power are like a happily married couple that rarely argues. It was clear that the reason the

Japanese Residency-General's Ministry of Finance commissioned Sekino to survey ancient Korean architecture in 1909 was to search for sites to build the shrine Chōsen jingū and the new Government-General Building.[253] Some suspect that the survey in 1902 was performed for the very same purpose.[254] The fact that the Korean imperial government particularly issued visas for Sekino's survey team and arranged for it to be well received by the governors and officials of each area hints at the reality behind the Kwangmu Reform that changed the Korean emperor's era name in the hopes of achieving national prosperity and military power.[255] In any case, such empirical investigations became a frame of reference for "modern" views of history like the *Mimana Nihonfu* theory, which argued that ancient Japan once ruled over southern Korean for more than two centuries. Memories of a bygone dynasty vanished into fading descriptions of history or dark corners of museums.

The Japanese Government-General of Korea created an office called Yiwangjik, and from February 1, 1911, Yiwangjik was charged with managing the affairs of the Korean royal household, deprived of authority. The office took over all the work the Department of the Royal Household used to handle and approached the task as if it were managing cultural artifacts.[256] Having adopted active assimilation since the Korea-Japan Annexation Treaty of 1910, the Government-General declared, at least officially, that it would consider the traditions, historical remains, and ancient architecture of Korea cultural artifacts of the Japanese Empire and offer them due protection. However, the decision to protect or demolish was driven strictly by the needs of Japan and caused damage to many ancient buildings in Korea. Cultural heritage, regardless of whether it survived, all lost its vitality and was left to fade into the mists of time.

The damage Kyŏngbokgung Palace sustained revealed the truth about what the Government-General meant by "managing cultural artifacts." Even after a majority of the eastern section was demolished to make room for halls for the Chōsen Industrial Exhibition, destruction continued to take place throughout the entire palace. Under the pretext of rebuilding the sleeping quarters damaged by the great fire of 1917 at Ch'angdŏkkung Palace, many buildings at Kyŏngbokgung, including the king and queen's sleeping quarters, were demolished. As a result, what used to be around three hundred thirty buildings in total when King Kojong rebuilt the palace dropped sharply to thirty-six. Sŏnwŏnjŏn, which housed the portraits of former Chōsen kings, was sold to the Pakmunsa Temple, built to pray for the repose of Itō Hirobumi, and was turned into a shrine belonging to the temple.[257] More than a few cases of such callous "management of cultural artifacts" were carried out in an impromptu fashion, but overall, they were based on a clear roadmap. The *Layout of the Kyŏngbokgung Palace Site and Buildings*, drafted in 1916 around the time the design for the new Government-General building was being finished, shows that the palace grounds were to be turned into a park with almost no trace of the facilities that once occupied the space. A closer look at the map reveals that a square was to be created to the west of the spot where the crown prince's sleeping quarters used to be. Flowerbeds were to occupy the section on the north side of the palace where Kŏnch'ŏnggung once was, as if Queen Min had never been assassinated there. A site for the Governor-General's residence was to be cleared at the foot of Mount Pugaksan where the Blue House, the Korean president's residence, is currently located. The map also included plans to create a fountain, amphitheater, and golf course on the palace grounds.[258]

Although not everything in the draft was realized, Kyŏngbokgung Palace was soon transformed into a space of an entirely different nature. The Government-General Building settled at the forefront of the palace grounds, and the museum built in the eastern section for the Chōsen Industrial Exhibition was later reopened as a museum for the Government-General. The rest of the palace grounds was turned into a resting area for officials working at the Government-General, just like Hibiya Park adjacent to the Kasumigaseki district of government offices in Tokyo. The dignified main palace of the Chōsen dynasty was demoted to an old backyard full of cherry blossoms for the Government-General.[259] Pure beauty is, after all, nothing but a product of cold-heartedness that glosses over the harshness of reality.

After the Government-General Building was completed and the Kwanghwamun Gate was removed, the walls connected to the gate on the palace's south side were removed, as well as the left side of the watchtower Tongsipchagak at the corner of those walls. Another watchtower named Sŏsipchagak was removed altogether later on, leaving nothing to function as the palace boundary.[260] Kyŏngbokgung no longer stood as a royal palace. Most of the other palaces and sanctuaries in Keijō met a similar fate. The altar of soil and grain Sajikdan, the first facility built when the Chōsen dynasty relocated its capital to Hanyang, was turned into a park. The shrine Mongmyŏk sinsa dedicated to the guardian spirit of the Chōsen dynasty was forced to relinquish its original spot because of the Shinto shrine Chōsen jingū. Part of the Kyŏnghŭigung palace grounds was appropriated to build a school for Japanese settlers, while another part of the palace was cleared to make way for roads. Ch'anggyŏnggung Palace became a case pathetic beyond ridicule. Under the pretext of providing consolation to King Sunjong, a zoo and botanical garden were built on the palace grounds. The name of the palace was changed to "Ch'anggyŏngwon Garden," indicating that the place had fallen to the state of a public recreational facility. According to *The Guide to Keijō* published in 1929, Ch'anggyŏngwon had "many exotic Korean animals that do not live in Japan such as wild cats, wolves, Korean pheasants, tigers, roe deer, and leopards." The palaces Ch'angdŏkkung and Tŏksugung were about the only places that retained a minimum degree of their original form. This was possible because Ch'angdŏkkung was the residence of King Sunjong, while Tŏksugung was the residence of King Kojong, though reduced to nothing like its original state when the palace used to be called Kyŏng'ungung. The palace's name had been changed from Kyŏng'ungung to Tŏksugung, as King Sunjong presented the title *Tŏksu*, which meant "virtuous longevity," to King Kojong when he was forced to abdicate in favor of his son.[261]

The Japanese rulers succeeded in drawing the past of colonial natives into a new spatio-temporal order. Zones forbidden during the dynastic times were travestied into museums, parks, zoos, and botanical gardens. However, there was an aspect the Japanese had not been aware of. If the Government-General Building in Korea, the largest building in the Japanese Empire, was like a salute celebrating the Japanese modern civilization's historic victory over other Southeast Asian civilizations nearby, the historical remains at colonies were like a mirror reflecting the past of the Japanese, a past they wished to cast aside! The acts the Japanese rulers committed at colonies may not have been aimed squarely at destruction, but still exhibited an aversion deep enough to believe that such acts could not have been based purely on reason. Had they instead been based on a secret desire to erase their own past and roots as Asians? The Japanese enthusiasm toward Western modern civilizations can in fact only be regarded as a cause and outcome of animosity against their Asian neighbors. This is because Asia was the other name of an actuality the Japanese were unwilling to come face to face with.

Whatever the reason, the colonial rulers eventually accomplished their goal. Sajik Park, Changch'ung Park, and Hyochang Park were all major parks formed in Keijō under Japanese colonial rule at sites that were once sanctuaries during the Chōsen dynasty.[262] The colonial rulers' voracious appetite for destruction provoked national antagonism, but it was far more pertinent to the matter of breeding "modern citizens" than the Korean Empire's urban renewal of Hansŏngbu. That appetite had been responsible for establishing a new spatial order through roads, land, transportation, and buildings as well as an entirely new temporal order for history, which formed a special topology called "modernity."[263]

The explosive reaction Koreans showed toward the 1915 Chōsen Industrial Exhibition is too significant to be considered simply an outcome of having been dazzled by Japanese propaganda. The number of visitors amounted to a total of more than 1.16 million, according to the authorities,[264] an unimaginable number for colonial Korea in the early twentieth century even after excluding the number Japanese and foreign visitors. Destroying Kyŏngbokgung Palace was an act of oppression against the pride and tradition of Koreans, but it also served as an occasion for Koreans to witness their own circumstances as "modern citizens." Though not held with good intentions, the exhibition did contribute to transforming the closed antiquated palace into a modern public space.[265] For Japan, the process of achieving cultural hegemony had been a process through which colonial natives were assimilated to a "modern" time and space. Colonization and modernization were like two sides of the same coin.[266]

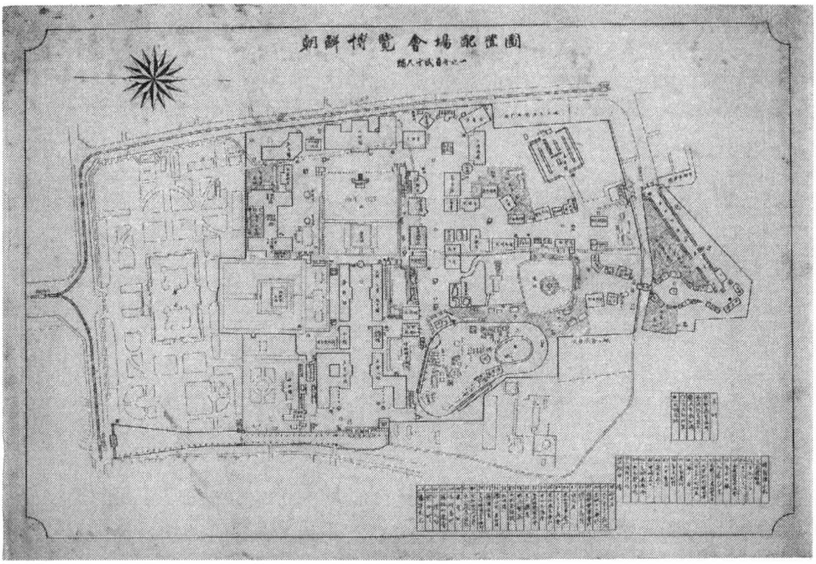

Figure 3.10 Layout of the Chōsen Industrial Exhibition (1929).

Source: Courtesy of the National Archives of Korea, management no. DJB0001382.

World fairs were originally events through which Western powers publicized their capitalist developments and professed the legitimacy of colonial rule. It was therefore standard to display not only cutting-edge technological inventions but also products from colonies as samples representing uncivilized cultures. A typical example of this was the display of Filipino aboriginals at the 1904 Louisiana Purchase Exposition.[267] At the fifth National Industrial Exhibition held the previous year in Osaka, Japan, Ainu and Ryukyuans were displayed as exhibits. So as not to be outdone by Western imperialism that deemed non-Western colored races "the others," the Japanese did not hesitate to otherize its neighboring nations.[268] In colonial Korea, since the 1907 Keijō Exhibition was hosted by the Japanese Residency-General, a series of exhibitions were held at Kyŏngbokgung Palace: the 1915 Chōsen Industrial Exhibition to celebrate the first five years of Japanese rule, the 1923 Chōsen Exhibition for Sideline Products, the 1923 Statistics Exhibition, the 1925 Chōsen Poultry Exhibition, the 1926 Chōsen Exhibition, the 1929 Chōsen Industrial Exhibition to celebrate the twentieth year of Japanese rule, the 1935 Chōsen Industrial Exhibition to celebrate the twenty-fifth year of Japanese rule, and the 1940 Chōsen Exhibition. These exhibitions consumed traditional Korean culture out of curiosity toward the exotic whether it was related to Korean royal customs, folklore, Confucianism, or shamanism. Even if the exhibitions had focused on displaying the indigenous nature of Korean cultures instead of disparaging them as uncivilized,[269] they all shared the common thread of taxidermizing the past of Korea and leaving it to fade into the mists of time. What is more important is that fact that people in colonial Korea went along with such a change of their own accord. Even when a national funeral for King Sunjong took place during an exhibition in 1926 ahead of the Emperor Taishō's silver wedding, the exhibition was still successful enough to extend its duration to welcome a total of nearly six hundred thousand visitors.[270]

The events held at Kyŏngbokgung Palace started out as fairs and evolved into larger exhibitions over time. The exhibition of 1929 served as a turning point in terms of the scale and nature of such events. The industrial exhibition to celebrate the twentieth year of Japanese rule was held over a period identical to the one held a decade earlier, but instead of remaining a domestic occasion, the 1929 exhibition was turned into an international event participated in by major Japanese cities as well as Taiwan. Considering the fact that Japan established Manchukuo soon after in 1932, the exhibition is likely to have been a chance to parade the imperial aspects of Japan and promote mutual cooperation and trade. The 1929 exhibition made different use of the space at Kyŏngbokgung Palace. Kwanghwamun Gate, relocated to the east side of the palace by that point, served as the main entrance to the event, and the exhibition halls were arranged along an east–west axis, crossing through the north side of Kŭnjŏngjŏn and leading up to Kyŏnghoeru Pavilion. What was also different about this exhibition was that special halls were created to feature certain regions in Japan as well as other Japanese colonies so as to place the Japanese Empire's imaginative geography on full display.[271] Korean visitors at the exhibition would have immersed themselves in the modern phantasmagoric portrayal that taxidermized their past as relics in a museum and sought to guide them toward civilizational progress. They would have soon found themselves in a singular spatio-temporal prison created by the Japanese Empire, a prison from which the prisoners did not wish to escape.

In "An Elegy for a Bygone Palace," published in the October 1931 issue of the monthly magazine *Samch'ŏlli*, the author spirals into "heartrending nostalgia" and "sorrow" during a quiet autumn stroll around the palaces Ch'angdŏkkung, Tŏksugung, and Kyŏngbokgung.[272] The description conveyed a sentiment commonly shared among the intellectuals of colonial Korea at the time. The editorial "Devastation of Kwanghwamun Gate" anonymously published in the August 11, 1926, edition of the daily *Dong-a Ilbo* attempted a sentimental approach by personifying the gate as "you" and using apostrophe.

> Oh, Kwanghwamun Gate, for five hundred years of wind and rain, you have seen loyal subjects come and go, traitors come and go, the reactionary faction come and go, and the enlightenment faction

Figure 3.11 Mount Paegaksan on an Early Spring Morning by An Chung-sik, watercolors on silk, 125.9 × 51.5 cm (1915).

Source: Public domain via Wikimedia Commons.

> come and go! . . . You were destined to greet and send them off, born to guide and show them the way. . . . They say the Government-General will dismantle you and have you rebuilt. Yet, the rebuilt person would not be the same one who wore a topknot, the spot the person moves to would not be the same one with Mount Pugaksan to its back, and the direction you are to face would not the same one directly facing Kyŏngbokgung Palace.[273]

The editorial had a heavily sentimental undertone but also revealed a clear awareness of national identity. Hostility toward foreign forces could definitely be sensed from the belief that Kwanghwamun Gate would never be the same after having been forced by Japan to move. Yet protest against a strategy for colonial rule does not necessarily have to be regarded as a rejection of the topology provided by the Japanese. The editorial defines the gate not as the symbol of a dynasty but as the symbol of a nation and the site of a long national history. After all, is nationalism not an ideological manifestation of modern time and space?

A similar case can be found through a painting by An Chung-sik, an artist known as a pioneer in modern Korean literary paintings. His work from 1915 titled *Mount Paegaksan on an Early Spring Morning* adopts a bird's-eye view to feature Kwanghwamun Gate swathed in the early morning mist. Unlike the title of this modern painting of real scenery, Kwanghwamun Gate and the buildings behind it surrounded by trees in Kyŏngbokgung Palace occupy the center of the canvas instead of Mount Paegaksan, and the season appears to be autumn instead of spring. A silence is in the air while the gate remains shut tight. A pair of statues shaped into the mythical beast Haet'ae stand at either corner of the square, adding to the weight of silence. The atmosphere hints at the fall of a dynasty. Yet a closer look at the ink strokes reveals an incongruity between the mountain and buildings at its foot. It almost seems as though two different paintings have been pasted together. Kwanghwamun Gate, the symbol of a dynasty, turns itself into a vanishing point instead of conforming to its natural background. Only when the gate of glory and shame disappears and is replaced by the Japanese Government-General Building can the colonial primate city Keijō be complete.

4. The Historicist Buildings of Keijō

The appearance of a modern capital would have been impossible without the installation of modern facilities for governance. Various government offices, courthouses, prisons, police stations, hospitals, and public schools rapidly disintegrated the traditional order in downtown Keijō to form a new urban layout and landscape.[274] The term "public" would mainly be used to indicate the city's new infrastructure,[275] which distinguished itself from its surroundings through Western architectural features adopted by modern Japan. Their sky-piercing height, staggering size, and geometric proportions and symmetry clearly engraved an image of modernity in people's minds. The basic trend of Japanese public architecture had been wholly transplanted to the heart of the colonial primate city Keijō.

The Ministry of Finance's Architectural Bureau and Its Adoption of Prussian Classicism

Since Japan turned Korea into its protectorate through the 1905 treaty, it was able to distribute throughout Korea a standardized blueprint for government offices. This "universal blueprint" preferred strong symbolic elements such as domes and spires, as well as central and corner protrusions with a gable above the entrance. Such preferences dominated the landscape in major cities of colonial Korea until modernism grew predominant in the 1930s.[276] Duplicating and spreading the same authoritarian, rigid spaces was a physical manifestation of an imperial "modern" order of governance. However, what was actually at play is not likely to have been the modernity of power but its coloniality, because those new identical spaces were based on ostentation and discrimination instead of rationality.

The universal blueprint began to be created by the Architectural Bureau under the Korean Ministry of Finance, which was by then under the control of the Japanese Residency-General of Korea. The Bureau was the first permanent modern architectural organ established to replace both the Yŏngsŏndogam in charge of constructing and repairing palace buildings and Kongjo in charge of public works until September 1906. The Bureau was large enough to oversee the engineering work on all major ports.[277] After Japan's annexation of Korea, an extensive reshuffle of the Korean administrative system merged the Bureau into the Civil Engineering Bureau of the Japanese Government-General's secretariat. In 1912, as preparations were being made for the new Government-General headquarters' construction and the Keijō City Improvement Project, the Bureau was placed under the supervision of the Building and Repairs Division within the Civil Engineering Bureau of the Government-General's secretariat. Then, in 1924, the Bureau name was changed to the Architectural Department under the Bureau of Interior Affairs. The fact that "architecture," a term with an overtone more proactive than "building and repairs," was chōsen for the department's new name indicates that the construction of government offices was at its height in the 1920s. Once the construction of core facilities, including the new Government-General headquarters and the Keijō Prefectural Government Building, were completed, the Architectural Department was merged back into the Building and Repairs Section under the Accounting Department of the Government-General's secretariat in 1928.[278]

Like the imperial capital Tokyo, the colonial primate city Keijō turned into an arena for competition among historicist styles under the unilateral leadership of Japanese bureaucracy. As in the imperial homeland, the neo-Renaissance and neo-Baroque styles became mainstream. Domes and orderly arranged columns of the Renaissance style had the decorative effect of creating an imposing, ostentatious aura, and the epitome of that happened to be the new Government-General Building. This style was widely adopted at facilities Japan established in Korea after it became a Japanese protectorate and throughout the early years of Japan's colonial rule. Among such facilities were the Institute of Industrial Training (1907), the office of the Ministry of Finance and its Architectural Bureau (1907), the Court of Cassation (1908), the Kwangt'onggwan Building (1909), the office of the Ministry of Agriculture and Commerce (1910), and the Oriental Development Company (1911).[279] At a glance, the neo-Baroque style may have appeared somewhat similar to the Renaissance style, but it flaunted imperial power more explicitly, was excessively decorative, and was composed of undulating forms. In addition, an antique mannerism was adopted as a decorative element to supplement the neo-Renaissance and neo-Baroque styles. Early on in the twentieth century, the abstraction and simplification of historicist architecture was a global trend during the transition from historicism to modernism. However, compared to Europe or Japan, the neo-Renaissance and neo-Baroque styles demonstrated an especially overpowering presence in colonial cities like Keijō.[280]

Representative among historicist buildings raised by the Architectural Bureau under the Residency-General's Ministry of Finance would be the Taehan Clinic building. Working at the Bureau around the time the construction project was launched was Yabashi Kenkichi. Yabashi was an engineer known as the right-hand man of Tsumaki Yorinaka who led the pro-German faction in the Japanese architectural realm and headed the Temporary Architectural Department of the Japanese Ministry of Treasury. This is perhaps why the Architectural Bureau in Korea almost functioned like an accessory to the Temporary Architectural Department in Japan. Yabashi had also studied under Tsumaki Yorinaka's rival Tatsuno Kingo so that his connection to the two masters placed him within the mainstream of Japan's architectural realm. Yabashi came to Korea to work as an engineer at the Ministry of Finance's Architectural Bureau, during which time he was placed in charge of designing and supervising the construction of Taehan Clinic's main building.[281] To carry out this assignment, Yabashi commissioned eight different Japanese experts and had Tsumaki Yorinaka visit Keijō as a consultant for the project. In fact, public buildings in early Keijō were directly influenced by Tsumaki's German-style historicism. It was natural for such buildings at a Japanese colony to first come under the influence of Tsumaki since he was an architect who represented the governmental rather than the academic side of architecture.

The site for Taehan Clinic's main building designed by the Ministry of Finance's Architectural Bureau was to be upon a hill called Madubong for resembling the shape of a horsehead. Considered a "blue dragon" spot in feng shui, the site just outside the east side of Ch'anggyŏnggung Palace was once occupied by a garden called Hamch'unwŏn. The idea of building modern medical facilities on a spot that overlooks an old palace demonstrated the authority of a new power. Originally under the direct control of Ŭijŏngbu, which was the Korean Supreme Council of State, Taehan Clinic was a national medical center in charge of the administration, research, and education on health and hygiene matters in Korea. The clinic's main building was completed in November 1907, and in October 1908, the clinic was opened. In September 1910, the clinic was renamed the Clinic of the Japanese Government-General of Korea, and its staff was completely replaced with Japanese members. And in 1928, the clinic was turned into the Keijō Imperial University Hospital.[282]

The architectural style of the main building wholly reflected the fundamental nature of Taehan Clinic. The symbolic clock tower in the center of the two-story brick building seemed to stretch down to the building's protruding entrance, and the left and right corners of the triangular roof were slightly protruding. Such features were typical of the north German neo-Renaissance style, which could be witnessed in buildings like the city hall of Hamburg. Yet, using the color and textural contrast between bricks and granite to add decorative bands above the semi-circular arched window frames on the ground floor was a feature of the Victorian Gothic Revival notably practiced by William Burges. The contrast between the arched porch with round pillars and the miniature temple-like façade placed above it was neo-Palladian. Such features are likely to have originated from the influence Yabashi had received from Tatsuno Kingo. The various degrees of protrusions and segmented flanks across the building, the bold rows of vertical windows, and the four-story-high rhombic clock tower were unmistakably neo-Baroque features.[283] This eclectic historicism exhibited the hybrid nature of colonial architecture as well as hints of the "empire style" popular in the West near the end of the nineteenth century.

Once the Ministry of Finance's Architectural Bureau was established, the construction of residences for government officials also gained momentum. In terms of importance, aesthetic completion, and the architect's reputation, the most prominent among such residences was the one for the Japanese Resident-General of Korea. After the Residency-General's establishment, Japan was as eager to build official residences as it was to build government offices. The Residency-General was, of course, in urgent need of an office to carry out administrative tasks. The building immediately available was the former Japanese legation. The two-story wooden building was built at the foot of Mount Namsan on the site of the Japanese fortress Waesŏngdae, which the Empire of Korea had ceded to Japan through the 1885 Treaty of Hansŏng, concluded as a result of the Kapsin Coup of 1884. Upon an adjacent hill, a two-story brick building covered with whitewash was built as an office for the Residency-General in early 1907. Unlike the office, however, the construction of

Figure 3.12 Front View of the Taehan Clinic Main Building.

Source: Photo by author (2016).

the Resident-General's residence ran into some setbacks. The two-story rectangular Renaissance-style building designed by Tatsuno Kingo and Kataoka Yasushi, leaders respectively in the Japanese realms of architecture and urban planning, was not realized due to financial reasons. After deferring the project for a while, a masterpiece emerged from Katayama Tōkuma, another Japanese expert known as the "court architect." The residence of the Resident-General built in Yongsan in 1908 is said to have been financed by funds left over from the Russo-Japanese War. The building went on to be used as the residence of seven different Japanese Governor-Generals of Korea, from Terauchi Masatake to Minami Jirō. The building was thereafter left almost unattended without any specific function when a new residence for the Governor-General was built in September 1939 at the northern end of Kyŏngbokgung Palace, a spot that would later house the Korean presidential residence Kyŏngmudae.[284]

The Resident-General's residence designed by Katayama was a French neo-Baroque style building with a gabled roof and windows. The façade and back side of the two-story rectangular building each had slight protrusions on the left and right corners, while the protrusion at the center extended much further out to the back. The ground plan showed a carriage porch placed at the center of the façade and a large hall past the porch and main entrance. The large hall stretched out left and right into a wide corridor, while the back section accommodated a couple of small offices. At the corridor's left end was a staircase, and the dining room was on the opposite end of the corridor. The large space between this elegant French-style building and the property's front gate was to accommodate a lavish garden generally modeled after the one at Château de Vaux-le-Vicomte in Maincy, France.[285] Katayama happened to admire Louis le Vau, the first architect to work for Louis XIV. Le Vau had been responsible for redesigning the château and later participated in designing the Palace of Versailles. Although the Resident-General's residence did not look anything like the Château de Vaux-le-Vicomte, it did share similarities such as a central section and corners shaped in the Baroque style, a lantern upon a round roof, vertical windows, and a geometrical garden.

To better draw a connection between the two buildings, it is necessary to discuss another work by Katayama completed in 1909. It is the Hyōkeikan, situated to the left of the Tokyo National Museum's main building. As its name suggests, the building was raised as a municipal gallery using the monetary gifts Tokyo citizens offered to celebrate the marriage of Prince Yoshihito, or the future Emperor Taishō.[286] The left and right corner protrusions and segmented flanks were similarities

Figure 3.13 Top Left: View of the Japanese Resident-General's Residence (1911). Top Right: Ground Plan of the Japanese Resident-General's Residence (from the 1920s to 1930s). Bottom Left: View of the Château de Vaux-le-Vicomte's Southern Façade, 2013. Bottom Right: View of Hyōkeikan.

Source: Top Left: Courtesy of the Seoul Museum of History, artifact no. seo17305. Top Right: Courtesy of the National Archives of Korea, management no. DJB0001190. Bottom Left: Photo: Jean-Pol GRANDMONT/CC BY-SA (https://creativecommons.org/licenses/by-sa/3.0). Bottom Right: From *Meiji-Taisho Architectural Photography Collection* (1936), no. 147. Courtesy of the Library of the Architectural Institute of Japan.

the Hyōkeikan shared with the Japanese Resident-General of Korea's residence, whereas the Ionic pilasters and dome were similarities the Hyōkeikan shared with the Château de Vaux-le-Vicomte. Aside from their similarities and differences, the three buildings definitely shared a familial resemblance in that their grandiose Baroque façades topped with domes and lanterns were all dedicated to the most powerful individual in their respective societies. Power was indeed elegant. For his contributions, Katayama Tōkuma was awarded the Order of the Eight Trigrams in the first class not by the Japanese Resident-General of Korea but by the Korean Emperor Kojong in June 1908.[287]

Whereas the residence of the most powerful authority featured the aristocratic elegance of the French Baroque style, Prussian authoritativeness and rigidity were pursued for public offices in Keijō. A typical example would be the Keijō branch office of the Oriental Development Company completed in 1911. Mention of the company is bound to bring back the sorrow Korean farmers felt from being deprived of their land under Japanese colonial rule. Modeled after the East India Company of Britain, the Oriental Development Company in fact mainly engaged in acquiring land and gained tremendous profits through farming, forestry, irrigation projects, and financial business in colonial Korea. The company's Keijō branch was the very target of a bomb the Korean patriotic martyr Na Sŏk-ju threw near the end of 1926.[288] The building possessed an exterior as imposing as the company's nature. This mutation of Prussian classicism was built along Hwanggŭmjŏng 2-chŏngmok near the Namch'on area dominated by the Japanese.

It is unknown who designed the Keijō branch of the Oriental Development Company, which seemed to be made of stone but was in fact a wooden construction.[289] One of the square building's protruding corners was turned into the main entrance with a pair of pillars placed to its left and right, a formation that was mirrored above it on the second floor beneath a rather formulaic pediment. A cupola with bull's-eye windows and lantern was placed on top of the building. Overall, the building was close to the Renaissance style, with hints of the neo-Baroque style, such as the rather conspicuous main entrance. It largely resembled the Yokohama Specie Bank building, a representative work of Tsumaki Yorinaka. This dignified bank building completed in 1904 eloquently reflected Tsumaki's German-style neo-Baroque tastes. A large dome with bull's-eye windows was placed above the main entrance at a corner of the square-shaped three-story bank building finished with thick slabs of granite. The differences that distinguished the bank building from the Oriental Development Company's Keijō branch were the Corinthian pilasters placed beneath the pediment, the Palladian gabled windows on the second floor, and the balustrade on the rooftop.[290] Despite their stylistic differences, the two buildings both conveyed a certain message about the Japanese empire's wealth

Figure 3.14 Left: The Keijō Branch of the Oriental Development Company (1930). Right: The Yokohama Specie Bank.

Source: Left: Courtesy of the Seoul Museum of History, artifact no. seo27650. Right: From *Meiji-Taisho Architectural Photography Collection* (1936), no. 133. Courtesy of the Library of the Architectural Institute of Japan.

in its mainland and colony. That wealth did not signify abundance or comfort but represented Prussian discipline devoted to national interests, thoroughly consistent regulations, and a grand view of an expanding empire.

The Emergence of Sŏnŭnjŏn Square

The Oriental Development Company's Keijō branch, the symbol of colonial exploitation, was at Hwanggŭmjŏng, an area dominated by the Japanese. All the major buildings the Government-General directly built or kept within its purview eventually appeared one by one within a 1-kilometer radius of Hwanggŭmjŏng: the Oriental Development Company (1911), the Bank of Chōsen (1912), the Keijō Post Office (1915), the Keijō Daily Building (1924), Keijō Station (1925), the Keijō Prefectural Government Building (1926), the Keijō Courthouse (1928), the Keijō Electric Company Building (1928), the Japanese Government-General's Commerce and Industry Promotion Hall (1929), and the Keijō Public Hall (1935).[291] Like the Chiyoda district in central Tokyo, downtown Keijō turned into a space where major administrative agencies, public offices, a courthouse, train station, and park were gathered. Of course, just as Forum Japanum never materialized to fulfill the ideals of Forum Fridericianum, Forum Koreanum never emerged to completely replace the old Street of Six Ministries. For more than half of Japan's colonial rule of Korea, the center of Keijō remained bifurcated between the area surrounding the new Government-General headquarters and the Namch'on area full of Japanese residents, thereby creating a division between the political center and economic center of the city.[292]

The Bank of Chōsen, currently the Money Museum of the Bank of Korea, was a definite landmark of Namch'on. "Sŏnŭnjŏn gwangjang," which literally means "square in front of the Bank of Chōsen," featured an image representative of modern Keijō during Japan's colonial rule of Korea. The bank itself was a Pan-Asian operation with four branches in Japan, sixteen in Manchuria, four in China, two in Primorsky Krai, and one in the United States. Originally created by the Residency-General in 1909 under the name "Bank of Korea," the bank was actually run by the Keijō branch of Japan's Dai-Ichi Bank. Then, as Japan annexed Korea in 1910, the bank became the central bank of colonial Korea and changed its name to the Bank of Chōsen. The building started to be built in November 1907 as the Dai-Ichi Bank's head office in Korea but was finished in January 1912 to house the Bank of Chōsen. The building situated to the north of Namdaemun Gate was where Chŏgyŏnggung used to be for the purpose of enshrining the ancestral tablet of Lady Kim Inbin, the concubine of King Sŏnjo and the grandmother of King Injo.[293] Under Japanese colonial rule, the site was part of an area called Hasegawa-chō after the second Governor-General Hasegawa Yoshimichi.

The Bank of Chōsen signified that Tsumaki's predominant influence upon public buildings in colonial Korea was being challenged. Like Tokyo, the power struggle between government and academia was not over in Keijō. As if to make up for his unfulfilled design of the Resident-General's residence, Tatsuno Kingo gave birth to an individual French style neo-Baroque building at the heart of Keijō, one that distinguished itself from those designed by Katayama Tōkuma. Finished in 1912, the stone building with two underground floors maintained a symmetrical façade while displaying nonconforming, distinctively Baroque features.

Figure 3.15 Left: The Bank of Chōsen (1915, Currently the Money Museum of the Bank of Korea). Right: The Keijō Post Office and Sŏnŭnjŏn Square.

Source: Left: Courtesy of the Seoul Museum of History, artifact no. seo11477. Right: From a postcard image (before 1945). Unknown – presumably Japanese government/public domain via Wikimedia Commons.

The elevation for the Bank of Chōsen showed the central porch formed out of a canopy supported by four granite entasis columns and a half-barrel shaped structure sitting on the roof above the main entrance. Cupolas in the Renaissance palazzo style were settled upon the corner pavilions to the left and right, which was a signature of Tatsuno's design to make the building stand out better from the street. Yet what stood out the most was the absence of emphasis on the central part of the façade. Aside from formalizing the protruding entrance, more emphasis was placed on either side of the building, subduing the symmetrical layout and securing horizontal proportions. The building's adequate size and rather nonconforming layout had a touch of familiarity compared to the Keijō branch of the Oriental Development Company.[294] Could the Bank of Chōsen have been Tatsuno's liberalistic answer to Tsumaki's nationalism? However, the bank building's resemblance to a château built in the Second Empire style made it appear more as a symbol of privilege than liberty.

In fact, it was colonial privileges instead of liberal communication that ruled over Sŏnŭnjŏn Square, intensely developed by the Japanese.[295] The Keijō Post Office that opened opposite the Bank of Chōsen in September 1915 had the imposing, rigid air of the north German neo-Renaissance style. Although the building's designer remains unknown, its presence appeared to be similar to the Oriental Development Company building rather than the Bank of Chōsen. Initially created by the Japanese government in 1888 inside the Japanese legation in Hansŏng as a branch of the Japanese Post Office in Inch'ŏn, the post office was expanded and restructured into the Keijō Post Office by 1905. And by 1915, a new building was raised for the post office in Honmachi, the area with the largest Japanese population in Keijō at the time. This massive three-story building with one underground floor was made of brick and stone and provided a floor space of 4,363.6 square meters, enough to fit twenty-three reception counters. The building's appearance was just as impressive as its size. It exhibited the neo-Renaissance style through its arched window frames and a balance formed between the corner protrusions and the accentuated central protrusion topped with a dome. Yet the horizontal white bands repeatedly woven into the brick walls upon the stone stylobate added an exotic Islamic touch. The arched entablature decorating the top parts of the left and right corner pavilions, the pairs of square pilasters beneath them, and the round dormer windows adorning what could have been a bland gabled roof all contributed to uplifting the building's level of architectural completion. From appearance to function, the Keijō Post Office was worthy of representing a new age with Imperial Japan at the vanguard.[296]

Sŏnŭnjŏn Square where the Keijō Post Office was located and Hasegawa-chō where the Bank of Chōsen was located both offered sights representative of modern Keijō. A view of Hasegawa-chō photographed from Mount Namsan around 1925 shows the façade of the Bank of Chōsen, the back

Figure 3.16 View of Hasegawa-chō From Mount Namsan (1925).

Source: Courtesy of the Seoul Museum of History, artifact no. seo27617.

side of the Keijō Post Office standing opposite the bank, the façade of Chōsen Hotel near the upper-right corner, and a straight boulevard between the buildings stretching north toward the Government-General Building. This modern sight lies in stark contrast to the random traditional tile-roofed houses populating the background along the top. Although Sŏnŭnjŏn Square was an economic rather than political center of Keijō, it was nevertheless a strategic space as it was occupied by an array of distinctive historicist buildings that created a modern phantasmagoria. In the long run, passing through such a space would have had an immeasurable impact on the collective identity and political awareness of people in Keijō.

Historicist Architecture of the 1920s

Under Japanese colonial rule, a modern layout and landscape materialized to a certain degree in downtown Keijō by the end of the 1910s, but the area truly began to look the way it was expected to by the mid-1920s. Above all, the Government-General Building began to serve its purpose from 1926. During the previous year, Keijō Station, the infrastructure most central to the city, was opened at the spot where Seoul Station stands today. And only a few days later, the Shinto shrine Chōsen jingū was finished upon a spot halfway up Mount Namsan that offered a complete view of downtown Keijō. The core axis of Keijō running along the boulevard from Kwanghwamun to Namdaemun was finished.

The location of Keijō Station used to be a sparsely populated area outside the town walls during the Chōsen dynasty until it emerged as a transportation hub as Japanese residences branched out from Yongsan to Honmachi. The wooden Namdaemun Railway Station built there in 1900 as part of the Kyŏngbusŏn Line was renamed Keijō Station even before the new station building was completed in September 1925. Railway stations started to be built in tandem with the launch of the Kyŏnginsŏn Line. However, because railway operations were more focused on transporting cargo than passengers, stations including those in Inch'ŏn, Namdaemun, and Yongsan were all small and equipped with the bare minimum facilities necessary to serve their immediate purpose.[297] The direct need for larger, multifunctional stations arose as the Kyŏngwŏnsŏn Line began operating in 1914 and Sŏdaemun Station was shut down. The addition of railway lines and the rearrangement of downtown Keijō required a new gateway into the city. Like the way railway stations generally came to replace the role castle gates once played, Keijō Station also pushed aside Namdaemun, the gateway to the Chōsen capital Hanyang, and established itself as the new gateway to a modern city.

Yet the construction of Keijō Station was also a matter directly linked to the interests of Imperial Japan. Although the project was carried out by the architectural team within the Public Works Division under the Government-General's Bureau of Railway Management, the station was to be the property of the South Manchuria Railway Company, or Mantetsu. Keijō Station was to be an advanced node that would serve Imperial Japan's expansion throughout Korea and Manchuria. The construction that began in June 1922 was supposed to be finished by 1923, but due to the Great Kantō earthquake and budgetary cuts, its completion was delayed until September 30, 1925. The massive two-story station with a floor space of 6,631 square meters including the underground floor was designed by Tsukamoto Yasushi, a professor at the Tokyo Imperial University's Department of Engineering. A student of Tatsuno Kingo, who designed the Tokyo Central Railway Station, Tsukamoto was serving as president of the Architectural Institute of Japan at the time Keijō Station was being built. Tsukamoto was also known for designing the Department of Engineering's auditorium and lecture rooms at the Tokyo Imperial University where he taught.[298]

The view of Keijō Station in a photo album Shimizu Corporation published in October 1925 to celebrate the completion of its work on the station exhibited the grand and powerful aura that came with the station's newly gained status. The large mass stretching out sideways had a protruding center to serve as the main entrance, upon which a dome and lantern was placed. Short spires were installed on either side of the dome to further accentuate the station's main entrance. The building also showed traces of the classicist yet liberal aesthetics Tatsuno Kingo featured through the Tokyo Central Railway Station. Overall, it adopted the French Renaissance style, but its heavily segmented layout and division between the flanks and central section were reminiscent of the neo-Baroque variation that had been attempted through the Taehan Clinic's main building. The station looked like a massive rock pressed from the front and back to rise at the center and spread out sideways.

Keijō Station remained the largest building in the city until the new Government-General Building was finished the following year. The ferroconcrete and reinforced masonry structure formed a single-story auxiliary wing on either side of a two-story main wing. The outer wall was finished with red bricks and a horizontal band of granite to separate the two stories. Decorations were added to the quoins to invigorate the station's exterior. The steel framed structure used for the roof was covered with natural slates and copperplates. The lower part of the ground floor was rusticated to give a sense of stability. The upper part of the main entrance was shaped into a vault fronted by a large semi-circular window with a clock hanging from its center. Positioned at the vanishing point of the station, the clock suggested that railway stations had turned into the headquarters to dictate modern times. Still, as if to soften the clock's stern message, the eaves of the vault shared the same semi-circular outline as the window. The most eye-catching feature of Keijō Station was the domed roof surrounded by semi-circular windows. This dome supported by pendentives was a structure that originated from Byzantine architecture and thereby demonstrated the station's international nature. The vertical formation of the dome finished with copperplates and topped with a lantern could be considered an architectural accoutrement to offset the station's lengthy horizontal expansion to its left and right.[299] Nevertheless, domes as a form language were political symbols associated with empires, which made Keijō Station no different from the Tokyo Central Railway Station.

According to the floor plan from when Keijō Station was built, a large hall occupied the building's central section beyond the protruding two-story-high main entrance and led to a two-story space on either side. This hall just inside the entrance served as the ground floor waiting room, with a display of Dorian columns and natural rays coming in through the semi-circular windows on the domed roof. The spaces attached to the central hall's left and right each provided room for administrative tasks and luggage transport. The V.I.P. lounge and restaurant on the second floor were less accessible from the central hall frequented by commoners, whereas the platform on the underground floor was more accessible from the central hall with an elevator that directly linked the hall to the

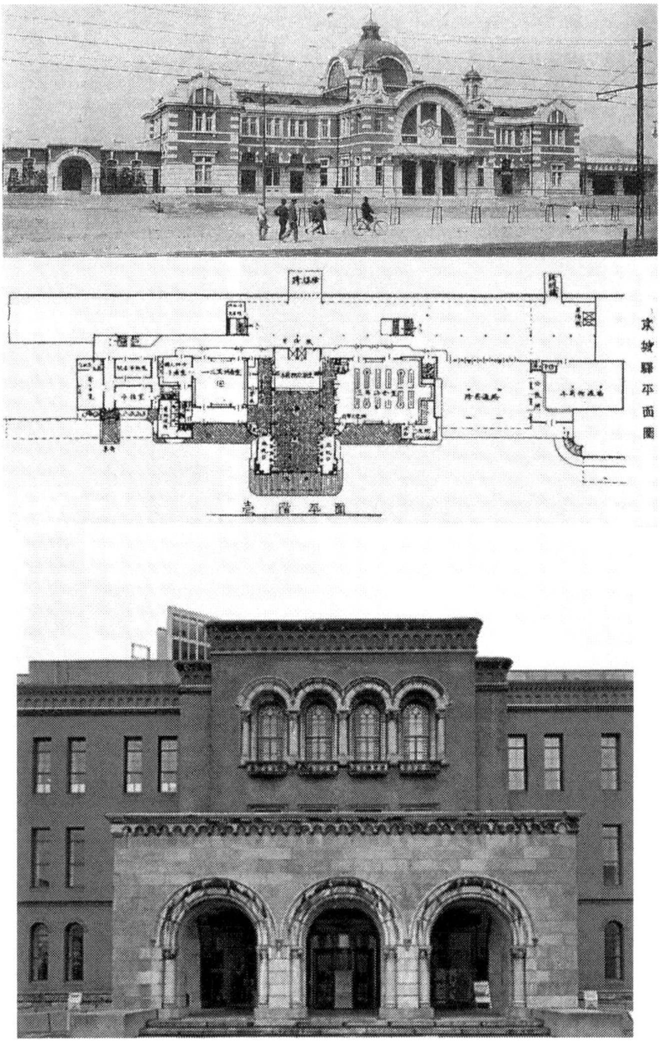

Figure 3.17 Top: View of Keijō Station From the Celebratory Photo Album (1925). Middle: First-Floor Plan of Keijō Station (1925). Bottom: Front View of the Keijō Courthouse (Currently the Seoul Museum of Art).

Source: Top: From KORAIL, *Sajinŭro ponŭn haebang ijŏnŭi ch'ŏlto yŏksa* (2003). Courtesy of the Korea Railroad Corporation (KORAIL). Middle: From KORAIL, *Sajinŭro ponŭn haebang ijŏnŭi ch'ŏlto yŏksa* (2003). Courtesy of the KORAIL. Bottom: Photo by author (2015).

platform.[300] The clear spatial division according to function seemed to be a miniature reflection of Keijō as an up-and-coming international city.

In terms of both form and function, Keijō Station revealed the genuine aspects of modern civilization. Common neo-Renaissance elements such as arches and brick walls were instruments employed to uplift the civilizational authority of public offices during Japan's colonial rule of Korea. The degree of emphasis on the image of a new civilization or power differed depending on the purpose of each building, but the difference between the two was unclear. Second to none in terms of demonstrating a ruling ideology, the Keijō Courthouse embodied aspects of both a new civilization and power. The courthouse, completed in November 1928, was situated upon the highest point in the middle of Jŏng-dong where diplomatic offices were concentrated. The site had previously accommodated P'yŏngniwŏn, a court of cassation and Korea's first modern court established in 1899. Through the Residency-General, Japan soon dominated the Korean judicial system and transformed it into a three-trial system. It took a long time to build a courthouse at Sŏsomunjŏng that could accommodate the district court, court of review, and high court all in one building. The one placed in charge of building the massive courthouse with a floor space of 6,164 square meters was Iwai Chōzaburō, head of the Architectural Department under the Government-General's Home Ministry. The engineers Sasa Keiichi and Iwatsuki Yoshiyuki were entrusted with designing the building. Iwai, Sasa, and Iwatsuki were all graduates of the Department of Architecture at the Tokyo Imperial University.[301]

From an architectural standpoint, the Keijō Courthouse maximized authoritative formality by adopting a protruding, triple-arched entrance. The three-story building with one underground floor was a combined structure of ferroconcrete and brick finished with soft, sandy brown tiles. Granite was attached to the porch's brick walls, creating the solemn impression stone buildings tend to give. The building's style could be classified as Gothic for its general outline reminiscent of a solid medieval castle, but a series of Renaissance palazzo features were present as well. The central section behind the protruding entrance was raised. The rows of doors and windows on the upper part were elaborately decorated by imitating the uniform series of arches at the main entrance, and the decorative parapet lining the entrance was replicated along the central section of the third floor. In the end, the building's features placed it between Renaissance and Gothic styles. However, the simplification of details such as the plain vertical windows and smooth walls had reason to be classified as modernist elements, which makes it possible to define the building's style as a modernist variation of the neo-Renaissance style. Some have been able to detect hints of the British neo-Palladian style from the triple-arched entrance paired with the arched windows along the third floor. Built in the late 1920s, the Keijō Courthouse seemed to signify the end of historicist architecture that had taken root in the city.[302]

The 1920s was when the landscape of Keijō changed markedly. Previous plans were realized to a certain degree, while new plans were conceived. Once the 1919 Urban Planning Act was established in Japan, a discourse on urban planning began in colonial Korea by the early 1920s and extensively transformed the arrangement of urban spaces. However, such changes exhibited more continuity than discontinuity. The completion of the Government-General Building in 1926 shifted the center of Keijō toward the north of Namch'on, prompting the dual urban structure of Namch'on and Pukch'on to be reorganized according to a stronger tectonic totality. The gap between the administrative and commercial centers remained but at least not intentionally. The vibrant urban planning movement in the 1920s aimed for a total restructuring of the city, and public support for this was gathered from officials of the Government-General, civil servants, Japanese civilians, and influential pro-Japanese Koreans.[303]

In terms of the cityscape of Keijō, the tide of change brought heavily historicist, authoritative-looking buildings to the commercial center Sŏnŭnjŏn Square, while the spaces north of the square were left to experiment with more postauthoritarian, functionalist architecture. The conversion from historicist architecture that emphasizes decorative façades to modernist architecture that values functionality was not a transfer of leadership from political to commercial forces[304] but rather part of a strategy to rationalize urban spaces and establish tectonic rule. Stark evidence of this was the modern Keijō Prefectural Government Building built to the northwest of Sŏnŭnjŏn Square.

Architectural Modernism in Keijō

After its annexation of Korea, Japan continued to reorganize the administrative system of its colony, which consisted of twenty-two prefectures. Early on, Isach'ŏng, or regional offices of the Residency-General that handled administrative affairs for Japanese settlers, were also utilized to perform administrative tasks at the prefectural level. Keijō Prefecture took advantage of the former Japanese consulate at Sŏnŭnjŏn Square until discussions about constructing a new building for the prefectural government finally began around 1920. Soon after Keijō Prefecture moved out, the old consulate building was torn down to make room for a branch of the Mitsukoshi Department Store headquartered in Tokyo. Sŏnŭnjŏn Square was thus reborn as a symbolic platform for new trends in Keijō.[305]

The new office for the Keijō Prefectural Government, currently Seoul City Hall, was established at a node along the diagonal road linking Kwanghwamun Boulevard to Sŏnŭnjŏn Square. The spot was also a dividing point between Hwanggŭmjŏng and Honmachi. This site across the street from the heart of the Korean Empire Tŏksugung had been occupied by the Government-General's bulletin *Keijō Daily*. Choosing such a site, however, does not seem to have been a decision primarily aimed at obliterating memories of the Empire of Korea.[306] By the 1920s, at least the downtown area of Keijō had already been transformed into a new urban space. The Keijō Urban Planning Research Society took the lead in proposing the construction of a new office for the Keijō Prefectural Government and in choosing its location.[307] Ahead of completing the new Government-General Building, the society was basically interested in expanding urban development projects from Namch'on to its north, not in undermining Koreans. The Government-General's goal for the Keijō Prefectural Government Building was indeed to create an impressive edifice in an open space. However, defining the project as the "Haussmannization of Keijō Prefecture"[308] based on that goal bears the shortcoming of fixating too much on the project's modernity. Instead, how about considering the project the "Ende-Böckmannization of Keijō Prefecture"? Does there not seem to be a desire to overcome the divide between administration and economy and achieve tectonic totality, even though it was never realized? If traces of an attempt like the one in Tokyo to concentrate government offices can be found from building an office for the Keijō Prefectural Government between the Government-General Building and Sŏnŭnjŏn Square, those traces would be closer to a manifestation of coloniality than modernity. Because the urban totality the Government-General and the ruling class of colonial Korea sought to realize in the name of modern civilization in fact engendered a "colonial difference," or the continuation of a dual city.

The Keijō Prefectural Government Building, constructed between 1925 and 1926, contributed to solidifying the diagonal, horizontal axis central to colonial rule. Such spatial planning was intimately related to changes in architectural style. The aspiration to form structural unity throughout an entire city caused more of a focus on individual building structure. Architectural modernism drew closer to the true province of Schinkelian tectonics by rejecting the historicist emphasis on decorative exteriors and assuming a "monumental classicist" aspect that was extremely abstract. Such changes were also caused by the change in construction methods. After the Great Kantō earthquake of 1923, buildings in Japan were sturdier ferroconcrete structures instead of the red brick structures that were used during the Meiji period to feature a Westernized cityscape. This provided buildings with internal force, allowing them to rely less on walls to sustain themselves and greatly diversify their façades. Corner windows were a characteristic of architectural modernism and a visual accoutrement demonstrating that walls were no longer crucial to sustaining a building's structure. Designs based on horizontal and vertical configurations were features of modernism that replaced the decorativeness of historicism. Façades with large or continuous horizontal windows surrounded by steel sashes, even and continuous walls, and cantilevered balconies appeared to create a new cityscape.[309]

Modernist architecture was introduced to Keijō in the mid-1920s through magazines like *Chōsen to kenchiku*.[310] The Keijō Prefectural Government Building was a pioneering case that certainly deposed the premise that modernist architecture possessed functionalist characteristics suitable for commercial buildings. Starting with the Keijō Prefectural Government Building, modernist buildings that emerged in Keijō, such as the Japanese Government-General's Commerce and Industry Promotion Hall (1929) and the Keijō Public Hall (1935), displayed a superiority no different from historicist buildings, or the "coloniality of power" that obliterated the homes and memories of colonial natives.

Finished in September 1926, the Keijō Prefectural Government Building's front, left, and right wings had four stories and a tower rising six stories high from the center of the front wing. The three-story-high rear wing consisted of meeting rooms. This massive building housed a total of ninety-seven rooms across a floor space of 6,783 square meters. It adopted a reinforced concrete beam-column frame and used bricks to fill the space between columns. The building was designed by Iwai Chōzaburō, the head of the Architectural Department under the Government-General's Home Ministry, with the assistance of his subordinates Sasa Keiichi and Iwatsuki Yoshiyuki. Although the exterior was simple compared to its political importance, the building was tall enough to overlook Tŏksugung Palace, and its long horizontal walls divided by vertical windows formed

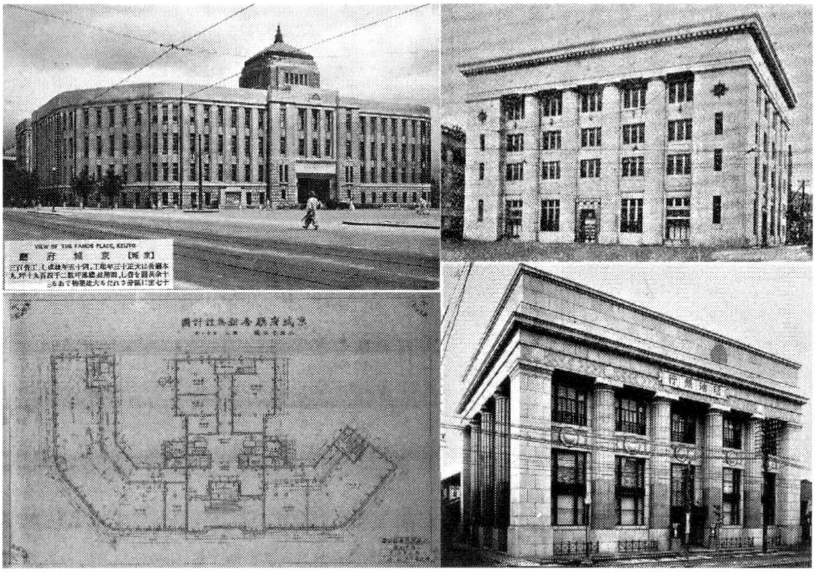

Figure 3.18 Top Left: Front View of the Keijō Prefectural Government Building (1930s). Bottom Left: Two-Story Floor Plan of the Keijō Prefectural Government (From Between 1922 and 1926). Top Right: Front View of the Chōsen Savings Bank (1938). Bottom Right: The Meiji Bank in Nagoya, Japan.

Source: Top Left: Courtesy of Busan Museum, collection no. guib2962. Bottom Left: Courtesy of the National Archives of Korea, management no. DJB0001821. Top Right: Courtesy of the Seoul Museum of History, artifact no. seo14407. Bottom Right: From *Meiji-Taisho Architectural Photography Collection* (1936), no. 219. Courtesy of the Library of the Architectural Institute of Japan.

the imposing presence usually found in government offices. Vertical windows in particular was an architectural element commonly adopted by major government offices built during the Japanese colonial rule, such as the Government-General Building. The central section of such offices tended to be accentuated with a large entrance and maintained a left–right symmetry. Domes and window frames were indicators that such offices had clearly been influenced by the Japanese Diet Building under construction at the time.[311]

What stood out about the Keijō Prefectural Government Building was its frontality as it faced the square bordering the main road T'aep'yŏng-ro. Although it eventually adopted a slightly asymmetrical layout to fit the shape of the site, the building maintained a strong left–right symmetry by compensating with an ascending central tower and windows and doors arranged in an orderly fashion upon a granite stylobate. This modernist transformation of Renaissance form language maximized the building's frontality. According to the building's ground plan, a staircase leading to the second floor was placed at the center past the main entrance and spacious hall. On the second floor was another hall with an elevator, stairs, and washroom at the center as well as a corridor stretching toward the building's left, right, and rear wing. As much as its stylistic form, the building's spatial layout stressed functionality.[312]

Historicism in Keijō entered a new stage in the 1930s. With the establishment of Manchukuo, fascism grew politically pronounced and had a great impact upon the society and culture of Imperial Japan. Keijō was no exception to this trend. The promulgation of the 1934 Chosŏn Urban Planning Ordinance launched the construction of new cities, as well as projects to reorganize or expand existing cities. This gave birth to "Greater Keijō," a colonial primate city belonging to the Greater East Asia Co-Prosperity Sphere. To more deeply imprint imperial greatness and powerfulness in the minds of people, Renaissance or Baroque elements of design mostly disappeared, and fascist, extremely neo-classical vestiges came to dictate the form of buildings. Fascist aesthetics actually had much in common with modernist aesthetics. They both valued function over ornamentation, structure over exterior, and unity over pluralism. As internationalism originating from the West started to be more readily accepted in the 1930s, the left–right symmetry of historicist architecture was replaced with a function-oriented surface reflecting the advantages of ferroconcrete structures.[313]

A work representative of fascist modernism was the Chōsen Savings Bank that appeared in Keijō in 1935 and later served as the headquarters of Cheil Bank. According to the Ordinance on Savings Banks, promulgated in 1928, the bank, aimed at improving people's finance, was established by acquiring part of the Chōsen Industrial Bank's savings and operations in July 1929. What was unique about the Chōsen Savings Bank was that an international design competition was held for the bank's new headquarters once the decision to build it was made in 1931. After the call for submissions was made in June 1932, the competition lasted for only a few months until the results were announced in September.[314] The building near Sŏnŭnjŏn Square, the economic center of Keijō, started to be built in October 1933 and was completed in November 1935. The competition awarded first prize to the plan by Hirabayashi Kingo, who also designed the Osaka Prefectural Government Building. The review on Hirabayashi's design noted how well it blended in with the Western-style buildings gathered around Sŏnŭnjŏn Square and lived up to the grand, trustworthy appearance expected from a bank.[315] The five-story building with one underground floor had a steel-framed, reinforced concrete structure and offered a floor space of 7,038 square meters. Granite was carefully attached to the external walls, and four weighty columns rose up to meet the entablature. Doric columns without an entasis were fluted to make them appear as classical as possible. A vertical row of three windows each lined the façade's left and right side to add to the building's verticality.[316]

As he designed the Nagoya City Hall and other buildings in the 1930s, the architect Hirabayashi Kingo pursued the Japanese fascist style known as the Imperial Crown Style. This was the very style featured in his design for the headquarters of the Chōsen Savings Bank. The form language of neoclassicism was assumed on the forefront to blend in well with the historicist buildings nearby, but fascist or modernist simplifications or exaggerations were made to that form language. Left–right symmetries or the transposition of horizontal and vertical surfaces were geometrically simplified, which accentuated unity, strengthened the level of concentration, and even seemed to ridicule the principle of tectonics. The repetition of vertical windows and columns almost looked like soldiers being inspected in line. The harmony and grandeur unique to Prussian classicism and found in the Government-General Building were replaced by a stiff lump of stone for the Chōsen Savings Bank.[317]

The façade of the Chōsen Savings Bank looked fairly similar to that of the headquarters of the Meiji Bank built in Nagoya, Japan in 1922. The Meiji Bank was designed by Nagano Uheji, a student of Tatsuno Kingo who built his reputation from designing the Japanese Government-General Building in Taiwan.[318] Nagano had experience working on projects in Korea, including the Busan Station he designed with his teacher Tatsuno. Most of all, he was known as a master of bank buildings for designing the Bank of Japan branches, so his designs are likely to have served as a reference in designing a headquarters for the Chōsen Savings Bank. The fact that Shimizu Corporation, the constructor for the Meiji Bank, handled the construction of major landmarks in Keijō, such as the Bank of Chōsen and Keijō Station, supports the suggestion that certain connections were at work in designing and carrying out such large-scale projects. The two-story Meiji Bank building was different from the Chōsen Savings Bank in terms of size and details involving the roof and corners. However, the two buildings both had four fluted stone columns, similarly shaped entrances, and rectangular façades. More stories were added to the neoclassical façade of the Meiji Bank in the 1920s in addition to modern vertical windows near the left and right corners in order to give birth to the Chōsen Savings Bank of the 1930s that exhibited fascist grandeur.

A building that featured modernism rather than fascism in Keijō was the Keijō Public Hall built along T'aep'yŏngt'ong in 1935. In June 1933, Keijō Prefecture received a donation from the Keijō Electric Company to help build infrastructure for the city. After much consideration, a multipurpose hall was constructed for the citizens of Keijō. Across a floor space of 5,676 square meters stood a three-story ferroconcrete structure with one underground floor. The architect behind the building's design was a student of Itō Chūta named Hagiwara Kōichi who later began to work as an engineer for the Government-General in 1937. The Keijō Public Hall, now serving as the Seoul Metropolitan Council building, was a landmark at the heart of Keijō where Kwanghwamunt'ong turned onto T'aep'yŏngt'ong. The building was bent at a ninety-degree angle to fit the shape of the site. Its three-story-high main hall could accommodate one thousand eight hundred people for lectures, plays, concerts, or screenings, while two smaller halls were added to serve a variety of other purposes.[319]

The façade dominated by straight lines and no decorations made the Keijō Public Hall a building representative of modernism at the heart of Keijō. The most eye-catching part was the 44-meter-high clock tower on the southeast corner, which displayed an ostentatious verticality that could be considered a tremendously modernist architectural expression. Placing the tower at a corner instead of its usual position at the main entrance maximized its verticality and helped the building stand out. The shadows created by the long, slit windows beside the clock tower, followed by mechanically placed rows of extremely simple, vertical windows, and the light-colored exterior formed a distinct, razor-sharp impression that made its modernist mark on the heart of the city.[320]

Cultural facilities in Japan are likely to have served as a reference in designing the Keijō Public Hall,[321] and considering the hall's central location in the capital, one of such reference must have been the Tokyo Metropolitan Hibiya Public Hall. Like the Keijō Public Hall, the Tokyo Metropolitan Hibiya Public Hall was built as a multipurpose cultural space annexed to the Municipal Research Building, a roadside landmark at a corner of Hibiya Park. Opened in 1929, the hall was the work of Satō Kōichi, a professor at the Tokyo Imperial University who later established the Waseda University's Department of Architecture. Satō mixed the form languages of the Renaissance and Gothic styles to create a modernist building.[322] The hall thereby shared modernist architectural details with the Keijō Public Hall in terms of the stark contrast between the horizontal outline and the explicit verticality of the clock tower and vertical windows.

Figure 3.19 Left: Façade of the Keijō Public Hall Along T'aep'yŏngt'ong (Currently Occupied by the Seoul Metropolitan Council). Middle: Current View of the Municipal Research Building, 2018. Right: Current View of the Rotes Rathaus, 2005.

Source: Left: Courtesy of Busan Museum, collection no. guib2804. Middle: Photo: Lombroso/CC BY-SA (https://creativecommons.org/licenses/by-sa/4.0). Right: Photo: Andreas Steinhoff.

The reason for assuming that the two halls share a "familial resemblance" is because of the Berlin City Hall. Often referred to as the "Rotes Rathaus," this red building designed by Hermann Friedrich Waesemann and completed in 1869 was basically formed in the Cinquecento style. Although it is generally classified as neo-Renaissance, the Berlin City Hall displays a highly unique combination of a Roman arched entrance, elements of the northern Italian Palazzo style such as the four wings upon a rectangular ground plan, and north German red brick walls. Considering its location in central Berlin, the old form language of the German round-arched style seems to complement the monumental, abstinent beauty of Schinkelian classicism.[323] At a glance, the Berlin City Hall may not appear anything like the Tokyo Metropolitan Hibiya Public Hall, but the two buildings both have red walls, tall central clock towers, and are shaped like a cube. Also, they are both "municipal establishments" at the heart of their cities and landmarks visible from afar because of their tall clock towers. The Berlin City Hall, the Tokyo Metropolitan Hibiya Public Hall, and the Keijō Public Hall can all be considered attempts to create a civic center in their respective capital or colonial primate city where a national center was absent.

Like the Tokyo Metropolitan Hibiya Public Hall, the Keijō Public Hall was a performance venue that looked as modern as the multiple purposes it aimed to serve, such as lectures, concerts, and film screenings. This demonstrated a departure from the yoke of historicism and an entry into the course of modernism. It was not, however, a signal of liberty but one of extreme control and oppression. The heavy, artificial contrast between horizontal and vertical lines and a clock tower too tall compared to the rest of the building's size made the Keijō Public Hall appear much larger and more imposing than it actually was. The hierarchy inherent in neoclassicism had grown iron strong from being geometrically simplified and condensed. Modernism had been none other than a fascist reinterpretation of neoclassicism.

The relationship between fascism and modernism resembled that between the omnipotent ruling power symbolized by the Government-General Building and "modern civilization" symbolized by Sŏnŭnjŏn Square. While fascism and modernism were connected through a shortcut called autolatry and dogmatism, the boulevards Kwanghwamunt'ong and T'aep'yŏngt'ong prevented people from freely crossing back and forth between the Government-General Building and Sŏnŭnjŏn Square. Like a film set, everything was prearranged, and political intervention was completely precluded. The radial Sŏnŭnjŏn Square seemed to be brimming with vigor on the surface, but the boisterousness was but a sad theater of the absurd, like the protagonist in Yi Sang's story *The Wings*, who yearned to spread his wings upon the rooftop of the Mitsukoshi Department Store. What seemed far more real were the dramatic scenes in which the patriotic martyr Na Sŏk-ju threw a bomb at the Oriental Development Company and confronted the police.[324]

Melancholy City

Having turned into an arena of competition for historicism under Japanese colonial rule, the colonial primate city Keijō was approaching the completion of plans its colonial ruler had formed early on. The emergence of modernist architecture was not a disconnection from such plans but rather a comprehensive step closer to their completion. This persistence was in fact a manifestation of coloniality, because arguments that relied on a certain context in mainland Japan were enforced as ironclad rules at colonies. Hence, it should come as no surprise that colonial natives found modern urban spaces a symbol of hopelessness. For instance, new urban spaces were rarely described in novels, which played an influential role in Korean culture during Japanese colonial rule. Even when they were mentioned, the descriptions were mostly consumed by frustration and melancholy and often reduced to a fragment of the novelist's personal psychological experience.[325] Even the novelist Yi Kwang-su, one of most renowned figures in Korean literature at the time, who later turned pro-Japanese and served as a "puppet that upholds the reign and ideas of another," was not enthusiastic about the changes in Keijō and conveyed a sense of transience in stating that he "wept in longing for the old, dark, smelly Seoul and Korea of two decades ago."[326]

The melancholy Koreans felt, however, fails to prove that the spatiotemporal impact Japan caused was not as great as it was assumed to have been. A symbol of hopelessness tends to explicitly induce antagonism but implicitly induce despairing admission. By the 1930s, the "large buildings soaring up to the capital's sky" were no longer gazed upon with amazement but often perceived as "reasonable and normal."[327] This process of accepting modern time and space as an irreversible trend was no different from the process of how melancholy grew prevalent. Melancholy is in fact a sentimental effect created by a modern order of time that separates the past from the present. The moment the past loses direct connectivity with the present and is relabeled as "history" or "tradition," the existence of modern urban spaces is accepted as a fait accompli.

Since Aoyagi Tsunatarō published *The Latest Guide to Keijō* in 1915, various guides on Keijō were made available, primarily for Japanese tourists. Such guides usually introduced the transportation system, government offices, hospitals, schools, and libraries as a testament to Japan's "benevolent rule" of the city. They would also feature museums, parks, a zoo, and other cultural and entertainment facilities so as to cater to a wide spectrum of tourists. As the history and traditional culture of colonial Korea were drawn into stark comparison with the present status of the Japanese empire, they were reclassified and reorganized and thus relegated to no more than goods to be consumed by curious tourists.[328] A Western-style landscape with native historical remains turned out to be a good pair of decorations for a modern city.

A highly symbolic example of such a pairing would be the Japanese Government-General Museum, which stood in the eastern section of Kyŏngbokgung Palace. Built as a space to display works of art during the 1915 Chōsen Industrial Exhibition, the museum was located where the building Kyejojŏn used to be near the palace gate Kŏnch'unmun. All buildings raised for the exhibition were demolished afterwards except for the museum building, which was reopened on December 1 of the same year as a permanent museum for the Japanese Government-General of Korea.[329] Like the other buildings constructed temporarily for the exhibition, the façade was arranged in the Renaissance style, and the mortar finish over a brick structure made the museum look like a stone building.[330] According to the *Guide to Keijō* published in 1929 by the Sponsors of the Chōsen Industrial Exhibition, the Government-General Museum housed a broad collection, including "items from the time of Nangnang and the Three Han States," as well as "lacquerware and paintings from the Chōsen dynasty."[331] For a museum displaying Chōsen dynasty relics to have a typically Western exterior was no coincidence. The idea of bundling together hundreds and thousands of relics between the Three Han States period and the Chōsen dynasty under the name of tradition demonstrated compliance to a Western, modern spatio-temporal order.

To blend in with the Government-General Building to be raised at the foreside of Kyŏngbokgung Palace, the Government-General Museum assumed an utterly classical appearance. The central section of the façade protruded to create the main entrance. Wide stone stairs led up to two pairs of Corinthian columns supporting the portico. The curve of the alcove softened the look of the massive wall on either side of the portico.

The symmetrical left and right wing were raised up to a height slightly lower than the central section and featured pilasters, which clearly revealed the building's hierarchical nature. Above the pilasters was a common entablature and a low rooftop balustrade. Along the rear wall inside the central hall were stairs leading to the second floor so that the two-story building's left and right wings would offer a total of six exhibition rooms. In other words, the Government-General Museum was practically a textbook case of adhering to the grammar of Western classical architecture. At the museum, the traditions of Chōsen had settled into a modern spatio-temporal order.[332]

Figure 3.20 Top: Complete View of the Government-General Museum at Kyŏngbokgung Palace (Before 1945). Bottom: Western Annex of Sŏkcho Hall (1938, Currently the Tŏksugung Branch of the Korean National Museum of Modern and Contemporary Art).

Source: Top: Unknown author/Public domain via Wikimedia Commons. Bottom: From the Collection Database of the National Museum of Korea, plate 30406. Korea Open Government License.

Japan certainly made political use of the museum. There is no doubt that the Japanese tried to establish their superiority as the civilized guardian of an otherized colony.[333] Besides exerting a particular political effect, however, building the museum was also about attempting to realize a new world view. In 1934, the Government-General planned to build a new museum to celebrate the upcoming twenty-fifth anniversary of its colonial rule the following year. Although it was never realized, the plan was to build a comprehensive museum featuring art, science, and resources by merging the existing Government-General Museum with the former Government-General Building serving as a science museum.[334] Japanese colonialism had sought to apply the generalities of natural science to ruling the Japanese empire and thereby sublimate such colonial rule as a universal truth no one could defy. Due to practical reasons, the dream of building a comprehensive museum had to be scaled down drastically to a museum only for exhibiting ancient relics, but the underlying purpose was not abandoned. Opened in 1938, the Yi Royal Family Museum of Art inside Tŏksugung Palace replaced the Yi Royal Family Museum that had existed since 1908 inside Ch'anggyŏnggung Palace. This placed colonial Korea's ancient works of art under a more structured historical order that isolated them from the present. The Yi Royal Family Museum of Art went on to serve as an exemplum virtutis after Korea's liberation for its national museum.[335]

Currently functioning as a branch of the National Museum of Modern and Contemporary Art, the Yi Royal Family Museum of Art was built as the western annex of Sŏkchojŏn, or Sŏkcho Hall. The hall was a British-style neoclassical granite building constructed inside Tŏksugung far earlier in June 1910, shortly before Japan's annexation of Korea. At the time, Tŏksugung was a secondary palace where King Kojong resided as a powerless supreme king, which is why it suffered less damage than other palaces. However, once the last Korean king, Sunjong, passed away, Japan formulated plans to turn Tŏksugung into a park by 1931. When the palace was opened to the public in 1933, Sŏkcho Hall was turned into an art museum that mainly exhibited modern Japanese works of art, leaving no room for traditional traces of the palace. The hall's western annex was built to accommodate the original purpose of the Yi Royal Family Museum of Art. Hence emerged the colonialist dual system, with the hall serving as the east building for modern Japanese art and the new annex serving as the west building for ancient Korean art.[336]

Built in 1938, the western annex of Sŏkcho Hall was designed by Nakamura Yoshihei. Nakamura built his career in Manchuria, where he designed branches of the Bank of Chōsen in Dalian and Changchun. Once he began serving as supervisor for the construction of the Seoul branch of Japan's Dai-Ichi Bank in 1907, Nakamura opened an architectural firm in Seoul and designed as well as supervised the construction of many buildings in the city, including the head office of the Chōsen Industrial Bank (1918), the Central Temple of Ch'ŏndogyo (1921), and the west (1921) and east (1923) annexes of Chungang High School. In 1922, he returned to Tokyo and continued to work as an architect. The western annex of Sŏkcho Hall was a project Nakamura worked on long after he left Korea. The building's framework and Corinthian columns basically adopted the neo-Renaissance style but possessed modernist features such as the minimally decorated vertical windows and the simple flat roof with no gables. Such abstract classicism could also be found in his design for the Bank of Chōsen's Dalian branch, completed earlier in 1920. As a matter of fact, compared to the Victorian classicism of the museum's east building beside it, the western annex of Sŏkcho Hall had the rigid, imposing presence of Prussian classicism. This was not a coincidence. While Nakamura ran an architectural firm in Keijō, the firm had a staff member from Austria named Anton Feller who made it possible for the firm to experiment with the German Secession style through projects like the Central Temple of Ch'ŏndogyo.[337] Hence, instead of a glorious Victorian palace left by a five-hundred-year-old dynasty, the traditions of Korea found a new home inside a Prussian fortress called the Yi Royal Family Museum of Art strictly guarded by sturdy columns.

5. Between the Japanese Government-General Building and Kyŏngbok Palace

Compared to the waves of shock the construction of new spaces sent, Japanese colonial rule did not last long. The laboriously constructed Government-General Building ended up serving its original purpose for less than two decades. On September 9, 1945, U.S. forces entered Seoul. That day, in Meeting Room no. 1 of the building, an instrument of surrender was signed between John Reed Hodge, the commanding general of the 24th corps, and Abe Nobuyuki, the Japanese Governor-General of Korea. The American flag was immediately hung outside the building, which had turned into an office for the U.S. military government's rule of Korea. It was around this time when the building started to be referred to by the more neutral-sounding name Capitol Hall, or Chungangch'ŏng in Korean.[338] Three years later, the same building housed the Korean constitutional assembly and once more began to serve a central government, when the establishment of the Republic of Korea's government was announced in front of the building. The former Government-General Building thus managed to maintain its central status even after the fall of the empire responsible for its creation. One cannot help but notice the historical irony from the fact that a photo of the Korean flag being raised in front of the building during the Korean War was once considered a national portrait meant to inspire patriotism.

Seoul, the Battlefield of Modernity and Coloniality

How was it possible for this headquarters of colonial rule to overcome all sorts of historical hardships and still stand firm at the top of a spatial hierarchy? The answer was surprisingly simple. It was because the building did not have a Japanese appearance. The building's Western exterior kept it alive as its greatest shield of protection. Rather than being reminded of their shameful colonial past, passersby in Seoul saw no reason to hasten the demolition of this seemingly Western modern building. Likewise, despite having been designed by Japanese architects, the Bank of Chōsen's head office, Keijō Station, and the Keijō Prefectural Government Building were each able to relabel themselves as the Bank of Korea's head office, Seoul Station, and Seoul City Hall, whereas buildings that explicitly looked Japanese, such as Chōsen jingū at Mount Namsan, were not able to survive.[339]

By the time the nation regained its sovereignty, Koreans were already used to the spaces Japanese colonial rulers had created, and despite drastic political changes, those spaces did not easily change. The citizens of Seoul had long accepted as a natural part of their daily lives the modern structures and straight roads from late Chōsen and Japanese colonial rule.[340] At the same time, they generally believed that Kwanghwamun Gate and Kyŏngbokgung Palace had to be restored at some point. Such contradictory sentiments can only be explained through the entanglement of colonization and modernization. Koreans abhorred colonial rule but were keen on the modernization it entailed. One might dare say that a certain consensus in terms of aiming for modernization was perhaps formed between the ruler and its subjects during colonial rule. If restoring Kwanghwamun and Kyŏngbokgung was the completion of a long-term project for modernization, that restoration should be regarded as a logical consequence of, rather than disconnection from, unavoidable colonialism. This view, of course, deeply involves a new dimension of time and space.

An almost shamanistic belief in the myth called modernity originates foremost from passively yet autonomously experiencing the built environment of a colonial city. Such a belief is none other than dissociation caused by contradictory experiences. In colonial cities, natives are harshly regulated, segregated, and excluded from public life, which is an oppressive, destructive process that simultaneously conceives new possibilities. Because cities have been places of exchange for humans in all ages, colonialist powers have never managed to wholly enforce their original intentions. Colonial subjects may seem to blindly accept modern civilization, or a new way of life and perception, but there is a rather strategic aspect to that acceptance. Through endless delays and dislocations, colonial subjects imprint themselves upon systematically formed urban spaces. And all too soon, the governmentality that had been enforced far more furtively and persistently in a colony than a metropole reaches a critical point. This process is utterly contradictory in that it corrupts colonialism yet allows colonialism to subsist.

When an empire dissolves, the spatiotemporal order of a colonial city makes an even louder rupturing sound. Through new social solidarity and economic, cultural, and political practices, the citizens of a postcolonial city transcend the spatio-temporal order previously established by the colonial ruler. Examples of this include natural time as opposed to Western capitalism's mechanical time or the ruralization of urban spaces due to a massive influx of a farming population.[341] Nevertheless, it is easy for decolonization to turn into a process of strengthening an already firmly internalized colonialism. Modernization projects carried out by nascent elites attempt to use postcolonial cities as the driving force of national development until they run into the contradiction of relying on a logic increasingly similar to that of former colonialists.[342] Postcolonial cities may appear to be filled with hope, but they are in fact inevitably traumatic spaces. New sovereign spaces experience endless fissure between past and present, or between territorial sovereignty and peripheral status. Such spaces are not the land of promise where anything can be newly attempted, nor are they a homeland people can return to at any time.

Such phases reveal the abyss of an experience that cannot be encompassed under the concept of colonial modernity. Imperial Japan presented a phantasmagoria of Prussian classicism to establish its modern identity, which seemed fairly plausible, at least when it paraded itself in front of its neighbors. However, colonial Korea faced a reality too wretched to be immersed in that phantasmagoria. In an attempt to offer an active appraisal of the history of colonial subjects, suggesting that colonial Koreans "autonomously" appropriated modern values such as civilization, freedom, equality, rights, and progress under circumstances different from the Japanese empire would be turning a blind eye to the truth. The extent of discrimination, violence, and coercion was too severe to be covered up by specious success stories.[343] "Postcolonial modernity" was not an alternative modernity but the tragic outcome of oppressing and obliterating the cultures and values of countless "others." Hence, a blind obsession over modernization perhaps requires historical oblivion. Although seemingly the complete opposite, an obsession over national traditions is none other than a display of colonial schizophrenia incapable of finding the true self. Despite the traditional appearance of old palaces or birthplaces of great men that came to decorate the liberated postcolonial city of Seoul, those "sites of memory" merely represented a situation devoid of substantial memories due to a fissure in memory, or deep-rooted "environments of memory" that have turned into vestiges of colonialism. Traces of a shameful past were neatly packaged like a souvenir on display.

Instead of seriously reflecting upon such a tragic situation and trying to devise a solution, the Republic of Korea unfortunately chose to conceal and distort the situation. The easiest, most antinomic means of doing so was to utilize anticommunism. The photo of the Korean flag being hung in front of Capitol Hall on the day Seoul was reclaimed exhibits an anticommunist rhetoric that glosses over Korea's entire colonial past and feigns indifference.[344] Such an approach causes colonialism to be confused with communism and reframes the bothersome contradiction between modernization and colonization into a simpler conflict between modernization and communism. Anticommunist states thoroughly suppressed memories of their colonial past and promoted national modernization as the only value. However, no matter how much it tried to suppress the memories of its colonial past, South Korea could not escape the accusation of being an anti-national state that failed to put colonialism past itself. Anticommunism was instead declared an extension of colonialism. Amid such bizarre circumstances, the contradiction between modernization and colonization has not been resolved at all. In fact, since Japanese colonial rule, to be both modern and national has been challenging, because, far from being a symbol of national glory, modernity has been a symbol of sorrow from being ruled by foreigners. The modern, anti-Korean Government-General Building thus became an object of ambivalent feelings that created schism in Seoul.

The National Assembly Building in Yŏŭido: A Travesty of Tectonics

South Korea's first president, Rhee Syngman, is known as the first to publicly argue for the Government-General Building's demolition. After the Korean War, he is said to have refused to restore the building partly destroyed by the North Korean People's Army and instead asked Commander Taylor of the Eighth United States Army to blow the building up.[345] The veracity of this story involving President Rhee is relatively less important because he was the one who turned the building into the site of the Republic of Korea's foundation. In 1950, at the beginning of the Korean War, the North Korean People's Army used the building as a temporary office until its inside was completely destroyed by a fire the army set upon its retreat. Kyŏngbokgung Palace also sustained heavy damage at the time. Kwanghwamun Gate, relocated to the north of Kŏnch'unmun Gate by then, was bombarded, leaving only the gate's arched foundation intact.[346] As the heart of the Republic of Korea turned into a heap of ashes, the "largest stone building in the Orient" was left at a crossroads of existence.

Securing a government office after the war was a matter more urgent than the decision to demolish or restore Capitol Hall. In 1954, the South Korean government established plans to use government funds and U.S. aid money to build two new government office buildings at the former site of a police academy. One building was to be used by departments related to economic aid, while the other was to house the United States Operations Mission to the Republic of Korea (USOM) in charge of aid-related affairs. USOM oversaw the construction project, which resulted in two minimalist modern buildings by October 1961. Although internally furnished with the latest facilities at the time, the simple box-shaped buildings appeared too modest to be government offices.[347] They didn't particularly have anything in common with the progressive image of modern architecture in vogue near the end of Japanese colonial rule and merely served as a reminder of the abject reality Korea was in after the war. Naturally, the desire arose for government offices capable of properly displaying state authority.

Even before these American-style buildings were raised, plans were already being made for a new office for the South Korean central government. Once Park Chung-hee and his allies carried out the military coup d'état on May 16, 1961, extensive repairs were done on Capitol Hall, which had been neglected for nearly a decade. The repair work that began in September 1961 was mostly finished by the following year, enough for an opening ceremony to be held in November. Beginning then, the building was the South Korean central government office, although it took another two years to complete the repairs. The South Korean flag was firmly set in the place that once bore the Japanese flag, the American flag, and even the North Korean flag.[348] Utilizing the Government-General Building cannot simply be considered a practical choice made under poor fiscal circumstances. The choice revealed the basic nature of the Park Chung-hee administration and, at the same time, was an inevitable consequence of South Korea's innate aporia.

The anticommunist state Rhee Syngman launched and Park Chung-hee completed actually aimed for antinational modernization. As Park Chung-hee's personal history demonstrates, the specter of Manchukuo haunted the center of the Korean state. The modern exterior of Capitol Hall bespoke the nature of the state. The building was an instrument that used its transcendent impression based on Prussian tectonics to conceal the devastations of a colonial past and thus ensure the smooth operation of the state's governmentality. The Prussia of Asia had in fact been a phantasmagoria created by a dark shadow called Imperial Japan. When such a phantasmagoria misleads reality, frustration and displacement are bound to occur in reality. The more an almost irresistible authority of modernity suppresses the cries of memory, the deeper the chasm of coloniality becomes. This is the context that explains why Seoul, the capital of the Republic of Korea, has endlessly attempted to destroy and forget under the pretense of becoming a modern international city but has never managed to dispel the compulsively repetitive specter of the past.

The Urban Planning Law and Building Law for Seoul was established and promulgated just six months after Park Chung-hee's military regime seized power. On January 20, 1962, laws no. 983 and 984 were passed around the same time the first five-year national development plan was launched. Seoul stepped back into the boundaries of urban planning nearly three decades after the Chosŏn Urban Planning Ordinance was enacted under Japanese colonial rule in 1934. Although a plan for Seoul's rehabilitation from war damage had been established on March 2, 1952, inadequate circumstances during a time of war forced the plan to be scaled down significantly. Considered the beginning of a full-scale urban renewal since the Republic of Korea's foundation, the 1962 Urban Planning Law tended to inherit aspects of the land readjustment carried out near the end of Japanese colonial rule. The difference, albeit minor, was that urban planning was partially delegated to local administrators, greenbelts were introduced, and education and hygiene districts were added instead of discipline districts. Nevertheless, it would be a mistake to overlook the changes in social circumstances that took place over a span of several decades. The South Korean capital's population of nine hundred thousand in 1945 when Japan withdrew plummeted during the Korean War but rose back to nearly 2.5 million by 1960. Due to these changes, the Land Readjustment Project Act was separated from the Urban Planning Law in 1966 so as to permit readjustment through private initiatives. The first few years that followed brought a distinct change to the landscape of Seoul. Trams disappeared, the Ch'ŏnggye Overpass was built, and modernist buildings such as the Seun Arcade and an affordable housing option called the "citizen apartment" appeared. Additionally, the development of the Han River was indeed groundbreaking. This, of course, did not mean change had caught up with the climate of centralized urban planning that had been around since Japanese colonial rule.[349]

Urban planning in postcolonial Seoul did not originate from middle-class efforts to preserve themselves. Its origin had been carried in the seed of colonialism from the beginning. The 1963 Southern Seoul New Town Project the Korean capitalist Pak Hŭng-sik ambitiously planned to clear his name as a pro-Japanese entrepreneur was a private initiative that induced foreign capital to build a road network and residential area. The project's success was, however, unlikely from the outset considering the reality of Korea at the time. Despite aiming to develop the current Gangnam area as well as Kwach'ŏn just outside Seoul, which amounted to an area of approximately 79,338,850 square meters, or thirty times the size of Yŏŭido, the project failed to meet the basic requirements of urban planning, such as preparing a transportation plan and alternatives for actual landowners. More fundamentally, it was highly unlikely for privately initiated projects to be carried out smoothly because they were at the mercy of the authorities of the military regime back then. Even if such a project had been launched at the military regime's behest, it could be canceled at any time depending on changes in the military regime's interests or preference.[350] The military regime did favor construction projects that required extensive manpower and fiscal resources, but road networks and monumental government offices that suited military purposes clearly had more appeal to the regime than residential areas for civilians.

In 1965, the Seoul Metropolitan Government began to work on urban planning for districts below the Han River and a plan to build the third bridge across the river. Once appointed as the mayor of Seoul in April 1966, Kim Hyŏ-nok established an urban master plan for the city before the end of that same year.[351] On September 22, 1967, a Comprehensive Development Plan for the Han River was announced. The plan was to basically build a 15-meter-high embankment along the entire river, use the reclaimed land as housing lots, and construct driveways above the embankment.[352] The curtain had risen on the so-called period of "developmental dictatorship."

The administrative boundary of Seoul had already expanded to below the Han River during Japanese colonial rule, but further expansions occurred after the Republic of Korea's foundation. As of January 1, 1963, parts of Kyŏnggi Province were incorporated into Seoul according to Law no. 1171, which greatly enlarged Seoul's administrative boundary.[353] The formation of the Han River embankment began with the construction of a circle levee planned for Yŏŭido in 1967. Yŏŭido was a river island located south of the Map'o Pier on the lower Han River. After serving as an airfield under Japanese colonial rule, the island turned into the scene of a grand project in 1968, one heavily supported by President Park Chung-hee. Developing Yŏŭido had been key to the Comprehensive Development Plan for the Han River.[354]

Not long after the circle levee's construction began, a fundamental change was demanded of the Comprehensive Development Plan for the Han River overseen by Mayor Kim Hyŏ-nok. In February 1968, Yŏŭido was selected as the site for the National Assembly building, which meant the island's layout had to be rearranged so that the building would occupy its center. The decision came quite unexpectedly. From the constitutional assembly up to the seventh National Assembly, the South Korean National Assembly wandered about without a building of its own. After the Keijō Public Hall, also known as the "assembly building along T'aep'yŏng-ro," was turned into an annex of the Seoul Civic Center, the national assembly still used part of the building, but it proved inconvenient due to the lack of hall space and infrastructure. Calls for a new building had been made continuously since the Liberty Party's dictatorship, but the matter kept experiencing complexities. At one point, President Rhee Syngman designated the spot where Chōsen jingū used to be as the site for the new building. Only after the military coup d'état could the national assembly building project move forward with the opening of the sixth National Assembly.[355]

Launched in February 1966, the National Assembly Building Construction Committee finished devising a master plan by 1967 for a building capable of accommodating bicameralism in case the two Koreas were to be united. The reason Yŏŭido surfaced as a site for government offices was because it was located within a 5-kilometer radius from the government offices along Sejong Boulevard in downtown Seoul. The river island was close enough so that it would only be a ten-minute drive from the boulevard but also distant enough from the bustling downtown area, quietly offering views of all the major mountains in Seoul, including Inwangsan, Namsan, Tobongsan, and Kwanaksan. Moreover, the river island's ground turned out to be firmer than expected.[356] In any case, apart from these official reasons, the most crucial reason was probably because Yŏŭido provided an empty space near the downtown area for the realization of new ideas.

The Yŏŭido and Han Riverside Development Plan, drafted in May 1969 under the leadership of Kim Su-kŭn, the then–vice president of the Korea Engineering Consultants Corporation, ambitiously aimed at building a new multifunctional town upon an artificial island surrounded by a 16-meter-high embankment. Having a six-lane highway serve as a central axis running between Map'o, the Seoul Bridge (currently Map'o Bridge), and the Yŏngdŭngp'o area, the plan also sought to form new districts around the National Assembly building, the City Hall, and the Supreme Court, as well as a residential district in order to redistribute the city's functions that had been concentrated in downtown Seoul. The plan to build the National Assembly building and an area for embassies to the west and place the city hall, supreme court, and residential areas to the east required a burdensome investment of one hundred billion Korean won over a period of twenty years. The plan ran into further difficulties a few months later near the end of October 1969, when the president ordered for a treeless 396,694–square meter asphalt square to be built at the center of Yŏŭido. Because there were fairly unrealistic aspects to this massive plan at a time when the downtown area above the Han River had been accommodating most of the city's functions for Seoul, the plan had to be entirely reconsidered.[357]

Kim Su-kŭn's plan to develop Yŏŭido was reminiscent of the project to concentrate government offices in Tokyo from a century ago. The expansive "May 16 Square" and the major government offices lined on either side of the square were a sight Wilhelm Böckmann would have described as a projection of "Forum Koreanum." The grand dream the extremely suppressive Japanese Government-General failed to realize, a desire to establish state tectonics or the "nucleus" of a national polity, had moved beyond the downtown area haunted by its colonial past to unravel in an empty space. It was therefore no surprise that the National Assembly building's construction was considered a priority along with building embankments and roads. Compared to the various difficulties the architectural firm Ende & Böckmann encountered when it tried to build the Japanese Diet building near the imperial palace, the National Assembly building to be raised at Yŏŭido was a far more feasible project, heavily supported by a military regime none dared to challenge.

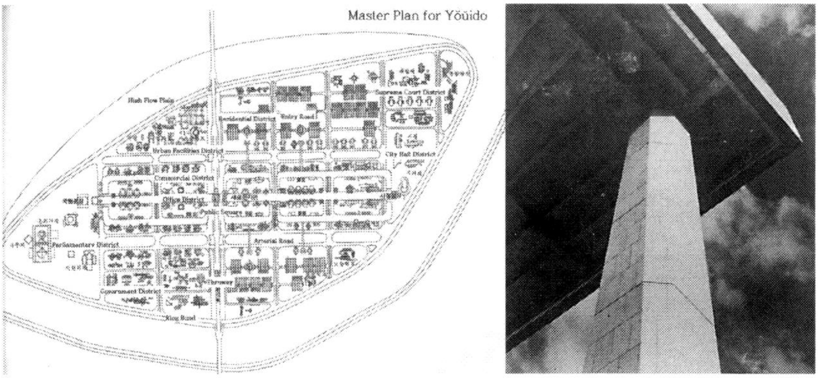

Figure 3.21 Left: Kim Su-gŭn's Master Plan for Yŏŭido. Right: The Weighty Columns Supporting Crossbeams and Slabs at the National Assembly Building in Yŏŭido.

Source: Left: From Seoul Metropolitan Government's Han River Construction Office, *Yŏŭido and Han Riverside Development Plan* (1969), YP (Yo-i do master pan) 02. Right: From *SPACE* 101 (1975), October/November Special Issue: For the Urgent Order of Korean Eclecticism of the National Assembly: 39. Courtesy of *SPACE* Magazine.

The seemingly untroubled construction of the National Assembly building nevertheless proved challenging. The greatest problem had to do with the proprietor of the project. Having too much power is bound to make something go awry. A design competition was newly held when Yŏŭido became the building's site instead of Mount Namsan in 1968. However, the excessive bureaucracy involved in the competition angered architects. The competition was neither strictly open nor invited, which meant it would only be used to gather ideas for a master plan, and while the preliminary and detailed designs would be based on the master plan, it would be a collaborative process. A mere two months was given to complete the design. This was the result of bureaucratic thinking that regarded architects as working-level technicians without a voice. The competition ended with no first-prize winner and six second-prize winners who were leading architects, such as Kim Su-kŭn and Kim Chung-ŏp. The Korean Institute of Architects submitted a petition in protest, and after some anguish, the architects Kim Chung-ŏp, Yi Kwang-no, and An Yŏng-pae finished the preliminary design under Kim Chŏng-su's lead by the end of 1968. The groundbreaking took place in December 1969, and on September 1, 1975, the National Assembly building of the Republic of Korea was completed.[358]

The 70-meter-tall, 21,881–square meter National Assembly building was built upon an approximately 330,580–square meter site where Mount Yangmalsan once was. A Renaissance-style dome with a diameter of 64 meters was added later to make the building taller than Capitol Hall. The classicism this ferroconcrete building featured was so abstract that it was virtually impossible to place the building under a specific stylistic category. Granite was used to finish the entire building except for the rooftop. The twenty-four columns decorating the façade were 32.5 meters tall and 20 meters apart from one another. The stereobate supported seven stories above ground and two stories below ground. The main spaces, such as the assembly hall, rotunda, and the chairman's room, were located on the second floor. The building's interior design was focused on creating a Korean atmosphere, which was why the central rotunda's marble mosaic floor featured a pattern modeled after that on the ceiling of the famous cave temple Sŏkkuram. The twenty-four columns along the façade were modeled after the stone pillars of Kyŏnghoeru Pavilion, representing the twenty-four solar terms of the year. The office building for assembly members was situated to the left of the assembly building, and to its right was the National Assembly Library.[359]

The National Assembly building was a monument of power that a centralized regime's determination erected in an empty space. Mixing extremely abstract Western classicism with Korean patterns to accommodate a modern institution such as the national assembly undoubtedly demonstrated the state's desire to modernize and express its national identity. Despite the exaggerated, monumental display, a shadow from the colonial days was cast upon the National Assembly building. The omnipotent state haphazardly forced its desire upon the building's construction process and architectural form, which ended up exhibiting a colonialist travesty of tectonics or national polity.

The Construction of the National Assembly Building, published in 1976 by the National Assembly Secretariat, explained that the massive columns and dome symbolized the nature of parliamentary politics to have conflicting opinions amicably arrive at a single conclusion.[360] This explanation was quite contrary to the architects' view at the time. The 1975 October/November issue of the architecture magazine *Space* specially featured the National Assembly building. Through the issue, the architect Kim Wŏn sharply criticized that the building's architectural form was from top to bottom "a stage set of unknown nationality." In Kim Wŏn's opinion, the columns and dome were pure decoration that was completely unnecessary. The sturdy columns were merely supporting crossbeams and thin slabs. To disguise this lightness, a 5-meter-high balustrade finished with light gray granite was installed above the eaves. This, however, turned out to be an inconvenient decoration, blocking the view from the rooftop. The rotunda "resembling an enormous chimney" and the Korean patterns that didn't seem to belong were the "product of a rational obsession" with including Korean features. This plainly demonstrates the "rashness of Korean culture as it attempts to create a physical connection between the East and West instead of trying to lay a spiritually sublimated bridge between the two."[361] Should the opinion of professional architects carry more weight than the National Assembly Secretariat's bureaucratic opinion, the monumentality of the National Assembly building can only be considered an illusion of tectonic solidity created by bold mixtures of the horizontal and vertical without adhering to the basic principle of tectonics in pursuit of harmony between form and function.

Due to limited fiscal resources and insufficient architectural awareness at the time, "Forum Koreanum" was unable to be realized in Seoul. The National Assembly building, an extensive public square, and a new town were built at Yŏŭido but only to reveal extreme instances of incoherence and pragmatism lacking ideology. Even if Kim Su-kŭn's original plan had been wholly realized alongside President Park Chung-hee's orders, the outcome would have still been no more than a (post)colonial parody of Forum Japanum or Forum Fridericianum. As the highlight of the development plan for Yŏŭido, the National Assembly building was built more as a symbol of state power than democracy. This could also be sensed from the building's secluded location on the riverside at one end of the island that seemed to welcome the sunset rather than the people. Yet even welcoming the sunset appeared to be a challenge for the building's flat slab roof and the random dome above it. This Parthenon wearing a beret did not possess enough authority to host the specter of Prussian classicism. That specter, which seemed to have disappeared amid the turmoil of modern Korean history, resurfaced before Capitol Hall instead of at an island on the Han River.

The Republic of Korea's Cultural Nationalism

Around the time the plan to build a large government office district upon the sandy fields of Yŏŭido was abandoned, the area around Sejong Boulevard started to attract public attention again. The construction of a new government complex had already begun in July 1967 and was nearing completion by the end of 1970. According to an article in the January 17, 1970, edition of the daily *Dong-a Ilbo*, another government office building of the same size as well as an annex nearby was supposed to be built opposite the government complex. That would have turned the area into a government office district, but the plan was postponed indefinitely due to financial reasons. While this plan to concentrate government offices remained at a standstill, a suggestion was made to disperse government offices as a means of preventing the concentration of population in the metropolitan area. This suggestion focused on the distribution and efficiency of government offices instead of the office buildings themselves.[362] No further discussions took place on concentrating government offices to increase administrative performance and ultimately form a true nucleus for South Korea. Although Capitol Hall was situated at a central location, the new, more modern government complex assumed the functions a building central to power was expected to perform. While the National Assembly building's construction was in full swing at Yŏŭido, the government complex's main building along Sejong Boulevard was completed in late December 1970. This modern building with nineteen stories above ground and three stories underground was nothing like the previously built government offices.[363] It grew even more difficult for Capitol Hall to justify itself as a central government office when the second government complex in Kwach'ŏn was completed in December 1981. Eventually, after undergoing repairs for almost two years starting in 1983, Capitol Hall began to serve an entirely different purpose as the National Museum of Korea from August 21, 1986.[364]

The Government-General Building's surprising transformation into the National Museum of Korea showed that the specter of Prussian classicism had not disappeared. The building lost its purpose as a government office but found an altogether new way back into the nation's center. It was perhaps the only way for such a symbol of national shame to survive for as long as it did in the Republic of Korea. What sort of connection was there between the Government-General Building and the National Museum of Korea, which seemingly had nothing in common? Was the connection strong enough to transcend a history of shame?

What the Government-General Building embodied back when it was being designed was the superiority of modern civilization. The Japanese colonialists who built it underscored modern civilization as part of Japan's identity and an inherent mission the Japanese had to undertake for Asia. Pan-Asianism launched in Japan suggested a possibility to proactively deal with the deluge of modern civilization from the West, and such a possibility resonated widely with Korean intellectuals beginning in the late Chōsen. The old "Sinosphere" was replaced with a modern "East" steered by Japan.[365] There was, however, an irreconcilable gap between the colonial reality and the ideals of modernization represented by the Government-General Building's conspicuous exterior, and from that gap budded a stem of nationalism. Rather than restoring a bygone dynasty, Korean independence movements that fought against Japan's two-faced policy of "cultural assimilation" and socioeconomic discrimination instead autonomously appropriated Japan's colonialist ideals.[366] Korean nationalists had been modernists from the outset. The Korean linguist Ch'oe Hyŏn-pae was no exception. He criticized that observing the four ceremonial occasions was an old-fashioned practice from the Chōsen dynasty and lamented that the Korean upper-class was preoccupied with holding ancestral rites for their deceased parents.[367] Therefore, it was imperative for Korean nationalism to develop a path toward modernization without being drawn into the logic of colonial authorities. What would allow a logic to be modern and Korean?[368] The solution was the logic of "national culture." The glorious "culture" Koreans cultivated over a period of five thousand years set the ideals of modernization free from the temptation of colonialism.

That solution was, however, not genuine. On the surface, the Republic of Korea's cultural nationalism may have appeared to be a manifestation of strong anti-Japanese sentiments, but it was actually an extension of the Prussian/German cultural nationalism that had influenced Japan. As it did in Japan and Germany, cultural nationalism tends to use a "systemic misrecognition" of the past to create a stereotypical image of a nation's origin and source culture.[369] This naturally conceals the incongruity between reality and the pressure to modernize, which is but a highly unstable discursive formation. That discursive formation may sometimes support modernization's unilateral logic or blindly support tradition but never allows itself to be challenged. Such a forcibly consecrated discourse of national culture becomes prone to serving authoritarian states. Incarnations of this included the Government-General Building and National Museum of Korea. They both considered themselves sacrosanct and exercised omnipotent central power in their respective fields of politics and culture. In other words, they were relatives to each other.

Instead of the leftist Sin Ch'ae-ho, it was the center-rightist Ch'oe Nam-sŏn who suggested a model of cultural nationalism for the Republic of Korea. Before turning pro-Japanese in the 1930s, Ch'oe Nam-sŏn defined the research field of Korean studies called *Chosŏnhak* and strived to uncover elements native to Korean culture that were on par with those of China and Japan. Through the publications *Discourse on Purham Culture* and *Korean Buddhism*, Ch'oe Nam-sŏn presented a unique interpretation of the Korean progenitor Tan'gun in order to conceptualize a Northeast Asian cultural sphere revolving around Koreans. His broad view was owing to the railroad trip he took across Korea and Japan in the 1910s. He was never simply a traditionalist.[370] Yet his strength also proved to be his fatal weakness. *Discourse on Purham Culture* portentously named the Indo-European, the Chinese, and the *Purham* as the world's three major cultural spheres. What was notable about his classification was that Korea and Japan belonged to the same cultural sphere. This could be viewed as a logic aimed at challenging the Japanese theory "Nissen dōsoron," which suggests that the Japanese and Koreans shared common ethnic origins and that ancient Japan used to rule over Korea. At the same time, the concept of a Purham cultural sphere had an affinity with the Japanese concept of a Greater East Asia Co-Prosperity Sphere. Thus, depending on political developments, it was more than possible for the core of the Purham cultural sphere to shift from Koreans to the Japanese. In fact, this concept readily coincided with the Japanese policy of "cultural rule," which tolerated the cultural independence of different ethnicities within the Japanese Empire.[371]

Ch'oe Nam-sŏn was a typical example that revealed the conflicts cultural nationalism ran into between modern universality and national identity. Korean nationalism sprang from the crevice between modernity and coloniality and branched out in various directions, serving at times as a logic of resistance and at others as a logic to defend the existing system.

It continued to shift its position and strategically reorganize itself according to changes in the ruling power. National identity always carried the potential for discord. In that sense, the surge of cultural nationalism could indicate an overall reformist or rightward shift of nationalism triggered by Japan's accommodationist policy of cultural rule.[372]

An invaluable clue to understanding the cultural nationalism that long wielded omnipotent power in the Republic of Korea can be found in "A Study on the History of Korean Art" by a young Korean philosopher named Pak Chong-hong, which was serially published in the magazine *Kaebyŏk* between 1922 and 1923. Through the first installment of the series, Pak Chong-hong stated that by attempting to describe "the history of our art," he hoped to uncover the origin and unique characteristics of Korean art within the context of a world history of art. Pak argued that Gandharan Buddhism's northern spread played a decisive role in the development of Korean art, hinting at a connection between Korean art and the Greek civilization. This view no doubt had Itō Chūta's architectural theory of Hōryū-ji in mind. Pak's understanding of Korean art history shared the same baseline as Okakura Kakuzō or Itō Chūta's understanding of Japanese art history. Pak Chong-hong explained that art was transmitted from Greece to India, synthesized in China, and finally brought to fruition on the Korean peninsula. The features of Korean art grew distinct when the fall of the Korean dynasties Paekche and Koguryŏ resulted in the cessation of exchange with Tang China. Yet the basis of such features had already been formed during the Three Kingdoms period of Korea. Proof of this was the murals of the golden hall Kondō at Hōryū-ji temple, which were supposedly the work of a Buddhist priest named Damjing (J. Donchō) who traveled from Koguryŏ to Japan and introduced Korean art.[373] Although this interpretation's baseline is similar to that for the architectural theory of Hōryū-ji, Pak's emphasis on the role Damjing played suggests that his understanding of Korean art history can be regarded as a Korean appropriation of Japanese cultural nationalism. This series by Pak Chong-hong failed to make an impact on formal studies of art history, but the suggestion it made about the role Damjing played eventually came to occupy a place with the collective memory of Koreans, enough for it to be mentioned in elementary textbooks after Korea's liberation.[374]

Nevertheless, it is necessary to take a closer look at Pak Chong-hong's view of the murals of the golden hall Kondō at Hōryū-ji. The sixth installment of Pak's series, published in the twenty-seventh issue of *Kaebyŏk* on September 1, 1922, delved further into Koguryŏ art. Pak highlighted the sublime spirit in Koguryŏ art and severely criticized Yanagi Muneyoshi's interpretation of Korean art history or similar interpretations. Because the Koguryŏ people "possessed a great spirit and remarkable abilities," they absorbed and internalized Buddhist ideas from India as well as Western techniques originating from Greece and eventually took the lead in Oriental art. According to Pak, emphasizing pathos was an error caused from being "controlled by a modern preconception in terms of appearance," while emphasizing the murals' dryness was a result of the inability to understand that such dryness was an outcome of the idea that "calligraphy and painting are one." To confront such "unjust reviews from the outside," Pak stressed that it was up to Koreans to elevate Korean art to the stature it deserves.[375]

The philosopher Pak Chong-hong thereby instantly unraveled the knot that Korean cultural nationalism had been entangled in and made the task of modernization synonymous to Korea's national identity. Considering the fact that the same philosopher played a leading role in drafting the National Charter of Education under President Park Chung-hee's *Yushin* regime, his exploration of ideas in the early 1920s is too significant to write off as youthful indiscretion. His ideas in some ways preceded the state ideology of Manchukuo that came ten years later. The desire to build a new state that had overcome the contradictions between modernization and national identity or between the most Eastern and the most Western had traveled through Manchukuo and come back to life in Park Chung-hee's anti-communist state.

Park Chung-hee's military regime discovered from history a new pivot for the nation. Of course, instead of traditional folk religion or customs, history at the time referred to the leading culture of the ruling class, or the "spirit of our forefathers." Hence, the past had to be selectively edited and intensively rearranged. The Korean nation's tradition was not sought in the past but was newly created for the future.[376] There was no need to hang onto Korea's dark colonial past. The Bureau of Cultural Property, currently the Cultural Heritage Administration, was established in October of the same year the military coup was successfully carried out. A few months later, in late December, the National Assembly Standing Committee swiftly passed the Cultural Properties Preservation Act. These developments show how strong the military regime's desire to control history had been.

The way the Park Chung-hee administration treated Capitol Hall and Kyŏngbokgung Palace clearly demonstrated the administration's view of history. Before using Capitol Hall as a government office again from 1962, the grounds of Kyŏngbokgung Palace, which remained severely damaged due to the Korean War, were used to host cowboy shows or international wrestling contests and even to operate an ice rink. In May 1962, the palace grounds were used to host an industrial exhibition to celebrate the "first anniversary of the May 16 Military Revolution," an event reminiscent of similar occasions during Japanese colonial rule.[377] What marked the pinnacle of these extraordinary uses of the palace was the construction of a new ferroconcrete Kwanghwamun Gate in 1968. The gate was restored roughly in its original position in front of Capitol Hall to give an impression of national retribution against Japan. Moreover, the extensive use of materials like ferroconcrete and stone that were symbolic of industrialization was an attempt to ingrain in people's minds an ideology of national regeneration.

The wooden signboard depicting the Korean President's handwriting highlighted the newness of this national monument. However, building the new gate in a hurry without conducting historical research on its original form made it look like an incorrectly produced replica. Restored at an angle still at odds with the palace's central axis, the new gate seemed more like the front gate to Capitol Hall instead of Kyŏngbokgung.[378] The new gate's construction therefore incited much criticism and debate from the very beginning.[379] Such developments indicated that the Park Chung-hee administration took advantage of history strictly as an instrument of power. Parts of the past could readily be deleted or doctored if they went against the spirit of the forefathers or national regeneration.

Park Chung-hee's practice of cultural nationalism erased Korea's dark colonial past and freely associated modern with national, leaving more distinct traces upon Sejong Boulevard in front of Capitol Hall. Next to the government complex where the Bureau of Postal Services used to be during Japanese colonial rule, the Sejong Center for the Performing Arts was built based on a modified version of Ŏm Tŏk-mun and Chŏn Tong-hun's winning design. The building that started to be constructed in 1974 and was completed in 1978 was specially featured in Volume 131 of the architecture magazine *Space* in May 1978. Through the magazine, the building's architect Ŏm Tŏk-mun described that his own work had achieved a "balance between tradition and function." As a steel-framed reinforced concrete structure finished with granite, the six-story Sejong Center for the Performing Arts with three underground stories offered a total floor space of 53,295 square meters. With a courtyard at the center, a conference space was placed between smaller halls to the left and the larger halls to the right. Featuring a traditional Korean architectural style with a modern touch, the building's façade facing Sejong Boulevard was decorated with a patterned window grille using the shape of the Chinese character *wan* (卍) installed behind a dignified granite colonnade flanked by two reliefs of a flying aspara on either side.[380] To include a grand hall with an unprecedented four thousand two hundred seats was a decision conscious of the capacity of the Mansudae Art Theatre in P'yŏngyang and also with the intention of housing the National Council for Unification, which was an elective body newly formed under the Yushin regime.[381]

Meanwhile, in the very same volume of *Space*, voices criticizing the Sejong Center for the Performing Arts were also introduced through an article titled "An Introspection on Inheriting Traditions and Modern Korean Architecture," which relayed a roundtable discussion held to share reflections about modern Korean architecture. Not only was the performing arts center adjacent to the dreary "government complex disturbing the skyline of Mount Pugaksan," it seemed to represent an "authority beyond the human scale" and its "concrete rafters and capital" seemed to reveal an "obsession with seeking something that has inherited Korean traditions." What was also pointed out as problematic was the west-side exit left open, which failed to

Figure 3.22 Façade of the Sejong Center for the Performing Arts.

Source: From *SPACE* 131 (1978), May Special Issue on the Sejong Center for the Performing Arts: 10. Courtesy of *SPACE* Magazine.

secure an exclusive yard for the facility.[382] In many ways, the Sejong Center for the Performing Arts was the most certain expression of Park Chung-hee's cultural nationalism. It was worthy of being called a Korean "Imperial Crown" style building. The combination of the granite colonnade and flying aspara reliefs showed a vivid mixture of East and West, or modern and national. Such contradictory elements were forced to be united through the building with no exception. There was no middle ground. The arrangement, allowing no space for people to stop and rest, could be considered an extreme application of tectonics. As if too intimidated to make eye contact with a man of power, most of the pedestrians passing by the building were likely to hasten their steps past the massive colonnade towering above the sidewalk instead of climbing the tall staircase to reach the courtyard in front of the building's entrance. To borrow the words of the architect Chŏng Ki-yong, the Sejong Center for the Performing Arts with "rafters emphasized to the point of weighing down like rocks" was indeed a distorted self-portrait of the Yushin regime imposing top-down obedience as it approached its end.[383]

Rectification of History?

When a "civilian administration" replaced the military regime that prescribed the "regeneration of the nation" as the ultimate purpose for achieving modernization, modern and national returned to being at odds with one another. On August 9, 1993, President Kim Young-sam ordered the demolition of Capitol Hall, which had been turned into the National Museum of Korea under the previous military regime led by Chun Doo-hwan. The demolition date was to be August 15, 1995, the fiftieth anniversary of Korea's liberation and the six hundredth anniversary of the beginning of Kyŏngbokgung Palace's construction. Opinions differed greatly on the demolition's timing, considerable cost, and educational importance, but the government unsparingly tore down the building's iconic dome and completed its demolition by the end of 1996.[384]

This demolition made it inevitable for the civilian administration to be criticized for failing to host a social debate on such an important national matter that was instead peremptorily decided by the president. Despite attempting to justify the demolition as an act to restore the pride and spirit of Korea, everyone knew that the administration made the strategic choice to take advantage of the prestige of independence or democratic movements so that it could gain the legitimacy it lacked from being born out of political collusion. Creating a spectacle by having a crane tear the building's dome off and hurl it on the ground during the celebration of the fiftieth anniversary of Korea's liberation in 1995 only proved that the administration was indeed vulnerable. After rushing to demolish the building, the government tried to pick up the pieces by creating a temporary space for visitors to explore the building in ruins before the demolition's completion. It also presented a plan to preserve some of the remains, such as the steeple, and use them to create a park for history education, but none of those efforts could undo the damage already done.[385]

Dismantling this lingering symbol of colonialism had actually been planned since the previous administration. The Roh Tae-woo administration wished to demolish that symbol in an attempt to stop the administration from being perceived as a military dictatorship. The only reason for not carrying out the demolition was because of the financial burden it entailed.[386] The Kim Young-sam administration, on the other hand, treated the demolition as part of a comprehensive policy dubbed the "Rectification of History," which was devised to actualize the administration's proposal for a "new Korea." This civilian administration declared that the policy was a "notable innovation" that would "rectify the distorted history of Korea and revitalize the nation's spirit." The tasks listed under this policy represented some long-deferred issues for the nation and could be grouped into four different categories. Tasks under the first category were aimed at upholding and developing the spirit of Korean independence movements, which included uncovering and rewarding patriots who contributed to such movements, repatriating the remains of deceased patriots, collecting historical sources related to independence movements, and publishing studies based on such sources. The second category of tasks involved demolishing the former Government-General Building, restoring Kyŏngbokgung Palace, removing the iron stakes the Japanese had driven into Korean mountains, and recovering original Korean place names. The third category of tasks had to do with the April 19 Movement, such as amending relevant ordinances in order to uphold and develop the movement's democratic ideas, redefining the movement as a "revolution" and reflecting the new definition in curricula, and designating as a historic site and expanding the cemetery for the lives sacrificed in the revolution. The fourth category of tasks included investigating the December 12 Incident, defining the incident as a military insurrection, and enacting a special law regarding the May 18 Democratic Uprising. During a cabinet meeting at the Blue House on December 21, 1995, President Kim Young-sam eagerly declared that rectifying history would lead to the "rebirth of Korea as a nation."[387] Although the policy's plans were grandiose, they turned out to lack substance. An example was the Sŏdaemun Prison, opened as a museum in 1998 as part of the project to preserve historic sites central to Korean independence movements. However, pairing the prison that used to hold people persecuted by the Japanese with the nearby Independence Gate that the Japanese erected in support of Korean reformists and designating the two as a single historic site made the government policy seem less convincing, since the designation had been based only on the locational proximity between the prison and the gate.[388]

Despite all this farce, there was no doubt that the tide of the times was changing. What was the explanation for such change? Why rush to tear down a building that once served as an icon of the Republic of Korea? Was it because of a single administration's political bravado? Did the citizens of Seoul truly wish for the demolition? South Korea's rapid economic development gradually but surely dissipated illusions about modernization and modern urban spaces. Meanwhile, the dark side of Korea's colonial past tended to be underlined. Capitol Hall was thus identified as a detestable remnant of a shameful past. The phantasmagoria of modernity could no longer obscure the emerging politics of representation and its corresponding collective memory.

As an indication of the nature of this change, an unusual alternative logic toward modern urban spaces resurfaced, which was none other than *feng shui*, or geomancy. All of a sudden, theories based on geomancy gained appeal, suggesting that the Japanese built the Government-General Building on the grounds of Kyŏngbokgung to quash the energy of the Korean royal family, drove iron stakes into major mountains across Korea to cut off the vein of energy coursing through them, or distorted and changed place names on purpose.[389] Along with these rather speculative theories, calls for the recovery of a unique Korean identity or "national spirit" suddenly became mainstream. A new type of cultural nationalism had emerged. Through a contribution he wrote in 1995, the veteran art historian An Hwi-jun argued that the Government-General Building had to be torn down, equating the "demolition of the ugly building" to "pulling out a nail stuck in the middle of our forehead." This well-respected Korean scholar highlighted the importance of a "deep understanding of and consideration for our national culture along with the unwavering determination to wipe out Japanese remnants."[390]

It was most natural for this trend to lead to calls for Kyŏngbokgung's restoration. After having remained a backwater of modern civilization until the end of Park Chung-hee's regime, the palace was soon reborn as a symbol of Korea's national culture. Under the Roh Tae-woo administration, a ceremony to launch Kyŏngbokgung's restoration took place at the palace on June 5, 1991. Once the Government-General Building was completely removed by October 1996, the restoration project started to pick up steam. The construction of Kwanghwamun Square also turned into a full-blown project after a proclamation ceremony for the "Restoration of Kwanghwamun" was held on December 4, 2006.[391] These developments were not surprising but not particularly axiomatic either. Kyŏngbokgung and Kwanghwamun were not considered sacred until Koreans were ravaged by the Japanese. In other words, Japan's imperialist intrusion and colonial rule turned them into sacred grounds. The moment when the nonexistent centrality of Kyŏngbokgung officially disappeared was precisely when that imaginary center was reborn as a modern state's vanishing point. And as if the palace's fate served as a metaphor for the tragedy Koreans had to suffer, the history of Korean dynasties was soon relabeled as the national history of Korea.[392] This was no more than turning inside out the trick Park Chung-hee's military regime used by slipping the history of Koreans into its logic of modernization. The tricks were practically two sides of the same coin for obscuring some aspect of the gap between modern and national. Meanwhile, the power pulling the wires from behind remained unaffected without suffering much.

Standing firm but hidden at the center of that power while the fate of the Government-General Building and Kyŏngbokgung oscillated was the Korean presidential residence called the Blue House. The building was located at a spot that used to be the back garden of Kyŏngbokgung, which included a couple of pavilions and buildings such as Yungmudang where state examinations were held during the Chōsen dynasty. During the palace's reconstruction in 1868, the fifth year of King Kojong's reign, the garden was remodeled into a site called Kyŏngmudae for enjoying martial art demonstrations. The site was later selected as the location for the new Governor-General's residence when the seventh Japanese Governor-General Minami Jirō turned the old residence at the fortress Waesŏngdae into a memorial hall for municipal governance. After tearing down the buildings at Kyŏngbokgung's back garden, the construction of the new Governor-General's residence was completed in July 1939 and began serving its purpose a few months later in September. Across a 171,902–square meter site including uninhabited hills, the two-story red brick masonry structure provided a total floor space of 1,861 square meters. The porch had four thick columns, and the roof was covered with blue tiles. The building's design was left to the Building and Repairs Section under the Government-General Secretariat's Accounting

Figure 3.23 Left: Front View of Kyŏngmudae. Right: Plot Plan of the Grounds of Kyŏngmudae (approx. 1938).

Source: Left: From Korean Presidential Secretariat, *Ch'ŏngwadae kŏnsŏlchi* (1992). Right: Courtesy of the National Archives of Korea, management no. DJB0001498.

Division and Professor Sano Toshikata of the Tokyo Imperial University was appointed as a design consultant for the project.[393]

The building served as residence to the seventh, eighth, and ninth Japanese Governor-Generals. During President Rhee Syngman's administration, it was again referred to as Kyŏngmudae until President Yun Bo-sun changed the building's name in 1961 to Ch'ŏngwadae, meaning the Blue House, and lived there for nine months.[394] In 1989, a plan to newly build the Blue House was established so that the construction of the new presidential residence was finished on October 25, 1990, while the Blue House's main building was finished on September 4, 1991. In August 1993, President Kim Young-sam demolished the old Governor-General's residence. Yet nothing had fundamentally changed. The site was still at the center of actual power.

A plot plan of the grounds of the Governor-General's residence offers a detailed view of the building's surroundings. The wall to the far south was the north-side wall of Kyŏngbokgung, and the door along that wall was the gate Sinmumun.[395] Right outside this gate was a road leading to the foot of Mount Pugaksan. A couple of official residences were situated near the beginning of that road, which thereafter gently bent toward the northeast until it ended at the entrance of the Governor-General's residence. A garden with a pond was placed on the south side of the residence. In essence, this residence was the embodiment of a power observing all things from a most covert location, unaffected by historical turmoil. Could the splendid phantasmagoria of the Government-General Building and Kyŏngbokgung have been nothing but a smokescreen to cover up that very place? Behind an unattainable imaginary center was an unexpected, all-too-realistic power, lurking like a snake in the woods.

Notes

1. André Sorensen, *The Making of Urban Japan: Cities and Planning From Edo to the Twenty-First Century* (New York, NY: Routledge, 2002), 81–84; David B. Stewart, *The Making of a Modern Japanese Architecture: 1868 to the Present* (Tokyo: Kodansha International, 1987), 75 ff.
2. K. Yamamura, "The Japanese Economy, 1911–1930: Concentration, Conflicts, and Crises," in *Japan in Crisis: Essays in Taisho Democracy*, ed. B. S. Silberman and H. D. Harootunian (Princeton, NJ: Princeton University Press, 1974), 299–328, esp. 327–328.
3. Ishida Yorifusa, *Nihon kindai toshi keikaku no hyakunen* (Tokyo: Jichitai kenkyūsha, 1987), 110.
4. Ibid., 112.
5. Yi Myŏng-kyu, "Ilbonbon'gukkwa chosŏnch'ongdokpu toshigyehoekpi gyoyŏn'gu: Toshigyehoekpŏmnyŏngŭl chungshimŭro," in *Chosŏnch'ongdokpu toshigyehoek kongmunsŏwa kirokp'yŏnggaron*, ed. Han'gukkukkagirokyŏn'guwŏn (Seoul: Chillit'amgu, 2008), 272–281.
6. Koshizawa Akira, *Tōkyō no toshi keikaku* (Tokyo: Iwanami shoten, 1991), 11–34; Son Chŏng-mok, *Ilche kangjŏmgi toshigyehoek yŏn'gu* (Seoul: Ilchisa, 1990), 279; Stewart, *The Making of a Modern Japanese Architecture*, 119–121.
7. Koshizawa, *Tōkyō no toshi keikaku*, 19–20, 30–31; Stewart, *The Making of a Modern Japanese Architecture*, 110.
8. Okata Junichiro, "Kŭndae tok'yoŭi toshigyehoek: Kyooehwawa toshibyŏnshin," in University of Seoul Sŏurhakyŏn'guso, *Sŏul, peijing, sanghai, tok'yoŭi taedoshiroŭi sŏngjanggwajŏng pigyoyŏn'gu*, vol. 1 (Seoul: Sŏurhakyŏn'guso, 2006), 108–110.
9. Fujimori Terunobu, *Meiji no tōkyō keikaku* (Tokyo: Iwanami shoten, 2012), 248.
10. Sorensen, *The Making of Urban Japan*, 58.
11. Yasuo Nishiyama, "Western Influence on Urban Planning Administration in Japan: Focus on Land Management," *Urban Development Policies and Programmes, Focus on Land Management*, ed. Nagamine Haruo (Nagoya: United Nations Centre for Regional Development, 1986), 331; Ishida Yorifusa, "Nihon ni okeru tochi kukaku seiri seidoshi gaisetsu 1870–1980," *Sōgō toshi kenkyū*, 28 (1986): 54–55.
12. Koshizawa, *Tōkyō no toshi keikaku*, 53–56; Nagamatsu Sakae, *Zusetsu toshi to kenchiku no kindai: Pure-modanizumu no toshi kaizō* (Kyoto: Gakugei shuppansha, 2008), 194–196; Peter Nakamura, "A Legislative History of Land Readjustment," in *Land Readjustment: The Japanese System*, ed. Luciano Minerbi et al. (Boston, MA: Oelgeschlager, Gunn & Hain, 1986), 17–32.
13. Shun-Ichi J. Watanabe, "Metropolitanism as a Way of Life: In Case of Tokyo, 1868–1930," in *Metropolis 1890–1940*, ed. Anthony Sutcliffe (Chicago, IL: University of Chicago Press, 1984), 416–417; Yi, "Ilbonbon'gukkwa chosŏnch'ongdokpu," 273.
14. Shun-Ichi J. Watanabe, "Garden City Japanese Style: The Case of Den-en Toshi Company Ltd., 1918–28," in *Shaping an Urban World*, ed. Gordon E. Cherry (London: Mansell, 1980), 129–143; Koshizawa, *Tōkyō no toshi keikaku*, 123–141.
15. Stewart, *The Making of a Modern Japanese Architecture*, 133–136; Bak Chin-han, "Osak'a, tok'yorŭl nŏmŏ tongbugaŭi chungshimŭro," in Yi Yŏngsŏk et al., *Toshinŭn yŏksada* (Paju: Sŏhaemunjip, 2011), 64–89; Bak Chin-han, "Kŭndae toshi osak'aŭi toshigyehoengnon'gwa toshigyehoeksaŏp," in Bak Chin-han et al., *Cheguk ilbon'gwa shingminji chosŏnŭi kŭndae toshi hyŏngsŏng* (Seoul: Shimsan, 2013), 52–80; Pak Se-hun, "1920nyŏndae kyŏngsŏngŭi toshigyehoekkwa toshigyehoegundong," in *Cheguk ilbon'gwa shingminji chosŏnŭi kŭndae toshi hyŏngsŏng*, 87–90.

16. Koshizawa, *Tōkyō no toshi keikaku*, 13–19. See also Koshizawa Akira, *Tōkyō no toshi kenkyūkai* (Iwanami shoten, 1991).
17. Watanabe Shun'ichi, *'Toshi keikaku' no tanjō: Kokusai hikaku kara mita Nippon kindai toshi keikaku* (Tokyo: Kashiwa shobō, 1993), 170–171.
18. Pak Se-hun, "1920nyŏndae kyŏngsŏngdoshigyehoegŭi sŏnggyŏk: Kyŏngsŏngdosh igyehoekyŏn'guhoewa toshigyehoegundong," *Sŏurhakyŏn'gu* 15 (2000): 174–175; Stewart, *The Making of a Modern Japanese Architecture*, 133–136.
19. Koshizawa, *Tōkyō no toshi keikaku*, 11–12; Koshizawa Akira, *Gotō Shinpei: Daishinsai to teito fukkō* (Tokyo: Chikuma shobō, 2011). On *Mantetsu fuzokuchi*, see Guō Tiěchūn et al., *Ilbonŭi taeryŏn shingmint'ongch'i 40nyŏnsa*, vol. 2, trans. (from Chinese into Korean) Sin T'ae-kap et al. (Seoul: Sŏnin, 2012), 285–304; William Shaw Sewell, *Japanese Imperialism and Civic Construction in Manchuria: Changchun, 1905–1945* (Vancouver: The University of British Columbia Press, 2000), 65–67.
20. Koshizawa, *Gotō Shinpei*, 87 ff.
21. Koshizawa Akira, *Tok'yo toshigyehoek tamnon*, trans. (from Japanese into Korean) Chang Chun-ho (Seoul: Kumisŏgwan, 2007), 8; Sewell, *Japanese Imperialism and Civic Construction in Manchuria*, 67–68. However, Beard's middle-class libertarian viewpoint displayed fundamental differences from Gotō's bureaucratic viewpoint. See the argument in Watanabe, "Metropolitanism As a Way of Life," 421.
22. Gotō Shinpei, "Toshi keikaku to hōsei hitsuyō," *Toshi kōron* 2, no. 2 (1919): 1; Gotō Shinpei, "Toshi no kaizen to shimin no kakugo," *Toshi kōron* 3, no. 1 (1920): 3.
23. Mizuno Rentarō, "Toshi kairyō mondai," *Toshi kōron* 2, no. 2 (1919): 2–16; Sano Toshikata, "Daitoshi no kenchikubutsu," *Toshi kōron* 3, no. 3 (1920): 18–28.
24. Okada Shūzō, "Toshi keikaku to toshi no fūchi bikan," *Toshi kōron* 9, no. 9 (1926): 2–16; Koshizawa, *Tōkyō no toshi keikaku*, 149–154.
25. Watanabe, *'Toshi keikaku' no tanjō*, 219.
26. Koshizawa, *Tōkyō no toshi keikaku*, 34–53; Son Chŏng-mok, "Shingmindoshigyehoekkwa kŭ yusan," in Sŏulshijŏnggaebaryŏn'guwŏn, *Sŏul 20segi konggan pyŏnch'ŏnsa* (Seoul: Sŏulshijŏnggaebaryŏn'guwŏn, 2001), 470–471; Sorensen, *The Making of Urban Japan*, 69–71; André Sorensen, "Urban Planning and Urban Sprawl in the Tokyo Metropolitan Area," *Urban Studies* 36, no. 13 (1999): 2333–2335.
27. Koshizawa, *Gotō Shinpei*, 199 ff.
28. Stewart, *The Making of a Modern Japanese Architecture*, 127 ff.; Koshizawa, *Tok'yo toshigyehoek tamnon*, 16–27, 118–119; Wolfgang Schwentker, "Die Doppelgeburt einer Megastadt: Tokyo 1923–1964," in *Megastädte im 20. Jahrhundert*, ed. Wolfgang Schwentker (Göttingen: Vandenhoeck & Ruprecht, 2009), 146–151.
29. Koshizawa, *Tōkyō no toshi keikaku*, 68–73.
30. Louis Frédéric, *Japan Encyclopedia* (Cambridge, MA: Harvard University Press, 2005), 264.
31. Koshizawa, *Tok'yo toshigyehoek tamnon*, 109–125.
32. Mark R. Peattie, "The Japanese Colonial Empire, 1895–1945," in Volume 6 of *The Cambridge History of Japan: The Twentieth Century*, ed. Peter Duus (Cambridge: Cambridge University Press, 1989), 264; Stewart, *The Making of a Modern Japanese Architecture*, 142–144; Carola Hein, "The Transformation of Planning Ideas in Japan and Its Colonies," in *Urbanism: Imported or Exported?* ed. Joe Nasr and Mercedes Volait (Chichester: Wiley-Academy, 2003), 54, 67 ff.
33. Regarding Japanese Empire's spatial domination of East Asia, see, notably, Muramatsu shin, "Tōbatsu shihai no bunpō," *Gendai shisō* 23, no. 10 (1995): 8–21.
34. Hashiya Hiroshi, *Ilbonjegukchuŭi, shingminji toshirŭl kŏnsŏrhada*, trans. (from Japanese into Korean) Kim Che-chŏng (Mot'ibŭ puk, 2005), 72–75, 87 ff.; Hein, "The Transformation of Planning," 54.

35. Hashiya Hiroshi defines this process as "orthogenetic transformation" rather than as "heterogenetic transformation." See Hashiya, *Ilbonjegukchuŭi*, 117 ff.
36. Ibid., 87–107, 138–139.
37. Nezar AlSayyad, ed., *Forms of Dominance: On the Architecture and Urbanism of the Colonial Enterprise* (Aldershot: Avebury, 1992), 5.
38. Anthony King, *Urbanism, Colonialism and the World-Economy* (New York, NY: Routledge, 1990), 9.
39. Fujimori Terunobu, Volume 1 of *Nihon no kindai kenchiku: Bakumatsu-Meiji-hen* (Tokyo: Iwanami shinsho, 2010), 36–43; Sorensen, *The Making of Urban Japan*, 79; Kim Paek-yŏng, "Sangjinggongganŭi pyŏnyonggwa chip'apkiŏgŭi palmyŏng: Sŏurŭi shingminji kyŏnghŏmgwa minjogŭi changsosŏng chaegusŏng," *Konggan'gwa sahoe* 28 (2007): 197.
40. Chu Wanyo (Zhou Wanyao), *Taeman: Arŭmdaun sŏm, sŭlp'ŭn yŏksa*, trans. (from Chinese into Korean) Son Chun-sik and Sin Mi-chŏng (Busan: Shin'gumunhwasa, 2003), 160–161; Chu-joe Hsia, "Theorizing Colonial Architecture and Urbanism: Building Colonial Modernity in Taiwan," *Inter-Asia Cultural Studies* 3, no. 1 (2002): 8–10; Sorensen, *The Making of Urban Japan*, 60–84.
41. Guō, *Ilbonŭi taeryŏn shingmint'ongch'i 40nyŏnsa*, 125 ff.; Hashiya, *Ilbonjegukchuŭi*, 164 ff.; Louise Young, *Japan's Total Empire: Manchuria and the Culture of Wartime Imperialism* (Berkeley, CA: University of California Press, 1999), 3–20.
42. Yi Kyŏng-ch'an and Hŏ Jun, "Shimyangŭi toshigonggan'gujo pyŏnch'ŏn'gwajŏnge taehan kyehoeksajŏk koch'al," *Han'gukchŏnt'ong jogyŏnghak'oeji* 24, no. 4 (2006): 93–94; Kim Chŏng-tong, *Nama innŭn yŏksa, sarajinŭn kŏnch'ungmul* (Seoul: Taewŏnsa, 2000), 28–39; Hashiya, *Ilbonjegukchuŭi*, 45–48; Hein, "The Transformation of Planning Ideas," 69 ff.
43. Kim Yŏng-sin, "Kaehang, choch'awa kŭndae manju shinhŭngdoshiŭi hŭnggi," in Yu Chi-wŏn et al., *Kŭndae manju toshi yŏksajiri yŏn'gu* (Seoul: Tongbugayŏksajaedan, 2007), 85–91; Koshizawa Akira, *Chunggugŭi toshigyehoek: Manjuŭi toshiron*, trans. (from Japanese into Korean) and ed. Chang Chun-ho (Busan: T'aerimmunhwasa, 2000), 99–114; Guō, *Ilbonŭi taeryŏn shingmint'ongch'i 40nyŏnsa*, vol. 2, 233–255.
44. Nishizawa Yasuhiko, *Nippon shokuminchi kenchikuron* (Nagoya: Nagoya University Press, 2008), 77–78; Guō, *Ilbonŭi taeryŏn shingmint'ongch'i 40nyŏnsa*, 251–261. On the city hall of Hamburg, see, notably, Hermann Hipp, "Das Rathaus der freien und Hansestadt Hamburg," in *Das Rathaus im Kaiserreich: Kunstpolitische Aspekte einer Bauaufgabe des 19. Jahrhunderts*, ed. Ekkehard Mai et al. (Berlin: Mann, Gebr., 1982), 179–231.
45. Nishizawa, *Nippon shokuminchi kenchikuron*, 134–136; Nishizawa Yasuhiko, "Kenchikuka Nakamura Yoshihei no keireki to kenchiku katsudō nitsuite," *Nippon kenchiku gakkai keikakukei ronbun hōkokushū* 450 (August 1993): 151–160; Kim Yŏng-chae, "Nak'amura yoshiheiŭi sŏyang kŏnch'ukyangshigŭi suyonggwajŏnggwa kŭ ŭimi," *Taehan'gŏnch'uk'ak'oenonmunjip kyehoekkye* 29, no. 5 (2013): 159–170.
46. Yi Ha-nŭl and Kim T'ae-yŏng, "20segi ch'o han'gugesŏ hwaltonghan ilbonin kŏnch'ukkaŭi chojikkwa kyeboe kwanhan yŏn'gu," *Taehan'gŏnch'uk'ak'oeyŏn hamnonmunjip* 11, no. 3 (2009): 59–61.
47. Sewell, *Japanese Imperialism and Civic Construction in Manchuria*, 64–65; Koshizawa, *Chunggugŭi toshigyehoek*, 76 ff.; Guō, *Ilbonŭi taeryŏn shingmint'ongch'i 40nyŏnsa*, vol. 1, 209–243; Nishizawa Yasuhiko, "Kenchiku no ekkyō to shokuminchi kensetsu," Volume 8 of *Teikoku Nippon no gaku chi: Kūkan keisei to sekai ninshiki*, ed. Yamamuro Shinichi (Tokyo: Iwanami shoten, 2006), 255–258.
48. Koshizawa, *Chunggugŭi toshigyehoek*, 80, 133.

49. Ibid., 73–75; Sewell, *Japanese Imperialism and Civic Construction in Manchuria*, 76–77, 107, 154.
50. Yamabe Hagane, "Shin Kyō ni tsuite," *Manshū kenchiku kyōkai zasshi*, 12, no. 6 (1932): 50.
51. Koshizawa, *Chungguŭi toshigyehoek*, 115–124.
52. Onoki Toshiharu, "Manshūkoku shuto kensetsu ni tsuite," *Manshū kenchiku kyōkai zasshi* 12, no. 6 (1932): 3. On Onoki Toshiharu, see Sewell, *Japanese Imperialism and Civic Construction in Manchuria*, 32.
53. Koshizawa, *Chungguŭi toshigyehoek*, 125–133.
54. Sewell, *Japanese Imperialism and Civic Construction*, 162–164; Nishizawa, *Nippon shokuminchi kenchikuron*, 138.
55. Nakazawa Kiyoshi, "Shin kokudō keikaku ni taisuru shoken," *Manshū kenchiku kyōkai zasshi*, 12, no. 6 (1932): 33.
56. Onoki, "Manshūkoku shuto kensetsu ni tsuite," *Manshū kenchiku kyōkai zasshi*, 2.
57. Sewell, *Japanese Imperialism and Civic Construction*, 155, 174.
58. Ueki Shigeru, "Manshūkoku shin shuto kensetsu toshi keikaku ni tsuite," *Manshū kenchiku kyōkai zasshi* 12, no. 6 (1932): 16–17.
59. Yumoto Saburo, "Shin koku shuto no kensetsu," *Manshū kenchiku kyōkai zasshi* 12, no. 6 (1932): 5–6.
60. Onoki, "Manshūkoku shuto kensetsu ni tsuite," *Manshū kenchiku kyōkai zasshi*, 1.
61. "Manshūkoku kokudō kensetsu keikaku gaiyō," *Manshū kenchiku kyōkai zasshi* 13, no. 11 (1933): 34–35.
62. Prasenjit Duara, *Sovereignty and Authenticity: Manchukuo and the East Asian Modern* (Lanham, MD: Rowman & Littlefield, 2004), 250; Young, *Japan's Total Empire*, 254–303.
63. Duara, *Sovereignty and Authenticity*, 98–102.
64. Fujimori Terunobu, Volume 2 of *Nihon no kindai kenchiku: Taisei-Shōwahen* (Tokyo: Iwanami shinsho, 2010), 21–23; Nishizawa, "Kenchiku no ekkyō to shokuminchi kensetsu," 248–250; Nishizawa, *Nippon shokuminchi kenchikuron*, 386–390; Hashiya, *Ilbonjegukchuŭi*, 122–124.
65. "Manshūkoku dai ni chōsha shinchiku kōji gaiyō," *Manshū kenchiku kyōkai zasshi* 13, no. 11 (1933): 41–42.
66. Nishizawa, *Nippon shokuminchi kenchikuron*, 95–102.
67. Ibid., 103–107.
68. Onoki, "Manshūkoku shuto kensetsu ni tsuite," *Manshū kenchiku kyōkai zasshi*, 2.
69. Oka Ōji, "Manshū ni okeru shinkō kenchiku taibōsu," *Manshū kenchiku kyōkai zasshi* 13, no. 11 (1933): 1–3.
70. Nishizawa, *Nippon shokuminchi kenchikuron*, 137–142; Fujimori, *Nihon no kindai kenchiku*, vol. 2, 100–101.
71. Sewell, *Japanese Imperialism and Civic Construction*, 180–181.
72. Duara, *Sovereignty and Authenticity*, 23–24.
73. Koshizawa, *Chungguŭi toshigyehoek*, 134–157.
74. Yi Sŏng-si, "Chosŏnwangjoŭi sangjing konggan'gwa pangmulgwan," in *Kuksaŭi shinhwarŭl nŏmŏsŏ*, ed. Yim Ji-hyŏn and Yi Sŏng-si (Seoul: Humanist, 2004), 273–275; Kim Yong-ch'ŏl, "Ok'ak'ura t'enshin'gwa ilbon misulsaŭi sŏngnip," *Ilbonsasang* 7 (2004): 181–182, 189–190.
75. Tanaka Akira, *Meijiyushin'gwa sŏyang munmyŏng: Iwak'ura sajŏltanŭn muŏsŭl poannŭn'ga*, trans. (from Japanese into Korean) Hyŏn Myŏng-ch'ŏl (Seoul: Somyŏngch'ulp'an, 2006), 140–154.
76. Kashiwagi Hiroshi, "On Rationalization and the National Lifestyle: Japanese Design in the 1920s and 1930s," in *Being Modern in Japan: Culture and Society From the 1910s to the 1930s*, ed. Elise K. Tipton and John Clark (Honolulu, HI: University of Hawai'i Press, 2000), 70–73; Sewell, *Japanese Imperialism and Civic Construction*, 156.

77. Gottfried Feder, *Die neue Stadt: Versuch der Begründung einer neuen Stadtplanungskunst aus der sozialen Struktur der Bevölkerung* (Berlin: Julius Springer, 1939). Regarding Japanese adoption of Feder's idea, see Carola Hein, "Visionary Plans and Planners," in *Japanese Capitals in Historical Perspective: Place, Power and Memory in Kyoto, Edo and Tokyo*, ed. Nicolas Fiévé and Paul Waley (New York, NY: Routledge, 2003), 333–341.
78. Satō Takeo, "Manshūkoku no kenchiku ni yorisu," *Manshū kenchiku zasshi* 22, no. 11 (1942): 8; Sewell, *Japanese Imperialism and Civic Construction*, 160–161.
79. Satō, "Manshūkoku no kenchiku ni yorisu," *Manshū kenchiku zasshi*, 8.
80. Duara, *Sovereignty and Authenticity*, 119–120.
81. David Tucker, "City Planning Without Cities: Order and Chaos in Utopian Manchuko," in *Crossed Histories: Manchuria in the Age of Empire*, ed. Mariko Asano Tamanoi (Honolulu, HI: University of Hawai'i Press, 2005), 53–81; Sewell, *Japanese Imperialism and Civic Construction*, 194.
82. Yu Chin-o, "Shin'gyŏng," in *Yu Chin-o tanp'yŏnjip*, ed. Chin Yŏng-pok (1942; Seoul: Chishikŭlmandŭnŭnjishik, 2012), 3–38, quoted from 8, 10.
83. Todd A. Henry, *Assimilating Seoul: Japanese Rule and the Politics of Public Space in Colonial Korea, 1910–1945* (Oakland: University of California Press, 2014), 22–61.
84. Kim Kwang-u, "Taehanjeguk shidaeŭi toshigyehoek: Hansŏngbu toshigaejo saŏp," *Hyangt'o sŏul* 50 (1991): 95–122.
85. Yi T'ae-chin, "1896–1904nyŏn sŏul toshigaejo saŏbŭi chuch'ewa chihyangsŏng," *Han'guksaron* 37 (1997): 181–206.
86. Yim Sŏk-chae, *Sahoemihakŭro ingnŭn kaehwagi-ilchegangjŏmgi sŏul kŏnch'uk* (Seoul: Ewha Womans University Press, 2011), 163 ff.
87. Pak Hŭi-yong, "Chosŏnhwangjeŭi aedalp'ŭn yŏksarŭl chŭngmyŏnghada: Wŏn'gudanŭi ch'ŏlgŏwa chosanhot'erŭi kŏnch'uk," in *Kunggwŏrŭi nunmul, paengnyŏnŭi ch'immuk: Chegugŭi somyŏl paengnyŏn*, ed. U Tong-sŏn and Pak Sŏng-jin (Seoul: Hyhyŏngch'ulp'an, 2009), 48–78; An Ch'ang-mo, *Tŏksugung* (Seoul: Tongnyŏk, 2010), 59–147.
88. Andre Schmid, *Korea Between Empires, 1895–1919* (New York, NY: Columbia University Press, 2002), 72–80; Todd A. Henry, "Respatializing Chŏson's Royal Capital," in *Sitings: Critical Approaches to Korean Geography*, ed. Timothy R. Tangherlini and Sallie Yea (Honolulu, HI: University of Hawai'i Press, 2008), 18–22.
89. Sŏult'ŭkpyŏlshi shisap'yŏnch'anwiwŏnhoe, trans. and ed., *Kukyŏk kyŏngsŏngbusa* [Keijō fushi], vol. 1 (1934; Seoul: Yemaek, 2012), 672–673; Aoyagi Tsunatarō, *Paengnyŏn chŏn ilboninŭi kyŏngsŏng yŏtpogi*, trans. (from Japanese into Korean) and ed. Ku T'ae-hun and Bak Sŏn-ok (1915; Seoul: Chaep'aellisŏch'i 21, 2011), 139–143. At the time, Emperor Kojong granted concessions to develop infrastructure to American entrepreneurs in the hopes of gaining political support from the United States government. Unfortunately, history shows that his political gesture failed to bear fruit.
90. Yi Hye-ŭn, "Sŏul 20segi kyot'ongŭi paltal," in *Sŏul 20segi konggan pyŏnch'ŏnsa*, ed. Sŏulshijŏnggaebaryŏn'guwŏn (Seoul: Sŏulshijŏnggaebaryŏn'guwŏn, 2001), 165; Ch'oe In-yŏng, "Ilcheshigi kyŏngsŏngŭi toshigongganŭl t'onghae pon chŏnch'anosŏnŭi pyŏnhwa," *Sŏurhakyŏn'gu* 41 (2010): 33.
91. Yi Sun-u, *T'onggamgwanjŏ: It'yŏjin kyŏngsulgukch'iŭi hyŏnjang* (Seoul: Hanŭlchae, 2010), 196–203, argues that Kyoto was the earliest city in East Asia to be equipped with an electric tram line. Ahead of the Fourth National Industrial Exhibition, a 6.6-kilometer tramway was laid in the Japanese city, and operations were launched on January 31, 1895, four years faster than Seoul. As for Tokyo, a tram line was introduced four years later than Seoul because the widespread operation of horse tramcars gave Tokyo no reason to rush. Numbers and dates carry even less meaning considering the fact that the technicians and operators for the

tramway construction in Seoul were procured from the Kyoto Electric Tramway Company. For further details, see Aoyagi, *Paengnyŏn chŏn ilboninŭi kyŏngsŏng yŏtpogi*, 139–143.

92. Yi, "Sŏul 20segi kyot'ongŭi paltal," 164, 167.
93. Bruce Cumings, *Korea's Place in the Sun: A Modern History* (New York, NY: Norton, 1997), 132–133.
94. Schmid, *Korea Between Empires*, 76–78.
95. Yŏm Pok-kyu, *Sŏurŭn ŏttŏk'e kyehoektoeŏnnŭn'ga* (Seoul: Sallim, 2005), 8, footnote 3. For further details, see Yi Kyu-ch'ŏl, *Taehanjegukki hansŏngbu toshigongganŭi chaep'yŏn*, Ph.D. diss. (Seoul National University, 2010).
96. Song Sŏk-ki, "Kunggwŏre tŭrŏsŏn kŭndae kŏnch'ungmul," in *Kunggwŏrŭi nunmul, paengnyŏnŭi ch'immuk*, 254–257; Yun Il-chu, *Han'guk yangshikkŏnch'uk 80nyŏnsa: Haebangjŏn p'yŏn* (Seoul: Ch'ijŏngmunhwasa, 1966), 63–66; Kim Chŏng-tong, *Kojonghwangjega saranghan chŏngdonggwa tŏksugung* (Seoul: Parŏn, 2004), 180; An, *Tŏksugung*, 174–185; Chungangilbo (Korea Joongang Daily), "Tŏksugung sŏkchojŏn 1898nyŏn sŏlgyedo wŏnbon ch'ajatta," August 19, 2011, p. A1.
97. Kim, *Nama innŭn yŏksa, sarajinŭn kŏnch'ungmul*, 174; Song, "Kunggwŏre tŭrŏsŏn kŭndae kŏnch'ungmul," 253–254.
98. Yi Sun-u, *Sont'ak'ot'el* (Seoul: Hanŭlchae, 2012).
99. Kim Chŏng-tong, "Toraehan sŏyangin kŏnch'ukkae kwanhan yŏn'gu (1): Sŏuresŏŭi yŏk'algwa yŏnghyangŭl chungshimŭro," *Taehan'gŏnch'uk'ak'oenonmunjip kyehoekkye* 5, no. 4 (1989): 84–85; Hashiya, *Ilbonjegukchuŭi*, 150–157.
100. Sŏult'ŭkpyŏlshisap'yŏnch'anwiwŏnhoe, ed., *Sŏulgŏnch'uksa* (Seoul: Sŏult'ŭkpyŏlshi, 1999), 707–709.
101. Nishizawa, *Nippon shokuminchi kenchikuron*, 130.
102. Kim, *Nama innŭn yŏksa, sarajinŭn kŏnch'ungmul*, 17–19.
103. *Kukyŏk kyŏngsŏngbusa* [Keijō fushi], vol. 2 (1936; Seoul: Yemaek, 2013), 270.
104. *Chōsen sōtokufu kanpō* 28, "Choku rei, no. 375: Chōsen sōtokufu chihōkan kansei," September 30, 1910, p. A3–4; *Chōsen sōtokufu kanpō* 29, "Chōsen sōtokufu rei, no. 6, no. 7," October 1, 1910, p. A13–14. See the argument in Yi Hye-ŭn, "Chosŏnshidae ihu sŏurŭi t'ojiiyonggwa kyŏnggwanbyŏnhwa," in Yi Hye-ŭn et al., *Sŏurŭi kyŏnggwanbyŏnhwa* (Seoul: Sŏurhakyŏn'guso, 1994), 200–201; Yi Kwang-hŭ, "Ilche kangjŏmgi toshihaengjŏngŭi ijungsŏnge taehan yŏn'gu," in *Chosŏnch'ongdokpu toshigyehoek kongmunsŏwa kirokp'yŏnggaron*, ed. Han'guk kukkagirokyŏn'guwŏn (Seoul: Chillit'amgu, 2008), 231–263; Son Chŏng-mok, *Han'guk chibangjedo chach'isayŏn'gu: Kkabogyŏngjang-ilchegangjŏmgi*, vol. 1 (Seoul: Ilchisa, 1992), 80–124.
105. *Chōsen sōtokufu kanpō* 174, "Chōsen sōtokufu keikidō rei, no. 3: Keijōfubukyūmen no meishōkyū kuiki," April 1, 1911, p. A3; Son, *Han'guk chibangjedo chach'isayŏn'gu*, 154–155.
106. *Chōsen sōtokufu kanpō* 449, "Chōsen sōtokufu keikidō rei, no. 1: Keijōfu, inchonfu, koyangun kyū kagetakegun naimen no kuiki henkō," January 30, 1914, p. A2; *Chōsen sōtokufu kanpō* 520, "Chōsen sōtokufu keikidō kokuji, no. 7: Keijōfu machihora no meishōkyū kuiki," April 27, 1914, p. A6–9.
107. *Chōsen sōtokufu kanpō* 56, "Chōsen sōtokufu kunre, no. 9," October 7, 1912, p. A1.
108. *Chōsen sōtokufu kanpō* 81, "Chōsen sōtokufu kokuji, no. 78: Keijō shiku kaishū yotei keikaku rosen," November 6, 1912, p. A1. On the Keijō City Improvement Plan, see Pak "1920nyŏndae kyŏngsŏngŭi toshigyehoekkwa toshigyehoegundong," 81; Kim Yŏng-kŭn, "Toshigyehoekkwa toshigongganŭi pyŏnhwa," in *Ilcheŭi shingminjibaewa ilsangsaenghwal*, ed. Yŏnsedaehakkyo kuk'akyŏn'guwŏn (Seoul: Hyean, 2004), 49; Kim Paek-yŏng, "Wangjo sudorobut'ŏ shingmindoshiro: Kyŏngsŏnggwa tok'yoŭi shigu kaejŏnge taehan pigyoyŏn'gu," *Han'guk'akpo* 112 (2003): 82. More generally, see Yŏm Pok-kyu, *Sŏurŭi kiwŏn, kyŏngsŏngŭi t'ansaeng: Shingminji sudonŭn ŏttŏk'e met'ŭrop'ollisŭga toeŏnna* (Seoul: Idea, 2016).

109. Son, *Ilche kangjŏmgi toshigyehoek yŏn'gu*, 102; Son, "Shingmindoshigyehoekkwa kŭ yusan," 464; Yi, *T'onggamgwanjŏ*, 264–267; Kim Ki-ho, "Ilchesidae ch'ogiŭi Toshigyehoege taehan yŏn'gu: Kyŏngsŏngbu sigukaejŏngŭl chungsimŭro, *Sŏurhakyŏn'gu* 6 (1995): 41–66.
110. Son, *Ilche kangjŏmgi toshigyehoek yŏn'gu*, 98–114; Kim Yŏng-kŭn, "Ilcheha kyŏngsŏngjiyŏgŭi sahoegonggan kujoŭi pyŏnhwawa toshigyŏnghŏm: Chungshimchubyŏnŭi chiyŏkpunhwarŭl chungshimŭro," *Sŏurhakyŏn'gu* 20 (2003): 152.
111. Pak, "1920nyŏndae kyŏngsŏngŭi toshigyehoekkwa toshigyehoegundong," 93; Yŏm, *Sŏurŭn ŏttŏk'e kyehoektoeŏnnŭn'ga*, 12.
112. According to Kim Paek-yŏng, the construction of the current Yulgok-ro, an arterial road cutting through Ch'angdŏkkung Palace and Chongmyo Shrine, was reactivated by the demise of the last Korean King Sunjong in 1926. Despite the constant resistance, it was completed in 1930. See Kim, "Sangjinggongganŭi pyŏnyonggwa chip'apkiŏgŭi palmyŏng," *Konggan'gwa sahoe*, 213–214; Yŏm Pok-kyu, *Ilche ha Kyŏngsŏng tosi kyehoekŭi gusangkwa silhang*, Ph.D. diss. (Seoul National University, 2009), 63–68.
113. *Kukyŏk kyŏngsŏngbusa*, vol. 2, 217.
114. Kim Dae-ho, "Ilchegangjŏm ihu kyŏngbokkungŭi hwech'ŏlgwa 'hwaryong' (1910 – hyŏnjae)," *Sŏurhakyŏn'gu* 29 (2007): 92.
115. Son, *Ilche kangjŏmgi toshigyehoek yŏn'gu*, 98–114; Yi Myŏng-kyu, "Han'gung kŭndae toshigyehoekchedoŭi paltalgwa soul," in Ch'oe Sangch'ŏl et al., *Tongyang toshisa sogŭi soul* (Seoul: Sŏulshijŏnggaebaryŏn'guwŏn, 1994), 438; Pak, "1920nyŏndae kyŏngsŏngŭi toshigyehoekkwa toshigyehoegundong," 101–108. Some argue that city improvement is only effective under colonial rule because it would be impossible to force landowners to donate land for such a purpose under any other circumstances. See Aoi Akihito, "Kyehoegŭi shingminji/ilsangŭi shingminji: Toshisaŭi shigak," trans. (from Japanese into Korean) Kim Hana and U Tong-sŏn, *Kŏnch'ukyŏksa yŏn'gu* 16, no. 2 (2007): 195.
116. Yi Kyu-mok, "Sŏul kŭndae toshigyŏnggwan ikki," in *Sŏul 20segi konggan pyŏnch'ŏnsa*, 121; Son, "Shingmindoshigyehoekkwa kŭ yusan," 454–456; Kim Paek-yŏng, "Rŏilchŏnjaeng chik'u sŏurŭi shingmindoshihwa kwajŏng: Pigyoshingmindoshisajŏk koch'al," *Chibangsawa chibangmunhwa* 8, no. 2 (2005): 95–101.
117. *The Veritable Records of Emperor Sunjong* (Sunjongshillok), vol. 1, "Naegangnyŏng, no. 1: Sŏngbyŏkch'ŏriwiwŏnhoee kwanhan kŏn," July 30, 1907.
118. *Kukyŏk kyŏngsŏngbusa*, vol. 2, 271, 69–70.
119. Cho Chae-mo, *Kunggwŏl, chosŏnŭl marhada: Kunggwŏllo ingnŭn chosŏnŭi chedowa inyŏm* (Seoul: Artbooks, 2012), 111; Kim, *Kojonghwangjega saranghan chŏngdonggwa tŏksugung*, 33.
120. *The Veritable Records of Emperor Sunjong*, vol. 4, "Irhanbyŏnghapchoyak sŏng," August 22, 1910.
121. Cho Byŏng-no, "Shingminji shigi torojŏngch'aekkwa chaejoilboninŭi taeŭng," in Cho Byŏng-no et al., *Chosŏnch'ongdokpuŭi kyot'ongjŏngch'aekkwa torogŏnsŏl* (Seoul: Kuk'akcharyowŏn, 2011), 22–23.
122. *Chōsen sōtokufu kanpō* 186, "Seirei, no. 3: Tochi shūyō rei," April 17, 1911, p. A1.
123. *Kukyŏk kyŏngsŏngbusa*, vol. 2, 270–271.
124. *Chōsen sōtokufu kanpō* 169, "Chōsen sōtokufu rei, no. 11: Shigaichi kenchiku torishimari kisoku," February 25, 1913, p. A1–2.
125. Son, "Shingmindoshigyehoekkwa kŭ yusan," 467; Yi Wang-mu, "Ilcheshidae kyŏngbokkung chubyŏndoroŭi pyŏnhwawa Kungjangŭi hwech'ŏl: Ch'ongdokpu shinch'ŏngsa wan'gong chŏnhurŭl chungshimŭro," in Cho, *Chosŏnch'ongdokpuŭi kyot'ongjŏngch'aekkwa torogŏnsŏl*, 83.
126. Yi, "Han'gung kŭndae toshigyehoekchedoŭi paltalgwa soul," 427.
127. Ch'oe, "Ilcheshigi kyŏngsŏngŭi toshigongganŭl," *Sŏurhakyŏn'gu*, 33.

128. Chŏng Chae-chŏng, *Ilchech'imnyakkwa han'gukch'ŏlto* (Seoul: Seoul National University Press, 1999), 164–165.
129. *Chōsen sōtokufu kanpō* 2062, "Keijō shiku kaishū yotei keikaku rosen kaisei," June 25, 1919.
130. Yi, "Han'gung kŭndae toshigyehoekchedoŭi paltalgwa soul," 428–429, 444–445; Yŏm, *Ilche ha Kyŏngsŏng tosi kyehoekŭi gusangkwa silhang*, 52–60.
131. *Maeil sinbo*, "Sasŏl: Shigugaejŏng," November 7, 1912, p. A1.
132. *Kukyŏk kyŏngsŏngbusa*, vol. 2, 270, 274–275.
133. Aoyagi, *Paengnyŏn chŏn ilboninŭi kyŏngsŏng yŏtpogi*, 16–17.
134. *Kukyŏk kyŏngsŏngbusa*, vol. 2, 279 Son, "Shingmindoshigyehoekkwa kŭ yusan," 466; Yi, "Sŏul kŭndae toshigyŏnggwan ikki," 121.
135. Son, *Ilche kangjŏmgi toshigyehoek yŏn'gu*, 105.
136. Pak, "1920nyŏndae kyŏngsŏngŭi toshigyehoekkwa toshigyehoegundong," 90.
137. For a discussion of the Japanese Government-General's "cultural rule," see, notably, Henry, *Assimilating Seoul*.
138. Son, *Ilche kangjŏmgi toshigyehoek yŏn'gu*, 115; Pak, "1920nyŏndae kyŏngsŏngŭi toshigyehoekkwa toshigyehoegundong," 96–101; Mun Chŏnghŭi and Yi Pyŏng-ryŏl, "Toshigyehoek hwaltonggwa inyŏm: Chosŏnshidae min ilcheshidaeŭi toshigyehoekŭl chungshimŭro," *Kukt'ogyehoek* 25, no. 2 (1990): 22–24; Yamabe Kentaro, *Ilbonŭi shingminji chosŏnt'ongch'i haebu*, trans. (from Japanese into Korean) Ch'oe Hye-chu (Seoul: Ŏmunhaksa, 2011), 163 ff.
139. Son, *Ilche kangjŏmgi toshigyehoek yŏn'gu*, 170–176; Son, "Shingmindoshigyehoekkwa kŭ yusan," 469 ff.
140. Keijōfu, ed., *Keijō toshi keikaku shiryō chōsasho* (Keijō: Yamaguchi insatsusho, 1927).
141. Yi Song-sun, "Chosŏnch'ongdokpu toshigyehoek kwallyŏn chojing mit kigu punsŏk," in *Chosŏnch'ongdokpu toshigyehoek kongmunsŏwa kirokp'yŏnggaron*, ed. Han'gukkukkagirokyŏn'guwŏn (Seoul: Chillit'amgu, 2008), 303–304; Pak, "1920nyŏndae kyŏngsŏngŭi toshigyehoekkwa toshigyehoegundong," 90, 96–101; Kim Chu-ya and Ishida Jun'ichiro, "Kyŏngsŏngbu t'ojiguhoeksaŏbe issŏsŏ shingmindoshisŏnge kwanhan yŏn'gu," *Taehan'gŏnch'uk'ak'oenonmunjip kyehoekkye* 25, no. 4 (2009): 170–171; Son, *Ilche kangjŏmgi toshigyehoek yŏn'gu*, 115, 170–176.
142. Kim Pae-kyŏng, *Chibaewa konggan: Shingminji toshi kyŏngsŏnggwa cheguk ilbon* (Seoul: Munhakkwajisŏngsa, 2009), 68.
143. Fiscal issues were most likely the direct cause behind the Government-General's hesitation in proceeding with urban planning proposals. To more realistically gauge the execution of urban planning, the Government-General conducted extensive surveys in the cities of Keijō, P'yŏngyang, Taegu, and Busan in 1926. That same year, the survey results were reported at the year-end Japanese Imperial Diet but failed to help garner financial aid for the urban planning projects scheduled for 1927. For further details, see Son, *Ilche kangjŏmgi toshigyehoek yŏn'gu*, 170–176.
144. *Kukyŏk kyŏngsŏngbusa*, vol. 2, 707.
145. In this sense, Todd A. Henry's argument that defines the Japanese Government-General's rule as "draconian forms of social control" is convincing. See Henry, *Assimilating Seoul*, 16.
146. *Chōsen sōtokufu kanpō* 2232, "Chōsen sōtokufu seirei, no. 18: Chōsen shigaichi keikakurei," June 20, 1934, p. A1–3; *Chōsen sōtokufu kanpō* 2264, "Chōsen sōtokufurei, no. 78: Chōsen shigaichi keikakurei shikō kisoku," July 27, 1934, p. A1–4; *Chōsen sōtokufu kanpō* 2593, "Chōsen sōtokufurei, no. 105: Chōsen shigaichi keikakurei shikō kisoku chū kaisei," September 2, 1935, p. A1–10. On the Chosŏn Urban Planning Ordinance, see Son, *Ilche kangjŏmgi toshigyehoek yŏn'gu*, 151–157, 195–200; Yŏm, *Ilche ha Kyŏngsŏng tosi kyehoekŭi gusangkwa silhang*, 97 ff.

147. Yi, "Ilbonbon'gukkwa chosŏnch'ongdokpu toshigyehoek pigyoyŏn'gu," 282–283; Son, *Ilche kangjŏmgi toshigyehoek yŏn'gu*, 184–186.
148. *Maeil sinbo*, "Sasŏl: Chosŏnshigajigyehoengnyŏng kongp'o," June 21, 1934, p. A2.
149. Son, *Ilche kangjŏmgi toshigyehoek yŏn'gu*, 187, 195–200.
150. Kim Hŭng-sun, "Ilchegangjŏmgi toshigyehoegesŏ nat'anan kŭndaesŏng: Chosŏnshigajigyehoengnyŏngŭl chungshimŭro," *Sŏultoshiyŏn'gu* 8, no. 4 (2007): 165.
151. Yi, "Ilbonbon'gukkwa chosŏnch'ongdokpu toshigyehoek pigyoyŏn'gu," 290–295; Son, *Ilche kangjŏmgi toshigyehoek yŏn'gu*, 106 ff., 186–194.
152. Kim Kyŏng-nam, "1930nyŏndae ilcheŭi toshigŏnsŏlgwa pusanshigajigyehoegŭi t'ŭksŏng," in *Yŏksamunhwahak'oe haksultaehoe palp'yo charyojip* (2004), 156, 173; Yŏm, *Sŏurŭn ŏttŏk'e kyehoektoeŏnnŭn'ga*, 49–50.
153. *Maeil sinbo*, "Kisŏngshigaŭi t'ongjeboda shinshigabaltare ch'ijung," June 21, 1934, p. A1.
154. Yi, "Ilbonbon'gukkwa chosŏnch'ongdokpu toshigyehoek pigyoyŏn'gu," 291–295; Yŏm Pok-kyu, *Sŏul ŭi kiwŏn, Kyŏngsŏng ŭi tansaeng 1910–1945* (Seoul: Idea, 2016), 161–175; Son Chŏng-mok, "'Ilche kangjŏmgi toshigyehoek yŏn'gu'rŭl chungshimŭro," *Han'guksayŏn'gu* 149 (2010): 413; Son, *Ilche kangjŏmgi toshigyehoek yŏn'gu*, 253–281, 383; Kim, "1930nyŏndae ilcheŭi toshigŏnsŏlgwa pusanshigajigyehoegŭi t'ŭksŏng," 171. More generally, see Kim Ki-ho, *Sŏul namch'on: Shigan, changso, saram* (Seoul: Sŏurhakyŏn'guso, 2003).
155. *Chōsen sōtokufu kanpō* 3506, "Chōsen sōtokufurei, no. 193: Chōsen shigaichi keikakurei shikō kisoku chū kaisei," September 21, 1938, p. A1–14. See the argument in Yi Song-sun, "Chosŏnch'ongdokpu shigajigyehoek kwallyŏn kongmunsŏŭi pullyuwa p'yŏngga," in *Chosŏnch'ongdokpu toshigyehoek kongmunsŏwa kirokp'yŏnggaron*, 200.
156. *Chōsen sōtokufu kanpō* 2758, "Chōsen sōtokufu kokuji, no. 180: Keijō shigaichi keikaku kuiki," March 26, 1936, p. A2.; Seoul Metropolitan Government, *T'ojiguhoekchŏngni paeksŏ* (Seoul: Ŭn'gwangsa, 1990), 36; *Chōsen sōtokufu kanpō* 2796, "Chōsen sōtokufu keikidō kokuji, no. 44: Shōwa 11 nen chōsen sōtokufurei dai 8 ni yorifu gun no kankatsu kuiki henkō," May 12, 1936, p. A12; Yŏm, *Sŏul ŭi kiwŏn*, 119–132; Son, "Shingmindoshigyehoekkwa kŭ yusan," 480 ff.
157. Kim Paek-yŏng, "1920nyŏndae taegyŏngsŏnggyehoekŭl tullŏssan shingmin'gwŏllyŏgŭi kyunyŏlgwa kaltŭng," in *Shingminjiŭi ilsang chibaewa kyunyŏl*, ed. Kong Jeug and Chŏng Gŭnshik (Seoul: Munhwagwahaksa, 2006), 259–300.
158. Seoul Metropolitan Government, *Sŏulshi t'ojiguhoekchŏngni yŏnhyŏkchi* (Seoul: Sŏult'ŭkpyŏlshi, 1984), 73–76, Sŏul tŭkbyŏlsi, *Tojiguhoekjŏnri yŏnhyŏkji* (1984), 73–76; Yŏm, *Sŏul ŭi kiwŏn, Kyŏngsŏng ŭi tansaeng 1910–1945*, 192–216, 247–282; Kim and Ishida, "Kyŏngsŏngbu t'ojiguhoeksaŏbe issŏsŏ shingmindoshisŏnge kwanhan yŏn'gu," 171–177; Chŏn Nam-il et al., *Han'guk chugŏŭi sahoesa* (Seoul: Tolbegae, 2009), 134 ff.; Chŏn Nam-il, *Han'guk chugŏŭi gonggansa* (Seoul: Tolbegae, 2011), 94–98.
159. On this point, see Yŏm, *Sŏurŭn ŏttŏk'e kyehoektoeŏnnŭn'ga*, 30–41.
160. Yi Sŭng-il, "Chosŏnch'ongdokpu kongmunsŏŭi kirok'akchŏk p'yŏngga: Chosŏnch'ongdokpu toshigyehoek kwallyŏn kongmunsŏgunŭl chungshimŭro," in *Chosŏnch'ongdokpu toshigyehoek kongmunsŏwa kirokp'yŏnggaron*, 63; Yi, "Chosŏnch'ongdokpu toshigyehoek kwallyŏn chojing mit kigu punsŏk," 302–327.
161. Yŏm, *Sŏurŭn ŏttŏk'e kyehoektoeŏnnŭn'ga*, 26.
162. Kim, "Ilchegangjŏmgi toshigyehoegesŏ nat'anan kŭndaesŏng," 155–173; Kim, "Toshigyehoekkwa toshigongganŭi pyŏnhwa," 57–60.
163. Kim, "Ilcheha kyŏngsŏngjiyŏgŭi sahoegonggan," 167–171. See also Busan National University Han'gungminjongmunhwayŏn'guso, Volume 2 of *Han'gung kŭndaeŭi p'unggyŏnggwa chiyŏgŭi palgyŏn: Kyŏngsŏng I*; Volume 3

of *Han'guk kŭndaeŭi p'unggyŏnggwa chiyŏgŭi palgyŏn: Kyŏngsŏng II* (Seoul: Kuk'akcharyowŏn, 2013).

164. *Chōsen sōtokufu kanpō* 520, "Chōsen sōtokufu keikidō kokuji, no. 7: Keijōfu machihora no meishōkyū kuiki," April 27, 1914, p. A6–9.
165. *Kukyŏk kyŏngsŏngbusa*, vol. 2, 272; Henry, "Respatializing Chosŏn's Royal Capital," 23–29.
166. Hŏ Yŏng-ran, Ryu Chun-pŏm and Kim Che-chŏng, "Han'gung kŭnhyŏndae sogŭi kŏrigwanggomulgwa karogyŏnggwan: Sŏul toshimŭi kanp'anŭl chungshimŭro," in *Sŏul 20segi saenghwal-munhwabyŏnch'ŏnsa*, ed. University of Seoul Sŏurhakyŏn'guso (Seoul: Sŏulshijŏnggaebaryŏn'guwŏn, 2001), 611–668; Yi Kyŏng-t'aek, *Sŏurŭi toshigyŏnggwan hyŏngsŏnggwa pyŏnhwae kwanhan tongin yŏn'gu*, Ph.D. diss. (Korea University, 2012), 328–330.
167. Yano Hosino and Morikawa Kiyohito, eds., *Daikeijō annai*, new edition (Keijō: Keijō toshibunka kenkyūjo, 1936), 12; Ha Sang-pok, "Kwanghwamunŭi chŏngch'ihak, yesulgwa kwŏllyŏgŭi chaehyŏn," *Han'gukchŏngch'ihak'oebo* 43 (2009): 84 ff.; Chang Kyu-sik, *Sŏul kongganŭro pon yŏksa* (Seoul: Hyean, 2004), 72–73; Yi Kyŏng-su, *Ilcheshigi kyŏngsŏngbuŭi karojŏngbigyehoege ŭihan karo pyŏnhwae kwanhan yŏn'gu*, Master's thesis (Yonsei University, 1991), 69–70; Kim, "Wangjo sudorobut'ŏ shingmindoshiro," *Han'guk'akpo*, 93–94, 100.
168. Yi Kwang-hŭi, "Ilche kangjŏmgi toshihaengjŏngŭi ijungsŏnge taehan yŏn'gu," in *Chosŏnch'ongdokpu toshigyehoek kongmunsŏwa kirokp'yŏnggaron*, 250–257.
169. For a critique about the account of colonial city as a dual city, see Kim Chong-kŭn, "Shingmindoshi kyŏngsŏngŭi ijungdoshirone taehan pip'anjŏk koch'al," *Sŏurhakyŏn'gu* 38 (2010): 1–68. Likewise, Todd A. Henry argues that in contrast to Japanese settler associations requiring ethnic and social discrimination for their own benefit the Japanese Government-General rather contrived to promote assimilation. See Henry, *Assimilating Seoul*, 28–42.
170. *Kukyŏk kyŏngsŏngbusa*, vol. 2, 458, 542–544.
171. Kim, "Ilcheha kyŏngsŏngjiyŏgŭi sahoegonggan," 139; Yi, "Sŏul kŭndae toshigyŏnggwan ikki," 123.
172. Kim Sa-ryang, "Ch'ŏnma," *Kim Sa-ryang, chakp'umgwa yŏn'gu*, vol. 2, ed. Kim Chae-yong and Kwak Hyŏng-tŏk (1940; Yŏngnak, 2009), 19.
173. Kim, "Ilcheha kyŏngsŏngjiyŏgŭi sahoegonggan," 148, 158.
174. Yŏm Pok-kyu, "Shingminji toshigyehoegŭi yusan'gwa kŭe taehan inshik"; Son, "'*Ilche kangjŏmgi toshigyehoek yŏn'gu*'rŭl chungshimŭro," *Han'guksayŏn'gu*, 406–407. In that sense, it is difficult to agree with Pak Hyŏng-yong's view only highlighting oppressive, exploitative aspects by stating that "while ports were being opened, urban planning merely existed as part of what appeared to be a modern legislative system and then became controlled by the interests of foreign powers under Japanese colonial rule" until it finally "came to anchor Korea's industrialization in tandem with other development policies after the nation's liberation." See Pak Hyŏng-yong, "Han'gugŭi kŭndae toshigyehoek hyŏngsŏng," *Konggan'gwa sahoe*, special vol. 9 (1997): 74–93, quoted from 91.
175. Kim, "Ilchegangjŏmgi toshigyehoegesŏ nat'anan kŭndaesŏng," 171.
176. Chŏn Sang-suk, "Ugak'i ch'ongdogŭi naesŏnyunghwa ideollogiwa nonggongbyŏngjin chŏngch'ael: Ugak'i chōsen ch'ongdokchŏngch'iŭi chibaejŏngch'aeksajŏk ŭimie taehan chaegoch'al," *Hyŏnsanggwa inshik* 34 (2010): 43–47.
177. Kim, "1920nyŏndae taegyŏngsŏnggyehoekŭl tullŏssan shingmin'gwŏllyŏgŭi kyunyŏlgwa kaltŭng," 260–262.
178. Yi, "Sŏul kŭndae toshigyŏnggwan ikki," 122.
179. Song Chak-saeng, "Oraein pŏngŏri: Chongno in'gyŏngŭi shinset'aryŏng," *Pyŏlgŏn'gon* 23 (1929), in Busan National University, *Han'gung kŭndaeŭi p'unggyŏnggwa chiyŏgŭi palgyŏn*, 244–251, quoted from 250.

180. *Taehanmaeilshinbo*, "Kyŏngbokkung ŏpsyŏjine," May 15, 1910, chappo, p. A2.
181. *The Veritable Records of Emperor Sunjong*, vol. 2, May 17, 1911, Appendix.
182. *The Veritable Records of Emperor Sunjong*, vol. 2, February 20, 1911, Appendix.
183. *The Veritable Records of Emperor Sunjong*, vol. 1, October 19, 1907.
184. *Taehanjegung kwanbo*, vol. 4014, March 5, 1908, p. A15–16.
185. Kim, "Ilchegangjŏm ihu," *Sŏurhakyŏn'gu*, 90–92. According to Kim Dae-ho, the number of buildings marked on the layout for Kyŏngbokgung Palace were five hundred nine, corresponding to an area of 6,806 kan. That number dropped to three hundred ninety-six, the equivalent of 5,505 kan, until the completion of the Government-General Building. Now only forty original buildings (857 kan) remain. See also Kim Chŏng-dong, *Nama innŭn yŏksa, sarajinŭn kŏnch'ungmul*, 183–227; Hong Sun-min, "Ilcheŭi shingminch'imt'algwa kyŏngbokkung hweson: T'ongch'igwŏllyŏgŭi sangjingsŏng t'alch'wi," *Munmyŏngyŏnji* 5, no. 1 (2004): 5–34; Yi Wang-mu, "Ilcheshidae kyŏngbokkung chubyŏndoroŭi pyŏnhwawa Kungjangŭi hwech'ŏl," 71–72. More generally, see Chŏng Gyu-hong, *Uri munhwajae sunansa: Ilchegi munhwajae yakt'algwa yurin* (Seoul: Hakyŏnmunhwasa, 2005).
186. *Maeil sinbo*, "Kongjinhoerŭl kaech'oehanŭn mokchŏk," September 4, 1915; Kang Sang-hun, *Ichegangjŏmgi kŭndaeshisŏrŭi modŏnijŭm suyong*, Ph.D. diss. (Seoul National University, 2004), 40.
187. Bak Sŏng-chin, "P'yŏngyangŭi hwanggŏnmuni namsanŭro naeryŏon kkadalgŭn?" in *Kunggwŏrŭi nunmul, paengnyŏnŭi ch'immuk*, 156–158; Kim, "Ilchegangjŏm ihu," *Sŏurhakyŏn'gu*, 92 ff.; Cho, *Kunggwŏl, chosŏnŭl marhada*, 253; Kang, "Ichegangjŏmgi kŭndaeshisŏrŭi modŏnijŭm suyong," 41, 48.
188. *Maeil sinbo*, "Kongjinhoe Kaehoeshik," October 2, 1915, p. A2; *Kukyŏk kyŏngsŏngbusa* [Keijō fushi], vol. 3 (1941; Seoul: Yemaek, 2014), 262–263.
189. Yi Sang-hae, "P'ungsu," in *Han'gukkŏnch'ukkaenyŏmsajŏn*, ed. Han'gukkŏnch'ukkaenyŏmsajŏn kihoegwiwŏnhoe (Seoul: Tongnyŏk, 2013), 841–846.
190. Kang Yŏng-hwan, *(Saero ssŭn) Han'guk chugŏmunhwaŭi yŏksa* (Seoul: Kimundang, 2013), 129 ff.
191. Yim Tŏk-sun, "Chosŏnch'ogi hanyang chŏngdowa sudoŭi sangjinghwa," in Yi, *Sŏurŭi kyŏnggwanbyŏnhwa*, 18–19, 34; Yi Sang-ku, "Sŏurŭi toshi hyŏngsŏng," in Ch'oe, *Tongyang toshisa sogŭi soul*, 313–361.
192. Yi, *Sŏurŭi toshigyŏnggwan hyŏngsŏnggwa pyŏnhwae kwanhan tongin yŏn'gu*, 39–41.
193. Nam Yŏng-u and Kwak Su-chŏng, "Kodaedoshi changansŏngŭi ipchijŏk ŭimiwa toshigujo," *Han'guktoshijirihak'oeji* 140, no. 1 (2011): 1–16; Yi, *Sŏurŭi toshigyŏnggwan hyŏngsŏnggwa pyŏnhwae kwanhan tongin yŏn'gu*, 39–41; Yim, "Chosŏnch'ogi hanyang chŏngdowa sudoŭi sangjinghwa," 45 ff.
194. Yi Kyu-mok and Kim Han-pae, "Sŏul toshigyŏnggwanŭi pyŏnch'ŏn kwajŏng yŏn'gu," *Sŏurhakyŏn'gu* 2 (1994): 3–19; Yi, *Sŏurŭi toshigyŏnggwan hyŏngsŏnggwa pyŏnhwae kwanhan tongin yŏn'gu*, 43–46; Han Yŏng-u, *Wangjoŭi sŏlgyeja Chŏngdojŏn* (Paju: Chishiksanŏpsa, 1999).
195. Yi, "Sŏurŭi toshi hyŏngsŏng," 336.
196. Cho, *Kunggwŏl, chosŏnŭl marhada*, 131; Yim, "Chosŏnch'ogi hanyang chŏngdowa sudoŭi sangjinghwa," 55–58; Kim, *Nama innŭn yŏksa, sarajinŭn kŏnch'ungmul*, 186 ff.
197. Kim Tong-uk, "Chōsen ch'ogi ch'anggŏn kyŏngbokkungŭi konggan'gusŏng: Koryŏgunggwŏlgwaŭi kwan'gyee taehaesŏ," *Kŏnch'ukyŏksa yŏn'gu* 7, no. 2 (1998): 15–21. According to the architectural historian Yim Sŏk-chae, asymmetries can actually be discovered all over Kyŏngbokgung, even though its main buildings may appear to be symmetrical from the front. Nevertheless, the palace is representative of Korean aesthetics for minimizing the display of sharp vertical lines while preserving the unique features of each building as they stand in harmony with one another. On this point, see Yim Sŏk-chae, *Sahoemihakŭro ingnŭn*

kaehwagi-ilchegangjŏmgi sŏul kŏnch'uk (Seoul: Ewha Womans University Press, 2011), 25 ff.

198. Yi Sun-u, *Kwanghwamun yukchoapkil* (Seoul: Hanŭlchae, 2012), 19 ff.; Yim, "Chosŏnch'ogi hanyang chŏngdowa sudoŭi sangjinghwa," 45–49; Son, *Ilche kangjŏmgi toshigyehoek yŏn'gu*, 102.
199. Yim, "Chosŏnch'ogi hanyang chŏngdowa sudoŭi sangjinghwa," 51–52.
200. Cho, *Kunggwŏl, chosŏnŭl marhada*, 118–122; Yang T'aek-kyu, *Kyŏngbokkunge taehae araya hal modŭn kŏt: Ch'injŏrhamyŏnsŏdo kkomkkomhan kyŏngbokkung tapsagi* (Seoul: Ch'aekkwahamkke, 2007), 28–41.
201. Yang, *Kyŏngbokkunge taehae araya hal modŭn kŏt*, 42–50.
202. Sŏult'ŭkpyŏlshisap'yŏnch'anwiwŏnhoe, ed. *Sŏulgŏnch'uksa*, 603.
203. Hong Sun-min, "Kojongdae kyŏngbokkung chunggŏnŭi ŭimi," *Sŏurhakyŏn'gu* 29 (2007): 57–82.
204. Koen de Ceuster, "The Changing Nature of National Icons in the Seoul Landscape," *The Review of Korean Studies* 4 (2000): 81; Ha Sang-pok, *Kwanghwamun'gwa chŏngch'igwŏllyŏk* (Seoul: Sogang University Press, 2010), 142–148.
205. Michael Kim, "Collective Memory and Commemorative Space: Reflections on Korean Modernity and the Kyŏngbok Palace Reconstruction 1865–2010," *International Area Review* 13, no. 4 (2010): 7–8; An Ch'ang-mo, "Kojongsamch'ŏnjigyo ch'angdŏkkungesŏ kyŏngbokkungŭl kŏch'yŏ tŏksugungkkaji," *Kunggwŏrŭi nunmul, paengnyŏnŭi ch'immuk*, 23; Sŏult'ŭkpyŏlshisap'yŏnch'anwiwŏnhoe, ed. *Sŏulgŏnch'uksa*, 603–608.
206. Kim, "Ilchegangjŏm ihu," *Sŏurhakyŏn'gu*, 83–131, esp. 85.
207. Kim, *Chibaewa konggan*, 344–349; Kim, "Sangjinggongganŭi pyŏnyonggwa chip'apkiŏgŭi palmyŏng," *Konggan'gwa sahoe*, 215.
208. Plan no. 1 for Kyŏngbokgung Palace is documented by the Cultural Heritage Administration (Munhwajaech'ŏng), *Kyŏngbokgung pyŏnch'ŏnsa: Kyŏngbokgung pyŏnch'ŏn kwajŏng mit chihyŏngpunsŏk haksulchosa yŏn'guyongyŏk*, vol. 1 (2007), 82, figure 15. Online access to this research report is available, www.albummania.co.kr/gallery/view.asp?seq=82946&path=&rpage=5 (accessed January 15, 2020).
209. National Museum of Korea, *Ku ch'ongdokpu kŏnmul shilch'ŭk mit ch'ŏlgŏ pogosŏ*, vol. 1 (Seoul: National Museum of Korea, 1997), 341.
210. *The Records on the Construction of the Japanese Government-General Building in Korea* (*Chōsen sōtokufu jōsha shineishi*), published by the Japanese Government-General in 1926, did not mention the person who played a leading role in making such decisions. See also its Korean translation, *Chosŏnch'ongdokpu ch'ŏngsa shinyŏngji*, trans. Kim Tong-hyŏn (Seoul: National Museum of Korea, 1995). It was claimed by Kim Chŏng-tong that who played a major role in determining the location of the Japanese Government-General Building in Korea was Itō Chūta. See Kim, *Nama innŭn yŏksa, sarajinŭn kŏnch'ungmul*, 196; Yun Hong-ki, "Kyŏngbokkunggwa ku chosŏnch'ongdokpu kŏnmul kyŏnggwanŭl tullŏssan sangjingmul chŏnjaeng," *Konggan'gwa sahoe* 15 (2001): 295.
211. Itō Chūta, "Jinja kenchiku ni dai suru kōsatsu," *Chōsen to kenchiku* 5, no. 1 (1926): 3–19.
212. Kim Dae-ho, "1910–1920nyŏndae chosŏnch'ongdokpuŭi chosŏnshin'gung kŏllipkwa unyŏng," *Han'guksaron* 50 (2004): 312–313; Kim Paek-yŏng, "Sangjinggongganŭi pyŏnyonggwa chip'apkiŏgŭi palmyŏng," *Konggan'gwa sahoe*, 199, 203–206; Kim Chŏng-dong, *Nama innŭn yŏksa, sarajinŭn kŏnch'ungmul*, 193–196; Henry, *Assimilating Seoul*, 62–91.
213. *Kukyŏk kyŏngsŏngbusa*, vol. 2, 217.
214. Yi Kŭm-to, *Chosŏnch'ongdokpu kŏnch'ukkiguŭi kŏnch'uksaŏpkwa ilbonin ch'ŏngbuŏpchae kwanhan yŏn'gu*, Ph.D. diss. (Busan National University, 2007), 51; Son Chŏng-mok, *Ilchegangjŏmgi toshisahoesang yŏn'gu* (Seoul: Ilchisa, 1996), 520–528; Yi and Kim, "20segi ch'o han'gugesŏ hwaltonghan ilbonin," *Tae han'gŏnch'uk'ak'oeyŏnhamnonmunjip*, 62.

215. Kim, *Nama innŭn yŏksa, sarajinŭn kŏnch'ungmul*, 199.
216. Takehiko Hirose, *Königlich preußischer Baurat Georg de Lalande* (Borsdorf: winterwork, 2012), 234 ff.
217. Hŏ Yŏng-sŏp suspects that although this German architect may have pretended to be Prussian in Japan, he actually claimed to be from Poland under Prussian rule and must have felt a sense of shame from working for a colonial ruler. Hŏ also suggests that such internal torment may have been what caused the architect's early death. See Hŏ Yŏng-sŏp, *Ilbon, chosŏnch'ongdokpurŭl seuda* (Seoul: Ch'aeryun, 2010), 105–109. But this view is contrary to the content of Takehiko Hirose's *Königlich preußischer Baurat Georg de Lalande*, the book detailing the life and activities of the German architect.
218. Son, *Ilchegangjŏmgi toshisahoesang yŏn'gu*, 529–530; Michiko Meid, *Europäische und nordamerikanische Architektur in Japan seit 1542* (Cologne: Abteilung Architektur des Kunsthistorischen Instituts Köln, 1977), 266–268; Ha, *Kwanghwamunŭi chŏngch'ihak*, 87.
219. Pak, "Chosŏnhwangjeŭi aedalp'ŭn yŏksarŭl chŭngmyŏnghada," 80–81; Chŏng Yŏng-hyo, "Chosŏnhot'el: Chegugŭi isanggwa shingminji chosŏnŭi p'yosang," *Han'gugŏmunhakyŏn'gu* 55 (2010): 320; Kim Chŏng-dong, "Toraehan sŏyangin kŏnch'ukkae kwanhan yŏn'gu," *Taehan'gŏnch'uk'ak'oenonmunjip kyehoekkye*, 84; Yi, *Sont'ak'ot'el*, 115–120; Nishizawa, *Nippon shokuminchi kenchikuron*, 269.
220. Kon Wajirō, "Sōtokufu shinchōsa wa rokotsu sugi," *Chōsen to kenchiku* 2, no. 4 (1923): 17–19.
221. Yi Hyo-sŏk, "Pyŏkkongmuhan," *The Complete Works of Yi Hyo-sŏk*, vol. 5 (1941; Seoul: Ch'angmisa, 1983), 186; Yu Chin-o, *Hwasangbo* (Seoul: Hansŏngdosŏjushik'oesa, 1941). See the argument in Chŏng, "Chosŏnhot'el: Chegugŭi isanggwa shingminji chosŏnŭi p'yosang," 317–348.
222. Kim, "Toraehan sŏyangin kŏnch'ukkae kwanhan yŏn'gu," *Taehan'gŏnch'uk'ak'oenonmunjip kyehoekkye*, 84–85.
223. Hirose, *Königlich preußischer Baurat Georg de Lalande*, 23–24.
224. On the comparison between General-Government buildings in Taiwan and Korea, see Chu-joe Hsia, "Theorizing colonial architecture and urbanism," *Inter-Asia Cultural Studies*, 10–12.
225. Son, *Ilchegangjŏmgi toshisahoesang yŏn'gu*, 520–557; Hashiya, *Ilbonjegukchuŭi*, 117–120; Kim, *Nama innŭn yŏksa, sarajinŭn kŏnch'ungmul*, 183–252, 217; *Chosŏnch'ongdokpu ch'ŏngsa shinyŏngji*, 56.
226. Son, *Ilchegangjŏmgi toshisahoesang yŏn'gu*, 552.
227. *Chōsen to kenchiku* reported that the building was located at a distance of 46 kan from the Kwanghwamun Gate and 17 kan from the front of Kŭnjŏngmun Gate. See Fujioka Shigekazu, "Shinch'ŏngsaŭi kyehoekkaeyo," in *Chosŏn'gwa kŏnch'uk, che5ho: Chosŏnch'ongdokpuch'ŏngsaho*, trans. (from Japanese into Korean) Kim Tong-hyŏn (1926; Seoul: National Museum of Korea, 1995), 31.
228. Chŏng Un-hyŏn, *Sŏulshinae ilcheyusandapsagi* (Seoul: Hanul, 1996), 56; Cho, *Kunggwŏl, chosŏnŭl marhada*, 117–118; Yi, *Kwanghwamun yukchoapkil*, 192–194; Hong, *Ilcheŭi shingmin ch'imt'algwa kyŏngbokkung hweson*, 25–26.
229. Fujioka, "Shinch'ŏngsaŭi kyehoekkaeyo," 31; *Chosŏnch'ongdokpu ch'ŏngsa shinyŏngji*, 56.
230. *Chosŏnch'ongdokpu ch'ŏngsa shinyŏngji*, 60–67.
231. Yim Kyŏng-il, "Munhwagigwan'gwa kyŏngsŏng," *Chogwang* 6, no. 9 (1940), in Busan National University, *Han'gung kŭndaeŭi p'unggyŏnggwa chiyŏgŭi palgyŏn*, 117; Yi, *T'onggamgwanjŏ*, 51–56.
232. National Museum of Korea, *Ku Ch'ongdokpu kŏnmul shilch'ŭk mit ch'ŏlgŏ pogosŏ*, 39; *Chosŏnch'ongdokpu ch'ŏngsa shinyŏngji*, 57; Ha, "Kwanghwamunŭi chŏngch'ihak," 88.
233. Iwai Chōzaburō, "Shinch'ŏngsaŭi kyehoege taehayŏ," in *Chosŏn'gwa kŏnch'uk, che5ho*, 29.

234. *Chosŏnch'ongdokpu ch'ŏngsa shinyŏngji*, 57.
235. Chang Gi-in, "Chosŏnch'ongdokpu ch'ŏngsa," *Kŏnch'uk* 35, no. 2 (1991): 44–50; Song, "Kunggwŏre tŭrŏsŏn kŭndae kŏnch'ungmul," 240–279. Georg de Lalande originally designed a thoroughly German roof, but the design was later modified into the shape of a Japanese-style cupola. See Kim, *Nama innŭn yŏksa, sarajinŭn kŏnch'ungmul*, 210.
236. Nishizawa, *Nippon shokuminchi kenchikuron*, 80–86.
237. Kim, *Nama innŭn yŏksa, sarajinŭn kŏnch'ungmul*, 200.
238. Yim, *Sahoemihakŭro ingnŭn kaehwagi-ilchegangjŏmgi sŏul kŏnch'uk*, 191.
239. *Chosŏnch'ongdokpu ch'ŏngsa shinyŏngji*, 63; "Hikarikamon iten to sono ato kōji," *Chōsen to kenchiku* 5, no. 9 (1926): 39–40; "Kyongbokku, Hikarikamon no iten kōji," *Chōsen to kenchiku* 5, no. 10 (1926): 56; Yi, "Ilcheshidae kyŏngbokkung chubyŏndoroŭi pyŏnhwawa Kungjangŭi hwech'ŏl," 67–88.
240. The column was published in five installments between August 24 and 28, 1922. The full column, including parts that were edited out from *Dong-a Ilbo*, was published through the Japanese monthly magazine *Kaizō* in September of the same year. See Yanagi Muneyoshi, "Changch'a ilk'edoen chosŏnŭi han kŏnch'ukŭl wihaya 1–5," *Dong-a Ilbo* 726–730 (1922), p. A1. This column was also published in his work *Chōsen to geijutsu* (1922). See Yanagi Muneyoshi, "Ah, kwanghwamuniyŏ," in *Chosŏn'gwa yesul* (Seoul: Pŏmumun'go, 1989), 99–111.
241. On this point, see, notably, Yŏm Un-ok, "Yanagi muneyoshiwa orient'al orient'allijŭm," *Yŏksawa munhwa* 14 (2007): 235–252. For an overall view on Yanagi's thought, see Ōkubo Takaki, *Ilbonmunhwaronŭi kyebo*, trans. (from Japanese into Korean) Song Sŏk-wŏn (Seoul: Sohwa, 2012), 101–120, quoted from Yanagi, "Changch'a ilk'edoen chosŏnŭi han kŏnch'ukŭl wihaya 1," *Dong-a Ilbo* 726, p. A1.
242. Ha, *Kwanghwamun'gwa chŏngch'igwŏllyŏk*, 172.
243. Yi, "Sŏul kŭndae toshigyŏnggwan ikki," 18.
244. For a similar argument, see Kim, "Collective Memory and Commemorative Space," *International Area Review* 9.
245. Yoshimura Tadashi, *Keijō annai* (Keijō: Chōsen hakurankai keijō kyōsankai, 1929), 25.
246. Yi, *Kwanghwamun yukchoapkil*, 173 ff., 195 ff.
247. Yi, "Ilcheshidae kyŏngbokkung chubyŏndoroŭi pyŏnhwawa Kungjangŭi hwech'ŏl," 87; Ch'oe, "Ilcheshigi kyŏngsŏngŭi toshigongganŭl t'onghae pon chŏnch'anosŏnŭi pyŏnhwa," *Sŏurhakyŏn'gu*, 45.
248. Kim Paek-yŏng, "Shingmin'gwŏllyŏkkwa kwangjanggonggan: Ilcheha sŏulshinae kwangjangŭi hyŏngsŏnggwa hwaryong," *Sahoewa yŏksa* 90 (2011): 298.
249. Pak Se-hun, "Tongwŏndoen kŭndae: Ilcheshigi kyŏngsŏngŭl t'onghae pon shingminji kŭndaesŏng," *Han'gukkŭndaemisulsahak* 13 (2004): 119–149, focuses on the colonial aspect of mobilization. On the urban development centered on Sŏnŭnjŏn Square, see notably Yŏm, *llche ha Kyŏngsŏng tosi kyehoekŭi gusangkwa silhang*, 34 ff.
250. *Kukyŏk kyŏngsŏngbusa*, vol. 2, 265; Yi, *T'onggamgwanjŏ*, 320–335.
251. Yi Sun-ja, *Ilchegangjŏmgi kojŏkchosasaŏm yŏn'gu*, Ph.D. diss. (Sookmyung Women's University, 2007), 26, 45; U Tong-sŏn, "Sek'ino tadashiŭi han'gung kogŏnch'uk chosawa pojone taehan yŏn'gu," *Taehan'gŏnch'uk'ak'oenonmunjip kyehoekkye* 22, no. 7 (2006): 135–146. See also Inaga Shigemi, *Kaiga no rinkai: Kindai Higashiajia bijutsushi no shikkoku to meiun* (Nagoya: Nagoya University Press, 2014), 355–372.
252. Takagi Hiroshi, "Ilbon misulsawa chōsen misulsaŭi sŏngnip," in *Kuksaŭi shinhwarŭl nŏmŏsŏ*, ed. Yim Ji-hyŏn and Yi Sŏng-si (Seoul: Humanist, 2004), 170–175. According to Takagi, the lecture on Japanese art history that Okakura Kakuzō gave at the Tokyo School of Arts had not yet been published into a book at the time. The lecture was first published in 1922 as part of *The*

Collected Works of Okakura Tenshin (Okakura Tenshin zenshū) by the Japanese visual arts academy *Nihon Bijutsuin*. Ibid., 172, 175.

253. Arai Shinichi, *Yakt'almunhwajaenŭn nuguŭi kŏshin'ga: Ilcheŭi munhwajae panch'ulgwa shingminjuŭi ch'ŏngsanŭi kil*, trans. (from Japanese into Korean) Yi T'ae-chin and Kim Ŭn-chu (Paju: T'aehaksa, 2014), 63–79; Cultural Heritage Administration (Munhwajaech'ŏng), ed., *Kyŏngbokkung pyŏnch'ŏnsa: Kyŏngbokkung pyŏnch'ŏn kwajŏng mit chihyŏngbunsŏk haksulchosa yŏn'guyongyŏk*, vol. 2 (2007), 28–29.
254. Kim, *Nama innŭn yŏksa, sarajinŭn kŏnch'ungmul*, 190–192.
255. Kuksap'yŏnch'anwiwŏnhoe, ed., Volume 5 of *Kojongshidaesa: Kwangmu 4–7nyŏn*, July 17, 1902 (Seoul: Kuksap'yŏnch'anwiwŏnhoe, 1971).
256. *The Veritable Records of Emperor Sunjong*, vol. 2, February 1, 1911, Appendix.
257. National Museum of Korea, *Ku Ch'ongdokpu kŏnmul shilch'ŭk mit ch'ŏlgŏ pogosŏ*, 342; Son Chŏng-mok, *Han'guk'yŏndaedoshiŭi palchach'wi* (Seoul: Ilchisa, 1989), 66–69. On the construction and utilization of the Pakmunsa Temple, see Mizuno Naoki, "Shingminji chosŏnesŏŭi it'o hirobumiŭi kiŏk: Sŏurŭi pangmunsarŭl chungshimŭro," in *Han'gukkwa it'o hirobumi*, ed. Yi Sŏng-hwan and Itō Yukio (Seoul: Sŏnin, 2009), 369–401.
258. *Dong-a Ilbo*, "'Ilche kyŏngbokkung ŏpsaeryŏ haetta': Chŏngbugirokpojonso 'sŏlgyedomyŏn' palgyŏn," December 28, 1995, p. A47. *Layout of the Kyŏngbokgung Palace Site and Buildings* (1916) is documented by the Cultural Heritage Administration (Munhwajaech'ŏng), *Kyŏngbokgung pyŏnch'ŏnsa: Kyŏngbokgung pyŏnch'ŏn kwajŏng mit chihyŏngpunsŏk haksulchosa yŏn'guyongyŏk*, vol. 2 (2007), 171. Online access to this layout is available, www.albummania.co.kr/gallery/view.asp?seq=82948&path=&rpage=183 (accessed January 15, 2020).
259. Kim, *Nama innŭn yŏksa, sarajinŭn kŏnch'ungmul*, 201–202; Kim, "Ilchegangjŏm ihu," *Sŏurhakyŏn'gu*, 107–115.
260. Yi, "Ilcheshidae kyŏngbokkung chubyŏndoroŭi pyŏnhwawa Kungjangŭi hwech'ŏl," 77–80; Yi Sun-u, *T'erauch'i ch'ongdok, chosŏnŭi kkoch'i toeda* (Seoul: Hanŭlchae, 2004), 124–134.
261. Quoted from Yoshimura, *Keijō annai*, 16–17, 31. See also Cho, *Kunggwŏl, chosŏnŭl marhada*, 250–251; Hwang Ki-wŏn, "Sŏul 20segi kongwŏnt'mnokchiŭi pyŏnch'ŏn: Chayŏn sogŭi toshiesŏ toshi sogŭi chayŏnŭro," in *Sŏul 20segi konggan pyŏnch'ŏnsa*, 396–400; Chŏng Chae-chŏng, *Tŏksugung chubyŏn kŭndaehwaŭi chach'wi: Sŏurŭi munhwayusan t'ambanggi* (Seoul: Sŏurhakyŏn'guso, 1997), 264.
262. Kang Sin-yong and Chang Yun-hwan, *Han'gukkŭndae toshigongwŏnsa* (Seoul: Taewangsa, 2004), 165–205.
263. Henry, "Respatializing Chŏson's Royal Capital," 23.
264. Chu Yun-chŏng, "Chosŏnmulsan'gongjinhoewa shingminjuŭiŭi shisŏn," *Munhwagwahak* 33 (2003): 159.
265. Sin Chu-paek, "Pangnamhoe, kwashi, sŏnjŏn, kyemong, sobiŭi ch'ehŏmgonggan," *Yŏksabip'yŏng* 67 (2004): 357–394; Kim Yŏng-hŭi, "Chosŏnbangnamhoewa shingminji kŭndae," *Tongbanghakchi* 140 (2007): 221–267; Yoshimi Shun'ya, *Pangnamhoe kŭndaeŭi shisŏn*, trans. (from Japanese into Korean) Yi T'ae-mun (Seoul: Nonhyŏng, 2004), 210–248.
266. Jong-Heon Jin, "Demolishing Colony: The Demolition of the Old Government-General Building of Chosŏn," in *Sitings: Critical Approach to Korean Geography*, ed. Timothy R. Tangherlini and Sallie Yea (Honolulu, HI: University of Hawai'i Press, 2008), 43; Nakane Takayuki, *Chōsen p'yosangŭi munhwaji: Kŭndae ilbon'gwa t'ajarŭl tullŏssan chiŭi shingminjihwa*, trans. (from Japanese into Korean) Konkuk University graduate school ilbonmunhwaŏnŏhakkwa (Seoul: Somyŏngch'ulp'an, 2011).
267. Carol Breckenridge, "The Aesthetics and Politics of Colonial Collecting: India at World Fairs," *Comparative Studies in Society and History* 31, no. 2 (1989):

195–216, esp. 200–201; Yoshida Kenji, *Bunka no hakken* (Tokyo: Iwanami shoten, 1999), 35. According to Yoshida, Tokyo National Museum's ethnographic collection reflects the duality of "looked" and "looking" accompanied by empire's colonial rule. Quoted from *Bunka no hakken*, 94.

268. Chu, "Chosŏnmulsan'gongjinhoewa shingminjuŭiŭi shisŏn," *Munhwagwahak*, 145–160.
269. Kim Che-chŏng, "Shingminjigi pangnamhoe yŏn'gu shigakkwa chiyŏksŏng," *Toshiyŏn'gu: Yŏksa, sahoe, munhwa* 9 (2013): 7–32.
270. Yi, *T'onggamgwanjŏ*, 53.
271. Kim Yŏng-hŭi, "Chosŏnbangnamhoewa shingminji kŭndae," *Tongbanghakchi* 140 (2007): 224–228; Ch'oe Sŏk-yŏng, *Han'gung kŭndaeŭi pangnamhoe, ppangmulgwan* (Seoul: Sŏgyŏngmunhwasa, 2001), 49–60; Kang, *Ichegangjŏmgi kŭndaeshisŏrŭi modŏnijŭm suyong*, 62–86.
272. "Kugungaesa," *Samch'ŏlli* 3, no. 10 (1931), in Volume 3 of *Han'gung kŭndaeŭi p'unggyŏnggwa chiyŏgŭi palgyŏn*, 252–256.
273. *Dong-a Ilbo*, "Hŏllyŏjinnŭn kwanghwamun," vol. 2129, August 11, 1926, p. A3.
274. Regarding the formation of colonial rule system and introduction of modern facilities, see Chu Sang-hun, *Chosŏnch'ongdokpuŭi kŭndae shisŏl kŏllipkwa kŏnch'ukkyehoegŭi t'ŭkching*, Ph.D. diss. (Seoul National University, 2010), 70–152.
275. Sin Ye-kyŏng and Kim Chin-kyun, "20segi ihu sŏul toshim nae chuyo konggonggŏnch'ugŭi hyŏngsŏng mit kongganjŏk t'ŭksŏng: Sŏulshich'ŏng, sŏulchunganguch'eguk, sŏuryŏkŭl chungshimŭro," *Taehan'gŏnch'uk'ak'oenonmunjip kyehoekkye* 25, no. 4 (2009): 109.
276. Chu, *Chosŏnch'ongdokpuŭi kŭndae shisŏl*, 255–363.
277. *(Ku han'guk) Kwanbo*, "Ch'ingnyŏng 55: Kŏnch'ukso kwanje," September 28, 1906, p. A16; Nishizawa, *Nippon shokuminchi kenchikuron*, 38–41.
278. Yi, *Chosŏnch'ongdokpu kŏnch'ukkiguŭi kŏnch'uksaŏpkwa ilbonin*, 51, 32–39; Yi Kŭm-to, "Chosŏnch'ongdokpu yŏngsŏn chojik," in *Han'gukkŏnch'ukkaenyŏmsajŏn*, 736–738; Yi Kŭm-to and Sŏ Ch'i-sang, "Chosŏnch'ongdokpu kŏnch'ukkiguŭi chojikkwa chigwŏne kwanhan yŏn'gu," *Taehan'gŏnch'uk'ak'oenonmunjip kyehoekkye* 23, no. 4 (2007): 138; Kim T'ae-chung, "T'akchibu kŏnch'ukso," in *Han'gukkŏnch'ukkaenyŏmsajŏn*, 808–810.
279. See the argument in Kang, *Ichegangjŏmgi kŭndaeshisŏrŭi modŏnijŭm suyong*.
280. Yim, *Sahoemihakŭro ingnŭn kaehwagi-ilchegangjŏmgi sŏul kŏnch'uk*, 191 ff.
281. Yi and Kim, "20segi ch'o han'gugesŏ hwaltonghan ilbonin," *Taehan'gŏnch'uk'ak'oeyŏnhamnonmunjip*, 60.
282. Yi Sun-ja, *Chosŏnŭi sumgyŏjin wangga iyagi* (Seoul: P'yŏngdanmunhwasa, 2013), 139–141; Yun, *Han'guk yangshikkŏnch'uk 80nyŏnsa*, 84–85.
283. Yim, *Sahoemihakŭro ingnŭn kaehwagi-ilchegangjŏmgi sŏul kŏnch'uk*, 163 ff.; Yim Sŏk-chae, *Sŏul, kŏnch'ugŭi toshirŭl kŏtta*, vol. 1 (Seoul: Inmulgwasasangsa, 2010), 400–405; Nishizawa, *Nippon shokuminchi kenchikuron*, 203–204.
284. Yi, *T'onggamgwanjŏ*, 12–37; Kim, *Nama innŭn yŏksa, sarajinŭn kŏnch'ungmul*, 194.
285. Stewart, *The Making of a Modern Japanese Architecture*. 62.
286. Dallas Finn, *Meiji Revisited: The Sites of Victorian Japan* (New York, NY: Weatherhill, 1995), 185–186. As the construction was delayed by the Russo-Japanese War, the prince postponed accepting the gift.
287. Kim, *Nama innŭn yŏksa, sarajinŭn kŏnch'ungmul*, 194.
288. Cho Tong-kŏl, *Shingminji chosŏnŭi nongminundong* (Seoul: Yŏksagonggan, 2010), 134 ff., 210 ff.
289. Yun In-sŏk, "Namch'onŭi kŭndae kŏnch'ungmul," in Kim, *Sŏul namch'on*, 134.
290. Finn, *Meiji Revisited*, 192–194; Nishizawa, *Nippon shokuminchi kenchikuron*, 166–168. Tsumaki Yorinaka designed the Yokohama Specie Bank's Dalian branch between the completion of the Yokohama Specie Bank building and the Oriental

Development Company's Keijō branch. Built at Zhongshan Square in 1909, the Yokohama Specie Bank's Dalian branch Tsumaki jointly designed with Ota Tsuyoshi assumed a more simplified German neo-Renaissance style compared to the buildings raised to its front and back. On this point, see Nishizawa, *Nippon shokuminchi kenchikuron*, 131–135.

291. Son, *Ilche kangjŏmgi toshigyehoek yŏn'gu*, 110–111.
292. Kim, *Chibaewa konggan*, 66–67.
293. *Kukyŏk kyŏngsŏngbusa*, vol. 2, 252–253; Yi, *Chosŏnŭi sumgyŏjin wangga iyagi*, 160–165, 169–171; Song, "Kunggwŏre tŭrŏsŏn kŭndae kŏnch'ungmul," 275.
294. Yim, *Sahoemihakŭro ingnŭn kaehwagi-ilchegangjŏmgi sŏul kŏnch'uk*, 218–223; Nishizawa, *Nippon shokuminchi kenchikuron*, 124–131.
295. Chŏng Chae-chŏng, *Sŏul kŭnhyŏndae yŏksagihaeng* (Seoul: Sŏurhakyŏn'guso, 1996), 164–166.
296. Sin and Kim, "20segi ihu sŏul toshim nae chuyo konggonggŏnch'ugŭi hyŏngsŏng," *Taehan'gŏnch'uk'ak'oenonmunjip kyehoekkye*, 110–111; Yun, *Han'guk yangshikkŏnch'uk 80nyŏnsa*, 109–110.
297. Kim Chong-rok, *Kŭndaerŭl sanch'aek'ada* (Paju: Tasanch'odang, 2012), 300–309; KORAIL, *Sajinŭro ponŭn haebang ijŏnŭi ch'ŏlto yŏksa* (Seoul: Ch'ŏltoch'ŏng, 2003), 90.
298. Yun, *Han'guk yangshikkŏnch'uk 80nyŏnsa*, 112–113.
299. Yim, *Sahoemihakŭro ingnŭn kaehwagi-ilchegangjŏmgi sŏul kŏnch'uk*, 228–233; Nishizawa, *Nippon shokuminchi kenchikuron*, 240–241.
300. Sin and Kim, "20segi ihu sŏul toshim," *Taehan'gŏnch'uk'ak'oenonmunjip kyehoekkye*, 113, 117.
301. Sŏult'ŭkpyŏlshisap'yŏnch'anwiwŏnhoe, ed., *Sŏulgŏnch'uksa*, 637–638; Yi and Kim, "20segi ch'o han'gugesŏ hwaltonghan ilbonin," *Taehan'gŏnch'uk'ak'oeyŏn hamnonmunjip*, 60.
302. Chu, *Chosŏnch'ongdokpuŭi kŭndae shisŏl*, 234, 238–251; Yim, *Sahoemihakŭro ingnŭn kaehwagi-ilchegangjŏmgi sŏul kŏnch'uk*, 209–217, defines this building's style as "neo-Romanesque" on account of its unique combination of arches and orders. See esp. 212.
303. Yŏm, "Shingminji toshigyehoegŭi yusan'gwa kŭe taehan inshik"; Son, "'*Ilche kangjŏmgi toshigyehoek yŏn'gu*'rŭl chungshimŭro," *Han'guksayŏn'gu*, 408.
304. Kim, *Chibaewa konggan*, 123.
305. Nishizawa, *Nippon shokuminchi kenchikuron*, 244–246.
306. Chŏng, *Sŏulshinae ilcheyusandapsagi*, 170–171.
307. Yŏm Pok-kyu, "Shingminjigŭndaeŭi konggan hyŏngsŏng: Kŭndae sŏurŭi toshigyehoekkwa toshigongganŭi hyŏngsŏng, pyŏnyong, hwakchang," *Munhwagwahak* 39 (2004): 197–219.
308. Kim, "Sangjinggongganŭi pyŏnyonggwa chip'apkiŏgŭi palmyŏng," *Konggan'gwa sahoe*, 208.
309. Kim, *Chibaewa konggan*, 123; *Sŏulgŏnch'uksa*, 597–601.
310. Modernist architecture was introduced for the first time in Seoul by Fujishima Kaijiro, a professor of Keijō High Technical School. In 1925, he published a series of architectural notes in *Chōsen to kenchiku*. See the argument in Kim Yong-pŏm, "1920–1930nyŏndae kyŏngsŏngŭi kŭndae kŏnch'uk'waltonge kwanhan kich'oyŏn'gu: *Chōsen to kenchiku*ŭi chappogisarŭl chungshimŭro," *Sŏurhakyŏn'gu* 42 (2011): 1–48.
311. *Sŏulgŏnch'uksa*, 637; Yim, *Sahoemihakŭro ingnŭn kaehwagi-ilchegangjŏmgi sŏul kŏnch'uk*, 193 ff.; Sŏult'ŭkpyŏlshisap'yŏnch'anwiwŏnhoe, ed., *Sŏul yukpaengnyŏnsa*, vol. 4 (1977), 353–357.
312. *Chōsen to kenchiku* 5, no. 10, Keijōfuchōsa shinchiku kinenhen (1926): 2–41; Kim Myŏng-sŏn and Bak Chŏng-tae, "Ilchegangjŏmgi toch'ŏngsa, puch'ŏngsa kŏllibŭi paegyŏnggwa sŏnggyŏk," *Taehan'gŏnch'uk'ak'oenonmunjip kyehoekkye* 24, no. 2 (2008): 199–205; Son, *Ilchegangjŏmgi toshisahoesang yŏn'gu*, 557–587.

313. Chu Sang-hun, "Shingminji t'ongch'i shisŏl," *Han'gukkŏnch'ukkaenyŏmsajŏn*, 591.
314. Kim, "1920–1930nyŏndae kyŏngsŏngŭi kŭndae kŏnch'uk'waltonge kwanhan kich'oyŏn'gu," *Sŏurhakyŏn'gu*, 44.
315. Yun, "Namch'onŭi kŭndae kŏnch'ungmul," 138–139; Jung-gu District of Seoul, ed., *Yet cheilŭnhaeng ponjŏm: Chŏngmil shilch'ŭkchosa pogosŏ* (Seoul: Jung-gu, 2010), 87, 73.
316. Jung-gu District of Seoul, ed., *Yet cheilŭnhaeng ponjŏm*, 90, 120.
317. Yim Sŏk-chae, *Sahoemihakŭro ingnŭn kaehwagi-ilchegangjŏmgi sŏul kŏnch'uk*, 237, evaluates the Chōsen Savings Bank as "totalitarian."
318. Fujimori Terunobu, Volume 2 of *Nihon no kindai kenchiku: Taisei-Shōwahen* (Tokyo: Iwanami shinsho, 2010), 87–92, 99–100; Sawai Reiichi, "Hirokōji ni sobieru matenrō," *Nagoya hirokōji mono gatari dai*, 4. Lecture of Taishō jidai no hirokōji, dai4kai, Web site, http://network2010.org/article/1103 (accessed January 15, 2020).
319. Son Chŏng-mok, "I. T'aep'yŏngno ilkaŭi kyŏngsŏng pumin'gwan," in Sejongmunhwahoegwan chŏnsa p'yŏnjibwiwŏnhoe, *Sejongmunhwahoegwan chŏnsa* (Seoul: Sejong Center for the Performing Arts, 2002), 71; Hagihara Kōichi, "Fuminkan no kōji ni tsuchōte," *Chōsen to kenchiku* 15, no. 3 (1936): 6.
320. Yim, *Sahoemihakŭro ingnŭn kaehwagi-ilchegangjŏmgi sŏul kŏnch'uk*, 238–241; *Sŏulgŏnch'uksa*, 725–727.
321. Kim Ho-yŏl, "1930nyŏndae sŏul chuminŭi munhwasuyonge kwanhan yŏn'gu: Pumin'gwanŭl chungshimŭro," *Sŏurhakyŏn'gu* 15 (2000): 201.
322. The Waseda University Ōkuma Memorial Hall is a geometric abstraction of historicism that Satō Kōichi designed in 1927. The tower at one corner of the building bears a great resemblance to the Keijō Public Hall. For further details on the memorial hall, see Fujimori, Volume 2 of *Nihon no kindai kenchiku*, 110–111.
323. Thomas Nipperdey, *Deutsche Geschichte 1866–1918: Arbeitswelt und Bürgergeist* (Munich: C. H. Beck, 1990), 718; Christa Schreiber, "Das Berliner Rathaus: Versuch einer Entstehungs-und Ideengeschichte," in *Das Rathaus im Kaiserreich: Kunstpolitische Aspekte einer Bauaufgabe des 19. Jahrhunderts*, ed. Ekkehard Mai et al. (Berlin: Mann, Gebr., 1982), 91–150.
324. On the colonial nature of such squares, see Kim, "Shingmin'gwŏllyŏkkwa kwangjanggonggan," *Sahoewa yŏksa*, 271–311, esp. 300–301.
325. Yun Tae-sŏk, "Kyŏngsŏngŭi kongganbunhalgwa chŏngshinbunyŏl," *Kugŏgungmunhak* 144 (2006): 91–112; Cho Ŭn-ae, "Shingmindoshiŭi sangjinggwa chanyŏ: Yŏm Sang-sŏp sosŏrŭi chaegyŏngsŏng ilbonin, kŭ chaehyŏn(pul) kanŭngŭi changsodŭl," *Han'gungmunhang iron'gwa pip'yŏng* 57 (2012): 454–459.
326. Yi Kwang-su, "Taegyŏngsŏnghoesanggok: Chuinjotch'a kŭriun ishimnyŏnchŏnŭi kyŏngsŏng," *Pyŏlgŏn'gon* 18 (1929), in Volume 3 of *Han'guk kŭndaeŭi p'unggyŏnggwa chiyŏgŭi palgyŏn*, 163–168, quoted from 168.
327. "Taegyŏngsŏngŭi kŭndaegŏnch'ungmul chŏnmang," *Samch'ŏlli* 7, no. 8 (1935): 129–130; "Taegyŏngsŏng ppilting kŏnch'ukp'yŏng," *Samch'ŏlli* 7, no. 9 (1935): 178–182.
328. Todd A. Henry, "Sanitizing Empire: Japanese Articulations of Korean Otherness and the Construction of Early Colonial Seoul, 1905–1919," *The Journal of Asian Studies* 64, no. 3 (2005): 664–666; Hyung Il Pai, "Navigating Modern Keijō: The Typology of Reference Guides and City Landmarks," *Sŏurhakyŏn'gu* 44 (2011): 1–40.
329. *Kukyŏk kyŏngsŏngbusa*, vol. 3, 265; Yi Sŏng-si, "Chosŏnwangjoŭi sangjing konggan'gwa pangmulgwan," 265–295, confirms that the museum building was designed by Georg de Lalande, who also designed the Government-General Building. Governor-General Terauchi Masatake was the one who ordered the building to be built in the first place and designated it as a permanent museum after the exhibition. See esp. 278 and footnote 29.

330. *Sŏulgŏnch'uksa*, 720.
331. Yoshimura, *Keijō annai*, 26. On the exhibitions of the Government-General Museum, see Mok Su-hyŏn, *Ilcheha pangmulgwanŭi hyŏngsŏnggwa kŭ ŭimi*, Master's thesis (Seoul National University, 2000), 44–50.
332. Nishizawa, *Nippon shokuminchi kenchikuron*, 225–226; Song, "Kunggwŏre tŭrŏsŏn kŭndae kŏnch'ungmul," 266–267.
333. Ch'oe, *Han'gung kŭndaeŭi pangnamhoe, ppangmulgwan*, 105–109.
334. *Dong-a Ilbo*, "Chonghappangmulgwan kŏnsŏlgyehoengnaeyong," September 5, 1934, p. A1; Nishizawa, *Nippon shokuminchi kenchikuron*, 225–226.
335. Mok Su-hyŏn, "Ilcheha iwanggabangmulgwanŭi shingminjijŏk sŏnggyŏng," *Misulsahakyŏn'gu* 227 (2000): 99–101; Song, "Kunggwŏre tŭrŏsŏn kŭndae kŏnch'ungmul," 257–258.
336. Kim, *Kojonghwangjega saranghan chŏngdonggwa tŏksugung*, 108–109, 235; Yi, "Chosŏnwangjoŭi sangjing konggan'gwa pangmulgwan," 285–292.
337. Nishizawa, "Kenchikuka Nakamura Yoshihei," *Nippon kenchiku gakkai keikakukei ronbun hōkokushū*, 154–157; Nishizawa, *Nippon shokuminchi kenchikuron*, 226–229; Kim, "Nak'amura yoshiheiŭi sŏyang kŏnch'ukyangshigŭi suyonggwajŏnggwa kŭ ŭimi," *Taehan'gŏnch'uk'ak'oenonmunjip kyehoekkye*, 163–164, 167–168.
338. Kim, *Nama innŭn yŏksa, sarajinŭn kŏnch'ungmul*, 227–231. The name "Chungangch'ŏng" is known to be the translation of American Capitol Hall by Chŏng In-bo, a representative intellectual of the time. See Kim, "Ilchegangjŏm ihu," *Sŏurhakyŏn'gu*, 116–117.
339. Hashiya, *Ilbonjegukchuŭi*, 137–139.
340. Yi and Kim, "Sŏul toshigyŏnggwanŭi pyŏnch'ŏn kwajŏng yŏn'gu," *Sŏurhakyŏn'gu*, 34–37.
341. Alfred Ndi, "Metropolitanism, Capital and Patrimony," in *Postcolonial African Cities: Imperial Legacies and Postcolonial Predicaments*, ed. Fassil Demissie (New York, NY: Routledge, 2013), 11–23; Jane M. Jacobs, *Edge of Empire: Postcolonialism and the City* (New York, NY: Routledge, 1996), 29–34.
342. Chungmoo Choi, "The Discourse of Decolonization and Popular Memory: South Korea," in *Formations of Colonial Modernity in East Asia*, ed. Tani E. Barlow (Durham, NC: Duke University Press, 1997), 349–372; Fassil Demissie, "Imperial Legacies and Postcolonial Predicaments: An Introduction," in *Postcolonial African Cities*, ed. Demissie, 1–9.
343. To Myŏn-hoe, "Omkiniŭi kŭl: T'alminjokchuŭi kwanjŏmesŏ parabon shingminji shigi yŏksa," in *Han'gugŭi shingminji kŭndaesŏng: Naejaejŏk palchŏllon'gwa shingminji kŭndaehwaronŭl nŏmŏsŏ*, ed. Gi-Wook Shin and Michael Robinson, trans. To Myŏn-hoe (Seoul: Samin, 2006), 16–20. See also Yi Sŭng-il et al., *Ilbonŭi shingminji chibaewa shingminjijŏk kŭndae* (Seoul: Tongbugayŏksajaedan, 2009); Keith Pratt, *Everlasting Flower: A History of Korea* (London: Reaktion Books, 2007), 218–223.
344. Jong-Heon Jin, "Demolishing Colony," 53.
345. Kim, *Nama innŭn yŏksa, sarajinŭn kŏnch'ungmul*, 233; Son, *Ilchegangjŏmgi toshisahoesang yŏn'gu*, 558.
346. Kim, "Ilchegangjŏm ihu," *Sŏurhakyŏn'gu*, 117.
347. *Sŏulgŏnch'uksa*, 940–944; Yi, *Kwanghwamun yukchoapkil*, 371–373.
348. Yi, *Kwanghwamun yukchoapkil*, 369.
349. An Ch'ang-mo, "Haebang ihu sŏurŭi toshigyehoekkwa toshi-kŏnch'ugŭi pyŏnhwa," in *Sŏul, peijing, sanghai, tok'yoŭi taedoshiroŭi sŏngjanggwajŏng pigyoyŏn'gu I*, 75–77, 54–55, 82–83; *Sŏulgŏnch'uksa*, 818–824, 827–829; Son Chŏng-mok, *Sŏul toshigyehoeg iyagi: Sŏul kyŏktongŭi 50nyŏn'gwa naŭi chŭngŏn*, vol. 1 (Paju: Hanul, 2003), 89–138, 252–286. On the population change of Seoul, see Kwŏn Yong-u, *Sudogwŏnŭi ihae* (Seoul: Posŏnggak, 1999), 73;

Son Chŏng-mok, *Sŏul toshigyehoeg iyagi*, vol. 4 (Seoul: Hanul, 2003), 289; Kim Ŭi-wŏn, "Urinara Tojiguhoekjŏngrisaŏbŭi doib kwa jŏn'gae," *Tosimunje* 18, no. 2 (1983): 20.

350. Son, *Sŏul toshigyehoeg iyagi*, 167–205.
351. Son, *Sŏul toshigyehoeg iyagi*, 201–203, 221–225.
352. An, "Haebang ihu sŏurŭi toshigyehoekkwa toshi-kŏnch'ugŭi pyŏnhwa," 58–60; Son, *Sŏul toshigyehoeg iyagi*, 301–308. Son Chŏng-mok deplores that the indiscriminate development of the Han River "deprived it of easy accessibility and hydrophilicity." The loss of its large sandy beaches, in particular, meant "the elimination of its idyllic landscapes and the eradication of artistic mood." Ibid., 326–327.
353. An, "Haebang ihu sŏurŭi toshigyehoekkwa toshi-kŏnch'ugŭi pyŏnhwa," 52–53.
354. Sŏulshisap'yŏnch'anwiwŏnhoe, *Han'gangsa* (Seoul: Sŏult'ŭkpyŏlshi, 1985), 874–877; *Sŏulgŏnch'uksa*, 830 ff.; An, "Haebang ihu sŏurŭi toshigyehoekkwa toshi-kŏnch'ugŭi pyŏnhwa," 60–61; Son, *Sŏul toshigyehoeg iyagi*, 309–316; Seoul Metropolitan City, *Han'gang chonghapkaebalsaŏm kŏnsŏlchi* (Seoul: Sŏult'ŭkpyŏlshi, 1988).
355. Son, *Sŏul toshigyehoeg iyagi*, 247–251; On the plan to build a national assembly building on Mount Namsan and the plan's eventual disposal, see Kang and Chang, *Han'gukkŭndae toshigongwŏnsa*, 279–283.
356. Taehanmin'gukkuk'oesamuch'ŏ, *Kuk'oeŭisadanggŏllipchi* (Seoul: Taehanmin'gukkuk'oesamuch'ŏ, 1976), 89.
357. *Sŏulgŏnch'uksa*, 831–834.
358. Song Ki-hyŏng, *Yŏŭido kuk'oeŭisadangŭi kŏllippaegyŏnggwa kŏnsŏlgwajŏnge kwanhan yŏn'gu*, Master's thesis (Hanyang University, 2007), 18–21; Chŏng In-ha, "Kuk'oeŭisadang hyŏnsangsŏlgye," in *Han'gukkŏnch'ukkaenyŏmsajŏn*, 197–199; *Sŏulgŏnch'uksa*, 944–950.
359. "T'ŭkchip: Kuk'oeŭisadang," *SPACE* 101 (1975): 28–42; Taehanmin'gukkuk'oesamuch'ŏ, *Kuk'oeŭisadanggŏllipchi*, 31–68, 89–90.
360. Taehanmin'gukkuk'oesamuch'ŏ, *Kuk'oeŭisadanggŏllipchi*, 90.
361. Kim Wŏn, "Han'gukchŏk chŏlch'ungjuŭiŭi shigŭp'an chŏngdonŭl wihayŏ," *SPACE* 101 (1975): 39–41.
362. *Dong-a Ilbo*, "Kwanch'ŏngga punsanŭi hŏshil," January 17, 1970, p. A3.
363. Yi, *Kwanghwamun yukchoapkil*, 375–376; *Sŏulgŏnch'uksa*, 942–944.
364. Kim, *Nama innŭn yŏksa, sarajinŭn kŏnch'ungmul*, 240.
365. Gi-Wook Shin, *Ethnic Nationalism in Korean: Genealogy, Politics, and Legacy* (Redwood City, CA: Stanford University Press, 2006), 25–40.
366. Henry, "Respatializing Chŏson's Royal Capital," 36. Like Pan-Asianism or Orientalism, Korean nationalism was also based on social Darwinism. On this point, see Shin, *Ethnic Nationalism in Korean*, 27–30, 40.
367. Ch'oehyŏnbae, "Chosŏnminjok kaengsaengŭi to," Volume 1 of *Oesol Ch'oehyŏnbae chŏnjip: Chosŏnminjok kaengsaengŭi to, Dong-a Ilbo yŏnjaebon* (1926; Seoul: Yonsei University Press, 2012), 33.
368. Schmid, *Korea Between Empires*, 73–74, 118–121; Michael E. Robinson, "Nationalism and the Korean Tradition, 1896–1920: Iconoclasm, Reform, and National Identity," *Korean Studies* 10 (1986): 35–53.
369. Duara, *Sovereignty and Authenticity*, 25, 30–33.
370. Ryu Si-hyŏn, *Ch'oe Nam-sŏn yŏn'gu: Chegugŭi kŭndaewa shingminjiŭi munhwa* (Seoul: Yŏksabip'yŏngsa, 2009), 109–124, 149 ff.
371. Ryu Si-hyŏn, *Ch'oe Nam-sŏn p'yŏngjŏn* (Seoul: Han'gyŏrech'ulp'an, 2011), 163–166.
372. Kim Myŏng-ku, *Hanmal ilchegangjŏmgi minjogundongnon'gwa minjokchuŭi sasang*, Ph.D. diss. (Busan National University, 2002), 131–163; Gi-Wook Shin and Michael Robinson, "Sŏron: Shingminji shigi han'gukŭl tashi

saenggak'amyŏ," in *Han'gugŭi shingminji kŭndaesŏng*, 42–59; Michael Edson Robinson, *Cultural Nationalism in Colonial Korea, 1920–1925* (Seattle, WA: University of Washington Press, 2014), 73 ff. Historian Gyan Prakash denounces the arguments that essentialize national culture or national identity as a form of representation at odds with colonial reality. See Gyan Prakash, "Introduction: After Colonialism," in *After Colonialism: Imperial Histories and Postcolonial Displacements*, ed. Gyan Prakash (Princeton, NJ: Princeton University Press, 1995), 3–17.

373. Pak Chong-hong, "Chosŏnmisurŭi sajŏk koch'al," *Kaebyŏk* 22 (1922): 13–21.
374. The first textbook to mention Damjing's name was *The New Korean History Textbook* (Sae kuksa kyobon), which Yi Pyŏng-to authored for elementary school students in 1948, but the basis for doing so remains unclear. See Kim Ŭn-suk, "Chungkodŭnghakkyo kuksakyogwasŏŭi kodae hanilgwan'gyesa sŏsul naeyong kŏmt'o," *Yŏksagyoyuk* 74 (2000): 240–242.
375. Pak Chong-hong, "Chosŏnmisurŭi sajŏk koch'al," *Kaebyŏk* 27 (1922): 13–26, quoted from 26.
376. Jin, "Demolishing Colony," 47; Ŭn Chŏng-t'ae, "Pak Chŏng-hŭi shidae sŏngyŏk'wa saŏbŭi ch'uiwa sŏnggyŏk," *Yŏksamunjeyŏn'gu* 15 (2005): 241–277.
377. Kim, "Ilchegangjŏm ihu," *Sŏurhakyŏn'gu*, 119–120.
378. Yun, "Kyŏngbokkunggwa ku chosŏnch'ongdokpu kŏnmul," *Konggan'gwa sahoe*, 300; Kim, "Ilchegangjŏm ihu," *Sŏurhakyŏn'gu*, 122–123; Ha, *Kwanghwamunŭi chŏngch'ihak*, 90–91; Ha, *Kwanghwamun'gwa chŏngch'igwŏllyŏk*, 224.
379. *The Kyunghyang Shinmun*, "Kwanghwamun pogwŏne iron," March, 20, 1968, p. A5.
380. "T'ŭkchip: Sejongmunhwahoegwan," *SPACE* 131 (1978): 11.
381. Yi, "Sŏul kŭndae toshigyŏnggwan ikki," 137.
382. "T'ŭkchip: Chŏnt'ong kyesŭnggwa han'guk hyŏndaegŏnch'ugŭi pansŏng," Kongdongt'oron II, *SPACE* 131 (1978): 31–37.
383. Chŏng Ki-yong, "Kwanghwamunesŏ namdaemunkkaji," *Munhwagwahak* 5 (1994): 56.
384. Ha, *Kwanghwamunŭi chŏngch'ihak*, 92; Ha, *Kwanghwamun'gwa chŏngch'igwŏllyŏk*, 258–277.
385. National Museum of Korea, *Ku Ch'ongdokpu kŏnmul shilch'ŭk mit ch'ŏlgŏ pogosŏ*, 385–386.
386. Jin, "Demolishing Colony," 51 ff.
387. Kongboch'ŏ, Volume 1 of *Pyŏnhwawa kaehyŏk, Kim Yŏng-sam chŏngbu kukchŏng 5nyŏn charyojip: Chŏngch'i, oegyo, t'ongil, kukpang* (Seoul: Samhwa, 1997), 71–91, quoted from 71, 77; Ha, *Kwanghwamun'gwa chŏngch'igwŏllyŏk*, 251 ff.
388. Kim, "Sangjinggongganŭi pyŏnyonggwa chip'apkiŏgŭi palmyŏng," *Konggan'gwa sahoe*, 190.
389. On the theory that Japanese imperialism contrived to cut off the energy of the Korean royal family in a mystical way, see Kim, "Sangjinggongganŭi pyŏnyonggwa chip'apkiŏgŭi palmyŏng," *Konggan'gwa sahoe*, 192–194.
390. An Hwi-chun, "Chosŏnch'ongdokpu (Kungnipchungangbangmulgwan) kŏnmurŭi ch'ŏlgŏ shibi," in An Hwi-chun, *Han'gugŭi misulgwa munhwa* (1995; Seoul: Sigong Art, 2001), 392–394.
391. Ha, *Kwanghwamun'gwa chŏngch'igwŏllyŏk*, 291 ff.; Michael Kim, "Collective Memory and Commemorative Space," *International Area Review*, 16–18.
392. Koen de Ceuster, "The Changing Nature of National Icons in the Seoul Landscape," *The Review of Korean Studies*, 99.
393. Korean Presidential Secretariat, *Ch'ŏngwadaegŏnsŏlchi* (Seoul: Taet'ongnyŏngbisŏshil, 1992), 138–146.
394. Kim, *Nama innŭn yŏksa, sarajinŭn kŏnch'ungmul*, 193.
395. On the north gate Sinmumun, see Yang, *Kyŏngbokkunge taehae araya hal modŭn kŏt*, 386–391.

Epilogue

Sites of Memory, Spaces of Hope

Demolishing and building is not such a difficult matter.
That is precisely what the president must carefully consider.
Chŏn Chin-sam, A Letter About Architecture to President
Roh Tae-woo, *SPACE* 281 (January 1991)

1. The Revival of Spree-Athens

In November 1989, the border between East and West Berlin was opened, and Potsdamer Platz instantly went from being a vacant lot to a focal point of the city. Despite the word "plaza" in its name, Potsdamer Platz was originally an intersection. One of busiest downtown areas in Europe, with a variety of commercial facilities, Potsdamer Platz represented all the buzz, pace, and movement typical of a contemporary metropolis and even gained the banal nickname "German Chicago."[1] In the 1830s, a railway section was built in the area, which led to the emergence of the station Potsdamer Bahnhof. The addition of an urban railway in the 1870s hatched a busy metropolitan scene in which different means of transportation competed with pedestrians. However, the place was soon swept away in historical turmoil and turned into a terrifying "death strip." Surrounded by a poisoned minefield, watchtowers, ferocious dogs, barbed wire, and armed guards, the strictly surveilled Berlin Wall (Berliner Mauer) was actually and metaphorically built upon the ruins of war, terrorism, and division. East Germany, which built this "Great Wall of Europe" and split a city in two, considered the wall an "anti-fascist protective rampart." To West Germany, however, it was a "wall of shame." As buildings damaged during the world war mostly collapsed in the 1950s, the areas around the wall turned into desolate, vacant spaces.[2] The Berlin featured in the 1987 film *Wings of Desire* by Wim Wenders is a bleak, gray city tormented by poverty. A bizarre scene shows the spaces surrounding the wall, riddled with weeds and haunted by memories of the past.

A New Berlin?

On June 20, 1991, the German federal parliament decided to relocate reunified Germany's capital from the West Germany capital Bonn to Berlin. The decision was made based on the belief that Berlin would be the best place to bring divided Germany together, heal its wounds, and establish a new national identity.[3] The capital city's relocation sparked debates about historical identity and its relation to a capital's appearance. From where would reunified Germany find its legitimacy? Would it be possible to uncover a trend in the history of the German nation that had absolutely nothing to do with the Nazi fascist regime or the East German communist regime? What would it take to reinvent the historically scarred Berlin as a new site of memory? Would it be better to assume an imposing monumental look or completely expose the traces of a tumultuous past and allow the city to appear fragmented?[4] As any visitor would be able to recognize, the cityscape of Berlin was a mess to the point that it could almost be called schizophrenic. There was no consistency in terms of urban planning or architectural style that could be witnessed at the capitals of other Western states. Berlin therefore had to be entirely reinvented as a capital.

Once the Berlin Wall was demolished as the result of a lengthy debate, Potsdamer Platz came back to life. Although it had remained a vacant lot for so long, part of it began to change even before German reunification. In the 1960s, the authorities of West Berlin started to carry out a long-term plan to turn the area back into an international attraction. With the completion of the Berlin Philharmonic Hall (Berliner Philharmonie) designed by Hans Scharoun in 1963, the New National Gallery (Neue Nationalgalerie) designed by Ludwig Mies van der Rohe in 1967, and the new Berlin State Library building (Haus Potsdamer Straße) in 1978 as a twin of the philharmonic hall, the Kulturforum's international, avant-garde aspect had begun to settle ahead of German reunification.[5] The project to revive Potsdamer Platz initiated by the West Berlin government gained momentum after reunification. Because the city's new look had already manifested on the plaza's west side, changes mainly occurred in places that used to be closed off by the wall as part of East Berlin. The authorities of Berlin attracted large-scale investments from leading corporations around the world to turn Potsdamer Platz into a hub of business and entertainment so as to shake off its former gloomy image and display a new aspect of Berlin.[6]

Potsdamer Platz's reconstruction basically aimed for the recovery of Berlin's "original" title as an international European city. Reinstating the tradition prior to when the Nazi regime seized power in 1933 involved, on the one hand, reviving the classical modernism at the turn of the century and during the time of the Weimar Republic and, on the other hand, allowing a limited number of postmodern glass buildings to be constructed. This was the result of adopting "critical reconstruction," a principle suggested by the architectural historian Dieter Hoffmann-Axthelm. Critical reconstruction was based on the diagnosis that postwar reconstruction in both East and West Berlin destroyed the city's organic nature by neglecting many buildings that could be restored from war damage and instead choosing to indiscriminately build high-rises, parking lots, expressways, and monotonous residential areas. For a city to possess pluralistic, organic connectivity, it was necessary to critically inherit the city's original traditions. Critical reconstruction ultimately professed a principle that aimed at invigorating the city's economy while restricting disorderly development through urban planning.[7] Potsdamer Platz reborn according to critical reconstruction seemed future oriented at a glance, but that rebirth had in fact been invented from selective memories, depicting a certain period of the past like a lost golden age. Memories of Berlin as an open international city and the capital of the Weimar Republic were the result of intentionally casting into oblivion the Berlin Wall, which had most recently existed for several decades. Although its reconstruction was meant to support the union and prosperity of East and West Germany, Potsdamer Platz ended up erasing the traces of East Germany and became devoted to propagating the rule of West Germany's capitalist system.

Critical reconstruction was based on the neo-traditionalism that widely influenced Western architecture at the time. Neo-traditionalism in architecture was a conservative reaction to drastic changes in modern society and attempted to revive a former royal capital or a modern urban tradition that had already turned into a classic. Hans Stimmann, named a "city architect" by the Berlin City Council in 1991, adopted the principle of critical reconstruction to suggest a set of guidelines for the reconstruction of central Berlin. According to Stimmann's guidelines, the Prussian state architect Schinkel's classical style was fit to represent the unique architectural identity of Berlin. Stimmann claimed that early modernists such as Peter Behrens or Ludwig Mies van der Rohe had wholly inherited the simplicity and restraint featured in Schinkel's works so that the works of such early modernists were valid exemplars for Berlin's reconstruction. Stimmann's guidelines recommended the stylistic features of classicist architecture, such as an imposing façade with conspicuous columns or granite that gave a sense of permanence. Such guidelines appealed to an idealized tradition to establish a new Berlin but ran the risk of limiting Berlin's identity and creating authoritarian regulations, which could lead to the error of sealing off the diverse heritage the city had formed over time amid contradictions and conflicts.[8]

The Return of the Berlin Palace

The debate surrounding the reconstruction of the Berlin Palace (Berliner Schloß) proved to be a case that dramatically demonstrated the potential for error in Stimmann's guidelines. Between 1993 and 1994, a life-size simulation of the palace was installed along the boulevard Unter den Linden in central Berlin. The installation was a symbolic event hinting at what the city would look like as the capital of reunified Germany. The palace's ghostly return shifted the public's attention from collecting fragments of the recently torn-down Berlin Wall to the Berlin Palace that had disappeared long ago.

A gem of Baroque architecture in northern Germany, the Berlin Palace was designed by Andreas Schlüter near the end of the seventeenth century as an extension of the old palace of the House of Hohenzollern. Under the Prussian king's rule, this extension gained further authority when it was topped with a massive dome designed by Schinkel's pupil Friedrich August Stüler. The Berlin Palace facing the Lustgarten thus practically served as a spatial pivot at the eastern end of Unter den Linden. This beautiful palace, alas, was a victim of historical turmoil.[9]

Almost eighty percent of the Berlin Palace was destroyed by the Allied Forces' air raids during World War II, but its main framework and a couple of wings were still in usable shape. Nevertheless, the German Democratic Republic led by Walter Ulbricht detonated dynamite there starting September 6, 1950 and completely blew up the palace over the next few months.[10] Bombing the Berlin Palace was, of course, not a manifestation of an iconoclastic impulse. Proof of this lies in the fact that other Prussian legacies were mostly restored and continued to be used. The reason for taking the trouble to blast the palace was because it was impossible to procure enough funds for the palace's restoration when there were other more urgent matters at stake, nor could the center of the capital be left in ruins.[11] However, after taking the desperate measure of destroying the palace, the site remained as a parking lot for decades due to cost issues until the Palace of the Republic (Palast der Republik) designed by Heinz Graffunder finally appeared in 1976. The building accommodated the ruling Socialist Unity Party's conventions as well as State Council sessions. Although it was erected upon the site of the Berlin Palace, the rectangular Palace of the Republic was not as large and adopted a modernist style, featuring a façade covered with white marble and bronze-mirrored windows. Such a stylistic choice reflected the wishes of East Germany's new leader Erich Honecker.[12]

The Berlin Palace's former location once more attracted public attention after German reunification. The reunified German government cast a doubtful gaze at the state council building of East Germany. On the surface, the city's aesthetics was given as the excuse for finding fault with the building, but in actuality, political judgment on the East German state was involved. The movement calling for the Berlin Palace's reconstruction started to gain support. In 1993, the Berlin municipal government decided to tear down the Palace of the Republic and reconstruct the Berlin Palace because not only did Berlin need to shake off its dismal past and assume a uniform cityscape befitting the capital of reunified Germany but because the Palace of the Republic could not be left untouched in its state full of asbestos and covered with soot due to the building's shoddy heating system. The decision, however, incurred serious resentment from the citizens of East Berlin. They kept filing petitions and organizing groups in opposition. They questioned why a palace was necessary for a democratic state. Was it simply because of commercial demand? No king meant no need for a palace! The Berlin municipal government's logic was in fact no different from that East Germany applied to destroy the Berlin Palace. People against the decision argued that the idea of seeking German historical continuity was purely based on the logic of a winner aimed at excluding the history of East Germany from German national history.[13]

The debate surrounding the Berlin Palace's reconstruction involved various subjects such as architectural aesthetics, urban planning, civil and national identity, the preservation of historical remains, and historical justice. The life-size simulation of the Berlin Palace in place for two years greatly contributed to gathering public support for the palace's reconstruction. The problem with the installation was, however, that it was irrational and biased for several reasons. One of them was that it completely disregarded the opinion of former East German citizens. To them, the Palace of the Republic was not at all a symbol of the East German state's repression. The main hall the state council used to hold sessions used to often serve as a venue for concerts featuring popular music, including those performed by Western pop musicians. The restaurant and café in the building used to be frequented as places for socializing with friends. The former citizens of East Berlin therefore each had cheerful memories related to the Palace of the Republic. Demolishing the building was enough to make them feel devastated that they would never become equal citizens of reunified Germany. Even from the standpoint of preserving history, destroying an intact building on purpose to reconstruct an older building was no more than a bad decision from allowing political judgment to take precedence. The Palace of the Republic has since been demolished, and in its place the construction of the Berlin City Palace (Stadtpalast) is underway.[14]

The arrival of the Berlin City Palace (currently Humboldt Forum) is likely to reinforce the trend of neo-traditionalism in rebuilding Berlin. With the Berlin City Palace at one end, the historic boulevard Unter den Linden was where Karl Friedrich Schinkel's neoclassical ideals came to life. From the Neue Wache, which has been transformed into a "central memorial" for reunified Germany, to the Museum Island, home to five prime museums, including the Altes Museum designed by Schinkel, many of the buildings along Unter den Linden underwent extensive repair work to internally and externally display the deep-rooted historical identity of reunified Germany. Yet fundamental questions remain. Did Germans have a national identity to begin with? Is it possible to skip the Nazi and Cold War era and discover such an identity among Prussian traditions?

Interestingly enough, the East German government made efforts of its own in the 1980s in terms of urban regeneration. Many buildings were historically rediscovered and restored long after having been ruined. In order to place the German working class within, not separate from, the developments of national history, East German historians strived to uncover from Prussia the values of bourgeois revolution rather than militarism.[15] This trend could be witnessed early on in East Germany. The buildings raised along the boulevard Stalinallee in celebration of Stalin's seventieth birthday in 1949 adopted the rather embellished, imposing architectural style of the Soviet Union. Depending on the viewer, their neoclassical entrances, pilasters, and window ornaments seemed to be reminiscent of the buildings by Schinkel. However, West German critics suggested that the wide street, overly large buildings, and classical elements of design were similar to the buildings designed by the Nazi war criminal Albert Speer.[16] The East German government embraced a traditionalist approach, while West Berlin went on to present modernist buildings by architects such as Hans Scharoun.[17] The Baroque-style arsenal on Unter den Linden was turned into the German Historical Museum to hold exhibitions about the progressive heritage of German laborers since the French Revolution.[18] The Neue Wache by Schinkel sustained serious damage during World War II and was restored into a "memorial for victims of fascism and world wars." And the historic Forum Fridericianum was reborn as Bebelplatz, named after the socialist revolutionary August Bebel.[19]

These developments must have had something to do with why old-fashioned residences and shops were built for the reconstruction of Nicholas' Quarter (Nikolaiviertel) not far from Unter den Linden once the quarter was highlighted as the origin of medieval Berlin. West German architects scorned such medieval-looking constructs built with concrete and called them kitschy,[20] but it made no difference to the fact that the constructs represented East and West Germany's respective preoccupation with establishing identities of their own.[21] Gaining exclusive possession of a nation's historical identity originating from Prussia, the Weimar Republic, and West Germany was as good as a trophy awarded to the winner in a contest of state systems.

2. Spaces of Hope

Berlin shows how an urban space can be divided by differing memories/oblivion and unified by unilateral memory/oblivion. The case is not so different for the South Korean capital Seoul, still haunted by the specter of Japanese colonial rule. If Berlin has been obsessed with erasing memories of the Nazi regime and East Germany, Seoul has been obsessed with erasing memories of colonial rule and war. Although those memories involve an aggressor and reunification for one city while involving a victim and division for the other, such a difference is not great enough to mask the far more significant commonality between the two cities. Both Berlin and Seoul are capitals suffering from a discord magnified by memories and oblivion. Remembering a certain past amid the vicissitudes of history inevitably accompanies forgetting the rest of the past, which leaves no agreed-upon guidelines for making correct judgments. Imagining the original state of something that never existed is as risky as it is ambitious. The spatial center of the cities is always being created, and their urban identities revolve around a hollow center. Such endless rotation has resulted in national "sites of memory" such as Potsdamer Platz, the Neue Wache, the Berlin Palace, Kyŏngbokgung Palace, and Kwanghwamun Gate, which testify to the future rather than the past. They are memories with only posterity in mind.

Impossible Tectonics in Postcolonial Seoul

The eerie specter of Athena created a glorious phantasmagoria of monumental buildings as it traveled from Berlin to Qingdao, Tokyo, and on to Seoul and Changchun, but all it ultimately did was cast a cold shadow called coloniality. Nowhere did it achieve tectonic unity. In a heterogeneous space called Seoul, the phantasmagoria of Prussian classicism with a scent of Pallas Athena only serves as a camouflage for the city's dramatic past. That phantasmagoria featuring the resplendent beauty of history may have a silhouette as dignified as Capitol Hall, but a closer look reveals serious cracks in each part where boundaries haphazardly overlap with one another. Lost, fragmented memories seem to be clinging onto the edge of that silhouette like sparse ivy. In any case, Prussian classicism can hardly rise to the status of a normal "cultural heritage" due to its inseparable association with traces of Seoul's colonial past. It instead continues to hover at the heart of the city like a specter and obstructs the discursive formation of history. There is, of course, no need to jump to the conclusion that this has nothing to do with Prussian classicism itself. Its phantasmagoria has clearly exposed the pitiable rear view of this higher idea that had remained invisible in Europe.

Modernity and coloniality's extended encroachment of Seoul is indeed different from the reality of other (post)colonial cities packed with illegal residences and slums. The South Korean capital has long escaped the wretched circumstances of being forced to "either stay put and die or leave and suffer," like the popular saying in an area in Brazil when it experienced a drought.[22] Should Seoul's escape be considered an achievement of state tectonics or national polity? Should the ultramodern transformation of Seoul City Hall or Tongdaemun Stadium be regarded as the completion or overcoming of a ceaseless pursued modernization? Could they instead be a manifestation of insuppressible trauma or an appeal to the extreme oblivion caused by such trauma? In the end, what matters is not a building's architectural style or artistic design but tending to the city as a home to the citizens and their collective memory, as well as having the political propriety to tend to such issues.

Berlin and Seoul are both entangled in multilayered modernity. The coexistence of avant-garde modernism under the Weimar Republic and reactionary modernism under the Nazi regime as well as the coexistence of East German socialist modernity and West German capitalist modernity suggested order and hope for Berlin and left indelible traces upon the city. It was the same for Seoul, where Prussian classicism under Japanese colonial rule and colorless modernism under military dictatorships coexisted in addition to the coexistence of post-1990s neo-traditionalism and American postmodernism.[23] Could this mixed memory, which cannot be reduced to a single identity, be forming the basis of Berlin and Seoul's respective urban identities? How, then, can the cities overcome the trauma caused by history and create civil identities suitable for democratic societies?

It is difficult to suggest a clear-cut solution, but it may be worth introducing a small beam of hope flickering at a corner of the South Korean capital Seoul. *Kkummaru*, designed by Joh Sung-Yong, sits placidly on the grounds of Seoul Children's Grand Park, with a name coined from the Korean words *kkum*, which means "dream," and *maru*, which means "lounge." The construct was originally designed as a clubhouse at the Seoul Country Club by a first-generation architect named Na Sang-jin of South Korea.[24] Not long after its completion in 1969, the building began to serve as an education center when the golf course was suddenly turned into a children's park. The fact that the building used to be part of a facility on the outskirts of Seoul only accessible to the privileged and that the facility's purpose was instantly changed at the order of the president inevitably leads to the conclusion that the space had been a product of power. The building's realization of modernism presents more conspicuous functionality than openness. After having its purpose changed to an education center, the original architect's name was slowly forgotten, until the architect Joh Sung-Yong saved the building on the verge of demolition by suggesting that it be remodeled into a completely different space.

Figure 4.1 Left: Kkummaru, Designed by Joh Sung-Yong Architectural Office + Choon Choi. Right: The Picnic Garden Inside Kkummaru.

Source: Left: Photo by Kim Jae-Kyeong (2011). Courtesy of Kim Jae-Kyeong. Right: Photo by Kim Jae-Kyeong (2011). Courtesy of Kim Jae-Kyeong.

Unique memories of the forgotten architecture of Na Sang-jin were what led to the production of Kkummaru. Rather than restoring the building to its original form, the remodeling project was about newly remembering Na Sang-jin's architectural idea and, by extension, the act of building itself. This kind of approach toward a building on the verge of destruction seems worthy of being dubbed an archaeological exploration. "Archaeological" here refers not to an academic field but an approach to the past per the words of Foucault. The French philosopher argued that trimming the past into a linear order of historical continuity the way existing historical research did was to commit the ideological violence of subordinating the past to the interests of the present. He thus suggested an alternative methodology centered on historical discontinuity, which was modeled after the archaeological method of digging through one stratum at a time. The Foucauldian sense of archaeological exploration excavates irregular networks from a particular time and space, thereby disintegrating the historical/historicist notion that it is possible to "restore" without "prejudice" the original form of a past in which time and space are one.[25]

Instead of restoring it per Na Sang-jin's original design, taking the approach of archaeological exploration to remodel the building uncovered a stratum of time between the building's past and present. The glass outer wall that blocked views into the building, the roof over the front hall, the floor plates, and part of the roof on the third floor were removed to empty the central space and plainly reveal the building's framework. Traces of damage over time were left untouched, and by choosing not to apply extra coats of paint, the building material's natural color was brought to the fore. The concrete beams newly inserted into the central space at regular intervals serve as a tool to assist in archaeologically exploring the building. The rays of sunlight flowing into the open building seem to make the strata of time appear like archaeological strata.

Kkummaru clearly visualizes not only the clubhouse's architectural framework but the principle of tectonics at the foundation of modern architecture. As the Prussian state architect Schinkel demonstrated, the transition from neoclassicism to modernism in modern (and contemporary) architecture certainly had a power-oriented aspect. Its emphasis on functional rationality and tight-knit unity coincided with a political formula based on rules and regulation. The modernism realized through the Seoul Country Club's clubhouse was as power-oriented and exclusive as the temporal circumstances at the time of its construction. Kkummaru visualizes the principle of tectonics running throughout the clubhouse in a dramatic fashion that inspires new memories and reflections about building. Kkummaru is in itself an archaeological exploration. It is a memory like a shovel digging into a modern spatio-temporal order. Creating a space through memory may basically satisfy the needs of power to specifically establish and differentiate that space, but, as in the case of Kkummaru, memory is bound to question such differentiation and incite critical reflections over it, which would inevitably go against the needs of power. The modernist utopia created by power was reborn into an entirely new space by adopting a different way to remember.

Kkummaru as a Heterotopia

Foucault once pointed out the harmful effects of indiscriminately yearning for a utopia. Utopia literally sketches a fictional future that cannot take root in the ground of reality and therefore has the potential to enforce a one-sided, self-centered idea. Foucault instead suggests "heterotopias" (hétérotopies) that value choice, diversity, and difference. It involves a strategy of recreation which acknowledges the reality that clearly exists while disintegrating its structure from within.[26] For instance, spaces carrying traces of the past, such as libraries, historic sites, memorial parks, and cemeteries, have always made political use of memory to help legitimize the dominant reality of a nation-state or imperialism. Yet by becoming involved in a politics of memory, such spaces have transformed themselves into spaces portraying historical discontinuities, conflicts between dissimilar memories, or incurable wounds, thereby firmly establishing themselves within reality and tearing down the existing reality's authority and hierarchy.

Kkummaru is basically a place not for the privileged but for ordinary citizens to relax. Anyone who visits can take the stairs, ramps, or elevator to roam about the place, stop by the book café or cafeteria inside, or settle down on a bench in the picnic garden featuring trees, a pond, and the sky, resting to their heart's content before they leave for a performance nearby or head back to the children's park. The space literally serves as a lounge, one that is open from top to bottom with no division between indoor and outdoor. The space once monopolized by the privileged now differentiates itself as a rare lounge in a dreary city.

Then, can this spatial openness and fluidity realized through Kkummaru be considered an indicator of a truly different space? David Harvey, a progressive American geographer, once argued that entertainment venues like Disneyland or cozy suburban shopping malls are "degenerate utopias."[27] The issue is, of course, not limited to entertainment venues or shopping malls. At some point, it grew easier to witness many ordinary spaces around us being refashioned and consumed in the name of history and tradition. Such a phenomenon has even been dubbed the "heritage industry." However, there is something different about Joh Sung-Yong's Kkummaru. The place has a memory fundamentally different from history and tradition, a memory that does not neatly package the past for current political or commercial purposes and encourages people to seek the open potential of time and space.

An alternative society can be built only by resisting the source of social power, which is the basic framework of time and space. Such a society would not, of course, involve blind resistance but the formation of different heterotopias here and there based on the material conditions of modern society without being dominated by those conditions. It would be necessary to realize that the phantasmagoria called "modernity" was ultimately a reflection of ourselves, and, rather than regarding it as a futile utopia, it can be used as a source of energy to advance at least one step further from where we now stand. With relieved hearts, we can now sit and chat at the lounge. We no longer have to be dictated to by the agenda of established politics. What would be able to stop us from picturing our future against those corrugated walls of a lounge where we are free to stay for a while and daydream? Places like Kkummaru are what David Harvey would call "spaces of hope." Through the lounge, hope is finally nurtured underneath the murky Seoul sky.

Notes

1. Brian Ladd, *The Ghosts of Berlin* (Chicago, IL: University of Chicago Press, 1997), 117.
2. Ibid., 7–39; Andreas Huyssen, "The Voids of Berlin," *Critical Inquiry* 24 (1997): 57–81; Hans-Hermann Hertle, *The Berlin Wall: Monument of the Cold War* (Berlin: Christoph Links Verlag, 2008); Edgar Wolfrum, *Die Mauer: Geschichte einer Teilung* (Munich: C. H. Beck, 2009). The "wall of shame" (Schandmauer) is a term the German Chancellor Willy Brandt used while serving as the mayor of Berlin. For further details, see Ch'oe Ho-kŭn, "Perŭllin, naengjŏnŭi sangjingesŏ yurŏbŭi chungshimŭro," in *Toshinŭn yŏksada*, ed. Yi Yŏng-sŏk et al. (Paju: Sŏhaemunjip, 2011), 215–219.
3. Christoph Stölzl, "Bonn oder Berlin?" in *Hauptstadt: Historische Perspektiven eines deutschen Themas*, ed. Hans-Michael Körner and Katharina Weigand (Munich: dtv, 1995), 269–275; Ladd, *The Ghosts of Berlin*, 224 ff.
4. Laurence McFalls, "Living with Which Past? National Identity in Post-Wall, Postwar Germany," in *A User's Guide to German Cultural Studies*, ed. Scott Denham et al. (Ann Arbor, MI: University of Michigan Press, 1997), 297–308.
5. Philipp Meuser et al., *Berlin: The Architecture Guide* (Berlin: Braun Publishing, 2007), 172–173.
6. Karen E. Till, *The New Berlin: Memory, Politics, Place* (Minneapolis, MN: University of Minnesota Press, 2005), 31–35; Meuser, *Berlin*, 261 ff.
7. Dieter Hoffmann-Axthelm, "Ein Niemandsland, das nur der Geschichte gehört: Zum Wettbewerb 'Topographie des Terrors' in Berlin," *Frankfurt Allgemeine Zeitung*, January 26, 1993, p. A30; Ladd, *The Ghosts of Berlin*, 229–231. At the root of the policy for Potsdamer Platz's reconstruction was a project in the 1980s called the International Building Exhibition Berlin (IBA Berlin) aimed at the reconstruction of West Berlin. To improve the residential circumstances of areas around the Berlin Wall, architects, urban planners, and historians came together to study and rediscover the modern building tradition of Berlin and construct new urban spaces. While the project was based on the progressive idea of improving the lives of the underprivileged, the argument for critical reconstruction did not share the same social agenda, even as it actively embraced the technological design elements of IBA Berlin. On this point, see Till, *The New Berlin*, 45–51.
8. Meuser, *Berlin*, 250–251; Till, *The New Berlin*, 46–47, 36–38, 50.

9. Goerd Peschken and Johannes Althoff, *Das Berliner Schloß* (Berlin: Bebra Verlag, 2000).
10. Rudy Koshar, *Germany's Transient Pasts: Preservation and National Memory in the Twentieth Century* (Chapel Hill, NC: The University of North Carolina Press, 1998), 205. Only one building in the Berlin Palace survived the detonation. It was the same building where Karl Liebknecht proclaimed the German Free Socialist Republic, the precursor to East Germany, on November 9, 1918, ahead of the proclamation of West Germany's precursor Weimar Republic.
11. Rudy Koshar, *From Monuments to Traces: Artifacts of German Memory 1870–1990* (Berkeley, CA: University of California Press, 2000), 157–161.
12. Kirsten Heidler, ed., *Von Erichs Lampenladen zur Asbestruine: Alles über den Palast der Republik* (Berlin: Argon Verlag, 1998).
13. Wilhelm von Boddien and Helmut Engel, eds., *Die Berliner Schloßdebatte: Pro und Contra* (Berlin: Wissenschafts-Verlag, 2000); Svetlana Boym, *The Future of Nostalgia* (New York, NY: Basic Books, 2002).
14. Moritz Holfelder, *Palast der Republik: Aufstieg und Fall eines symbolischen Gebäudes* (Berlin: Ch. Links Verlag, 2008).
15. Mitchell Ash, "Geschichtswissenschaft, Geschichtskultur und der ostdeutsche Historikerstreit," *Geschichte und Gesellschaft* 24 (1998): 283–304; Chŏn Chin-sŏng, "Nach'i kwagŏ haesŏgŭi chudogwŏn kyŏngjaeng," in *Pundanŭi tu ŏlgul*, ed. Kim Sŭng-ryŏl et al. (Seoul: Yŏksabip'yŏngsa, 2005), 317–334.
16. Werner Durth, Niels Gutschow and Jörn Düwel, *Architektur und Städtebau der DDR* (Berlin: Jovis, 1998), 126–193; Bernd Wilczek, ed., *Berlin-Hauptstadt der DDR 1949–1989: Utopie der Realität* (Zürich: Elster Verlag, 1995), 33–50.
17. On architectural modernism in Berlin, see, notably, Gabi Dolff-Bonekämper, *Das Hansaviertel: Internationale Nachkriegsmoderne in Berlin* (Berlin: Verlag Bauwesen, 1999).
18. H. Glenn Penny III, "The Museum für deutsche Geschichte und German National Identity," *Central European History* 28 (1995): 343–372.
19. The Brandenburg Gate's restoration was a highly unusual affair. The old entrance and symbol of Berlin located at the starting point of Unter den Linden suffered damage during World War II, and by the late 1950s, East and West Berlin managed to reach an agreement on the gate's restoration. West Germany was to repair the quadriga, while East Germany was to install the repaired masterpiece by Johann Gottfried Schadow above the refurbished gate. West Germany kept its end of the agreement, but East Germany damaged the delivered quadriga by cutting the iron cross and imperial eagle off the top of the lance the goddess of victory held. This was because the socialist republic regarded the iron cross originally designed by Schinkel as an intolerable symbol of Prussian militarism. On this point, see Jürgen Reiche, "Symbolgehalt und Bedeutungswandel eines politischen Monuments," in *Das Brandenburger Tor 1791–1991: Eine Monographie*, ed. Willmuth Arenhövel and Rolf Bothe (Berlin: Willmuth Arenhövel Verlag, 1991), 304.
20. Koshar, *Germany's Transient Pasts*, 226.
21. Regarding memory culture of West Germany, see, notably, Charles Maier, *The Unmasterable Past: History, Holocaust, and German National Identity* (Cambridge, MA: Harvard University Press, 1988), 121–159.
22. Joel Kotkin, *The City: A Global History* (New York, NY: The Modern Library, 2006), 132–133.
23. Till, *The New Berlin*, 51.
24. Yi Haeng-ch'ŏl and Yun In-sŏk, "Kŏnch'ukka Na Sang-jinŭi chakp'um hwaltonge kwanhan yŏn'gu," *Taehan'gŏnch'uk'ak'oenonmunjip kyehoekkye* 21, no. 2 (2001): 577–580.

25. Michel Foucault, *The Archeology of Knowledge and the Discourse on Language* (Stockton, CA: Barnes & Noble Books, 1993).
26. Michel Foucault, "Different Spaces," in Aesthetics, Method, and Epistemology: Essential Works of Foucault, 1954–1984, vol. 2, ed. James D. Faubion, trans. Robert Hurley (New York, NY: The New Press, 1998), 175–185. Ahead of Foucault, Henri Lefèbvre suggested heterotopias as spaces of difference and others through *The Urban Revolution* (La révolution urbaine) (Paris: Gallimard, 1970). On the conceptual difference between Lefèbvre and Foucault's suggestions, see Chang Se-ryong, "Het'erot'op'ia: (T'al) kŭndaegonggan ihaerŭl wihan shiron," *Taegusahak* 95 (2009): 285–317.
27. David Harvey, *Spaces of Hope* (Berkeley, CA: University of California Press, 2000), 164.

Index